FUZZY LOGIC
for Business and Industry

LIMITED WARRANTY AND DISCLAIMER OF LIABILITY

FUZZY LOGIC

for Business and Industry

EARL COX

The Metus Systems Group
Chappaqua, New York

Foreword by Bart Kosko

CHARLES RIVER MEDIA, INC.
Rockland, Massachusetts

Publisher: David F. Pallai
Production: Solstice Communications
Cover Design: The Vision Group
Printer: InterCity Press, Rockland, MA.

CHARLES RIVER MEDIA, INC.
P.O. Box 417
403 VFW Drive
Rockland, Massachusetts 02370
617-871-4184
617-871-4376 (fax)
chrivmedia@aol.com

This book is printed on acid-free paper.

"Icons" and "Topic Symbols (and their descriptions)" appearing throughout the book are reprinted with permission from AP PROFESSIONAL, Cox, Earl D., The Fuzzy Systems Handbook, (1994).

Earl Cox. *Fuzzy Logic for Business and Industry.*
Foreword and Appendix by Bart Kosko
ISBN: 1-886801-01-0

Printed in the United States of America
95 96 97 98 99 7 6 5 4 3 2 First Edition

CHARLES RIVER MEDIA titles are available for site license or bulk purchase by institutions, user groups, corporations, etc. For additional information, please contact the Special Sales Department at 617-871-4184.

Requests for replacement of a defective diskette must be accompanied by the original diskette, your mailing address, telephone number, date of purchase and purchase price. Please state the nature of the problem, and send the information to CHARLES RIVER MEDIA, INC., P.O. Box 417, 403 VFW Drive, Rockland, Massachusetts 02370. CRM's sole obligation to the purchaser is to replace the diskette, based on defective materials or faulty workmanship, but not on the operation or functionality of the product.

People who like this sort of thing will find this the sort of thing they like.

Abraham Lincoln
(1809–1865)
Critique of a book
G.W.E. Russel,
Collections and Recollections, Chap. 30

E quindi uscimmo a riveder le stelle. . .
Thence we came forth to rebehold the stars. . .

Dante Alighieri
(1265–1321)
Divine Comedy, Inferno, xxxxiv. 139

Dedication

Like the one before it, this book is also for my wonderful wife Marilyn, as well as my daughters Diana and Laura; without their support, tolerance, patience, and nagging ("when *will* you be finished with this book?!!") it would not have been possible.

Table of Contents

```
Initial;
Parms[0]
Parms [1
sprint(s)
strncpy(;
FDBptr[M
if(*stat;
Part Dom
Part Dom
(*FDBcnt,
```

List of Figures

13

Acknowledgments

```
Initiali
Parms[0]
Parms [1
sprint(s
strncpy(
FDBptr[M
if(*stat
Part Dom
Part Dom
(*FDBcnt
```

This book provides a synthesis of many ideas about and actual work developed from real-world fuzzy models. For their contributions to my philosophy of fuzzy logic model building, the nature of approximate reasoning, and the integration of fuzzy logic with conventional decision support aparata, I need to thank David Brubaker of The Huntington Group, Karl Wiig of The Wiig Group, Gary S. David of Impact Enterprises, Dr. Frederick W. Hegge, Director of the Office of Military Performance Assessment, Walter Reed Army Hospital, Steve Marsh, Director of Strategic Operations at Motorola, Farhad Sadighi, Manager of the Artificial Intelligence Unit at Travelers Insurance, and Cort Wrotnowski of Yankee Publications.

For their support and encouragement I want to thank Lotfi and Fay Zadeh.

For permission to use his organizational dynamics model and his insights into the use of policies for adaptive and feed-back fuzzy models I want to thank my friend and pioneer in the field of fuzzy logic business systems, Peter Llewelyn Jones.

I also want to thank Dr. Rod Taber of Ring Technology for permission to use his managed health care fuzzy cognitive map. Rod also provided invaluable assistance in guiding my way through the concepts underlying FCMs and how they are used in knowledge acquisition and policy analysis.

No man is an island, and the pragmatic business of building and supporting complex business systems rests both on knowledge and craftsmanship. For their contributions to knowledge and fine tuning of my craft, I want to especially thank Dr. Ron Yager, Director of the Machine Intelligence Institute at Iona College, Guido DeBoeck of The World Bank, Casey and Jane Klimasauskas of Neuralware, Martin McNeill of Fuzzy Systems Engineering, Michael and Nadja O'Hagan of Fuzzy Logic, Incorporated, Fred Watkins of HyperLogic, and Bill Siler of the Kemp-Carraway Heart Institute.

Finally, I want to thank Dr. Bart Kosko of USC not only for his kind foreword, but for his advice, occasional badgering, and continued insistence that I actually learn the mathematics behind and the meaning of such concepts as the Standard Additive Model.

Foreword

Earl Cox has written an important and much needed book on fuzzy systems. The book applies these "intelligent" systems to a wide range of problems in finance and scheduling and management information systems. The book covers these topics with a minimum of math and comes with enough software code to apply the fuzzy techniques to real problems.

The book is much needed in part because it helps show that fuzzy systems are universal function approximators. They are smart black boxes or model-free systems that apply just as well to finance and quantum mechanics as to the engineering fields of control and signal processing that have helped popularize them. The user need not build a math model of how the process turns inputs to outputs. The fuzzy black box builds it for him. This holds for the many embedded systems of the business world and for the many commercial successes of fuzzy systems in Japan and Korea: camcorders, washing machines, microwave ovens, car transmissions, suspension systems, traffic lights, and hundreds of others.

The device applications all too often suggest that fuzzy logic is a mere gadget technology for turning sensor measurements into control actions. Instead they show that a black box with just a few fuzzy rules can model a system that we might otherwise have to guess at with complex and brittle nonlinear equations. And the device applications show but a small part of the approximation power of fuzzy systems. These trees of parallel if-then rules have the same approximation status that neural networks and polynomials have. They too give a universal way to compute. And it is high time the business world adds them too to its tool kit of decision aids.

The book is also much needed because it shows how to map the vague language of the business world to the smart black boxes of fuzzy systems. It shows how to turn sentences into rules and paragraphs into systems. The humble vague or fuzzy set acts as the atom of the knowledge-based system. The terms low price and high demand are fuzzy terms. All prices are low and not low to some degree. All demands for goods or services are high and not high to some degree. These words or noun phrases stand for fuzzy sets. The user draws the sets as curves or lets a neural network draw them for him. Wider triangles and trapezoids tend to stand for more vague and less sure sets or concepts. Rectangles stand for binary concepts.

A fuzzy rule associates two or more fuzzy sets in a sentence: *If price is low then demand is high*. The rule also mates the two set curves to give a rule patch. The rule patch is the basic geometric unit of a fuzzy system and its size defines the conceptual granularity of the system. Larger rule patches are less certain than smaller rule patches. Patches shrink in the limiting case to the points of binary certainty. A standard math model defines a locus or surface of such binary points and thus casts the model at too fine a level. More often than not a user can build a more accurate system with the cookie-cutter approach of fuzzy rule patches. Brains did not evolve to guess at the equations that best fit the swirling non-linear world around us.

A fuzzy system is a set of such sentences or rules or rule patches that turns inputs to outputs. The paragraph of rules stands for a set of rule patches that cover some underlying surface in the state space or set of all system outcomes. Fuzzy systems work well when the rule patches cover the control or decision surface well. Theorems show that the rule patches are always out there if only we can find them. The best a fuzzy system can do is to patch the bumps and cover the peaks and valleys of the surface with rule patches and fill in with rule patches between the bumps as the rule budget allows.

One problem is that no one knows what the decision surface looks like in most cases. So the designer must guess at the rules and the thus guess at the turning points of the surface. Or the designer must appeal to training data and let a neural or statistical learning scheme guess for him. Learning forms the first rule patches and then moves them as more training data pours in. Better learning schemes quickly move the patches toward the bumps in the decision surface.

The bigger problem is rule explosion in high dimension. It takes too many rule patches to cover most surfaces or to approximate most functions or systems. The number of rules grows exponentially with the number of inputs and outputs in the system. More inputs mean more causes and often a more realistic model of a system or process. But the cost may be a fuzzy system that needs more rules than it can get from brains or neural nets. Sooner or later every formal system crashes on the rocks of this curse of dimensionality. At least with fuzzy systems we know in theory where the best rules should lie. Complex systems of high dimension may have more bumps in their surfaces than a fuzzy system will ever have rules. Then the goal is to estimate these bumps or extrema and allocate rule patches to the largest bumps first.

Business problems tend to have more variables than control problems have. Systems for stock market prediction may use dozens or even hundreds of input variables. These may range from interest rates and currency exchange ratios to measures of insider trading and benchmarks of firms and industries. Markets are among the most nonlinear, noisy, asynchronous, ill-measured, time-varying, and multi-dimensional systems known to man. The user must often break the problem into smaller systems of fewer dimensions. Even then the user may find little help in the quasi-linear math models of econometrics or portfolio analysis. Fuzzy systems offer a practical way to transfer the vague judgments and wisdom of the user to a quantitative and nonlinear approximation model. The math of the fuzzy system is not fuzzy but the user need not know the math to use or tune the fuzzy system. The user can program the system in words and sentences.

Earl Cox tackles many of these complex business problems in this book. The applications range from risk and financial analysis to digital ID matching. Some systems help manage a structured database while others help draw the fuzzy line between whether to buy or sell. Earl Cox has built real fuzzy systems for over a decade for many skeptical business clients and has managed to do quite well at it. This gives the book a hands-on feel and a practical insight that more academic books lack. It also shows how decision problems in business have begun to yield to the fuzzy method.

Professor Bart Kosko
Director
Signal and Image Processing Institute
Electrical Engineering Department
University of Southern California
Los Angeles, California

Preface

```
Initializ
Parms[0]
Parms [1,
sprint(s;
strncpy(:
FDBptr[M;
if(*stat;
Part Dom;
Part Dom,
(*FDBcnt:
```

There is a tide in the affairs of men,
Which, taken at the flood, leads on to fortune;
Omitted, all the voyage of their life
Is bound in shallows and in miseries.
On such a full sea are we now afloat,
And we must take the current when it serves,
Or lose our ventures.
William Shakespeare,
(1564–1616)
Julius Caesar, iv,iii. 217

Scope and Objectives of this Book

In *The Fuzzy Systems Handbook* (AP Professional, 1994), I took up the issues associated with understanding the basic concepts of fuzzy logic and approximate reasoning as well as the more pragmatic issues of building, using, and interpreting fuzzy models. In this book we turn our attention to the integration of fuzzy reasoning with the ideas of general machine intelligence, the way in which fuzzy systems approximate and represent arbitrary functions as well as the application of more advanced approximate reasoning systems such as fuzzy database operations, adaptive and feed-back systems, and decision models with multiple constraints and multiple experts. In a wider context, this book addresses many issues outside fuzzy logic. In an attempt to bring the ideas of fuzzy systems into a more meaningful framework, I have also included general discussions about rule-based machine reasoning, the nature of relational database systems, and strategic and tactical management decision-making. The presentation of the material is, I hope, clear and concise without being unduly cluttered with mathematical and other symbolic notations. In fact, as a book for practicing technical managers, business analysts and knowledge engineers, I have excluded much of the underlying mathematical theory associated with fuzzy set theory. To a much larger extent than *The Fuzzy Systems Handbook*, this is a book for the technical business reader. While I have included a library of fuzzy programs that illustrate many of the concepts developed in the book, the actual code has been moved out of the main text.

A Perspective on Fuzzy Modelling

There has been a steady rise of interest in fuzzy systems over the past several years and the term *fuzzy* now has a certain panache that was missing only a year or two ago. In fact, the word *fuzzy* has become a technical adjective used to describe anything that is not absolutely precise.

In October, 1991, I presented a paper on fuzzy database queries at the *First International Conference on Artificial Intelligence Application on Wall Street.* My first paper was rejected since it used the words *Fuzzy Logic* in the title. Only after changing the title to *A Company Acquisition Analysis: Formulating Queries with Imprecise Domains* was the paper accepted. I had the only paper on fuzzy logic. Eighteen months later, at the second conference, it seemed as though everyone had a fuzzy system. I was delighted to find my self in the midst of a fuzzy system renaissance. Yet, as I wandered around the conference, I found nearly all of these systems simply employed some variation of the fuzzy set concept to generate membership values for model parameters. These membership values were used in various ways throughout the system. In most of these cases the designers employed a form of interval arithmetic to generate a scaling or ordinal ranking of parameters values. Few of these systems used the techniques of approximate reasoning such as the evaluation of rules in parallel, the combining of output fuzzy regions, and the defuzzification of the final combined fuzzy region to produce a result.

Recently I have encountered fuzzy database search programs that were vaguely fuzzy only in the sense you could adjust the scope of their proximity comparisons or use a phonetic search based on some form of the soundex algorithm. And I have seen a fuzzy trading systems advertised that employes the same "powerful fuzzy logic techniques used in MYCIN[1]." Within the technical marketplace, the term "fuzzy" has become as common as "object oriented" and "client server." Clearly the designers of these systems as well as their marketing organizations have only a dim understanding of fuzzy logic. Because of this, a new notion of fuzzy logic is slowly emerging replacing the old world order of fuzzy set theory and approximate reasoning with a new definition:

Fuzzy Logic (n.) Any system of computation where the values are not precisely predetermined or where confidence in the system or its data can be called into dispute or where statistical, probabilistic, or ad-hoc certainty measurements are used to develop one or more parameters.

---

1. For a discussion of the MYCIN expert system see Bruce G. Buchanan and Edward H. Shortliffe, *Rule-Based Expert Systems: The MYCIN experiments of the Stanford Heuristic Programming Project* (Addison-Wesley, Reading, Mass, 1984) MYCIN did not use fuzzy logic in any form, but employed an uncertainty system that combined a form of probabilistic reasoning into a form of "certainty factors."

The question that naturally arises from this is, what is the correct definition of fuzzy logic? This has proven to be an elusive quest. I answered some parts of this question in *The Fuzzy Systems Handbook,* but the larger issues of the mechanisms in fuzzy business models remains largely unexplored. In this book, I want to continue the inquiry into the meaning of fuzzy systems by examining the use of fuzzy logic in a wide spectrum of business and industry applications. Ignoring the popular, but inaccurate, definition of fuzzy logic, I focus on the real issues of how fuzzy systems are designed, how they work, and how we can make accurate and precise predictions from their results.

Too many books and articles on fuzzy logic are concerned with engineering applications—balancing pendulums, backing up trucks, digital signal processing, and so forth. While this emphasis has been beneficial to the fuzzy logic community in general, the idea that fuzzy logic can significantly contribute to better business and scientific models is still not generally accepted. I have included working models of many complex fuzzy systems although, in the interest of exposition and comprehension they have been reduced to their basic architecture. I have removed some important constructs necessary for commercial durability and robustness such as error detection and recovery, memory management, overlay segmentation, and graphical user interfaces.

Organization of the Book

Chapter 1. The book begins with an introduction to the features and benefits of fuzzy systems, exploring how they provide enhanced capabilities for the modelling of highly nonlinear systems, the use of multiple conflicting experts, the accumulation of evidence, and the improvement in system robustness and intelligence.

Chapter 2. Provides an extensive look at rule-based machine reasoning techniques, both fuzzy and crisp. We explore the nature of backward and forward chaining and opportunistic forward firing, as well as fuzzy reasoning. The Fuzzy Approximation Theory developed by Bart Kosko is explored, showing how a fuzzy reasoning system can approximate any continuous function.

Chapter 3. Addresses the use of fuzzy logic in relational database systems. After reviewing the underlying concepts of relational theory—relations, normalization, joins and projections—we look at `FuzzySQL`, a form of the Structured Query Language using fuzzy predicates; the use of composite truth rankings, the role of hedges in fuzzy queries, the methods for implementing fuzzy join operations, and the design of a fuzzy secondary indexing scheme.

Chapter 4. Covers the concept of generating a fuzzy system from the data itself. Using a technique developed by Li Xi Wang and Jerry Mendel based on the work of Kosko and Specht, we see how a set of input and output data elements are used to automatically decompose variables, or database columns, into multiple fuzzy regions, discover the rule relationships, and finally produce a working Fuzzy Associative Memory.

Chapter 5. Explores the use of fuzzy logic in complex business decisions where the constraints of the problem often involve multiple, dynamic constraints and the knowledge is partitioned among multiple experts. We look at the ways in which objective ranking and weighting can lead to solutions among many alternatives. This chapter also addresses the ways in which multiple fuzzy systems can be combined.

Chapter 6. Concerns both adaptive and feed-back fuzzy systems. We look at such models as Just-in-Time inventory systems and organizational dynamic models of work effectiveness and supervision. Using the concept of the Fuzzy Cognitive Map (FCM) we also look at adaptive, multi-state fuzzy systems that are in and out of equilibrium.

Chapter 7. This concludes the main theme of the book with a discussion on the nature of fuzzy models, the planning and organization of fuzzy projects (with application to any business project involving advanced technologies), and a look at the inherent problems with fuzzy systems.

Chapter 8. Contains the full listings of all the demonstration and application code used in the book.

Appendices. Contains a review of the basic operations in fuzzy set theory, a guide to available fuzzy logic modelling software, a mathematical treatment of the Standard Additive Model by Bart Kosko, a glossary of terms, and a bibliography.

Fuzzy Models and Application Examples

This book contains many real-world fuzzy models drawn from a diverse range of industries and businesses. I have attempted to remain faithful to the actual design and implementation constraints associated with the fuzzy systems but, in some cases, for reasons of simplicity, space, confidentiality, and protection of a client's trade secrets or the intellectual property rights some case example details have been omitted or altered. A few of the more detailed applications and page numbers in this book include:

Because fuzzy systems draw on a variety of different technologies and, in fact, use various kinds of fuzzy reasoning within the same modelling infrastructure (such as fuzzy database queries and fuzzy rule discovery and knowledge mining) the application descriptions often encompass much more than the topic of a particular chapter or section. In this way I have tried to place the model design and operation "in perspective." Thus, as an example, the Portfolio Suitability and Safety Advisor, which appears in the chapter on rule discovery and knowledge mining, covers a wider ranging discussion of the system architecture, the organization and use of policies, as well as the task dispatching and communication protocol established through a blackboard control facility.

Using and Exploiting the C++ Code Libraries

Chapter 8 contains the source listing of all the programs, and the machine readable form of this code is also available on the accompanying diskette. In addition to the source code for the application examples, the diskette also contains a set of object libraries that must be compiled with these programs. These object libraries contain the fuzzy logic, fuzzy system modelling, and utility programs that were included in source code form with *The Fuzzy System Handbook*. All of the demonstration and application programs in this book have been compiled under the Microsoft Visual C++ 1.5 Professional compiler, but with some few exceptions (see the `readme.1st` file on the diskette) should compile on any standard C++ compiler that can produce a DOS ".exe" file. The programs are targeted to run under DOS and they use the basic C input/output routines (*printf* and *fprintf*). No compilation guidance is included with this book except that all programs should be compiled with the `LARGE` memory model. In order to create executable files from the enclosed programs you should be an experienced C/C++ programmer and understand the project and memory management options in your compiler system. Additionally, these programs are provided as examples only, and they may or may not be suitable for any particular business, scientific, or engineering purpose.

Analysts and programmers familiar with the C++ language will find the enclosed program code much closer to standard C. This is intentional. I have attempted to provide application systems that are accessible by a wide audience. While C++ is emerging as the language of choice in the design and development of complex systems, the exclusive use of C++ could have unnecessarily restricted the book's audience. The C++ components of the code rests primarily in the nature of comments (//) and in the use of the **new** and **delete** operators to allocate and release memory.

Fuzzy Set Graphics and Output Listings

Many of the applications and demonstration programs in this book display fuzzy sets both as part of the basic vocabulary and as dynamic sets created or manipulated during model execution. I have elected to display these fuzzy sets in the character-based graphics used by the software. These graphs appear in the following format:

```
PROFIT.LOSS
Domain [UofD]:      -500.00 to     500.00
     1.00..              *     .     *      .      *        ..
     0.90 ...               *  *          .    .      * *          ...
     0.80  ..            .     *       .   * *      *        ..
     0.70    .          *       .          .      *          .
     0.60      .          *.            .          *.          .
     0.50      .          *          .          *          .
     0.40
     0.30        .          *.        .          *.          .
     0.20        .. *                .        .        *. ..
     0.10            ..     .   *      .          *  .        .
     0.00.............................................*************
         0---|---|---|---|---|---|---|---|---|---|---|---|---|---|---0
       -500.00 -375.00 -250.00 -125.00    0.00  125.00 250.00 375.00 500.00
       .   FuzzySet:     BIG.LOSS
           Support :      -500.00,     -350.00,    -200.00
       *   FuzzySet:     MODERATE.LOSS
           Support :      -200.00,      100.00
       .   FuzzySet:     SMALL.LOSS
           Support :      -100.00,      100.00
       *   FuzzySet:     BREAK.EVEN
           Support :         0.00,       50.00
       .   FuzzySet:     SMALL.GAIN
           Support :       100.00,      100.00
       *   FuzzySet:     MODERATE.GAIN
           Support :       200.00,      100.00
       .   FuzzySet:     BIG.GAIN
           Support :       200.00,      350.00,     500.00
```

The fuzzy sets are drawn alternating with a dot (.) and as asterisk (*). The fuzzy set names appear below the graph and are read from left to right. The name of the owning variable (if any) appears at the top left of the graph, followed by the actual Universe of Discourse for the variable. The domain of each fuzzy set is drawn from this universe.

The actual output from many of the demonstration and application programs also appears in this book. This is printed in a special monotype print (Letter Gothic) in small, seven point type. The following is an example, from the chapter on fuzzy database operations, of how computer output appears,

```
FuzzySQL Database Processor
---------------------------
AlphaCut Threshold    : .1
AND operator Type     : AVERAGE
select company
  from MfgDBMS
  where:
Company Age is       : somewhat RECENT
----Applying the hedge 'somewhat'
Annual Revenues are : very MODERATE
----Applying the hedge 'very'
Product Count is     : //
Employee Count is    : //
Profit or Loss is    : //
Retained EPS is      : //
Ranking   15 Rows.
Ranking Complete.
```

In some instances I have modified the actual output to remove clutter, highlight some important points, reorganize the output sequence, or to economize on space. This means, of course, in some cases your output from the demonstration and application programs may be slightly different from the output that appears in the book (also refer to "Fuzzy Models and Application Examples" on page 28.)

Icons and Sidebar Topics

In *The Fuzzy Systems Handbook* and also in this book, I have adopted a uniform convention for presenting material that is tangential to the main topic of the current section. These comments, warnings, cross-references, and philosophical wanderings appear in a series of sidebars. Each topic is set off from the main text and is introduced by a specific icon.

Code Discussion and Cross-reference. The diskette icon indicates this section deals with code models, programs, and software in general. This icon usually means that a concept discussion is being tied back to the actual supporting code in one or more of the libraries.

System Internals. The plumbing icon indicates this section discusses system internals. System internals refer to the data structures, control blocks, interprogram linkages, process flow, and other details associated with the way fuzzy modeling systems work.

Key Topics. A key icon indicates a detailed discussion on some important aspect of the system. The nature of key topics covers a broad spectrum from hints and techniques that may not be obvious to detailed and off-line explorations of concepts and philosophies.

System Construction. The hammer icon represents discussions centered around the construction of models, applications, and high-level software systems.This topic is not specifically concerned with function code or data structures.

Practical Hints and Techniques. The wingnut ("nuts and bolts") icon indicates a discussion about the practical considerations of the current topic. This includes programming techniques, system design considerations, and methodology approaches.

Mathematical Topics. The ruler icon indicates a discussion of mathematical, logical, or algorithmic topics. This includes the underlying mathematics of fuzzy set theory, technical computer algorithms, topics in stability and verification, as well as discussions of performance metrics. The icon is only used for detailed discussed outside the main manual text.

Danger! Warning! The lightning bolt icon indicates a topic that could be potentially dangerous to model integrity, validation, or data. The danger icon is also used to highlight harmful side effects that are not obvious. You should read every danger topic carefully.

Important Point. The pointed finger is used to draw attention to an important comment related to the text. This is the most common sidebar icon and often takes the place of a discussion that would otherwise be placed in a footnote or chapter endnote.

Reminders and Warnings. The reminder icon indicates a discussion of important, but generally not obvious, points that the user must consider when exploiting some portion of the fuzzy modeling technology.

Special Symbols

The following symbols are used throughout this book in mathematical and logical expressions and equations.

Symbol	Use
~	set NOT (also complement or inversion)
$\cap$	set AND (also intersection operator)
$\cup$	set OR (also union operator)
$\aleph$	higher-dimensional fuzzy space
[x,x,x]	indicates a fuzzy membership value
$\in$	member of a set (general membership)
poss(x)	the possibility of event x
prob(x)	the probability of event x
{x}	crisp or Boolean membership function
•	dyadic operator
$\xi(x)$	The expected value of a fuzzy region
μ	fuzzy membership function
$\propto$	proportionality
$\mu[x]$	membership or truth function in fuzzy set
$\Re$	element from domain of fuzzy set
$\otimes$	Cartesian product or space
$\varnothing$	empty or null set
$\supset$	implication
$\wedge$	logical AND
$\vee$	logical OR
Σ	summation

About this Book

This book was composed and produced on a Power Macintosh 8100/80AV using Frame Technologies's FrameMaker 4.0. The text was formatted in Times Roman and Stone fonts, with Symbol font used for the mathematical and logical elements, and Letter Gothic used for the code and program output. The drawings and figures were produced with Aldus SuperPaint. The formal charts and graphs were produced by Microsoft Excel.

Contacting the Author

If you would like to send comments on this book, error notices, or recommendations, I can be reached through both Compuserve and directly via the internet at the following addresses:

Compuserve   `72700.2615@compuserve.com`
Internet   `ecox@paltech.com`

The Metus Systems Group maintains a World Wide Web page on fuzzy systems and computational intelligence. Metus also manages an anonymous FTP site for abstracts, shared software, and technical publications. You can access the Web page through the following URL address:

`http://www.paltech.com/metus/metus.htm`

The Web page provides a subscription service for businesses and consultants involved in building operational fuzzy, neural, and genetic systems in information technology. This page also provides access to a quarterly newsletter on the applications of fuzzy systems to business.

Introduction

. . . γηρασκω δ' αιει πολλα διδασκομενος
. . . I grow old ever learning many things.

Poetae Lyrici Graeci,
Solon, 18
(c. 640–c. 558 B.C.)

Fuzzy logic has emerged as a powerful tool in process engineering where its ability to model highly nonlinear problems (such as the double-stage inverted pendulum and the truck backer-upper problem) with a minimum of micro-control code makes it an important technology. Yet process engineering is simply the tip of the iceberg in the application of fuzzy logic. The real benefits and power of fuzzy logic, in the form or a broader representation known as approximate reasoning, lie in the domain of information technology—the design of highly intelligent and adaptive knowledge-based systems. Few managers, analysts, and knowledge engineers recognize the benefits of fuzzy logic in solving a wide spectrum of difficult, computationally complex, and semantically imprecise problems.

Artificial Intelligence and Fuzzy Models

The terms *artificial intelligence*, *AI*, and, in particular, *expert system* have fallen out of favor in the business community. Over the past few years project after project has failed to build and deliver systems that live up to the expectations of both the end user and senior management. In fact, among consultants in the field, the phrase "expectation management" has become all too common. Part of this decline in the fortunes of expert systems can, indeed, be attributed to over-optimistic expectations brought on by the somewhat romantic name of Artificial Intelligence. Part of the problem lies with the tools used to construct these new intelligent systems.

35

Managers today are in a frenetic search for the silver bullet. They are aided and supported by an increasingly vast cadre of unemployed chief executives and management professors from the leading business schools (with their fresh insights untainted by actual work experience) following along with the latest clever buzzwords in illuminating tomes with titles like *Thriving in the Ninth Chaotic Virtual Discipline of the Systematically Reengineered Intrapreneurial Organization.*

What is this silver bullet? It's the magical way to regain productivity and technological preeminence without pain. Yet, in today's transitional society businesses are moving from a goods and services to a knowledge-producing organization. Old fashioned leadership has fallen out of favor and reliance on people is being replaced with reliance on size and structure. No simple solution can guide a senior executive painlessly through this maze of neologisms into a solid and achievable plan for strategic growth. At the core of every corporation planning to compete in the next century lies a process of integrating the corporation's architectural knowledge, its proprietary processes, and the intellect of its technology officers and their staff with the fundamental and intuitive marketing skills of its executives. The emerging technology that provides the underlying tool for this fusion is the evolution of intelligent and adaptive system models.

In the future, even more than today, intelligence will be the key asset of the organization. While knowledge is power, intelligence is the ability to effectively use that power. And, of course, most business knowledge is perishable, that is, it is time dependent. If we cannot act on a piece of knowledge when we have proprietary use of that information, if we cannot leverage this knowledge with intelligence, if we cannot adequately assess the risk and confidence of the opportunity, then our position will be that of a follower rather than a leader. In this future, as the time between the acquisition of knowledge and its use becomes shorter and shorter, decision makers will rely heavily on machine intelligence.

True machine intelligence, in the form of models with great predictive strength under rapidly changing conditions, will be quite different from the conventional expert systems of today. These systems, coupled with the everyday availability of massively parallel computers, will employ a fusion of technologies such as fuzzy logic and cellular automata (often called *artificial life*) to make real-time simulations of highly complex non linear problems.

The Problem

> *If all you have is a hammer, everything looks like a nail.*
> —attributed, at various times, to Dionysis of Agapunta (fl. A.D. 300),
> Abraham Maslow, and Lotfi Zadeh

The expert system industry in the United States is in a severe state of disrepair. Analysts and knowledge engineers, frustrated with their inability to effectively model complex business applications, have been turning to other forms of knowledge representation and intelligence. This turning away has seen the rise of natural computing paradigms such as neural networks and genetic algorithms. Yet, for all their power and representational breadth, these technologies, in their turn, have often proven unsatisfactory. This resistance stems from the intrinsic complexity of such emergent intelligence systems. In these technologies the engineer must confront a wide array of highly complex and often mathematically intimidating parameters and structures the interplay of which can have significant implications for the performance of the model. Such difficult to articulate and deploy factors include the definition of satisfactory objective functions, the composite architecture of the system (neural layers, training algorithms, and mitosis and mutation rates), the mathematics associated with constructing reasonable and workable systems, the selection of suitable component structures (gnomes, neurons, connectivity webs, and so forth), the filtering and transformation of raw data, and the means of representing knowledge in the system.

Knowledge engineers planning the design of advanced expert and decision support systems are continuously faced with decisions about how to represent the problem. And how they represent the problem—how they construct their models—often determines whether or not they are successful. Choosing a representation scheme because it is the newest "hot" technology, enhances our own skill set, or because the supporting technology sits at the top of our current skill set is the usual way of selecting a modelling approach. Of these, only the last has any real merit.

But there is a deeper consideration that, as information systems scientists, we must address: What exactly do we know about representational modeling in today's complex world of object orientation, neural networks, rule-based systems, and fuzzy logic? Perhaps the reason behind the high prototype-to-production failure rate in our industry lies not in the tools but in our understanding of what the tools can and cannot do. It is a fact of life that many of us had our apprenticeships tied to specific commercial packages and vendor training courses. Our knowledge of client server models reflects this conditioning. We see the world in terms of forward or backward chaining problems, back propagation opportunities, or exemplars in a case-based repository.

Fuzzy Systems

Fuzzy systems, on the other hand, combine the high level flexibility and knowledge representation of conventional decision support and expert systems with the power and analytical depth of natural computing paradigms. Their proven ability as universal approximators coupled with their ability to handle complex, non linear, and often noisy systems with a minimum of rules makes them a powerful tool in the design and construction of the next generation of intelligent, information decision support systems. How these intrinsic features translate into bottom-line benefits for senior and middle managers, and how they translate into a significant technological edge for project managers, designers, analysts, and knowledge engineers is the topic of this chapter.

Fuzzy System Capabilities

The intrinsic benefits of fuzzy logic as a modeling technique can be summarized in three statements:

1. Reduced application development costs.
2. Reduced application execution costs.
3. Reduced application maintenance costs.

Since 60% to 80% of the software activities in most organizations are centered around maintenance, this last benefit is very important. These benefits cover a variety of sins and there is no clear demarcation between the development and the maintenance benefits. In general, when compared to conventional expert and decision support systems, fuzzy logic models have the following properties. Fuzzy models:

- Are easier to build.
- Are easier to understand.
- Are easier to verify, validate, and tune.
- Are more intrinsically stable.
- Are more resilient and robust. They work well with missing rules.
- Can approximate highly nonlinear problems.
- Can automatically measure their degree of "intelligence."
- Can be adaptive and self-organizing.
- Can be prototyped in significantly reduced time.
- Can explain their behavior.
- Can handle uncertain, vague and imprecise information.
- Can incorporate knowledge from conflicting experts.
- Have a more powerful reasoning engine.
- Require fewer rules.

A fuzzy information model has significantly higher computational capabilities than corresponding symbolic expert systems due to its:

1. Parallel processing nature.
2. Ability to accumulate evidence for and against target propositions.
3. Ability to work at a high "set theoretic" level instead data element by data element.
4. Ability to deal with imprecise information with a high degree of precision.
5. Ability to produce results consistent with both the preponderance of evidence and the compatibility between data and the underlying rules.

Fuzzy models are much more compact, encode a higher degree of knowledge, usually execute faster, are less prone to error, work well with missing decision points, and can be maintained much more easily. On the whole, these benefits mean:

- Less experienced knowledge engineers can build more complex models.
- Less time is needed to extract intelligence from experts.
- Less time is required to design and prototype the model.
- Less time is required to find and repair errors.
- Less time is used to code and extend the mode capabilities.
- Less time is needed to verify and fine tune the model.

The benefits of fuzzy models mean, in general, that more models can be maintained with a smaller high-technology staff, more extensive capabilities exist for improving model performance, better, more natural knowledge representations are available, an enhanced capability exists for encoding common sense into the model, and a better, visual understanding of the model properties is usually available.

Reduced Cognitive Dissonance

Cognitive dissonance is the difference between the way an expert visualizes or expresses a problem and its solution and the way it is coded in the expert/decision support system. A fuzzy model dramatically reduces this difference by encoding knowledge at a much higher level. The encoding is done very close to the equivalent English language expression. Cognitive dissonance is built into conventional decision/expert systems in two ways:

1. State transitions in a model must be expressed in crisp variables so the division is often arbitrary and not in accordance with the true semantic meaning of the state.
2. In conventional models, complex problem states must be decomposed into many different rules that state the predicates and actions for each combination of problem states.

We can see this in a simple financial analyst's statement of how profitability is related to other factors:

When price is high but demand is low, and quantity-on-hand is excessive, then profitability will be correspondingly reduced.

This can be expressed in the following fuzzy rule almost exactly as stated:

if price is high
    and demand is low
    and quantity-on-hand is excessive
      then profitability is severely reduced.

where *high, low, excessive,* and *severely reduced* are fuzzy sets. However, in a conventional model the problem states associated with *high, low, excessive,* and *reduced* must be expressed as mathematically precise expressions or relationals. Thus, one formulation of the rule might be:

if price > 25.00
    and demand < 1200
    and quantity-on-hand > 4200
      then profitability=
        profitability-(QOH*unitprice)

Now this looks like a fairly straight-forward conversion between the imprecise statement of the expert and the crisp expression in conventional systems. But appearances are deceiving. The fuzzy rule is much more expressive and powerful than the crisp rule since the value of profitability is proportionally[1] adjusted according to the various truth states of the three antecedent propositions. This is because, unlike conventional systems, the truth of the action is related to the truth of the antecedent as a function of the fuzzy sets. In a conventional rule the antecedent is either true or false, thus the action (the value of profitability) is either equal to the assignment statement or no assignment is done!

If price is only slightly high then profitability is only slightly reduced. This behavior is not present in the conventional rule. In fact, we would have to introduce many, many conventional rules to encapsulate the behavior of a single fuzzy rule. As we add these conventionally crisp rules, the distance between what the expert said and what the model encodes becomes greater and greater. At some point, usually very soon, the mapping between the visualization of the expert and the logic of the model becomes disjointed and difficult to follow. The degree to which this mapping is altered determines how well the model reflects the expert's actual problem statement and solution.

Use of Multiple Conflicting, Cooperating, and Collaborating Experts

A common assumption in nearly all expert systems (at least those that appear in the literature) is there is a single expert or the underlying experts are all in close agreement. In the real world this is hardly ever the case for anything except toy problems. Since a conventional model can only partition its solution space into true or false, this creates signifi-

---

1. This does not mean linear proportionality, of course. In fact, the truth transfer function in approximate reasoning provides a facility to describe arbitrarily complex, non linear relationships between the fuzzy antecedent spaces and the fuzzy consequent (output) spaces.

cant difficulties when the problem and solution states have fuzzy properties. And many, if not most, real world problems certainly have fuzzy characteristics. This is most evident where we have conflicting experts. Conventional expert and decision support systems are unable to handle directly opposing views. As an example, consider the rules:

> *the product.price must be low*
> *the product.price must be high*

In all conventional systems a statement can not be both true and false (this is Aristotle's *Law of Non-Contradiction* and the *Law of the Excluded Middle*.) The above rule is like saying:

> *product.price = 0*
> *product.price = 36*

Most people would say this is nonsense since the price cannot be both zero and 36 at the same time. Yet in the real world, when we are developing a new product pricing model, the marketing and sales manager may say the price should be low to gain market share, while the finance manager might say the price should be high to cover costs and accelerate the pay back. This inability to be in two (or more) states at the same time is due to the Boolean nature of conventional systems. In a fuzzy model, with its partial degrees of membership, the statement: *the product.price must be low* has a degree of truth x, while the statement the *product.price must be high* has another degree of truth y. In general the separate degrees of truth for all concurrent states must equal the total possibility for finding the model in all the states (that is [1]). This is the specific requirement of a two state machine. Equation 1.1 shows the more general requirement for an array of x data points mapped into P fuzzy regions.

$$\sum_{n=0}^{P} \mu_n[x] \equiv 1$$

Equation 1.1 The Sum of Fuzzy Possibility States

In this way a fuzzy model can accommodate the differing points of view from many experts. These are combined to produce the over-all model recommendation. As an example the following are rules from an actual product pricing model:

> *the product.price must be high*
> *the product.price must be low*
> *the product.price be around 2*mfgCosts*
> *if the competition.price is not very high*
>   *then the product.price*
>   *must be near the competition.price*

Why does this work? Because in a fuzzy model all of the rules are effectively run in parallel and fuzzy rules are not absolute. The affect of running rules in parallel is the final result depends on the combined output from each individual rule. However, since fuzzy rules do not indicate absolutes, this final output reflects the melding of knowledge from each expert. In essence, fuzzy rules accumulate evidence. Each rule enters into evidence a set of facts with varying degrees of truth. Although the process of aggregating this evidence is not done by simple addition, the net effect is to weight clusters of evidence based on the truth associated with the rule and the expertise franchise or ranking of the expert.

Improved Knowledge Representation

In conventional expert systems nearly all the knowledge is encoded in the rules. These are executed serially. Each rule acquires knowledge until either some goal has been determined (in backward chaining) or no more rules can execute (in forward chaining.)

In a fuzzy reasoning system, however, the knowledge is embedded in several representations: rules, fuzzy sets, hedges and the methods of implication and defuzzification. Rules take data elements and find their memberships in fuzzy sets (a rule can also create a fuzzy set if necessary). The shape, density, and overlap of the fuzzy sets indicates the semantics of the model data spaces. Hedges intensify, dilute, and otherwise dynamically modify the shape of a fuzzy set. In any event, this distribution of knowledge across a set of inter dependent and inter related structures allows a designer to construct a much more flexible, powerful, and extensible model infrastructure. Models can be more finely tuned, represent a wider variety of fundamental data types, be in a greater number of problem states, and handle a more effective collection of goals.

Improved and More Powerful Uncertainty Calculus

Traditional expert and decision support system usually rely on one of two uncertainty management schemes: subjective probability in the form of Bayes Theorem or some form of confidence factors. Bayes Theorem suffers from two fundamental weaknesses. First, the total probability state of the model is organized in terms of the odds for an event. Once the odds for an event is known the event space is partitioned along crisp lines. The overlapping idea of partial membership states is not supported. And second, probabilities are not the same as possibilities. Confidence factors also suffer from their general ad-hoc nature. In both cases, probabilities and confidence factors are external to the model logic. In a fuzzy model the uncertainty measurement is an intrinsic component of the reasoning engine. As a specific example, the following rule with its certainty factor, *if height > 6.0 then weight = height*3 with CF=.75* says nothing about the relationship between height and weight. The certainty factor is "tacked" on to the consequent assignment. In a fuzzy model, the degree of confidence is generated by the inference process.

Reduced Rule Set

Since fuzzy models are parallel processors, the knowledge-handling activities in the rules are4343 done at a set theoretic level. Rules combine fuzzy states to produce a composite output fuzzy state. Each rule contributes evidence to the final solution. As a result, the Cartesian Product of all of the states is evaluated at once. This has the affect of drastically reducing the number of rules needed to represent a given model state[2]. When rules are reduced, model comprehension is improved, mean-time-to-repair (referred to as MTTR) to reduced, mean-time-between-failure (referred to as MTBF) is increased, model maintenance is improved, and model extensibility is increased with less risk in introducing new faults.

More Robust Models

Model robustness is tied to the corresponding engineering term. A robust model is one with predictable and stable behaviors. A value of x+n as input consistently yields y+m as output. As **n** changes, **m** also changes. This is a steady and predictable relationship but not necessarily a linear relationship (See "Modeling of Highly Complex, Nonlinear Problems" on page 44.) Many large expert and decision support systems are not robust due to the large number of rules and the rather "ad-hoc" nature of how rules are executed. In most cases, the number of rules in a fuzzy system are significantly and profoundly smaller than the number of rules in a conventional system for the same problem (large, complex systems may need to be decomposed into smaller packages called policies to handle the growth of fuzzy rules. See "Modelling Systems with Large Numbers of Input and Output Variables" on page 56.) This means the model flow state is more accurately predicted. We can understand its behavior in terms of the standard input-process-output model. Consequently, we can build models with predictable and stable robustness. Such robustness means that fuzzy models lend themselves to easier validation and verification. We can place much more confidence in a fuzzy model because we know its operating characteristics and can predict its long term behavior. That is, we can assure ourselves that the model is reliable.

More Intelligent Models

Fuzzy models not only handle uncertainty, possibilities, usualities, and frequencies better than conventional models, but they provide the model builder with performance measurement tools that insure the model is operating intelligently. This built-in metric is called the *compatibility index* and measures the degree to which the model data, the rule system, and the fuzzy sets are in agreement. A very low or a very high compatibility index means the model data lies at the extreme edges of the fuzzy sets or at the maximal point of

---

2. Assuming the problem states are fuzzy. A fuzzy model applied to Boolean or discrete value variables collapses to a crisp or first order predicate representation. No saving in rule depth is then realized.

the fuzzy sets. In either case, it indicates the fuzzy model is assuming binary properties and not properly evaluating the data.

Reduced Development and Validation Times

Due to all of these previously discussed properties, fuzzy models can be constructed in much less time, with fewer rules, and with less time devoted to testing and validation than conventional expert and decision support systems. The protocycling time for fuzzy models is often 20% or less that of conventional systems. Significantly reduced development time is reflected in two ways: through the ability to deliver working systems to end users in less time and through the ability to deliver more sophisticated and complex systems with a generally fewer staff involvement.

Modeling of Highly Complex, Nonlinear Problems

Nonlinearity is a property of complexity. In a linear system the model behavior is proportional to the initialization constraints. In a nonlinear model, the behavior of the model can vary drastically given even very minor changes in initialization values. Nonlinear system are related to fractals and chaos theory through their natural complexity and self-referential (feed-back) architecture. Many business problems involve nonlinear, time-dependent and stochastic (apparently random) relationships. These include market predictions, portfolio asset allocations, econometric modelling, inventory control, production scheduling, transportation route planning, container loading, corporate stability analysis, and so forth. Since fuzzy systems are universal approximators they can model any continuous function, both linear and nonlinear. The intrinsic nonlinearity of many outwardly simple business problems has lead to the general failure of conventional expert systems. They cannot "scale up" to highly complex, adaptive, and feed-back type systems. Fuzzy models break this complexity barrier by directly representing such systems in terms of their behavior rather than their mathematical equations.

Limitations of Fuzzy System Models

Fuzzy systems are not a panacea for the problems encountered in the real world of information and process modeling. They have limitations and representational constraints that make them difficult to use in some situations. Further, some developers, unfamiliar with fuzzy logic, believe this technology is a way of handling missing data or a way of calculating confidences from arbitrarily noisy or missing data. We now look at some of the limitations found in fuzzy models. In discussing limitations, we will also examine some of the more suitable applications of fuzzy logic in related areas.

Linear Systems with a Well-Understood Mathematical Model

We start with a limitation that is often *not* a limitation. Fuzzy systems are heuristic by nature. That is, they represent the intelligence of an expert in approximating some process. When this process is a well behaved, well understood linear function that can be described mathematically, the use of fuzzy logic or any other expert system technology is often more expensive and less precise. Knowing for example that a time-dependent function follows the mathematical function:

$$x(t) = a + mB(t - 1)$$

we can write a simple and straight forward mathematical model that solves x(t) for each of the independent variables. A fuzzy rule-based model that represented the same process may be more difficult to construct and more difficult to maintain. Thus, for linear systems of modest complexity, for which we can write (or discover) a mathematical model, fuzzy systems are a "second best" solution. There are however, some considerations in deciding when to apply fuzzy logic to such systems. (As you might suspect, the point at which fuzzy logic begins to offer a payback is somewhat fuzzy.) A few of the important points to consider in using a fuzzy model where a mathematical model is known include the following.

The Model Involves Fuzzy Variables

A surprising number of models in economics, finance, urban planning, manufacturing, sales, and transportation involve fuzzy variables. Model designers, unaccustomed to using approximate variables, write their models using traditional mathematical techniques. As an example, in a capital budgeting model we might find a statement like the following:

> *if CashOnHand < MinimalReserves do*
> *   Dept=Debt(t-1)+MininalReserves-CashOnHand*
> *   CashOnHand=MinimalReserves*
> *enddo*

Indicating that, if cash balances (CashOnHand) fall below the minimum capital reserve level (MinimalReserves), the corporation's credit line (Debt) is automatically increased by the amount of the shortfall. This is from an actual capital budgeting system used in urban redevelopment. In any real-world model that is tolerant to changes in corporate economics, we would like to increase or trigger actions as our cash reserves fall. As an example, we might restate the control part of this rule as:

> *if CashOnHand is quite LOW do...*

Waiting until a variable's value reaches some threshold is a reactionary process. In models using crisp variables, we are often forced to raise the threshold ("buffer" the process) so actions are triggered well before the actual level would be recognized by the human expert. In a fuzzy model, we can track such dynamic process and invoke model actions based on the degree to which a variable is in some state.

The Model May Use Noisy or Imprecise Data

Some seemingly simple linear models have, on closer examination, a data space that involves imprecise information. That is, they use fuzzy data. Due to the constraints of conventional computer languages and expert systems, imprecise data is often grouped into precise sets and thus this condition often goes unrecognized. As an example, a criminal identification system receives such factors as the suspect's age, weight and height. A conventional system receives crisp values and searches for suspects that match these factors. As an example, an identification session might appear as:

```
ENTER THE FOLLOWING:
SEX:      MALE
AGE:        45
WEIGHT:    180
HEIGHT:    6.2
```

In such a conventional model, the value for AGE is used to screen the database for suspects that fall within a specified range around the specified value. The range of values might be 45±10 so we can select individuals within the inclusive age spectrum of 35 to 55. Figure 1.1 shows how this set of values exists in the conventional system.

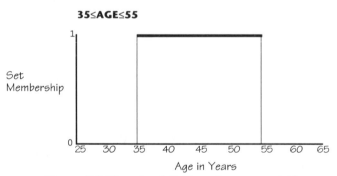

Figure 1.1 The crisp definition of age around 45

With this approach, a typical file-screening system is used to loop through the suspects table in the criminal records database. A partial set of commands for this process might appear as:

foreach suspect where sex="MALE";
candidate=0;
if suspect.age >=(AGE-10) or suspect.age =< (AGE+10) then candidate++;
•
•

In fact, the age of the suspect is not actually a numeric value, but a conceptual framework defined by a a series of fuzzy sets, such as: YOUNG, MIDDLE AGED, OLD. Following this logic, we would like to respond to the suspect screening system using these semantic categories,

```
ENTER THE FOLLOWING:
SEX:      MALE
AGE:      MIDDLEAGED
WEIGHT:   HEAVY
HEIGHT:   TALL
```

In this approach we replace crisp values with the names of fuzzy sets. Each fuzzy set defines the range of values for the concept as well as the degree of membership for any suspect characteristic value. Figure 1.2 shows how the fuzzy set for MIDDLE AGED is defined.

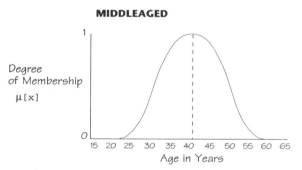

Figure 1.2 The fuzzy definition of middle aged

With this approach, we can use a file screening system to loop through the suspects table in the criminal records database. For each suspect record selected, the database value is mapped against the specified fuzzy set. The truth of this mapping (its compatibility with the fuzzy set) is saved and used to give a composite value for how well this suspect matches the complete fuzzy description. A partial set of commands for this process might appear as:

```
foreach suspect where sex="MALE";
candidate=0;
if suspect.age is MIDDLEDAGED then do
    candidate++
    membership[candidate]=truth
enddo
```

- •
- •

The prototype criminal identification system is typical of many systems that accept crisp input data but are actually processing fuzzy variables. Models in econometrics, marketing, sales forecasting, manufacturing, inventory control, urban planning, and so forth typically process imprecise variables. In these cases, even where the behavior of the system is well understood (and even routine), the use of fuzzy logic can provide a significant increase in intelligence and flexibility.

The Model Will Be Revised Regularly

If the model is subject to regular revisions due to such factors as regulatory changes, operating policy shifts, economic sensitivity, mergers and acquisitions, international monetary fluctuations, or if a base version of the model is shipped into significantly different geographic areas where the model performance is influenced by environmental factors (temperature, vibration, dust, wind, and so forth) then the robustness, ease of maintenance, and fault tolerance of fuzzy systems may provide a better alternative to "hard coding" the model as a mathematical or conventionally crisp system. In these cases, the extra work necessary to develop and deploy a fuzzy model is offset by the mean time to repair or mean time to revise profile of the rule-based system.

The Model Benefits from an Explanatory Facility

A fuzzy system, like most expert systems, provides an audit capability tracing its decision making process. This audit trail provides a mechanism for explaining its reasoning. An explanatory facility enables the end user to find out how the system came to its conclusions. This is important if the system recommendation is unexpected (such as a portfolio mix advisor recommending 5000 shares of an unknown, declining stock.) For some systems, especially those that make recommendations involving large cash movements, affect the welfare of human beings, or can significantly increase the risk of a planned enterprise, the explanatory facility out weights any other considerations of performance, development costs, and maintainability.

The Model Designer Is not Available for Maintenance

Even if a well behaved linear model exists, the choice of its representation can be influenced by the availability of the original knowledge engineers, developers, and documentalists. For models of even modest complexity, a rule based fuzzy system is usually easier to understand, maintain, and enhance than a corresponding system written as a mathematical model or as a conventional program module. When the system must be maintained by either the end user or by a technical staff that was not initially responsible for the model, a fuzzy rule based system can be understood more easily than most conventional systems (including programming as well as other expert system languages.)

Natural Language Processing

Much attention has been directed toward the use of fuzzy logic in natural language processing as well as database queries to reduce or eliminate semantic ambiguity. While, at first, this seems a natural application of fuzzy logic, given the inherent ambiguity of language, fuzzy logic is of little use in this area. Unlike the ambiguity associated with the numeric domain of continuous model variables, the ambiguity of language is noncomputational. Take the natural language database query:

How many bakers are in marketing?

Does the word "bakers" refer to an individual's last name or an occupation? Does "in marketing" refer to the marketing department or to a job description (such as a product manager that is also performing product marketing) or to a special marketing assignment? This ambiguity can be resolved through an analysis of the sentence structure if the word "baker" begins with a capital, the parser might take this as a hint that the object refers to a name) through context (marketing might be interpreted as a department if previous queries dealt with departments or marketing is not in the personnel database's skill set), or from special knowledge about the query domain. And, while there is a high degree of ambiguity in natural languages, this ambiguity is not necessarily fuzzy in the approximate reasoning sense. We can ask ourselves, what is the fuzzy set that underlies the baker-as-name versus baker-as-skill ambiguity? The answer is: none. This kind of ambiguity is not quantifiable as a computational set.

Textual and Bibliographic Searches

There *are* ways in which fuzzy logic can be of considerable help in database and natural language querying systems. This has to do with relevance sets and frequency counts. In constructing Keyword In Context (KWIC) indices for terms in large lexicographic and textual databases, we can assign these terms to fuzzy sets depending on how well they map to various concepts. An extended fuzzy SQL request that accesses the relevance descriptors in a cancer research database might appear as:

select oncology.studies
where relevence(interferon) is high
and relevence(clinical.studies) is moderate

This type of query processing is often called *meta-analysis*, meaning we are reasoning about the material rather than with the contents of the material. Meta-analysis requires that the system designers extract and organize information describing the contents and the structure of the documents. As an simple example, in a medical bibliographic database, a fuzzy SQL statement such as:

rank drug.interdiction.studies
where count(&id.citations) are large
and date is recent
and count(kwic(heroin)) is frequent

chooses studies that have a large number of citations in other database articles (this measures the importance or significance of the article), that were published in the recent past, (this insures the article is still relevant; a highly cited article from 20 years ago might not be valid today) and where the keyword *heroin* appears frequently.

Keyword and Content Searches

Fuzzy logic can improve but not markedly revolutionize the way conventional text engines search databases. The most common methods of searching large textual databases combine the concepts of keyword in context, keyword proximity analysis, and phonetic recognition. Search engines that use keyword and proximity techniques can benefit from fuzzy logic through the concept of distance mapping. In most engines, the distance between related terms is specified, such as:

find FUZZY + LOGIC within 1

This means find the term "fuzzy" followed by "logic" within one word of the predicate ("fuzzy"). The search mechanism generally provides a scope of search, say within n words, within the same sentence or within the same paragraph. Fuzzy logic replaces the distance metric with a fuzzy or approximate metric. Figure 1.3 illustrates how the idea of word proximity can be expressed as a set of fuzzy sets over the variable PROXIMITY.

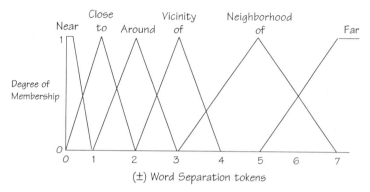

Figure 1.3 Fuzzy proximity measures

These fuzzy sets provide the foundation for a more flexible and more easily understood search engine. From this base of vocabulary terms we can use text search criteria like:

find LOGIC near FUZZY
find LOGIC close to FUZZY
find LOGIC close to OR around FUZZY

The use of fuzzy qualifiers in keyword proximity searches also enhances our ability to move the search into different contextual frameworks where the acceptable or mandatory distance between words is different. By changing the definition of *near, close to,* and other fuzzy sets we can accommodate changes in the search requirement while preserving the linguistic nature of the search system itself. Once again, however, we are not resolving any ambiguity or imprecision in the meaning of the text or the definition of the keywords. We are simply addressing the ambiguity and imprecision associated with the user's meaning of the search space itself (what do we mean by *near, close to, far from,* and so forth.)

Phonetic Recognition and Fuzzy Logic

Using fuzzy logic to find similar or related keywords is not generally a fuzzy mechanism, although, in the common meaning of the word fuzzy or imprecise, it often appears as an ideal candidate for fuzzy logic. The reason, once more, is tied to the idea of computational utility and the underlying mechanism at work in fuzzy reasoning. Generally, this attack on recognizing related terms (and, by analogy, related concepts) focuses on the idea of phonetic identification or similarity classes. The most popular method uses some form of the Soundex algorithm to convert words into a restricted set of codes (See "mttlpan.cpp (The Phonetic Analyzer)" on page 385.) This method is based on an algorithm that attempts to assign the same code to similar sounding names (or any arbitrary strings). The algorithm has the following general steps:

Remove all nonalphabetic characters
Remove all vowels
Convert all lower case letters to upper case letters
Remove frequently unvoiced consonants H and W
Change dipthongs and doubles to singles, such as:
    "X" to "Z" when first character
    "PH" to "F"
    "CH" to "G"
Save first letter of string
Replace all other letters with following numbers:

Labials	*B,F,P,V*	*1*
Gutterals,sibilants	*C,G,J,K,Q,S.X.Z*	*2*
Dentals	*D,T*	*3*
Long Liquids	*L*	*4*
Nasals	*M,N*	*5*
Short Liquids	*R*	*6*

Combine two or more identical digits
Concatenate first three digits of result to first letter of string

Since the Soundex algorithm maps words that sound alike into the same code, this method is used quite broadly in banking, insurance, and other financial services industries to find policies, financial instruments, and documents that have been misfiled due to irregular spellings in the client's name. As an example, Table 8.1 shows the soundex classification for a set of names.

Table 8.1 Phonetic (Soundex) Name Classifications

Name	Soundex
SMITH	S253
SMYTH	S253
SMOOT	S253
SCHNIEDER	S253
SCHIMMLER	S254
SAMSON	S252
SHAFFER	S216
SOREL	S264

But the Soundex code is a poor choice for use in fuzzy name searches. The lack of continuity between adjacent Soundex codes makes it difficult to apply fuzzy logic analysis to this kind of phonetic analysis. In fact, this adjacency distance is rather arbitrary and is not continuous. In Table 8.1 we can see that the step from SMITH with a soundex code of S253 to SAMSON with a soundex code of S252 is a single digit, but the phonetic space between the two source strings is quite large.

> We are restricting our discussion of fuzzy logic limitations in phonetic and proximity searches to techniques that are commonly available in the business community. Fuzzy logic has proven itself *very* adept at recognizing phonetic patterns (voices, songs, industrial noises, etc.) and has been used, as an example by *Infobased Systems, Inc.* in their proprietary real-time ScannTech™ methodology, to recognize songs played over commercial radio stations in a system that audits royalty payments.

Handling Missing Information.

There seems to be a common notion that fuzzy logic deals in imprecise information, where imprecision is based on gaps and holes in the underlying data. Fuzzy logic is not a clairvoyant technology. It has only limited abilities to handle data that is missing or incomplete. Without some mechanism to relate the missing data to a general description of the current context, fuzzy logic in and of itself is unable to make any reliable prediction about missing information.

Noisy (Uncertain) Instead of Missing Data

Certainly data that is noisy can be handled through the assumption that the data points are fuzzy numbers. Fuzzy numbers represent noise or uncertainty in the actual value of a data element (or a set of data points). The data are not missing, but are diffused around a central possible value. Figure 1.4 shows the underlying concepts associated with INCOME.

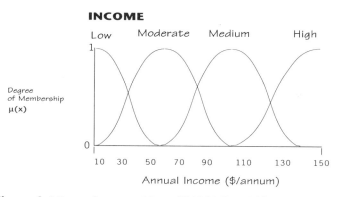

Figure 1.4 Fuzzy decomposition of INCOME variable

By evaluating where in the underlying domain of fuzzy sets the piece of noisey data lies, an estimate is made of its possible value. Figure 1.5 shows a fuzzy number representing an annual income. The number is uncertain due to such factors as the method of collection, the documentation support, the validity of the source, the age of the data, and so forth. The width of the fuzzy curve around the number defines the degree to which we are uncertain of this information. The narrower the bell curve, the lower its fuzziness, and consequently, the higher our belief the data represents a single number.

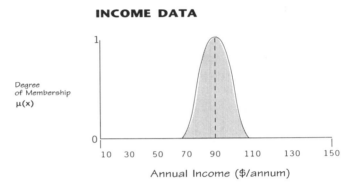

Figure 1.5 A noisy or fuzzy piece of income data

Resolving fuzzy data involves finding a fit between the underlying fuzzy regions of a variable and the maximum truth membership of the fuzzy data elements. Figure 1.6 illustrates how the noisy or fuzzy annual income around $90,000/year is converted to a precise value of $94,700/year with a confidence of [.93].

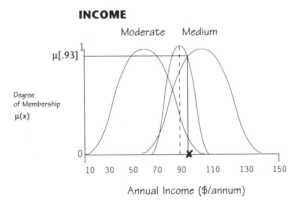

Figure 1.6 Finding the expected value of a fuzzy data point

In Figure 1.6 the fuzzy term set that has the maximum intersection value with the input data is used as the specifier. But the noise around the income value is sufficiently broad to intersect significantly with more than one fuzzy set. In this case, we can use a weighted averaging technique that balances the value between the several fuzzy term spaces. Equation 1.2 illustrates how this weighted mean of the intersecting fuzzy regions is calculated.

$$\bar{x}_w = \frac{\sum\limits_{i=1}^{n} x_i \cdot m_i}{\sum\limits_{i=1}^{n} m_i}$$

Equation 1.2 Weighted Average of Possible Fuzzy Values

Equation 1.3 shows how the precise value for an income data point is calculated using the weighted average of the MODERATE and MEDIUM fuzzy sets.

$$\bar{x}_w = \frac{94.7 \cdot [.93] + 82.3 \cdot [.80]}{[.93] + [.80]} = \frac{153.911}{1.73} = 88.96$$

Equation 1.3 The weight average for a fuzzy income data point

The weighted average moves the actual data point to the left, centering it between the two fuzzy term sets. The value is less than the central measure of the income fuzzy number, but seems to represent a good fit based on the degree of overlap with the income variable fuzzy sets. If the missing data falls within (below) the noise level of the data, then fuzzy logic can be used to compensate for missing elements. In general, however, other more conventional techniques should be used to project a data series across a gap in the data.

Missing and Unknown Data

Given clearly unknown reference points, fuzzy logic does little in assessing the possible domain space for a data point. While this seems obvious, it is often a criteria in selecting fuzzy logic as modelling approach. The following model objective was voiced by a manager in a large chemical manufacturing company.

> *How much of product X should we produce, given that we don't know our competition's plans, the seasonal market demand, or the cost of production?*

Although fuzzy qualifications provides a valuable extension to sensitivity or goal seeking analysis, it is not, of and by itself, a methodology for handling a complex set of unknowns. With sufficient historical information, a fuzzy model can, when combined with techniques for time series prediction, help discover the probable values for missing model parameters. Fuzzy Logic is concerned with expressing and using the uncertainty and imprecision associated with the description of a parameter, not with the absence of information about a parameter (as is often the case in such fields as tolerance analysis.)

Discovering Trends and Relationships

The close relationship between the modelling domains of fuzzy logic and neural networks has caused some confusion over the aims of these two technologies. Neural networks are modelless systems that learn from the underlying relationships of the data. Data elements in many neural network schemes can belong to more than one output class with differing degree of intensity in each class (equivalent to degrees of membership.) A fuzzy system operates on a wide spectrum of data having imprecise descriptive properties. The system designer specifies the data relationships through a set of rules that are run in parallel to accumulate evidence for or against a solution state. Although rule discovery techniques exist that can be used to generate a fuzzy system from the underlying data, such techniques are external to the operation of the fuzzy system whereas such self-organizing and self-tuning properties are an internal and intrinsic part of neural networks.

Modelling Systems with Large Numbers of Input and Output Variables

As a rule, fuzzy systems are sensitive to combinatorial explosions as the number of input and output variables grows beyond a reasonable number. This is a more-or-less direct reflection on the underlying complexity of the model itself. We should note the combinatorial problem is associated with the semantics of the model variables. A model of 10 variables with two underlying fuzzy sets (such as HIGH and LOW) has a low level of granularity and a corresponding low level of complexity. On the other hand a model of 10 variables with an average of eight fuzzy sets per variable has a relatively high level of granularity and a fairly high level of complexity. In simple fuzzy systems, the number of rules grows exponentially with the number of input and solution variables. In general, for a system with a behavior:

$$f : R^n \rightarrow R^p$$

where there are **k** fuzzy sets underlying the variables, it takes

$$k^{(n+p)-1}$$

rules to completely cover the surface of *f*. The exact number of rules depends on the nature of the function, the degree to which high level (low granularity) approximation is satisfactory, and the placement of rules in the function.

Control Engineering Systems

This type of combinatorial problem occurs most frequently in control applications where the fuzzy model must closely approximate (to the point of *representation*) a known or partially known function. We can overcome the combinatorial problem by carefully selecting the domain of our model and, if the function is sufficiently well understood, by modeling the surface with a minimum number of rules. Bart Kosko has shown that, for a well understood function, the optimal fuzzy rules cover the extrema of the function[3]. Figure 1.7 shows the idea behind this process.

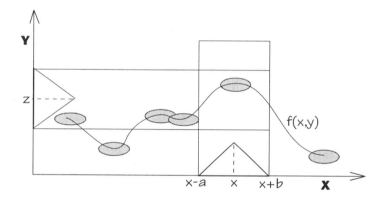

Figure 1.7 Patches covering the extrema of function f(x,y)

Fuzzy systems approximate a function by covering its surface with areas of fuzzy rules. The fuzzy rules describe the behavior of the function in these areas or, in Kosko's terms, *patches*. Where the patches overlap, we average them. For complex, highly nonlinear functions of higher dimensions, the number of patches necessary to cover the function graph grows exponentially. By concentrating the function representation at the points where the function changes, we can minimize the number of rules necessary to describe what we hope are the important behaviors of the function.

---

3. Kosko, Bart, Optimal Fuzzy Rules Cover Extrema, *International Journal of Intelligent Systems*, Vol 10. John Wiley & Sons, Inc. (1995)

Information and Business Systems

Business problems are not nearly as compact and clear as control problems. Nor are information decision models constructed and run in the same fashion as control models. Business systems are often built around goal focusing architectures where variables are acquired through traditional machine reasoning facilities such as backward and forward chaining. Fuzzy components are isolated in packages called *policies*. With the use of intermediate blackboard systems, and the functional decomposition of the model into a set of policies, business systems can handle very complex fuzzy systems.

Models Constrained by Regulations or Boolean Factors

When selecting and evaluating a project for fuzzy modeling, you should insure a fuzzy solution is not only feasible (doable within the processing capabilities of the system) but also acceptable. A fuzzy model for vehicle underwriting risk assessment was designed and built for a large insurance company. The knowledge engineering team spent a considerable amount of time with the underwriters, field agents, and policy managers to completely understand how the model would work. The current risk assessment model took nearly 180 rules in a conventional expert system. The fuzzy model, by translating these rules to fuzzy statements, required only 12 rules to derive the same answer. As an example, Figure 1.8 shows how the risk associated with a driver's age was encapsulated into a singe fuzzy set.

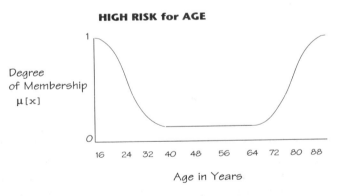

HIGH RISK for AGE

Figure 1.8 The high risk fuzzy set based on policy Holder's Age

The semantics of the fuzzy set show that perceived risk (from an underwriter's perspective) is very high for both very young and very old drivers. The risk is low (but not zero) for early to late middle aged drivers. Using this fuzzy set, one rule maps the correspondence between age and the risk in vehicle underwriting:

if age is HIGHRISK then PolicyRisk is INCREASED

Other rules in the risk assessment policy evaluated risk for distance to work, number of chargeable accidents in the past 2 years, number of moving traffic violations in the past 5 years, any driving while under the influence of alcohol or drugs, and so forth. Each rule updated the POLICYRISK output fuzzy set by adding or subtracting the cumulative risk in the fuzzy sets INCREASED or DECREASED along a psychological scale from zero (no risk) to 100 (absolute risk.) Figure 1.9 shows how this fuzzy set reflected the increase in Risk.

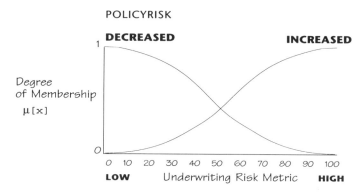

Figure 1.9 Policy risk on a psychometric scale

The new model not only gave the correct answer, it also provided a measure of the confidence between the policy data and the risk rating. There was just one problem: the model could not be deployed. State insurance underwriters developed a rating for policies from a set of regulations prescribed through a set of state regulations. They failed to mention this fact to the unwary knowledge engineering team until the system was demonstrated to a group of middle and senior executives. The regulations defined classes of risk along crisp category lines, such as "if AGE is between 16 and 22 then assign 8 risk points to the policy." Since the knowledge infrastructure in this project was well understood and thoroughly codified, it was easily transferred to a conventional expert or decision support system. But the hard boundary lines enforced by the state regulations made this an inappropriate model for a fuzzy system. Similar types of problems exist in industry, business, and the government.

Fuzzy Logic and Machine Reasoning

"I am inclined to think—" said I.
"I should do so," Sherlock Holmes remarked, impatiently.

Sir Arthur Conan Doyle
(1859–1930)
The Valley of Fear

Fuzzy systems are a form of rule-based models. In this chapter we explore the nature of the fuzzy rule system and the methods used by fuzzy systems to approximate arbitrary functions. We also examine two other forms of conventional machine reasoning paradigms: backward and forward chaining along with their fuzzy logic versions.

Machine Reasoning Techniques

How does a computer program evaluate a proposition and decide whether or not some action should be the consequent of this proposition? Ignoring for a moment the actual syntax and semantics of a formal rule system, we can view this reasoning as a logical expression in the form:

$$\text{If } P_1 \bullet P_2 \bullet P_3 \ldots P_n \text{ then } A_1 \ldots A_n$$

where P_i is a proposition expressed in either Boolean or fuzzy logic, "$\bullet$" represents a dyadic operator (such as AND or OR), and A_i is an action that results from the truth of the predicate proposition evaluation. The total collection of predicates is called the *Proposition set* (P_s) and the set of actions is the *Action set* (A_s). The machine reasoning process thus follows a form of *modus ponens* expressed as:

$$P_s \supset A_s$$

it is the objective of a reasoning system to isolate and construct the necessary syllogistic relationships and then prove the problem state P_s as true so the implication logic can establish A_s as true (so each A_i can be executed).

Now proposition (P_i) represents a bounded (restricted) relationship between two problem spaces in the control surface. The orthogony of the proposition can be expressed in either Boolean or fuzzy logic. In Boolean logic, the proposition has the form:

$$g(exp) \bullet g(exp)$$

In this instance $g(x)$ means a general functional evaluation of an expression (exp) with the standard arithmetic operators. The dyadic "•" is a relational operation such as equal, less than, greater than, is contained in, is a member of, is a substring of, and so forth. Examples include:

if (costs*volume)*discount > minimum_margins
and volume > retailminimum
and customercredit= "OK"
then order is APPROVED;
else order is REJECTED;

if region.city is member_of CITYLIST
then perform ComputeCosts(region.city, CITYLIST[&loc]);

if substr(clientid, length(clientid), 1)='X'
then action = 'Refer to Credit Department';

Formal propositions in a reasoning system may also include imprecise or fuzzy relations. These have the connonical form:

$$g(exp) \bullet Ls$$

where $g(x)$ is also a general functional evaluation, but L_s is a linguistic variable in the current state space. In fuzzy predicate relations only the membership operator (IS) or the exclusion operator (IS NOT) is permitted. Examples include:

if sales are high then inventory must be increased;

if (mfg.costs*1.8)+overhead is very low
then our price should be around avg(competition.price);

if voltage_spike is steep and decay_time is rapid
then intruder_probability is high;

So an automated reasoning system evaluates the truth of the *predicate* proposition set, and, if the predicate (also called the *premise*) is true, then some action is taken. Since this action is taken as a consequent of the premise, it is also called the *consequent*.

Variables

The individual data elements of a proposition or consequent are called *variables* and they come in two flavors: control and solution. Generally, *solution variables* appear in the left-hand side of consequent action statements. *Control variables* appear in the premise or on the right-hand side of the consequent action. In some cases, a control or solution variable can also be used as a "goal" in the reasoning process. A goal is an important semaphore of the automated inference process since it is used to actually construct a reasoning syllogism and sometimes tells the reasoning process when it is done. A variable has an implicit or explicit dimensionality.

Reasoning Methods

Backward and Forward Chaining

There are two principal kinds of reasoning machines in a conventional expert or knowledge based system: *backward* and *forward chaining*. In backward chaining the reasoning engine is presented with a goal and asked to find all the relevant, supporting processes that lead to this goal. Thus, given a broken radio transmitter and the observed symptoms (static, no power light, broken antenna, etc.), what are the probable causes of the breakage and what actions can we take to repair the transmitter? In forward chaining we collect data and try to build a sustainable problem state and, eventually, a solution state. Thus, given a series of tasks and their resource requirements, precedence order, and costs, a forward chaining system builds a viable assembly schedule or a least cost shipping order, or a workable project network.

Backward and forward chaining are the two principal inference engines used in intelligent systems. Together they provide the tools necessary to construct systems that can conduct deep diagnostics, multiple policy evaluations, scenario screening, configuration planning, project management, resource allocations, production planning, material requirements planning, and general task scheduling.

Fuzzy Reasoning

A third kind of reasoning system, *fuzzy* or *approximate reasoning*, combines knowledge representation in rules as well as fuzzy sets. Fuzzy reasoning systems deal with imprecise or ambiguous information. In fuzzy reasoning the rules are effectively run in parallel. Every solution variable is resolved by accumulating evidence for or against its possible value. Each rule contributes to the final shape of the consequent solution variable. When all the rules have been fired, the resulting fuzzy sets representing each output variable are defuzzified to find an expected value. This value is based on a preponderance of evidence.

Backward Chaining Inference Strategy

The GOAL ANALYZER determines the current goal state. On entry into the inference engine this goal is selected from the model's execution protocol. If we are searching for the value of a variable, the variable is made the current goal (often called a "*sub-goal*") and we recursively enter the reasoning protocol. The Goal Analyzer is also invoked after each rule is executed. If the goal has been satisfied the backward chaining engine exits.

Figure 2.1 illustrates a high level schematic of a reasoning system called an *inference engine* supporting backward chaining.

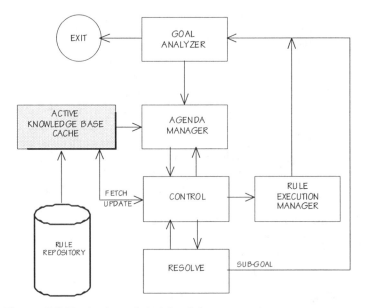

Figure 2.1 The backward chaining inference engine

The AGENDA MANAGER builds a list of those rules that have the current goal in the left-hand side of one or more of their consequent actions or have the goal variable as one of the rule's "exposed variables". The rules are stored on the agenda in their execution order. This order is based on three factors: their stated priority, their "depth-first probabilistic execution cost," and their rule description. A priority is assigned by the designer. The lower the number the higher the priority. The execution cost is based on the amount of work the inference engine might be expected to perform in order to make this rule eligible for firing. This cost is calculated from the number of unresolved variables in the rule, the minimum truth threshold for the rule, the rule's structural complexity (rules with **else** parts or nested *if-then-else* statements increase the rule's complexity), and the probability that firing this rule resolves the goal value. When all the rules on the top most agenda have been executed, the backward chaining engine exits.

The CONTROL process selects, prepares, and instructs the RULE EXECUTION MAN-
AGER to execute each rule. It is also responsible for fetching variable values from the
knowledge base and updating the knowledge base with newly resolved values. When a
rule has been successfully fired, the controller may also initiate forward firing (See
"Opportunistic Forward Firing" on page 69). This concept is discussed shortly. The controller also terminates execution of the backward chaining engine when the goal has been
resolved or the rules in the top level agenda have been executed. As the control processor
selects a rule, it calls Resolve to find the value for any uninstantiated variable.

The RESOLVE process is the heart of the backward chaining engine. It takes an uninstantiated variable and attempts to find its value. To do this it makes the variable a goal
and calls the entire backward chainer recursively. If the variable is still unresolved when
the inference engine returns to the Resolve process then either the knowledge base contains no rules that establish a value for the goal or those fired failed to instantiate the goal.
In this case, the Resolver simply asks the user for a value.

The following figures illustrate how backward chaining is used to find the value for a
goal variable. Figure 2.2 shows the rules in the policy and the agenda management process:

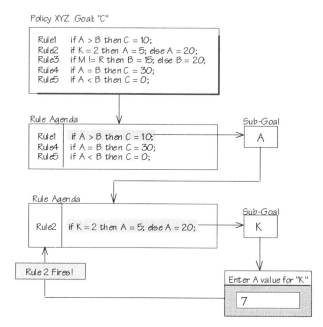

Figure 2.2 Backward chaining and finding the value of goal "C"

The inference engine selects all the rules in the policy that specify the variable "C" on
the left-hand side of their consequent assignment statement. These rules are then placed on
a backward chaining conflict resolution agenda. Although not important in this simple

example, rules have priorities and execution costs that determine their actual order in the agenda. Once the agenda has been formed, the rules are executed in top to bottom order[1].

Figure 2.2 illustrates how Rule1, at the top of the agenda, is evaluated. In order to fire Rule1, we must decide whether or not its premise is true. This means evaluating the expression "A>B". Since, at the start of the evaluation, variables "A" and "B" do not currently have values, the Controller calls the Resolver to find values for these variables. This involves making each variable a goal (called a *sub-goal*) and finding all the rules that have the sub-goal on the left-hand side of their consequent assignment statements. In this case only one rule, Rule2, specifies the sub-goal "A". We now must resolve its premise expression "K=2". This means finding a value for the variable "K". The Controller calls the Resolver for "K", but, since no rules, specify the value of "K", its value is requested from the user.

Figure 2.3 continues this process and also shows the current state of the active Knowledge Base Cache for the policy. This is the set of variables that have values (showing only the values in the current time frame.) We now find all the rules that specify "B" on the left-hand side of their consequent assignment statement.

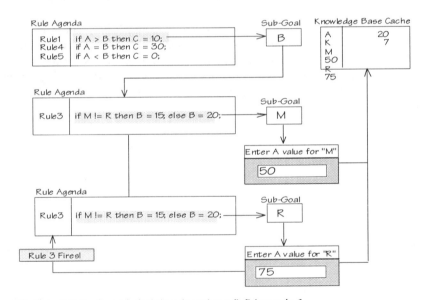

Figure 2.3 Backward chaining (continued) firing rule 1

As Figure 2.3 shows, Rule3 is the only rule that specifies "B". But, in order to set this variable, we need to resolve the value of "M" and "R". Since these variables are not specified in any other rules, the system prompts for their values. These values are added to the active knowledge base cache. As Figure 2.4 shows, we now have values for variables "A" and "B" in the top most rule agenda.

---

1. In fact, the agenda controller reorders the conflict agenda each time a rule is executed since the probable execution costs of rules within their priority classes changes as variables are instantiated. We have omitted this detail from the backward chaining example.

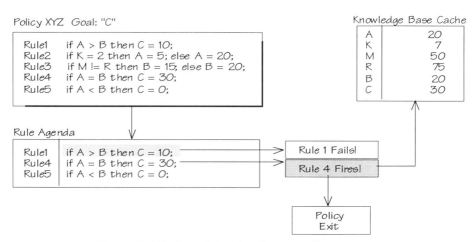

Figure 2.4 Backward chaining (continued)

Rule1 in the agenda is now evaluated. Its premise is false so the rule fails. The agenda manager moves to the second rule, Rule4, and test its premise. The premise is true so the rule fires and the value for the goal "C" is added to the active knowledge base cache. Since the goal has been resolved, backward chaining terminates. The final agenda rule, Rule5 is never tested.

Forward Chaining Inference Engine

A forward chaining engine is driven by its sensor system. These sensors, analogous to sensors and actuators in physical control devices, read data from the outside world, find rules that match the data, and then fire these rules. Thus a forward chaining system collects information about the current environment and builds a configuration space that matches one or more problem states.

A high level schematic of a reasoning system supporting forward chaining is illustrated in Figure 2.5.

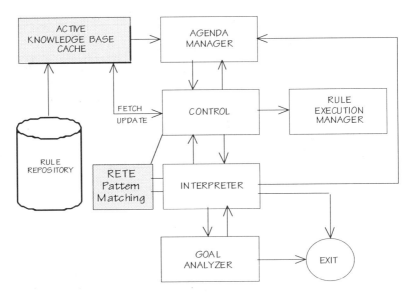

Figure 2.5 The forward chaining inference engine

The INTERPRETER examines the status of the rules and the variables in order to control the engine's next action. The forward chaining engine keeps looping through its rule set (the Agenda) until no more rules fire or until any optional goal is satisfied. Each loop is called a *cycle*. As a rule fires, additional variables are instantiated. This means additional rules might fire on the next cycle. When a rule fires it is normally removed from the active agenda. If another rule changes a variable that appears in the predicate of an inactive rule, the inactive rule is returned to the active agenda.

Unlike backward chaining, a forward chaining engine does not require a goal. The reasoning process is initiated by the sensing of data. The engine matches the current data state against the predicate (premise) of each rule to find the one's that are eligible for firing. These rules are fired and the data state is updated. Another pass is made through the rule set and any new rules are fired (eligible by virtue of new data instantiated by the executed rules or from new data collected by any methods associated with the agenda). When a pass through the rule set is made without firing a single rule, the engine terminates. Of course, the engine also terminates if, during any cycle, the optional goal variable is instantiated.

The RETE Algorithm

The general problem with forward chaining inference engines is the time required to find and apply rules that match to specific instances of data. For large systems (say with 2000 or more rules) this matching time increases almost geometrically. To solve this problem, Charles Forgy devised the RETE Algorithm in 1979 as part of his doctoral thesis. Using the RETE approach, the antecedents of each rule are maintained in a multi-directional network or *plex structure*. This network keeps status information about how data changes from one cycle to the next. Only those rules whose antecedent propositions contain altered data are scheduled for execution. Figure 2.5 shows how the RETE algorithm is integrated into a forward chaining system. Note the network is updated and used by both the Controller in finding the rules and the Interpreter in modifying the association threads that identify each candidate node for the next cycle.

The RETE algorithm significantly improves performance on medium to large systems. On smaller systems the over-head of maintaining the RETE network usually costs more than the speed gained by finding the altered nodes. Of course the RETE facility assumes the input to the forward chainer has a relatively high level of variability.

Opportunistic Forward Firing

By now it might have occurred to you that backward chaining converges on the top level goal by recursively establishing sub-goal states. This piecemeal approach means the solution space is narrowed by a process of (possibly) slow hill-climbing. Backward chaining is not only memory and computer instruction-cycle intensive, but, in its basic form, is not very intelligent. We can improve its performance in many problem states by taking advantage of the knowledge we elicit through each agenda's cycle. As we fire a rule, new variables are instantiated and added to the active knowledge cache. What if we now looked into the premise of still unfired rules and, if the newly resolved variables occur in these rules, we take this opportunity to fire these additional rules? Well, these new rules will add more information to the knowledge base and may cause other rules to fire. This process can significantly improve our chances of moving to the current goal state. In fact, experience shows it can significantly improve your chance of finding the global goal state! Figure 2.6 shows how this hill climbing process accelerates the backward chaining engine.

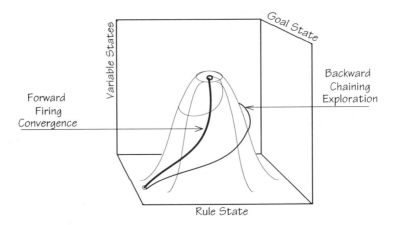

Figure 2.6 Backward chaining hill climbing to the goal state

Adding opportunistic forward firing to the backward chaining engine improves its performance and broadens its ability to tackle a wider variety of problems. Figure 2.7 shows how this component is integrated into the process schematic.

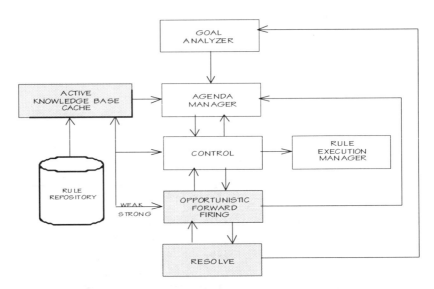

Figure 2.7 Opportunistic forward firing mechanism

There are two modes of forward firing: *strong* and *weak*. In the strong mode, a rule is only placed on the forward fire agenda if all its predicate variables have been resolved—

that is, the rule is now ready for immediate execution. In the weak mode, a rule is placed on the agenda even if some premise variables are still unresolved (the forward firing mechanism must invoke Resolve to find these values.)

Fuzzy Reasoning Inference Engine

The AGENDA MANAGER in a fuzzy system builds a list of all the rules in the policy. The rules are stored on the agenda according to their proposition class: unconditionals first and conditionals second. Since all rules in the policy are evaluated, the agenda order is minimal. Rules are ordered, within proposition class, only by priority. When all the rules on the agenda have been executed, the fuzzy reasoning engine terminates.

Figure 2.8 illustrates the schematic operation of the fuzzy reasoning inference engine. This engine implements a high level, sophisticated approximate reasoning system that combines fuzzy logic with fuzzy function approximation.

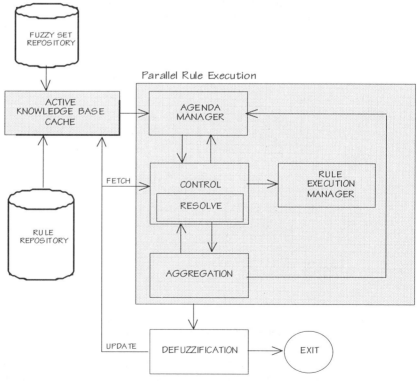

Figure 2.8 Fuzzy reasoning (approximate reasoning) inference engine

The `CONTROL` process selects, prepares, and instructs the `RULE EXECUTION MAN-AGER` to execute each rule. It is also responsible for fetching variable values and fuzzy sets from the knowledge base. The controller also terminates execution of the fuzzy reasoning engine when all the rules have been executed. As the control processor selects a rule, it calls Resolve to find the value for any uninstantiated variable.

The `RESOLVE` process is the backward chaining engine (See "Backward Chaining Inference Strategy" on page 64). It takes an uninstantiated variable and attempts to find its value. To do this it makes the variable a goal and calls the entire backward chainer recursively. If the variable is still unresolved when the inference engine returns to the Resolve process then either the knowledge base contains no rules which establish a value for the goal or those that fired failed to instantiate the goal. In this case, the Resolver simply asks the user for a value. Since all the rules in a policy are executed by the fuzzy inference strategy, a fuzzy model cannot perform backward chaining through the current policy. Instead, each variable can have an associated *acquisition policy*. When the model needs a value, it backward chains through this remote policy. Many variables can, of course, have the same acquisition policy.

The `AGGREGATION` process handles the correlation and management of solution fuzzy sets. For each solution variable, the fuzzy modelling system creates a corresponding fuzzy set with the same name. This fuzzy set region is updated by each rule that specifies the solution variable in its consequent. Thus, fuzzy rules contribute to the final shape and strength of the solution fuzzy set. Aggregation correlates the consequent fuzzy set (the fuzzy set appearing on the right-hand side of the consequent) with the truth of the rule's premise and then, according to the current implication method, updates the solution variable's fuzzy set. More details on this process are discussed in the next section, "*Fuzzy System Reasoning*."

When all the rules have been fired, the `DEFUZZIFICATION` process is invoked for each of the solution variables. Defuzzification is the process of finding the expected value for the solution variable. There are several methods of defuzzifying a fuzzy set (such as composite moments or centroid, composite maximum, or average maximum), but the general theme is finding a single (scalar) value that best represents the fuzzy set. Along with the expected value, a measure of the solution variable's degree of validity, called the *compatibility index*, is computed and saved.

Fuzzy System Reasoning

Unlike conventional expert systems that use bivalent logic, fuzzy systems take a significantly different approach to machine intelligence and reasoning. A fuzzy system employs rules that accumulate evidence for (or against) a specific set of solution variables. Instead of isolating a point on the function surface, a fuzzy rule localizes a region of space along the function surface. When multiple rules are executed, multiple regions are combined in the same local space to produce a composite region. The final point on the surface is found through defuzzification. In this section we examine the way a fuzzy model applies its rule set to a problem. Figure 2.9 illustrates the general organizational and flow schematic of a fuzzy modelling system.

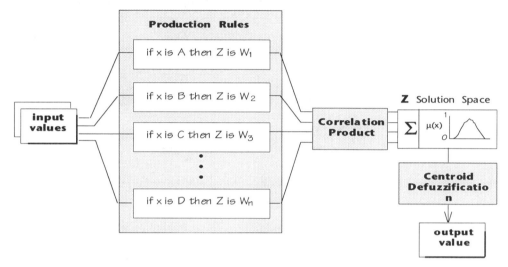

Figure 2.9 The fuzzy modeling system

Input values (scalars, vectors, and other fuzzy sets such as fuzzy numbers) are read into the system. Each rule is potentially executed. Some rules do not fire because their premise truth falls below the alpha threshold. Each rule that executes contributes some evidence about the value of its solution variable. This evidence, in the form of a fuzzy set, is correlated to agree with the truth of the premise and then aggregated into the on-going solution variable's fuzzy region. When all the rules have been fired, the composite solution variable's fuzzy set is defuzzified. This produces a number, the expected value for the solution variable.

Additive and Min/Max Fuzzy Systems

The general mechanics of how a fuzzy system works has been introduced in "Fuzzy Reasoning" on page 63. The basic principles of fuzzy reasoning are the same during rule evaluation and execution. The reasoning methods diverge in two respects after the predicate has been evaluated: in how the consequent fuzzy region is correlated with the truth of the rule's premise and in how this correlated fuzzy region is aggregated into the solution variable "under generation" fuzzy region. This divergence of methods classifies fuzzy systems into two broad classes:

1. Those that use an additive method to accumulate evidence.
2. Those that use a combination of minimum truncation with maximum membership (equivalent to ORing two fuzzy regions).

The correlation and aggregation techniques play an important part in the design and processing of fuzzy model. In particular, the additive fuzzy model forms the core of the universal approximation capabilities of the fuzzy model (See "Fuzzy Systems as Universal Approximators" on page 113.)

Correlation Techniques

As we have seen a fuzzy rule has two principle parts:

1. The predicate also called the *premise*.
2. The consequent also called the *action*.

In executing a fuzzy rule, we must first determine the truth of the predicate. As an example, consider the following fuzzy rule:

if price is HIGH then profits are near MfgCosts;

where `price` and `profits` are variables and `HIGH` and `near  MfgCosts` are fuzzy sets (the latter is a fuzzy number formed by applying the hedge `near` to the scalar value of the manufacturing costs). We must evaluate the degree to which `price` is a member of the fuzzy set `HIGH`. Figure 2.10 illustrates how a value of price—in this case $24.00—has a degree of membership in the fuzzy set `HIGH` (for `price`).

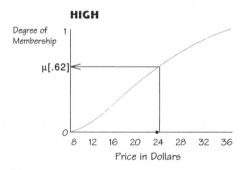

Figure 2.10 Grade of membership for price ($24) in HIGH

This yields a grade of membership value (in this case, μ[.62]). Given some truth exists in the premise, this rule can be executed. In executing the rule, we must take the consequent fuzzy set (the set name appearing at the right in the consequent action) and update the solution variable's fuzzy region (the fuzzy set name appearing at the left in the consequent action). When we accumulate evidence by combining the near MfgCosts consequent fuzzy set with PROFITS—the solution variable's fuzzy set[2]—the shape of near Mfg-Costs must be temporarily modified. This is the process of correlation. Near MfgCosts is a bell shaped fuzzy regions formed by approximating the manufacturing costs. Figure 2.11 shows how this fuzzy set appears centered around a value of $16,000.

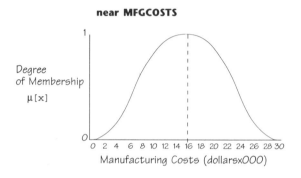

Figure 2.11 The near MfgCosts fuzzy set

Correlation insures that the inference truth transfer function obeys a simple law of approximate reasoning:

> *The truth of the consequent can not be any greater than the truth of the predicate.*

To insure this, some modification to the consequent fuzzy region must be made. There are two approaches to this modification: *correlation minimum* and *correlation product*.

---

2. Remember that a fuzzy reasoning system creates a temporary fuzzy region for each of the solution variables (see the comments on aggregation in "Fuzzy System Reasoning" on page 72). This means that a fuzzy set PROFITS will exist for the variable profits. This new, temporary fuzzy set is independent of any fuzzy sets forming the term set for the variable profits and contains the correlated, aggregated fuzzy sets that are specified by all the rules that provide some evidence for the value of profits.

Correlation Minimum

Correlation minimum, as Figure 2.12 illustrates, works by truncating the consequent fuzzy set at the truth of the premise.

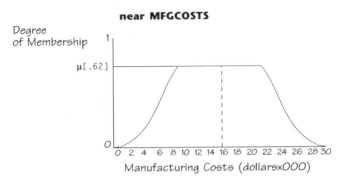

Figure 2.12 near MfgCosts adjusted by correlation minimum

The correlation minimum clips the top of the consequent fuzzy set. Equation 2.1 shows how the minimum operation is used to truncate the incoming fuzzy set (μ_{ci}) using the premise truth (μ_p) to produce the outgoing fuzzy set (μ_{co}).

$$\mu_{co}[x]_i = \bigvee_{i=0}^{n} \min(\mu_{ci}[x]_i, \mu_p)$$

Equation 2.1 The correlation minimum process

Correlation Product

The second method, correlation product, takes a different approach to reducing the truth of the consequent. As Figure 2.13 shows, the consequent fuzzy set is scaled by multiplying each truth membership by the premise truth.

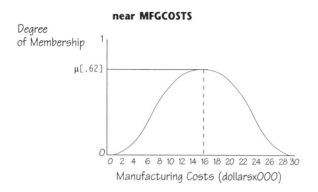

Figure 2.13 near MfgCosts adjusted by correlation product

The correlation product preserves the over-all shape of the fuzzy region by, in effect, shrinking the fuzzy set so its maximum height equals the height of the predicate truth. Equation 2.2 shows how the multiplication operator is used to scale the consequent fuzzy region.

$$\mu_{co}[x]_i = \overset{n}{\underset{i=0}{\forall}} \mu_{ci}[x]_i \cdot \mu_p$$

Equation 2.2 The correlation product process

Selecting the appropriate correlation method depends on both the nature of the fuzzy model as well as the economics of the hardware platforms. In general, for information models, the correlation product technique appears to work better than the minimum since it tends to preserve the most information. Further, the mathematics and reasoning underlying function approximation (see "Fuzzy Systems as Universal Approximators" on page 113 for complete details) require the use of correlation product. On the other hand, some work by Jones and Graham in their book, *Expert Systems: Knowledge, Uncertainty, and Decision*[3], suggests business models can benefit from the plateaus created by the correlation minimum method. These plateaus produce interval values along the solution fuzzy space instead of the continuous values produced by the correlation product technique. This means slight variations in the model center on the same output value. Such grouping can be important in risk assessment, asset and resource allocation, production and inventory planning, and similar applications.

Economic factors also play a role in selecting the correlation method. This is especially true in process engineering where the fuzzy system is resident in firmware or has use of a microprocessor's limited instruction set. These real-time fuzzy systems often use the correlation minimum technique since finding the lesser of two real (floating point) numbers is considerably faster and requires less memory overhead than multiplying two

---

3. Ian Graham and Peter Llewelyn Jones, *Expert Systems: Knowledge, Uncertainty, and Decision*,1988, Chapman and Hall, London.

real numbers. In business models that are generally not time-dependent and are executed on powerful workstations, the economics of selecting one correlation technique over another is out weighed by the necessity of finding the best representational technique for the model at hand.

Aggregation and Implication Techniques

Aggregation is the process of combining correlated fuzzy sets to produce a composite fuzzy region that represents the target solution variable. This is the core of the evidential reasoning method used in fuzzy systems. Like the correlation process, there are also two different ways of aggregating consequent fuzzy regions: the additive and the Min/Max methods. While the correlation method involves an action on one fuzzy set at a time, the aggregation process works on many fuzzy sets. Its purpose is to create a final fuzzy region that represents the combined interaction of all the rules. Consider the following small fuzzy pricing model:

> [R1] our price must be LOW;
> [R2] our price must be HIGH;
> [R3] if MfgCosts are ELEVATED then price must be a PREMIUM;
> [R4] if SpoilageRates are LARGE then price must be near 1.5*MfgCosts;

This model involves both conditional and unconditional fuzzy propositions. How they are handled depends on the aggregation techniques used in the model. In general, unconditionals are treated as a separate inferencing strategy in a fuzzy model and are only "felt" by the model if the degree of truth in all the conditionals is less than the maximum degree of truth resulting from applying the minimum operator to all the unconditionals.

Unconditional Fuzzy Propositions

An unconditional fuzzy proposition implies a minimum constraint on the model solution. These propositions are handled using the minimum operator. Since an unconditional fuzzy rule lacks any predicate it is applied to the solution fuzzy region without any correlation. The following figures illustrate how this process works. Figure 2.14 shows the basic HIGH for price fuzzy set. Figure 2.15 shows the LOW for price fuzzy set.

HIGH

Figure 2.14 High for price fuzzy set

LOW

Figure 2.15 Low for price fuzzy set

Although these fuzzy sets are complements, neither the fuzzy model nor the rules of fuzzy logic impose this requirement.When we execute the first rule:

[R1] our price must be LOW;

the temporary fuzzy region for the solution variable price is updated with the consequent fuzzy set LOW. Since this region is empty it is made as true as possible constrained by the membership function of LOW. This is equivalent to copying LOW into the price fuzzy set. The second rule:

[R2] our price must be HIGH;

is applied using the rule of unconditional propositions that involves taking the minimum of the current solution fuzzy region and the consequent fuzzy set at each point in the output. Figure 2.16 shows the results of applying rule [R1] and rule [R2] in the model.

HIGH and LOW

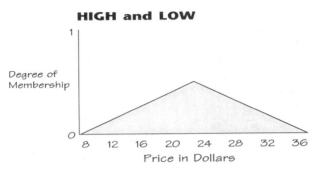

Figure 2.16 High and low fuzzy sets unconditionally aggregated

Equation 2.3 shows how the minimum operator is applied for each incoming consequent and solution fuzzy membership value. This process transforms the solution region.

$$\mu_{sol}[x]_i = \bigvee_{i=0}^{n} \min(\mu_{sol}[x]_i, \mu_{ci}[x]_i)$$

Equation 2.3 Aggregation process for unconditional propositions

Unconditional fuzzy propositions provide a means of insuring a model produces some
reasonable, default result even if none of the conditional rules execute. Although uncom-
mon in process engineering models, business models can often have executions where
none of the conditional rules have a truth above the current alpha threshold. Without
unconditionals, the results of such models are undetermined.

> The order in which rules are entered into a fuzzy modelling system is not usu-
> ally important. This changes, however, when both conditional and uncondi-
> tional rules are found in the same model. *You must run all the unconditionals
> before or after all the conditionals.* Running the unconditionals first establishes
> a default result space. Running the unconditionals last constrains the under
> generation solution space produced by the conditionals—that is, it restricts the
> solution space.

Conditional Fuzzy Propositions

Conditional fuzzy propositions or rules are the most frequently used productions in
expert and decision support systems. These productions have the traditional *if-then* syntax.

Some fuzzy modelling systems also provide for *else* extensions to the rule syntax (where the truth of the *else* branch is 1-[*then* truth]). There are two general methods of aggregating fuzzy consequents in conditional rules: the min/max method and the additive method. Both of these techniques take the results of many rules and combine them into a final fuzzy regions for each solution variable, but each differs in the way this combined region is formed. Each method also has limitations and constraints on the way in which different defuzzification methods work. Conditional rules start with an **if** term. The following two rules from the sample fuzzy model are conditional rules.

[R3] if MfgCosts are ELEVATED then price must be a PREMIUM;
[R4] if SpoilageRates are LARGE then price must be near 1.5*MfgCosts;

In order to follow the reasoning mechanism aligned with fuzzy set aggregation, we need to look at the fuzzy sets associated with the rule productions. These are the sets describing the semantic spaces underlying manufacturing costs, spoilage rates, and the product effective price. Figure 2.17 shows the term set for the variable MfgCosts.

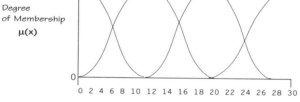

Figure 2.17 The manufacturing costs fuzzy term set

Figure 2.18 shows the term set associated with the SpoilageRate variable. This is the percentage of the warehouse stackage that is unusable for any reason (damaged in manufacturing or in-transit).

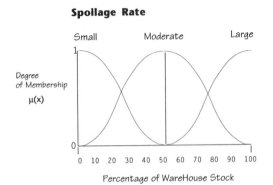

Figure 2.18 The spoilage rate fuzzy term set

Figure 2.19 completes the term set for the Price variable. In addition to the HIGH and LOW fuzzy sets introduced when we discussed unconditional fuzzy rules, the PREMIUM fuzzy set is added as a price that is positioned between the two extremes.

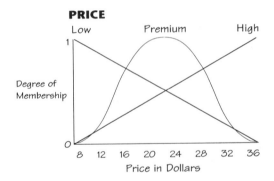

Figure 2.19 The price variable fuzzy term set

Min/Max Aggregation

The min/max technique[4] effectively ORs the correlated consequent fuzzy set with the contents of the solution variable's output fuzzy region. The process takes the maximum of the consequent fuzzy set and the solution fuzzy set at each point along their mutual mem-

---

4. The Min/Max nomenclature comes from the early days of fuzzy models when the correlation minimum and aggregation maximum technique was used almost exclusively. By this same reasoning, an addtive model should be called the Product/Additive technique.

bership functions. Figure 2.20 illustrates the min/max process when the first conditional rule is executed.

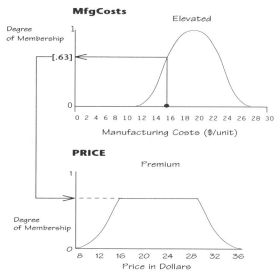

Figure 2.20 Executing rule [R3] (setting the value of Price)

[R3] if MfgCosts are ELEVATED then price must be a PREMIUM;

The premise of the rule is evaluated by finding the compatibility between the current value for MfgCosts and the fuzzy set ELEVATED. A manufacturing cost of $16.00 per unit has a membership of μ[.63] in this fuzzy set. This membership value is used to reduce the value of the PREMIUM fuzzy set (using correlation minimum). This correlated fuzzy set is aggregated into the under-generation PRICE.

Since the maximum membership of the consequent fuzzy set PREMIUM is greater than the [.50] membership of the current PRICE region formed by the intersection of HIGH and LOW, these rules do not contribute to the final value of PRICE. This is precisely the behavior we expect of unconditional rules: they should only contribute to the final solution when the truth of all the conditionals is very low.

The second conditional rule:

*[R4] if SpoilageRates are LARGE then price must be near 1.5*MfgCosts;*

must now be executed and its results combined with the previous conditional rule. We examine this process in two steps. Figure 2.21 shows the minimum correlation component of the rule execution.

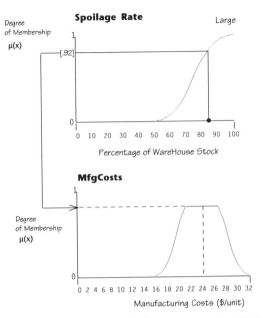

Figure 2.21 Executing rule [R4] (correlating consequent with Premise)

We have selected a relatively large spillage rate of 85%. This has a μ[.92] membership in the underlying fuzzy set LARGE. The consequent of the rule specifies an approximate number found by fuzzifying the value of 1.5 times the current manufacturing costs
(which is $16.00). We produce a bell shaped number centered broadly around the value
$24.00 and then truncate this fuzzy set at the [.92] membership level.

Figure 2.22 shows the second phase of the rule evaluation: aggregating the correlated
fuzzy set near 1.5*MfgCosts into the current fuzzy region for the solution variable
price.

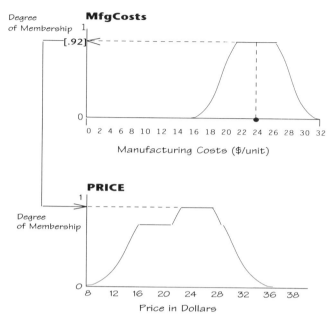

Figure 2.22 Executing rule [R4] (aggregating the correlated fuzzy sets)

The min/max aggregation method involves an aggregation using the fuzzy union operation. That is, we take the maximum of the truth membership values for the current PRICE fuzzy set and the truncated fuzzy number 24.00 at each point in the output fuzzy region. The result of this operation is the dual plateau fuzzy region shown in Figure 2.22.

Equation 2.4 shows how the Min/Max Aggregation process works when applied to all the conditional rules in a model (or model policy).

$$\mu_{out}[x]_i = \bigvee_{i=0}^{n} \max(\mu_{out}[x]_i, \mu_{co}[x]_i)$$

Equation 2.4 The Min/Max aggregation process

From this we can see that each membership value in the solution fuzzy region ($\mu_{sol}[x]$) is found by taking the maximum of the current solution fuzzy region ($\mu_{sol}[x]$) and the correlated consequent region ($\mu_{co}[x]$).

Additive Aggregation

The additive technique effectively adds the correlated consequent fuzzy set to the contents of the solution variable's output fuzzy region. The process adds the truth membership values of the consequent fuzzy set and the solution fuzzy set at each point along their mutual membership functions. The addition is the bounded sum operation so that the composite membership value can never exceed [1.0]. In this section we examine the same fuzzy model using the additive aggregation method. Figure 2.23 illustrates the additive process when the first conditional rule is executed.

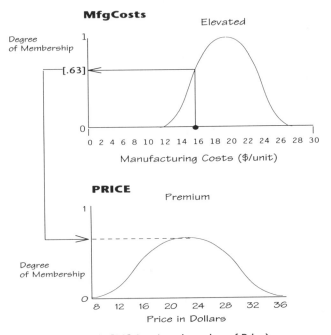

Figure 2.23 Executing rule [R3] (setting the value of Price)

[R3] if MfgCosts are ELEVATED then price must be a PREMIUM;

The premise of the rule is evaluated by finding the compatibility between the current value for MfgCosts and the fuzzy set ELEVATED. A manufacturing cost of $16.00 per unit has a membership of μ[.63] in this fuzzy set. This membership value is used to reduce the value of the PREMIUM fuzzy set (using correlation product). This correlated fuzzy set is aggregated into the under-generation PRICE.

In same manner as the min/max model, since the maximum membership of the consequent fuzzy set PREMIUM is greater than the [.50] membership of the current PRICE region formed by the intersection of HIGH and LOW, these rules do not contribute to the final value of PRICE. This is precisely the behavior we expect of unconditional rules: they should only contribute to the final solution when the truth of all the conditionals is very low.

Unconditional rules are handled in the same manner for both the min/max and the additive aggregation models. The underlying unconditional fuzzy memberships are **not** added into the solution output space. Only conditional (*if-then*) rules contribute to the solution space through the bounded sum addition technique.

The second conditional rule:

[R4] if SpoilageRates are LARGE then price must be near 1.5*MfgCosts;

must now be executed and its results combined with the previous conditional rule. We also examine this process in two steps. Figure 2.24 shows the product correlation component of the rule execution.

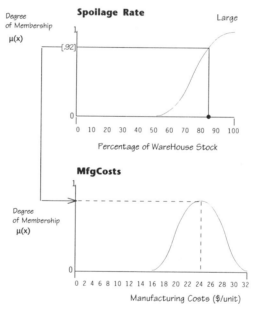

Figure 2.24 Executing rule [R4] (correlating consequent with Premise)

We have selected the same large spillage rate of 85%. This has a μ[.92] membership in the underlying fuzzy set LARGE. The consequent of the rule specifies an approximate number found by fuzzifying the value of 1.5 times the current manufacturing costs (which is $16.00). We produce a bell shaped number centered broadly around the value $24.00 and then scale this fuzzy set using the [.92] membership level.

Figure 2.25 shows the second phase of the rule evaluation: aggregating the product fuzzy set `near 1.5*MfgCosts` into the current fuzzy region for the solution variable price.

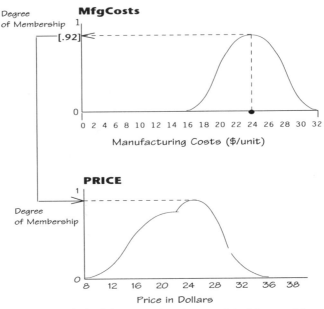

Figure 2.25 Executing rule [R4] (aggregating the correlated fuzzy sets)

The additive method involves an aggregation using the bounded sum operation. That is, we add the truth membership values for the current `PRICE` fuzzy set and the scaled fuzzy number `24.00` at each point in the output fuzzy region. The result of this operation is the smooth fuzzy region shown in Figure 2.25.

Equation 2.5 shows how the additive aggregation process works when applied to all the conditional rules in a model (or model policy).

$$\mu_{out}[x]_i = \overset{n}{\underset{i=0}{\forall}} \min((\mu_{out}[x]_i + \mu_{co}[x]_i), 1)$$

Equation 2.5 The additive aggregation process

From this we can see each membership value in the solution fuzzy region ($\mu_{sol}[x]$) is found by adding the current solution fuzzy region ($\mu_{sol}[x]$) and the correlated consequent region ($\mu_{co}[x]$). If the sum exceeds [1.0], it is truncated at the [1.0] level (no membership value can exceed one).

Refer to Appendix C, *The Fuzzy Standard Model*, by Bart Kosko, for a complete mathemaical treatment of this important modeling capacity.

Defuzzification

Defuzzification is the process of finding a single number that properly represents the information contained in the output fuzzy set. This is called the *expected value* of the solution variable. Defuzzification is necessary in most models since we are obliged, under most circumstances, to work with numbers rather than fuzzy sets. Thus, deciding on how to convert an arbitrary fuzzy region into a representative number is an important aspect in fuzzy system modeling. While many approaches to defuzzification appear in the literature, there are essentially two prevailing methods: composite moments and composite maximum. These techniques are also known as the centroid (or center of gravity) and the mean of the maxima methods.

The techniques for fuzzy system inferencing interact with the defuzzification schemes in a variety of ways; however, we can generally tie a method of defuzzification with a method of implication in a straight forward manner. Table 2.1 shows this cross relationship.

Table 2.1 Implication and defuzzification techniques

Implication method	Defuzzification methods
Correlation minimum and Min/Max Inference	Composite maximum
Correlation product and additive inference	Composite moments

This table describes the two most frequently used fuzzy reasoning methods. Other combinatons are possible, such as correlation minimum and the additive inference. However, it is the expected morphology of the output fuzzy set that actually determines which defuzzification method is most appropriate. The correlation minimum and additive inference, as an example, is best resolved with the composite moments since the additive inference tends to smooth out the plateaus caused by the correlation minimum technique. In the remainder of this section we look at the two principle methods of defuzzification.

Composite Maximum

As Table 2.1 suggests, models using correlation minimum with the min/max inferencing technique should use the composite maximum defuzzification method. This recommendation follows from the type of topology produced by the correlation method. Models with this kind of structure have a number of plateaus in the output fuzzy set. These plateaus are a result of the truncation process used in correlation minimum. In Figure 2.26 we can see how the composite maximum defuzzification method is applied to the price solution fuzzy set. The expected value is determined by finding the plateau with the largest grade of membership value.

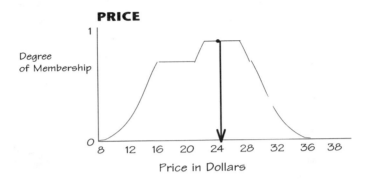

Figure 2.26 Composite maximum at middle of plateau

When a two edged plateau is found, the middle of the plateau is used. Sometimes, however, the edge of the solution fuzzy set domain clips or cuts the consequent fuzzy set. This can result in a single-edged plateau. In these cases, a different defuzzification method is used to find an expected value. Figure 2.27 shows how a single-edged plateau with the edge at the left of the solution area is handled.

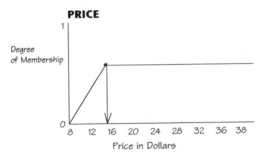

Figure 2.27 Composite maximum at the left edge of plateau

Figure 2.28 shows show how a single-edged plateau with the edge at the right of the solution area is handled.

Figure 2.28 Composite maximum at the right edge of plateau

When only a single edge exists in the solution fuzzy region we take the value at the edge of the plateau. Together these three approaches provide a method of defuzzification that finds a single position on the maximum plateau best representing the value of the fuzzy set. When two or more plateaus exist having the same maximum truth value (that is, when the output has a saddle or sinusoidal appearance) the mean of the center of the plateaus is used.

Composite Maximum selects a point on the output where the fuzzy set reaches its maximum value. Thus, it is influenced by the single rule that generates the maximum strength in the production set. As a consequence of this behavior, systems that use composite maximum are often subject to sudden transition states in the output. The solution values tend to jump from one value to another as one rule or another gains control during subsequent model executions. This is not necessarily a bad thing. In many decision models, the plateau created by the dominant rule represents an action class. Selecting the center point in this class is the required model solution. Class solutions are common in models that handle groups or packages such as resource and asset allocations, just-in-time (JIT) inventory models, project or product risk assessments, and related applications.

Although the correlation minimum and the min/max implication method are generally associated with composite maximum defuzzification, this is not a hard and fast rule. In fact, due to economies of memory and restrictions on the speed of certain instructions, most real-time process control applications use correlation minimum and min/max along with the composite moments defuzzification method. Controllers use the composite moments method in order to derive continuous output values for the host device. They also, to some extent, rely on the composite moments as a result of the more tightly compacted fuzzy term sets associated with fuzzy logic controllers.

Composite Moments

Table 2.1 also suggests models using correlation product with the additive inferencing technique should use the *composite moments* defuzzification method. This recommendation also follows from the type of topology produced by the correlation method. The additive method coupled with the correlation product scaling tends to produce output fuzzy regions that are smooth with few, if any, plateaus. In Figure 2.29 we can see how the composite moments defuzzification method is applied to the price solution fuzzy set. The expected value is determined by finding the center of gravity of the fuzzy set.

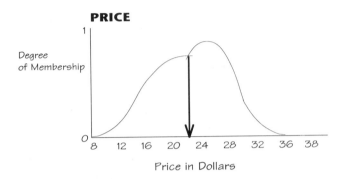

Figure 2.29 Composite moments defuzzification

The composite moments method, also called the *center of gravity* or *centroid* technique, finds the point on the output membership curve where the fuzzy set is evenly "balanced." For most business applications the composite moments method provides the best method of defuzzification. This technique, in effect, considers the *number of votes* for a solution value by placing more emphasis on the region of the output that has been covered by several fuzzy sets (that is, the region supported by the majority of the rules). Figure 2.30 shows how the underlying fuzzy sets in the PRICE solution fuzzy set contribute to the defuzzified value.

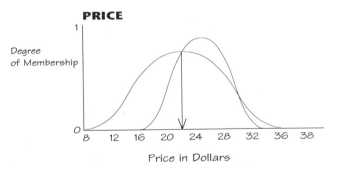

Figure 2.30 Composite moments as a region of multiple votes

Composite Moments finds the center of gravity of the output fuzzy set. This is the weighted average of the fuzzy set found by weighting each domain value that has a non-zero membership grade by that membership value. Equation 2.6 shows how the composite moments is calculated.

$$x = \frac{\displaystyle\sum_{i=0}^{n} d_i \mu_S(d_i)}{\displaystyle\sum_{i=0}^{n} \mu_S(d_i)}$$

Equation 2.6 Calculating the composite moments (centroid)

The sum of each domain value (d_i) times its membership grade (μ_S) is divided by the sum of all the membership grades. In effect, then, the contributions from all the fired rules are added together rather than being combined with the fuzzy union operation. This keeps the composite moments method from being influenced by a single rule. The expected values from this kind of defuzzification tends to move smoothly across the output fuzzy region so small changes in the data make continuous changes in the solution values. As a general rule, the composite moments defuzzification provides the best "first estimate" approach to solving a fuzzy model.

Performance Compatibility and Undecidable Models

At the point of defuzzification, a composite fuzzy region exists for each solution variable. The robustness of this fuzzy set determines the amount of information contained in the solution variable. By this we mean the expected value derived from defuzzification can lack support in the underlying fuzzy space. Support is missing because the degree of membership truth in the solution fuzzy region is very low. We run into problems with finding an acceptable expected value in a model because the defuzzification process is essentially insensitive to the degree of truth in the output fuzzy set. As an example, consider the following fragment from a materials planning system:

> *if MillDiameter is WIDE then Volume is LARGE;*
> *if MillDiameter is NARROW then Volume is SMALL*
> *if MillDiameter is THIN then Volume is TINY*
> *if MillDiameter is MEDIUM then Volume is MODERATEl*
> *if PartLength is LONG then Volume is LARGE*
> *if PartLength is SHORT then Volume is SMALL*
> •
> •

These rules define the volume of material needed in the current sub-assembly for a part with a specific milled diameter and part length. Figure 2.31 shows the VOLUME solution fuzzy set after executing the model rules.

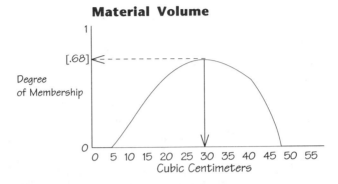

Figure 2.31 Defuzzification at [.68] membership level

The defuzzified volume of slightly more than 30 cubic centimeters is supported with a truth membership of [.68]. This means one or more rules fired with a reasonably strong predicate truth. Figure 2.32 shows the same execution with a different set of data points.

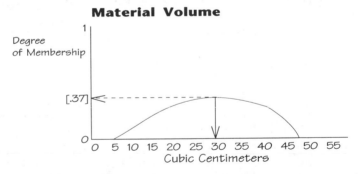

Figure 2.32 Defuzzification at [.37] membership level

In this case the same expected volume of slightly more than 30 cubic centimeters is supported with a reduced truth membership of [.37]. The height of the solution fuzzy region is reduced since the predicates of the contributing rules fire less strongly than the rules that created the output in Figure 2.31. Finally, Figure 2.33 shows the same rules executed with a new set of data points.

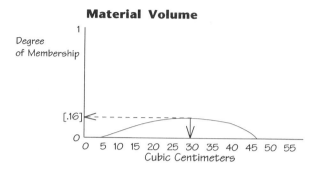

Figure 2.33 Defuzzification at [.16] membership level

Again we have an expected VOLUME of slightly more than 30 cubic centimeters but with a seriously low truth membership value of [.16]. This means the contributing rule predicates fired with very little truth. Indeed, the material volume fuzzy set, VOLUME, can have an extremely small membership truth, say [.087], and still defuzzify to a value around 30 cubic centimeters. This shows both the composite maximum and composite moments defuzzification methods are relatively insensitive to the height of the output fuzzy region. A maximum defuzzification simply centers on the largest truth membership without applying a qualitative analysis to that height. The weighted average used in the composite moments is also centered on the point that was, essentially, midway across the fuzzy set. Center of gravity defuzzification turns out to be sensitive to the width of the fuzzy set but not especially responsive to varying heights.

Compatibility Measurements

From another perspective, the height of the output fuzzy set can be used to measure the fitness of the model itself. This measurement is both specific to a single execution of the model as well as the historical modelling process itself. Since the height of the output fuzzy set is a measure of how strongly the rule predicates fired, we can visualize the value as an indicator of how well the current data points fell within the domains of the predicate fuzzy sets. If the rules fired weakly, then the data lay at the edges or outside of the fuzzy sets. If the rules fired strongly, then the data lay well within the fuzzy sets—that is, the data was more representative of the sets than data that caused the rules to fire weakly. In other words, the data for a strongly firing rule set is more compatible with the semantics and process of the model than data causing the rules to fire weakly. This yields the idea of using the height of the output fuzzy set as a compatibility measurement. We call this value the *compatibility index*.

Compatibility Types

There are two kinds of compatibility measurements: unit and statistical. The unit compatibility reflects the height of the output fuzzy region on a single execution of the model. The statistical compatibility, and by far the most important, reflects the mean unit compatibility over a large number of model executions. The statistical compatibility index is a measure of how well the model itself fits with the underlying data. To see how this measure works, consider the fuzzy profit forecasting system schematically shown in Figure 2.34.

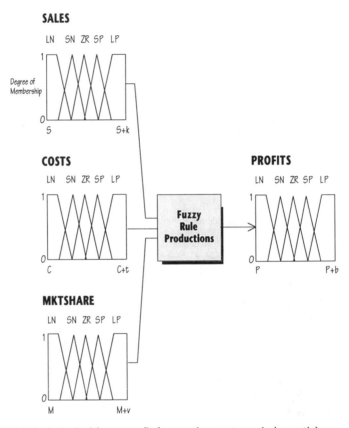

Figure 2.34 A Prototypical fuzzy profit forecasting systems (schematic)

In this simple model of market dynamics, we forecast a profit based on changes in the previous quarter's sales, cost of sales, and marketshare. The fuzzy sets represent positive and negative changes from the last period (from LN, Large Negative, through ZR, Zero change, to LP, a Large Positive Change.) Some of the rules might appear as,

> *if sales are SN then profits are SN*
> *if costs are ZR then profits are SP*
> *if mktshare is SN then profits are ZR*

As Figure 2.35 shows, when the values for `sales`, `costs`, and `marketshare` fall well within the fuzzy regions, the truth membership is relatively large. This large membership value is reflected in a sizeable height in the output `PROFITS` fuzzy region.

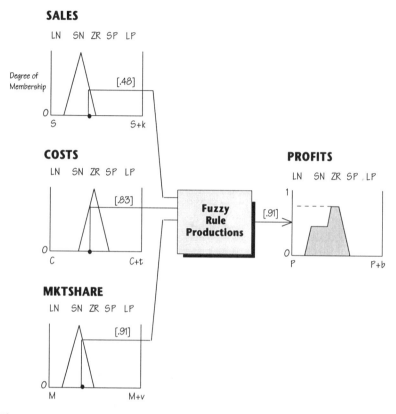

Figure 2.35 Model execution with a high compatibility values

On the other hand, Figure 2.36 shows a model execution where the compatibility index is quite low. This is understandable when we examine the fit between the predicate fuzzy sets and the incoming data. When data lies at the edges of the fuzzy sets (or, for the marketshare variables, lies outside the control domain) the model and the data are weakly fitted. This model execution could produce the same expected value from defuzzification; however, the data does not support this interpretation.

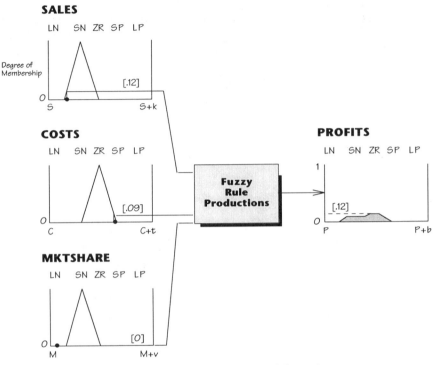

Figure 2.36 Model execution with a low compatibility values

We might suppose, in models like the profit forecasting system, a lack of membership in one fuzzy set is compensated for by a more representative membership in one of the neighboring fuzzy sets in the term set. Thus, a low membership in Small Negative (SN) might have a high membership in Large Negative (LN). Although this is often the case, the compatibility metric measures the actual outcome of the model. A symptom of low degrees of membership in the solution fuzzy region can reflect several problems such as: an improper decomposition of the variable into meaningful fuzzy sets, incorrect overlapping of fuzzy sets, improper domains (the data consistently lies at the extremes of the variable's term set), a lack of rules covering one or more fuzzy regions in the model, and incorrect contribution weights on the rules. The problem of incompatibility arises frequently in models where the variables have sparse or weakly defined term sets. In these cases, data can easily cluster around regions of the model state that are not covered by sufficient rule productions or have more problems states than the knowledge engineer initially anticipated.

Compatibility as a Measure of Change

Models with generally high unit and consistently high statistical compatibility can decay over time as the relationship between the model and the real world begins to change. Figure 2.37 is an example of one such case. The Price variable is decomposed into two fuzzy regions, LOW and HIGH. Much of the data is centered around the LOW end of the data information spectrum.

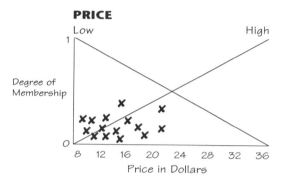

Figure 2.37 A skewed compatibility distribution on a sparse term set

If this (very simple) model has a rule base such as:

if price is LOW then marketshare is INCREASED
if price is HIGH then marketshare is DECREASED

then the model would have consistently high compatibility index values in its prediction that the market share would increase. As inflation, the cost of materials, and competition begins to over-take the company's product line, however, the product price edges upward. The membership of price in the fuzzy set LOW begins to decline. As the price drifts toward the right, its membership in LOW declines, but its membership in HIGH does not automatically compensate for this decline.

Statistical Compatibility

An individual unit compatibility can indicate the reliability of an single model prediction. In all real-world models, however, the random nature of data generally insures that even the best models have occasional executions where the unit compatibility is very low. A more revealing and important measurement is the *statistical compatibility index*.

This basic measurement, as indicated in Equation 2.7, is the mean of the unit compatibility index values for N runs of the model[5].

$$CI_{stat} = \frac{\sum\limits_{t=0}^{N} CI_t{}^{unit}}{N}$$

Equation 2.7 Calculating the statistical compatibility index

The mean value of the unit compatibility measurements reflects model robustness in terms of its flexibility in handling data. The unit compatibilities should be evenly spread through the model decision space. Figure 2.38, a two dimensional scatter plot, illustrates how a model with good compatibility should appear. The 36 unit values are spread with a mean value of [.53].

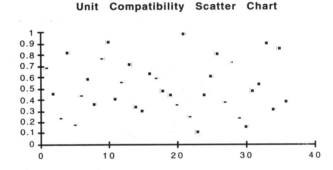

Figure 2.38 Unit compatibility values (with a mean of [.53])

---

5. In some time-series models the change in the compatibility unit values as the sum of the square differences across time is also an important measurement. Equation 2.8 illustrates how this metric is calculated.

$$CI_{ssq} = \frac{\sum\limits_{t=1}^{N} (CI_t{}^{unit} - CI_{t-1}{}^{unti})^2}{N}$$

Equation 2.8 The Sum-of-the-Squares Difference in Coimpatibility

The directionless change in the model compatibilty provides an insight into how well the current production rules relfect the external work (in terms of the data point mapping to the predicate fuzzy sets.)

You should note the objective of the statistical compatibility measurement is not to find a model with a value approaching [1.0]. In terms of the model execution space, statistical measurements close to zero or close to one indicate a fundamental flaw in the model logic. Figure 2.39 is a fuzzy set describing the meaning of an acceptable or good statistical compatibility.

STATISTICAL COMPATIBILITY

Good

Degree
of Membership
μ[x]

Average Unit Compatibility Index

Figure 2.39 The limits of acceptable (good) statistical compatibility

A model that consistently generates a unit compatibility near [1.0] has all its predicate rules firing with the maximum degree of truth. This means the data points are clustered tightly in a narrow band at the centers of all the fuzzy sets. Statistical compatibilities should range (as a general guideline) between [.40] and [.80], although, in true fuzzy logic fashion, these are only approximate figures.

Figure 2.40 and Figure 2.41 illustrate statistical spreads for models with problems in their over-all unit compatibilities.

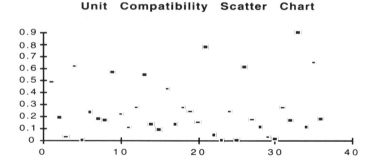

Figure 2.40 Unit compatibility values (with a mean of [.33])

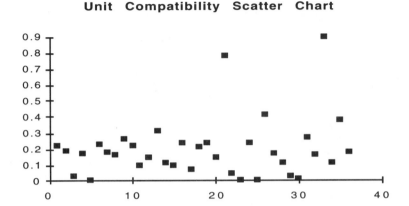

Figure 2.41 Unit Compatibility Values (with a mean of [.20])

These models have a few outliers that rise above the general behavior of the model, but both the average unit compatibility and the visual sense of the apparent performance trend shows these systems have a compatibility problem in the rule predicates and the domain data.

> Resolving an incompatibility between the model and the data is not a simple task since the source of the problem can be interwoven among the rules, the fuzzy sets, the variable declarations, and the techniques for fuzzy reasoning (correlation and implication.) In some fuzzy modelling system we can ask the software to track the execution of rules. By providing statistics on rule execution (including, perhaps, frequency histograms) we can begin to find areas in the models that are not behaving as expected.

Undecidable Models

In addition to problems with compatibility, the model designer and knowledge engineer must be aware that fuzzy systems can produce undecidable results. A model is undecidable if its information content is either ambiguous or non-existent. Undecidable models have one or more solution variables with under-generation fuzzy regions that are either all zeros or all ones. As an example, consider a fuzzy model with a single rule:

if costs are HIGH then profits are LOW

If this rule does not fire, then the PROFITS under-generation solution fuzzy set is left in its empty state (all the membership values are zero). Figure 2.42 shows how an empty fuzzy set appears.

Figure 2.42 An undecidable solution variable (empty fuzzy set)

This model is undecidable. We cannot make any predictions from the output state. We can also have an undecidable model when the non-zero membership plateau of the solution fuzzy set extends completely across the underlying domain. This is called an *infinite plateau*. Figure 2.43 shows how this appears in the PRICE solution set.

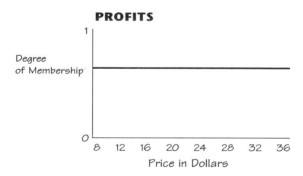

Figure 2.43 An undecidable solution variable (infinite plateau)

Infinite plateau solutions present an difficult problem in model interpretation. The best approach is to define them as undecidable. When the entire domain of the output fuzzy set has a single non-zero value, we cannot say precisely where the boundaries of the decision space lie. Applying a defuzzification operator to this kind of solution might produce an apparently reasonable result, but the underlying support for that answer is absent. This kind of solution space indicates a significant problem in the design of the model that must be addressed and repaired.

A model can also be undecidable if it is ambiguous. While fuzzy logic was designed to handle linguistic ambiguity, the existence of model solution state ambiguity in the system is very serious. Figure 2.44 illustrates a classical case of solution ambiguity. The model presents to equally well supported values for the PROFITS variable.

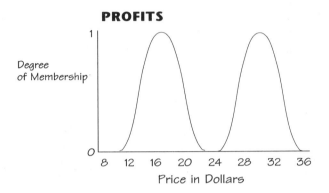

Figure 2.44 An undecidable solution variable (ambiguous solutions)

In order to have an undecidable model, the amount of ambiguity must be high, but not necessarily absolute (as in Figure 2.44). Even output fuzzy regions that have overlapping fuzzy regions can be ambiguous. Figure 2.45 illustrates a solution space for PROFITS that has a combined space but is still sufficiently ambiguous to be undecidable.

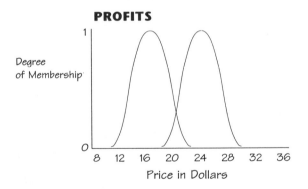

Figure 2.45 An undecidable solution variable (mostly ambiguous solution)

Fuzzy Backward Chaining

Fuzzy backward chaining follows the same general strategy for resolving a goal as the crisp *backward chaining* methodology. The central difference is the way in which the goal is resolved. During crisp backward chaining, a value is assigned to the goal variable by one or more rules. These rules are located in the same policy. In fuzzy reasoning, evidence is accumulated for a goal by firing all the rules in the policy, and a final value is determined through defuzzification. Figure 2.46 shows how a fuzzy model backward chains through a series of policies (sub-expert systems) to find the value of `profits` in the current rule.

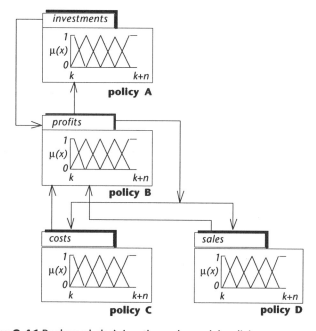

Figure 2.46 Backward chaining through model policies

When **policy A** requires a value for the variable `profits`, it looks for another policy that has `profits` as one of its solution variables. This is **policy B** and contains the following rules:

> *[R1] if costs are very high then profits are reduced*
> *[R2] if costs are quite low then profits are positively increased*
> *[R3] if costs are unchanged the profits are unchanged*
> *[R4] if sales are near mfgCosts then profits are low*
> *[R5] if sales are significantly above costs then profits are increased*
> *[R6] if sales[t] are much greater than sales[t-1] then profits are high*

In order to execute these rules, the policy needs a value for the variables costs and sales. Using the backward chaining strategy, **policy B** execution is interrupted so that the rules in **policy C** can be run to find a value for costs, and **policy D** can be run to find a value for sales. The order in which these policies are performed depends on the model agenda manager (which resolves conflicts among processes).

These policies, in turn, can contain fuzzy statements that must be resolved. As an example, **policy C** contains rules that are used to compute the estimate for the costs variable and contains the following rules:

> [R1] if expenses are increased then costs are near expenses
> [R2] if spoilage is large the costs are around spoilage
> [R3] if chargebacks are high then costs are near 1.2*chargebacks
> [R4] if backorders are above seasonalAvg then costs are decreased
> [R5] if inventory is large then costs are increased

These rules are resolved using fuzzy logic. A temporary output fuzzy set is established for the costs variable. When all the rules have been executed, an output fuzzy set exists that must be defuzzified to find a value for the variable costs. Figure 2.47 shows how a value for costs of $63.50 is found.

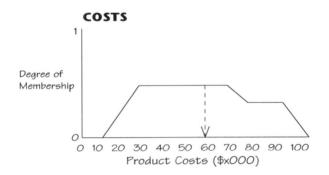

Figure 2.47 The fuzzy regions for costs solution variable

This value of $63,500 for costs and the value for sales from **policy D** is returned to **policy B** so that a value for the variable profits can be determined. When these rules are executed, a fuzzy region for profits is created (this is the fuzzy set PROFITS). The final or expected value for profits is derived through defuzzification. Figure 2.48 shows the expected value of +54 percent increase in profits.

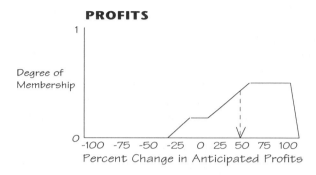

Figure 2.48 The fuzzy region for profits solution variable

Propagation of Fuzzy Entropy

Since defuzzification reduces a large fuzzy region to a single number, there is always some small loss of information. This loss of information increases disorder in the model. A result of this disorder is an increased loss of information. Measuring this loss of information between successive policy execution requires finding the amount of information lost when the expected value is assigned. In some cases we can reduce the amount of information loss by delaying the defuzzification process until the variable's value is actually required. This works to our advantage if the solution fuzzy set is explicitly used in another, subsequent policy. By passing the solution fuzzy region instead of the defuzzified value, we keep intact the morphology of the output fuzzy region.

Reduction of Entropy Through Evidence

The amount of disorder associated with a fuzzy model is somewhat dependent on the amount of evidence we can find to support the expected value of a solution variable. This is reflected in several model state measurements: the number of term or fuzzy sets that define the semantic of conceptual domain of the variable, the number of rules that execute on these fuzzy regions, and the degree of truth in the aggregate rule space.

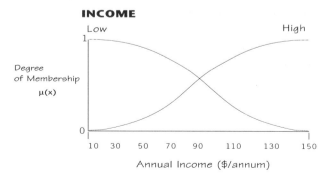

Figure 2.49 Income with sparse fuzzy definitions

Measurement of Model Entropy

With each defuzzification process the uncertainty associated with the expected result increases. We can see this in the backward chaining process that lead to the value for profits and finally to a value for the investments strategy. When a value for costs is determined, we discarded the remainder of the fuzzy region. No information about the degree of fitness (the compatibility index, as an example) is carried forward to the next reasoning level. Since defuzzification is generally insensitive to the strength of the output fuzzy set, repeated defuzzifications in a chain of inferencing can lead to an ill-supported value. This causes a general increase in the model entropy (disorder).

We can account for an increase in model distorter during successive backward chaining processes by measuring the steady-state fuzziness associated with each policy execution. This fuzziness is reflected in the unit compatibility index, that is, the degree of membership strength in the output fuzzy region.

Fuzzy Conditions in Conventional Rules

A fundamental and rather profound difference exists between the use of fuzzy sets in conventional reasoning mechanisms and their use in pure fuzzy or approximate reasoning models. Some general confusion exists about this issue. Pure fuzzy models combine evidence from many rules executed in parallel to produce a composite fuzzy region for each solution variable that is defuzzified to produce an answer. The answer is related to the degrees of truth in the consequent propositions of all the rules that contribute to the solution variable. When fuzzy sets are used in conventional rules, we simply replace the YES and NO dichotomy of a Boolean relational with the interval truth value of the fuzzy set. This has some far reaching implications for conventional expert systems.

Independent Relationships

The consequent action of a conventional rule is not proportionally linked to the truth of the antecedent. This might seem a little strange since we can easily conceive of conventional rules where the outcome is proportional to the antecendent. As an example:

```
if trafficflow is HEAVY
    then green signallight is increased.
```

so that, by some built-in extrapolation mechanism we might extend the duration of the green light based on the degree to which traffic flow is considered heavy. Equation 2.9 shows one possible extrapolation mechanism.

$$D(green) = D(green)_{base} \times (1 + \mu_{HEAVY}[x])$$

Equation 2.9 Extrapolating the duration of a green traffic light

In Equation 2.9 the duration of the green light ($D(x)$) is extended by a percentage that is proportional to the traffic flow's membership in the fuzzy set HEAVY. When traffic flow is not HEAVY (membership is zero) the duration is not changed, and when the traffic flow is absolutely HEAVY (membership is one), the duration is doubled. But this is **not** fuzzy reasoning. As an example, the rule:

```
if stresslevel is HIGH then perform medical.exam
```

measures *stresslevel* on a scale of 0 to 100. The fuzzy set HIGH is a sigmoid curve that indicates the degree of membership of a particular stress level in this fuzzy set. If there is any truth in the proposition (*stresslevel is HIGH*) then we perform a medical exam. But what is the meaning of this rule? When the stresslevel has a membership in HIGH of [.4], do we perform, say, only 40% of the medical exam. It doesn't make sense to perform a partial medical exam based on the degree of stresslevel. Consider another rule:

```
if bloodpressure is HIGH then take temperature
```

How can we take a temperature to some partial degree? Or does this mean the time we allow for a temperature reading should be proportional to the patient's blood pressure. Regardless of the interpretation, the consequent is an all or nothing proposition.

The disconnect between pure fuzzy reasoning and the use of fuzzy sets in conventional models is illustrated clearly when we consider the range of crisp consequents allowed in conventional rules. As an example:

```
if portfolio.dollars are LARGE
    and prime.rate is HIGH then do;
        AccountFlag="CRITICAL"
        exec SafetyAnalysis(safetylevel);
        sendmsg "Account "+portfolio.id+" is "+safetylevel
    end;
```

Clearly the degree to which the consequent actions in this rule are executed is unrelated to the degree of truth in the predicate (except the aggregate truth in the predicate must be above the current alpha threshold for rule execution). On the other hand, it is possible to effectively use fuzzy antecedents by applying explicit alpha cut thresholds to the fuzzy propositions. This sets a minimum truth in the fuzzy relationship before the rule can be fired. As an example:

```
if portfolio.dollars are LARGE [.4]
    and prime.rate is HIGH [.7]
        then AccountFlag="CRITICAL"
```

Of course, this simply sets a crisp boundary on the interval arithmetic associated with the fuzzy proposition. We must know *a priori* where along the domain of the underlying LARGE and HIGH fuzzy sets their values becomes of interest. The previous rule is equivalent to the conventional rule:

```
if portfolio.dollars > 13200
    and prime.rate > 5.2
        then AccountFlag="CRITICAL"
```

since any excess degree of truth above the alpha threshold does not affect the rule outcome. The only advantage we have in using fuzzy propositions in otherwise crisp rules is the ease with which knowledge representation can be accommodated. This is not a minor advantage and can significantly contribute to both model maintainability and knowledge acquisition.

Execution Ambiguity

The use of fuzzy predicates can lead to ambiguity problems in backward and forward chaining engines. Consider a simple backward chaining rule set:

```
[R1] if A = B then C = 1
[R2] if A > B then C = 2
[R3] if A < B then C = 3
```

If the values for the variables "A" and "B" are unknown, the inference engine backward chains through the rule set looking for rules that specify "A" and "B" in their consequents. When these are found, they are collected and executed. If any unresolved variables exist in the antecedent of the new rules, the engine backward chains to discover the value for the variables. This continues until the variables are given a value or until all the rules are exhausted. If the variables are still without values, the engine prompts the user for the values. Eventually, the inference engine winds its way back up to the original rule set. With values for "A" and "B" now firmly in hand, one of the three rules are fired and a value for the solution variable "C" determined. A complete discussion of this technique is found in the section "Backward Chaining Inference Strategy" on page 64.

A problem arises, however, if the antecedent propositions involve fuzzy sets or hedges that convert numbers to fuzzy sets[6]. Since fuzzy sets represent regions that have over-lapping domains, some truth might exist in propositions that we would ordinarily consider mutually contradictory. Consider the following rules that uses fuzzy sets instead of conventional relational operators.

---

6. The approximation and restriction hedges can convert numbers into bell or triangular shaped fuzzy sets. The rule set would appear as something similar to:
```
    if A is around        B then C is 3
    if A is above around  B then C is 2
    if A is below around  B then C is 3
```
In this version of the rule set, the variable "B" becomes a fuzzy number. The value for "B" is determined through conventional backward chaining.

```
if A is MEDIUM   then C is 1
if A is HIGH     then C is 2
if A is LOW      then C is 3
```

Figure 2.50 shows how the antecedent fuzzy sets are mapped onto the domain for variable "A". Within the central region of the variable's domain, all the fuzzy sets overlap. Although not a common practice, it occurs relatively frequently in some business models.

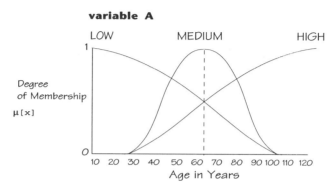

Figure 2.50 The LOW, MEDIUM and HIGH Fuzzy Sets for Variable "A"

If a value for "A" does not exists, conventional backward chaining is used to instantiate the variable. When we find a value of "A" the inference engine can begin the evaluation of the conflict agenda and fire the appropriate rules. Figure 2.51 shows the various memberships associated with a domain value of 40.

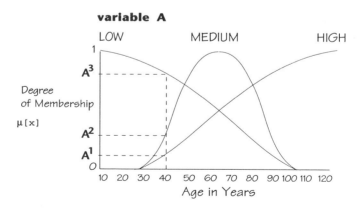

Figure 2.51 Multiple membership grades for a domain value of "40"

Because of this overlap in the fuzzy sets, many values for "A" have degrees of truth in several fuzzy sets. Thus, more than one rule on the agenda executes. In the previous rule set, for a value of 40, all three rules execute. Depending on the priority of the rules, and other factors such as their execution costs, the final value for "C" can be 1, 2, or 3. In fact, for anything but the most simple agenda, the final value of the solution variable may appear to be randomly chosen from the possible data space. Thus, rules using fuzzy sets in their antecedent can introduce a high level of ambiguity into the machine reasoning process.

Lack of Evidential Reasoning

Unlike pure fuzzy rules, the consequent actions of a conventional rule are definitive rather than suggestive. This means that fuzzy sets can not be used on the right-hand side of a consequent assignment statement. As an example, if the following is a conventional rule:

```
if project.duration is LONG
    then monitorlevel is ELEVATED;
```

we immediately encounter a problem in its interpretation. While the antecedent or predicate can be evaluated to determine the membership of project.duration in the fuzzy set LONG, with the exception of fuzzy monotonic reasoning, there is no corresponding or analogous action that maps the fuzzy set ELEVATED into the variable monitorlevel. The monotonic reasoning approach provides a serviceable mechanism when the solution variable is specified in only a single rule, but is not adequate when we want to accumulate evidence for a variable from many individually executed rules. As an example, the following conventional rules assess the need for closely monitoring a project.

```
if project.duration is LONG then monitorlevel is ELEVATED;
if project.budget is LARGE then monitorlevel is HIGH;
if project.timesrevised is BIG
        then monitorlevel is MODERATE;
```

While these rules make perfect sense in a pure fuzzy reasoning model, a conventional backward or forward chaining engine cannot process them correctly. Assuming we employ a form of monotonic reasoning, each rule independently sets a value for the variable monitorlevel. This means that we are not accumulating evidence for the value of monitorlevel. When the previous set of rules complete execution, monitorlevel has the value associated with the last rule.

Naturally, if we take liberties with the syntax of our hypothetical expert system, an extended reasoning mechanism can be constructed that aggregates the monotonic reasoning relationships among several predicates. Following is an example of such a statement.

```
monitorlevel = AVG(
    {(project.duration,LONG),ELEVATED},
    {(project.budget,LARGE),HIGH},
    {(project.timesrevised,BIG),MODERATE})
```

Using this approach we take the average or mean of the individual monitorlevels produced in each of the subordinate clauses. Note we are solving a particular and restricted class of problems by abandoning the rule architecture of the expert system in favor of a functional system.

Fuzzy Systems as Universal Approximators

An important attribute of a fuzzy system is its ability to model any continuous function within a bounded domain (that is, within a reasonable scope of the function dimensions.) This critical capability is derived from the Fuzzy Approximation Theorem (FAT) developed and subsequently proved by Dr. Bart Kosko. In his 1994 paper[7], Kosko says:

> *An additive fuzzy system can uniformly approximate any real continuous function on a compact domain to any degree of accuracy.*

In this section we examine the way a fuzzy system can approximate, to any degree of accuracy, an arbitrary function. Although we are looking at continuous functions, this same approach can also be applied to noncontinuous, lattice, and step functions. The ability to approximate an arbitrary continuous function is an important capability. In the everyday world of business and industry—in finance, insurance, medicine, manufacturing, retailing, transportation, biotechnology, petrochemicals, just to name a few—models are predominately based on continuous variables. We start by examining the additive fuzzy system and the way a conventional rule-based system can define a function.

The Additive Fuzzy System

The ideas underlying the additive fuzzy method have been discussed in "Additive Aggregation" on page 85. This type of fuzzy reasoning system is based on the bounded sum. When correlated consequent fuzzy sets are aggregated, the incoming fuzzy regions are added to the solution fuzzy region. Equation 2.10 is the basic process of the additive fuzzy system.

$$S = \min(\sum_{i=1}^{n} w_i C_i, 1)$$

Equation 2.10 The additive fuzzy system mechanism

This process shows that the additive system accumulates the consequent fuzzy sets (C_i) scaled by the adaptive contribution weights (w_i). When the summed membership value at any point across the solution domain exceeds one [1.0], it is constrained to a maximum of [1.0]. For nonadaptive and nonself-organizing systems, the contribution weight is set to one [1.0] indicating it has no impact on the reasoning process.

Rule-Based Function Approximation

A rule defines a space in the current problem state. Rules also tell the model how to find the next state in the problem resolution process. This is equivalent to moving along the function surface. Figure 2.52 illustrates this concept for an arbitrary function **f(x,y)**.

---

7. Kosko, Bart, *Fuzzy Systems as Universal Approximators*, IEEE Transactions on Computers, Vol 43, No. 11, Nov. 1994

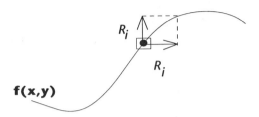

Figure 2.52 Moving over the surface of a function

At any arbitrary point in the function, P_n, a rule, R_i, specifies how to move over the surface. Figure 2.53 shows how this state change is made by a rule. In a two dimensional function, as an example, the state specified by point P_1 is moved to point P_2 by executing a rule (R_i) that specifies the movement along the *x-y* coordinates.

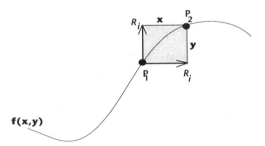

Figure 2.53 Moving from point-to-point along a function

As each rule is executed, it accumulates data. This data defines the nature of the underlying process. As an example, the following small set of rules, using time-series variables:

> *if X is P(t) then Y is S(t-m)*
> *if X is B(t) then Y is S(t-n)*
> *if X is W(t) then Y is S(t-r)*

sets a value for Y for each value of X (this is the f(x,y) function.) With these kinds of rules we can step across the surface of a function. Figure 2.54 shows how three rules can identify four points—P_1, P_2, P_3 and P_4— on the function surface.

In this way, as illustrated in Figure 2.55, we can construct a piecewise linear interpolation of the function surface. In general, the more rules we have in our system, the better our approximation becomes.

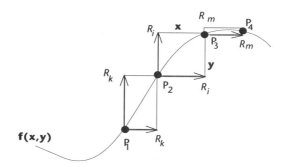

Figure 2.54 Crisp approximation of a function surface

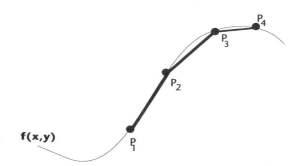

Figure 2.55 The approximated curve for function f(x,y)

From this you can see that even a conventional expert system using binary logic can approximate a bounded function. Kosko comments directly on this in his paper, *[A] large enough AI expert system can approximate any bounded measurable function and fuzzy rules reduce in the bivalent case to expert-system rules.*

The caveat here, of course, is the necessity that the expert system rule set be "large enough" to cover all R^n dimensions in the function space. A requirement that is difficult to meet for even moderately sized knowledge-based systems. Large, conventional expert systems are well known for their brittleness and the frequency with which a model execution finds *holes* in the logic— a problem state exists that is not covered by the rules.

This is seldom surprising in business application were the processes are highly non-linear, have high dimensionality, and an underlying mathematical model is seldom known. In process and control engineering problems such as balancing a double stage pendulum, detecting an infrared signal profile, controlling the movement of a crane, and so forth, the mathematical model is usually well known. These problems are typically and regularly implemented using proportional, integral, differential (PID), state space, and H∞ techniques. Fuzzy systems are regularly used to implement a wide spectrum of process control applications. They are also important modelling tools for an even wider array of hard to model business problems.

Fuzzy Rule and State Spaces

A fuzzy system differs from a conventional expert system in the method used to cover the surface of a function. A fuzzy system accumulates evidence for a state in the function space. As an example, consider a simple function with one dependent and one independent variable. A chemical manufacturing process suffers a loss of material through evaporation that is proportional to the temperature of the liquid. Figure 2.56 shows this functional relationship.

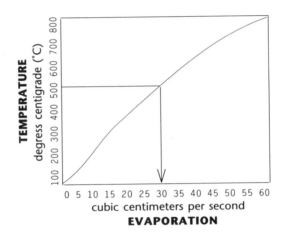

Figure 2.56 Functional relationship between temperature and evaporation

How does a fuzzy system go about approximating this function. We know this 1x1 fuzzy model can be expressed as a simple rule: as the temperature rises, the rate of evaporation also rises. This rise is not quite linear. To begin the approximation process, we need to decompose the variables TEMPERATURE and EVAPORATION into a set of fuzzy regions that can be addressed by our rules. Figure 2.57 shows the term set for the TEMPERATURE independent variable.

The temperature ranges from COLD to HOT (in terms of the sublimation threshold for the chemical substance). Figure 2.58 shows the term set for the EVAPORATION RATE dependent variable.

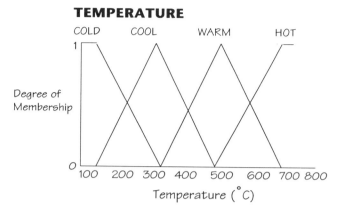

Figure 2.57 The temperature independent variable

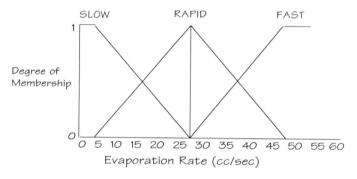

Figure 2.58 The evaporation dependent variable

The rate of evaporation is measured in terms of cubic centimeters per second at the specified temperature and has a term set that goes from SLOW to FAST. Using these two variables with their fuzzy regions, we want to build a system that predicts the evaporation rate for a particular temperature. The following set of rules describe part of this model,

> *[R1] if temperature is HOT then evaporation is FAST*
> *[R2] if temperature is WARM then evaporation is RAPID*
> *[R3] if temperature is COOL then evaporation is SLOW*

These rules describe the behavior of the system as the temperature changes. With this concept in mind, Figure 2.59 shows the over-all frame work for how a fuzzy system can represent the relationships between TEMPERATURE and EVAPORATION.

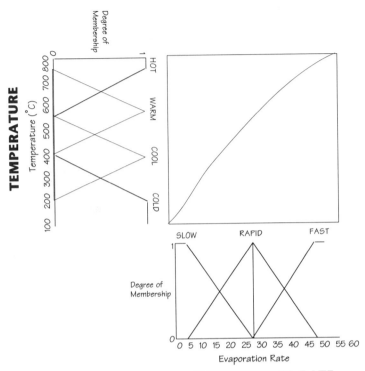

Figure 2.59 The framework for approximating the evaporation function

One or more fuzzy regions in the TEMPERATURE variable domain, corresponds, in some degree, to one or more fuzzy regions in the EVAPORATION variable domain. Figure 2.60 shows how these overlapping fuzzy regions cover parts of the temperature to evaporation function curve. As we will see shortly, these overlapping regions are critical in converging on a close approximation to the function.

In Figure 2.60 we can see an area subtended by the rule:

[R2] if temperature is WARM then evaporation is RAPID

any individual value of temperature in the WARM fuzzy region falls somewhere in the triangular region defined by the fuzzy set RAPID. The large domain sizes of the underlying fuzzy sets means the level of granularity in this approximation is not very high. But, since fuzzy system accumulate evidence for the nature of the function's shape, additional rules provide a better and better approximation. Figure 2.61 illustrates how two adjoining regions define more regions on the curve.

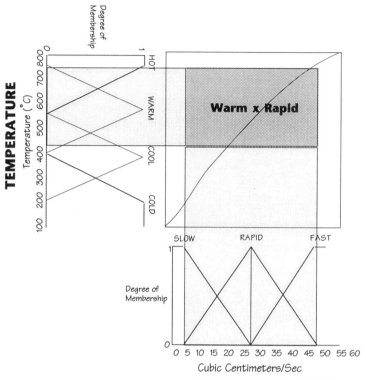

Figure 2.60 The warm temperature and rapid evaporation region

In the example shown in Figure 2.61, we are looking at the two regions refined by adding another rule,

> *[R2] if temperature is WARM then evaporation is RAPID*
> *[R3] if temperature is COOL then evaporation is SLOW*

And the region between them defines a part of the curve that is in transition between COOL and WARM. This transition also induces a change in predicted evaporation rate from SLOW to RAPID. When a fuzzy system model executes, it accepts data for each of the independent variables. These values are checked against each rule's premise. A premise is TRUE when a data value has some nonzero membership in one or more of the fuzzy sets. As an example, Figure 2.62 shows how a Temperature of 460°C is processed.

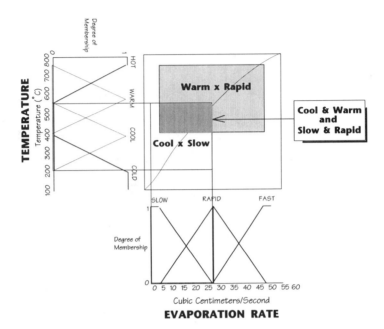

Figure 2.61 Overlapping region on the temperature and evaporation curve

A temperature of 460°C has a μ[.88] degree of membership in the fuzzy set WARM. This means that any rule with WARM in its predicate will fire. Thus:

[R2] if temperature is WARM then evaporation is RAPID

executes, inducing some evidence the evaporation rate should be somewhere in the RAPID region. The exact value for the rate is unknown. Figure 2.63 shows how the rule causes the fuzzy state associated with the evaporation rate to take on a partial value of RAPID.

The RAPID fuzzy set from the TEMPERATURE variable's term set is applied to the solution region after it is adjusted to account for the truth of the rule's premise. In this case, the height of the RAPID triangular set is scaled by the μ[.88] membership level. Since, however, 460°C also has some degree of truth in the COOL fuzzy region, the rule:

[R3] if temperature is COOL then evaporation is SLOW

is also selected for execution. This temperature has a μ[.32] degree of membership in the COOL fuzzy set. When rule [R3] executes we accumulate some small amount of evidence that 460°C should be locate somewhere in the SLOW evaporation rate region. Figure 2.64 shows how executing this rule adjusts information about the SLOW evaporation rate.

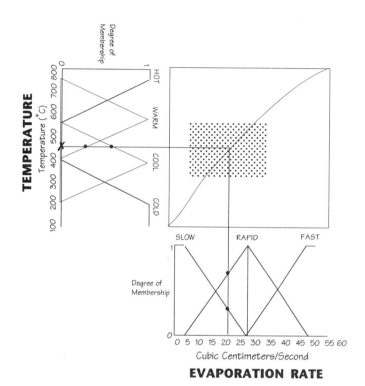

Figure 2.62 Locating a temperature point on the function curve

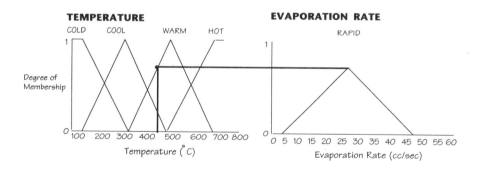

Figure 2.63 Model state when temperature of 460°C is in WARM region

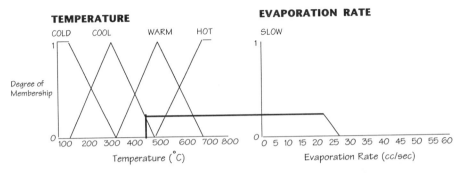

Figure 2.64 Model state when temperature of 460°C is in COOL region

There are two general methods of adjusting the consequent fuzzy region with the degree of truth in the rule premise. These are called *correlation minimum* and *correlation product*. Correlation Maximum truncates the consequent fuzzy set at the premise truth while correlation product "scales" the fuzzy set by multiplying each membership value by the premise truth. The Fuzzy Approximation Theorem (FAT), requires the correlation product form. This insures that the centroid method (the weighted average of the membership functions) of defuzzification falls correctly within the combined consequent fuzzy sets. For a complete discussion of correlation methods and their affects on fuzzy reasoning see "Correlation Techniques" on page 74.

When the SLOW region, adjusted for the truth of rule [R3], is merged with the accumulated evidence already in the evaporation rate solution region, it is added to the existing truth membership values. As Figure 2.65 shows, this causes a slight bulge in the left triangular region. This is the way an additive fuzzy system combines output (consequent) fuzzy regions.

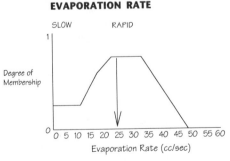

Figure 2.65 Finding a value on the evaporation function curve

When all the rules have been executed, the resulting fuzzy output region represents the approximation of the function solution. A precise value is found by defuzzifying the fuzzy set (represented by the downward arrow in Figure 2.65).

Approximation and the Additive System

In the previous section we saw how a system is modeled by finding its behavior within regions defined by a set of fuzzy relations. These relations are defined by a set of production rules. The output of these relations—the region of the system behavior or function—is also a fuzzy set. We can view this region as a "patch" on the underlying function. Fuzzy approximation is based on the idea of *adding* together the fuzzy patches on a function graph and *averaging* the patch regions that overlap. We can see how this works in Figure 2.66 where a series of patches cover the principle surface of the function.

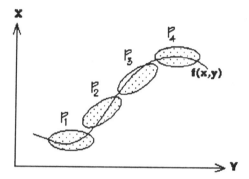

Figure 2.66 Fuzzy patches on the function surface

These four patches, P_1 through P_4 define the behavior of the function in these regions of the problem space. Now these patches are actually fuzzy sets produced through the rule system. As an example, we can view Figure 2.66 as a series of fuzzy patches produced by the interaction of the fuzzy rules. This kind of relationship is illustrated in Figure 2.67.

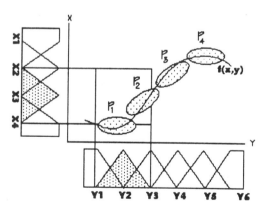

Figure 2.67 Fuzzy patches defined by fuzzy relations

Patches and Fuzzy Relations

Each fuzzy patch is actually a space representing the possible position of a point along the function surface. The patch itself derives from the idea of the *Cartesian product*. Cartesian products are the combinations that result from combining elements from many different sets. If we have set X with **a** elements and set Y with **b** elements, then the Cartesian product of set X⊗Y is **axb**. Figure 2.68 illustrates this relationship.

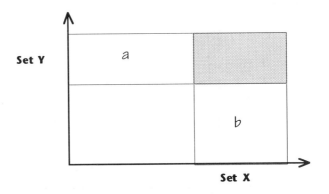

Figure 2.68 Cartesian product of two crisp sets

When set Y contains five elements and set X contains three elements then the Cartesian product X⊗Y is 15. Figure 2.69 illustrates this concept as a lattice of elements in both sets.

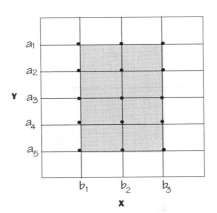

Figure 2.69 Element-wise Cartesian product of sets Y and X

The Cartesian product of two fuzzy sets, on the other hand, is quite different. The number of elements in a fuzzy set are not discrete and elements have varying degrees of membership in the set. We can envision the Cartesian product as a three dimensional surface reflecting the combination of the set elements as well as their degree of membership in the set. Figure 2.70 shows the Cartesian Product of two fuzzy regions Y⇔X.

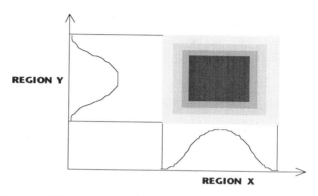

Figure 2.70 Cartesian product of two fuzzy sets

As we see, this Cartesian space has the same properties as a "patch" lying along the function surface and is, in fact, produced in the same manner. These Cartesian product spaces describe degrees of intensity in the relationships between fuzzy spaces. When many fuzzy sets are involved, the patches combine to produce an approximation of the function's general form.

Approximation, Patch Granularity, and Overlap

A function k=f(x,y), can be approximated with a fuzzy rule based system by decomposing the dependent and independent parameters (variables) x, y, and k into a set of fuzzy regions. The rules specify the behavior among these fuzzy regions for any locus on the function (for any value within the domain of the function). This behavior is defined by patches on the function that is generated by the Cartesian product of the independent fuzzy sets. But correct approximation depends on more than decomposing the variables into a set of fuzzy sets. It also depends on the number of underlying fuzzy sets and their overlap. In particular, approximation depends on two principles: The fine grain description of the variables through their term set, and the appropriate degree of overlap between the neighboring fuzzy sets.

Fuzzy Set Granularity and Density

Granularity is the key to approximation. The more fuzzy sets we have, the more rules we can write. The more rules we can write, the finer we can describe the behavior of the system (or function.) Figure 2.71 illustrates this situation. Here we have a fuzzy system where the variables X and Y are defined by three fuzzy sets.

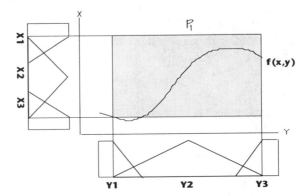

Figure 2.71 A fuzzy system with few fuzzy sets

When the level of granularity is very low, as in Figure 2.71, the patch size of the Cartesian product between region **X2** and **Y2**, Y⇔X, is extremely large. Although we can describe the function is broad terms—we can certainly define the general area of the systems—none of the fine grain detail such as its sinusoidal nature is observed. When we increase the number of fuzzy sets, more of the underlying behavior can be described. As Figure 2.72 illustrates, increasing the fuzzy sets for each variable's term set, increases our ability to describe the system's over-all behavior.

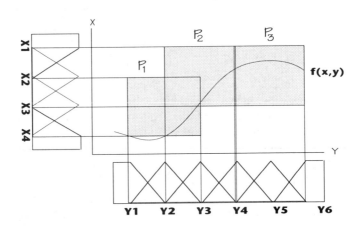

Figure 2.72 A fuzzy system with many fuzzy sets

The fuzzy regions overlaying the function in Figure 2.72 only describe the space subtended by the major fuzzy sets in the variable term set. But fuzzy sets do not have sharp boundaries (hence the name "fuzzy"). In fact, the patches on a function are combined from not only the region described by a principal fuzzy set, but also from the regions that over-lap from neighboring fuzzy sets. This contribution increases the granularity of the system. Figure 2.73 shows how the same fuzzy system is defined using the Cartesian products of **X1** and **X2** with **Y4** and **Y5**.

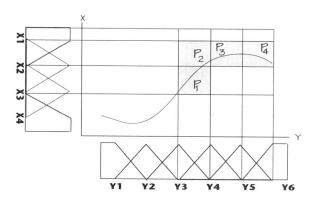

Figure 2.73 A fuzzy system with fine grain patches

By increasing the number of fuzzy sets in the model, our ability to refine the system approximation increases. As an example, Figure 2.74 shows the same function when the number of fuzzy sets are significantly increased. The regions defined by patches on the function are smaller and its wave-like behavior is clearly visible.

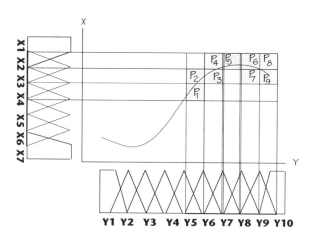

Figure 2.74 A fuzzy system with high degrees of fuzzy set resolution

Fuzzy Set Overlap

In addition to the decomposition of a variable's domain space into fuzzy sets, system approximation also depends on the overlap of neighboring fuzzy sets. This overlap, in fact, is necessary to support the combination of evidence and to correctly define the system behavior. Figure 2.75 illustrates a fuzzy system where the term sets contain fuzzy sets that do not overlap.

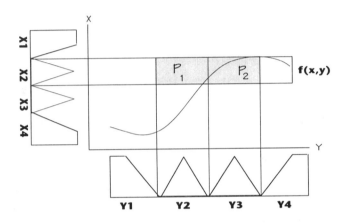

Figure 2.75 A fuzzy system without term set overlaps

The overlap between fuzzy sets causes the function surface to "smooth out" across the domain of each underlying fuzzy region. Without overlap, only a single rule can contribute to the definition of a function surface for any Cartesian product space such as Y3⇔X2. As an example, in the following rule:

[R1] if x is X2 and y is Y2 then s is P$_1$
[R2] if x is X2 and y is Y3 then s is P$_2$

the domain value **y** cannot have a partial membership in both Y2 and Y3. This means, if rule [R1] fires, rule [R2] will not fire, and if rule [R2] fires, then rule [R1] will not fire. In a proper fuzzy system, of course, **y** could have a partial membership in both Y2 and Y3. Then rule [R1] would fire to a degree $\mu[i]$ and rule [R2] would fire to a degree $\mu[j]$ (where, normally, $\mu[i]+\mu[j]=1$). This lack of overlap means that the approximation process makes a sharp jump between each fuzzy region. These jumps are the result, as we have seen, of discontinuities in the fuzzy sets that lead to corresponding discontinuities in the output fuzzy sets.

Approximating a Drug Concentration Model

Fine grain function approximation depends on the number of fuzzy sets and the overlap the fuzzy sets in the term set. However, we can gain a significantly rich approximation of a fuzzy system with a moderate population of fuzzy sets. This is the nature of fuzzy systems. When we want to increase approximation detail, we can increase the level of granularity in the underlying fuzzy sets. To illustrate how function approximation works in fuzzy systems, we look at a simple blood dosage concentration model. Equation 2.11 describes this model.

$$C(t) = Dte^{-(t/3)}$$

Equation 2.11 The blood dosage model

A given drug with dosage **D** diffuses to a level **C(t)** in the blood after time **t**. The model is a nonlinear bell-shaped function. The blood concentration increases rapidly at first and then begins to decay over time. Figure 2.76 shows how the blood concentrations varying according to time at various initial dosages.

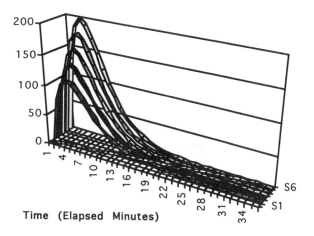

Figure 2.76 Drug blood concentrations at various initial dosage levels

In this model Figure 2.76 shows several concentration levels associated with various initial dosage levels. The initial dosages are 100, 120, 140, 160, and 200 units. The initial blood concentration is close to zero and rapidly rises toward the initial dosage level. The blood concentration then decays quickly toward zero. The code that generates this mathematical model is found in "dcmodel1.cpp (The Drug Concentration Model)" on page 389.

The Preliminary Concentration Model

The fuzzy drug concentration model is essentially a 1x1 model. Given a particular initial dosage, the blood concentration is simply a function of time. Our model operates on a fuzzy associative memory that indicates a relative change in the blood concentration given the current time period. Figure 2.77 shows the plot of values from the preliminary fuzzy estimation model for an initial dosage of 120 units.

Drug Concentration (in units) Across Time

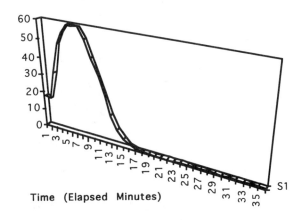

Figure 2.77 The fuzzy dosage concentration model (first approximation)

Model Design

This model does not perform particularly well, but it does capture the basic growth and exponential decay properties of the function. The low level of granularity in both the time periods and the concentration fuzzy sets does not provide a good approximation of the system. The complete code for this model is located in "dcfuzzy1.cpp (The Fuzzy Drug Concentration Model)" on page 390.

In this next section we examine the way this first drug concentration model was designed and the affects the fuzzy set descriptions have on model precision. The rules for the model are held in a two dimensional Fuzzy Associative Memory (FAM). For any particular time period the FAM indicates which fuzzy set is used to determine the period's change in drug concentration. Figure 2.78 shows the actual FAM for the preliminary model.

TIME PERIOD	CHANGE IN CONCENTRATION
T0	LN
T1	LP
T2	SP
T3	ZR
T4	SN
T5	MN
T6	LN
T7	ZR

Figure 2.78 Fuzzy associative memory (FAM) for preliminary dosage model

Interpreting this FAM is the same as executing a set of rules in the form:

if timeperiod is T_i then ConChange is C_i

where T_i is a fuzzy set defining a time period in the model, and C_i is a directional change in the concentration. This change goes from LN, a Large Negative, through ZR, a zero change in the concentration, to LP, a Large Positive change in the concentration. The model itself steps through 36 clock periods (minutes). At any one time, a clock period can be one or more fuzzy time periods thus causing more than one rule in the FAM to execute. The combined action of these multiple rules create the output concentration fuzzy set. This set is defuzzified to find the dosage concentration in that particular clock period.

The Variable Term (Fuzzy) Sets

The first step in understanding how to approximate the drug dosage model is the definition of the underlying fuzzy sets for the independent and dependent variables. Figure 2.79 shows the organization of the TIME.PERIOD variable. It is decomposed into eight fuzzy set regions.

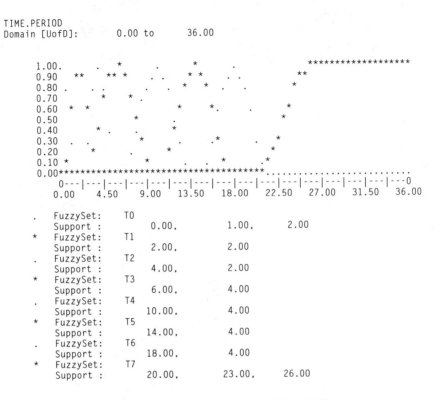

Figure 2.79 The term set for the TIME.PERIOD variable

Figure 2.80 is the blood drug dosage value and is model dependent (since it must have a universe of discourse that spans the minimum and maximum possible drug concentrations.) The dosage amounts are supported by five fuzzy sets.

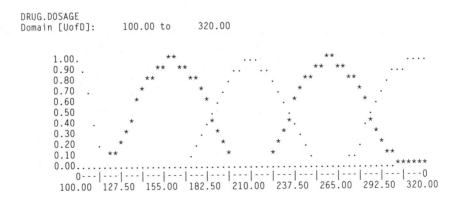

```
     .   FuzzySet:     SMALL
         Support :       100.00,      110.00,      120.00
     *   FuzzySet:     MEDIUM
         Support :       160.00,       50.00
     .   FuzzySet:     MODERATE
         Support :       210.00,       50.00
     *   FuzzySet:     LARGE
         Support :       260.00,       50.00
     .   FuzzySet:     COPIOUS
         Support :       260.00,      285.00,      310.00
```

Figure 2.80 Term set for the DRUG.DOSAGE variable

Figure 2.81 shows the change in concentration from one time period to the next. This is the solution variable—the output from the fuzzy model in each clock time period. The change runs in a percentage of the current blood dosage from -100% to +100%. This variable's term set is decomposed into seven fuzzy sets grouping the concentration change in regions from Large Negative (LN) through Zero (ZR) to Large Positive (LP).

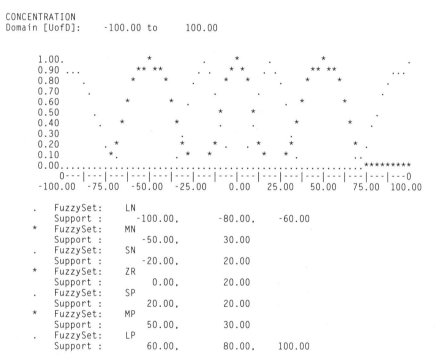

```
CONCENTRATION
Domain [UofD]:     -100.00 to      100.00


     1.00.                    *            .     *       .         *             .
     0.90 ...              ** **         .   *   *     . .       ** **          ...
     0.80  .            *      *        .    *   *         *      *         .
     0.70  .
     0.60             *        *     .       *   *      .     *         *
     0.50          .                     *      *                    .
     0.40       .     *        *         .      .           *        *        .
     0.30                         .                     .
     0.20      .  *           *      *    .   *        *          *    .
     0.10       *.                .  *   *         *   *  .              ..
     0.00.................................................................*********
          0---|---|---|---|---|---|---|---|---|---|---|---|---|---|---|---0
       -100.00  -75.00  -50.00  -25.00   0.00   25.00   50.00   75.00  100.00


     .   FuzzySet:     LN
         Support :      -100.00,      -80.00,      -60.00
     *   FuzzySet:     MN
         Support :       -50.00,       30.00
     .   FuzzySet:     SN
         Support :       -20.00,       20.00
     *   FuzzySet:     ZR
         Support :         0.00,       20.00
     .   FuzzySet:     SP
         Support :        20.00,       20.00
     *   FuzzySet:     MP
         Support :        50.00,       30.00
     .   FuzzySet:     LP
         Support :        60.00,       80.00,      100.00
```

Figure 2.81 Term set for the CONCENTRATION variable

Model Results

The preliminary drug dosage model captures the bell-shaped organization of the model but does not provide sufficient granularity over time to correctly approximate the degree of this curve. Figure 2.82 shows the output from the preliminary model.

```
BLOOD DOSAGE CONCENTRATION
Time      +/-Chg      Concentration
---       --------    -------------
  0.       -0.89          17.50
  1.       -0.02          17.09
  2.        0.88          32.18
  3.        0.51          48.52
  4.        0.13          54.58
  5.        0.09          59.27
  6.        0.00          59.27
  7.        0.00          59.27
  8.       -0.09          53.72
  9.       -0.17          44.48
 10.       -0.20          35.45
 11.       -0.27          26.03
 12.       -0.38          16.07
 13.       -0.47           8.54
 14.       -0.51           4.20
 15.       -0.54           1.94
 16.       -0.63           0.71
 17.       -0.78           0.16
 18.       -0.89           0.02
 19.       -0.89           0.00
 20.       -0.88           0.00
 21.       -0.85           0.00
 22.       -0.01           0.00
 23.       -0.01           0.00
 24.       -0.01           0.00
 25.       -0.01           0.00
 26.       -0.01           0.00
 27.        0.00           0.00
 28.        0.00           0.00
 29.        0.00           0.00
 30.        0.00           0.00
 31.        0.00           0.00
 32.        0.00           0.00
 33.        0.00           0.00
 34.        0.00           0.00
 35.        0.00           0.00
```

Figure 2.82 Output from the drug concentration model

In essence we have not sliced the curve into enough time frames so the rule base can move the function surface properly. The time slicing is also too coarse to manage the small decay of the dosage along the tail of the curve. We can see this by examining some of the fuzzy reasoning at several time periods along the clock time frame.

Model Execution

Figure 2.83 shows the model output from the first two clock time periods in the function. Each clock time period is annotated in the output followed by the Fuzzy Associative Memory [FAM] rule that fired along with its truth. You can see which rules are executed by examining the FAM display which indicates the fuzzy sets as:

FAM[*time,Δconcentration*]

where time is the TIME.PERIOD fuzzy set, and *Δconcentration* is the CONCENTRATION fuzzy set. This FAM display is followed by the degree of truth in the rule predicate.

```
-----------------------PERIOD:    0-----------------------------
FAM[  0,LN] mem( 1.000)
---RULE FIRED--Premise truth of:1.0000

        FuzzySet:     Concentration
        Description:
        1.00.
        0.90 ...
        0.80    .
        0.70     .
        0.60
        0.50     .
        0.40      .
        0.30
        0.20       .
        0.10          ..
        0.00          .....................................................
          0---|---|---|---|---|---|---|---|---|---|---|---|---|---|---|---0
        -100.00  -75.00  -50.00  -25.00   0.00   25.00   50.00   75.00  100.00
          Domained:          -100.00 to      100.00
          AlphaCut:          0.10

---'CENTROID'    defuzzification. Value:     -89.063, [0.8505]

-----------------------PERIOD:    1-----------------------------
FAM[  1,LN] mem( 0.516)
---RULE FIRED--Premise truth of:0.5155

        FuzzySet:     Concentration
        Description:
        1.00
        0.90
        0.80
        0.70
        0.60
        0.50.......
        0.40         .
        0.30
        0.20        .
        0.10          ..
        0.00          .....................................................
          0---|---|---|---|---|---|---|---|---|---|---|---|---|---|---|---0
        -100.00  -75.00  -50.00  -25.00   0.00   25.00   50.00   75.00  100.00
          Domained:          -100.00 to      100.00
          AlphaCut:          0.10

FAM[  1,LP] mem( 0.484)
```

```
---RULE FIRED--Premise truth of:0.4845

        FuzzySet:    Concentration
        Description:
        1.00
        0.90
        0.80
        0.70
        0.60
        0.50.......
        0.40       .                                  ........
        0.30
        0.20       .                              .
        0.10       ..                             .
        0.00       ..  .................................  ..
            0---|---|---|---|---|---|---|---|---|---|---|---|---|---|---|---0
          -100.00  -75.00  -50.00  -25.00   0.00   25.00   50.00   75.00  100.00
            Domained:        -100.00 to       100.00
            AlphaCut:           0.10

---'CENTROID'     defuzzification. Value:       -2.344, [0.0000]
```

Figure 2.83 Dosage concentration approximation in Periods [0] and [1]

As you can see, the lack of detail in the fuzzy model means an abrupt change occurs in the second time period. The approximation of the curve surface—dipping to zero initially and then rising toward the full concentration level—results in a bifurcation of the control space yielding a small increase in concentration in the second time frame. Once we reach a certain rise point in the model, the approximation converges to a normal fuzzy model. Figure 2.84 shows how the model rules begin to work together in clock period four.

```
----------------------PERIOD:    4-----------------------------
FAM[ 4,SP] mem( 0.998)
---RULE FIRED--Premise truth of:0.9980

        FuzzySet:    Concentration
        Description:
        1.00                                     .
        0.90                                   . .
        0.80                                     .
        0.70                                  .
        0.60                                   .
        0.50
        0.40                             .
        0.30                                .
        0.20                          .
        0.10                                 .
        0.00.................................     ....................
            0---|---|---|---|---|---|---|---|---|---|---|---|---|---|---|---0
          -100.00  -75.00  -50.00  -25.00   0.00   25.00   50.00   75.00  100.00
            Domained:        -100.00 to       100.00
            AlphaCut:           0.10

FAM[ 4,ZR] mem( 0.469)
---RULE FIRED--Premise truth of:0.4692
```

```
      FuzzySet:      Concentration
      Description:
     1.00                                                .
     0.90                                            .  .
     0.80                                              .
     0.70                                          .
     0.60                                              .
     0.50
     0.40                                  . . . . . . .
     0.30                                                .
     0.20                                  .
     0.10                              .                .
     0.00. . . . . . . . . . . . . . . . . . . . .        . . . . . . . . . . . . . . . . . . . . . . .
        0---|---|---|---|---|---|---|---|---|---|---|---|---|---|---|---|---0
     -100.00   -75.00    -50.00   -25.00    0.00    25.00    50.00   75.00  100.00
      Domained:          -100.00 to     100.00
      AlphaCut:             0.10

  ---'CENTROID'     defuzzification. Value:       12.500, [0.7188]
```

Figure 2.84 Dosage concentration approximation in Period [4]

The Enhanced Concentration Model

An obvious improvement to the drug concentration model involves increasing the granularity of the TIME.PERIOD term set so we can specify, in finer detail, the movement of the function surface. In fact, this change gives us a markedly improved version of the model toward the left of the curve. Figure 2.85 shows the new approximation curve for the drug concentration model.

Drug Concentration (in units) Across Time

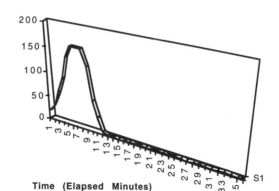

Figure 2.85 The fuzzy dosage concentration model (second approximation)

Model Design

This model performs fairly well, it captures the basic growth and exponential decay properties of the function as well as the magnitude of the curve. The higher level of granularity in the time periods allows us to divide the surface of the curve into small units and thus improves the approximation. The complete code for this model is located in "dcfuzzy2.cpp (The Fuzzy Drug Concentration Model)" on page 395. In this section we examine the way this second drug concentration model was designed and the affects the fuzzy set descriptions have on model precision.

The rules for the model are also held in a two dimensional Fuzzy Associative Memory (FAM). For any particular time period the FAM indicates which fuzzy set is used to determine the period's change in drug concentration. Figure 2.86 shows the actual FAM for the enhanced model.

TIME PERIOD	CHANGE IN CONCENTRATION	TIME PERIOD	CHANGE IN CONCENTRATION
T0	LN	T7	ZR
T1	LP	T8	SN
T2	LP	T9	MN
T3	MP	T10	MN
T4	MP	T11	LN
T5	SP	T12	LN
T6	ZR	T13	LN

Figure 2.86 Fuzzy associative memory (FAM) for enhanced dosage model

The TIME.PERIOD Term (Fuzzy) Sets

There are two degrees of freedom in the drug dosage model and we are free to change both the granularity of the time periods and the change in blood concentration. In this enhanced version of the model, we have changed the time periods, increasing the level of detail by nearly doubling the size of the term set. Figure 2.87 shows the organization of the TIME.PERIOD variable. It is decomposed into fourteen fuzzy set regions.

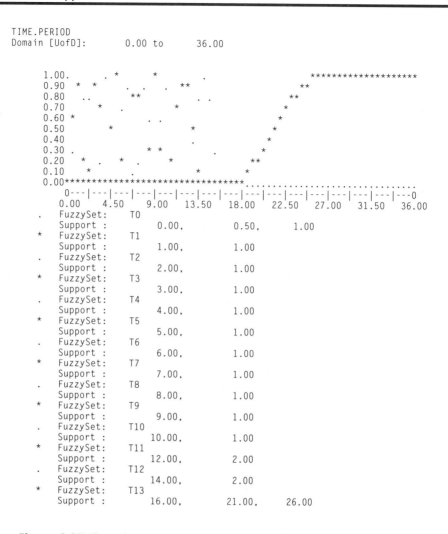

```
TIME.PERIOD
Domain [UofD]:        0.00 to      36.00


    1.00.      . *        *          .                    ********************
    0.90  *  *       .    .       **                  **
    0.80  ..        **      . **       ..              **
    0.70   *    .              *          ..          *
    0.60 *                 . .                        *
    0.50     *                   *                   *
    0.40                      .                      *
    0.30 .              * *          .            *
    0.20   *     *    .      *              **
    0.10   *          .                      *
    0.00********************************....................................
     0---|---|---|---|---|---|---|---|---|---|---|---|---|---|---|---0
      0.00    4.50    9.00   13.50   18.00   22.50   27.00   31.50   36.00
    .  FuzzySet:   T0
       Support :        0.00,       0.50,      1.00
    *  FuzzySet:   T1
       Support :        1.00,       1.00
    .  FuzzySet:   T2
       Support :        2.00,       1.00
    *  FuzzySet:   T3
       Support :        3.00,       1.00
    .  FuzzySet:   T4
       Support :        4.00,       1.00
    *  FuzzySet:   T5
       Support :        5.00,       1.00
    .  FuzzySet:   T6
       Support :        6.00,       1.00
    *  FuzzySet:   T7
       Support :        7.00,       1.00
    .  FuzzySet:   T8
       Support :        8.00,       1.00
    *  FuzzySet:   T9
       Support :        9.00,       1.00
    .  FuzzySet:   T10
       Support :       10.00,       1.00
    *  FuzzySet:   T11
       Support :       12.00,       2.00
    .  FuzzySet:   T12
       Support :       14.00,       2.00
    *  FuzzySet:   T13
       Support :       16.00,      21.00,      26.00
```

Figure 2.87 The enhanced term set for the TIME.PERIOD variable

This change in the granularity of the TIME.PERIOD variable's term set improves our ability to approximate the function by slicing the time frame into a large number of fuzzy sets each covering a small region of time. This smaller time increment means we can specify the change in function surface with much finer detail.

Model Results

The enhanced drug dosage model captures both the bell-shaped organization of the model and the proper magnitude of the curve height, but does not provide sufficient granularity over time to correctly approximate the right-hand tail of this curve. Figure 2.88 shows the output from the enhanced model.

```
Time      +/-Chg     Concentration
---       --------   -------------
  0.       -0.89          17.50
  1.        0.88          32.95
  2.        0.88          62.04
  3.        0.49          92.57
  4.        0.49         138.13
  5.        0.20         160.00
  6.        0.00         160.00
  7.        0.00         160.00
  8.       -0.20         127.50
  9.       -0.51          62.75
 10.       -0.51          30.89
 11.       -0.88           3.86
 12.       -0.89           0.42
 13.       -0.88           0.05
 14.       -0.89           0.01
 15.       -0.88           0.00
 16.        0.00           0.00
 17.        0.00           0.00
 18.        0.00           0.00
 19.       -0.85           0.00
 20.       -0.86           0.00
 21.       -0.88           0.00
 22.       -0.88           0.00
 23.       -0.89           0.00
 24.       -0.89           0.00
 25.       -0.89           0.00
 26.       -0.89           0.00
 27.       -0.89           0.00
 28.       -0.89           0.00
 29.       -0.89           0.00
 30.       -0.89           0.00
 31.       -0.89           0.00
 32.       -0.89           0.00
 33.       -0.89           0.00
 34.       -0.89           0.00
 35.       -0.89           0.00
```

Figure 2.88 Output from the enhanced drug concentration model

Model Execution

Figure 2.83 shows the model output from the first two clock time periods in the function. Each clock time period is annotated in the output followed by the Fuzzy Associative Memory [FAM] rule that fired along with its truth. You can see which rules are executed by examining the FAM display.

```
------------------------PERIOD:    0-------------------------------
FAM[  0,LN] mem( 1.000)
---RULE FIRED--Premise truth of:1.0000


        FuzzySet:    Concentration
        Description:
     1.00.
     0.90 ...
     0.80    .
     0.70    .
     0.60
     0.50      .
     0.40      .
     0.30
     0.20        .
     0.10          ..
     0.00           ...................................................
        0---|---|---|---|---|---|---|---|---|---|---|---|---|---|---|---0
      -100.00  -75.00  -50.00  -25.00   0.00   25.00   50.00   75.00  100.00
        Domained:      -100.00 to       100.00
        AlphaCut:          0.10

---'CENTROID'    defuzzification. Value:    -89.063, [0.8505]

------------------------PERIOD:    1-------------------------------
FAM[  1,LP] mem( 1.000)
---RULE FIRED--Premise truth of:0.9995


        FuzzySet:    Concentration
        Description:
     1.00                                                           .
     0.90                                                          ...
     0.80                                                         .
     0.70
     0.60                                                       .
     0.50
     0.40                                                     .
     0.30                                                    .
     0.20                                                 .
     0.10                                               ..
     0.00...................................................
        0---|---|---|---|---|---|---|---|---|---|---|---|---|---|---|---0
      -100.00  -75.00  -50.00  -25.00   0.00   25.00   50.00   75.00  100.00
        Domained:      -100.00 to       100.00
        AlphaCut:          0.10

---'CENTROID'    defuzzification. Value:     88.281, [0.8283]
```

Figure 2.89 Dosage concentration approximation in Periods [0] and [1]

This new model provides a better control surface for the function. The switch from curve decay to curve growth is explicit and definite producing the marked increase in the dosage concentration in the first full time period. From this increase in the Cartesian space around the dosage concentration function we provide, as least within the main portion of the function, an better estimation of its behavior. Figure 2.90 shows the output from the approximation model during clock period five through nine. As you can see we have improved our ability to define the curve surface so that the final approximation is fairly close to the actual function surface (Refer to "Drug blood concentrations at various initial dosage levels" on page 129 for the output from the mathematical model).

```
-----------------------PERIOD:   6------------------------------
FAM[  6,ZR] mem( 0.982)
---RULE FIRED--Premise truth of:0.9824

        FuzzySet:    Concentration
        Description:
        1.00
        0.90                                        ...
        0.80                                    .    .
        0.70
        0.60
        0.50                                .          .
        0.40
        0.30
        0.20                            .          .
        0.10                        .          .
        0.00.........................        ...........................
          0---|---|---|---|---|---|---|---|---|---|---|---|---|---|---0
        -100.00  -75.00   -50.00   -25.00     0.00   25.00    50.00    75.00  100.00
        Domained:        -100.00 to     100.00
        AlphaCut:          0.10

---'CENTROID'    defuzzification. Value:       0.000. [0.9824]


-----------------------PERIOD:   7------------------------------
FAM[  7,ZR] mem( 0.976)
---RULE FIRED--Premise truth of:0.9761

        FuzzySet:    Concentration
        Description:
        1.00
        0.90                                        ...
        0.80                                    .    .
        0.70
        0.60
        0.50                                .          .
        0.40
        0.30
        0.20                            .          .
        0.10                        .          .
        0.00.........................        ...........................
          0---|---|---|---|---|---|---|---|---|---|---|---|---|---|---0
        -100.00  -75.00   -50.00   -25.00     0.00   25.00    50.00    75.00  100.00
        Domained:        -100.00 to     100.00
        AlphaCut:          0.10

---'CENTROID'    defuzzification. Value:       0.000. [0.9761]


-----------------------PERIOD:   8------------------------------
FAM[  8,SN] mem( 0.969)
---RULE FIRED--Premise truth of:0.9688
```

```
        FuzzySet:    Concentration
        Description:
     1.00
     0.90                                    ...
     0.80                                  .
     0.70                                    .
     0.60                                 .
     0.50
     0.40                                .
     0.30                              .
     0.20                                 .
     0.10                            .
     0.00...................         ...............................
        0---|---|---|---|---|---|---|---|---|---|---|---|---|---|---|---0
       -100.00  -75.00  -50.00  -25.00   0.00   25.00   50.00   75.00  100.00
        Domained:        -100.00 to      100.00
        AlphaCut:          0.10

---'CENTROID'    defuzzification. Value:     -20.313, [0.9688]


-----------------------PERIOD:    9-----------------------------
FAM[  9,MN] mem( 1.000)
---RULE FIRED--Premise truth of:1.0000


        FuzzySet:    Concentration
        Description:
     1.00                    .
     0.90                 .. ..
     0.80              .       .
     0.70
     0.60            .          .
     0.50
     0.40           .           .
     0.30
     0.20          .            .
     0.10         .
     0.00........              ...............................
        0---|---|---|---|---|---|---|---|---|---|---|---|---|---|---|---0
       -100.00  -75.00  -50.00  -25.00   0.00   25.00   50.00   75.00  100.00
        Domained:        -100.00 to      100.00
        AlphaCut:          0.10

---'CENTROID'    defuzzification. Value:     -50.781, [0.9986]
```

Figure 2.90 Dosage concentration approximation in Periods [6] through [9]

As consequence of the Fuzzy Approximation Theorem (FAT) and the ability of fuzzy systems to universality approximate complex, nonlinear functions, we can build production business systems that are capable of handling the high degree of complexity found in all but the most trivial problems. For a more complex approximation model see "dcfuzzy3.cpp (Weight-biased Drug Concentration Model)" on page 400. This is a 2x1 model that considers body weight and time as concentration control parameters.

FuzzySQL and Database Systems

Initiali₂
Parms[0]
Parms [1₂
sprint(s₹
strncpy(₂
FDBptr[M₹
if(⌐)t₁
Par⌐om₹
Part⌐m₁
(*⌐nt₂

3

Fallentis semita vitae...
The untrodden paths of life...

Horace (65–8 B.C.)
Epistles, xviii, 103

In this chapter we explore the world of relational database systems and the use of fuzzy logic in formulating imprecise queries against database tables. The majority of databases in commercial use today, in such areas as financial services, manufacturing, retail, transportation, pharmaceutical and biotechnology, are constructed around the relational model. We begin with a review of the nature and organization of relational systems, the development and nature of SQL, the Structured Query Language, and then the use of approximate queries in the relational database environment. This chapter is not intended as complete examination of relational databases and database query languages, but only as a foundation so the introduction of fuzzy query predicates can be understood in context.

Relational Database Concepts

An Historical Perspective

In the late 1960's Edgar Codd, then at the IBM Santa Terresa research facilty in San Jose, California proposed a new organization for commercial databases[1]. In this new model the hierarchical and network database organizations with their explicit and internal links between data elements, the principal structural component of then existing databases, are

---

1. See E.F. Codd, "A Relational Model for Large Shared Data Banks", *Commun. ACM* 13, 377 (June 1970)

145

replaced by a much simpler and more direct data model based on the mathematical principle of the relation. In the pure relational model each table or relation consists of several *domains*. Domains are organized in rows or, more formally, *tuples*. New tables are formed by connecting tables that share common domains. This connection process is called a *join*. Joins come in many flavors. The most common is the equi-join, meaning the join is made on equal values. An important property of a join is called *closure*, indicating that the result of a join is always a new table. Subsets of tables are produced by selecting a set of rows through the process of *projection*. Projection also shares the property of closure.

By the early 1970's D. D. Chamberlin, M. M. Astrahan and others had developed a formal method of defining and manipulating a relational database. This language, SEQUEL[2]—Stuctured English Query Language—provided a cohesive and comprehensive method of using a relational database, thus turning relational theory into a practical implementation. As an example, the SEQUEL instruction to retreive the project manager names for all projects in the engineering department would look something like:

```
SELECT PROJMGR
FROM PROJECTS
WHERE DEPARTMENT = "ENGINEERING";
```

This language, in the shortened form of SQL—the Structured Query Language—formed the basis for the ORACLE relational database system from Oracle Corporation[3] as well as IBM's initial database offerings: SQL/DS on their VM/CMS machines, and DB2 on their MVS machines. With IBM's endorsement (a strong impetus for adoption in the late 1970's and 1980's) SQL emerged as the *de facto* standard for relational database access and maintenance.

Through the mid-1970's other important relational database languages and organizations began to emerge, most notable among these is INGRES, designed and developed by Michael Stonebraker. Unlike the relational calculus foundations of SEQUEL and SQL, the INGRES system, using its QUEL[4] language, takes a more relational algebra approach to database access and maintennace. The same project manager retreiveal in QUEL would look like the following,

```
RANGE OF P IS PROJECTS
RETRIEVE (P.PROJMGR) WHERE P.DEPARTMENT = "ENGINEERING"
```

---

2. See Chamberlin, D.D., Astrahan, M.M, et alia, "SEQUEL 2: A Unified Approach to Data Definition, Manipulation, and Control", *The IBM Journal of Research and Development*, Vol 20, No. 6, (November 1976).

3. Known as RTI, Relational Technology Incorporated when it released its initial UNIX version of the ORACLE database in the early 1980's.

4. QUEL is the interactive version of the language, while EQUEL (embedded QUEL) is intended for integration into application software.

The relational algebra orientation provides a lower level instruction base for relational operations thus allowing a finer control over database operations. Although QUEL is superior to SQL in many important ways (it is a more uniform language, supports explicit closure, allows nested aggregation, and provides capabilities for cross-table updates), the success of SQL-based database products has not made this language popular outside the INGRES community.

Relational Systems

A Relational Database System (RDBMS) consists of many independently created and maintained tables. Tables are added or removed from the database or have their structures changed without reorganizing or redesigning the entire facility. In production database systems there are other facilities needed to improve performance and extend capabilities. These additional facilities include secondary indexes, explicit domains, security controls, access permissions, checkpoint and restart monitoring, database reorganizaton and compression facilities, and similar management controls.

Databases, Tables, Rows, and Columns

A Database consists of tables. Tables consist of rows. Rows consist of columns. Each table is designed and maintained independently of other tables in the database (momentarily disregarding the concepts of domain enforcement and referential integrity). Figure 3.1 shows the basic organization of a relation.

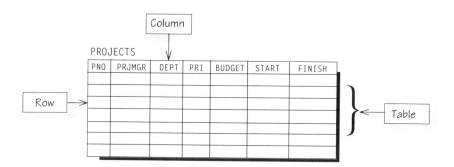

Figure 3.1 Organization of a relation

A database is a collection of related tables. These tables share a common support function in the underlying application. A project management system, as an example, might have tables that hold project information, resources and their availabilities, project task or event data, precedence network links for critical path analysis, cost allocations, and so forth. Inventory databases contain tables holding part information, part quantity-on-hand counts, backorders, suppliers, shipments, and warehouse bin inventories. Each table in a database is defined by a *schema*. The schema is a schematic defining both the high-level organization of the table as well as the individual columns. The following is a sample schema.

> *table=projects, file="c:\projdata",password=socrates*
> *compressed=YES,encrypted=YES;*
> *column=projno, data=ch, len=16;*
> *column=description, data=ch, len=80;*
> *column=department,data=ch, len=12,*
> *index="projdept", domain=depts;*
> *column=budget, data=double;*
> *column=priority, data=integer, default=5;*

A schema is compiled into the working image of the table. A set of compiled schema definitions collectively form the database's data dictionary.

Database tables consist of rows. A table can be empty, that is, it contains no rows. A table row is also called a *tuple* and consists of an ordered collection of columns. Each column has a definite set of attributes including a name, a description, a data type, a possible domain, a default value, and a formal report label. A row can consist of any number of columns so long as their total length does not exceed the physical page size of a relation.

The relationships in a database are established dynamically by connecting tables that share common data elements. This connection process is called a join. Joins can be made between any columns that share the same kind of data. Figure 3.2 illustrates some of the relationships in a simple project management database.

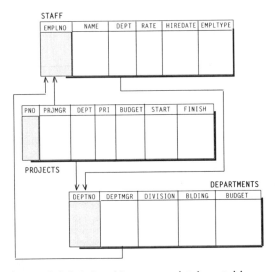

Figure 3.2 Relationship among database tables

These relationships not only allow a clear and consistent method of generating inter-table relationships, they also provide the underlying support structure for column domain enforcement. As an example, the project manager column (PRJMGR) in the PROJECTS table must also be a valid employee number (EMPLNO) in the STAFF table. The department columns in the staffing and projects table must contain valid department number (DEPTNO) values from the DEPARTMENTS table. Thus, a relational database usually contains a number of tables that are used only to enforce data integrity.

> Despite popular belief, it is not the ability to 'relate' tables that gives relational databases their name. A true relational database has the following properties: (1) all information is maintained in mathematically coherent structures called relations, (2) all relationships are maintained through the data, and (3) all synthesizing processes applied to relations result in new relations (the property called *closure*). This misunderstanding of relational technology and the meaning of a relation has resulted in many commercial databases that are not true relational systems.

Normalization

The design of a relational database is centered around the concept of normal forms. A relation is in a particular normal form when it obeys a specific set of ever stricter constraints. A complete exploration of normalization is not possible, but this section examines the nature of the three principle normal forms.

First Normal Form

A pure relational database must have all its tables in normal form. While there are several orders of normalization, a minimal normal form called *first normal form* (abbreviated 1NF) means each column in a table consists of a single value. That means that any row and column intersection in a table contains a single data element. Figure 3.3 illustrates a table—sales by product within region—that is *not* in first normal form.

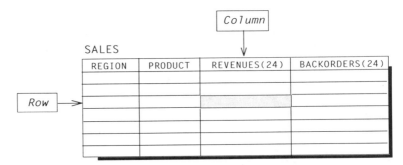

Figure 3.3 A table NOT in first normal form

In this table the sales revenues and backorders for the previous 24 months are maintained as an array. The REGION and PRODUCT columns form the unique key or identifier for this table. The Revenue and Backorders columns violate first normal form. We can convert this to first normal form by making the index values of these column explicit and converting them to part of the unique key extent for the table.

Figure 3.4 shows how the table can be reorganized so it is now in first normal form. Each separate monthly value of sales revenues and backorder amounts is stored in a separate row.

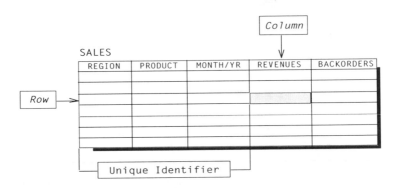

Figure 3.4 A table in first normal form (1NF)

Figure 3.5 shows a small portion of the SALES table with the regional revenues and backorders broken down by month and year. Notice how the implicit array index has become a right-hand key part and uniquely idenfies a region, product, and month combination.

SALES

REGION	PRODUCT	MONTH/YR	REVENUES	BACKORDERS
EAST	WIDGET	JAN94	19765.44	17
EAST	WIDGET	FEB94	23005.83	8
EAST	WIDGET	MAR94	24335.91	5
EAST	WIDGET	APR94	24506.04	0
EAST	WIDGET	MAY94	23811.92	0
EAST	WIDGET	JUN94	23527.88	7
EAST	WIDGET	JUL94	20053.49	2

Figure 3.5 A SALES table in first normal form (Eastern Region Widget Sales)

This is the simplest form of normalization. There are at least four different levels of relational nomalization (first through fourth normal form) each specifying a different relationship between data and the table structure (many of the higher order normalizations address issues associated with key dependencies, dependencies along non-key data elements, autocorrelation between data elements, and the isolation of intersectional relationships.)

Second Normal Form

A table is in 2NF when it is also in 1NF and every nonkey column is fully dependent on the primary key. Failure to restrict tables to second normal form is an even more common problem than failure to place tables in first normal form. Figure 3.6 shows a PROJECTS table that is not in second normal form.

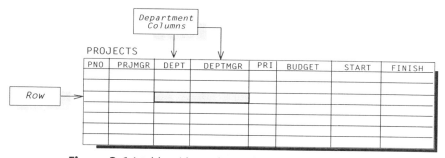

Figure 3.6 A table with a column dependency problem

Failure to place a table in second normal form leads to serious forms of maintenance anomaly. In the example of Figure 3.6 the department manager for the project's owning department is kept in each row. If the department manager changes, then every occurrence of department manager in every affected row and table must be found and changed. In second normal form, the DEPT column is used to find the department in a DEPARTMENTS table. This departments table contains one entry for each department along with the current department manager. Figure 3.7 shows the PROJECTS table in second normal form.

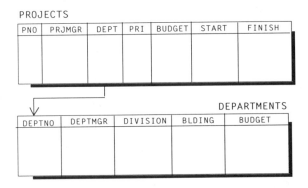

Figure 3.7 The PROJECTS table in second normal form (2NF)

Third Normal Form

Third normal form is a refinement on second normal form. A table is in 3NF when each nonkey column is mutually independent and also fully dependent on the table's primary key. The PROJECTS relation shown in Figure 3.7 is in both 2NF and 3NF. Note third normal form is a semantic property of the relation. In order to assure yourself that a table is, in fact, in 3NF you must understand the meaning of each column and the intensional meaning of the primary key collection.

Secondary Access Paths (Keys)

In addition to primary keys used to maintain row uniqueness, a table can have many secondary indexes[5]. These index structures provide access to sets of rows in the table based on generally non-unique occurrences. As an example, in the PROJECTS table, we might like to find all the projects that belong to a paticular group of departments (DEPT) or are assigned to a a specific set of project managers (PRJMGR). These are not components of the primary key. Thus, to find a set of rows that contain projects in the ENGINEERING department or assigned to MILLER as the project manager we must read every record in the table. We would like someway to locate all the rows with these attributes without reading the entire physical file. A secondary index serves this purpose.

---

5. From a purist viewpoint, I suppose I should say *indices*.

Alternate Index Concept

A secondary index contains each unique value for a column and, attached to this value, the primary keys[6] of all the records in the file that have this value in the corresponding column. In this way we can find a value for project manager, say MILLER, and then directly access every row that has this value in the PRJMGR column. Figure 3.8 shows how the secondary index for the PRJMGR and DEPT columns are arranged.

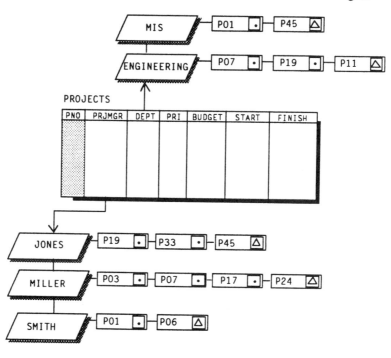

Figure 3.8 Secondary index paths on project manager and department

The secondary index manager returns a count of the multiple occurrences as well as the identifier lists. These lists allow the system to perform logical operations. Thus, keyed access expressions (in a hypothetical search language) such as:

find projects where prjmgr is "MILLER" and dept is "ENGINEERING";

produces two lists—one containing all the project identifiers managed by MILLER, the other containing all the project identifiers for the ENGINEERING department. The AND of the two lists are the project identifiers that appear in both lists (in Figure 3.8 this is the single project P07). The secondary indexes can be used to select arbitrarily complex lists, such as:

---

6. This may not, in fact, be an actual record key but some tag that can be translated into a record address. Some indexing schemes use a special "symbolic" address for the record. Other implementations use page and offset values in the table (for records that cannot be dynamically moved)

find projects where projmgr has ("SMITH", "MILLER")
and dept is "MIS"
and costcenter is "ENGR1"

In this example a list of all project identifiers for projects managed by SMITH or MILLER is retrieved from the secondary PROJMGR index. A second list containing all the projects in the MIS department is created from the DEPARTMENT secondary index. A third list containing all the projects charged to the ENGR1 cost center is created from the COSTCENTER secondary index. The intersection (AND) of all three lists is performed to find a list of the project identifiers satisfying the selection criteria. The index processor generally selects items in the index based on equality, contents (such as dept contains "ENG"), or comparisons for greater or less than a specific value. You usually cannot use airthmetic, logical, or string expressions in the index selection statement.

The Index Architecture

The unique values and multiple occurences lists are maintained in a separate hash-addressed files, in essence, standard database relations. This means we can quickly locate any unique value since this value is simply a primary key in a relation. Once a unique value has been found, the chain of multiple occurrences can be retreived. Figure 3.9 shows the general schematic of a hash-based secondary index.

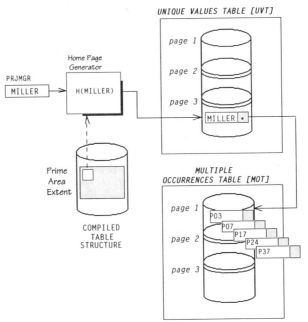

Figure 3.9 The architecture of a FuzzySQL secondary index

Each row in the Unique Values Table [UVT] contains a value from the associated column, a count of the multiple occurrences, and some other statistical and control information. The key is the unique value itself. The Multiple Occurrences Table [MOT] contains the actual cross-reference index. This relation is keyed by the unique value and the primary key from the associated table. The relation is clustered on the unique value. All of the index values for a value are located in the same region of the table space and can be retreived quickly.

B*Tree versus Hash-Based Indexing Schemes

B*Trees are balanced, multi-way trees that, since their orginal invention by Bayer and McCreight[a] in the early 1970s, have become the standard method for implementing secondary indexes in large commercial databases. This prediliction for the use of B*Trees stems from their compactness, controlled growth strategies, and the ability to traverse a B*tree symmetrically (in ascending lexigraphic order). On the other hand, B*tree structures are complex and difficult to maintain. Deletion of nodes from a B*Tree is particularly difficult.

FuzzySQL uses another, simpler, indexing scheme that incorporates the speed and flexibility of B*Trees without the internal complexity. In return for this increase in speed and ease of maintenance FuzzySQL makes a trade-off in storage space and growth flexibility. In a B*Tree the unique key is kept in a leaf node with the multiple occurrences kept below the leaf. FuzzySQL indexes repeat the unique key value for each multiple occurrence in a clustered relation. This increases the amount of disk storage required for the index. A B*Tree grows dynamically and acquires storage as required. The FuzzySQL Hash Index has an initial prime area based on the estimated record population. The Index performance is a function of how well this estimate corresponds to the actual size of the table. On the otherhand, FuzzySQL Index tables allow very easy insertion and deletion. Unique keys can be located without the recursion associated with B*Trees. Since FuzzySQL Indexes are standard relations, no special file access methodologies are needed.

a. Bayer, R. and McCreight, E.,"Organization and Maintenance of Large Ordered Indexes," *Acta Informatica*, 1, No. 3 (1972), pp. 173-89.

Database Query Concepts with SQL

The Structured Query Language, or SQL, provides a complete set of instructions for accessing and maintaining a relational database. Access is done through the SELECT statement while maintenance is performed through the DELETE, INSERT and UPDATE statements. Our concern is with the use of fuzzy logic in the qualification of queries against the underlying relational tables and we are primarily addressing the use of the SELECT statement (although much of this discussion might just as easily apply to qualifications used in the DELETE and UPDATE statement as well).

The SELECT statement

The complete language syntax for a SQL SELECT statement can be quite complicated and extensive, involving, as an example, mutiple table joins, "outer" joins, recursive SELECT statements called *subqueries*, set grouping and group screening (GROUP BY and HAVING), as well as alias tags for statements that make joins on the same table. In this chapter we will use only the very basic syntax to explore the implications of fuzzy queries on the retreival model. The basic syntax of the SQL database query is:

```
SELECT col_1, col_2, col_3,..., col_n
FROM tableid_1, tableid_2, ... tableid_k
WHERE expression_1 [ANDIOR] expression_2 ... expression_j;
```

Where:

SELECT   A set of column names from the specified tables written in the order you want them to appear in the query. If some ambiguity exists in the column names (such as a column with the same name existing in two or more specified tables) then the column name is prefixed with the name of the table.

FROM   A list of the tables. The columns are drawn from this list of tables. The order in which the tables are specified is not important, but all the tables must be included.

WHERE   The core of the database query process and is also the center of focus in fuzzy database operations. The WHERE statement in SQL performs two functions:

1. It selects rows from a table that meet a specific condition

2. It connects or joins tables based on specific comparison conditions.

When an expression is screening records, it must result in a **true** answer. As an example,

```
FROM PROJECTS
WHERE BUDGET > 1000
AND COSTCENTER = "MKTG";
```

selects only rows that have a BUDGET column greater than 1000 and have a COSTCENTER column with a string value of "MKTG". If either of the columns has an index, SQL automatically uses this to reduce the search space (see "Secondary Access Paths (Keys)" on page 152 for additional details on this concept.) When the expression is specifying a table join, it indicates the conditions under which the two tables are joined. As an example,

```
FROM PROJECTS,STAFF
WHERE PROJECTS.PROJMGR=STAFF.NAME;
```

joins the PROJECTS table with the STAFF table by comparing the PROJMGR column in the first column with the NAME column in the second table. Only rows in each table that have matching values are returned by the join[7].

Selection Intentionality and Logic

Clearly this kind of high-level language provides a powerful tool for querying relational database repositories. However, although SQL can easily capture the mechanical intent of a query, it lacks the ability to capture the semantics of a query. We can group and slice up collections of data in a variety of ways, but each division of the record collection proceeds along crisp lines. These crisp lines, like the crisp bifurcations in expert system rules, cause us to make arbitrary decisions about the membership of concepts that are

---

7. Commercial implementations of SQL also support more complex types of joins such as the outer-join (essentially, a join with missing data), the relational UNION, and joins on arithmetic and logical expression (often called *virtual joins* since they use dynamically created or *virtual columns*).

intrinsically imprecise. Thus database access methods share the same kind of constraints on expression and encounter the same kinds of complexity boundary limitations as conventional knowledge-based systems that use crisp rules.

In SQL the logic of the request resides in the WHERE statement. The results of this expression evaluation, as we noted previously, must be **true** in order to select a row. However, the logic of a SQL qualification is not Boolean as many people assume. Since a column in a database can have the NULL value (that is, no value has been assigned this column), the Structured Query Language supports a three-valued logic: true, false, and unknown. Columns with no assigned value—they are NULL—return an unknown state. The unknown statement results in a three value logic, since a value of unknown has a higher logical precedence than either true or false. Figure 3.10 shows the AND truth table for the SQL logic.

$$P_2$$

	TRUE	FALSE	UNKNOWN
TRUE	TRUE	FALSE	UNKNOWN
FALSE	FALSE	FALSE	UNKNOWN
UNKNOWN	UNKNOWN	UNKNOWN	UNKNOWN

$$P_1$$

Figure 3.10 The AND table for SQL's three valued logic

From our previous discussion of logic we know trivalent logics were among the earliest attempts to improve the rigid dichotomizations imposed by Boolean logic. Fuzzy logic is an outgrowth of this evolution, and we now turn our attention to examining how a extension of the SQL's three valued logic into fuzzy's infinite valued logic provides an important improvement on database access. In particular, stating fundamental queries as fuzzy predicates gives SQL the ability to express the intention as well as the mechanics of the query.

Fuzzy SQL Operations

We now turn our attention to the use of fuzzy logic in the formulation of queries against a standard relational database. To illustrate the differences between fuzzy and conventional (crisp) queries we use a small company profile database. It is similar to the kind of databases, but on a much smaller scale, as those maintained by Dunn and Bradstreet, Standards and Poor's, and ValueLine. Table 3.1 shows the database contents.

Table 3.1 The FuzzySQL financial database of small manufacturing companies

Company	Year Founded	Annual Revenues	No. of Products	No. of Employees	Profit or Loss	Earnings per Share
CompA	1948	570	1	16	3	0.2
CompB	1972	478	3	27	243	1.77
CompC	1982	401	9	58	17	1.02
CompD	1987	321	3	8	25	3.11
CompE	1988	650	5	33	-87	0.44
CompF	1994	550	16	9	99	0.79
CompG	1992	597	4	11	-13	0.04
CompH	1990	602	7	41	33	2.14
CompI	1991	498	5	15	207	1.33
CompK	1994	501	2	57	133	2.83
CompL	1985	920	8	5	201	1.55
CompM	1983	555	2	9	509	1.05
CompN	1988	1050	10	25	427	2.94
CompO	1990	530	14	12	22	0.3
CompP	1988	522	4	21	62	1.28
CompR	1959	900	3	5	-8	0
CompS	1964	659	2	7	0	0.1
CompT	1979	619	5	17	280	3.17
CompU	1967	1233	2	28	322	2.4
CompW	1964	973	11	48	422	2.88

The Intentionality Problem

The main focus behind the use of fuzzy logic is the addition of intentional structure to the query process itself. We can use fuzzy predicates to broaden the qualification specification in the WHERE statement to include approximate boundaries. This gives us what we *intend* to retrieve instead of what we must retrieve due to the mechanical and arbitrary nature of the crisp WHERE statements. Intentionality is concerned with improving the semantics of the query so that we capture more of the underlying meaning in the query. As an example, consider a search of the small manufacturing database for companies with high revenues. We decide that the boundary between high and not high is $600 million in revenues. Figure 3.11 shows the results of issuing an SQL request to find these companies.

```
SELECT COMPANY, REVENUES
    FROM MFGDBMS
        WHERE REVENUES > 600;
```

Company	Revenues
CompE	650
CompH	602
CompL	920
CompN	1050
CompR	900
CompS	659
CompT	619
CompU	1233
CompW	973

Figure 3.11 Companies with revenues > 600

But does this request actually capture the intent of our query? Did we really mean that high revenues start precisely at $600 million? In all likelihood, Companies CompG at $597 and CompA at $570 would also be of interest. Including these companies in the request output—perhaps with an indication that they are close to our cutoff point—would have captured the intention of the query.

Changing the lower boundary of the selection criteria is not a solution to this problem. In our sample database, reformulating the request as:

```
            SELECT COMPANY, REVENUES
            FROM MFGDBMS
               WHERE REVENUES > 585
```

will certainly pick up the close outliers to the $600 boundary, but at what price? We have now implicitly redefined our meaning of high. Now, however, near outliers to this value, such as $584, will still be excluded from the request. We can, of course, continue to lower our selection threshold, but at some point the entire concept of high in respect to revenues disappears. Thus a change in boundary points is not a solution for two reasons, first, it fails to maintain the central idea behind our request, and second, it fails to distinguish between candidates that are highly representative of our intention and those that are marginally or only partially representative of our intention.

A Simple FuzzySQL Query

To capture the intention instead of the mechanics of the request, we would like to issue SQL statements that select records based on a broader interpretation of our WHERE expression. Fuzzy sets provide a solution to this problem since, in their role as linguistic variables, they let us define the conceptual rather than the mechanical domain of the query. Thus, to make fuzzy queries against a relational database we need to decompose the domain of database columns into their underlying term sets. Figure 3.12 shows the fuzzy sets for HIGH and LOW.

```
REVENUES
Domain [UofD]:     500.00 to     1200.00
     1.00*
     0.90 *******                                                .
     0.80       ******                                        ......
     0.70            ******                              .......
     0.60                 *******                  .......
     0.50                       ******.....
     0.40                       ......*******
     0.30                 .......            ******
     0.20            ......                        *******
     0.10       .......                                  ******
     0.00......                                                ******
         0---|---|---|---|---|---|---|---|---|---|---|---|---|---|---0
       500.00  587.50  675.00  762.50  850.00  937.50 1025.00 1112.50 1200.00

     .   FuzzySet:    HIGH
         Support :       500.00,      1200.00
     *   FuzzySet:    LOW
         Support :       500.00,      1200.00
```

Figure 3.12 Fuzzy sets for HIGH and LOW revenues

The fuzzy set HIGH has a zero grade of membership below $500 and rises in a smooth linear curve toward a maximum of $1200. The fuzzy set LOW is the complement of HIGH. This new semantic interpretation of high, makes use of the compatibility measurement capabilities of fuzzy logic by starting slightly to the left of $600, and assigning values to the right of $600 various degrees of compatibility with the idea of high. The fuzzy set

HIGH becomes a vocabulary element in our SQL query language. Figure 3.13 shows exactly how this fuzzy set can be used in an approximate query (see "FzySQL0 (A Fuzzy SQL database processor [version 0])" on page 402 for the actual code supporting this query).

```
alphaCut: .1
select company
from MfgDBMS
where  Annual.Revenues are HIGH;

Company            CompIDX
----------------   ----------
CompU                1.000
CompN                0.782
CompW                0.669
CompL                0.595
CompR                0.568
CompS                0.226
CompE                0.210
CompT                0.167
CompH                0.144
CompG                0.136
Record Selected           :          10
Rejected due to AlphaCut  :           5
Percent (%) Found         :       50.00
```

Figure 3.13 A simple FuzzySQL query for HIGH revenues

The fuzzySQL query produces a ranked list of the selected companies in descending order of their CompIDX, the query compatibility index (which in this case, since only a single fuzzy set is involved, is simply the grade of membership for ANNUAL.REVENUES in the fuzzy set HIGH). From this query we see that the retrieval has captured more of our intent in the request. Companies are arrayed along the domain of the fuzzy set HIGH, providing us with information about how well each candidate meets our notion of high revenues. Companies CompU, CompN, and CompW are ranked as highly compatible with the idea behind the request. At the bottom of the list is company CompG, ranked as weakly compatible with the request's intention.

Alpha Cut Thresholds

We can also see some companies that have revenues between $500 and $1200 were not included in the list (as an example, company CompA). This is due to the alpha cut threshold specified in the fuzzySQL query. Any membership less than this threshold is excluded from the candidate list. In essence, the alpha cut sets any membership below its threshold to zero. Figure 3.14 shows the evaluation of the membership grade for ANNUAL.REVENUES in the fuzzy set HIGH for each database record. The actual value of revenues is followed by the truth membership.

```
  1. CompA
     ANNUAL.REVENUES      in 'HIGH' ( 570.00,0.097)
     Alpha Cut Rejection: 0.097 < 0.100
  2. CompB
     ANNUAL.REVENUES      in 'HIGH' ( 478.00,0.000)
  3. CompC
     ANNUAL.REVENUES      in 'HIGH' ( 401.00,0.000)
  4. CompD
     ANNUAL.REVENUES      in 'HIGH' ( 321.00,0.000)
  5. CompE
     ANNUAL.REVENUES      in 'HIGH' ( 650.00,0.210)
  6. CompF
     ANNUAL.REVENUES      in 'HIGH' ( 550.00,0.070)
     Alpha Cut Rejection: 0.070 < 0.100
  7. CompG
     ANNUAL.REVENUES      in 'HIGH' ( 597.00,0.136)
  8. CompH
     ANNUAL.REVENUES      in 'HIGH' ( 602.00,0.144)
  9. CompI
     ANNUAL.REVENUES      in 'HIGH' ( 498.00,0.000)
 10. CompK
     ANNUAL.REVENUES      in 'HIGH' ( 501.00,0.000)
 11. CompL
     ANNUAL.REVENUES      in 'HIGH' ( 920.00,0.595)
 12. CompM
     ANNUAL.REVENUES      in 'HIGH' ( 555.00,0.078)
     Alpha Cut Rejection: 0.078 < 0.100
 13. CompN
     ANNUAL.REVENUES      in 'HIGH' (1050.00,0.782)
 14. CompO
     ANNUAL.REVENUES      in 'HIGH' ( 530.00,0.039)
     Alpha Cut Rejection: 0.039 < 0.100
 15. CompP
     ANNUAL.REVENUES      in 'HIGH' ( 522.00,0.031)
     Alpha Cut Rejection: 0.031 < 0.100
 16. CompR
     ANNUAL.REVENUES      in 'HIGH' ( 900.00,0.568)
 17. CompS
     ANNUAL.REVENUES      in 'HIGH' ( 659.00,0.226)
 18. CompT
     ANNUAL.REVENUES      in 'HIGH' ( 619.00,0.167)
 19. CompU
     ANNUAL.REVENUES      in 'HIGH' (1233.00,0.996)
 20. CompW
     ANNUAL.REVENUES      in 'HIGH' ( 973.00,0.669)
```

Figure 3.14 The fuzzy membership analysis for the fuzzySQL query

Five records were eliminated from consideration due to the weakness of their membership strength. The rejection message appears in bold following each record. This threshold is an important component of a fuzzy SQL query. An alpha cut is applied to the composite truth value of the complete WHERE statement (which may contain many fuzzy propositions) and acts as a hurdle for inclusion in the candidate list. As an example, raising the alpha cut threshold to .5 produces a much smaller list of candidates as shown in Figure 3.15.

```
AlphaCut: .5
select company
  from MfgDBMS
    where  Annual.Revenues are HIGH;


Company           CompIDX
- - - - - - - - - - -   - - - - - - - -
CompL                 0.595
CompN                 0.782
CompR                 0.568
CompU                 0.996
CompW                 0.669
Record Selected           :          5
Rejected due to AlphaCut  :         10
Percent (%) Found         :      25.00
```

Figure 3.15 FuzzySQL query with Alpha cut of .5

A high alpha cut filters out records that are not highly compatible with the intention of the query while a low alpha cut allows records even weakly compatible with the query intent.

Measuring Compatibility with Complex Predicates

In practice, database queries involve more complex predicates than the one illustrated in the previous example. A FuzzySQL request might involve many columns in the database. As an example:

```
SELECT COMPANY
    FROM MFGDBMS
        WHERE COMPANY.AGE IS MATURE
          AND REVENUES ARE HIGH
          AND PRODUCT.COUNT IS FEW;
```

When complex predicates are used, the compatibility of the query is measured by evaluating the composite truth of all the fuzzy propositions in the WHERE statement. This raises an additional issue about how we compute this aggregate truth membership. There are two techniques that appear to work well in practice. These involve taking either the fuzzy AND (intersection) of all the predicate expressions or taking the average of all the predicate expressions[8].

---

8. In this discussion we are, for simplicity, treating all the WHERE predicate as through they are connected by the logical AND. When the logical OR is used, the expression is evaluated by taking the minimum of the maximums produced by the OR propositions.

The Fuzzy AND Method

The fuzzy AND technique treats each predicate as an inter-dependent statement. A query is satisfied only if all the component expressions contribute, and the compatibility index can not be any stronger than the weakest membership. The contribution to the complete query is computed by taking the minimum of the truth memberships for each predicate expression. Equation 3.1 shows how this result is computed for the complete query.

$$\mu_{query}[X] = \bigvee_{i=0}^{N} MIN(\mu_{\exp_i}[x]_i)$$

Equation 3.1 The FuzzySQL WHERE evaluation (fuzzy AND)

A significant difficulty with the fuzzy AND approach is its sensitivity to expressions with zero membership (including those that fall below the alpha cut threshold). If any individual expression is zero, the entire composite truth membership is zero. Depending on the nature of the request, this might be too strong a restriction on the semantics of the query.

The Average of Memberships Method

The average truth membership of all the WHERE predicates treats the entire query as a thematic unit with each WHERE predicate is an independent expression. A weakness in the contribution of one expression can be compensated by an increase in strength of the remaining expressions. The contribution to the complete query is computed by taking the average of the truth memberships for each predicate expression. Equation 3.2 shows how this result is computed for the complete query.

$$\mu_{query}[X] = \frac{\sum_{i=0}^{N} \mu_{\exp_i}[x]_i}{N}$$

Equation 3.2 The FuzzySQL WHERE evaluation (average)

The average method is generally insensitive to complex query predicates where one of the sub-expressions has a zero membership. On the other hand, the average technique tends to flatten the query compatibility index. Thus, a strongly compatible expression along with many weakly compatible propositions can yield a higher membership than you might expect. On the other hand, the average query can induce a skewed candidate population in the query if one or more of the predicate has a consistent zero membership value. As an example:

```
SELECT COMPANY
   FROM MFGDBMS
        WHERE COMPANY.AGE IS RECENT
        AND ANNUAL.REVENUES ARE HIGH;
```

If, as an example, the fuzzy proposition *annual.revenues* are HIGH has few representatives in the database, the aggregate truth on averaging are generally nonzero, assuming that the proposition *company.age is RECENT* has a moderate amount of truth for a significant number of records.

The AVERAGE aggregation method is, of course, a functional form of the logical OR (union) between several fuzzy sets. The average method also avoids the weaknesses of the dyadic operator type of averaging where the truth is reduced by each connecting operator. Equation 3.3 shows how the averaging process works as an expression $a \bullet b \bullet c \bullet d$ where $\bullet$ is the average operator.

$$ t = \left[\frac{\left[\frac{\left[\frac{a+b}{2} \right] + c}{2} \right] + d}{2} \right] $$

Equation 3.3 The Average process as a dyadic function

In this kind of protocol, the last expression's truth contributes most to the over-all truth of the expression. The functional averaging method solves this biasing function by performing a truth average of the individual memberships.

FuzzySQL with Complex Predicates

We now turn to an examination of queries involving complex predicates. This complexity arises in two areas: from the compound nature of the WHERE propositions and from the increased population of fuzzy sets underlying the database columns. In this section we look at the same query using both types of aggregation and make some observations about how well they implement the intended query.

Creating the Fuzzy Set Vocabulary

In the previous example, we established a small term set for the REVENUES column. This term set defines the vocabulary used in the query. In more realistic terms, the domains of a database systems, like variables in a fuzzy model, are decomposed into a set of overlapping fuzzy sets. The vocabulary for the complex SQL queries consists of the semantics underlying company age, annual revenues, the product count, the employee count, the change in profit (or loss), and the retained earnings per share.

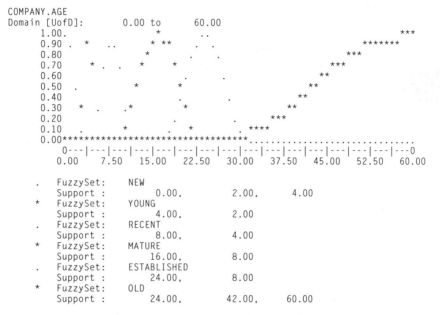

```
COMPANY.AGE
Domain [UofD]:      0.00 to     60.00
     1.00.                  *            ..                          ***
     0.90 .   *    ..       * **      . .                  *******
     0.80              *         .   .                 ***
     0.70    *  .   *        *          .           ***
     0.60                           .            **
     0.50 .          *         *              **
     0.40                  .        .        **
     0.30    *   .    .*        *          **
     0.20                   .        .    ***
     0.10 .        *        *        . ****
     0.00*********************************.............................
        0---|---|---|---|---|---|---|---|---|---|---|---|---|---|---0
        0.00   7.50  15.00  22.50  30.00  37.50  45.00  52.50  60.00

     .    FuzzySet:   NEW
          Support :       0.00,       2.00,      4.00
     *    FuzzySet:   YOUNG
          Support :       4.00,       2.00
     .    FuzzySet:   RECENT
          Support :       8.00,       4.00
     *    FuzzySet:   MATURE
          Support :      16.00,       8.00
     .    FuzzySet:   ESTABLISHED
          Support :      24.00,       8.00
     *    FuzzySet:   OLD
          Support :      24.00,      42.00,     60.00
```

Figure 3.16 The term set for COMPANY.AGE

Figure 3.16 is the underlying term set for the company age column. In the database, the founding year of the company is stored. An actual age is found by subtracting that date from the current year. The fuzzy term sets are compacted toward the left of the domain where we are concerned with more fine grain detail on the age of the company. After a larger number of years, the age of a company does not segment semantically—the company is simply OLD.

```
ANNUAL.REVENUES
Domain [UofD]:     100.00 to    1800.00
     1.00.      **        .       *         ..............................
     0.90      *  *     . .     ** *       ..
     0.80 .                .     .   *        .
     0.70    *      *         . *           .
     0.60                .                .
     0.50    *        *         *        *
     0.40 .          .        .        .
     0.30    *        *        *        .
     0.20          .        .        .
     0.10 *          *      *        .. *
     0.00.........................*********************************
        0---|---|---|---|---|---|---|---|---|---|---|---|---|---|---0
        100.00  312.50  525.00  737.50  950.00 1162.50 1375.00 1587.50 1800.00
```

```
 .    FuzzySet:    NONE
      Support :      100.00,     150.00,    200.00
 *    FuzzySet:    LOW
      Support :      300.00,     200.00
 .    FuzzySet:    MODERATE
      Support :      500.00,     200.00
 *    FuzzySet:    MEDIUM
      Support :      700.00,     200.00
 .    FuzzySet:    HIGH
      Support :      700.00,     850.00,   1000.00
```

Figure 3.17 The term set for ANNUAL.REVENUES

Figure 3.17 shows the distribution of annual revenues from $100,000 to $1.8 million. Since we are concerned with small manufacturing companies the fuzzy term set defines in particularly fine detail the semantic regions between $300,000 and $700,000. The complete Universe of Discourse for the annual revenues column extends out to $1,800,000 although the descriptive part of the fuzzy sets end at $1,000,000. This is a common feature of building fuzzy query models. The large right-hand domain provides space to change the descriptive geometry of the term set without altering the domain of the entire variable (which might alter the semantics of the variable itself.)

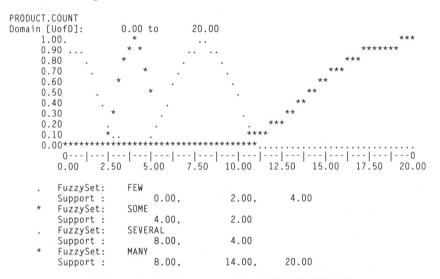

```
PRODUCT.COUNT
Domain [UofD]:        0.00 to      20.00
      1.00.            *           ..                               ***
      0.90 ...         *  *          ..  ..               *******
      0.80      .        *         .          .              ***
      0.70      .          *        .          .          ***
      0.60      .    *         .          .            **
      0.50      .         *        .          .        **
      0.40      .         .          .            **
      0.30      .   *        .          .        **
      0.20      .         .          .      ***
      0.10      .   *..       .          ****
      0.00*********************************.............................
        0---|---|---|---|---|---|---|---|---|---|---|---|---|---|---|---0
        0.00    2.50    5.00    7.50   10.00   12.50   15.00   17.50   20.00

 .    FuzzySet:    FEW
      Support :        0.00,       2.00,      4.00
 *    FuzzySet:    SOME
      Support :        4.00,       2.00
 .    FuzzySet:    SEVERAL
      Support :        8.00,       4.00
 *    FuzzySet:    MANY
      Support :        8.00,      14.00,     20.00
```

Figure 3.18 The term set for PRODUCT.COUNT

Figure 3.18 shows the fuzzy term set for the count of products sold by the company. This kind of information is important because it helps differentiate (perhaps normalize) the revenues produced by the company. A company with FEW products and HIGH revenue might be better positioned than a company with SEVERAL (or MANY) products and an equally HIGH revenue.

```
EMPLOYEE.COUNT
Domain [UofD]:       0.00 to      60.00
    1.00.              *           ..                            ****
    0.90 ..        *        ..  .                       *******
    0.80 .      *   *       .       .                 ***
    0.70 .                          .          ***
    0.60         *      .        .        ***
    0.50     .  *        .               **
    0.40                      .        **
    0.30    .       .              **
    0.20    *         .        ****
    0.10*************************** .    ****
    0.00***************************         ..................................
       0---|---|---|---|---|---|---|---|---|---|---|---|---|---|---|---0
       0.00   7.50   15.00   22.50   30.00   37.50   45.00   52.50  60.00

    .    FuzzySet:    SMALL
         Support :        0.00,       5.00,     10.00
    *    FuzzySet:    MODERATE
         Support :       10.00,       5.00
    .    FuzzySet:    MEDIUM
         Support :       20.00,      10.00
    *    FuzzySet:    LARGE
         Support :       20.00,      35.00,     60.00
```

Figure 3.19 The term set for EMPLOYEE.COUNT

Figure 3.19 shows the fuzzy term set associated with the number of employees in the company. Like the number of products sold by the company, the total number of employees also provides an indirect metric for discriminating between companies. The revenue per employee is a standard measurement in the software industry for measuring productivity and effectiveness. Thus, a company with a SMALL employee count, but HIGH revenues has a generally higher productivity than a company with a LARGE employee count and HIGH revenues.

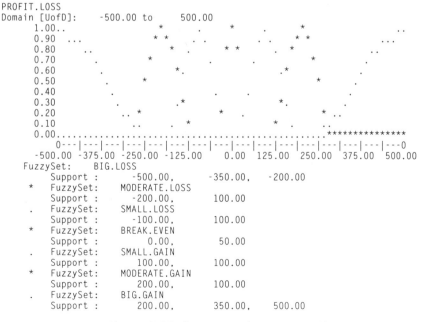

```
PROFIT.LOSS
Domain [UofD]:    -500.00 to     500.00
    1.00..               *       .      *     .       *         ..
    0.90 ...            * *     . .    * *    .     * *        ...
    0.80 ..          *       .     . *    .       * .
    0.70 .          *       .        .          *     ..
    0.60 .       *.      .           .*
    0.50 .      *                   *        .
    0.40
    0.30    .        .*          *.
    0.20    .. *        *    .       *    . ..
    0.10         ..     .  *        *    .   ..
    0.00...............................***************
       0---|---|---|---|---|---|---|---|---|---|---|---|---|---|---|---0
      -500.00 -375.00 -250.00 -125.00    0.00  125.00  250.00  375.00  500.00
    FuzzySet:    BIG.LOSS
         Support :     -500.00,    -350.00,   -200.00
    *    FuzzySet:    MODERATE.LOSS
         Support :     -200.00,     100.00
    .    FuzzySet:    SMALL.LOSS
         Support :     -100.00,     100.00
    *    FuzzySet:    BREAK.EVEN
         Support :        0.00,      50.00
    .    FuzzySet:    SMALL.GAIN
         Support :      100.00,     100.00
    *    FuzzySet:    MODERATE.GAIN
         Support :      200.00,     100.00
    .    FuzzySet:    BIG.GAIN
         Support :      200.00,     350.00,    500.00
```

Figure 3.20 The term set for PROFIT.LOSS

Figure 3.20 shows the fuzzy sets associated with the company's profit and loss in the previous financial reporting period (normally the past fiscal year). Since we are looking at companies with annual revenues just above $100,000 to $1,800,000, the profit and loss categories span the range of a gain or loss of $500,000. If we make a half million dollars on sales of $1.8 million, this is certainly a BIG.GAIN. The idea of a BIG.LOSS is equally appropriate in the semantics of our query.

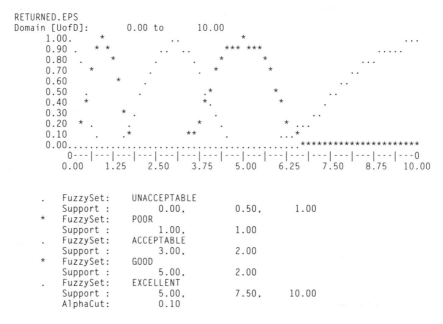

```
RETURNED.EPS
Domain [UofD]:         0.00 to      10.00
     1.00.     *              ..             *                                    ...
     0.90 .   * *              .. ..     *** ***                               .....
     0.80 .     *                  .      *        *                        ...
     0.70   *                   .           *         *                    ..
     0.60        *       .                                               ..
     0.50   .               .              *             *             ..
     0.40   *              .              *.            *             ..
     0.30         *  .                     .                        ..
     0.20   * .          .              *         .      *  ...
     0.10     .     .*              **         .       ...*
     0.00.....................................................**********************
         0---|---|---|---|---|---|---|---|---|---|---|---|---|---|---|---|---|---0
        0.00    1.25    2.50    3.75    5.00    6.25    7.50    8.75   10.00


     .    FuzzySet:    UNACCEPTABLE
          Support :         0.00,        0.50,        1.00
     *    FuzzySet:    POOR
          Support :         1.00,        1.00
     .    FuzzySet:    ACCEPTABLE
          Support :         3.00,        2.00
     *    FuzzySet:    GOOD
          Support :         5.00,        2.00
     .    FuzzySet:    EXCELLENT
          Support :         5.00,        7.50,       10.00
          AlphaCut:         0.10
```

Figure 3.21 The term set for RETAINED.EPS

Figure 3.21 shows the fuzzy term set for the returned earnings per share. This is the amount paid to investors based on the common stock dividends. The amount returned to investors is a measure of financial strength, so a company that has GOOD or EXCELLENT returned earnings per share (EPS) even when revenues are LOW (or MODERATE) has better performance than a company with HIGH revenues but a POOR or only slightly ACCEPT-ABLE return.

Approximating Fuzzy Regions with a Crisp Query

An SQL query involving multiple WHERE predicates evaluates the logical truth of the record selection criteria and returns each row in the table that has a TRUE value. When the query involves tests against crisp bifurcation points (greater than, less than, not equal to) the use of fuzzy predicates can capture more of the underlying meaning (refer to "The Intentionality Problem" on page 160 for additional details.) When we are using queries that specify a range of values, in a manner similar to a fuzzy set, the question we ask is: How does fuzzy logic provide us with a better answer?

In the ANNUAL.REVENUES column, the term set for the column includes a fuzzy set for MODERATE revenues. This is a PI curve centered around $500K with base diffusion width of $200K. Figure 3.22 shows this fuzzy set isolated from its neighboring sets.

```
ANNUAL.REVENUES
Domain [UofD]:      100.00 to     1800.00
        1.00                   .
        0.90                  . .
        0.80                 .   .
        0.70                     .
        0.60                .
        0.50
        0.40               .       .
        0.30
        0.20              .         .
        0.10
        0.00.........                ............................................
           0---|---|---|---|---|---|---|---|---|---|---|---|---|---|---|---0
        100.00  312.50  525.00  737.50  950.00 1162.50 1375.00 1587.50 1800.00

           FuzzySet:      MODERATE
           Support :      500.00,      200.00
```

Figure 3.22 The MODERATE fuzzy set of ANNUAL.REVENUES

This fuzzy set covers a region on the domain from $300K to $700K. Since this is a range of values, we can construct an SQL query to cover the same set of values. As an example:

```
SELECT COMPANY
    FROM MFGDBMS
        WHERE ANNUAL.REVENUES ≥ 300
        AND ANNUAL.REVENUES ≤ 700;
```

The AND insures that both conditions are true, thus forming a bracket around a range of values. Figure 3.23 shows the results of this query. These are companies with revenues in the range $300K to $700K inclusive.

```
select company,annual.revenues
   from MfgDBMS
   where  annual.revenues >= 300
      AND Annual.Revenues <= 700;

Company              Annual.Revenues
----------------     ----------------
CompA                            570
CompB                            478
CompC                            401
CompD                            321
```

```
CompE                         650
CompF                         550
CompG                         597
CompH                         602
CompI                         498
CompK                         501
CompM                         555
CompO                         530
CompP                         522
CompS                         659
CompT                         619
```

Figure 3.23 Results of crisp range selection on ANNUAL.REVENUES

Since our idea of moderate revenues is centered around $500K, this selection does not differentiate between revenues at the low or the high end of the spectrum. Company CompK with an ideal MODERATE value appears along with company CompD that is at the low end of the range and company CompS that is at the high end of the range. This means range selections do not correspond either semantically or functionally with fuzzy queries over the same domain. Naturally, we can refine the query to specify a tighter range on the selection, such as:

```
SELECT COMPANY
    FROM MFGDBMS
        WHERE ANNUAL.REVENUES ≥ 450
        AND ANNUAL.REVENUES ≤ 550;
```

This query restricts the data space for the idea of moderate. Figure 3.24 reflects the reduced table rows selected by this query.

```
Company              Annual.Revenues
----------------     ----------------
CompB                         478
CompF                         550
CompI                         498
CompK                         501
CompO                         530
CompP                         522
```

Figure 3.24 Reduced data space on a Crisp SQL Query

If we are interested in the broad conceptual foundations of revenues that map to our idea of moderate, but this reduction does not improve the quality of the query. We can see company CompM with revenues of $555K is eliminated even though its value is close to the new range of moderate. No matter how we move our range boundary, we exclude candidates that are just beyond the range horizon. A fuzzy query includes a wider number of candidates and ranks the selected company according to their compatibility with the fuzzy concept MODERATE, thus more information is returned by a fuzzy query. This, in turn, means that the query process has more intelligence.

A Fuzzy Query with Multiple WHERE Predicates

With the installed fuzzy set vocabulary, we can make approximate queries against the underlying database (refer to Table 3.1 on page 159 for the database contents). The second version of the FuzzySQL processor uses the full declared vocabulary (see "FzySQL1 (A Fuzzy SQL database processor [version 1])" on page 408 for details on the code model). Figure 3.25 shows the terminal session for the query.

```
FuzzySQL Database Processor
---------------------------
AlphaCut Threshold      : .1
AND operator Type       : MINIMUM
select company
  from MfgDBMS
  where:
Company Age is          : RECENT
Annual Revenues are     : MODERATE
Product Count is        : //
Employee Count is       : //
Profit or Loss is       : //
Retained EPS is         : //
```

Figure 3.25 Executing a FuzzySQL query with two predicates

In this query we initially specify the alpha cut threshold used to determine whether or not a row will participate in the query (see "Alpha Cut Thresholds" on page 162 for more details on how this option affects the query.) The type of composition method, MINIMUM or AVERAGE is also specified. The query then requests the fuzzy set domain for each of the columns. A double slash (//) is used to indicate this column should be ignored in the current query. If you enter a question mark (?) or the fuzzy set name you enter is not part of the term set for that column, a list of valid fuzzy set names is displayed and you are asked to re-enter the name.

Effects of the MINIMUM Truth Composition

Using the MINIMUM truth aggregation method is the most restrictive of the fuzzy query techniques. Figure 3.26 shows the results of combining the minimum of Company.Age is RECENT and Annual.Revenues are MODERATE.

```
select company
  from MfgDBMS
  where  Company.Age is RECENT
    AND Annual.Revenues are MODERATE;
Company          CompIDX      AvgIDX
----------------  ----------   ----------
CompP               0.819        0.901
CompE               0.154        0.486
CompH               0.106        0.313
CompO               0.106        0.537
Record Selected         :          4
Rejected due to AlphaCut :          2
Percent (%) Found       :      20.00
```

Figure 3.26 The MINIMUM of RECENT Age and MODERATE revenues

The query is ranked in descending order by the compatibility index (CompIDX). In this query only four rows were actually selected, representing 20% of the database. By examining the fuzzy membership analysis for each row (shown in Figure 3.27) we can see the aggregate membership is set to zero when either the age is not RECENT or the revenue is not MODERATE.

```
 1. CompA
    COMPANY.AGE          in 'RECENT' (   47.00,0.000)
    ANNUAL.REVENUES      in 'MODERATE' ( 570.00,0.790)
    CompIDX: 0.000, AvgGrade: 0.395
 2. CompB
    COMPANY.AGE          in 'RECENT' (   23.00,0.000)
    ANNUAL.REVENUES      in 'MODERATE' ( 478.00,0.960)
    CompIDX: 0.000, AvgGrade: 0.480
 3. CompC
    COMPANY.AGE          in 'RECENT' (   13.00,0.000)
    ANNUAL.REVENUES      in 'MODERATE' ( 401.00,0.488)
    CompIDX: 0.000, AvgGrade: 0.244
 4. CompD
    COMPANY.AGE          in 'RECENT' (    8.00,1.000)
    ANNUAL.REVENUES      in 'MODERATE' ( 321.00,0.018)
    CompIDX: 0.018, AvgGrade: 0.509
    Alpha Cut Rejection: 0.018 < 0.100
 5. CompE
    COMPANY.AGE          in 'RECENT' (    7.00,0.819)
    ANNUAL.REVENUES      in 'MODERATE' ( 650.00,0.154)
    CompIDX: 0.154, AvgGrade: 0.486
 6. CompF
    COMPANY.AGE          in 'RECENT' (    1.00,0.000)
    ANNUAL.REVENUES      in 'MODERATE' ( 550.00,0.899)
    CompIDX: 0.000, AvgGrade: 0.450
 7. CompG
    COMPANY.AGE          in 'RECENT' (    3.00,0.000)
    ANNUAL.REVENUES      in 'MODERATE' ( 597.00,0.582)
    CompIDX: 0.000, AvgGrade: 0.291
 8. CompH
    COMPANY.AGE          in 'RECENT' (    5.00,0.106)
    ANNUAL.REVENUES      in 'MODERATE' ( 602.00,0.519)
    CompIDX: 0.106, AvgGrade: 0.313
 9. CompI
    COMPANY.AGE          in 'RECENT' (    4.00,0.000)
    ANNUAL.REVENUES      in 'MODERATE' ( 498.00,0.997)
    CompIDX: 0.000, AvgGrade: 0.498
10. CompK
    COMPANY.AGE          in 'RECENT' (    1.00,0.000)


    ANNUAL.REVENUES      in 'MODERATE' ( 501.00,1.000)
    CompIDX: 0.000, AvgGrade: 0.500
11. CompL
    COMPANY.AGE          in 'RECENT' (   10.00,0.575)
    ANNUAL.REVENUES      in 'MODERATE' ( 920.00,0.000)
    CompIDX: 0.000, AvgGrade: 0.288
12. CompM
    COMPANY.AGE          in 'RECENT' (   12.00,0.000)
    ANNUAL.REVENUES      in 'MODERATE' ( 555.00,0.867)
    CompIDX: 0.000, AvgGrade: 0.434
    Alpha Cut Rejection: 0.000 < 0.100
13. CompN
    COMPANY.AGE          in 'RECENT' (    7.00,0.819)
    ANNUAL.REVENUES      in 'MODERATE' (1050.00,0.000)
    CompIDX: 0.000, AvgGrade: 0.410
```

```
14. CompO
    COMPANY.AGE          in 'RECENT' (    5.00,0.106)
    ANNUAL.REVENUES      in 'MODERATE' ( 530.00,0.969)
    CompIDX: 0.106, AvgGrade: 0.537
15. CompP
    COMPANY.AGE          in 'RECENT' (    7.00,0.819)
    ANNUAL.REVENUES      in 'MODERATE' ( 522.00,0.983)
    CompIDX: 0.819, AvgGrade: 0.901
16. CompR
    COMPANY.AGE          in 'RECENT' (   36.00,0.000)
    ANNUAL.REVENUES      in 'MODERATE' ( 900.00,0.000)
    CompIDX: 0.000, AvgGrade: 0.000
17. CompS
    COMPANY.AGE          in 'RECENT' (   31.00,0.000)
    ANNUAL.REVENUES      in 'MODERATE' ( 659.00,0.089)
    CompIDX: 0.000, AvgGrade: 0.044
18. CompT
    COMPANY.AGE          in 'RECENT' (   16.00,0.000)
    ANNUAL.REVENUES      in 'MODERATE' ( 619.00,0.336)
    CompIDX: 0.000, AvgGrade: 0.168
19. CompU
    COMPANY.AGE          in 'RECENT' (   28.00,0.000)
    ANNUAL.REVENUES      in 'MODERATE' (1233.00,0.000)
    CompIDX: 0.000, AvgGrade: 0.000
20. CompW
    COMPANY.AGE          in 'RECENT' (   31.00,0.000)
    ANNUAL.REVENUES      in 'MODERATE' ( 973.00,0.000)
    CompIDX: 0.000, AvgGrade: 0.000
```

Figure 3.27 The fuzzy membership analysis for the MINIMUM query

An additional two rows were rejected since their combined truths were greater than zero, but less than the current alpha cut threshold. The minimum truth aggregation provides the strongest restriction on the query contents. As the number of WHERE predicates increase, the probability that the resulting query is empty (every row evaluated to a zero aggregate truth value) increases rapidly. Figure 3.28, as an example, illustrates the reduction in the query space when the proposition *Product.Count is SOME* is added to the previous query.

```
select company
  from MfgDBMS
  where  Company.Age is RECENT
    AND Annual.Revenues are MODERATE
    AND Product.Count is SOME;
Company           CompIDX       AvgIDX
----------------  ----------    ----------
CompP                0.819         0.934
CompE                0.154         0.491
Record Selected        :             2
Rejected due to AlphaCut :            1
Percent (%) Found      :         10.00
```

Figure 3.28 Adding PRODUCT.COUNT to the MINIMUM query

Only two rows—ten percent of the records—are selected from the database with another row excluded due to the alpha cut threshold. Figure 3.29 shows part of the membership analysis when we add this third WHERE predicate to the query.

```
1. CompA
   COMPANY.AGE         in 'RECENT' (  47.00,0.000)
   ANNUAL.REVENUES     in 'MODERATE' ( 570.00,0.790)
   PRODUCT.COUNT       in 'SOME' (   1.00,0.000)
   CompIDX: 0.000, AvgGrade: 0.263
2. CompB
   COMPANY.AGE         in 'RECENT' (  23.00,0.000)
   ANNUAL.REVENUES     in 'MODERATE' ( 478.00,0.960)
   PRODUCT.COUNT       in 'SOME' (   3.00,0.469)
   CompIDX: 0.000, AvgGrade: 0.477
3. CompC
   COMPANY.AGE         in 'RECENT' (  13.00,0.000)
   ANNUAL.REVENUES     in 'MODERATE' ( 401.00,0.488)
   PRODUCT.COUNT       in 'SOME' (   9.00,0.000)
   CompIDX: 0.000, AvgGrade: 0.163
4. CompD
   COMPANY.AGE         in 'RECENT' (   8.00,1.000)
   ANNUAL.REVENUES     in 'MODERATE' ( 321.00,0.018)
   PRODUCT.COUNT       in 'SOME' (   3.00,0.469)
   CompIDX: 0.018, AvgGrade: 0.496
   Alpha Cut Rejection: 0.018 < 0.100
5. CompE
   COMPANY.AGE         in 'RECENT' (   7.00,0.819)
   ANNUAL.REVENUES     in 'MODERATE' ( 650.00,0.154)
   PRODUCT.COUNT       in 'SOME' (   5.00,0.500)
   CompIDX: 0.154, AvgGrade: 0.491
```

Figure 3.29 The fuzzy membership analysis for SOME product count

At the same time, this type of query enforces a semantic coherence among the predicates: every fuzzy set must contribute before the row is a valid candidate. The minimum functions as a true fuzzy AND by selecting the minimum strength from all the query predicates. This means that the strength of the query cannot be stronger than the weakest proposition in the WHERE statement.

Effects of the AVERAGE Truth Composition

An AVERAGE truth aggregation method is a softer form of the query. Each predicate fuzzy proposition is considered independently. By averaging the total truth, rows that have zero membership in one expression but a high membership in another predicate can be selected. Figure 3.30 shows the results of the same query in Figure 3.25 with the AVERAGE truth method.

Company	CompIDX	AvgIDX
CompP	0.819	0.901
CompO	0.106	0.537
CompD	0.018	0.509

```
CompK                    0.000        0.500
CompI                    0.000        0.498
CompE                    0.154        0.486
CompB                    0.000        0.480
CompF                    0.000        0.450
CompM                    0.000        0.434
CompN                    0.000        0.410
CompA                    0.000        0.395
CompH                    0.106        0.313
CompG                    0.000        0.291
CompL                    0.000        0.288
CompC                    0.000        0.244
CompT                    0.000        0.168
Record Selected           :            16
Rejected due to AlphaCut  :             1
Percent (%) Found         :         80.00
```

Figure 3.30 The AVERAGE of RECENT Age and MODERATE Revenues

The query is ranked in descending order by the average compatibility index of each column (AvgIDX). In this query sixteen rows were actually selected, representing 80% of the database. By examining the fuzzy membership analysis for each row (shown in Figure 3.27) we can see the aggregate membership is set to zero only when both the age is not RECENT or the revenue is not MODERATE. A single row was also excluded because of the alpha cut threshold.

Filtering Database Rows with the Compatibility Metric

Although the AVERAGE truth aggregation technique produces a larger number of candidate rows than the MINIMUM method, this increased number of records does not have an equal meaning to the query evaluator (meaning either the person issuing the query or the software system evaluating the set of returned physical records). We can apply a hurdle to the inclusion of rows in the query through the alpha cut threshold specified when the query was initiated. A very high alpha threshold enforces a high compatibility between the selected row and the query, while a low alpha threshold allows a broader interpretation of the query concept. As an example, Figure 3.31 shows the effect of raising the alpha threshold to [.5] and re-issuing the same query:

```
FuzzySQL Database Processor
- - - - - - - - - - - - - - - - - - - - - - - - - -
AlphaCut Threshold    : .5
AND operator Type     : AVERAGE
select company
  from MfgDBMS
  where:
Company Age is        : RECENT
Annual Revenues are   : MODERATE
Product Count is      : //
Employee Count is     : //
Profit or Loss is     : //
Retained EPS is       : //
```

```
Company            CompIDX     AvgIDX
- - - - - - - - - - - - - - -  - - - - - - - - - -  - - - - - - - - - -
CompP                0.819       0.901
CompO                0.106       0.537
CompD                0.018       0.509
CompK                0.000       0.500
Record Selected        :            4
Rejected due to AlphaCut    :            0
Percent (%) Found      :        20.00
```

Figure 3.31 An AVERAGE query with a high alpha cut threshold

The truth aggregation or composite membership value produced by the `fuzzySQL` process provides both the internal query mechanism as well as application program logic with a means of judging whether or not a particular set of candidate rows are compatible with the query. This is shown schematically in Figure 3.32.

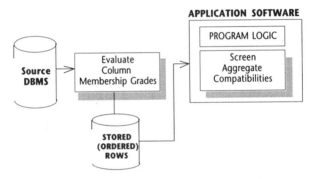

Figure 3.32 FuzzySQL and application logic filtering

When a `fuzzySQL` operation returns a candidate row to the user it automatically extends the row by adding a new column containing the composite membership value. This ordinal ranking number is then available for use in application software systems that read the candidate records.

FuzzySQL with Hedged Predicates

In the previous section we examined queries using fuzzy sets in the WHERE predicate. The fuzzy sets were defined as static members of the underlying vocabulary. We now turn our attention to more flexible and more expressive types of queries where the fuzzy sets can be dynamically modified through the use of hedges to produce new sets that either dilute, intensify, or restrict the candidate domain space. Hedges also provide a way of approximating *scalar values* (numbers) so that we can create fuzzy regions from known central measures in the column domain.

Hedges and Scalar Approximators

A *hedge* is an action that either changes the shape of a fuzzy set or produces a new fuzzy set. There are many different types and methods associated with hedges. Some hedges such as *very, extremely, somewhat, quite,* and *slightly* intensify or dilute the fuzzy set's membership function. Other hedges like *positively* and *generally* change the degree of fuzziness in a fuzzy set. Another group of hedges like *above, below,* and *not* (the fuzzy set complement) restrict the domain of an existing fuzzy set. And other hedges like *about, near,* and *around* either diffuse a fuzzy set or create a fuzzy set form a scalar numeric value.

In general, there are no "first principle" design foundations for the operation of a particular hedge. The action of a hedge is heuristic; it changes the shape of a fuzzy set in a way that seems to correspond closely the new semantic state. Some convincing psychological work[9] has gone into the use of many popular hedges (such as *very* and *somewhat* which we discuss in the next subsection), while other hedge transformations are considered well-educated "guesses" about the way a fuzzy region should be changed to reflect the new properties implied by the hedge (such as *positively* and *generally.*)

Hedges play the same role in approximate reasoning as adjectives and adverbs play in natural language. They modify the meaning of the fuzzy set on which they act. A single fuzzy set can be modified by any number of hedges, although, in practice, no more than two or three hedges are ever used. Like natural language, the order in which a hedge is applied is significant; thus *positively very HIGH* and *very positively HIGH* are two distinct and different fuzzy spaces. When hedges are combined with base fuzzy sets, we refer to the combined phrase as a linguistic variable. Linguistic variables are always actual fuzzy sets (through a process known as closure.)

A complete discussion of the philosophy, design and use of hedges appears in *The Fuzzy System Handbook* (Cox, AP Professional, 1994); consequently this section provides only a brief introduction to the ideas underlying the application of hedges.

---

9. See Smithson, Michael, *Fuzzy Set Analysis for Behavioral and Social Sciences* (Springer-Verlag,1986), page 67, *2.5* Linguistic Hedges and Fuzzy Modifiers.

The VERY Hedge

One of the earliest described and most frequently used hedges is very and is used in queries as a fuzzy set adjective. As an example:

```
SELECT COMPANY
...WHERE ANNUAL.REVENUES ARE VERY HIGH;
```

The very hedge intensifies the membership function of an existing fuzzy set by squaring each membership function. Equation 3.4 shows the process of producing very W from fuzzy set W.

$$\mu_{veryW}[x] = \mu_W^2[x]$$

Equation 3.4 Generating a very hedged fuzzy set

Since membership values lie in the range [0,1], squaring them reduces the truth at each point along the set (except for the values zero and one). This causes a slight bowing of the set. The very hedge also has the desirable property of respecting the original domain of the fuzzy set. Figure 3.33 shows the effect of applying the hedge very to the base fuzzy set HIGH.

Figure 3.33 Fuzzy sets HIGH and very HIGH

As Figure 3.34 illustrates, the net affect of the hedge is the reduction of membership for any given domain value that does not lie at the zero or one truth points. The price value 24 is moderately compatible with the concept of HIGH price, but is only slightly compatible with the ideas of very HIGH for price.

Figure 3.34 Domain value "24" at HIGH and very HIGH

In a fuzzy query, the application of a hedge such as very reduces the number of qualifying instances. The truth of the column value either falls below the alpha cut threshold or it tends to reduce the total aggregate truth of the composite columns in the WHERE predicate. As you can see in Figure 3.34 a particular column value must be much further to the right of the fuzzy set to have the same truth membership value.

The SOMEWHAT Hedge

Another early and frequently used hedge is somewhat. It is also used as a fuzzy set adjective. As an example:

```
SELECT COMPANY
...WHERE ANNUAL.REVENUES ARE SOMEWHAT HIGH;
```

The somewhat hedge dilutes the membership function of an existing fuzzy set by taking the square root of each membership function. Equation 3.5 shows the process of producing somewhat W from fuzzy set W.

$$\mu_{somewhatW}[x] = \mu_W^{\frac{1}{2}}[x]$$

Equation 3.5 Generating a somewhat hedged fuzzy set

Since membership values lie in the range [0,1], taking the square root increases the truth at each point along the set (except for the values zero and one). Like the very hedge, this causes a slight bowing the set. Figure 3.35 shows the effect of applying the hedge somewhat to the base fuzzy set HIGH.

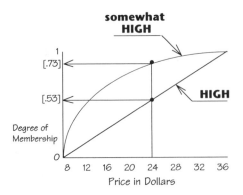

Figure 3.35 Fuzzy sets HIGH and somewhat HIGH

As Figure 3.36 illustrates the net affect of the somewhat hedge is an increase in membership for any given domain value that does not lie at the zero or one truth points. The price value 24 is moderately compatible with the concept of HIGH price, but is highly compatible with the ideas of somewhat HIGH for price.

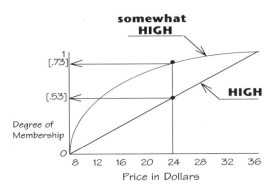

Figure 3.36 Domain value "24" at HIGH and somewhat HIGH

In a fuzzy query, the application of a hedge such as somewhat increases the number of qualifying instances. The truth of the column value either falls more often above the alpha cut threshold or it tends to improve the total aggregate truth of the composite columns in the WHERE predicate.

The ABOUT or NEAR Hedge

Another important class of hedges, characterized by the adjectives *about*, *around*, and *near* approximates the base fuzzy set. If the hedge is applied to a number, then the number is converted to a bell-shaped or triangular fuzzy set. As an example:

```
SELECT COMPANY
   WHERE ANNUAL.REVENUES ARE ABOUT MODERATE;

SELECT COMPANY
   WHERE RETAINED.EPS IS NEAR 2.00;
```

Figure 3.37 illustrates how the application of around to the fuzzy set MIDDLEAGED causes a general diffusion or broading of the membership function.

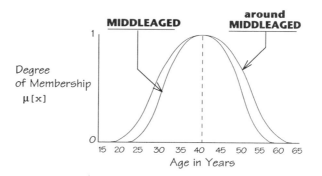

Figure 3.37 The fuzzy set MIDDLEAGED and around MIDDLEAGED

When the hedge *around* is applied to a number, it converts that number into a fuzzy set centered over the number's position in the domain. In fact, the initial fuzzy set for middle aged was created by applying the hedge *near* to the number 40. This creates a bell-shaped fuzzy number (alternately, of course, depending on the application and the needs of the model builder, the approximation process can produce either bell, triangular, or in rare cases trapezoidal shaped fuzzy sets).

Simple FuzzySQL Queries with Hedged Predicates

How do hedges affect the retrieval of records in a fuzzy query? We start by looking at simple query involving a base fuzzy set. All these queries use the MINIMUM truth composition method and an alpha cut threshold of [.1]. Figure 3.38 shows the results of a query that selects companies with LOW annual revenues.

```
select company
  from MfgDBMS
  where  Annual.Revenues are LOW;


Company             CompIDX
- - - - - - - - -   - - - - - - - - -
CompD                  0.982
CompC                  0.512
Record Selected        :         2
Rejected due to AlphaCut  :      3
Percent (%) Found      :     10.00
```

Figure 3.38 The set of LOW annual revenue companies

This query selects two records with an additional three rejected due to the alpha cut threshold. Perhaps the criteria for selecting companies is too restrictive. We increase the scope of the query by hedging the fuzzy set LOW. We ask for companies that are somewhat LOW. Figure 3.39 shows the FuzzySQL session for this request.

```
FuzzySQL Database Processor
---------------------------
AlphaCut Threshold    : .1
AND operator Type     : MINIMUM
select company
   from MfgDBMS
   where:
Company Age is        : //
Annual Revenues are   : somewhat LOW
----Applying the hedge 'somewhat'
Product Count is      : //
Employee Count is     : //
Profit or Loss is     : //
Retained EPS is       : //
Ranking    3 Rows.
.+++
.++
.
Ranking Complete.
```

Figure 3.39 Querying the database for somewhat LOW revenues

When the query processor detects the hedge somewhat associated with the base fuzzy set, it creates a new fuzzy set containing the hedged fuzzy region. Figure 3.40 shows the results of the hedging process.

```
ANNUAL.REVENUES
Domain [UofD]:      100.00 to      1800.00
     1.00          **
     0.90        *   *
     0.80      *       *
     0.70    *.        .*
     0.60
     0.50    *.        .*
     0.40
     0.30  *.            .*
     0.20                *
     0.10 *.            .
     0.00*.           .****************************************************
       0---|---|---|---|---|---|---|---|---|---|---|---|---|---|---|---0
       100.00  312.50  525.00  737.50  950.00 1162.50 1375.00 1587.50 1800.00

       .    FuzzySet:    LOW
       *    FuzzySet:    somewhat LOW
```

Figure 3.40 The LOW and somewhat LOW fuzzy sets

The somewhat hedge diffuses the bell-shaped LOW fuzzy set so it encompasses a slightly broader space across the underlying ANNUAL.REVENUES domain. This increases the number of candidate records. It also increases the membership values for the companies selected in the previous query. Figure 3.41 shows the results of the somewhat LOW query.

```
select company
  from MfgDBMS
  where  Annual.Revenues are somewhat LOW:

Company              CompIDX
----------------     ----------
CompD                   0.991
CompC                   0.715
CompB                   0.199
Record Selected        :         3
Rejected due to AlphaCut  :      2
Percent (%) Found      :     15.00
```

Figure 3.41 The set of somewhat LOW annual revenue companies

The hedged query selects an additional company. Company CompB which was just below the alpha cut threshold is now included in the query. The compatibility index also reflects the higher membership of each annual revenues column value in the hedged fuzzy region. The use of hedges can be compounded in a FuzzySQL query so that the linguistic space encompasses selectively broader or narrower regions. Suppose we decide that we want to examine the companies that are somewhere in the vicinity of somewhat LOW. One way to do this is to apply the hedge somewhat to the linguistic variable somewhat LOW. Figure 3.42 shows how this query is performed.

```
FuzzySQL Database Processor
---------------------------
AlphaCut Threshold    : .1
AND operator Type     : MINIMUM
select company
  from MfgDBMS
  where:
Company Age is        : //
Annual Revenues are   : somewhat somewhat LOW
----Applying the hedge 'somewhat'
----Applying the hedge 'somewhat'
Product Count is      : //
Employee Count is     : //
Profit or Loss is     : //
Retained EPS is       : //
Ranking   5 Rows.
.++++
.+++
.+++
.++
.
Ranking Complete.
```

Figure 3.42 Querying the database for somewhat somewhat LOW

In this case the FuzzySQL processor detects two hedges associated with the base fuzzy set. Hedges are resolved "from the inside out." This means the expression is interpreted as somewhat(somewhat(LOW)) and while, in this particular instance, the order is not important, the order is quite important for queries involving a mixture of hedges. Figure 3.43 shows the first step in this process—applying the hedge somewhat to LOW.

```
---Hedge 'somewhat' applied to Fuzzy Set "LOW"

ANNUAL.REVENUES
Domain [UofD]:      100.00 to      1800.00
        1.00        **
        0.90      *   *
        0.80      *     *
        0.70    *.     .*
        0.60
        0.50    *.      .*
        0.40
        0.30    *.        .*
        0.20             *
        0.10  *.          .
        0.00*.           .*************************************************
          0---|---|---|---|---|---|---|---|---|---|---|---|---|---|---|---0
        100.00  312.50  525.00  737.50  950.00 1162.50 1375.00 1587.50 1800.00

        .   FuzzySet:    LOW
        *   FuzzySet:    somewhat LOW

---Hedge 'somewhat' applied to Fuzzy Set "LOW"
```

Figure 3.43 Applying the hedge somewhat to the fuzzy set LOW

When the fuzzy set somewhat LOW is formed (more properly, this is a linguistic variable), the processor applies the hedge somewhat to this new fuzzy space. The result is a new linguistic variable somewhat somewhat LOW. It is this fuzzy region that is used by the query. Figure 3.44 shows the fuzzy set produced by this hedging operation.

```
ANNUAL.REVENUES
Domain [UofD]:      100.00 to      1800.00
        1.00        **
        0.90      **  **
        0.80    *.     .*
        0.70    *.     .*
        0.60    *        *
        0.50    .        .
        0.40  *           *
        0.30    .        .
        0.20             .
        0.10  .          *
        0.00*           .*************************************************
          0---|---|---|---|---|---|---|---|---|---|---|---|---|---|---|---0
        100.00  312.50  525.00  737.50  950.00 1162.50 1375.00 1587.50 1800.00

        .   FuzzySet:    somewhat LOW
        *   FuzzySet:    somewhat somewhat LOW
```

Figure 3.44 Applying the hedge somewhat to the fuzzy set somewhat LOW

This final query specification increases the over-all truth membership values for each of the candidate companies. Figure 3.45 shows the output from the FuzzySQL query.

```
select company
  from MfgDBMS
  where  Annual.Revenues are somewhat somewhat LOW;

Company           CompIDX
----------------  ----------
CompD               0.995
CompC               0.846
CompB               0.446
CompI               0.241
CompK               0.105
Record Selected        :          5
Rejected due to AlphaCut :         0
Percent (%) Found      :      25.00
```

Figure 3.45 The set of somewhat somewhat LOW annual revenue companies

With this fuzzy domain, all five companies in the query space are selected and none are rejected due to alpha cut threshold restrictions. The truth memberships have all been promoted above this cut off horizon and reflect their membership in the concept of companies with annual revenues somewhere around somewhat LOW.

Complex FuzzySQL Queries with Hedged Predicates

Hedged WHERE predicates can be combined in a FuzzySQL query to expand or restrict the query space in the same manner as the base fuzzy sets. We can see this by comparing hedged and unhedged complex queries across the same fuzzy regions. The query using RECENT company age and MODERATE revenues shown in the "Effects of the AVERAGE Truth Composition" on page 176 is a good illustration. Figure 3.46 shows the corresponding query with hedged fuzzy sets.

```
select company
  from MfgDBMS
  where  Company.Age is somewhat RECENT
    AND Annual.Revenues are very MODERATE;

Company           CompIDX     AvgIDX
----------------  ----------  ----------
CompP               0.905       0.936
CompO               0.326       0.632
CompD               0.000       0.500
CompK               0.000       0.500
CompI               0.000       0.497
CompE               0.024       0.464
CompB               0.000       0.461
CompN               0.000       0.453
CompF               0.000       0.404
CompM               0.017       0.384
CompL               0.000       0.379
CompA               0.000       0.312
CompH               0.270       0.298
CompG               0.000       0.170
CompC               0.000       0.119
Record Selected        :         15
Rejected due to AlphaCut :        2
Percent (%) Found      :      75.00
```

Figure 3.46 A query with multiple hedged fuzzy WHERE statements

Here we see the query is only slightly different, although the number of participating rows based on the minimum truth composition method would be much higher. In each example encountered so far the WHERE qualifiers have all been hedged or all been base fuzzy sets. We can also mix these concepts to produce queries that drive home the exact meaning of our intentions. Figure 3.47 shows a query with mixed linguistic variables.

```
FuzzySQL Database Processor
----------------------------
AlphaCut Threshold    : .1
AND operator Type     : AVERAGE
select company
  from MfgDBMS
  where:
Company Age is        : RECENT
Annual Revenues are   : extremely MODERATE
----Applying the hedge 'extremely'
Product Count is      : //
Employee Count is     : //
Profit or Loss is     : //
Retained EPS is       : //
Ranking   13 Rows.
.+++++++++++
.++++++++
.++++++
.+++++
.+++++
.+++
.++
.++
.++
.++
.++
.+
.
Ranking Complete.
```

Figure 3.47 Querying the database with mixed linguistic variables

This query combines the truth of RECENT in the company age column with the truth of extremely MODERATE in the annual revenues column. The extremely hedge is an intensifier like VERY except that the membership values are cubed instead of squared. This provides a tighter constraint on the output fuzzy space. Figure 3.48 shows the results of applying the extremely hedge.

```
ANNUAL.REVENUES
Domain [UofD]:    100.00 to    1800.00
     1.00                 *
     0.90               .  *
     0.80              .*   .
     0.70                  .
     0.60            .*    *
     0.50
     0.40          .       .
     0.30          *       *
     0.20        .        .
     0.10                 *
     0.00************     *************************************************
       0---|---|---|---|---|---|---|---|---|---|---|---|---|---|---|---0
       100.00 312.50 525.00 737.50 950.00 1162.50 1375.00 1587.50 1800.00

     .   FuzzySet:    MODERATE
     *   FuzzySet:    extremely MODERATE
```

Figure 3.48 The MODERATE and extremely MODERATE fuzzy sets

The `extremely MODERATE` fuzzy region sits well inside the space defined by the base `MODERATE` fuzzy set. It's sides are also sharply defined so the truth membership falls off rapidly. This restricts the annual revenues that have nonzero membership in the region. Figure 3.49 shows the results of this query.

```
select company
  from MfgDBMS
  where  Company.Age is RECENT
    AND Annual.Revenues are extremely MODERATE;

Company                CompIDX     AvgIDX
----------------       ----------  ----------
CompP                      0.819      0.885
CompO                      0.106      0.508
CompD                      0.000      0.500
CompK                      0.000      0.500
CompI                      0.000      0.495
CompB                      0.000      0.443
CompE                      0.004      0.411
CompN                      0.000      0.410
CompF                      0.000      0.363
CompM                      0.000      0.326
CompL                      0.000      0.288
CompA                      0.000      0.246
CompH                      0.106      0.123
Record Selected          :            13
Rejected due to AlphaCut :             4
Percent (%) Found        :         65.00
```

Figure 3.49 Set of companies with constrained with mixed fuzzy regions

Complex expressions involving base fuzzy sets, hedges, and general approximators significantly improve the mechanism for translating the intention of a query. Although not directly covered in the previous discussion, the use of approximator hedges that convert numerical values into fuzzy sets are also important capabilities in fuzzy query facilities. Since the approximator constructs a narrow fuzzy set around the numeric value, such dynamically formed sets can be used to restrict a query to a small region of a larger column domain. Approximations also provide a method for querying database columns that have not been further defined by a set of base fuzzy sets (assuming we know the general range of values in the column's underlying data space.)

Predicates with Usuality and Frequency Qualifiers

Another important class of operators in a fuzzy query facility involve what could be called second order fuzzy qualifiers[10]. These qualifiers modify the results of fuzzy propositions so we can map one fuzzy concept into the restricted domain of another fuzzy region. The primary second order qualifier is the usuality restriction. This concept is

---

10. This should not be confused with second-order fuzzy sets. A second-order fuzzy set has domain and membership values that are also fuzzy numbers.

implemented through qualifier terms such as *mostly, usually, often, always,* and *every.* In this respect they work as a form similar to hedges except they filter by insisting the truth membership meet certain minimum truth hurdle constraints. As an example, consider the following query:

```
SELECT COMPANY
    FROM MFGDBMS
        WHERE MOSTLY(ANNUAL.REVENUES ARE HIGH);
```

The intention of this query is to create a collection of companies where the annual revenues would be HIGH in most of the cases. We do this by mapping the membership of the proposition annual.revenues are HIGH into another fuzzy region that defines the idea of *mostly.* Figure 3.50 shows the organization of the MOSTLY fuzzy set.

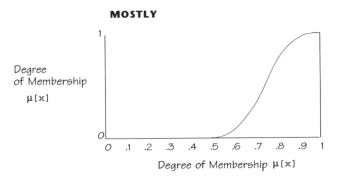

Figure 3.50 The MOSTY usuality fuzzy set

The value of the fuzzy proposition in the WHERE statement is used as a domain point in the MOSTLY fuzzy set. From this we can derive a compatibility membership in MOSTLY. It is this membership value that is returned to the fuzzy query facility. Figure 3.51 shows how this process works in a simple FuzzySQL request.

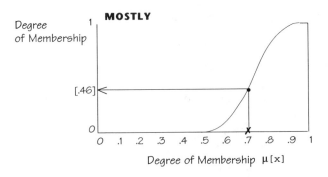

Figure 3.51 Classifying a domain value as MOSTLY(x)

As an natural extension of this process, the usuality and frequency operators evaluate any complex fuzzy expression. This means we can collect groups that reflect an aggregate truth as well as an individual truth. As an example:

```
SELECT COMPANY
   FROM MFGDBMS
   WHERE MOSTLY(COMPANY.AGE IS RECENT
        AND USUALLY(ANNUAL.REVENUES ARE VERY HIGH)
        AND PRODUCT.COUNT IS SOME);
```

this query involves a mostly qualification for the entire WHERE predicate as well as a usually qualification on the annual revenues predicate. Figure 3.52 shows how these two qualification fuzzy sets are related.

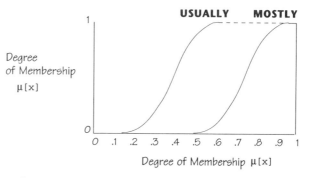

Figure 3.52 The USUALLY and MOSTLY fuzzy sets

Since usuality qualifiers are fuzzy operators we can view them as linguistic variables. A natural consequence of this approach is that a usuality space can also be hedged in the same manner as base fuzzy sets. Care must be taken that we understand the exact meaning of hedged usuality regions. As an example, consider this query request:

```
SELECT COMPANY
   FROM MFGDBMS
        WHERE POSITIVELY MOSTLY(ANNUAL.REVENUES ARE HIGH);
```

The positively hedge (this is a contrast intensifier) is applied to the MOSTLY fuzzy set before the target fuzzy proposition is evaluated. Hedging has the same affect on the underlying usuality qualifiers as it has on normal fuzzy sets. In the case of usuality sets, however, the outcome of this modification is felt through a second-order truth transfer process. Although the mechanism is quite different and the results are different, the use of alpha cut threshold instead of usuality hedging is often better understood and more predictable.

In a complete fuzzy query facility, the usuality and frequency components would include the complements of the qualifiers such as *never, hardly ever, infrequently,* and *seldom*. Figure 3.53 illustrates, as an example, the idea of MOSTLY as well as its complement, SELDOM.

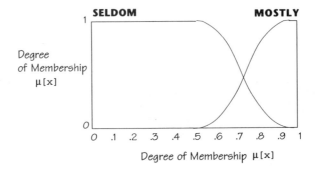

Figure 3.53 The SELDOM and MOSTLY fuzzy sets

Unlike the model-based context for fuzzy sets, the organization of usuality and frequency fuzzy sets are independent of the context. They represent the ideas behind our notions of what constitutes a preponderance of truth in a proposition, of how we understand proportionality, and the imprecision associated with these concepts.

Fuzzy Secondary Indexing Techniques

When the number of records in a database table is relatively small compared to the processing power of the machine (instructions per second), the machine task load (available cycles in a multi-tasking environment), the speed of the hard disk (latency time, head positioning time for the access arm, and the data transfer rate) and the number of tables involved in a single query is also fairly small a database query can use "brute force" to select a set of records that meet the WHERE predicates in a conventional or fuzzy SQL request. As the number of records or participating tables increase (or a combination of both), the response time for a query decays rapidly. Figure 3.54 illustrates the relationship between machine through-put capability and the number of records that must be processed.

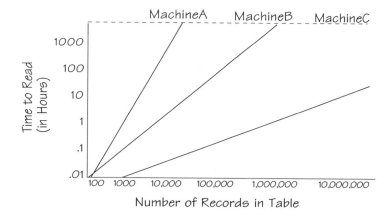

Figure 3.54 File read time as a function of machine performance

As the number of records (or rows) in a table increases sequential processing of the entire file becomes prohibitive. Not only does the processing time increase rapidly, but the utility of the knowledge itself declines as the time between the request and the result becomes longer and longer. Conventional database management systems include structures for improving performance. These are called *secondary indexes*. A secondary index is a search structure that allows the retrieval process to rapidly locate records associated with indentifiers that are used to actually store the record (they are not the primary identifier). Unlike primary indexes, a secondary index can retrieve entire collections of records associated with a single index value.

Using Conventional Index Schemes

The purpose of a *secondary index* is easy to understand. We examine a simple SQL query against a real-world database of financial information like those maintained by commercial credit and financial reporting companies such as Dunn and Bradstreet, Equifax, TRW, and Standards and Poor's. As an example, consider a query against the financial data profile table (FINDATA) containing roughly 20,000,000 records. We are looking for manufacturing companies on the east coast with revenues in excess of $600,000.

```
SELECT COMPANYID,TAXID,1994REVENUES,1994GROWTH
   FROM IEH004.FINDATA
      WHERE COMPANY_TYPE="MFG"
      AND LOCATION="EAST"
      AND REVENUES > 600;
```

Without a secondary indexing scheme, all twenty million records must be read to find the subset where the company type is manufacturing (MFG) and the location is the eastern United States (EAST). Even for a fast machine, the response time is large. When the COMPANY_TYPE and the LOCATION have secondary index structures, the search time can be dramatically reduced. To retrieve all the records that satisfy the WHERE conditions using the column secondary indexes we follow these steps:

1. Find COMPANY_TYPE index.
   Locate Unique Occurrence of "MFG".
   Read all Index Records that have this value into IDX1 list.

2. Find LOCATION index.
   Locate Unique Occurrence of "EAST".
   Read all Index Records that have this value into IDX2 list.

3. Create list IDX3 containing Intersection of IDX1 and IDX2.

4. Read all database records on list IDX3.

5. If REVENUE column > 600 then select record.

The two index lists are combined through the intersection operation and the company identifiers that exist on both lists are read from the database. The REVENUE column is then compared against $600,000. If, say, 10,000 manufacturing companies and 100,000 east coast companies exist, the total records read from the database are less than or equal to the minimum of both lists (10,000). For a more complete discussion of conventional secondary indexing schemes see "Secondary Access Paths (Keys)" on page 152.

A Fuzzy Secondary Index Scheme

Conventional secondary indexes find database records associated with column values. Fuzzy *secondary index structures* maintain a correspondence between fuzzy concepts and the underlying database records. Without such an indexing structure, FuzzySQL queries would require a search of an entire table. As an example, consider the following change in the previous crisp query:

```
SELECT COMPANYID,TAXID,1994REVENUES,1994GROWTH
   FROM IEH004.FINDATA
      WHERE REVENUES ARE HIGH
      AND COMPANYAGE IS RECENT;
```

without any qualification by conventional index columns (such as those used in the previous query) this request must also scan the entire table to find the records that satisfy the WHERE predicates. A fuzzy index, however, provides a mechanism for rapidly retrieving records that have values associated with one or more fuzzy regions. The index structure stores not only the fuzzy set relationship but the degree of membership as well. Figure 3.55 shows the basic architecture of a fuzzy index.

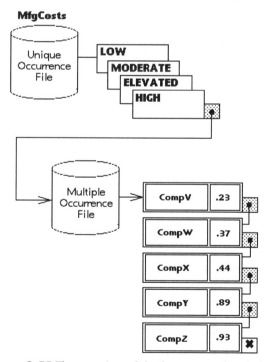

Figure 3.55 The overview of the fuzzy secondary index

Each indexed column has its own index. Like conventional data index structures, the fuzzy index consists of two components: the Unique Occurrence File containing the name of each fuzzy set in the column's underlying term set. The entry of a particular fuzzy set has a pointer into the Multiple Occurrence File. This file contains the actual index. The Multiple Occurrence File contains a list of database table records where the indexed column has a value in this fuzzy set. The entry contains the primary identifier (in this case, the company identifier) and its degree of membership. (The small shaded boxes in Figure 3.55 indicates pointer values.)

Overlapping Index Entries

A record can appear in more than one index chain. That is, for the manufacturing costs column *(MfgCosts)*, a record can have an index in both the ELEVATED and the HIGH fuzzy sets. Figure 3.56 shows how the index entries are ordered for the value 22.5 in the MfgCosts column.

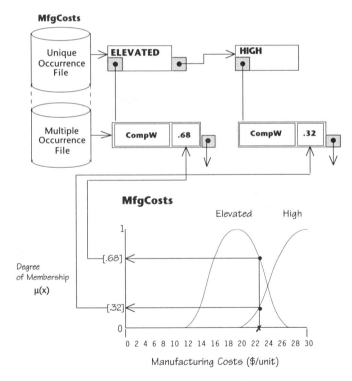

Figure 3.56 Indexing a value from the MfgCosts column

This cross indexing makes sense in the fuzzy environment since it reflects the way column values have grades of membership in neighboring term set regions. The index stores the primary identifier and the membership value. This allows the indexing process to skip memberships that fall below the alpha cut threshold. For database organizations where identifier hashing is not used to store the record, the actual index entries may need to carry the physical page (and/or offset) for the stored record.

This kind of indexing provides a method of slicing quickly through a large database when only fuzzy qualifications are specified. Consider the query:

```
SELECT COMPANYID,TAXID,1994REVENUES,1994GROWTH
   FROM IEH004.FINDATA
       WHERE REVENUES ARE HIGH
       AND COMPANYAGE IS RECENT;
```

To retrieve all the records that satisfy the WHERE conditions using the fuzzy secondary indexes we follow steps very close to those used in conventional indexing:

1. Find REVENUES fuzzy index
   Locate Unique Occurrence of fuzzy set HIGH
   for each Index Record where GradeofMembership > AlphaCut
   Insert Index Records into IDX1 list

2. Find COMPANYAGE fuzzy index
   Locate Unique Occurrence of RECENT
   for each Index Record where GradeofMembership > AlphaCut
   Insert Index Records into IDX1 list

3. Create list IDX3 containing Intersection of IDX1 and IDX2

4. Read all database records on list IDX3

The two index lists are combined through the intersection operation and the company identifiers that exist on both lists are read from the database. Naturally, if the retrieval process is qualified by conventional indexes, we can form a pool of these records first and then simply apply fuzzy membership qualification directly to this reduced set of records.

The FuzzySQL Data Flow

Figure 3.57 shows the general process flow within the FuzzySQL system. This is a high level schematic of the over-all process and does not show every step in the extraction and ranking process. The schematic only reflects the process flow for the fuzzy logic side of the query, the qualification using conventional crisp predicates is not shown.

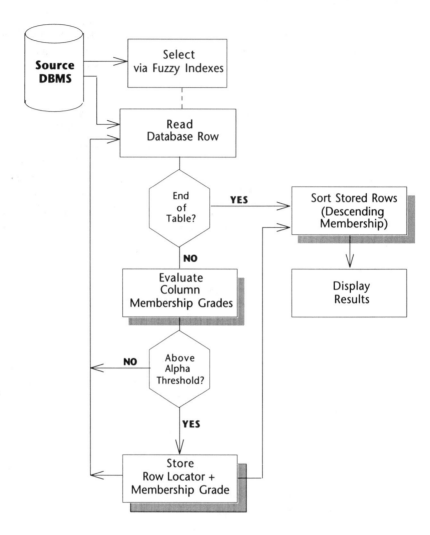

Figure 3.57 The fuzzySQL process flow schematic

Applications of Fuzzy SQL Systems

The use of fuzzy predicates in relational database queries has a broad range of applications. In nearly all cases, whenever a crisp selection is made, a fuzzy or approximate query produces a result closer to the intentionality of the user. In this section we look at three actual applications of fuzzy queries in a relational database environment.

Company Acquisition and Mergers

This multi-stage fuzzy logic system was designed and built in the late 1980's for the acquisitions and mergers division of a large international financial services institution. The complete model consists of three components: a fuzzy database query facility, a fuzzy financial statement analyzer, and a fuzzy model of the organizational behavior—a model of the expected management stability of the candidate company. Figure 3.58 shows a schematic representation of the company acquisitions system.

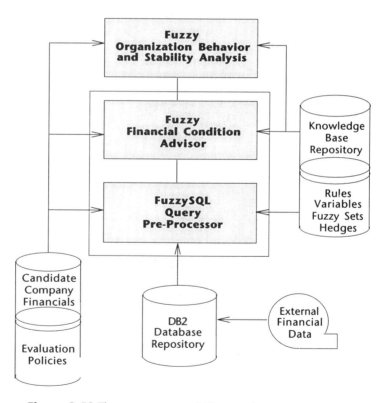

Figure 3.58 The company acquisitions and mergers systems

The DB2 database repository contains public credit and financial information extracted from such diverse sources as Equifax, TRW, Standards and Poor's, Dunn and Bradstreet, and Valueline. This public data is combined with semi-private information as well as market-place intelligence extracted from a variety of sources such as corporate annual reports, stock exchange tracking histories, and corporate management and meta-activity information from sources like *ComputerWorld* (a weekly trade newspaper for the computer industry), *The Wall Street Journal*, and *The New York Times*. This information—selected for relevance to the fuzzy database query—formed the information base used by the array of fuzzy rules to further evaluate the companies for the fitness as candidates for acquisition or merger.

The Fuzzy Database Component

The company acquisition system uses fuzzy database queries to locate and extract a set of candidate companies based on the broad meaning of the selection criteria expressed by the client. In this way, the retrieval covers and returns a set of companies that are much closer to the intent of the search[11]. The example database used in this chapter is based on this acquisition model that handles queries such as:

```
SELECT COMPANYID,FEDTAXID,COMPTYPE
   FROM IEH001.FINDATA
   WHERE COMPANYSIZE IS BELOW LARGE
      AND SALES ARE INCREASING
      AND ANNUAL.REVENUES ARE SIGNIFICANT
      AND PE_RATIO IS ACCEPTABLE;
```

The FuzzySQL query creates a new column in each retrieved record containing the truth of the predicate (using the average truth method.) The financial services organization has reported a number of important benefits from the use of the fuzzy database query facility in addition to its improved query scope capabilities. These are the principal four benefits:

1. By standardizing a common analytical vocabulary for their analysts, they insure company financial, marketing, product, and management evaluations are made against a uniform benchmark. This provides a consistent approach to candidate selection and in-

---

11. The description of the acquisition system has been somewhat simplified for this discussion. The actual application executes embedded SQL statements in a PL/1 application program running on an IBM mainframe (running the MVS operating system) under the CICS transaction processor. The results of this conventional (crisp) SQL query (a set of qualified records) are loaded into a SQL/DS database under the VM/CMS operating system. The interactive FuzzySQL software issues database API calls to fetch, evaluate, and rank these records.

sures a high level of quality work for their clients. Of course, analysts are free to specify crisp values in the WHERE predicate and FuzzySQL recognizes this as a special case[12]. As an example, the following are valid FuzzySQL requests,

```
WHERE ANNUAL.REVENUE IS HIGH
      AND PE_RATIO IS VERY SIGNIFICANT;

WHERE ANNUAL.REVENUE > 9500
      AND PE_RATIO IS VERY SIGNIFICANT;
```

In practice, however, the use of crisp values, occurring very frequently in the initial stages of system implementation, drops off rapidly as analysts gain confidence in the meaning and utility of the fuzzy vocabulary.

2. They are able to evaluate the degrees of membership for each candidate in some detail. This allows management to provide a more coherent and complete description to clients concerning how and why a particular company was either selected or (more important) omitted from the recommendations. By explaining ". . .you requested only 'highly profitable' companies. . ." or "if you relax (or tighten) what you mean by "large company" then . . ." they are better able to communicate the nature of the selection screening process.

3. The use of an interactively adjustable alpha cut threshold along with the compatibility index for each company provides an important mechanism for adjusting each client's query based on how tolerant or intolerant they are of diffusion around the centers of measurement for each fuzzy concept. By moving the alpha cut threshold upward, only highly compatible companies are selected; by moving the alpha threshold down, a wider but lest compatible collection of candidates is selected.

4. In some respects (according to the user) the most important benefit, is the ability to move the potential candidate screening process down to less experienced analysts. Since these junior analysts now have access to the semantic vocabulary used by the experts, they

---

12. Actually FuzzySQL simply converts crisp scalars into narrowly diffused fuzzy numbers using a bell-shaped (PI) fuzzy set.

can explore the database space linguistically and generally retrieve the same companies as an expert. Senior, expert analysts now have more time to evaluate marginal cases, refine the query vocabulary, and improve the rule base in the more important financial condition advisor. This ability to use less than senior analysts is important for the corporation in two critical ways, both affecting the bottom line: first, they can service, with the same staff and within the same time frame, a larger number of prospective clients thus increasing revenues, and second, they can use a mix of senior and junior analysts thus reducing their effective costs per project and therefore improving profitability on a project-by-project basis.

There is, of course, no free lunch in the business world. In some ways the benefits of the fuzzy database query are partially offset by several factors. The basic complexity of the system—using SQL queries issued from compiled program code and the migration of data between two different mainframe operating systems—makes increased coordination between the user and the corporate information services department critical. The issues of "who owns and who can see" the data also becomes significant when the data resides on a corporate data repository. Finally, the underlying relational database occupies several "spindles" (physical disk drives) of DB2 database pool space. An unstructured query against this database (of many gigabytes) takes an appreciable amount of time. Only the retrieved records in their own database can be accessed interactively. In spite of these logistical and management drawbacks, the fuzzy query facility has found continued and high profile use in the organization's marketing, sales, strategic planning, and site location planning departments.

The Fuzzy Financial Statement Analyzer Component

The fuzzy database operations are really only a filtering process for the actual work of the acquisitions and mergers recommendation system. When a set of candidate companies are stored in ranked order, the financial analysis model is invoked to determine whether or not the company is a good opportunity for acquisition or merger based primarily on its financials but also on ancillary information such as product line composition, expansion rate, principle service sectors, pending legal actions, and turbulence in senior management or executive turnover. While some issues associated with management are evaluated in more depth by the organizational behavior model, many aspects of management, such as the recent addition or departure of a chief executive, a high executive attrition rate, or a law suit involving senior corporate executives, are incorporated in the fundamental financial analysis component.

As Figure 3.59 illustrates, the financial statement advisor consists of several policies and a macro-economic modelling program.

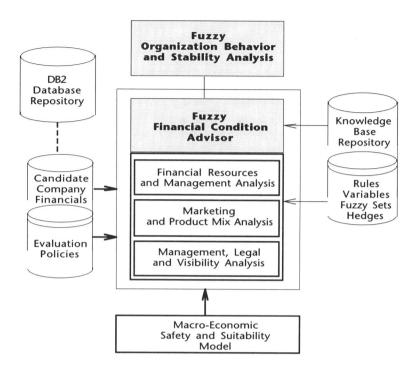

Figure 3.59 The financial analysis component of the acquisition model

From the accumulated financial, inventory, sales, and marketing information, the second component of the acquisitions and mergers system attempts to evaluate the capabilities and stability of the organization based on the management of is financial resources. In particular the model looks at such factors as changes in retained earnings or income, changes in net and undiscounted income, and changes in net property. The system uses balance sheets, source and application of funds reports, and available sales and on-hand inventory data to construct an estimated funds flow as well as profit and loss model of the organization. The model logic is particularly interested in assessing the impact of short-term notes, long-term debt (with payments extending for more than two years), the depletions of capital reserves, net profit to equity ratios, and minority stock ownership.

The model also makes use of an external fuzzy macro-economic model that communicates with the acquisitons and mergers systems through the message switching capabilities of a blackboard facility. The economic model contains information on the general trends of the stock markets, the movement of the prime rate, the change in revenues and profits for a wide range of industries, current unemployment rates, construction and new housing starts, mortgage rate changes. As an example, to retrieve the prime rate in model time period "t", the following request is made:

```
PrimeRate=GetFromECONOMICS("PRIMERATE",t);
```

or to find the average change in the treasure bond rate over the past six months as a fuzzy approximation, the following request is made:

```
DeltaBondRate=GetFromECONOMICS(
        AVG("CHG.BONDRATE"),t-6,CIX)
```

The economic model provides important external (exogenous) information about the state of the world. Since the model contains fuzzy sets and fuzzy rules that measure the movement of important economic indicators, we can request both crisp information (such as the prime rate) or fuzzy information, such as the average change in the bond rate over the past six months.

The marketing and product mix assessment policy in this component evaluates the current increase or decrease in sales revenues, the type and mix of products, and the management of the inventories. Using fuzzy estimation and fuzzy numerical techniques, the policy evaluates such factors as turnover ratios (using both gross and net assets) and inventory carrying costs and turnover. The marketing policy is intended to provide the acquisition and merger client with an analysis of potential problems as well as potential opportunities in the use of real and intangible assets and to define a broad evaluation of the marketing and production management skills of the candidate organization.

This system uses a multiple constraint and ranking model to match the properties of the candidate corporation against the client's acquisition or merger requirements. The underlying financial and marketing rules assimilate knowledge into categories with associated degree of compatibility among the category members (a measure of tightly or how loosely the cluster of data points are spread within the category.) For more detailed information refer to Chapter 5.

A final policy relies on supplemental information about the candidate company extracted from trade sources, legal databases (such as Lexus), and items of record found in credit analysis reports. The management, legal and visibility policy provides an analysis of the risks associated with actually selecting the company as a working candidate. The analysis considers such factors as the turn-over rate of senior and middle management, pending legal actions, possible legal actions (inferred from the nature of the company's business coupled with projections from the macro-economic model), and, finally, the "visibility" of the company both within its business sector and within the general press.

The core of the acquisitions and mergers system is the financial analysis component. From this evaluation, companies are ranked according to their potential and their risk. This potential ranking is within the inclusive psychometric scale of $[0, 100]$ while the risk is measured on a scale from zero to one $[0, 1]$ inclusive. In measuring candidate company potential (a measure of the best fit with the client's acquisition or merger criteria), 100 represents a perfect fit while 0 represents a complete lack of compatibility. For the risk associated with the company (a measure of the possibility the acquisition fails or the candidate can not perform as anticipated), 0 represents the highest risk and 1 represents the least risk. Equation 3.6 shows how a final satisfaction goal index is developed.

$$SIDX(company) = potential_{company} \cdot risk_{company}$$

Equation 3.6 The candidate company satisfaction index

The satisfaction index is created by taking the product of the two factors so that, in fact, the potential of the candidate company is scaled by the associated degree of risk. In the acquisition and mergers model, the screening of companies using this index is done by another small selection policy that evaluates satisfaction using a set of rules about what constitutes minimal, acceptable, and best satisfaction with rules such as,

```
if SatisfactionIDX is GOOD then candidate is ACCEPTABLE
if SatisfactionIDX is EXCELLENT then candidate is BEST
```

The analyst's alpha cut threshold determines which companies are finally placed on the agenda of actual candidates. When this agenda has been filled, the acquisitions model then calls another set of policies involved with evaluating the management dynamics of each corporation and assessing the robustness, so to speak, of the organization.

The Fuzzy Model of the Organizational Behavior Component

Using the final set of candidate companies, ranked by their satisfaction goals index, the organizational behavior component attempts to determine how an acquisition or merger affects the behavioral dynamics of the organization. To do this, it analyzes such factors as the internal interactions among the senior management team, the relationship between management and the work force, the maturity, depth, and competence of management throughout the organization. The utility of this system component depends on the availability of information about the infrastructure of the organization, about its management style, and about the type of management practices found in the particular company, in the industry in general, and among companies of similar size, in like demographic service areas, and similar geographic distribution. Figure 3.60 shows the schematic structure of the organizational behavior model.

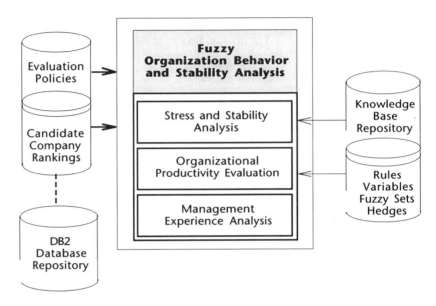

Figure 3.60 The organizational behavior component of the acquisition model

The three policies in this model component each evaluate a different perspective on the dynamics of the organization. A stress and stability policy examines the ways in which management is attempting to cope with changes in the marketplace (if any), the rise of competition, the changes in marketshare, the obsolescence curve for high technology products, and the movement from a specialty to a commodity driven production and pricing strategy. Based on the work of industrial management researches such as Alvin Gouldner, the organizational productivity policy creates a simulation of the adaptive feed-back associated with changes in management supervisory levels and worker productivity. This policy assesses the likely deterioration of the productivity, the rise in attrition rates, and the decline in customer support that follows changes in management policy enforcement, management style, and supervisory control. A final policy evaluates the depth of management experience by considering such factors as the average age of the management team, and the past experience of the senior executives.

Intelligent Project Management and Risk Assessment

This interactive enterprise modelling system combined project risk assessment and management, capital budgeting, and strategic decision support into a common framework based on its own proprietary relational database system. The design grew out of an awareness that the relational model not only provides a consistent method of storing the system components, but also provides a flexible and highly adaptive way of generating new views of information without the necessity of predefining all possible relationships. Figure 3.61 shows the general schematic of the project handling components of the enterprise modelling system.

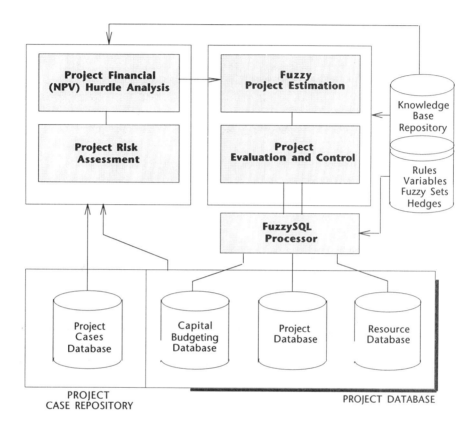

Figure 3.61 The project management and project risk assessment system

The model consists of three major components: risk assessment with a financial hurdling analysis based on the projected net present value of the project, a classical project network analysis facility that includes a task estimation module as well as a fuzzy critical path analysis module, and a project tracking and control facility that analyzes the underlying project database through a specialized fuzzy database system. The database facility contains not only all the project descriptions in a series of normal tables, but also a special database section containing structured historical projects or project "case" records.

A Case-Based Reasoning Facility

The risk assessment component is a nonlinear fuzzy model that evaluates the structure of a project based on such intrinsic factors as proposed budget, project duration, number of necessary resources, level of required technology support, experience and age of the project manager, and internal project complexity (number of phases and activities, as an example). The risk model also draws on a fuzzy Case-Based Reasoning facility to find similar projects done by the same organization. The risk assessment extrapolates from similar projects to gauge the risk of the current project. In the fuzzy case-based reasoning facility, a fuzzy similarity function is used to find projects with similar attributes. This similarity function treats each project attribute as a fuzzy quantity and measures the degree of compatibility between the areas of two projects (the current project and the case test project.) Thus the case-based reasoning module checks for similarity in tests such as,

```
SIMILARITY(PROJECT.DURATION,CASE[i].DURATION) > AlfaCut
```

When the degree of similarity (the degree to which the fuzzy areas are congruent) is greater than the alpha cut threshold, the case project is selected. By increasing the alpha cut value, the analyst can force a higher and higher degree of similarity comparison. An alpha threshold of [1.0], as an example, would require an exact match between parameters. Figure 3.62 shows the similarity analysis between two closely placed fuzzy numbers with different diffusions or band widths.

```
FUZZY.NUMBERS
Domain [UofD]:       0.00 to      100.00
       1.00                    .. **
       0.90                   .. **. **
       0.80                  ..  *  .  *
       0.70                 .   *    .
       0.60                          .  *
       0.50              .    *         *
       0.40              .           .
       0.30          .   *         *
       0.20          .  *        .  *
       0.10******************  .    *
       0.00*************       ..  ********************************
         0---|---|---|---|---|---|---|---|---|---|---|---|---|---|---0
         0.00  12.50  25.00  37.50  50.00  62.50  75.00  87.50 100.00

    .    FuzzySet:    NUM1
         Description: Number: '30.00' at 70.00% width spread
         Support :       30.00,       21.00
    *    FuzzySet:    NUM2
         Description: Number: '35.00' at 50.00% width spread
         Support :       35.00,       17.50

Number 1:     30.00 (0.7000)
Number 2:     35.00 (0.5000)
SIMILARITY:   30.00 to 35.00 at strength 0.5000 is: 0.9641
```

Figure 3.62 Similarity between two distributions of fuzzy numbers 30 and 35

These two numbers, at their current band widths, are similar to the [.96] membership level. We would need an alpha cut threshold above this grade to force a dissimilarity result. Numbers can be weakly similar. Figure 3.63 shows the similarity analysis between the fuzzy numbers 20 and 30 when these numbers have narrow band widths.

```
FUZZY.NUMBERS
Domain [UofD]:        0.00 to      100.00
      1.00                 .      *
      0.90               . .      *
      0.80                 .      *
      0.70               .
      0.60             .
      0.50                      *
      0.40           .
      0.30               *
      0.20             .
      0.10        .        *
      0.00****************.....******************************************
          0---|---|---|---|---|---|---|---|---|---|---|---|---|---|---0
          0.00   12.50   25.00   37.50   50.00   62.50   75.00   87.50  100.00

     .    FuzzySet:    NUM1
          Description: Number: '   20.00' at 40.00% width spread
          Support :       20.00,      8.00
     *    FuzzySet:    NUM2
          Description: Number: '   30.00' at 20.00% width spread
          Support :       30.00,      6.00

Number 1:      20.00 (0.4000)
Number 2:      30.00 (0.2000)
SIMILARITY:    20.00 to       30.00 at strength 0.1000 is: 0.1538
```

Figure 3.63 Similarity between fuzzy numbers 20 and 30 with narrow band widths

Fuzzy numbers of the same shape are similar to the degree that their fuzzy spaces overlap. The height of this overlap among conformal fuzzy sets is the degree of similarity between the sets. For fuzzy numbers that are not conformal, such as trapezoids compared to bell curves or triangles compared to bell-curves, a more complex approach is necessary. The similarity of nonconforming fuzzy sets is determined by finding the area of each fuzzy set, finding the area over the common domain, and determining the ratio (or percentage) of the area that is not subtended by the common area. See "cbrsiml.cpp (The CBR Similarity Function)" on page 433 for the fuzzy Case-Based Reasoning similarity function. Also refer to "similnum.cpp (Similarity Analysis Program)" on page 434 for the similarity analysis program.

The Net Present Value (NPV) Risk Hurdle Threshold

The computed project risk is also laid across an inclusive psychometric scale of [1,100]. The risk is used by the financial hurdle analysis in adjusting the required net present value (NPV) for the project. Equation 3.7 is the basic equation for calculating this quantity.

$$NPV = \sum_{t=1}^{n} \left[\frac{R^t}{(1+k)^t} \right] - I$$

Equation 3.7 Calculation of net present value

For each time period (**t**) across the life of the project (**n**), **R** is the cash flow from the project in that period, **k** is the cost of capital in that period, and **I** is the initial cost of the investment (the original cash outlay). The counter-balancing risk assessment model adjusts both the anticipated period cash flows and the cost of capital to decrease the net present value of the project[13]. Thus, the higher the risk, the higher the payback hurdle for a project—up to a reasonable point, when, regardless of potential payback, the risk of project failure exceeds the acceptance threshold for any project.

The Fuzzy Relational Algebra System

In the project management component of the enterprise system, the database access is done through an integrated relational algebra system instead of the relational calculus of the standard `FuzzySQL` query facility. This capability provides a method of looping through a table one row at a time. As each record is active, a join can be made to other tables through an explicit `SELECT` capability. As an example, the following is a database-driven rule from the expert project control component.

```
FOR EACH PROJECT
    WHERE DUATION IS LONG
        AND BUDGET IS LARGE
        AND COUNT(PROJECT.PROJID,PHASE) IS HIGH;
    SELECT RESOURCE VIA PROJECT.PROJMGR;
    PERFORM PROJECT_SLIPPAGE_ANALYSIS(PROJECT.PROJID);
```

This rule loops through the project table, selecting each project with a `LONG` duration, a `LARGE` budget, and a `HIGH` number of project phases. For each of these projects, the associated project manager is selected from the resource table in the database (this is a standard equi-join.) The rule then performs a slippage analysis policy for the project. The relational algebra approach provides a very controlled method of accessing a relational database. Unlike the `SQL` query that returns a complete set of records, the `FOR EACH` mechanism retrieves and activates one set of records during each of the cycles. This mechanism can support many very complex query operations. As an example:

---

13. In the actual project risk assessment model, the choice of whether the cost of capital was increased or the returned cash flow was decreased is selected by the analyst for a particular evaluation.

```
FOR EACH PROJECT AS P1 WHERE BUDGET IS HIGH;
   FOR EACH PROJECT AS P2
       WHERE P2.DEPT=P1.DEPT AND P2.BUDGET > P1.BUDGET;
   SELECT RESOURCE AS R1 VIA PROJECT.PROJMGR;
   SELECT DEPARTMENT VIA PROJECT.DEPT
       WHEN DEPARTMENT EXISTS
           SELECT RESOURCE R2 VIA DEPARTMENT.MANAGER;
   PERFORM STORE_PROJECT(P1,P2,R1,R2);
```

This query involves a nested FOR EACH loop (the PROJECTS table is joined with itself.) The outer FOR EACH loop selects each project where the budget is considered HIGH. This record instance is labeled P1 so it can be distinguished from project records in the nested loop. For each project record that has some degree of membership in HIGH, the query loops through the PROJECTS table again (with these records labeled as P2) looking for records that are in the same department at the record active in the outer FOR EACH and where the inner project's budget is greater than the outer project's budget[14]. Then for each of the matched project records, we select the project manager from the RESOURCE table and, if a record for the project's department exists in the DEPARTMENT table, we select the department manager's resource record. Finally a policy that stores this information is invoked with the tags (the addresses) for each of the active records.

Both approaches to database accesses—the relational algebra and the relational calculus—compute a computability index for any record retreived by a WHERE statement. However, the way in which individual compatibility index values (CIX) are used by the two methods are completely different. In the SQL query the set of retrieved records are collected and then sorted in descending order by the compatibility value. In the FOR EACH query, when a record is selected, its compatibility truth value is computed and available for use in the query itself but the order of retrieval is relatively random. Because the compatibility index is computed when the WHERE expression is processed, the algebra method can use this compatibility value as part of the query itself. As an example, consider the following variation on a previous query,

```
FOR EACH PROJECT WHERE DUATION IS LONG AND BUDGET IS HIGH;
   IF PROJECT.&CIX IS ACCEPTABLE
       THEN
           PERFORM PROJECT_SLIPPAGE_ANALYSIS(PROJECT.PROJID);
```

The slippage analysis is only performed when the compatibility index has some membership in the fuzzy set ACCEPTABLE. Figure 3.64 shows this fuzzy set.

---

14. This could have been turned into a fuzzy comparison by using the fuzzy relational operator ABOVE, thus: WHERE P2.BUDGET IS ABOVE P1.BUDGET;

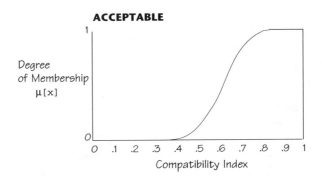

Figure 3.64 The ACCEPTABLE fuzzy set

The "&CIX" indicates a reference to a built-in component of the FOR EACH language rather than to a column in the PROJECTS table. In this query the actual rule body itself uses the compatibility index to decide whether or not to perform the slippage analysis. This value can be used like any other scalar in a rule's predicate, so we could formulate a rule with a premise such as if project.&cix is very acceptable.

Criminal (Suspect) Identification System

Initially developed for a European police force, this system provides a method of searching a large repository of known criminals based on a combination of fuzzy attributes. Although the database system includes digital photographic data, the production system does not directly involve graphical pattern matching, but relies on data pattern matching and the concept of "perspective shifting." This system has reduced the time to find a set of possible candidates from several hours to a few minutes. Figure 3.65 shows the schematic of this system.

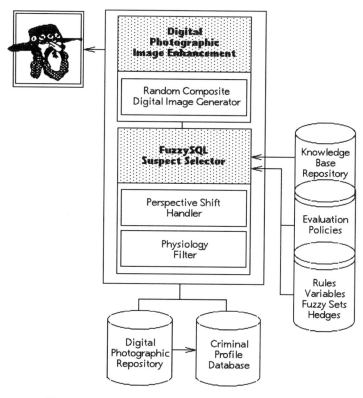

Figure 3.65 The Criminal Suspect Identification System

The process of searching through photographs of known criminals with their historical propensity for a particular kind of crime is time consuming and error prone. After the first few minutes, the ability to distinguish between photographs that share similar characteristics is significantly reduced. In order to improve the accuracy and speed of the search, a fuzzy identification system provides the victim with the ability to identify the characteristics of a criminal using approximate descriptors. As an example, for the characteristics of *height*, *weight*, *age*, and *build*, the criminal system provides a query such as the following.

```
SUSPECT IDENTIFICATION
select LastName, KPFserialNo, DigitPhoto
from ieh054.kpfdb.iehm002
Height:  somewhat TALL
Weight:  HEAVY
Age:     late MIDDLEAGED
Build:   STOUT
```

```
LastName        KPFserialNo    CIX
- - - - - - - - - - -  - - - - - - - - - -   - - - - - - - -
Carmichael      1896-88-044    .965
Smuthers        1397-63-308    .872
Wienmen         2443-79-114    .501
Embery          1053-11-820    .476
Bloomberg       7742-63-053    .441
Chambers        1208-55-297    .388
Huan            5729-34-772    .209
Holmes          1344-66-121    .187
  .
  .
```

Using the same fuzzy database techniques we examined in "The Intentionality Problem" on page 160 and explored in some detail in "FuzzySQL with Complex Predicates" on page 166, this query finds the candidate suspects that best match the victim's description. These are ranked by the compatibility measures and displayed along with the digital photograph. The criminal suspect identification system also allows more complex predicates than we have seen in the previous expression. The victim (or law enforcement official) can also qualify the physical attributes by creating a new linguistic variables with the union, intersection, or not operators. As an example:

```
SUSPECT IDENTIFICATION
select docitNo, KPFserialNo, DigitPhoto
from ieh054.kpfdb.iehm002
Height:   somewhat TALL but not very SHORT
Weight:   HEAVY
Age:      late MIDDLEAGED but not OLD
Build:    STOUT
```

The value for the candidate height is defined by the intersection of the hedged fuzzy set somewhat TALL and the complement of the hedged fuzzy set very SHORT. The operator BUT is the same as the fuzzy conjunctive AND.

Perspective Shifts Transformations

The criminal identification process is compounded by the variability in the observer's frame of reference, cultural preferences, and gender. While not all of this can be normalized by a fuzzy analysis system, some aspects of the victim's perceptions can be incorporated into the modelling and selection facilities. The basic mechanism for this is the perspective shift. The shift changes the underlying domain of the target fuzzy set based on the perspective fuzzy set's domain.

```
SUSPECT IDENTIFICATION
select LastName, KPFserialNo, DigitPhoto
from ieh054.kpfdb.iehm002
Height:   TALL from a SHORT perspective
Weight:   HEAVY
Age:      OLD from a YOUNG perspective
Build:    STOUT
```

```
LastName        KPFserialNo     CIX
- - - - - - - - - - -   - - - - - - - - - - -   - - - - - - - -
Nichols         4856-01-122     .989
Hogarth         3006-44-307     .940
Klien           1107-11-891     .903
Smuthers        1397-63-308     .882
Wienmen         2443-79-114     .571
Evans           5099-27-990     .486
```

The rationale behind perspective shifting is clear. What is *old* to someone eighteen years old is not the same as *old* to someone that is 45 years old. What is *tall* to someone under four feet is not the same as *tall* to someone over six feet. In order to effectively find the proper correlation between a fuzzy set and a data point in the suspect database, the domain of the fuzzy sets must be adjusted to accommodate the perspectives of the victim (or even the law enforcement officer).

Digital Photographic Enhancement

When a pool of candidate suspects are selected and ranked by the FuzzySQL system, the digital photograph of each suspect is displayed as the system user clicks on the candidate name. Photographic enhancement is available at this point to perform such modifications as general aging, removal or addition of facial hair, removal or addition of eye glasses, changes in hair, skin, and eye color, and grey-scale shading. The system contains a semi-autonomous "line up" facility—a random composite image generator creates a set of imaginary suspects and mixes these with those selected from the database. These images are drawn close to the fuzzy parameters specified by the user. In this way, the law enforcement agency can operate in a single or double blind mode to assess whether or not the victim is identifying an actual individual in the live database. In the double blind mode, neither the victim nor the law enforcement officers know which photographs are real and which are 'virtual' suspects.

Knowledge Mining and Rule Discovery

4

Ne in maximis quidem rebus quicquam adhuc inveni firmius,
quod tenerem aut quo iudicium meum dirigerem,
quam id quodcumque mihi quam simillimum veri videretur,
cum ipsum illud verum tamen in occulto lateret.
Even in the most important subjects,
I have never found anything more substantial to hold to or use
in forming my opinions than what seemed like truth
—yet the truth itself is hidden in obscurity.

Marcus Tullius Cicero
(106–43 B.C.)
Orator, 120

Corporations and government agencies often have large databases of data but an unclear understanding of the relationships represented in the data. This chapter examines a method used to create fuzzy systems from this data. Initially described by Jerry Mendel and Li-Xi Wang, the approach uses a training set of input and output data points in a manner similar to neural networks to generate a rule set that captures the underlying relationship. In the sense that the algorithm discovers relationships in the database, it provides a form of directed knowledge mining. In fact, the Wang-Mendel algorithm has been used by insurance, financial services, and large retail corporations to expose behavior patterns and data relationships in applications not directly connected with creating a fuzzy rule base.

The Ideas of Knowledge Mining and Discovery

Recently there seems to be a common theme among fuzzy researchers: how can we create a fuzzy system from the underlying databases of information. This approach, they reason, would solve several problems: it would discover and create the fuzzy sets and it would form and write the actual system rules. In this chapter an approach to these issues are discussed. The method is developed from the work done by Li-Xi Wang and Jerry Mendel at the University of Southern California on producing fuzzy sets and rules from a discovery set of model performance data. This technique, in turn, has some of its origins in the mathematical and analytical work of Bart Kosk and Donald Specht.

Benefits of Knowledge Mining

Fuzzy business systems can be complex and difficult to develop using the conventional approach to systems engineering and knowledge acquisition. By using the behavior of the system itself as reflected in the data, a fuzzy model can be developed that provides a first approximation of the final system. Figure 4.1 illustrates the general process of generating fuzzy sets and discovering the behavior rules.

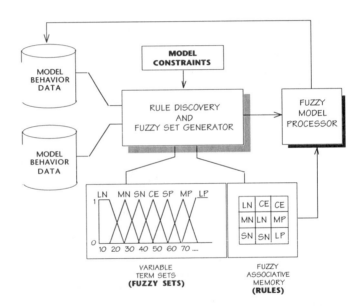

Figure 4.1 The over-all rule discovery model building process

From sets of behavior data and model structure constraints, the rule discovery mechanism generates all the necessary fuzzy term sets for each variable and then produces the rules that describe the model behavior. The model processor itself can influence this process by either changing one or more of the constraints or modifying the behavior data characteristics. This prototype is an important mechanism for structuring the over-all nature of the system. From this data-developed model a business analyst can direct much more effective knowledge acquisition from the expert team, can isolate irregularities in the described process flow, can discover missing control variables or refine the use of variables within the model, and can provide a data-driven feed-back mechanism that constantly tunes the system.

Problems with Knowledge Mining

The generation of fuzzy systems through knowledge mining has gained some convincing support in the control and process engineering field. Using combinations of neural networks and genetic algorithms, control system designers have managed to reduce the problem space to collections of fuzzy sets and the rules that reflect the system behavior within the domain of these sets. This seems to work well for engineering applications because the systems are generally fuzzy approximations of mathematical models rather than fuzzy interpretations of complex, database connected business systems. This does not detract from the power and effectiveness of producing fuzzy models from data, but it does address an important issue in fuzzy system development: the representation of the semantic meaning or intention of the model. When fuzzy sets are generated mechanically from the domain of a variable, they lack any semantic intentionality. They serve in a simply functional capacity—a way of decomposing the width of the variable's domain into a collection of fuzzy regions that can be addressed by the rules. Figure 4.2 illustrates how a variable (or a database column) can be arbitrarily divided into fuzzy sets,

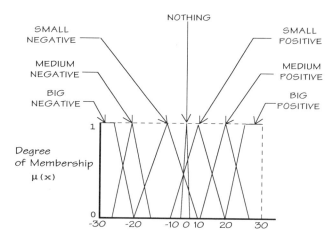

Figure 4.2 A Mechanical Partitioning into functional fuzzy sets

This kind of data discovering and mapping is common in the engineering disciplines due to the differential nature of model control variables. That is, many of the control parameters in common engineering problems—such as double stage pendulum balancing, navigation control, digital signal recognition—involve measuring the magnitude of changes in the variable state. The underlying fuzzy sets measure whether this is a big change, a moderate change, or a small change in either a positive or negative direction. However, when fuzzy sets are generated mechanically, as they are in most knowledge mining and rule discovery systems, there is very little relationship between the domain of a fuzzy set and the semantics of the model as might be understood by an expert.

Knowledge Mining Trade-Off Summary

Table 4.1 Knowledge mining benefits and trade-offs

Benefits	Draw Backs
Easy to use.	Arbitrary fuzzy set partitioning.
Generates a real production fuzzy logic system.	Lack of semantic meaning in rules.
Processes large amounts of data.	Lack of clear explanations
Handles nonlinear chaotic time-series data.	Difficult to maintain without re-generating entire system from data.
Machine and user rules can be in-tegrated	Needs lots of data.
System can be regenerated with new data.	Combinatorial explosion if not careful.
Use of adaptive rule weights.	Usually requires considerable amount of post-processing work.
Provisions for missing and noisy data.	

Table 4.1 summarizes some of the important benefits and disadvantages associated with creating a fuzzy system from rule discovery or knowledge mining techniques.

The Wang-Mendel Rule Discovery Method

In January 1991, Li-Xin Wang and Jerry M. Mendel at the Signal and Image Processing Institute of the University of Southern California in Los Angeles, published USC-SIPI Report Number 169, *Generating Fuzzy Rules from Numerical Data, with Applications.* This report detailed a step-by-step method of using model behavior data—similar to a training data set in supervised neural networks—to discover the relationships among data elements and produce the rules that describe these relationships.

> The general methods described by Wang and Mendel share a framework with much previous work done in the area of rule discovery and fuzzy system generation by Donald Specht and, in particular, Bart Kosko. In Kosko's **Neural Networks and Fuzzy Systems—A Dynamical Systems Approach to Machine Intelligence** (Prentice Hall, New Jersey, 1992) a detailed mathematical treatment of fuzzy associative memories [FAM's] and the generation of rules is given in Chapter Eight. See, as an example, the section *Adaptive FAM-Rule Generation*, page 328.

The central idea behind the Wang-Mendel Method is simple and straight forward (although its implementation is rather complex.) A model designer is often faced with a problem of quantifying model control and solution parameters in terms of their linguistic representation. If the model is well understood and mathematical descriptions are both robust and deterministic, then we can describe the system behavior with confidence. As an example, in an econometric system we might have a model of sales based on disposable income (D) and the cost of capital (k) in the consumer market. Equation 4.1 shows the basic function.

$$S = S(D,k)$$

Equation 4.1 The basic sales model function

From this, the rate of change in sales based on changes in the disposable income and the cost of capital (the interest rate on consumer loans), if the function is smooth and differentiable everywhere, is given by the partial differential equation in Equation 4.2.

$$dS = \frac{\partial S}{\partial D}\,dD + \frac{\partial S}{\partial k}\,dk$$

Equation 4.2 The change in sales as a total differential function

With this equation in hand, and knowing the changes in disposable income (ΔD) or the cost of capital (Δk) for any particular period, we can calculate a change in our projected sales volume. When one variable is fixed (it becomes a constant) and another is changing, a new partial differential provides a means of estimating the model's behavior under these conditions. Equation 4.3 shows the partial differential produced when the cost of capital (interest rates) are a constant.

$$\frac{\partial S}{\partial D} = \left(\frac{dS}{dD}\right)_{k \to constant}$$

Equation 4.3 Sales when cost of capital is a constant

Using these equations, we can provide exploratory values for each of the independent variables and observe the function's behavior. This is the essence of a system's mathematical model.

Quite frequently, however, the phenomenology of the model—its underlying causal relationships—are not well understood, highly non-linear, and subject to multiple interpretations by a family of experts. These problems are very difficult to model. In many instances, however, the case data for a model exists so we have a fundamental knowledge about the level of output when we have a series of inputs. Figure 4.3 illustrates this basic input, process, and output model.

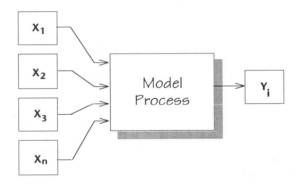

Figure 4.3 The input-process-output scheme of a fuzzy model

In this situation we have a mapping between an initial model state represented by the quantized data vector $\{x_{i1}...x_{in}\}$ and the problem solution state represented by the decomposed state variable $\{y_i\}$ for the i-th case of the model. This means, as shown in Figure 4.4, that some transfer function (g) probably exists between these states.

$$y_1 \leftarrow g(x_1,...,x_n)$$

.

.

.

$$y_k \leftarrow g(x_{k1},...,x_{kn})$$

Figure 4.4 The model transfer function problem state

The actual mechanics of the Model Process (see Figure 4.3) are unknown or, perhaps, only poorly understood. Using this relationship, we would like to derive a set of conditional fuzzy associations or rules in the form:

if x_1 is P_{i1} • x_2 is P_{i2} •... x_j is P_{ij} then y is C_i

where "P" is a predicate fuzzy region and "C" is a consequent fuzzy region. These fuzzy regions are generated directly from the data as approximations of the underlying domains. The rule discovery process finds the best combination of predicates and consequences consistent with the data points. This means it needs some method of comparing conflicting rules, consolidating redundant rules, and assigning rule precedence based on such factors as confidence in the data and membership in the underlying fuzzy sets.

The Rule Discovery Process

The Wang-Mendel rule discovery process consists of four basic steps (although the actual discovery software combines the rule generation and filtering into a single phase). Figure 4.5 shows and overview schematic of the process. The actual details of each step is discussed in the remainder of this section.

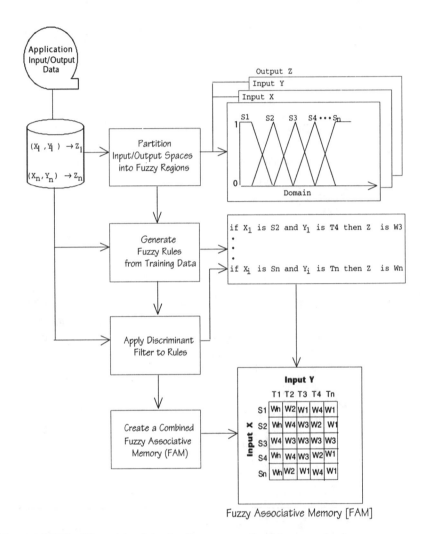

Figure 4.5 The Wang-Mendel rule discovery method (an overview)

The complete program source code (in C/C++) for the Wang-Mendel method is included in Chapter 8, C/C++ Code Listings. Refer to "wmdriver.cpp (The Wang-Mendel Main Program Driver)" on page 438 for the main program that drives the rule discovery process.

A Simple Price Sensitivity Model

In order to the follow the process of discovering the rules underlying a business process, we will use a simple (and admittedly unrealistic) sales volume to price sensitivity model. From a number of demographic regions we have the sales volumes as the retail price of our product steadily increases. The model has three variables: *time*, *price*, and *sales* with the relationship indicated in:

$$sales_{time} = f(price_{time}, time)$$

Equation 4.4 The sales volume to price functional relationship

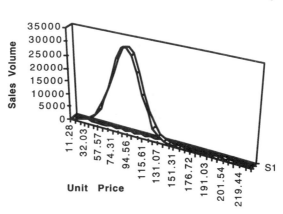

Figure 4.6 The sensitivity of sales to price function

Figure 4.6 shows the curve for one region. This data is derived from sales volume and price information across 36 months in one of four demographic regions (the actual data values are located in `sales.dat` and `nsales.dat`, the noisy data file, on the diskette). Sales appear relatively insensitive to product price until price reaches a threshold. Above this point, as price increases sales volume rapidly declines.

Representing and Using Model Behavior Data

The Wang-Mendel method uses the behavior of a system in terms of its underlying data in order to discover the descriptive fuzzy rules. This data is placed in a data file and read by the main driver program. The data file has a general format of:

```
x1, x2, x3, ... x4, y ; d
```

where "x_i" is an independent or control variable in the model, "y" is the dependent or solution variable, and "d" is the degree of contribution (data confidence factor) associated with the rule implied by the data elements. The data confidence factor can be omitted and is assumed to be [1]. As an example, Figure 4.7 shows a portion of the behavior file for the price sensitivity model discussed in the previous section.

```
//time     price       sales
//-----    ----------  ----------
     1,      11.28,        40.94
     2,      17.45,       336.82
     3,      28.75,       574.15
     4,      32.03,      1066.51
     5,      40.29,      2003.77
     6,      49.92,      3646.68
     7,      57.57,      6418.38
     8,      58.81,     10607.24
     9,      66.19,     15860.38
    10,      74.31,     21624.00
    11,      81.06,     27379.11
    12,      89.42,     31538.08
    13,      94.56,     32066.22
    14,     101.49,     29985.87
    15,     104.64,     23837.87
    16,     115.61,     16075.54
```

Figure 4.7 A model behavior training file

Lines that begin with a double slash (//) are comments and are ignored by the rule discovery system. The training file can contain any number of records. You can also specify a degree of contribution for the data elements as indicated in Figure 4.8.

```
//time     price       sales
//-----    ----------  ----------
     1,      11.28,        40.94 ; .4
     2,      17.45,       336.82 ; .4
     3,      28.75,       574.15 ; .4
     4,      32.03,      1066.51 ; .4
     5,      40.29,      2003.77 ; .4
     6,      49.92,      3646.68 ; .7
     7,      57.57,      6418.38 ; .7
     8,      58.81,     10607.24 ; .7
```

Figure 4.8 Model behavior training with degree of contribution

Each line in the behavior file implies a rule about the system behavior. The purpose of the rule discovery mechanism is to learn the model's aggregate behavior from the relationships among the independent and dependent variables.

Executing the Rule Discovery Process

Once a data file has been created, you can invoke the rule discovery with the wmdriver command. Figure 4.9 shows how such a session would appear using the sales.dat behavior file.

```
wmdriver
Enter name of Data File: sales.dat
 1.0--Partition Variables into Fuzzy Sets.
 1.1----Generating Term Set for 'time'.
 1.1----Generating Term Set for 'price'.
 1.1----Generating Term Set for 'sales'.
 2.0--Generate Intermediate Rules from Training Data.
 2.1----Learning Rules from Data File: 'sales.dat'
 2.2----Formed   144 Rules.
 3.0--Create Combined FAM and write Production Rules.
 3.1----Generating FAM from Rule File: 'B:WMrules.FIL'.
 3.2----Combined FAM contains    23 Rules.
```

Figure 4.9 Executing the rule discovery process

From an input file containing 144 lines (each line is an implicit rule), the discovery process creates a combined Fuzzy Associative Memory (FAM) containing just 23 actual rules. These rules can then be used by the fuzzy modelling system. During processing the rule discovery system creates a series of auditing log files containing detailed information about the state of the process in each phase. The program also creates intermediate files—such as the rule matrix—that are read by other parts of the system during subsequent steps. Figure 4.10 shows a high level schematic of the various program steps in the Wang-Mendel rule discovery program and the files that are written or read during execution.

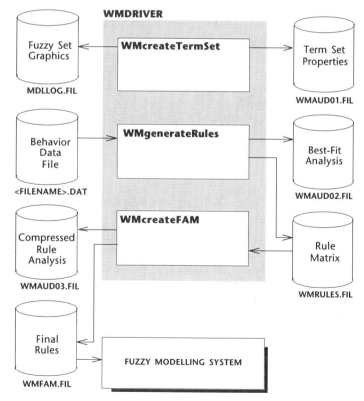

Figure 4.10 The process flow for the Wang-Mendel rule discovery method

You can use this kind of system to generate a fuzzy model from many different (but hopefully related) sets of data. In particular, the actual rule generation is driven by the contents of the uncompressed rule matrix (`wmrules.fil`). By saving this file across many rule discovery executions (with seasonal, regional, enhanced or new data as an example) you can create a combined rule matrix. Feeding this rule matrix into the **WMcreateFAM** program generates a rule set from the combined and updated information.

Step One. Decompose Variables into Fuzzy Sets

A rule discovery process begins with the generation of fuzzy sets for each of the input and output variables. The variable's complete Universe of Discourse is decomposed into a set of bell-shaped fuzzy sets (PI curves) with the left and right end points represented as shouldered fuzzy sets. This decomposition is directed by the analyst—the number of underlying fuzzy sets is based on the analyst's choice of how many regions would be necessary to correctly represent the variable's domain. This must be an odd number greater than three. There are always an odd number of fuzzy regions due to the way the decomposition process anchors a center fuzzy set and then moves out left and right to completely cover the rest of the variable's domain. The process starts, as illustrated by Figure 4.11, by creating a fuzzy set in the center of the variable's domain.

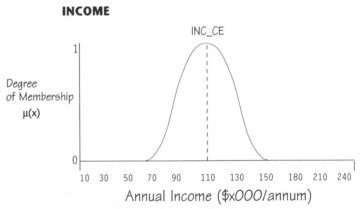

Figure 4.11 Generating the center fuzzy set in a variable's domain

Much of the decomposition intelligence is handled by the discovery process itself. After the analyst specifies the number of underlying fuzzy sets in the variable, the width of each bell-shaped fuzzy set, the degree of over-lap, and the inflection points of the S-curve sets used as the left and right shoulders are determined by the methodological process.

> The initial Wang Mendel algorithm specified triangular functions, with the center of the domain having a value of [1] and the edges linearly sloped to zero [0]. The end points were bisected trapezoids. However, PI distributions (or Gaussian curves) along with ending S-curves provide a better semantic decomposition for most real-world business problems. A more complete discussion of this issue is found in *The Fuzzy System Handbook* (Cox, AP Professional, 1994), in Chapter 3, Fuzzy Sets, pages 65 through 78.

When the center fuzzy set has been installed, the remaining fuzzy sets are added by moving right and left across the remainder of the variable's explicit domain. The ending fuzzy regions are installed as left and right facing S-curves. Figure 4.12 shows the first part of the process for the left-hand portion of the INCOME variable.

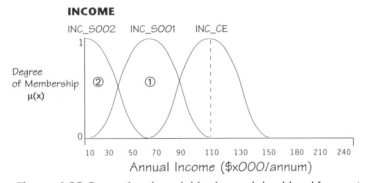

Figure 4.12 Generating the neighboring and shouldered fuzzy sets

The rule discovery decomposition process automatically labels the fuzzy sets to the left of the center, with S001 through S999 (indicating the values are Smaller than the center) and those to the right of the center with B001 through B999 (indicating the values are Bigger than the center.) In Figure 4.12 the fuzzy set INC_S001 (①) is added immediately to the left of center. It has a 50% over-lap meaning that its right edge with zero membership is at the INC_CE fuzzy set's center (the domain value with [1] membership.) Fuzzy set INC_S002 (②) is then added to the left of INC_S001. This is a shouldered fuzzy set in the form of an S-curve; it also has a 50% over-lap with INC_S001.

As noted in "Problems with Knowledge Mining" on page 219 this decomposition is unrelated to any explicit (or implicit) semantic structure in the variable. That is, the divisions do not correspond to such concepts as *low*, *moderate*, *medium*, or *high* incomes. This does not mean that the rule discovery process must be decoupled from such knowledge, only that the automatic generation of fuzzy sets is generally done without any meta-knowledge about the properties and semantic nature of the variable. The process would work equally well if the business analyst replaced the automatic fuzzy sets with those created by conventional knowledge acquisition.

Decomposition of the Sales Sensitivity Model

Variable decomposition is performed in the first phase of the rule discovery process using the fuzzy set counts provided by the systems or knowledge engineer. This number can be different for each variable. Refer to "wmpartv.cpp (Create the Fuzzy Set Term Set for Variable)" on page 440 for a the actual C/C++ code. The process of creating the fuzzy sets is annotated in an audit file (wmaud01.fil) while the fuzzy set graphical images are stored in the standard model log file (mdllog.fil). In the following figures the contents of the audit and the model log file have been combined (and re-arranged) to illustrate how the decomposition process is reflected in both files.

Figure 4.13 shows the process used by the rule discovery mechanism to decompose the variable TIME into nine underlying fuzzy sets.

```
---PI FuzzySet 'TIM_CE' created.
---PI FuzzySet 'TIM_B001' created.
---PI FuzzySet 'TIM_B002' created.
---PI FuzzySet 'TIM_B003' created.
---Growth S-Curve FuzzySet 'TIM_B004' created.
---PI FuzzySet 'TIM_S001' created.
---PI FuzzySet 'TIM_S002' created.
---PI FuzzySet 'TIM_S003' created.
---Decline S-Curve FuzzySet 'TIM_S004' created.
```

Figure 4.13 Creating the fuzzy sets for the variable TIME

The process creates the center of domain fuzzy set, completes the space to the right of center (the "B*xxx*" sets), and then completes the space to the left of the center (the S*xxx*) sets. A complete analysis of how the variable was decomposed is saved in the audit file. Figure 4.14 shows the contents of this report.

```
RD---[001]: Rule Discovery. Fuzzy Term Set Generation
        Variable  :    time
        Domain    :    0.00 to 36.00
        INITIAL PARAMETERS
        DomRange  :         36.00
        MidPoint  :         18.00
        Partitions:             9
        PartWidth :          6.00
```

		Curve Edges			Curve Surface Parameters	
	FuzzySet	Left	Right	P1	P2	P3
1.	TIM_S004	0.00	9.00	0.00	4.50	9.00
2.	TIM_S003	6.00	12.00	9.00	3.00	
3.	TIM_S002	9.00	15.00	12.00	3.00	
4.	TIM_S001	12.00	18.00	15.00	3.00	
5.	TIM_CE	15.00	21.00	18.00	3.00	
6.	TIM_B001	18.00	24.00	21.00	3.00	
7.	TIM_B002	21.00	27.00	24.00	3.00	
8.	TIM_B003	24.00	30.00	27.00	3.00	
9.	TIM_B004	27.00	36.00	27.00	31.50	36.00

Figure 4.14 The Audit Report detailing the Term Set properties for TIME

The DomRange (domain range) is the difference between the high and low values of the variable's domain. The MidPoint is the domain value that is midway across the domain and is the center of the middle fuzzy set (TIM_CE, in this instance). Partitions indicates the number of fuzzy sets in the variable's term set. This number is supplied by the knowledge engineer (if the number is even, it is incremented by one to make it odd.) The PartWidth is the partition width and indicates the base length of each bell-shaped fuzzy set. Half the PartWidth forms the extent of the PI curve. In the report, the Curve Edges indicate the left and right edges of the fuzzy sets while the Curve Surface Parameters indicate the specification parameters for each PI or S-curve fuzzy set. Figure 4.15 shows the actual fuzzy sets produced by this decomposition method.

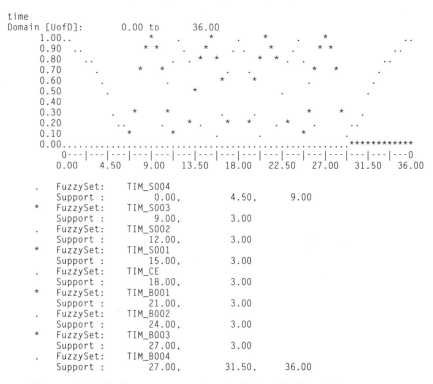

Figure 4.15 The fuzzy sets associated with the TIME variable

During this variable decomposition phase, each model variable is broken down into a collection of fuzzy sets. A fuzzy rule can only specify an action within a defined fuzzy region. The following figures show the way the rule discovery process decomposes the PRICE and SALES variables in the fuzzy term sets. Figure 4.16 is the audit file report on the PRICE variable.

```
RD---[001]: Rule Discovery. Fuzzy Term Set Generation
      Variable  :     price
      Domain    :       8.00 to      200.00
      INITIAL PARAMETERS
      DomRange  :       192.00
      MidPoint  :       104.00
      Partitions:             9
      PartWidth :        32.00
```

		Curve Edges		Curve Surface Parameters		
FuzzySet		Left	Right	P1	P2	P3
1. PRC_S004		8.00	56.00	8.00	32.00	56.00
2. PRC_S003		40.00	72.00	56.00	16.00	
3. PRC_S002		56.00	88.00	72.00	16.00	
4. PRC_S001		72.00	104.00	88.00	16.00	
5. PRC_CE		88.00	120.00	104.00	16.00	
6. PRC_B001		104.00	136.00	120.00	16.00	
7. PRC_B002		120.00	152.00	136.00	16.00	
8. PRC_B003		136.00	168.00	152.00	16.00	
9. PRC_B004		152.00	200.00	152.00	176.00	200.00

Figure 4.16 The audit report detailing the term set properties for PRICE

The domain of PRICE is $8.00 to $200.00 with a domain range of $192.00. We are also decomposing this variable into nine fuzzy sets. Figure 4.17 shows the fuzzy sets produced by the decomposition process.

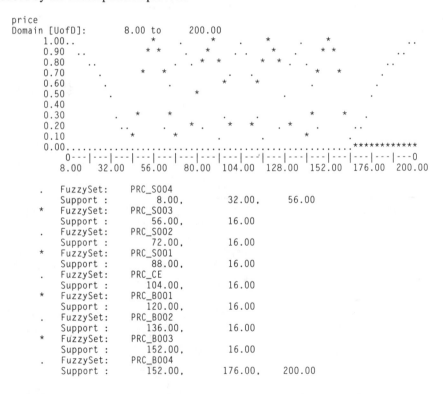

Figure 4.17 The fuzzy sets associated with the PRICE variable

Because the SALES variable is an output (solution) variable and the nature of the curve requires a moderate degree of granularity (see the section "Approximation, Patch Granularity, and Overlap" on page 125 for more details on this issue) the variable is decomposed into seventeen fuzzy sets. Figure 4.18 shows the audit report on the decomposition of sales into its term set.

```
RD---[001]: Rule Discovery. Fuzzy Term Set Generation
        Variable  :    sales
        Domain    :        0.00 to    90000.00
        INITIAL PARAMETERS
        DomRange  :      90000.00
        MidPoint  :      45000.00
        Partitions:          17
        PartWidth :       7941.18

                           Curve Edges           Curve Surface Parameters
        FuzzySet         Left      Right        P1          P2          P3
        ---------------  --------- ---------    ---------   ---------   ---------
     1. SAL_S008             0.00  17205.88         0.00     8602.94    17205.88
     2. SAL_S007         13235.29  21176.47     17205.88     3970.59
     3. SAL_S006         17205.88  25147.06     21176.47     3970.59
     4. SAL_S005         21176.47  29117.65     25147.06     3970.59
     5. SAL_S004         25147.06  33088.24     29117.65     3970.59
     6. SAL_S003         29117.65  37058.82     33088.24     3970.59
     7. SAL_S002         33088.24  41029.41     37058.82     3970.59
     8. SAL_S001         37058.82  45000.00     41029.41     3970.59
     9. SAL_CE           41029.41  48970.59     45000.00     3970.59
    10. SAL_B001         45000.00  52941.18     48970.59     3970.59
    11. SAL_B002         48970.59  56911.76     52941.18     3970.59
    12. SAL_B003         52941.18  60882.35     56911.76     3970.59
    13. SAL_B004         56911.76  64852.94     60882.35     3970.59
    14. SAL_B005         60882.35  68823.53     64852.94     3970.59
    15. SAL_B006         64852.94  72794.12     68823.53     3970.59
    16. SAL_B007         68823.53  76764.71     72794.12     3970.59
    17. SAL_B008         72794.12  90000.00     72794.12    81397.06    90000.00
```

Figure 4.18 The audit report detailing the term set properties for SALES

The left and right tails of the sales volume function have very low values while the central portion of the function have value between roughly 35,000 and 85,000 units. Thus the range of the SALES variables is quite wide, running from 0 through 90,000. Figure 4.19 shows the fuzzy sets associated with the SALES variable.

```
sales
Domain [UofD]:       0.00 to   90000.00
      1.00.            .   *       *   .  *        *   .     .
      0.90 ..             . **  ..      .. **  .     *        . ..
      0.80  .       *   *  .       *    *       . *   *           .
      0.70  .              .  .                  .               .
      0.60  .      *       *       *       *        *        *    .
      0.50  .                 . .                        .
      0.40  .                *   *             *  *            .
      0.30  .             .       .              .            .
      0.20  .       * *.         * *          .* *         .
      0.10     .   .       *       *    .  *        *        .
      0.00...............................................*********
        0---|---|---|---|---|---|---|---|---|---|---|---|---|---0
        0.00 1125.00 2250.00 3375.00 4500.00 5625.00 6750.00 7875.00 9000.00
        Scaling: 10x
```

```
    .   FuzzySet:     SAL_S008
        Support :          0.00,    8602.94,   17205.88
    *   FuzzySet:     SAL_S007
        Support :      17205.88,    3970.59
    .   FuzzySet:     SAL_S006
        Support :      21176.47,    3970.59
    *   FuzzySet:     SAL_S005
        Support :      25147.06,    3970.59
    .   FuzzySet:     SAL_S004
        Support :      29117.65,    3970.59
    *   FuzzySet:     SAL_S003
        Support :      33088.24,    3970.59
    .   FuzzySet:     SAL_S002
        Support :      37058.82,    3970.59
    *   FuzzySet:     SAL_S001
        Support :      41029.41,    3970.59
    .   FuzzySet:     SAL_CE
        Support :      45000.00,    3970.59
    *   FuzzySet:     SAL_B001
        Support :      48970.59,    3970.59
    .   FuzzySet:     SAL_B002
        Support :      52941.18,    3970.59
    *   FuzzySet:     SAL_B003
        Support :      56911.76,    3970.59
    .   FuzzySet:     SAL_B004
        Support :      60882.35,    3970.59
    *   FuzzySet:     SAL_B005
        Support :      64852.94,    3970.59
    .   FuzzySet:     SAL_B006
        Support :      68823.53,    3970.59
    *   FuzzySet:     SAL_B007
        Support :      72794.12,    3970.59
    .   FuzzySet:     SAL_B008
        Support :      72794.12,   81397.06,   90000.00
```

Figure 4.19 The fuzzy sets associated with the SALES variable

The decomposition process creates a set of evenly spaced fuzzy sets across the variable's domain (or Universe of Discourse). Each fuzzy set has a 50% over-lap with its adjacent neighbors so when membership in one fuzzy set is completely true the membership in an over-lapping neighbor is completely false. Several reasonable modifications to the fuzzy set generation process are useful in many modelling situations. One obvious change involves altering the way in which fuzzy sets are placed in the variable's domain. In many situations, especially when handling non-linear output variables, we might want the density of fuzzy sets around some central measure to be higher than the density or scope of fuzzy sets as we move away from this value. Supplying a vector of density or diffusion factors would allow the process to generate nonuniform fuzzy distributions. Another modification that often proves helpful is changing the type of fuzzy set installed at some points across the domain. Besides the obvious change to triangular shapes, the use of trapezoidal fuzzy sets is sometimes beneficial. Trapezoid fuzzy sets are well suited to represent abrupt fuzzy changes across the domain of a variable (especially step functions that have implicit dichotomies in their surface.) Finally, it is occasionally necessary to change the degree of over-lap among neighboring fuzzy sets. In some control and pattern matching applications, the edges of a control or image space can be better managed if the fuzzy set overlap is greater than fifty-percent.

Step Two. Generate Tentative Rules from Data

After the model variables have been decomposed into fuzzy sets, we can start the rule production process. The actual rule production is actually done in several steps, each step designed to find the best set of rules that reflect the over-all model behavior. In this step, the rule discovery process creates a matrix of tentative rules based on the maximal fit of data with the underlying fuzzy sets. This phase begins reading the model behavior or training data. Refer to "wmgenrl.cpp (Generate Intermediate Rule Set)" on page 445 for the program code that produces the intermediate rules. Figure 4.20 show part of the training data for the sales model.

```
//time     price        sales
//-----    ----------   ----------
     1,      11.28,         40.94
     2,      17.45,        336.82
     3,      28.75,        574.15
     4,      32.03,       1066.51
     5,      40.29,       2003.77
     6,      49.92,       3646.68
     7,      57.57,       6418.38
     8,      58.81,      10607.24
     9,      66.19,      15860.38
    10,      74.31,      21624.00
    11,      81.06,      27379.11
    12,      89.42,      31538.08
    13,      94.56,      32066.22
    14,     101.49,      29985.87
     .
     .
     .
```

Figure 4.20 A portion of the sale sensitivity behavior file

Each line in the training data file (as an example, `sales.dat`) contains a model input and output behavior. By convention, the last data element is the dependent or solution variable. The training behavior file represents a model process in the form of a fuzzy rule,

if time is TIM_xxxx and price is PRC_xxxx then sales are SAL_xxxx

where xxxx represents one of the fuzzy sets underlying the specified variable. It is, of course, the data points themselves that helps the discovery process decide which fuzzy set should be included in the rule. This phase of the rule discovery process forms a tentative rule for each line by finding the "best fit" relationship between each data value and a fuzzy set in the associated variable's term set. The idea of best fit simply means that fuzzy set where the data element has the maximum membership value. Thus, for each data element, *x*, associated with variable *V*, the best fit among the fuzzy sets in the partitions, *P*, is found. Equation 4.5 shows this process.

$$\mu(x)_{\max} = g(x_i, \overset{N}{\underset{j=0}{\forall}} P_j)$$

Equation 4.5 The data "Best-Fit" method for fuzzy set membership

As an example, for a given value of the PRICE variable, say $63.00, we can see in Figure 4.21 that it has a partial membership in fuzzy sets PRC_S003 and PRC_S002. The best fit, or its maximal fit, is in PRC_S003.

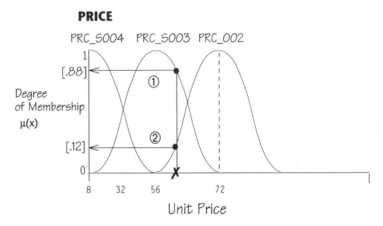

Figure 4.21 Finding the maximum ("Best Fit") for a data point

From this membership evaluation the rule discovery forms a tentative fuzzy proposition, price is PRC_S003 and also stores its degree of compatibility ([.88]). When each input and output data element is evaluated to find its maximum membership, a tentative rule is generated:

if time is TIM_S001 and price is PRC_S003 then sales are SAL_S001

This tentative rule, along with the degrees of membership for each of the predicates as well as the consequent propositions is stored in an intermediate matrix. The intermediate rule matrix forms the basis for all the rule discovery processing. As each record is read from the behavior data file, the data value is used to find the maximum membership in one of the fuzzy sets associated with the variable. These maximum memberships are used to calculate a Degree of Effectiveness and, finally, a Degree of Contribution. Rules are eventually filtered based on their relative degrees of contribution to the system behavior description.

Resolving an Effectiveness Degree for Each Rule

Since each line in the behavior data file generates an entry in the intermediate rule matrix, the discovery process creates many potential rules. Some of these rules specify conflicting actions and others have relatively weak contribution weights. In order to provide a mechanism that rule consolidation can use to select a rule based on its strength in describing model behavior, a degree of effectiveness is calculated for each rule. The basic effectiveness of a rule (designated Eff(x)) is the product of the maximum membership degrees for each rule component. Equation 4.6 is the definition of the effectiveness degree.

$$Eff(rule) = \bigvee_{i=0}^{N} \mu_P(x_i) \cdot \mu_C(y)$$

Equation 4.6 Definition for degree of effectiveness

This means we multiply the predicate membership and the consequent membership to derive a final effectiveness. As an example, consider the rule:

if x_1 is W and x_2 is Y and y is Z,

(where W, Y, and Z are fuzzy sets out of the variable term set) the effectiveness is computed as indicate in Equation 4.7.

$$Eff(rule) = \mu_W(x_1) \cdot \mu_Y(x_2) \cdot \mu_Z(y)$$

Equation 4.7 Calculating the degree of effectiveness

The degree of effectiveness is a conflict resolution weight, acting as a sieve that only allows rules with the highest effectiveness to participate in rule discovery. Using a measure of effectiveness exploits not only the maximum truth of the various rule components but also a measure of the rule's over-all utility. In lieu of an explicit weight assignment, we can reprocess the training set to find the rules that exhibit the best behavior under the restrictions imposed by the training set. In most real-world cases, the training data produces many rules with the same predicate and consequent. These rules contend for participation in the model. One simple way to discriminate among multiple rules is to assign a ranking degree to each rule and select the rule with the highest rank. This is the purpose of the Effectiveness metric.

Assigning and Using a Degree of Contribution

In some instances we might also want to adjust the rule production ranking using our knowledge of the data. Based on measurement precisions, our belief in the validity of the data, or some other metric, an index of believability (Bel) can also be assigned to the training pairs. Since the believability is assigned on a record by record basis, it is also known as the *Unit Confidence Weight*—specifying the over-all confidence we have in the data for this behavior entry. For highly believable data this factor moves toward [1] and for highly suspect data this factor moves toward [0].This believability index is combined with the rule degree of effectiveness to generate an over-all Degree of Contribution (Doc). The rule filtering equation, shown in Equation 4.8, then becomes:

$$Doc(rule) = Eff(rule) \cdot Bel(rule)$$

Equation 4.8 Calculating the degree of contribution

This process now incorporates factors that bias the data with the expert's experience, giving rise to a system that is responsive to different degrees of reliability in the data. In the actual model building world, data has varying degrees of noise, applicability, and importance. The contribution weight adjusts the rule based on how much trust we have in the underlying data. You should note that we can remove this human subjectivity or data usefulness relationship simply by setting all the Bel(rule$_i$) values to [1]. If a Believability Index is not specified with a behavior record, a value of [1] is always assumed.

Evaluating the Behavior Training Data

The primary rule generation facility (WMgenerateRules) reads the behavior file to construct a matrix of potential rules. This evaluation information, on a record-by-record basis, is stored in the best-fit analysis audit file (wmaud02.fil). Figure 4.22 shows the contents of this file.

```
RD---[002]: Rule Discovery. Initial Rule Generation
      Data  File :      sales.dat
      Rule  File :      b:WMrules.fil
      Audit File :      b:WMaud02.fil
   1. //time     price       sales

   2. //-----   ----------  ----------

   3.      1.       11.28.      40.94
RD---[003]: Rule Generation Statistics from Data:
      'time           ' (       1.00) has max m[0.9761] in termset 'TIM_S004      '
      'price          ' (      11.28) has max m[0.9922] in termset 'PRC_S004      '
      'sales          ' (      40.94) has max m[1.0000] in termset 'SAL_S008      '
            Unit ConfWeight: 1.0000, RuleDegree: 0.9684
   4.      2.       17.45.     336.82
RD---[003]: Rule Generation Statistics from Data:
      'time           ' (       2.00) has max m[0.9043] in termset 'TIM_S004      '
      'price          ' (      17.45) has max m[0.9297] in termset 'PRC_S004      '
      'sales          ' (     336.82) has max m[1.0000] in termset 'SAL_S008      '
            Unit ConfWeight: 1.0000, RuleDegree: 0.8407
   5.      3.       28.75.     574.15
RD---[003]: Rule Generation Statistics from Data:
      'time           ' (       3.00) has max m[0.7847] in termset 'TIM_S004      '
      'price          ' (      28.75) has max m[0.6440] in termset 'PRC_S004      '
      'sales          ' (     574.15) has max m[0.9992] in termset 'SAL_S008      '
            Unit ConfWeight: 1.0000, RuleDegree: 0.5049
   6.      4.       32.03.    1066.51
RD---[003]: Rule Generation Statistics from Data:
      'time           ' (       4.00) has max m[0.6172] in termset 'TIM_S004      '
      'price          ' (      32.03) has max m[0.5000] in termset 'PRC_S004      '
      'sales          ' (    1066.51) has max m[0.9925] in termset 'SAL_S008      '
            Unit ConfWeight: 1.0000, RuleDegree: 0.3063
   7.      5.       40.29.    2003.77
RD---[003]: Rule Generation Statistics from Data:
      'time           ' (       5.00) has max m[0.4106] in termset 'TIM_S004      '
      'price          ' (      40.29) has max m[0.2153] in termset 'PRC_S004      '
      'sales          ' (    2003.77) has max m[0.9791] in termset 'SAL_S008      '
            Unit ConfWeight: 1.0000, RuleDegree: 0.0866
   8.      6.       49.92.    3646.68
RD---[003]: Rule Generation Statistics from Data:
      'time           ' (       6.00) has max m[0.2363] in termset 'TIM_S004      '
      'price          ' (      49.92) has max m[0.6440] in termset 'PRC_S003      '
      'sales          ' (    3646.68) has max m[0.9165] in termset 'SAL_S008      '
            Unit ConfWeight: 1.0000, RuleDegree: 0.1395
   9.      7.       57.57.    6418.38
```

Figure 4.22 The record-by-record best-fit analysis from the sales behavior data

The analysis for each line calculates the Contribution Degree (`RuleDegree`). This is the product of the Effectiveness Degree and the unit Believability Index or Unit Confidence Weight (`Unit ConfWeight`). If a Unit ConfWeight factor is not specified for the record, a value of [1.0] is assumed and the Contribution Degree is simply the Degree of Effectiveness. To find the rule's effectiveness, the fuzzy set with the maximum degree of membership for the incoming data value is isolated. The product of these values is the effectiveness of the rule.

Understanding the Intermediate Rule Matrix

When the behavior data file has been completely processed, an intermediate rule matrix is created and saved (in file `wmrules.fil`). Figure 4.23 shows the partial contents of the rule matrix for the sales sensitivity model.

```
time, TIM_S004, 0.9761, price, PRC_S004, 0.9922, sales, SAL_S008, 1.0000, 0.9684
time, TIM_S004, 0.9043, price, PRC_S004, 0.9297, sales, SAL_S008, 1.0000, 0.8407
time, TIM_S004, 0.7847, price, PRC_S004, 0.6440, sales, SAL_S008, 0.9992, 0.5049
time, TIM_S004, 0.6172, price, PRC_S004, 0.5000, sales, SAL_S008, 0.9925, 0.3063
time, TIM_S004, 0.4106, price, PRC_S004, 0.2153, sales, SAL_S008, 0.9791, 0.0866
time, TIM_S004, 0.2363, price, PRC_S003, 0.6440, sales, SAL_S008, 0.9165, 0.1395
time, TIM_S003, 0.1763, price, PRC_S003, 0.9824, sales, SAL_S008, 0.7295, 0.1263
time, TIM_S003, 0.7188, price, PRC_S003, 0.9604, sales, SAL_S008, 0.2996, 0.2068
time, TIM_S003, 1.0000, price, PRC_S002, 0.6948, sales, SAL_S007, 0.7565, 0.5256
time, TIM_S003, 0.7847, price, PRC_S002, 0.9688, sales, SAL_S006, 0.9908, 0.7532
time, TIM_S002, 0.7637, price, PRC_S001, 0.5894, sales, SAL_S005, 0.5308, 0.2389
time, TIM_S002, 0.9995, price, PRC_S001, 0.9922, sales, SAL_S003, 0.5894, 0.5845
time, TIM_S002, 0.8047, price, PRC_S001, 0.6948, sales, SAL_S003, 0.8476, 0.4739
time, TIM_S001, 0.7417, price, PRC_CE,   0.9297, sales, SAL_S004, 0.9257, 0.6383
time, TIM_S001, 0.9980, price, PRC_CE,   1.0000, sales, SAL_S005, 0.6783, 0.6770
time, TIM_S001, 0.8237, price, PRC_B001, 0.8237, sales, SAL_S007, 0.7565, 0.5133
time, TIM_CE,   0.7188, price, PRC_B001, 0.9043, sales, SAL_S008, 0.3662, 0.2380
time, TIM_CE,   1.0000, price, PRC_B002, 0.6699, sales, SAL_S008, 0.8363, 0.5603
time, TIM_CE,   0.7847, price, PRC_B002, 0.8047, sales, SAL_S008, 0.9699, 0.6124
time, TIM_B001, 0.7637, price, PRC_B002, 0.8237, sales, SAL_S008, 0.9967, 0.6270
time, TIM_B001, 0.9995, price, PRC_B003, 0.9604, sales, SAL_S008, 1.0000, 0.9600
time, TIM_B001, 0.8047, price, PRC_B003, 0.9956, sales, SAL_S008, 1.0000, 0.8012
```

Figure 4.23 The intermediate matrix

Each line in this matrix consists of many *3-tuple* groups, one for each predicate and one for the consequent. The 3-tuple contains the name of the variable, the name of the fuzzy set that had the maximum value for the data element associated with that variable, and the degree of membership of that data element. The last entry in each line is the calculated *Contribution Degree* for the rule. This matrix is the set of rules produced from the behavior data. The next phase of the discovery process, forming the actual fuzzy rules, is generated from this intermediate rule matrix.

Step Three. Create the Combined Fuzzy Rules

As we can see in Figure 4.23, the intermediate rule matrix contains many redundant and conflicting rules. This is the natural consequence of the rule learning process associated with the behavior data. The final phase of rule discovery involves using the Contribution Degree to select those rules that best describe the system performance. Although the maximum membership values are carried with the rules, they are maintained for validation and analysis purposes, but do not participate in rule compression. Refer to "wmcrfam.cpp (Create the Consolidated FAM structure)" on page 451 for details on the program.

The Rule Compression Process

The rule combination involves inserting the temporary rules into the *MxN* fuzzy associative memory using the predicate fuzzy sets. At any combination of predicate fuzzy sets (such as those for TIME and PRICE) a solution fuzzy set exists (such as those for the dependent variable SALES). The rectangular fuzzy associative memory is used to consolidate the intermediate rules, but the discovery mechanism writes conventional if-then productions. Figure 4.24 shows the contents of the rule compression audit file (wmaud03.fil) for the sales model.

```
RD---[003]: Rule Discovery. Combined FAM Generation
     Audit File :    b:WMaud03.fil
     Rule  File :    B:WMrules.FIL
     FAM   File :    b:WMfam.fil


Record:     1. Rule ADDED:    TIM_S004xPRC_S004: SAL_S008 (0.9684)
Record:     2. Rule REJECTED: TIM_S004xPRC_S004: SAL_S008 (0.8407 versus 0.9684)
Record:     3. Rule REJECTED: TIM_S004xPRC_S004: SAL_S008 (0.5049 versus 0.9684)
Record:     4. Rule REJECTED: TIM_S004xPRC_S004: SAL_S008 (0.3063 versus 0.9684)
Record:     5. Rule REJECTED: TIM_S004xPRC_S004: SAL_S008 (0.0866 versus 0.9684)
Record:     6. Rule ADDED:    TIM_S004xPRC_S003: SAL_S008 (0.1395)
Record:     7. Rule ADDED:    TIM_S003xPRC_S003: SAL_S008 (0.1263)
Record:     8. Rule UPDATES:  TIM_S003xPRC_S003: SAL_S008 (0.2068)
Record:     9. Rule ADDED:    TIM_S003xPRC_S002: SAL_S007 (0.5256)
Record:    10. Rule UPDATES:  TIM_S003xPRC_S002: SAL_S006 (0.7532)
Record:    11. Rule ADDED:    TIM_S002xPRC_S001: SAL_S005 (0.2389)
Record:    12. Rule UPDATES:  TIM_S002xPRC_S001: SAL_S003 (0.5845)
Record:    13. Rule REJECTED: TIM_S002xPRC_S001: SAL_S003 (0.4739 versus 0.5845)
Record:    14. Rule ADDED:    TIM_S001xPRC_CE: SAL_S004 (0.6383)
Record:    15. Rule UPDATES:  TIM_S001xPRC_CE: SAL_S005 (0.6770)
Record:    16. Rule ADDED:    TIM_S001xPRC_B001: SAL_S007 (0.5133)
Record:    17. Rule ADDED:    TIM_CExPRC_B001: SAL_S008 (0.2380)
Record:    18. Rule ADDED:    TIM_CExPRC_B002: SAL_S008 (0.5603)
Record:    19. Rule UPDATES:  TIM_CExPRC_B002: SAL_S008 (0.6124)
Record:    20. Rule ADDED:    TIM_B001xPRC_B002: SAL_S008 (0.6270)
Record:    21. Rule ADDED:    TIM_B001xPRC_B003: SAL_S008 (0.9600)
Record:    22. Rule REJECTED: TIM_B001xPRC_B003: SAL_S008 (0.8012 versus 0.9600)
Record:    23. Rule ADDED:    TIM_B002xPRC_B003: SAL_S008 (0.5820)
Record:    24. Rule ADDED:    TIM_B002xPRC_B004: SAL_S008 (0.1759)
Record:    25. Rule UPDATES:  TIM_B002xPRC_B004: SAL_S008 (0.4119)
Record:    26. Rule ADDED:    TIM_B003xPRC_B004: SAL_S008 (0.5331)
Record:    27. Rule UPDATES:  TIM_B003xPRC_B004: SAL_S008 (0.8750)
Record:    28. Rule REJECTED: TIM_B003xPRC_B004: SAL_S008 (0.7295 versus 0.8750)
Record:    29. Rule REJECTED: TIM_B003xPRC_B004: SAL_S008 (0.2224 versus 0.8750)
Record:    30. Rule ADDED:    TIM_B004xPRC_B004: SAL_S008 (0.2153)
Record:    31. Rule UPDATES:  TIM_B004xPRC_B004: SAL_S008 (0.3828)
Record:    32. Rule UPDATES:  TIM_B004xPRC_B004: SAL_S008 (0.5894)
Record:    33. Rule UPDATES:  TIM_B004xPRC_B004: SAL_S008 (0.7637)
Record:    34. Rule UPDATES:  TIM_B004xPRC_B004: SAL_S008 (0.8901)
Record:    35. Rule UPDATES:  TIM_B004xPRC_B004: SAL_S008 (0.9688)
Record:    36. Rule UPDATES:  TIM_B004xPRC_B004: SAL_S008 (1.0000)
Record:    37. Rule REJECTED: TIM_S004xPRC_S004: SAL_S008 (0.9684 versus 0.9684)
Record:    38. Rule REJECTED: TIM_S004xPRC_S004: SAL_S008 (0.8171 versus 0.9684)
Record:    39. Rule REJECTED: TIM_S004xPRC_S004: SAL_S008 (0.4365 versus 0.9684)
Record:    40. Rule REJECTED: TIM_S004xPRC_S004: SAL_S008 (0.1976 versus 0.9684)
```

```
Record:    41. Rule REJECTED: TIM_S004xPRC_S004: SAL_S008  (0.0872 versus 0.9684)
Record:    42. Rule REJECTED: TIM_S004xPRC_S003: SAL_S008  (0.0789 versus 0.1395)
Record:    43. Rule REJECTED: TIM_S003xPRC_S003: SAL_S008  (0.0000 versus 0.2068)
Record:    44. Rule REJECTED: TIM_S003xPRC_S002: SAL_S008  (0.2588 versus 0.7532)
Record:    45. Rule UPDATES:  TIM_S003xPRC_S002: SAL_S002  (0.8215)
 .
 .
 .
RD---[003]: Rule Discovery. FAM Generation Complete
        Record Count  :          144
        Rule Used     :           23
        Rule Rejected :          121
        Rule Use Ratio:        15.97
```

Figure 4.24 Partial audit trail from the fuzzy rule generation

In this audit file, the compression action is shown for each rule. The temporary rules are shown in algebraic or rectangular form, thus, we interpret the rule specification:

TIM_B002xPRC_B003: SAL_S008

as the rule *if time is* TIM_B002 *and price is* PRC_B003 *then sales are* SAL_S008. The rectangular form shows the vertical and horizontal axis of the fuzzy associative memory with the solution fuzzy set occupying a cell at the intersection of the row and column.

There are several actions the rule compression logic can invoke when it encounters a new rule from the intermediate rule matrix. The rule can be ADDED, meaning that this is a new rule (the intersection of the TIME and PRICE fuzzy sets is empty). A new rule also UPDATES an existing cell if the Degree of Contribution is higher than the contribution weight of the rule already in that cell. And a new rule is also REJECTED if its Degree of Contribution is less than the contribution weight of the rule already in the cell (the audit analysis also shows the reason for this rejection by displaying the two confidence weights). When the complete rule matrix has been processed, a statistics report indicates the number of combined rules generated and the percentage this represents of the initial rule set.

Producing the Fuzzy Associative Memory

Figure 4.25 shows the final Fuzzy Associative Memory for the sales sensitivity model. The time fuzzy sets run along the vertical axis and the price fuzzy sets run along the horizontal axis. At the intersection of TIME and PRICE is the corresponding SALES fuzzy sets.

```
          PRC_S004 PRC_S003 PRC_S002 PRC_S001 PRC_CE   PRC_B001 PRC_B002 PRC_B003 PRC_B004
          -------- -------- -------- -------- -------- -------- -------- -------- --------
TIM_S004|SAL_S008 SAL_S008
TIM_S003|         SAL_S008 SAL_S002
TIM_S002|                  SAL_S007 SAL_S003
TIM_S001|                  SAL_S007 SAL_B002 SAL_S001 SAL_S007
TIM_CE  |                           SAL_S006 SAL_S008 SAL_S007 SAL_S008
TIM_B001|                                             SAL_S008 SAL_S008 SAL_S008
TIM_B002|                                                      SAL_S008 SAL_S008 SAL_S008
TIM_B003|                                                               SAL_S008 SAL_S008
TIM_B004|                                                                        SAL_S008
```

Figure 4.25 The final Fuzzy Associative Memory for the sales model

The Fuzzy Associative Memory (FAM) is sparse for this problem. This should be expected when small amounts of data are used to train the system or, as in the case of the sales model, we use repeating sets of 36 time periods, each running along the time axis from one to thirty-six. Larger spectrums of data describing more of the system behavior leads to a better saturation of the rule space and provides a closer approximation to the actual system.

Generating the Combined Fuzzy Rules

The rule discovery process terminates when the final rules have been generated from the Fuzzy Associative memory. These are stored in the file wmfam.fil. Each fuzzy rule is in the form if-then and is prefaced by a rule number enclosed in brackets. Figure 4.26 shows the rules produced for the sales model from the consolidated fuzzy associative memory.

```
[R001]: if time is TIM_S004 and price is PRC_S004 then sales is SAL_S008;
[R002]: if time is TIM_S004 and price is PRC_S003 then sales is SAL_S008;
[R003]: if time is TIM_S003 and price is PRC_S003 then sales is SAL_S008;
[R004]: if time is TIM_S003 and price is PRC_S002 then sales is SAL_S002;
[R005]: if time is TIM_S002 and price is PRC_S002 then sales is SAL_S007;
[R006]: if time is TIM_S002 and price is PRC_S001 then sales is SAL_S003;
[R007]: if time is TIM_S001 and price is PRC_S002 then sales is SAL_S007;
[R008]: if time is TIM_S001 and price is PRC_S001 then sales is SAL_B002;
[R009]: if time is TIM_S001 and price is PRC_CE   then sales is SAL_S001;
[R010]: if time is TIM_S001 and price is PRC_B001 then sales is SAL_S007;
[R011]: if time is TIM_CE   and price is PRC_S001 then sales is SAL_S006;
[R012]: if time is TIM_CE   and price is PRC_CE   then sales is SAL_S008;
[R013]: if time is TIM_CE   and price is PRC_B001 then sales is SAL_S007;
[R014]: if time is TIM_CE   and price is PRC_B002 then sales is SAL_S008;
[R015]: if time is TIM_B001 and price is PRC_B001 then sales is SAL_S008;
[R016]: if time is TIM_B001 and price is PRC_B002 then sales is SAL_S008;
[R017]: if time is TIM_B001 and price is PRC_B003 then sales is SAL_S008;
[R018]: if time is TIM_B002 and price is PRC_B002 then sales is SAL_S008;
[R019]: if time is TIM_B002 and price is PRC_B003 then sales is SAL_S008;
[R020]: if time is TIM_B002 and price is PRC_B004 then sales is SAL_S008;
[R021]: if time is TIM_B003 and price is PRC_B003 then sales is SAL_S008;
[R022]: if time is TIM_B003 and price is PRC_B004 then sales is SAL_S008;
[R023]: if time is TIM_B004 and price is PRC_B004 then sales is SAL_S008;
```

Figure 4.26 The actual fuzzy rules produced for the sales model

These rules represent the best fit between the raw behavior data and their implied functional or rule relationships taken collectively. One important aspect of the rule discovery process is the ability to combine machine generated and expert generated rules. This combination can come at either of two points: through inserting potential rules in the intermediate rule file (with corresponding degrees of contribution), or by inserting completed rules into the consolidated rule set shown in Figure 4.26. In this way, we can use the rule discovery method to enhance the knowledge acquisition process by keeping the mechanical process close to the knowledge of the domain experts.

Applications of Knowledge Mining Techniques

Rule discovery and knowledge mining techniques have found their way into a wide variety of business applications. Many business systems draw on large corporate databases containing not only in-depth data about the information infrastructure of the organization but extensive historical data about the way in which business is actually performed. This historical data plays a pivotal role in building fuzzy systems. By preprocessing (or post-processing) the data into the form of input and output process data model, the rule discovery facility can create a functional fuzzy model. In this section we examine some actual fuzzy systems that use knowledge mining or rule discovery as a crucial component of their underlying design and operation.

Managed Health Care Provider Fraud Detection

Estimates of provider fraud—fraud committed by doctors and other care givers—range between 10 and 12 percent of the $650 billion spent annually on health care in the United States. This is slightly less than 12 percent of the United States' adjusted Gross National Product (GNP). In fact, the National Healthcare Anti-Fraud Association (NHCAA) estimates that 10 percent of all health care claims contain an element of fraud or abuse.

Given the enormous amounts of money involved in the American health care industry, the shallowness of regulatory and business oversight, the complexity of today's medical services protocols, and the relative ease with which abusive behaviors can be disguised or buried in the high transaction volumes processed by most insurers, it is easy to understand how abusive and ultimately fraudulent behavior can arise. Fraud detection is further complicated by the dispersal of claims across many insurance companies so no single insurer has a complete picture of a provider's activities. Conventional analytical approaches to finding fraudulent providers are based on statistical and mathematical models, rule-base expert systems, and, more recently on the use of neural network technologies to "discover" patterns of abuse in the data. Yet no system today appears to satisfactorily address the enormous complexities of finding partial behavior patterns and correlating these into a cohesive picture of the provider's over-all claim profile.

The health provider abuse and fraud detection system was originally developed for a major insurance company. The fuzzy systems approach to isolating abusive and fraudulent healthcare providers is based on the concept of nonparametric anomaly detection within a population whose behavior characteristics are governed (we suppose) by the Law of Large Numbers and the Central Limit Theorem. In particular, the weak Law of Large Numbers says that for a sufficiently large population, the measurement of behavior characteristics approaches the mean for the population. Thus we can "look into the data itself" to find providers that have behaviors that are significantly at variance from their peers.

Fraud or abuse is detected by comparing the behavior of an individual provider of a certain specialty for a particular behavior against the behavior of his or her peers in the same specialty and geographic region. The fraud model is a time-series analysis system. It examines the incremental changes in behavior over time. Health care providers seldom move in an abrupt step from normal to anomalous behavior. They learn that some small changes in billing practices increase revenues and, at the same time, go undetected. Thus a fraud model must not only discover anomalous behavior but must detect a change in the direction of anomalous behavior. Insurance companies find it much more economical to interdict early irregular behavior than to prosecute a provider at a later date. Figure 4.27 shows the way provider peers are qualified for the model.

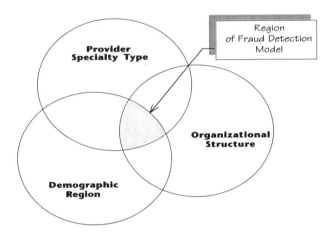

Figure 4.27 Provider peer qualification

The system evaluates the claim data of, as an example, all of the small clinic Osteopaths in the greater Chicago area. In order to find the correct peer ranking, providers are grouped in four organizational types: individuals, small clinics, large clinics, and hospitals. The claim data itself contains a variety of fundamental behavior patterns—average number of clients per week, mean billing dollars, degree of work outside immediate specialty, patients served on weekends or in evenings, and so forth. The number of behavior patterns varies according to specialty (an Osteopath, for example, has seventeen pronounced patterns.) The behavior patterns are identified by the insurance company's own fraud management department, but how these patterns govern the detection of abuse and fraud is found through the rule discovery process. Figure 4.28 shows a high-level schematic of the fraud detection system.

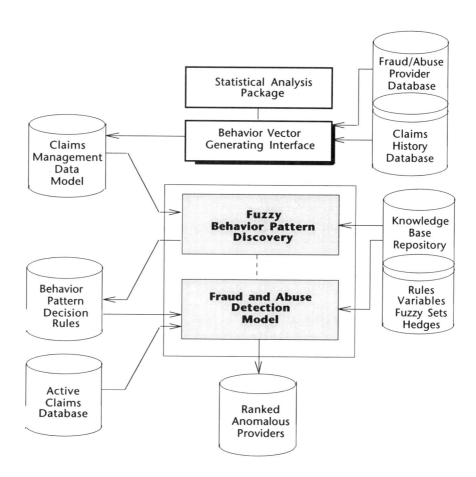

Figure 4.28 The abuse and fraud detection system

In order to discover the relationships between behavior patterns and abusive or fraud-ulent behavior, we need a training set that maps patterns in the claim data into a ranking of abusive behavior for known practitioners. This is done by matching the claims history database (a large repository of several million records) with the fraud and abuse database maintained by the organization's own fraud unit. The functional mapping makes a corre-spondence between the patterns in the claims data (B_i) and the degree of anomalous behavior (A_k) in the scaled ranking between 0 (well within the behavior of the peer group) and 100 (completely outside the behavior of the peer group). Equation 4.9 shows the nature of the functional mapping.

$$f : (B_1, B_2, B_3, ..., B_n) \rightarrow A_{[0, 100]}$$

Equation 4.9 The anomalous behavior function

A collection of behavior patterns are mapped into a degree of anomaly. The anomaly is represented as a fuzzy possibility space with the degree of anomaly scaled by the possibility the provider has committed fraud or abuse.

The Provider Behavior Patterns Dimension

Behavior patterns in the claim data are not simple data fields, but generally reflect statistical, fuzzy, and probabilistic profiles of the claim data. Such patterns include the type and degree of service provided, the frequency of service and billings, the cost of the service, the frequency and type of follow-up activities, the day and time of services, and the logical necessity of the service. In order to understand how the behavior patterns relate to the detection of anomalous behavior, we group them into Financial, Maintenance, Suitability, Utilization, Operational, and Type. The behavior vector for the provider is generated by coupling the raw data with a statistical analysis package. Using this package the system calculates the total number of data points for a provider, and, for each pattern, the mean for each provider, the over-all mean (independent of provider), the variance in each pattern as well as the over-all variance, and then the sum of square means, and the sum of squares within and between patterns. These statistical values measure the difference between the behavior of a single provider and the behavior of the peer population.

These values become fuzzy numbers in the rule discovery process. Each number is a central measure of the behavior. Figure 4.29 illustrates this concept with neighboring fuzzy sets representing regions outside (above and below) the behavior.

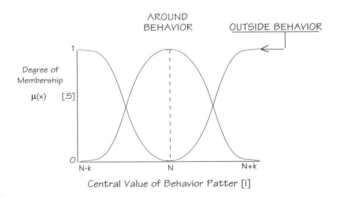

Figure 4.29 The behavior pattern as a fuzzy number

In building the fraud and abuse model, the behavior patterns play a crucial role in providing the insight into how the individual provider varies from the behavior of his or her peers. Behavior patterns include a wide variety of information about the way a provider services his or her patients. As an example, Figure 4.30 shows the term set decomposition for the change in the average patient work load per week.

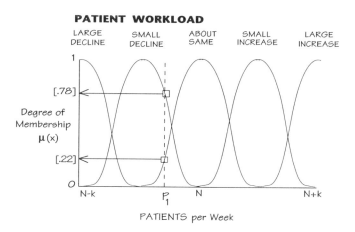

Figure 4.30 The patient work load change behavior pattern

As this figure illustrates, a particular patient work load value (P_1) has some degree of membership in the SMALL DECLINE and the ABOUT [the] SAME fuzzy sets. In evaluating the work load change, how we set the term set decomposition parameters determines the level of granularity and the number of rules. In this example, the variable's domain was divided into five fuzzy sets. Figure 4.30, like all the figures in this section, substitutes linguistic descriptions for the arbitrary fuzzy set names produced by the rule discovery process. Refer to "Step One. Decompose Variables into Fuzzy Sets" on page 228 for a complete discussion of this concept.

The actual fraud model combined automatic fuzzy set decomposition of many behavior patterns with "hand-crafted" fuzzy set decomposition performed by the knowledge engineer. Some patterns, especially those that were unrelated to measuring changes in a behavior's value, had a complex semantic structure that required a careful design of the fuzzy substructure. As noted in the section on term set decomposition (see page 228) the Wang-Mendel approach works well because it accommodates a mixture of machine generated and analyst generated fuzzy sets.

We can look at the peer values in the population as the boundary objectives in a constraint on the normal behavior among members of the population. Because the peer metrics are fuzzy numbers, the boundaries are not precise limitations, but represent a gradual degree of variance as the individual practitioner's behavior moves away form the center of the peer's behavior. As an example, Figure 4.31 shows how a provider's value for evening visits is positioned on the fuzzy set HIGH for Evening Visits as it moves away from the peer's normal value.

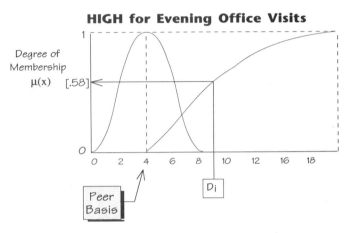

Figure 4.31 High evening visits versus the normal peer value

This peer value, of course, is not only a fuzzy boundary, but varies from one peer population to another. The HIGH fuzzy set is usually generated by applying the hedge ABOVE to the behavior's fuzzy set. The hedge approach allows the shape of the HIGH curve to be parametrically related to the bandwidth of the behavior's fuzzy set (which itself is determined by the variance of the population).

The Dollars Paid Dimension

Rightly or wrongly, the fraud model concentrates on providers that are receiving a significant amount of money from the insurance company. In this way the efforts of the fraud detection unit (which must ultimately evaluate the anomalous providers ranking generated by the model) can concentrate its efforts on the practitioners constituting the highest expense to the insurance company. When the peer behavior divergence policy has completed executing, the providers appear to have the most variance from their peers are isolated in the database. The model assesses the payment schedule for a provider according to the payment scales of both the insurance company and the peer population

Excessive payments for services is, in fact, one of the behavior patterns in the divergence policy. This excessive payment is based on the variance from the peer population for similar services. The actual dollar paid dimension of the fraud money reflects the absolute amount of money paid to the provider by the insurance company. The domain of this variable (its minimum and maximum dollar span) is adjusted for each peer population according to the patient demographics of the region (average income, median disposable income, etc.) Figure 4.32 illustrates the provider payments fuzzy sets (based on the Chicago metropolitan region).

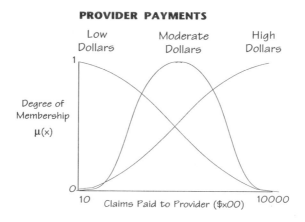

Figure 4.32 The dollar paid to provider fuzzy sets

In some demographic regions (especially those where the medium income is low) the shape of the curve as well as the domain of claims dollars paid must be altered to reflect an increased concern over claims dollars. This can bias the model toward selecting ranked providers at different thresholds of provider payments.

The Population Compatibility Dimension

The third component of the fraud and abuse detection system is a measure of the compatibility between the provider and the peer population in general. This is a type of meta-analysis. In measuring the distance between over-all peer behavior and the provider's behavior, the anomalous characteristics of a single pattern in a single time frame are not significant. Only when multiple patterns are significantly at variance, or when a single pattern increases its variance over time does the provider migrate toward the rank of anomalous providers. Instead, the system measures the number of anomalous behavior patterns and the degrees to which they are outside the peer population (their membership functions in the above or below fuzzy regions).

In the base model, we could simply assume the degree of abuse of fraud increases as the count of significant behavior patterns increases. This proportionality can be either linear or nonlinear. Thus, we can set a threshold of significance associated with the count. Figure 4.33 shows how, for one representation of significant counts, if one out of three patterns are anomalous we are at a [.5] membership level.

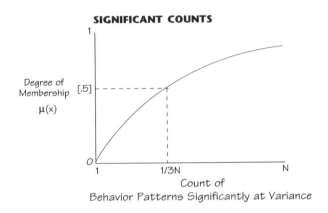

Figure 4.33 Count of significant anomalous behavior patterns

An alternate method of connecting the number of significant behavior patterns with the degree of fraud, is by computing a measure of compatibility between the provider and the population. Compatibility is the degree to which the provider "fits inside" the collection of behavior patterns for the peer group. This is essentially the weighted average of the distance from the central measure of each patter. Equation 4.9 shows the basic population compatibility index.

$$PopCIX = \frac{\sum_{i=0}^{N} \mu_B[x] \cdot i}{\sum_{i=0}^{N} \mu_B[x]}$$

Equation 4.10 Calculating the population compatibility index

The population compatibility index adjusts the system so a provider with one or two behavior patterns that are anomalous will not unduly bias the model. This means a few spikes in the manifold will not promote a provider to the first frontier of the anomaly curve. On the other hand, if the spikes are consistent across time, then the cumulative variance (an additive fuzzy model) exceeds the damping affect of the significant count fuzzy set. Conversely, it is possible that several behavior patterns were at variance, but not sufficiently to promote the provider to the anomaly curve. This count is also used to check for a provider that has many variances but none of them with a high profile.

Detecting Outliers in Fuzzy Space

The discovery model rests on three major static criteria metrics and one time-varying metric in the population space. Roughly these correspond to the insurer's exposure to fraudulent behavior (the total claims dollars paid to the provider), the degree of variance from the center of the peer population (the population compatibility number) for each behavior pattern, and the number of behaviors that are significantly at variance. The time-varying metric is the change in the behavior population dynamics over-time and is discussed later. Within the distribution analysis space the model can detect anomalous behaviors of several degrees. The first degree variances correspond to major variations from the peer population. Figure 4.34 illustrates the outliers that would be found by the gross model sieve. These are also the abusive or fraudulent providers we would expect the insurer's manual fraud investigators to uncover.

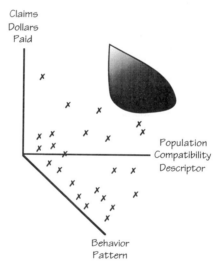

Figure 4.34 Finding first tier outliers in the fraud/abuse model

The fuzzy anomaly detection model, on the other hand, is designed to detect the second level of outliers, those that are not easily recognized by conventional abuse and fraud detection techniques. Figure 4.35 shows that these providers lie close to the edge of the acceptable domain. The fuzzy model isolates these behaviors by recognizing the degree to which they are at variance from the peer behaviors.

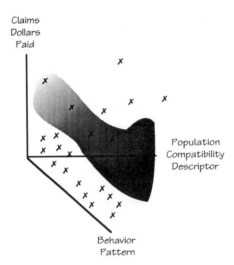

Figure 4.35 Finding the second tier outliers in the fraud/abuse model

The fuzzy model also provides an analysis of the provider behavior across time. This accomplishes two objectives.

1. It readjusts the system parameters to account for changes in regulatory requirements, economics, as well as social and cultural expectations.

2. It identifies anomalous behaviors early in the detection phase so that the behavior can be interdicted. Economically and socially it is usually better to correct a behavior rather than prosecute a provider.

Portfolio Safety and Suitability Advisor

In managing the investment portfolios of their clients, financial service organizations are often faced with difficult choices in an uncertain and volatile market. With the precision and clarity of hindsight, clients who suffer losses can often point to weakness in the investment strategies as actions that were totally (or partially) unsuitable for them in terms of their explicit investment strategy, their financial capacities, or their level of understanding of the implications and impact of various investment options. This is the issue of suitability. The question, then, becomes: How can we determine, *a priori*, whether a client's existing portfolio is suitable and whether a particular transaction is, *in vacuo*, suitable (realizing this may also change the over-all properties of the portfolio)?

Design Rationale

There was a sound rationale for approaching this problem from a fuzzy logic perspective. In analyzing the information used by analysts and branch managers to decide issues of safety and suitability, we immediately discovered that, while particular guidelines provided boundaries at crisp points (such as income and assets for option trading), the actual evaluation of suitability was far less precise. The conceptual understanding of suitability is concerned not so much with the actual transactions that occur across the portfolio, but rather with an imprecise analysis of the client's ability to sustain risk (react to adversity and absorb monetary loss) and comprehend the implications of a particular investment strategy. Collateral issues such as the client's previous trading history, the composite mixture of the portfolio, and the authority granted the financial consultant—the degree to which a client is personally involved in making day-to-day decisions—also plays an important part in suitability.

A fuzzy system model provides a way of representing the ambiguities and uncertainties in the suitability model. By encoding the issues of suitability in terms of degrees instead of absolutes, we can view and manage model states that fall on the boundaries between one state and another—just the regions where the issues of suitability and safety are the most difficult to determine. If such boundary conditions were rare, we might well apply conventional mathematical or statistical techniques. But, as the logic of suitability indicates, many of these model states involve highly complex, nonlinear manifolds of many interacting variables. Fuzzy representations are ideal for such models.

The General Model Design

The basic suitability model is built on a series of approximate and elastic relations between our knowledge of the client's background, holding, and trading history as well as the reputation and professionalism of the financial consultant. Figure 4.36 illustrates the high level model process schematic.

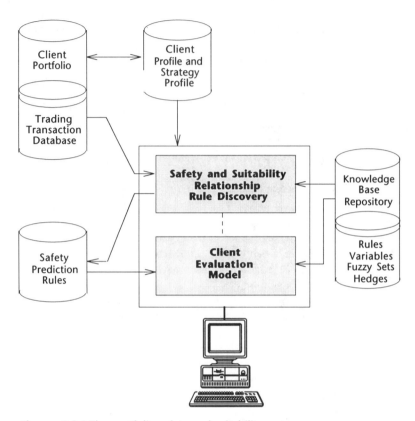

Figure 4.36 The portfolio safety and suitability system

An integrated rule discovery component of the safety and suitability model is used to find the relationship between the properties of a client's portfolio, his or her trading history, and the stated investment strategy. There are two objective functions in the rule discovery process, both measuring a degree of risk. The safety objective measures the risk that a client finds a particular investment strategy unsafe. The suitability objective (and the more important of two objectives) measures the risk that a client finds a particular investment strategy unsuitable. These are distinct objectives since a portfolio investment strategy can be safe but unsuitable—either because safety is not an investment objective or because the concentration mix of equities, bonds, and options does not map to the client's investment plan. From this we can see that an unsafe portfolio mix or investment strategy can also be very suitable from a client's perspective.

The client evaluation model is the actual core of the safety and suitability system. In this complex but integrated modeling environment, the safety and suitability prediction rules are combined with risk assessment rules acquired from portfolio managers, traders, and a random sample of clients. A model represents a computational interpretation of the cognitive processes underlying the evaluation of the issues associated with suitability, safety, and proper portfolio management. In constructing this model the logic has been organized into a set of functional policies. Each policy handles the evaluation of some important aspect of the system, such as determining the implicit risk tolerance associated with a client. In this section we explore the architecture of the suitability model. Figure 4.37 is a high-level schematic view of this system.

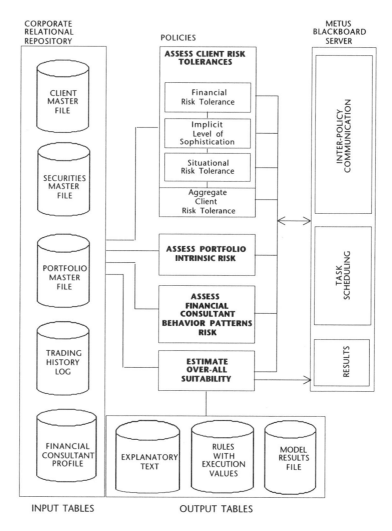

Figure 4.37 A high level schematic of the safety and suitability model

Suitability and Risk Factors

Many of the modules are concerned with calculating some form of risk tolerance. Risk itself is measured on an arbitrary psychometric scale from 1 to 1,000 in order to increase fine grain granularity. Figure 4.38 shows the fuzzy representation for different levels of risk.

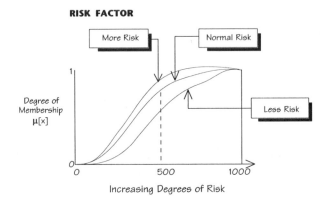

Figure 4.38 The risk measurement fuzzy set

The heart of the model is the concept of *proportional risk*. This risk is high for factors that suggest unsuitability and low for factors that are suitability neutral or indicate a higher compatibility with the company's business practices in this area. However, within a particular policy, whether we are examining high or low risk as a target depends on the semantics of the rules. As an example, the rule:

if client.AnnualIncome is LOW then FinancialRiskTolerance is LOW;

in the Financial Risk Tolerance policy measures the client's tolerance for financial risk. In this case, a low value indicates a substantially higher risk exists for suitability when problems exist in changes to the client's financial standing. It is the responsibility of the overall model to bring together risk appraisals from various policies in a meaningful and consistent manner.

The RISK fuzzy set is a sigmoid or S-curve between [1] and [1000]. The S-curve form insures that small degrees of risk do not contribute significantly to the model. As a rule measures a high degree of truth in its premise (the truth exceeds the 50% inflection point of the fuzzy set) the degree of risk increases in a proportional response. Figure 4.39 shows the nature of the basic RISK fuzzy set.

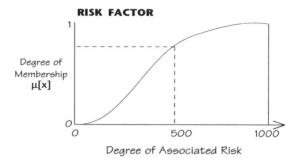

Figure 4.39 The RISK fuzzy set as a sigmoid curve

We can alter the degree or sensitivity of the policy risk by changing the shape of the RISK fuzzy set. When the solution fuzzy set is intensified or dilated, the correlation means the model responds with more risk or less risk. This is a primary way of tuning each policy to accommodate various types or degrees of risk.

These risks are calculated in a series of inter-communicating policies. The suitability model is composed of various fuzzy logic policies. These are self-contained knowledge-base systems that receive data, apply a set of rules to calculate some result, and place this output in an external file as well as on the system global blackboard facility. Figure 4.40 shows the schematic of a policy.

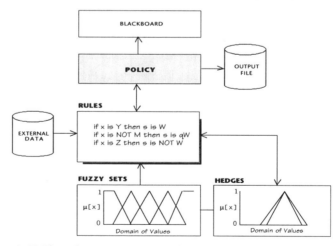

Figure 4.40 The schematic structure of a fuzzy logic policy

The central part of a policy is a set of rules and associated fuzzy sets. These rules generally have an `if-then` form. Each rule takes a data element and maps it to a fuzzy set. The results of this mapping is a truth value. These truth values are combined with the `AND` and `OR` operators. From this combined truth value, a final output fuzzy region is constructed that determines the degree of the solution variable, such as financial risk tolerance. Inside a policy all the rules are run in parallel. This is simulated in software so no special hardware is necessary. The parallel processing paradigm means all of the rules contribute to ("provide evidence for") the various solution variables. In this way the fuzzy model can accumulate information about the problem state and combine it with the current state in a consistent and meaningful manner. The following policies are used in the safety and suitability model.

- **Client risk tolerance**. This model component evaluates a client from three directions: the implicit ability to absorb financial losses measured in terms of over-all risk tolerance; the sophistication of the client measured in terms of the client's education, occupation, previous trading history, and similar factors; and, finally, the ability of a client to understand and deal with various levels of risk. This final ranking is partially synthesized from and uses input from the financial risk tolerance and sophistication policies.

  Financial risk tolerance. This policy examines the client's income and net worth (among other factors) to determine the degree to which we might suppose the client can absorb negative financial actions, independent of the client's own assertion. From this we can infer the risk of continuing with a strategy that has a high level of financial risk.

  Level of sophistication. Relying on observations of a client's education, job position, income, trading history, and related factors we calculate a level of sophistication. The higher the level of sophistication the more capable we assume a client is of understanding his/her risk position and the long term implication of particular strategies.

  Situational risk tolerance. This policy uses the level of sophistication found in the previous context to decide the client's adaptability to risk based on a wide spectrum of situational factors. To what degree, we ask ourselves, can a client tolerate risks based not only his/her financials, but on other less tangible factors such as time to retirement and family obligations.

- **Portfolio risk assessment.** This model component examines the client's actual portfolio as well as activity on that portfolio over the past two years. From this analysis we want to develop an understanding of how much implicit risk is associated with the portfolio, the kind of trading, transaction frequencies, and the inherent degree of technical difficulty associated with these transactions. In this analysis we are concerned with concentrations (by industry, by instrument type, and by exchange), types of stocks, cash movements, margins and margin interest payments, as well as gains and losses.

- **Financial Consultant Risk.** This policy examines the behavior patterns of the client's financial consultant. We are concerned here with the idea of active unsuitability rather than incidental or passive suitability. In looking at the behavior of the financial consultant the analysis evaluates such factors as the number of sales and non-sales related complaints, the number of litigations credited to the consultant, the amount of commissions earned, the turnover of the portfolio, and, for an operational model, the number of a consultant's clients that have also been ranked with suitability problems.

- **Ideal strategy generator.** In this module we combine principles of asset allocation with a general knowledge of the client's capabilities and objectives (both implicit and explicit) to produce an ideal suitability model. That is, we generate an optimal base-line investment strategy—considering the mix of instrument types (equities, bonds, options, cash) and industry classifications—that matches the client's financial resources, investment program, and over-all risk tolerance.

- **Aggregate suitability analysis.** The final analysis phase of the model combines the risk assessment knowledge developed by the other policies, the ideal investment strategy (an optional component), the client's stated investment strategies, and risk tolerance to produce a final ranking of overall suitability in two areas: to the client's explicit objectives and restrictions and to the clients implicit financial capabilities, sophistication, and risk tolerance.

- **Macro-economic/business intelligence [ME/BI].** Not so much an analysis component as an external intelligent data repository, the ME/BI facility combines a spread sheet of critical economic and business data with expert system technology. This facility uses goal-based reasoning and forward-chaining strategies to evaluate and forecast market movements, ideal product mixes, changes in technology, the effects of foreign government or foreign corporate activities on the U.S. economy, and so forth. This facility helps the model decide "what is suitable" in the near and reasonably far future.

The fuzzy model also carries an implicit measure of its own uncertainty. Each fuzzy analysis policy has an associated 'compatibility index' that measures the compatibility between the data and the knowledge base. Very large or very small numbers indicate problems with the model and bias the certainty of the result. In developing a final solution for the model, we adjust the risk factors according to the level of the compatibility index. This means that a compatibility index of [1] yields the original risk level, a compatibility of zero [0] eliminates the risk, and values in between scale the risk according to our confidence or compatibility with the underlying rules.

Understanding Fuzzy Rules in the Model

Rules in a fuzzy model are fundamentally different from rules in conventional expert and decision support systems where "rules" are often encoded as mathematical, statistical, or heuristic statements. In a conventional expert system statements establish the value of a variable although we can have degrees of confidence in this value. Thus the statement:

if concentration-by-options > .80 then risk = "LARGE"

evaluates the predicate (if) and determines whether it is true or false. The predicate can only have two values: true or false. If the predicate is true, the solution variable risk is set to the value LARGE. And while we might add a measure of our certainty in this statement, the fact remains the variable risk is assigned a discrete and absolute value by the rule.

This is not the case in fuzzy systems. In fuzzy systems the degree of truth in the predicate determines the degree of truth in the consequent (solution). These degrees of truth are determined by mapping predicate values to fuzzy sets and combining these with fuzzy operators, such as AND and OR. The solution variable does not have a single value, but is represented by a fuzzy set whose shape is determined by all the rules that reference the same solution variable. In the end, a solution value is found by 'defuzzifying' this output fuzzy set. Since the predicate and solution fuzzy sets can have any shape, highly complex, nonlinear problems can be easily modeled.

Statements of Evidence

A single fuzzy rule does not decide the outcome of a solution (or decision) variable, rather, it contributes evidence toward the final state of that variable. As example, the rule:

if concentration-by-option is HIGH then risk is LARGE

says, "to degree that the percentage of holdings in a portfolio are options is HIGH, the risk variable has a membership in the set of LARGE risk values." Note that the decision variable risk is not set to the value LARGE, nor does it have a 100% membership in the set of large risk values. A particular rule accumulates evidence for the state of the risk value. Thus, if we evaluate another rule:

if concentration-by-securities is HIGH then risk is LARGE

its truth can increase our confidence in the problem state RISK. That is, we accumulate evidence for a high risk portfolio. The first rule might contribute a small amount of evidence for risk and the second rule adds more evidence to the state of risk. Thus, a rule such as:

if concentration-by-bonds is HIGH then risk is SMALL

can contribute in such a way that the decision variable risk has less membership in the LARGE risk set and more membership in the SMALL risk set. Thus rules act to aggregate states of evidence for some particular problem state. The result of evaluating a set of rules that contribute to the same decision or solution variable is a fuzzy region that represents through numerical approximation the value of the final result.

Executing the Suitability Model

When the suitability model starts, a series of data acquisition and analysis policies are initiated, as shown in Figure 4.41. These policies use a forward chaining methodology to search through the Portfolio Line Items File and the Activity History File and develop the statistics necessary for the main model policies.

```
12/10/19xx 12.44pm
Fuzzy Suitability Model. (c) 19xx Metus Systems Group.
Client Account Identifier      : 999-76543-123
Client Name                    : John Smith
Rule Minium Truth Threshold    : 0.200
```

Figure 4.41 Starting the safety and suitability model

Figure 4.42 is a schematic representation of the safety and suitability model showing how the various components interact with the data sources and the output tables.

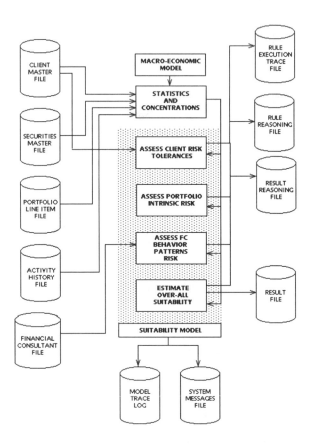

Figure 4.42 The process flow in the safety and suitability model

Portfolio Concentrations

This analysis program performs two services: the portfolio valuation and a determination of concentration ratios of various kinds. During the valuation phase a join is made with each symbol entry in the Securities Master File to find the symbol's current price. Figure 4.43 shows the output from the table and the analysis produced by this phase.

```
            C l i e n t      H o l d i n g s (Portfolio)     V a l u a t i o n

            Symbol       Qty      currPrice   currValue
     ----  ------------  -------  ----------  ----------
      1   GNE           200        40.00      8000.00
      2   IBM95         10000     104.50     10450.00
      3   IBMAJ         5           3.25      1625.00
      4   AAPL          50         38.50      1925.00
                                             ------------
                                        $   22000.00

     Current Value         :     22000.00
     Original Value        :     22600.00
     BetaWgtd Value        :         0.41
     QltyWgtd Value        :         0.34
     [%] in securities     :        45.11
     [%] in options        :         7.39
     [%] in bonds          :        47.50
     6mon average minimum  :        39.75
     6mon average maximum  :        55.00
     Avergae Beta          :         0.48
     [%] Beta              :        50.00
     [%] security holdings :        50.00
     [%] options holdings  :        25.00
     [%] bond holdings     :        25.00
     Turnover ratio        :         2.40
```

Figure 4.43 Portfolio valuation and concentration analysis

When the concentrations have been completed, a summary statistics report is also written to the model log indicating profile information. Some of the statistics displayed here include:

- BetaWgtdValue represents the factor which, if multiplied by the current portfolio value, yields a portfolio valuation adjusted for market volatility.

- QltyWgtdValue represents the factor which, if multiplied by the current portfolio value, yields a portfolio valuation adjusted for the quality of the holdings. Quality is a subjective judgement of the security's worth based on such tangibles as projected return and such intangibles as company reputation, stability, and perceived market growth.

- [%] in securities, options and bonds indicates the percentage of the portfolio valuation distributed among these kinds of holds.

- 6mon average minimum/maximum indicates the average minimum and maximum unit price of the portfolio holdings over the previous six month time frame.

- [%] Beta indicates the percentage of the portfolio that can be measured by the application of beta metrics.

- [%] security/options/bond holdings indicates the actual percentage by total line items held in each of the indicated security classes.

- Turnover ratio is the average turn-over for this portfolio from each of the past analysis periods. For the first time-analysis this is zero.

Following the valuation phase, the portfolio items are collected by various attributes to compute a concentration ratio. A concentration measures the percentage of the portfolio that is associated with one of these attributes. The Suitability model currently measures three types of concentrations:

1. Ticker symbol
2. An industry classification,
3. The Beta (volatility) value.

Concentrations are important measures of the general robustness of the portfolio since high concentrations in a particular stock, a particular industry, or with stocks that have relatively high sensitivity to market movement might indicate a problem in the investment strategy. The symbol concentration report is shown in Figure 4.44.

```
        H o l d i n g s  (Portfolio)      C o n c e n t r a t i o n s

Holdings Concentration [by Symbol]

        Item              ConRatio
        ---------------   ----------
     0. GNE                  0.36
     1. IBM95                0.47
     2. IBMAJ                0.07
     3. AAPL                 0.09
```

Figure 4.44 Concentrations by symbol

There are several other interesting concentrations that had been identified but not included in the production model. These include concentrations by quality code (a subjective judgement of the stock encapsulating its current marketability), by line item type (stock, option, bond), by type of exchange, and by amount margined.

Trading Activity History Statistics

The system reads the Activity History File to analyze the trading history behind the current portfolio. From this information the model acquires knowledge about the behavior of the client over an extended period of time, the types of buys and sells in the portfolio, the amount of income generated by the investments, the cash position, and the gains and losses incurred by the client. Figure 4.45 show an abbreviated version of the portfolio trading history report produced by the model.

```
              P o r t f o l i o    A c t i v i t y    S t a t i s t i c s

Total Income          :        563.00
Total Debits          :       1000.00
Total Credits         :      35000.00
Total Buys            :      22600.00
Total Sells           :          0.00
Total Commissions     :        583.00
Total Margin Int.     :          0.00
-----------------------------------
Average Value         :      34331.50
Change in Value       :       -386.00
Income/Comm Ratio     :       1.03552
TurnOver Ratio        :       0.65829
-----------------------------------
Buys                  :             4
Sells                 :             0
Credits               :             1
```

Figure 4.45 The trading activity history report

Note the Policy Activity analysis also calculates two other important factors:

1. The ratio of income to commissions paid.
2. The turnover ratio.

These factors become important parameters when the financial consultant evaluation is performed.

The Client Financial Risk Tolerance Policy

As an example of how a policy works, the client's financial risk tolerance analysis is briefly reviewed. This is one of several policies that evaluate risk. Each policy calculates one aspect of the Client's ability to tolerate risk. Together these constitute a complete evaluation of the client's probable psychological response to the risks associated with various investment strategies. The financial risk policy calculates the client's financial risk tolerance and is a measure of their probable reaction to an adverse financial position. In order to determine whether or not a client has a high or low risk tolerance we look at their annual income, the total net worth, and the total available or liquid net worth.

Context Prologue

The known facts in this context are derived directly from the Client Master File. We are concerned here with that portion of the Client Master File dealing with the financial solvency of the client. The rules are concerned with developing a measure, either high or low, of the client's basic tolerance to financial loss. Figure 4.46 shows an abbreviated version of output from the policy execution.

```
Known Facts:
    TAI--Total Annual Income   :    80000.00
    TNW--TOTAL Networth        :   190000.00
    LNW--Liquid Networth       :    50000.00
    TLR--Total/Liquid Ratio    :     0.263158


The Rules:
R1 if Client.TAI is loDAI then FinRiskTol is loFRT;
R2 if Client.TAI is hiDAI then FinRiskTol is hiFRT;
R3 if Client.LNW is somewhat hiCNW then FinRiskTol is hiFRT;
R4 if Client.TNW is very hiCNW then FinRiskTol is hiFRT;
R5 if Client.TNW is not hiCNW and Client.LNW is not near Client.TNW
       then FinRiskTol is loFRT;
R6 if Client.TAI is loDAI and [Client.LNW/Client.TNW] is hiRATIO
       then FinRiskTol is loFRT;

Context Parameters:
    Correlation Method       : Product
    Implication Method       : Minimum/Maximum
    Defuzzify   Method       : Centroid
    Rule Truth Threshold     :    0.20
```

Figure 4.46 Starting the financial risk tolerance policy

The policy displays its known facts and the rule set, only the first six rules are shown in this example. During execution, other facts are generally added to the policy through backward or forward chaining as well as the execution of methods associated with the policy.

Vocabulary Fuzzy Sets

During knowledge mining and rule discovery many of the model parameters are decomposed into fuzzy sets by the automatic fuzzy set generators. This provides an effective way of handling parameters for which the experts, the business analysis and traders, have no predefined semantic decomposition. On the other hand, many of the model controls have specific meanings within the boundaries of safety and suitability. For these factors, the knowledge engineer decomposes the variables into a predetermined and fixed collection of fuzzy sets. In this section we look at some of the fuzzy sets that have been predetermined. Figure 4.47 shows the basic dependent or solution variable for the policy—FRTTOL, the Financial-based Risk Tolerance.

```
FrtTol--Financial-based Risk Tolerance
Domain [UofD]:        0.00 to     1000.00

        1.00***                                                    .....
        0.90    ******                                   ...........
        0.80       ****                               .....
        0.70        ***                             .....
        0.60         ***                         ...
        0.50          **                      ....
        0.40          ***          ...
        0.30            ***..
        0.20             .....  ***
        0.10                ......       ****
        0.00..............           ****************************
            0---|---|---|---|---|---|---|---|---|---|---|---|---|---|---0
            0.00 125.00 250.00 375.00 500.00 625.00 750.00 875.00 1000.00

    .     FuzzySet:    hiFRT
          Description: High for Financial Risk Tolerance
    *     FuzzySet:    loFRT
          Description: Low for Financial Risk Tolerance
```

Figure 4.47 The financial risk tolerance solution fuzzy set

This is the risk metric used in the financial tolerance context. It is a standard nomographic fuzzy set ranging between [0] and [1000]. Zero indicates a complete lack of risk tolerance. One thousand indicates a complete tolerance for any kind of financial risk. The two fuzzy sets represent a high and a low tolerance to risk. Note these sets are not complements. Low risk tolerance drops off very quickly while high risk tolerance has a more gradual climb. In the production rules we balance the factors that indicate a low tolerance with those that indicate a high tolerance. This fuzzy set arrangement gives slightly more weight to low financial risk tolerance (thereby erring on the side of a conservative strategy).

```
Client.TAI--Total and Deciding Annual Income
Domain [UofD]:        25.00 to     100.00

        1.00***                                                    .......
        0.90    ******                                  ..............
        0.80       ****                              .......
        0.70        ***                            .....
        0.60         ***                       .....
        0.50          **                    ....
        0.40          ...***
        0.30            ....        ***
        0.20             .....          ***
        0.10           ....                ****
        0.00.....                    ****************************
            0---|---|---|---|---|---|---|---|---|---|---|---|---|---|---0
            25.00 34.38 43.75 53.12 62.50 71.88 81.25 90.62 100.00

    .     FuzzySet:    hiDAI
          Description: High for Deciding Annual Income
    *     FuzzySet:    loDAI
          Description: Low for Deciding Annual Income
```

Figure 4.48 The total annual income fuzzy sets

Figure 4.48 shows the term set for the `Client.TAI` or Total Annual Income parameter. In discussions with experts, the model builders found that total annual income is not the most important consideration in deciding whether or not to allow a specific type of investment strategy. Rather, the thresholding income for riskier forms of investment breaks at the $25,000 to $50,000 level. We therefore refer to a specific annual income spread as a "Deciding" annual income [DAI].

Like the over-all risk tolerance the fuzzy sets for high and low deciding annual income levels are not complements. The low annual income curve drops off quickly so after ≈$60,000 no income is considered low. The high annual income rises quickly with the $50,000 point resting at the 50% inflection point. The curve becomes absolutely true at $100,000, but has significant truth after the $70,000. These limits are skewed slightly above the normative $50,000 level to give the model some flexibility in classifying clients as having high or low income, thus taking a slightly conservative track.

```
FuzzySet:    hiCNW
Description: High for Composite Net Worth
1.00                                                                    .....
0.90                                                         ............
0.80                                              ......
0.70                                        .....
0.60                                   ....
0.50                              ...
0.40                         ....
0.30                    ....
0.20               .....
0.10          ......
0.00..........
     0---|---|---|---|---|---|---|---|---|---|---|---|---|---|---0
     15.00   163.12   311.25   459.38   607.50   755.62   903.75 1051.88 1200.00
   Domained:        15.00 to     1200.00
```

Figure 4.49 The high composite networth fuzzy set

The fuzzy set in Figure 4.49 represents the concept of a client with high net worth. This fuzzy set reflects the truth of the proposition *The client's networth is high* and is derived from the expert's appraisal of what constitutes a high networth. This is a composite since we map both total and liquid networth to the same metric. The curve says, in effect, that networth values below ≈$250,000 are low. That a moderate networth (at the 50 percent inflection point) is ≈$650,000 and a high networth begins to take serious truth values above $900,000.

```
FuzzySet:    nearTNW
Description: Near the Client's Total Net Worth
1.00
0.90            ..
0.80          .  .
0.70
0.60
0.50        .      .
0.40
0.30
0.20      .        .
0.10
0.00......          .....................................................
    0---|---|---|---|---|---|---|---|---|---|---|---|---|---|---|---0
    15.00  163.12  311.25  459.38  607.50  755.62  903.75 1051.88 1200.00
    Domained:        15.00 to    1200.00
```

Figure 4.50 The fuzzy set approximating the client's total net worth

Some vocabulary fuzzy sets are dynamically created by model parameter values. The NearTNW (Near or Close-to the client's Total Net Worth), shown in Figure 4.50, is a bell-shaped fuzzy set centered around the client's current total net worth. This is used in the rules to compute the truth of the proposition *X is close to TNW*. The spread or diffusion of the fuzzy set is 15% of the value. Changing the width of the diffusion (say, to 25 percent or 50 percent) has a significant impact on the model performance. The choice of the diffusion pattern in the fuzzy set was derived from the expert's view of what constitutes values that significantly neighbor the center amount.

```
Client.TNW--Client Total Net Worth
Domain [UofD]:      15.00 to    1200.00

   1.00                                                         .....
   0.90       **                                    ............
   0.80      *  *                          ......
   0.70                                   .....
   0.60                                .....
   0.50     *      *                  ...
   0.40                              .....
   0.30                            ....
   0.20     *        *        .....
   0.10              ......
   0.00******.....    **********************************************
       0---|---|---|---|---|---|---|---|---|---|---|---|---|---|---|---0
       15.00  163.12  311.25  459.38  607.50  755.62  903.75 1051.88 1200.00

   .   FuzzySet:    hiCNW
       Description: High for Composite Net Worth
   *   FuzzySet:    nearTNW
       Description: Near the Client's Total Net Worth
```

Figure 4.51 The client's total networth compared to high net worth

Once we have created the NearTNW fuzzy set, it is mapped to the fuzzy set metric that describes the total net worth. This mapping, shown in Figure 4.51, provides a visual check on the underlying semantics of the model both in terms of where the central value lies in relation to the Total Net Worth fuzzy set but also in terms of whether or not the set diffusion accurately represents the approximation concept[2].

```
FuzzySet:     hiLTNWRATIO
Description: High for Total to Liquid Networth Ratio
1.00                                                            ......
0.90                                                 ............
0.80                                          ......
0.70                                     .....
0.60                                 ....
0.50                             ...
0.40                         ....
0.30                     .....
0.20                 .....
0.10           .....
0.00..........
     0---|---|---|---|---|---|---|---|---|---|---|---|---|---|---0
     0.00    0.12    0.25    0.38    0.50    0.62    0.75    0.88    1.00
     Domained:          0.00 to        1.00
```

Figure 4.52 The fuzzy set for liquid net worth

Liquid net worth, shown in Figure 4.52, is always less than total net worth. In fact, since these two model parameters are related (liquid net worth is always a subset of total net worth) we must exercise care in specifying independent rules that affect risk based on LNW and TNW as if they were independent variables. But one important model factor is the ratio of liquid to total net worth. If this ratio is very low, then the client is not very liquid. An increase in financial risk might require him or her to convert some assets to available capital. This has implications for perceptions of suitability and safety. This fuzzy set measures the ratio of liquid to total net worth in terms of what is a high ratio. The inflection point is at the [.5] membership grade.

Executing Discovered and Engineered Rules

The underlying premise behind rule discovery is we find, among the input and output values of the data model, the relationships that establish changes in the model solution state (the dependent variable) when one or more of the control or independent variables change. The safety and suitability model, as we discussed earlier, uses the rule discovery process to find relationships in the data. These relationships, in the form of rules, are not applied directly to the model, but are reviewed by the business analysis, traders, and finan-

---

2. This is important. We do not want to create a specially tailored approximation fuzzy set for each client total net worth value. Seeing how the bell-shaped fuzzy set sits on the Total Net Worth fuzzy gives the model designer a feel for how the two semantics are matched.

cial analysts for correctness. From the discovered rules and the rules generated through conventional knowledge acquisition, the intelligence for each policy is created. In this section, some of the composite rules are executed to show how the reasoning underlying the model is performed. Figure 4.53 shows the first rule executed with the value for the client's total annual income.

```
R1 if Client.TAI is loDAI then FinRiskTol is loFRT;
12/10/19xx 12.44pm---Rule fails. Premise truth is below alpha threshold: 0.2000
12/10/19xx 12.44pm---Premise Truth= 0.0031
```

Figure 4.53 Executing rule [R1]

This rule is interpreted as,

if the client's total annual income is LOW then FinRiskTol is LOW

The annual income for this client is $80,000 which falls to the extreme right-hand side of the loDAI fuzzy set. Since the mapping of the annual income to the fuzzy set yields an almost completely zero truth value, the rule fails and is not executed. The alpha cut indicates a truth membership level equivalent to zero. Any value below this is automatically set to zero. Figure 4.54 now shows the execution of the second rule with the same annual income value.

```
R2 if Client.TAI is hiDAI then FinRiskTol is hiFRT;
12/10/19xx 12.44pm---Premise Truth= 0.9245


      FuzzySet:    RiskTol
      Description: UNDER GENERATION Financial Risk Tolerance
     1.00
     0.90                                                        .........
     0.80                                                 .........
     0.70                                          .....
     0.60                                    .....
     0.50                               ....
     0.40                           ...
     0.30                       ....
     0.20                  .....
     0.10             ......
     0.00..............
       0---|---|---|---|---|---|---|---|---|---|---|---|---|---|---|---0
       0.00 125.00  250.00 375.00  500.00 625.00  750.00 875.00 1000.00
      Domained:          0.00 to    1000.00
```

Figure 4.54 Executing rule [R2]

This rule is interpreted as:

if the client total annual income is HIGH then FinRiskTol is HIGH

The client's annual income falls in the upper part of the hiDAI fuzzy set with a truth membership value of μ[.92]. This rule executes by updating the solution fuzzy set (Risk-Tol). An image of the hiFRT fuzzy set is moved to the RiskTol output, but truncated at the [.92] truth level. Figure 4.55 shows the execution of the third rule in the policy.

```
R3 if Client.LNW is somewhat hiCNW then FinRiskTol is hiFRT;
12/10/19xx 12.44pm---Hedge 'somewhat' applied to Fuzzy Set "hiCNW"

Composite Net Worth--Normal and Hedged [Somewhat]
Domain [UofD]:      15.00 to    1200.00

     1.00                                                   ********
     0.90                                      ***************...
     0.80                              *******......
     0.70                        ******  .....
     0.60                   *****  ....
     0.50              *****   ...
     0.40          ****    ....
     0.30       ****    ....
     0.20    *****   .....
     0.10  ***     ......
     0.00***........
        0---|---|---|---|---|---|---|---|---|---|---|---|---|---|---|---0
        15.00  163.12  311.25  459.38  607.50  755.62  903.75 1051.88 1200.00
     .  FuzzySet:     hiCNW
        Description: High for Composite Net Worth
     *  FuzzySet:     hiCNW
        Description: somewhat hiCNW

12/10/19xx 12.44pm---Rule fails. Premise truth is below alpha threshold: 0.2000
12/10/19xx  0.45am---Premise Truth= 0.0694
```

Figure 4.55 Executing rule [R3]

This rule is interpreted as:

if the client liquid networth is somewhat HIGH then FinRiskTol is HIGH

The hedge somewhat dilutes the fuzzy set hiCNW so a value toward the left-hand side of the hiCNW has a higher truth membership value. This means we want to give added strength of any client that has a significant liquid net worth. In this case, the client's liquid net worth ($50,000) still falls below the alpha cut threshold for the fuzzy set. The rule fails and does not contribute to the solution. Figure 4.56 shows the results of executing the fourth rule in the policy.

```
R4 if Client.TNW is very hiCNW then FinRiskTol is hiFRT;
12/10/19xx  0.45am---Hedge 'very' applied to Fuzzy Set "hiCNW"
12/10/19xx  0.45am---Rule fails. Premise truth is below alpha threshold: 0.2000
```

```
Composite Net Worth--Normal and Hedged [very]
Domain [UofD]:      15.00 to    1200.00

     1.00                                                  .****
     0.90                                       .....******** 
     0.80                                  ......*****
     0.70                             .....  ****
     0.60                          ....   ***
     0.50                       ...   ***
     0.40                      ....  ***
     0.30                  ....   ***
     0.20               .....  ****
     0.10          ......  ******
     0.00********************** 
         0---|---|---|---|---|---|---|---|---|---|---|---|---|---|---0
         15.00  163.12  311.25  459.38  607.50  755.62  903.75 1051.88 1200.00

    .    FuzzySet:    hiCNW
         Description: High for Composite Net Worth
         Domained:        15.00 to    1200.00
    *    FuzzySet:    hiCNW
         Description: very hiCNW
         Domained:        15.00 to    1200.00

12/10/19xx  0.45am---Premise Truth= 0.0055
```

Figure 4.56 Executing rule [R4]

This rule is interpreted as:

if the client total networth is very HIGH then FinRiskTol is HIGH

The hedge `very` intensifies the fuzzy set `hiCNW` so a value toward the left-hand side of the `hiCNW` has a higher truth membership value. This means we want to give added strength of any client that has a very high total net worth. In this case, the client's total net worth ($190,000) still falls below the alpha cut threshold for the fuzzy set. The rule fails and does not contribute to the solution. The next rule contains a compound predicate involving the application of the negation operator to two fuzzy sets.

```
R5 if Client.TNW is not hiCNW and Client.LNW is not near Client.TNW
      then FinRiskTol is loFRT;
12/10/19xx  0.45am---Hedge 'ZADEH' NOT applied to Fuzzy Set "hiCNW"

High and NOT High Composite Net Worth
Domain [UofD]:      15.00 to    1200.00

     1.00***                                               .....
     0.90    ********                          ............
     0.80        ******                    ......
     0.70          *****              .....
     0.60           ****          ....
     0.50          ****  ..
     0.40         ....  ***
     0.30           ....   ****
     0.20           .....   *****
     0.10        ......      *******
     0.00...........                ***************
         0---|---|---|---|---|---|---|---|---|---|---|---|---|---|---0
         15.00  163.12  311.25  459.38  607.50  755.62  903.75 1051.88 1200.00
```

```
    .  FuzzySet:    hiCNW
       Description: High for Composite Net Worth
    *  FuzzySet:    hiCNW
       Description: ZADEH NOT hiCNW
```

Figure 4.57 Creating the NOT high composite net worth fuzzy set

Applying the hedge NOT to the hiCNW fuzzy set, as shown in Figure 4.57, creates the fuzzy set's complement. This is a symmetric fuzzy set that starts at [1] and falls to [0]. Before we can process the first proposition in the rule's premise this fuzzy set must be created and stored in the temporary knowledge base.

```
12/10/19xx  0.45am---Predicate 1 Truth= 0.9260
12/10/19xx  0.45am---Hedge 'ZADEH' NOT applied to Fuzzy Set "nearTNW"

Near and NOT near TNW
Domain [UofD]:       15.00 to    1200.00

     1.00*****            *****************************************************
     0.90     *    ..   *
     0.80          .  . *
     0.70     *
     0.60
     0.50      .      *
     0.40      *
     0.30
     0.20      .      .
     0.10        *  *
     0.00......    **  .................................................
         0---|---|---|---|---|---|---|---|---|---|---|---|---|---|---0
         15.00 163.12 311.25 459.38 607.50 755.62 903.75 1051.88 1200.00
     .  FuzzySet:    nearTNW
        Description: Near the Client's Total Net Worth
     *  FuzzySet:    nearTNW
        Description: ZADEH NOT nearTNW
```

Figure 4.58 Apply the negation operator (NOT) to the client's total net worth

Applying the hedge NOT to the nearTNW fuzzy set, as shown in Figure 4.58, creates its complement. This is also a symmetric bell-shaped fuzzy set centered around the total net worth value. We defer the creation of this fuzzy set until the first predicate proposition is evaluated (since, if FALSE, then the second proposition can be ignored). Figure 4.59 shows how the dependent variable RiskTol's fuzzy set region is updated by this rule.

```
12/10/19xx  0.45am---Predicate 2 Truth= 1.0000
12/10/19xx  0.45am---Premise Truth= 0.9260
```

```
FuzzySet:     RiskTol
Description: UNDER GENERATION Financial Risk Tolerance
1.00
0.90......                                                          .........
0.80      .....                                           .........
0.70          ...                                      .....
0.60            ...                                 .....
0.50              ...                            ....
0.40                ...                      ...
0.30                  .......
0.20
0.10
0.00
    0---|---|---|---|---|---|---|---|---|---|---|---|---|---|---|---0
    0.00  125.00  250.00  375.00  500.00  625.00  750.00  875.00 1000.00
 Domained:          0.00 to    1000.00
```

Figure 4.59 Updating RiskTol from the execution of rule [R5]

This rule is interpreted as:

>*if the client total networth is not HIGH*
>   *and client liquid net worth is not near the client's total net worth*
>   *then FinRiskTol is LOW*

The AND operator is applied by taking the minimum of the two predicate expressions. Thus min(1.0,.9260) is [.9260]. This means it is very true the client's total net worth is not high and the liquid and total net worths are not near each other. This causes the solution fuzzy set to be updated with the loFRT fuzzy set creating a saddle surface in the output. The saddle has the effect of dampening the risk tolerance, reducing the over-all client's financial risk tolerance. Thus, the client has a high risk tolerance by virtue of his/her salary, but a low risk tolerance by virtue of the total and liquid net worth standing. Figure 4.60 shows the execution of the next rule in the policy.

```
----------------------------------------------------------------
R6 if Client.TAI is loDAI and [Client.LNW/Client.TNW] is hiRATIO
      then FinRiskTol is loFRT;
12/10/19xx  0.45am---Predicate 1 Truth= 0.0000
12/10/19xx  0.45am---Predicate 2 Truth= 0.2252
12/10/19xx  0.45am---Rule fails. Premise truth is below alpha threshold: 0.2000
12/10/19xx  0.45am---Premise Truth= 0.0000
```

```
FuzzySet:    RiskTol
Description: FINAL Financial Risk Tolerance
1.00
0.90......                                              .........
0.80     .....                                    .........
0.70       ...                              .....
0.60        ...                        .....
0.50         ...                   ....
0.40          ...              ...
0.30           .......
0.20
0.10
0.00
    0---|---|---|---|---|---|---|---|---|---|---|---|---|---|---|---0
    0.00  125.00  250.00  375.00  500.00  625.00  750.00  875.00 1000.00
Domained:          0.00 to    1000.00
```

Figure 4.60 Executing rule [R6]

This rule is interpreted as:

> *if the clientannual income is LOW*
> *and the ratio of liquid to total net worth is HIGH*
> *then FinRiskTol is LOW*

The AND operator is applied by taking the minimum of the two predicate expressions. Thus min(0,.2252) is [.22520]. This means the client's annual income is definitely not low but the ratio of liquid to total net worth is moderately high. The combined affect is a zero truth value for this rule. The rule is not executed and does not contribute to the model.

Defuzzification and Explanation

When all the rules have been executed, the solution fuzzy set associated with financial risk tolerance must be defuzzified. This process produces a scalar that is the actual risk tolerance on a scale of zero to one thousand. Figure 4.61 shows the defuzzification using both the center of gravity (centroid) and the average of maximums.

```
- - - - - - - - - - - - - - - - - - - - - - - - - - - - - - - - -
Model Solution:
Centroid
    RiskTol   :     515.62
    CompIdx   :       0.49
Average of Maximums
    RiskTol   :     500.00
    CompIdx   :       0.70
- - - - - - - - - - - - - - - - - - - - - - - - - - - - - - - - -
CIX          :       0.93
```

Figure 4.61 Defuzzifying the risk tolerance fuzzy set

In risk assessment models of this type, the various maximum defuzzifications seldom produce reliable results. Since the loFRT curve applied to the output space has a higher membership value than the hiFRT curve, this curve produces the maximum value at the zero domain point. The centroid (center of gravity) is the default and preferred method of defuzzification. Figure 4.62 shows the final explanatory script for the policy execution.

```
EXPLANATIONS:
1   .75  .50  .25   0
|----+----+----+----+----------------------------R U L E S----|
   According to rule 5, we have definitely concluded that
   because the Client's Total Networth is certainly not High
the Client's Liquid Networth is definitely not Near Total New Worth
    so FinRiskTol is certainly Low

   Rule 2 states that we have definitely concluded that
   since the Client's Income is definitely High
    the FinRiskTol is certainly High

----------------------------------------S O L U T I O N S------

In Conclusion....From these rules we find that "FinRiskTol"
has a value of '515.625' which is, to some degree, supported.
This is a middle value.
```

Figure 4.62 The rule explanatory mechanism for the suitability model

The rule explanatory facility takes the logical structure of the rule (not its textual representation) and combines it with the truth values of the predicate and consequent expressions to make an intelligent, near-English statement of what the rule signifies. One explanation is offered for each rule and a final explanation is offered for the defuzzified solution space.

Fuzzy Multi-Criteria and Multi-Expert Decision Making

> *Chaos umpires sits,*
> *And by decision more embroils the fray*
> *By which he reigns: next to him high arbiter*
> *Chance governs all.*
>
> John Milton (1608–1674)
> *Paradise Lost*, bk. ii, l. 907

This chapter explores the ways in which fuzzy rule based systems can fuse the expertise of multiple conflicting, collaborating, and cooperating experts into a single model. We examine such techniques and capabilities as how fuzzy systems use the preponderance of evidence in deciding for and against a solution, how peer ranking can be used to control the degree of evidence in the rules, and the relationship of defuzzification to finding appropriate answers. In particular we take up the issues associated with an actual fuzzy pricing model to illustrate how conflicting rules can provide a much more realistic and robust model. The rapid prototyping capabilities of fuzzy rule-based systems with several experts is also explored.

Multi-Expert Systems

One of the principal benefits of a fuzzy reasoning system is its ability to use and assimilate knowledge from multiple experts (see "Use of Multiple, Conflicting, Cooperating and Collaborating Experts" in Chapter 1). This capability gives fuzzy modelling systems an expressiveness that is generally lacking in conventional expert and decision support systems. There are two general aspects of multiple expert systems that are of primary interest in business systems—models that involve conflicting experts, and models of collaborating experts where the results of a consultation must be combined. In some respects, of course, collaborating experts, to the degree that they may disagree on the fine details of the solution, are also conflicting experts. But, for the sake of exploration and clarity, we treat these as two separate but related cases.

Conflicting Expert Systems

A model solution often involves decisions from multiple disagreeing as well as blind, noncollaborating or co-operating, experts. This kind of conflict is common in complex business models where opinions about such important business factors as the state of the stock market, the movement of the prime interest rate, the affect of pricing decisions, the level of inventory stockage, or the rate of change in portfolio concentrations are fiercely debated. As an example, an individual investment planning model that adjusts the investment planning policy depending on whether interest rates are falling or rising might have conventional rules such as:

```
if (PrimeRate[t]-PrimeRate[t-1]) < 0
    then InvestmentPolicy = "AGGRESSIVE";

if (PrimeRate[t]-PrimeRate[t-1]) > 0
    then InvestmentPolicy = "CONSERVATIVE";
```

In this model, the InvestmentPolicy variable is assigned a string describing the investment strategy. These rules could, of course, also assign a numeric value to the variable. In any case, the assignment is made based on the truth of the premise which can be either TRUE or FALSE. Since the rules specify opposite policies, there is no conflict in resolving the proper investment strategy for any change in the prime rate. Suppose we now have two investment experts, Paul and Mary, who see opportunities in the market when the prime rate fluctuates in either direction. The same rules could reflect this:

```
[PAUL]     if (PrimeRate[t]-PrimeRate[t-1]) < 0
               then InvestmentPolicy = "AGGRESSIVE";

[MARY]     if (PrimeRate[t]-PrimeRate[t-1]) > 0
               then InvestmentPolicy = "AGGRESSIVE";
```

With this kind of approach to encoding investment knowledge, we have a conflict in the expert's perception of what a change in the prime rate means. The rule base contains and executes Paul's and Mary's rules. You can see the same aggressive strategy is followed no matter what the interest rate change. We can now replace the two rules with a single declarative rule:

```
        InvestmentPolicy = "AGGRESSIVE"
```

But this statement, in the context of an investment expert system, contributes nothing to our understanding of the expert's knowledge. The assignment statement simply indicates an unconditional aggressive policy. Now, suppose Mary and Paul are investment analysts that take opposite positions on strategy depending on the prime rate.

```
[PAUL]      if (PrimeRate[t]-PrimeRate[t-1]) < 0
                then InvestmentPolicy = "AGGRESSIVE";
                else InvestmentPolicy = "CONSERVATIVE"

[MARY]      if (PrimeRate[t]-PrimeRate[t-1]) < 0
                then InvestmentPolicy = "CONSERVATIVE";
                else InvestmentPolicy = "AGGRESSIVE";
```

When the prime rate is falling Paul indicates an aggressive policy while Mary indicates a conservative policy. How can we integrate these two approaches into a common strategy? In a conventional expert system, combining the rules is not easy. When the strategies are literal strings, the combination might be impossible and we are left with a logical conundrum. In most expert systems, the strategy actually recommended by the model depends on which rule was executed last. This means the strategy recommendation is unpredictable since the ordering of rules on the conflict agenda varies from one model execution to the next.

A Mathematical Model of Conflicting Experts

This conflict can be partially resolved in conventional systems by replacing the string attributes with numeric values. Using numbers we might devise some mathematical algorithm that combines the results of all the executed rules into a composite answer. As an example, consider these rules:

```
[PAUL]      if (PrimeRate[t]-PrimeRate[t-1]) < 0
                then InvestmentPolicy = 90;
                else InvestmentPolicy = -50

[MARY]      if (PrimeRate[t]-PrimeRate[t-1]) < 0
                then InvestmentPolicy = -40;
                else InvestmentPolicy = 70;
```

These numeric strategy values (S_i) are scaled by the peer ranking or contribution weights (W_i) of the expert to produce a weighted average of the proper strategy. Equation 5.1 shows how we can calculate the weighted average of the strategies for N experts.

$$I_{strategy} = \frac{\sum\limits_{i=0}^{N} W_i \cdot S_i}{\sum\limits_{i=0}^{N} W_i}$$

Equation 5.1 Calculating an investment strategy from multiple experts

In this model the investment strategy runs in a continuous range of values form -100 (conservative) to $+100$ (aggressive) with the zero point indicating that no strategy should be employed. The peer weights indicate the degree to which we value the expert's advice. This runs in a range from 0 to 1, inclusive. As an example, given a change in the prime rate, Mary (with a peer weight of $[.2]$) recommends a strategy of $[-40]$ while Paul (with a peer weight of $[.7]$) recommends a strategy of $[+90]$. Equation 5.2 shows how the investment strategy for a particular prime rate change scenario is calculated.

$$I_{strategy} = \frac{\sum\limits_{i=0}^{N} W_i \cdot S_i}{\sum\limits_{i=0}^{N} W_i} = \frac{(.2 \times -40) + (.7 \times 90)}{.2 + .7} = \frac{55}{.9} = 61.11$$

Equation 5.2 Calculating an investment strategy decision

If we now interpret $+100$ as a very aggressive investment strategy and -100 as a very conservative investment strategy, this scheme allows the expert system to recommend a strategy that is balanced by the recommendations of conflicting experts (refer to "invest1.cpp (The Peer-Ranked Investment Policy Advisor)" on page 460 for the program to compute the weighted average of the advisors.) Figure 5.1 shows the actual advisor session for the two investment experts following the schema shows in Equation 5.2.

```
Number of Experts       : 2
Enter Expert Rankings   :
1. Identification of Expert: Paul
   Ranking of Expert [0,1] : .7
2. Identification of Expert: Mary
   Ranking of Expert [0,1] : .2
Enter Expert Strategies :
1. Paul            Investment Strategy   :  90
2. Mary            Investment Strategy   : -40
```

```
Expert                 Peer Rank          Strategy
----------------       ------------       ------------
Paul                         0.70               90
Mary                         0.20              -40
Strategy Recommendation: 61.11
```

Figure 5.1 Executing the peer-ranked investment strategy advisor

The investment strategy recommendation is biased or weighted toward the expert with the highest peer ranking instead of centering around the simple arithmetic mean. With the scheme we can add any number of experts with differing peer rankings and recommendations. Figure 5.2 shows a session with five experts of varying ranks and recommendation strategies.

```
Expert                 Peer Rank          Strategy
----------------       ------------       ------------
Peter                        0.30              -33
Paul                         0.80               70
Mary                         0.50               10
Bill                         0.90               50
Nancy                        0.60              -17
Strategy Recommendation: 27.71
```

Figure 5.2 A peer-ranked advisor session with five experts

This approach to resolving problems of conflicting experts in an expert system is really a simplistic method of computing weighted averages across a fixed domain. Figure 5.3 shows how the advisor session in Figure 5.1 is represented on the strategy scale (in this figure, the dashed line is the ordinary average while the bold arrow to its right is the weighted average).

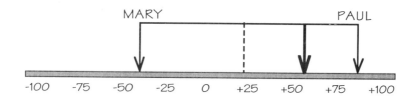

Figure 5.3 Finding the weighted average strategy recommendation

In fact this is the kind of scaled arithmetic that substitutes for the use of actual fuzzy logic processing in many hybrid intelligent systems (see "A Perspective on Fuzzy Modelling" on page 26 of the Preface for a discussion of this phenomenon.) The use of this mathematical infrastructure in expert systems to resolve conflicts in expert knowledge has some serious short-comings.

- If the mathematical relationships among experts are highly non-linear, the representation function can be very difficult to design and use. As more and more experts are added, the mathematical support can become extremely complex. This complexity leads to a brittleness in the reasoning process: new expert knowledge in the same class or expertise that is related and only indirectly influences the current knowledge goal "under focus" is often hard to represent and very difficult to correctly assess.

- The mean of the scaled expert weights provides a crisp and single evidential point in the spectrum of values. We have no way of approximating the judgement of an expert who reasons imprecisely. Combining crisp points yields another crisp point. The degree to which the recommendation reflects the certainty of the expert's knowledge or the degree to which the judgement is based on imprecision in the data is not reflected in the result. That is, the mathematical model does not rely on a reasoning mechanism where the outcome reflects the cognitive model of the experts.

Naturally, there are instances when the mathematical or the statistical approach to model formulation is not only appropriate but completely adequate to the task. In cases when the cumulative knowledge is independently derived and collected from a very large number of sources where the distribution of the population leads us to believe the responses are generally random, a statistical analysis method is preferable to either a conventional or a fuzzy a rule-based model. In this case each reference point in the population (each questionnaire, as an example) is considered an *expert*. If we asked the question,

When the Prime Interest Rate is increasing would you adopt:

1. An aggressive investment strategy.
2. A conservative investment strategy.
3. Don't know.
4. What's an investment strategy?

To a sufficiently large number of individuals we would find a distribution of answers: 67 percent of the population would pursue a conservative strategy, 18 percent would follow an aggressive policy, eight percent couldn't decide, and the remainder shop at Macy's instead of Neimann Marcus. The statistical approach does not actually tell us very much about the correct investment strategy (in the thirteenth century 97 percent of the European population thought the world was flat). The statistical and mathematical approach also can not tell us the reasoning behind the population trend, nor does it reflect the contribution weights of individuals in the population that are economists, investment brokers, and business analysts.

A Fuzzy Model of Conflicting Experts

Fuzzy logic provides a means of collecting the evidential reasoning from multiple experts and combining it into a coherent and consistent recommendation scheme. Fuzzy logic's ability to simultaneously represent complementary concepts allows the reasoning process to synthesize the views of several experts. As an example, consider the following rules that use fuzzy relational operators to measure the prime interest rate changes in successive time periods.

```
[PAUL]      if PrimeRate[t-1] is greater than PrimeRate[t]
                then InvestmentPolicy is Aggressive;

[MARY]      if PrimeRate[t-1] is less than PrimeRate[t]
                then InvestmentPolicy is Conservative;
```

In these rules to the degree to which the change is greater than or less than the interest rate in the previous period, the investment policy has some degree of membership in either the Aggressive or Conservative fuzzy sets. Although fuzzy relational operators are used in some advanced fuzzy modelling systems, we can restate the rules in simpler terms:

```
[PAUL]      if PrimeRate is MovingDOWN
                then InvestmentPolicy is Aggressive;

[MARY]      if PrimeRate is MovingUP
                then InvestmentPolicy is Conservative;
```

In order to evaluate these rules we need two collections of fuzzy sets. The first group of fuzzy sets must address the change in the prime rate by defining what is meant by the concepts of MovingDOWN and MovingUP. The model measures the prime interest movement as the percent difference between the two time periods[1]. Equation 5.3 is the method used to calculate this difference.

$$pctdiff = \frac{N_1 - N_2}{N_1} \times 100$$

Equation 5.3 Calculating the percent difference between terms

Although a percent difference can be any quantity (such as a 1500 percent change), the fuzzy model is only measures changes between -100 percent and +100 percent which seems a reasonable domain for changes in the prime interest rate. As Figure 5.4 shows, the concepts of MovingUP and MovingDOWN are represented by growth and decay S-curves.

---

1. A more realistic model, of course, would consider the average percent difference and the sum of the magnitudes and direction over the past N time periods (where N might be the last six quarters.)

```
PRIMERATE.CHANGE
Domain [UofD]:       -100.00 to        100.00
      1.00*****                                                       .....
      0.90       ***********                            ...........
      0.80                  *****                    .....
      0.70                       *****            .....
      0.60                          ***        ...
      0.50                            ****  ...
      0.40                            ... ***
      0.30                         ....        ****
      0.20                   .....              *****
      0.10            ......                      ******
      0.00..............                              **************
        0---|---|---|---|---|---|---|---|---|---|---|---|---|---|---|---0
      -100.00  -75.00  -50.00  -25.00    0.00   25.00   50.00   75.00 100.00

      .    FuzzySet:    MOVEUP
           Description: Prime Rate PctDiff in Upward Movement
      *    FuzzySet:    MOVEDOWN
           Description: Prime Rate PctDiff in Downward Movement
```

Figure 5.4 The change in prime rate fuzzy sets

The degree to which it is true that the prime rate has moved up or down between suc-
ceeding periods controls the investment policy. In this model the same psychometric scale
[-100 to +100] is used as a measure of the investment strategy. Figure 5.5 shows the fuzzy
sets associated with the solution variable. Like the change in interest rate, they are also
growth and decay S-curves.

```
INVESTMENT.POLICY
Domain [UofD]:       -100.00 to        100.00
      1.00.....                                         ***********  *****
      0.90       ...........                        ***********
      0.80                  .....                *****
      0.70                       .....        *****
      0.60                          ...      ***
      0.50                            ...****
      0.40                            ***  ...
      0.30                         ****        ....
      0.20                   *****              .....
      0.10            ******                      .....
      0.00**************                              ..............
        0---|---|---|---|---|---|---|---|---|---|---|---|---|---|---|---0
      -100.00  -75.00  -50.00  -25.00    0.00   25.00   50.00   75.00 100.00

      .    FuzzySet:    CONSERVATIVE
           Description: Conservative Investment Policy
      *    FuzzySet:    AGGRESSIVE
           Description: Aggressive Investment Policy
```

Figure 5.5 The investment strategy fuzzy sets

The output surface design provides a wide overlap between the aggressive and the
conservative strategies so they cross-over at the zero strategy point. A strategy close to
zero would indicate a high state of ambiguity in the decision process—the change in prime
rate was sufficiently small so the investment policy could go in either direction. Figure 5.6
shows how the fuzzy investment advisor is executed (refer to "invest2.cpp (The Fuzzy
Investment Strategy Advisor [version 2])" on page 462 for details on the program code.)

```
The Fuzzy Investment Policy Advisor
(c) 1995 The Metus Systems Group
There are   2 experts in this model.
Enter Expert Rankings   :
   1. Identification of Expert      : Paul
      Ranking of Expert [0,1]       : .7
   2. Identification of Expert      : Mary
      Ranking of Expert [0,1]       : .2
PctDiff Change in Prime Rate        : 20
```

Figure 5.6 Executing the fuzzy investment advisor

In this model the number of experts are determined by the rule set. The system then asks for the expert's identification and peer ranking. Finally, the model asks for the percent difference in the prime interest rate. In this case a positive 20 percent change occurred.

The Adaptive Peer Ranking Parameter

How does the peer ranking apply to fuzzy models? The crisp mathematical model used this ranking to scale the strategy and generate a weighted average. In a fuzzy model, the ranking is used in a slightly different manner. We view the ranking as a predicate truth amplifier. The truth of the rule's premise is modified by multiplying the base premise truth by one plus the peer ranking. Equation 5.4 shows the final predicate truth is computed.

$$P_{truth} = (1 + R_{peer}) \times P_{truth}$$

Equation 5.4 The peer ranking amplification calculation

In this way the correlation process (see "Correlation Techniques" on page 74) transfers more truth into the implication process for experts that have a higher ranking order. On the other hand, experts with lower ranking have their premise truths unbiased or only slightly biased by the additive coefficient. Not only does this improve the unit compatibility value for the model (an important consideration if the model results are further scaled by the compatibility value), but improves the performance of the model at higher alpha threshold levels. The alpha threshold is an important tuning metric in a multiple expert model. For additional details on the use of the adaptive rule coefficient see "The Additive Fuzzy System" on page 113. To see how this works, we can follow the basic fuzzy investment model. Figure 5.7 shows the execution of the first rule.

```
if PrimeRate is MovingDOWN then InvestmentPolicy is Aggressive;
Expert 'Paul'. Ranking:  0.70
[Base] PremiseTruth=        0.32
[Rank] PremiseTruth=        0.55
---RULE FIRED--Premise truth of:0.5504

        FuzzySet:    STRATEGY
        Description: Combined Investment Strategy
  1.00
  0.90
  0.80
  0.70
  0.60
  0.50                                                        ..............
  0.40                                             ..........
  0.30                                     .......
  0.20                              ......
  0.10                       ........
  0.00...................
       0---|---|---|---|---|---|---|---|---|---|---|---|---|---|---|---0
      -100.00  -75.00  -50.00  -25.00    0.00   25.00   50.00   75.00 100.00
        Domained:        -100.00 to      100.00
        AlphaCut:          0.10
```

Figure 5.7 Executing the first rule in the fuzzy investment model

The 20 percent change in the prime rate has a truth membership of [.32] in the Mov-ingDOWN fuzzy set. Paul's expert peer ranking is [.70]. This yields a 70 percent increase in the premise truth value so that the effective or rank premise truth is [.55]. As Figure 5.7 shows, the Aggressive fuzzy set is truncated at this level and moved into the STRATEGY solution fuzzy region. The second rule, as shown in Figure 5.8, is then executed.

```
if PrimeRate is MovingUP   then InvestmentPolicy is Conservative;
Expert 'Mary'. Ranking:  0.20
[Base] PremiseTruth=        0.68
[Rank] PremiseTruth=        0.81
---RULE FIRED--Premise truth of:0.8115

        FuzzySet:    STRATEGY
        Description: Combined Investment Strategy
  1.00
  0.90
  0.80........
  0.70        ..........
  0.60                  ......
  0.50                        .....                  ..............
  0.40                             ....    ..........
  0.30                                  .......
  0.20
  0.10
  0.00
       0---|---|---|---|---|---|---|---|---|---|---|---|---|---|---|---0
      -100.00  -75.00  -50.00  -25.00    0.00   25.00   50.00   75.00 100.00
        Domained:        -100.00 to      100.00
        AlphaCut:          0.10
```

Figure 5.8 Executing the second rule in the fuzzy investment model

The 20 percent change in the prime rate has a truth membership of [.68] in the Moving UP fuzzy set. Mary's expert peer ranking is [.20]. This yields a 20 percent increase in the premise truth value so the effective or rank premise truth is [.81]. As Figure 5.8 shows, the Conservative fuzzy set is truncated at this level and combined with the current STRATEGY fuzzy set through the fuzzy union operator (See "Additive and Min/Max Fuzzy Systems" on page 73.) Since the membership of the 20 percent change in prime rate already had a significant membership in the MovingUP fuzzy set, the small peer ranking of this expert contributes little—as we might expect—to the final result. The STRATEGY fuzzy region represents the combined recommendations of the two experts.

To find the actual recommended strategy the solution fuzzy set must be defuzzified. This involves taking the center of gravity or the centroid of the fuzzy set (refer to "Defuzzification" on page 89 for complete details.) Figure 5.9 shows how the solution fuzzy set is defuzzified to produce a combined recommendation.

```
---'CENTROID'     defuzzification. Value:    -10.938, [0.4896]
Model Solution:
   Strategy    =     -10.94
   Complex     =       0.49
   SurfaceHght =       0.81

       FuzzySet:    STRATEGY
       Description: Combined Investment Strategy
      1.00
      0.90
      0.80........
      0.70          ..........
      0.60              ......
      0.50                  .....              ..............
      0.40                     .x..    ..........
      0.30                      |    .......
      0.20                      |
      0.10                      |
      0.00                      |
          0---|---|---|---|---|---|---|---|---|---|---|---|---|---|---|---0
       -100.00  -75.00   -50.00  -25.00   0.00   25.00   50.00   75.00  100.00
          Domained:         -100.00 to    100.00
          AlphaCut:            0.10
```

Figure 5.9 Defuzzifying the STRATEGY solution fuzzy set

The fuzzy set surface represents the intersection of the MovingUP and MovingDOWN fuzzy sets. Because there is a preponderance of evidence toward the conservative investment strategy with a smaller mass of evidence toward the aggressive investment strategy, the center of gravity finds a point that balances the STRATEGY region. The scalar result of -10.94 [≈11] indicates a slightly conservative investment program. In Figure 5.9 the vertical line shows the point of defuzzification.

What happens as the change in prime rate decreases? We would suppose that the strategy of the expert(s) that specify investment programs when the prime rate is going down would dominate the recommendation. This is, in fact, what does happen. When the percent change is -40 percent the following execution session creates a new strategy. Figure 5.10 shows the execution of the first rule in this session.

```
if PrimeRate is MovingDOWN then InvestmentPolicy is Aggressive;
Expert 'Paul'. Ranking:  0.70
[Base] PremiseTruth=        0.82
[Rank] PremiseTruth=        1.00
---RULE FIRED--Premise truth of:1.0000

         FuzzySet:    STRATEGY
         Description: Combined Investment Strategy
     1.00                                                             .....
     0.90                                                   ...........
     0.80                                           .....
     0.70                                     .....
     0.60                                   ...
     0.50                                 ....
     0.40                               ...
     0.30                            ....
     0.20                         .....
     0.10                   ......
     0.00.............
        0---|---|---|---|---|---|---|---|---|---|---|---|---|---|---|---0
      -100.00  -75.00  -50.00  -25.00    0.00   25.00   50.00   75.00 100.00
         Domained:        -100.00 to     100.00
         AlphaCut:           0.10
```

Figure 5.10 Executing the first rule in the investment model (PctDiff is -40%)

The percent difference of -40 percent has a membership of [.82] in the MovingDOWN fuzzy set. With the [.70] expert ranking, the predicate truth is increased 70 percent to ≈1.4 [1.394]. This is truncated to the maximum membership value of [1.0]. The Aggressive fuzzy set at the [1.0] truth level is moved into the STRATEGY solution fuzzy set. Following this the next rule is executed. Figure 5.11 shows the results of this rule execution.

```
if PrimeRate is MovingUP then InvestmentPolicy is Conservative;
Expert 'Mary'. Ranking:  0.20
[Base] PremiseTruth=        0.18
[Rank] PremiseTruth=        0.21
---RULE FIRED--Premise truth of:0.2115

         FuzzySet:    STRATEGY
         Description: Combined Investment Strategy
     1.00                                                             .....
     0.90                                                   ...........
     0.80                                           .....
     0.70                                     .....
     0.60                                   ...
     0.50                                 ....
     0.40                               ...
     0.30                            ....
     0.20.............             .....
     0.10                   .....
     0.00
        0---|---|---|---|---|---|---|---|---|---|---|---|---|---|---|---0
      -100.00  -75.00  -50.00  -25.00    0.00   25.00   50.00   75.00 100.00
         Domained:        -100.00 to     100.00
         AlphaCut:           0.10
```

Figure 5.11 Executing the second rule in the investment model (PctDiff is -40%)

The percent difference of -40% has a membership of [.18] in the MovingUP fuzzy set. With the [.20] expert ranking, the predicate truth is increased 20 percent to [.21]. The Conservative fuzzy set at the [.21] truth level is combined with the STRATEGY solution fuzzy set using the fuzzy union operator.

```
---'CENTROID'     defuzzification. Value:      32.031, [0.7690]
Model Solution:
   Strategy    =        32.03
   CompIdx     =         0.77
   SurfaceHght =         1.00
```

Figure 5.12 Defuzzifying the STRATEGY fuzzy set (PctDiff is -40%)

In this case, only a small piece of evidence for the Conservative strategy is added to the model with the preponderance of the evidence supporting the Aggressive investment strategy. Figure 5.12 shows how the outcome was defuzzified. The center of gravity shifts to the right at [32.03] indicating a moderate but significant recommendation for an aggressive investment program. The unit compatibility index (*CompIdx*) of [0.77] means this recommendation is well supported by the underlying rule base.

Peer Ranking by Membership Modification

The adaptive rule weights in a fuzzy model involving multiple experts can also influence the combination of evidence (in terms of how the fuzzy sets are combined) in another manner. Using this technique, the peer ranking changes the shape of the fuzzy set so that values in the domain are either included or excluded from the final solution space. Modifications in this approach work very much like traditional hedges. For complete details on hedge transformations and how they change the shape of fuzzy sets see "Hedges and Scalar Approximators" on page 179. Also refer to Chapter 5. *Fuzzy Set Hedges* in *The Fuzzy System Handbook* (Cox, AP Professional, 1994).

A peer ranking membership modifier acts on the surface of the membership function in the same way as the very and somewhat hedges. But unlike the peer ranking in the previous section the membership transformer can assume a set of values between -1 and +1, inclusive. This value, subtracted from one, becomes the contrast exponent for the membership function. Equation 5.5 shows how this operation is applied to the fuzzy set.

$$\mu_A[x] = \mu_A^{1-R_i}[x]$$

Equation 5.5 Transforming a fuzzy set with peer surface modification

As the peer ranking approaches one ($R \rightarrow 1$) the transformation assumes the characteristics of the *somewhat* hedge. When the ranking is zero, no modification to the fuzzy set is made (the expert has neutral impact relative to all other experts) and when the ranking approaches minus one ($R \rightarrow -1$) the transformation assumes the characteristics of the *very* hedge. This idea is illustrated in the following investment strategy model.

```
if PrimeRate is MovingDOWN then InvestmentPolicy is Aggressive;
Expert 'Paul'. Ranking:  0.50

PRIMERATE.CHANGE
Domain [UofD]:     -100.00 to      100.00
      1.00*******
      0.90    ..***************
      0.80              .....*******
      0.70                 .....  *****
      0.60                   ...    *****
      0.50                    ....     ****
      0.40                     ...       *****
      0.30                        ....     ****
      0.20                         .....     *****
      0.10                            ......   ****
      0.00                                .........*****
         0---|---|---|---|---|---|---|---|---|---|---|---|---|---|---|---0
      -100.00  -75.00  -50.00  -25.00    0.00   25.00   50.00   75.00 100.00

      .   FuzzySet:    MOVEDOWN
          Description: Prime Rate PctDiff in Downward Movement
      *   FuzzySet:    MOVEDOWN
          Description: 'Paul'--Prime Rate PctDiff in Downward Movement

PremiseTruth=       0.43
---RULE FIRED--Premise truth of:0.4254
```

Figure 5.13 Executing the first rule in the membership modified investment model

The first expert, Paul, has a peer ranking of +.50. Figure 5.13 shows the results of applying this dialation operator (equivalent to applying the hedge somewhat) to the membership function associated with the MovingDOWN fuzzy set. The curve indicated by the asterisk (*) is the modified membership function. This change means that more domain values, at a slightly higher truth membership, fall within the scope of the curve at the equivalent alpha threshold level. In effect, we give added weight to the Aggressive investment policy by indicating that more percent changes are considered a movement down. Figure 5.14 shows the STRATEGY solution fuzzy set after this rule executes.

```
      FuzzySet:    STRATEGY
      Description: Combined Investment Strategy
      1.00
      0.90
      0.80
      0.70
      0.60
      0.50
      0.40                                              ..............
      0.30                                      ............
      0.20                              ........
      0.10                     ...........
      0.00...................
         0---|---|---|---|---|---|---|---|---|---|---|---|---|---|---|---0
      -100.00  -75.00  -50.00  -25.00    0.00   25.00   50.00   75.00 100.00
      Domained:      -100.00 to     100.00
      AlphaCut:         0.10
```

Figure 5.14 The STRATEGY solution fuzzy set after rule one

The `Aggressive` fuzzy set is truncated at the [.43] truth level and assigned to the `STRATEGY` solution fuzzy set. This indicates a moderate amount of evidence for an aggressive investment program. The second rule is now executed. The associated expert, Mary, has a peer ranking of -.50. Figure 5.15 shows the outcome of executing this rule.

```
if PrimeRate is MovingUP   then InvestmentPolicy is Conservative;
Expert 'Mary'. Ranking: -0.50

PRIMERATE.CHANGE
Domain [UofD]:    -100.00 to      100.00
    1.00                                                    .****
    0.90                                          ...*********
    0.80                                     ...*****
    0.70                                  ...****
    0.60                               ...***
    0.50                             ....***
    0.40                          ...  ***
    0.30                         ....****
    0.20                      .....  ***
    0.10                    ......******
    0.00********************************
       0---|---|---|---|---|---|---|---|---|---|---|---|---|---|---|---0
    -100.00  -75.00  -50.00  -25.00   0.00   25.00   50.00   75.00  100.00

     .    FuzzySet:     MOVEUP
          Description: Prime Rate PctDiff in Upward Movement
     *    FuzzySet:     MOVEUP
          Description: 'Mary'--Prime Rate PctDiff in Upward Movement

PremiseTruth=        0.82
---RULE FIRED--Premise truth of:0.8191
```

Figure 5.15 Executing the second rule in the membership modified investment model

The second expert, Mary, has a peer ranking of -.50. Figure 5.15 shows the results of applying this intensification operator (equivalent to the hedge `very`) across the membership function associated with `MovingUP`. The curve indicated by the asterisk (*) is the modified membership function. This change means that fewer domain values, at a slightly lower truth membership, fall within the scope of the curve at the equivalent alpha threshold level. In effect, we give less weight to the `Conservative` investment policy by indicating that fewer percent changes are considered a movement upward. Figure 5.16 shows the `STRATEGY` solution fuzzy set after this rule executes.

```
      FuzzySet:     STRATEGY
      Description: Combined Investment Strategy
    1.00
    0.90
    0.80.........
    0.70          .........
    0.60                  ......
    0.50                    .....
    0.40                       ....              ..............
    0.30                          ......  ...........
    0.20                                   .
    0.10
    0.00
       0---|---|---|---|---|---|---|---|---|---|---|---|---|---|---|---0
    -100.00  -75.00  -50.00  -25.00   0.00   25.00   50.00   75.00  100.00
      Domained:        -100.00 to      100.00
      AlphaCut:          0.10
```

Figure 5.16 The STRATEGY solution fuzzy set after rule one

The `Conservative` fuzzy set is truncated at the [.82] truth level and combined with the `STRATEGY` solution fuzzy set using the fuzzy union operator. This indicates a considerable amount of evidence for a conservative investment program. The entire solution fuzzy region is now skewed toward the `Conservative` fuzzy region and we would expect any defuzzification that considered the preponderance of evidence to indicate some degree of conservative investment program.

```
---'CENTROID'     defuzzification. Value:    -17.188, [0.5382]
Model Solution:
   Strategy    =     -17.19
   CompIdx     =       0.54
   SurfaceHght =       0.82
```

Figure 5.17 Defuzzifying the STRATEGY fuzzy set

As Figure 5.17 shows this is exactly what happens. The center of gravity for the combined expert recommendations lies slightly to the left of center with a moderate -17.2 investment strategy value. We can interpret this as mild recommendation for a conservative investment program. The advice is counterbalanced by the contribution of the aggressive strategy advice. If the first expert has a smaller positive peer ranking (say [0] or [.2]), the right-hand side of the solution fuzzy set would have been shallower and contributed less to the final center of gravity value (the expert's advice would not have been as significant).

A Conflicting and Cooperating Experts Application

How are knowledge-based systems that use multiple experts deployed in the real world of business planning and decision making? We can see an actual example of this in a new product pricing model developed in the middle 1980s for a major British retailer.

> The *Fuzzy Systems Handbook* (Cox, AP Professional, 1994) contains a much more detailed discussion of the new product pricing model and a set of variations on the model architecture. In this section we take up the issues of how the fuzzy rule-based system combines the intelligence from multiple conflicting and cooperating experts.

The model combines the expertise of financial, marketing, sales, and manufacturing management to develop a recommended initial pricing position for a new consumer product. This pricing model is an excellent example of how a fuzzy rule based system can combine the intelligence of several experts into a single, cohesive process. The model also demonstrates how conditional and unconditional fuzzy propositions work together to support a complex planning objective. The model consists of four rules:

```
[R1]   our price must be high;
[R2]   our price must be low;
[R3]   our price must be around 2*MfgCosts;
[R4]   if the CompetitionPrice is not very high
       then our price must be near the CompetitionPrice;
```

We immediately notice two unusual properties of this model (for those readers familiar with conventional expert and decision support systems).

1. The initial three rules are not in the form *if-then*. These are unconditional fuzzy propositions.
2. These first three rules are mutually exclusive.

Certainly the first two rules appear to prescribe contradictory model states. In fact, these are rules actually contributed by experts that collaborated in the model development. They are conflicting only in the sense they state unconditionally the value for the dependent variable price must be a specific value. Our concept of contradiction, however, centers around the mistaken idea that the rules actually assign a value to *price*. In fact, this is not the case. The right hand components of these fuzzy propositions are fuzzy sets. The first three rules are interpreted in the following manner:

consistent with any existing constraints:
price should be within the fuzzy region HIGH
price should be within the fuzzy region LOW
price should be within the fuzzy region formed by approximating
twice the manufacturing costs.

The phrase "*consistent with any existing constraints*" means the degree to which the fuzzy set representing the variable *price* assumes the shape of the right-hand fuzzy region is limited by the current state of the `price` fuzzy region. Unconditional propositions are applied using the fuzzy intersection operator when the solution fuzzy set is not empty. See "Unconditional Fuzzy Propositions" on page 78 for a complete discussion of these constraints.

The Basic Fuzzy Vocabulary

The underlying fuzzy vocabulary for the pricing model consists of static as well as dynamically created fuzzy sets. The static vocabulary defines the term set for the variable `price`, while the dynamic fuzzy sets describe fuzzy numbers associated with other model parameters. Figure 5.18 shows the fuzzy term set for price.

```
PRICE
Domain [UofD]:        4.00 to        48.00
       1.00*                                                      .
       0.90 *******                                        ......
       0.80          ******                          .......
       0.70              ******                 ......
       0.60                 *******        .......
       0.50                    ****** .....
       0.40                 ...... *******
       0.30          .......           ******
       0.20      ......                     *******
       0.10  .......                              ******
       0.00......                                       ******
         0---|---|---|---|---|---|---|---|---|---|---|---|---|---0
         4.00   9.50   15.00  20.50  26.00  31.50  37.00  42.50  48.00

     .  FuzzySet:    HIGH
        Description: High for Price
     *  FuzzySet:    LOW
        Description: Low for Price
```

Figure 5.18 The pricing model high and low fuzzy sets

The domain of the price variable—from a low of $4.00 to high of $48.00—defines the range of possible new product price values. These values must enclose not only the range of prices we would consider satisfactory for the product, but also covers the domain of the average competition prices in the demographic region. These are straight line fuzzy sets, indicating that the concept of HIGH or LOW changes linearly as the value of price changes. The two fuzzy sets are, in fact, complements although this relationship is not required by the model.

The dynamic fuzzy sets are created from parameter values that are not known until the model is executed. These are fuzzy numbers in the shape of PI (bell-shaped) curves. The dynamic sets are used in rules [R3] and [R4] as the linguistic variables near 2*Mfg-Costs and near CompetitionPrice. Figure 5.19 shows the fuzzy set representing near (or around) twice the manufacturing costs.

```
FuzzySet:    Near.2*MfgCosts
Description: Near (Around) Twice MfgCosts
1.00                                          .
0.90                                     .. ..
0.80                                   .     .
0.70                                 .         .
0.60                               .
0.50                                             .
0.40                             .
0.30                                               .
0.20                           .
0.10                         .                       .
0.00.................................         .................
   0---|---|---|---|---|---|---|---|---|---|---|---|---|---|---0
    4.00    9.50   15.00   20.50   26.00   31.50   37.00   42.50   48.00
Domained:              4.00 to      48.00
AlphaCut:              0.10
```

Figure 5.19 The pricing model near 2*MFGCosts fuzzy set

Each fuzzy number has its own band width or diffusion level. The band width as well as the sharpness of the slope specifies the compactness of the fuzzy number and constrains the fuzzy model. The manufacturing costs fuzzy number is created with a PI curve centered at twice the manufacturing costs and has a 25% band width. Figure 5.20 shows the fuzzy number created for a MfgCosts value of $15.00.

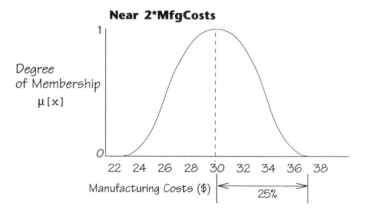

Figure 5.20 Forming a fuzzy number from the manufacturing costs

Figure 5.21 shows the fuzzy set representation for near the average competition price. This is also a PI shaped fuzzy number but has a 15 percent band width. The narrower width means the allowable range of price values are held closer to the region near the average competition price.

```
      FuzzySet:    Near.CompPrice
    Description: Near (Around) Competition Price
 1.00                                    .
 0.90                                   . .
 0.80                                  .
 0.70                                    .
 0.60
 0.50                                 .
 0.40                                    .
 0.30
 0.20                              .        .
 0.10
 0.00..................................    ..........................
    0---|---|---|---|---|---|---|---|---|---|---|---|---|---|---|---|---0
    4.00    9.50   15.00   20.50   26.00   31.50   37.00   42.50   48.00
    Domained:        4.00 to      48.00
    AlphaCut:        0.10
```

Figure 5.21 The pricing model Near.CompPrice

These dynamic fuzzy sets cannot be defined as part of the price variable's term set since their center values are unknown until the model executes. By controlling the rise rate of the bell-curve—using other Gaussian forms such as the beta distribution, as an example—as well as the band width of the fuzzy set the region of allowable price values can be controlled. The wider the width of the bell curves the softer the restriction on the price value. The narrower the width of the bell curves, the harder the restriction on the price value.

Executing the New Product Pricing Model

The pricing model uses a simple feed forward fuzzy reasoning strategy. The model itself is composed of a main driver and a reasoning module that handles the actual fuzzy rule execution. The separate reasoning module is called a *policy*. Refer to "Price1.cpp (The Fuzzy Pricing Model Main Module)" on page 472 for the actual C++ code. Refer to "price1pl.cpp (The Fuzzy Pricing Model's Reasoning Policy)" on page 475 for the program code associated with the fuzzy reasoning policy. Since this is a rather large complex program, the Microsoft Visual C++ make file is also included (see "price1.mak (The Visual C++ 1.5 Make File for Price1.cpp)" on page 478.) Figure 5.22 shows the initialization and start-up processing for the model. This session displays the control parameters, the rules, and the empty output fuzzy set associated with the price variable.

```
FUZZY NEW PRODUCT PRICING MODEL[1]. (c) 1995 Metus Systems Group.
[Mean] Competition Price:     28.00
Base Manufacturing Costs:     15.00
The Rules:
Rule1   our price must be HIGH
Rule2   our price must be LOW
Rule3   our price must be AROUND 2*MFGCOSTS
Rule4   if the competition.price is NOT VERY HIGH
        then our price must be AROUND the COMPETITION.PRICE
(Price1Policy) New Product Pricing Estimation Policy Begins....
---MetusNote(003): Fuzzy Work Area Initialized
---Empty FuzzySet 'PRICE' created.
---MetusNote(005): Output Variable 'PRICE' added to Model.

        FuzzySet:    PRICE
        Description: The Estimated Product Price
    1.00
    0.90
    0.80
    0.70
    0.60
    0.50
    0.40
    0.30
    0.20
    0.10
    0.00.............................................................
      0---|---|---|---|---|---|---|---|---|---|---|---|---|---|---0
      4.00    9.50   15.00   20.50   26.00   31.50   37.00   42.50   48.00
      Domained:            4.00 to      48.00
      AlphaCut:            0.10
```

Figure 5.22 Price model initialization and start

An empty solution fuzzy set region is created for each output variable in a fuzzy modelling system. Each rule that specifies one of the solution variables combines its knowledge with the existing fuzzy set shape in ways determined by the type of correlation and the method of implication. Figure 5.23 shows the state of the PRICE fuzzy region after the first rule has been executed.

```
Rule1   our price must be HIGH

        FuzzySet:    PRICE
        Description: The Estimated Product Price
    1.00                                                         .
    0.90                                                   ......
    0.80                                              .......
    0.70                                        ......
    0.60                                  .......
    0.50                            ......
    0.40                      ......
    0.30                .......
    0.20          ......
    0.10    .......
    0.00......
      0---|---|---|---|---|---|---|---|---|---|---|---|---|---|---0
      4.00    9.50   15.00   20.50   26.00   31.50   37.00   42.50   48.00
      Domained:            4.00 to      48.00
      AlphaCut:            0.10
```

Figure 5.23 Pricing model after executing Rule 1

Since this is an unconditional fuzzy proposition and the output fuzzy region is empty, the rule of inference attempts to make the PRICE fuzzy region maximally true at each point along the membership function. The membership function assumes the truth value of HIGH for each point along the curve. Figure 5.24 shows the fuzzy set for PRICE after executing the second rule.

```
Rule2   our price must be LOW


       FuzzySet:    PRICE
       Description: The Estimated Product Price
  1.00
  0.90
  0.80
  0.70
  0.60
  0.50                                      .
  0.40                            ......  .......
  0.30                     .......              ......
  0.20              ......                           .......
  0.10       .......                                      ......
  0.00......                                                   ......
      0---|---|---|---|---|---|---|---|---|---|---|---|---|---0
      4.00    9.50   15.00   20.50   26.00   31.50   37.00   42.50   48.00
      Domained:          4.00 to      48.00
      AlphaCut:          0.10
```

Figure 5.24 Pricing model after executing Rule 2

The fuzzy regions specified in unconditional propositions are combined by taking the minimum or fuzzy intersection of the respective membership functions. Figure 5.24 shows the triangular region formed by the intersection of HIGH and LOW. The third rule uses one of the dynamically created fuzzy sets. This is a fuzzy number centered over twice the manufacturing costs. Figure 5.25 shows where this region is positioned over the current solution fuzzy set for PRICE.

```
  Domain [UofD]:        4.00 to      48.00
       1.00                                            .
       0.90                                        .. ..
       0.80                                      .       .
       0.70                                   .            .
       0.60                                 .
       0.50                               *             .
       0.40                       ****** .*******
       0.30               *******               ******
       0.20        ******                    .*******
       0.10  *******                  .              ******
       0.00******.....................................  .........******
      0---|---|---|---|---|---|---|---|---|---|---|---|---|---0
      4.00    9.50   15.00   20.50   26.00   31.50   37.00   42.50   48.00

      .   FuzzySet:    Near.2*MfgCosts
          Description: Near (Around) Twice MfgCosts
      *   FuzzySet:    PRICE
          Description: The Estimated Product Price
```

Figure 5.25 Near 2*MfgCost fuzzy set overlaid with Price

The third rule is also an unconditional fuzzy proposition so its results are combined with the existing PRICE fuzzy set by taking the minimum of the membership functions. As Figure 5.27 shows, the edges of the bell curve slice through the legs of the triangular fuzzy set leaving an area bounded by the slope of the manufacturing costs fuzzy set and the cross-over points of the HIGH and LOW fuzzy sets.

```
Domain [UofD]:       4.00 to      48.00
      1.00                                          .
      0.90                                       .. ..
      0.80                                     .        .
      0.70                                  .             .
      0.60                                .
      0.50                                               .
      0.40                          *******
      0.30                                      *****
      0.20                       *                       *
      0.10                     *                           *
      0.00****************************                       *****************
        0---|---|---|---|---|---|---|---|---|---|---|---|---|---|---|---0
        4.00    9.50   15.00   20.50   26.00   31.50   37.00   42.50   48.00

   .   FuzzySet:    Near.2*MfgCosts
       Description: Near (Around) Twice MfgCosts
   *   FuzzySet:    PRICE
       Description: The Estimated Product Price
```

Figure 5.26 Constraining Price with Near 2*MfgCost fuzzy set

This leaves a constricted region in the solution fuzzy set bounded by twice the manufacturing costs. Figure 5.27 shows the PRICE fuzzy region after the third rule has been applied.

```
Rule3    our price must be AROUND 2*MFGCOSTS

       FuzzySet:    PRICE
       Description: The Estimated Product Price
      1.00
      0.90
      0.80
      0.70
      0.60
      0.50
      0.40                               ........
      0.30                                        .....
      0.20                          .                   .
      0.10                        .                       .
      0.00.............................                   .................
        0---|---|---|---|---|---|---|---|---|---|---|---|---|---|---|---0
        4.00    9.50   15.00   20.50   26.00   31.50   37.00   42.50   48.00
       Domained:          4.00 to      48.00
       AlphaCut:          0.10
```

Figure 5.27 Pricing model after executing Rule 3

The fourth and last rule contains conditional expert knowledge. This is the kind of if-then intelligence normally found in expert and decision support systems. In a fuzzy expert system the unconditional rules (as an example, rules one through three) provide a support or default solution if none of the conditional rules have sufficient truth to fire. Conditional rules can only influence the outcome of a model if, in the same region of the solution space, they have more truth than the unconditionals or if they specify a region outside the area covered by the unconditionals.

Conditional rules are combined with the existing PRICE fuzzy set using the fuzzy union or maximum operator. In order to apply a conditional rule, we need to evaluate the truth of the predicate and use this to adjust the truth of the consequent. The predicate of this rule: competition.price is not very high involves computing the linguistic variable not very high. Figure 5.28 shows the first step, applying the hedge very to the fuzzy set HIGH.

```
Rule4    if the competition.price is NOT VERY HIGH
             then our price must be AROUND the COMPETITION.PRICE

         FuzzySet:    HIGH
         Description: very HIGH
     1.00                                                                    .
     0.90                                                                  ...
     0.80                                                               ...
     0.70                                                           ....
     0.60                                                       ....
     0.50                                                    .....
     0.40                                              ....
     0.30                                         ......
     0.20                                   ......
     0.10                          .........
     0.00.....................
         0---|---|---|---|---|---|---|---|---|---|---|---|---|---|---0
         4.00    9.50   15.00   20.50   26.00   31.50   37.00   42.50   48.00
         Domained:          4.00 to      48.00
         AlphaCut:          0.10
```

Figure 5.28 Applying the hedge VERY to the fuzzy set HIGH

When this new fuzzy region is formed, the negation or NOT operator is applied. The negation operator is treated as another hedge. Figure 5.29 shows the results of applying not to very HIGH. This is the new linguistic variable not very HIGH.

```
         FuzzySet:    HIGH
         Description: ZADEH NOT HIGH
     1.00.......
     0.90            ...............
     0.80                          ........
     0.70                                 ......
     0.60                                       ......
     0.50                                            ....
     0.40                                               .....
     0.30                                                    ....
     0.20                                                       ...
     0.10                                                          ....
     0.00                                                             ...
         0---|---|---|---|---|---|---|---|---|---|---|---|---|---|---0
         4.00    9.50   15.00   20.50   26.00   31.50   37.00   42.50   48.00
         Domained:          4.00 to      48.00
         AlphaCut:          0.10
```

Figure 5.29 Applying the hedge NOT to the fuzzy set HIGH

The value of the competition price ($28.00) is now mapped to this new fuzzy region. The `CompPrice` parameter has a membership of [.71] in the fuzzy set `not very HIGH`. We will use this value to scale the truth of the consequent. The consequent fuzzy proposition `price must be around the competition.price` involves combining the fuzzy number represented by the competition price with the current solution fuzzy set representing `PRICE`. Figure 5.30 shows the position of competition price fuzzy region on the `PRICE` fuzzy set.

```
Domain [UofD]:      4.00 to      48.00
       1.00                                            .
       0.90                                          . .
       0.80                                     .
       0.70                                       .
       0.60
       0.50                                 .
       0.40                              ********
       0.30                                     *****
       0.20                         *        .      *
       0.10                      *              *
       0.00****************************.        .......*****************
          0---|---|---|---|---|---|---|---|---|---|---|---|---|---0
          4.00    9.50   15.00   20.50   26.00   31.50   37.00   42.50   48.00
        .   FuzzySet:     Near.CompPrice
            Description: Near (Around) Competition Price
        *   FuzzySet:     PRICE
            Description: The Estimated Product Price
```

Figure 5.30 The Near.CompPrice fuzzy set overlaid with Price

A conditional fuzzy proposition's evidence is combined with the current solution fuzzy set using the fuzzy union operator. However, before the consequent fuzzy set is used, it is correlated with the truth of the premise. In this case the model is using correlation product so the `Near.CompPrice` fuzzy set is scaled by multiplying each membership value by the premise truth ([.71]). Figure 5.31 shows the `PRICE` solution fuzzy set after executing the final rule.

```
---RULE FIRED--Premise truth of:0.7075

        FuzzySet:     PRICE
        Description: The Estimated Product Price
    1.00
    0.90
    0.80
    0.70                                      .
    0.60                                   . .
    0.50                               .      .
    0.40                                    ..
    0.30                                       .....
    0.20                             .            .
    0.10                            .            .
    0.00...........................           ..................
        0---|---|---|---|---|---|---|---|---|---|---|---|---|---|---0
        4.00    9.50    15.00   20.50   26.00   31.50   37.00   42.50   48.00
        Domained:         4.00 to      48.00
        AlphaCut:         0.10
```

Figure 5.31 Pricing model after executing Rule 4

Interpreting the Combined Model Results

Figure 5.31 is the final shape of the fuzzy set associated with the PRICE solution variable. In order to find a recommended price position based on the combined evidence from the four rules, the fuzzy set must be defuzzified. Defuzzification is performed by finding the weighted average or center of gravity of the fuzzy set. Figure 5.32 shows the model's recommended price of $29.44 with a reasonable compatibility index of [.54].

```
    ---'CENTROID'     defuzzification. Value:     29.438, [0.5417]
    Model Solution:
        Price      =      29.44
        CIX        =      0.54
        SurfaceHght =     0.71
```

Figure 5.32 The defuzzified results from the Pricing model

Along with the defuzzified scalar results, the model also displays both the unit Compatibility Index (CIX) and the maximum surface height of the final solution fuzzy set. The compatibility index is the truth of the fuzzy set at the point of defuzzification while the surface height is the maximum height of the solution fuzzy set. This index provides an important measure of how well the model is performing. A very low unit compatibility indicates the truth of the rule predicates for the solution fuzzy sets covering this region of the output space was very low. For more information on this see "Performance Compatibility and Undecidable Models" on page 93.

Using Undefuzzified Model Results

In many business models the output from a policy is not defuzzified, rather, the fuzzy set is passed to another model segment or policy that regards the solution fuzzy set from a previous policy as a base fuzzy set in its own reasoning. Sales and marketing models, for instance, commonly contain policies that determine the disposal income of a customer that does not hold a store credit card based on spending habits, frequency of store visits, and similar attributes. As an example, these are rules from the target marketing system built for a large New York retailer:

```
[R1] disposableINC is NORMAL
[R2] if avg(purchasedollars(*,t-6)) are HIGH
         and avg(storevisits(*,t-6)) are FREQUENT
             then disposableINC is ABOVE.NORMAL
```

In the absence of any other evidence the model concludes the shopper's disposable income is NORMAL. Otherwise, (and this is only one of seventeen rules) if the average purchase dollars over the last six quarters were HIGH and the shopper's store visits during the same period were FREQUENT, then there is some evidence the customer's disposable income is above normal. In this particular model, the solution fuzzy set representing the expected value for the above normal income shoppers is not defuzzified but used by the sales targeting system to segregate catalogs, credit card invitations, and other solicitations.

Rapid Multiple Expert Prototyping with Fuzzy Systems

Fuzzy reasoning provides a flexible and fluid environment for re-modelling the system constraints imposed by multiple expert intelligence and the restrictions imposed by multiple reasoning criteria. The pricing model is an excellent example of the way in which changes in expert reasoning can be quickly transferred into the rule base. Rapid application development or protocycling makes the knowledge engineer and business analyst highly responsive to end-user feed-back as well as changes in the model logic discovered during construction and testing. In the pricing model, as an example, the manufacturing cost constraint:

```
[R3] our price must be near 2*MfgCosts;
```

seems unduly restrictive. Feed-back from the manufacturing manager indicates that she did not mean, in the absence of other evidence, the price should be centered around twice the manufacturing costs, but that the price should be at least twice the manufacturing costs. This can be changed simply by adding the hedge above in front of the linguistic specification near 2*MfgCosts.

```
FUZZY NEW PRODUCT PRICING MODEL[2]. (c) 1995 Metus Systems Group.
[Mean] Competition Price:     28.00
Base Manufacturing Costs:     12.50
The Rules:
Rule1   our price must be HIGH
Rule2   our price must be LOW
```

```
Rule3    our price must be ABOVE AROUND 2*MFGCOSTS
Rule4    if the competition.price is NOT VERY HIGH
              then our price must be AROUND the COMPETITION.PRICE
(Price1Policy) New Product Pricing Estimation Policy Begins....
MetusNote(003): Fuzzy Work Area Initialized
Empty FuzzySet 'PRICE' created.
MetusNote(005): Output Variable 'PRICE' added to Model.
```

Figure 5.33 Starting a pricing model with new MfgCosts constraint criteria

The above hedge slices through a bell-shaped fuzzy set with a curve that starts at the center and moves upward. The membership of the above curve, as shown in Figure 5.34, is minimum at the target fuzzy set's center (which has [1.0] membership) and is maximum when the left edge of the slope is zero [0.0].

```
Domain [UofD]:       4.00 to     48.00
     1.00                                      ..            ***************************
     0.90                                  .  .        *
     0.80                                .     .     *
     0.70                              .          .
     0.60                                             *
     0.50                            .              .
     0.40                                         *
     0.30                          .            .
     0.20                                     *
     0.10                                   *
     0.00*********************************        .         ...........................
         0---|---|---|---|---|---|---|---|---|---|---|---|---|---|---|---0
         4.00    9.50   15.00   20.50   26.00   31.50   37.00   42.50   48.00

    .    FuzzySet:    Near.2*MfgCosts
         Description: Near (Around) Twice MfgCosts
    *    FuzzySet:    Near.2*MfgCosts
         Description: above Near.2*MfgCosts
```

Figure 5.34 Near.2*MfgCosts and Above Near.2*MfgCosts fuzzy sets

After applying the above hedge, the current PRICE solution fuzzy set is clipped by the new linguistic variable. This truncates the PRICE fuzzy set to the left of the center of the about 2*MfgCosts fuzzy set. Figure 5.35 shows how the complete curve for *above about twice the manufacturing costs* cuts the HIGH and LOW price fuzzy set.

```
Domain [UofD]:       4.00 to     48.00
     1.00                                                  ***************************
     0.90                                       *
     0.80                                     *
     0.70
     0.60                                   *
     0.50
     0.40                                *....
     0.30                                      ......
     0.20                              *           .......
     0.10                            *                       ......
     0.00*********************************                          ......
         0---|---|---|---|---|---|---|---|---|---|---|---|---|---|---|---0
         4.00    9.50   15.00   20.50   26.00   31.50   37.00   42.50   48.00

    .    FuzzySet:    PRICE
         Description: The Estimated Product Price
    *    FuzzySet:    Near.2*MfgCosts
         Description: above Near.2*MfgCosts
```

Figure 5.35 The Price fuzzy set clipped by Above about 2*MfgCosts

When the third rule has been executed, the PRICE solution fuzzy set has been truncated to the left so that the current preponderance of evidence for the price is located on the right of the PRICE fuzzy set's domain. Figure 5.36 shows how this new fuzzy set for PRICE appears.

```
Rule3   our price must be ABOVE ABOUT 2*MFGCOSTS

          FuzzySet:    PRICE
          Description: The Estimated Product Price
       1.00
       0.90
       0.80
       0.70
       0.60
       0.50
       0.40                                           .....
       0.30                                              ......
       0.20                                    .             .......
       0.10                               .                      ......
       0.00.................................               .           ......
          0---|---|---|---|---|---|---|---|---|---|---|---|---|---|---|---|---0
          4.00     9.50     15.00    20.50    26.00    31.50    37.00    42.50    48.00
          Domained:           4.00 to       48.00
          AlphaCut:           0.10
```

Figure 5.36 Price model after executing Rule 3

The final rule is executed in the same manner as the before, starting with the formation of the linguistic variable not very HIGH. The membership of the average competition price ($28.00) in the new fuzzy set is determined ([.71]). Using this value the consequent fuzzy proposition, price must be around the competition.price is scaled and combined with the current PRICE fuzzy set. Figure 5.37 shows how this appears.

```
Rule4    if the competition.price is NOT VERY HIGH
            then our price must be AROUND the COMPETITION.PRICE
---RULE FIRED--Premise truth of:0.7075

Domain [UofD]:        4.00 to       48.00
          1.00                                         .
          0.90                                        . .
          0.80                                      .
          0.70                                       .
          0.60
          0.50                                 .
          0.40                              *****
          0.30                                  ******
          0.20                      .    *      .     *******
          0.10*******************************   *            .    ******
          0.00*******************************        *            .................******
          0---|---|---|---|---|---|---|---|---|---|---|---|---|---|---|---0
          4.00     9.50     15.00    20.50    26.00    31.50    37.00    42.50    48.00

     .    FuzzySet:    Near.CompPrice
          Description: Near (Around) Competition Price
     *    FuzzySet:    PRICE
          Description: The Estimated Product Price
```

Figure 5.37 Overlaying the scaled around CompPrice with the PRICE fuzzy set

Figure 5.38, reflecting the new evidence from the manufacturing expert, shows the final fuzzy region produced by change in the third rule. The PRICE solution fuzzy set is skewed toward the right with a small counter-balance associated with the constraint criteria that the final price be near the average competition price.

```
FuzzySet:    PRICE
Description: The Estimated Product Price
1.00
0.90
0.80
0.70                                          .
0.60                                       . .
0.50                                    .  .
0.40                                       ..
0.30                              .        ......
0.20                                              .......
0.10                         .                    ......
0.00...................................                  ......
    0---|---|---|---|---|---|---|---|---|---|---|---|---|---|---|---|---0
    4.00    9.50    15.00   20.50   26.00   31.50   37.00   42.50   48.00
    Domained:          4.00 to      48.00
    AlphaCut:          0.10

---'CENTROID'    defuzzification. Value:      32.016, [0.3658]
Model Solution:
  Price      =      32.02
  CIX        =       0.37
  SurfaceHght =      0.71
---MetusNote(009): Fuzzy Work Area Closed.
```

Figure 5.38 The final PRICE fuzzy set and recommended price value

The center of gravity defuzzification generates a recommended product price of ≈$32.00. This value is balanced between the fuzzy regions showing evidence for a price near the competition and above twice the manufacturing costs. It is easy to see from these examples, that fuzzy models can combine the expertise and constraint criteria from many experts into a singe, robust model. The ability to add rules supporting additional criteria, as well as the ability to change existing rules to reflect peer rankings, new semantic meanings for model parameters, and changes in the criteria constraints on the model performance gives the business analyst and knowledge engineer a powerful analytical tool.

Combining Multiple Fuzzy Models

In the previous section we looked at multiple expert intelligence expressed as individual rules in a single fuzzy rule set (such as the new product pricing model). Complex business systems are often built around multiple fuzzy models representing the combined intelligence of several experts. Instead of individual rules, a package of rules, formulated by a single expert[2], evaluates the data space and produces a solution. These fuzzy systems consider the same set of data elements but produce different recommendations. Additionally, when several experts produce a package of knowledge, the value of that knowledge is tied to the peer ranking of the originating expert. In this section we examine ways in which fuzzy models themselves are combined and how this combination takes peer ranking into consideration.

The Project Risk Assessment System

Today's rapid changes in computer and industrial technologies, the inability to adequately capitalize research and development, and the high attrition rate of technically competent employees have far reaching implications for moderate to high technology projects. Indeed, project failure or extensive slippage has become commonplace and almost expected. Experienced project managers, technical analysts, and middle level corporate executives all have perspectives on what constitutes a high risk and a low risk project. Encoding this knowledge in a project risk assessment system would allow both senior executives and staff officers (not to mention project managers themselves) to evaluate and weigh the trade-offs between merit and risk in a collection of proposed projects. In fact, understanding the nature of risk is essential in prioritizing and capitalizing projects. The level of risk is often a factor in adjusting the hurdle threshold for a project's Net Present Value (NPV) requirement (see, as an example, "The Net Present Value (NPV) Risk Hurdle Threshold" on page 209). Calculating risk is an ideal fuzzy system since the nature of project risk involves many complex, highly nonlinear, and imprecise variables. Since risk is often tightly coupled to corporate culture as well as the ideas of macro-economic conditions, technological certainty, and available, stable skills, fuzzy reasoning provides the semantic flexibility, representational depth, and evidential reasoning needed to model this general class of problems. The idea of project risk assessment, as a component of a larger project and enterprise management system, was previously discussed in Chapter 3. Fuzzy SQL and Database Systems, "Intelligent Project Management and Risk Assessment" on page 206.

---

2. More precisely, the package represents a single expertise. This expertise may result from the combined knowledge of several individual experts, although the over-all effect is a rule set that reflects the common and consensual knowledge of the expert or set of experts.

The System Organization and Design

This project risk system supports a collection of independent fuzzy models (or *policies*). Each fuzzy model contains the cohesive expert judgment about the risk of funding a project with a particular set of properties. In the real world of decision support, the knowledge of one expert is often preferred to the knowledge of another expert. This is reflected in the peer standing of one expert over another. Thus, we would like the judgement of a favored peer to carry more weight than the judgement of a less experienced or less favored expert. The risk assessment model implements this concept by carrying an ordered vector of peer weights. This weighting, in the range [0,1] inclusive, is used to adjust the contribution strength of the fuzzy model. This weight is used in two different ways depending on the type of combination process. Figure 5.39 shows an overview schematic of the project risk assessment system using average weighting and its multiple expert system components.

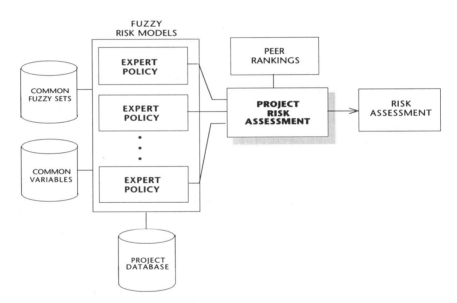

Figure 5.39 The weighted average project risk assessment system overview

Each expert system or fuzzy policy is executed as a stand-alone component. The results of the policy—the defuzzified value for risk—is used by the risk assessment manager to derive a final value on a scale between zero and one hundred. This is done by computing an average of the recommendations weighted by the peer ranking.

A second approach to risk assessment, shown in Figure 5.40, involves combining expert intelligence inside the model. In this architecture, the output from each fuzzy model is collected and aggregated using the additive method. The result of this aggregation, a final outcome fuzzy set, is then defuzzified using the center of gravity technique to produce a risk assessment measure.

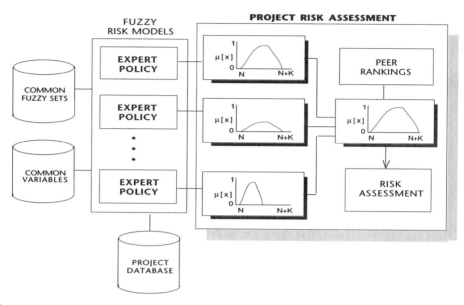

Figure 5.40 Project risk assessment the combined intelligence model overview

Our project risk system, simplified to illustrate the concepts of combining fuzzy models, considers three primary variables: the project duration in work days, the project budget in thousands of dollars, and the level of project staffing. The system is started by issuing the projrsk1 (weighted average) or the projrsk2 (combined intelligence) command. Refer to "projrsk1.cpp (The Weighted Average Risk Model)" on page 481 and "projrsk2.cpp (The Combined Intelligence Project Risk Model)" on page 490 for the complete program code. The peer weighting vector is entered at run-time after the module name. As an example:

```
projrsk2 .7 .4
```

One decimal value for each fuzzy policy in the system (in our example program, there are two project management experts). Executing the projrsk1 or projrsk2 module starts the model and asks for the project profile properties.

```
THE PROJECT RISK ASSESSMENT MODEL  (c)1995 Metus Systems
Enter Project Properties:
Enter the Project Duration    :100
Enter the Project Budget      :650
Enter the Project Staffing    :40
Model Finished.
```

The system output is written to the model log file (md1log.fil) on the work drive. This is normally the a: drive, but its destination can be changed by altering the specifications in the SysConnecttoMetus or the SysConnecttoFMS functions.)

The Project Risk Fuzzy Sets

Underlying the risk assessment model are the fuzzy sets for each of the variables. These fuzzy sets define the semantics of the model. Figure 5.41 shows the term set for the project duration variable. Project time spans are evaluated from zero to 200 working days, nearly a full year; there are approximately 220 working days in a typical year. Project times range from BRIEF, ten days or less, to LONG, projects over 90 days.

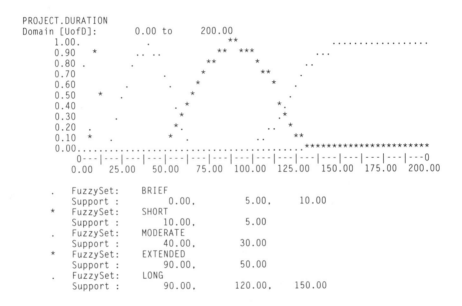

Figure 5.41 The project duration fuzzy sets

Another important factor in determining the over-all risk of a project is the allocated budget. Figure 5.42 shows the fuzzy sets associated with the project budget. Budgets range from MINOR, projects less than $100,000, to MAJOR, projects above $800,00 to one million dollars. Although the shouldering fuzzy sets are left and right facing S-curves, the main terms consist of narrowly flanged trapezoidal fuzzy sets. The trapezoidal nature of these sets reflects the organizational perception that budgeting allocation falls into clusters or ranges of committed dollars.

```
PROJECT.BUDGET
Domain [UofD]:        0.00 to    1200.00
     1.00.     *****   .............     *************            .............
     0.90 .    *       .               . *               *           . .
     0.80          *                                             .
     0.70 .
     0.60
     0.50      *        .              *              *        .
     0.40          *                                          .
     0.30 .
     0.20                                                   .
     0.10     *.    .  *            *  .                 .
     0.00......................................................*******************
         0---|---|---|---|---|---|---|---|---|---|---|---|---|---|---|---0
         0.00  150.00  300.00  450.00  600.00  750.00  900.00 1050.00 1200.00

    .    FuzzySet:    MINOR
         Support :         0.00,       50.00,     100.00
    *    FuzzySet:    LOW
         Support :        50.00,      100.00,     200.00,     250.00
    .    FuzzySet:    MEDIUM
         Support :       200.00,      250.00,     500.00,     550.00
    *    FuzzySet:    HIGH
         Support :       500.00,      550.00,     800.00,     850.00
    .    FuzzySet:    MAJOR
         Support :       800.00,      900.00,    1000.00
```

Figure 5.42 The project budget fuzzy sets

The third factor in the risk assessment model is the level of staffing associated with a project. Figure 5.43 shows the fuzzy sets for the staffing variable.

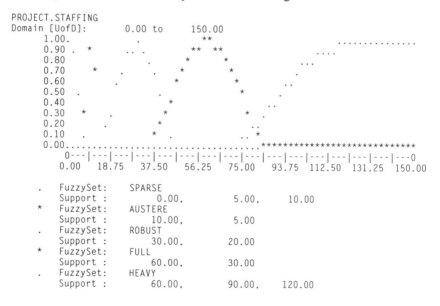

```
PROJECT.STAFFING
Domain [UofD]:        0.00 to     150.00
     1.00.          .          **                    .............
     0.90 .   *     . .       **  **                 . . . .
     0.80                 .       *       *              . . . .
     0.70     *      .        .    *         *           . . .
     0.60                .         *            *      . .
     0.50 .                    .              *
     0.40                      *                        . .
     0.30     *      .            *              *       . .
     0.20            .                *                 . .
     0.10 .                   *    .             .  *
     0.00.............................................****************************
         0---|---|---|---|---|---|---|---|---|---|---|---|---|---|---|---0
         0.00   18.75   37.50   56.25   75.00   93.75  112.50  131.25  150.00

    .    FuzzySet:    SPARSE
         Support :         0.00,        5.00,      10.00
    *    FuzzySet:    AUSTERE
         Support :        10.00,        5.00
    .    FuzzySet:    ROBUST
         Support :        30.00,       20.00
    *    FuzzySet:    FULL
         Support :        60.00,       30.00
    .    FuzzySet:    HEAVY
         Support :        60.00,       90.00,     120.00
```

Figure 5.43 The project staffing fuzzy sets

Too little staffing and the project risk is increased and, somewhat paradoxically, too much staffing and the project risk is also increased. Finally, the degree of risk associated with the project is measured on the psychometric scale of [0,100]. Figure 5.44 shows the fuzzy sets underlying the idea of risk. A value of zero indicates no risk, while a value of 100 indicates extremely high (intolerable) risk.

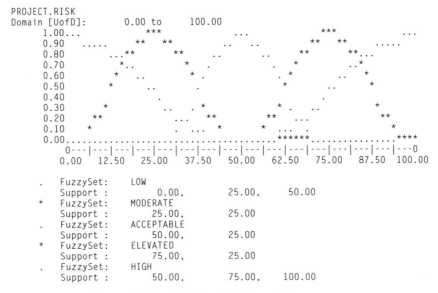

Figure 5.44 The Project Risk Fuzzy Sets

In this risk assessment model, all the sub-expert systems—the policies—share the same fuzzy set vocabulary. By sharing a common set of variable and fuzzy set definitions, the organization insures the experts are making their judgments on the same semantic foundation. Shared fuzzy sets are not a requirement of combinable fuzzy systems; in fact, each policy could have its own fuzzy vocabulary or just partly over-ride the common sets with its own definitions for specific rule sets.

Combination Through Weighted Output Averaging

Averaging fuzzy model output is the easiest and most straight-forward way of combining expert intelligence. We can combine the peer ranking of each fuzzy model to produce a biased or weighted average of the system results. Equation 5.6 shows the method used to calculate this weighted result.

$$R_i = \frac{\sum\limits_{i=1}^{N} S_i \times P_i}{\sum\limits_{i=1}^{N} P_i}$$

Equation 5.6 The weighted (biased) of combined fuzzy systems

The system result (R_i) is determined as the ratio of the scaled individual model results and the peer rankings. In particular, we sum the product of the individual model solutions (S_i) and the peer ranking of the model (P_i). This is then divided by the sum of the model peer rankings. When all P_i values are one [1.0], then the standard mean of the individual model solutions is computed.

Weighted Model Policy Execution

There are two experts and two policies in the project risk assessment model that determine the expected risk associated with capitalizing a project given its anticipated duration, budget, and staffing. The first policy, developed by Bill Smith, a senior project manager, contains four rules:

```
if project.duration is long then risk is acceptable;
if project.duration is extended then risk is elevated;
if project.budget is high then risk is elevated;
if project.staffing is full then risk is high;
```

These four rules adjust risk upward, placing more emphasis on the problem of over staffing. The second policy, developed by Mary Williams, the marketing division's research manager, contains three rules:

```
if project.duration is long then risk is elevated;
if project.budget is high then risk is acceptable;
if project.staffing is full then risk is elevated;
```

Mary's analysis of risk tends to put more emphasis on duration and less on other factors. As an example, while Bill Smith judges that a LONG duration presents an ACCEPT-ABLE risk, Mary Williams judges that the same LONG duration produces an ELEVATED risk. We observe when duration is slightly reduced, the first expert actually increases risk, following a general theory that shorter projects have less recovery time and thus involve increased risk.

> In discussing the ability to combine multiple fuzzy systems we annotate the execution of the rules for the initial policy executions. In subsequent sections, the model execution is previewed only where it is important to the current context. Note also that there is a slight difference between the rule contents in the weighted average and the combined intelligence models.

These policies are executed independently of each other and the results combined to produce a final system risk recommendation. Figure 5.45 shows the data elements in the weighted model execution. No ranking vector is specified so the expert weights are all set equal to one.

```
projrsk1

PROJECT DATA
   Duration     :      100.00
   Budget       :      650.00
   Staffing     :       40.00
```

Figure 5.45 Execution data summary

In Figure 5.46 we see the results of executing the initial two rules of the policy. The first rule fails since the membership of 100 work days in the fuzzy set LONG is extremely low and falls below the alpha cut threshold. The second rule, however, has a very high membership in the fuzzy set EXTENDED and updates the RISK solution fuzzy region with the ELEVATED term correlated at the [.92] membership grade.

```
-----------------------------------------------------------------
 Risk Assessment Policy [Expert: BILL.SMITH] begins.
-----------------------------------------------------------------
[R1]  if project.duration is long then risk is acceptable;
---RULE FAILS. Premise truth of 0.0556 is below alpha threshold: 0.1000
[R2]  if project.duration is extended then risk is elevated;
---RULE FIRED--Premise truth of:0.9200

       FuzzySet:     RISK
   1.00
   0.90                                        .....
   0.80                                     ..      ..
   0.70                                   .           .
   0.60                                 .               .
   0.50                                .                 .
   0.40                              .                     .
   0.30                            .                         .
   0.20                          .                             .
   0.10                        ..                                ..
   0.00........................                                    ....
       0---|---|---|---|---|---|---|---|---|---|---|---|---|---|---|---0
       0.00   12.50   25.00   37.50   50.00   62.50   75.00   87.50  100.00
       Domained:           0.00  to      100.00
```

Figure 5.46 Output risk fuzzy set after executing Rules [R1] and [R2]

Risk is now fairly high. Figure 5.47 shows the state of the RISK fuzzy set after executing the third rule. The consequent of this rule specifies the same output fuzzy set. Since the truth of this rule is greater than the previous rule, its effect is to re-enforce the risk at this domain level.

```
[R3]  if project.budget is high then risk is elevated;
---RULE FIRED--Premise truth of:1.0000

     FuzzySet:     RISK
  1.00                                                        ...
  0.90                                                     ..    ..
  0.80                                                  ..         ..
  0.70                                                 .             .
  0.60                                                .               .
  0.50                                               .                 .
  0.40                                              .                   .
  0.30                                             .                     .
  0.20                                           ..                       ..
  0.10                                          .                          ..
  0.00.......................................  .                            ....
     0---|---|---|---|---|---|---|---|---|---|---|---|---|---|---|---0
     0.00    12.50   25.00   37.50   50.00   62.50   75.00   87.50  100.00
     Domained:              0.00 to       100.00
```

Figure 5.47 Output risk fuzzy set after executing Rules [R3]

Figure 5.48 shows the state of the RISK solution fuzzy set after the last rule has been executed. Since the proposition project.staffing is full is only marginally true, the fuzzy set HIGH is correlated at the [.22] level. This is applied to the output RISK fuzzy set causing a slight right-hand skew.

```
[R4]  if project.staffing is full then risk is high;
---RULE FIRED--Premise truth of:0.2153

     FuzzySet:     RISK
  1.00                                                    ...
  0.90                                                 ..    ..
  0.80                                              ..         ..
  0.70                                             .             .
  0.60                                            .               .
  0.50                                           .                 .
  0.40                                          .                   .
  0.30                                         .                     .
  0.20                                       ..                       .......
  0.10                                      .
  0.00.......................................  .
     0---|---|---|---|---|---|---|---|---|---|---|---|---|---|---|---0
     0.00    12.50   25.00   37.50   50.00   62.50   75.00   87.50  100.00
     Domained:              0.00 to       100.00
```

Figure 5.48 Output risk fuzzy set after executing Rules [R4]

The final shape of the RISK solution fuzzy set is shown in Figure 5.48 after the execution of the last rule. This set must be defuzzified in order to derive an actual risk assessment value for the policy. The center of gravity or centroid technique is used to find the fuzzy set's expected value. Figure 5.49 shows that Risk has a value of 75.78 with a compatibility index of [1.0].

```
---'CENTROID' defuzzification. Value: 75.781, [0.9980]
Model Solution:
  Risk        =      75.78
  CompIdx     =       1.00
  SurfaceHght =       1.00
```

Figure 5.49 Defuzzifying RISK in the first policy

In a system of multiple fuzzy models, each model or policy is executed independently and the results saved for the aggregation process. Figure 5.50 shows the execution profile of the second policy in the risk assessment system. There are only three rules in this policy.

```
-----------------------------------------------------------------
Risk Assessment Policy [Expert: MARY.WILLIAMS] begins.
-----------------------------------------------------------------
[R1]  if project.duration is long then risk is elevated;
---RULE FAILS. Premise truth of 0.0556 is below alpha threshold: 0.1000
[R2]  if project.budget is high then risk is acceptable;
---RULE FIRED--Premise truth of:1.0000

        FuzzySet:    RISK
   1.00                                      ...
   0.90                                   ..    ..
   0.80                                 ..        ..
   0.70                               .            .
   0.60                                             .
   0.50                             .                .
   0.40
   0.30                           .                   .
   0.20                         ..                     ..
   0.10                        .                         .
   0.00...................    .                           ....................
       0---|---|---|---|---|---|---|---|---|---|---|---|---|---|---|---0
       0.00   12.50   25.00   37.50   50.00   62.50   75.00   87.50 100.00
       Domained:           0.00 to       100.00


[R3]  if project.staffing is full then risk is elevated;
---RULE FIRED--Premise truth of:0.2153

        FuzzySet:    RISK
   1.00                                      ...
   0.90                                   ..    ..
   0.80                                 ..        ..
   0.70                               .            .
   0.60                             .                .
   0.50                             .                .
   0.40
   0.30                           .                   .
   0.20                         ..                     ..........
   0.10                        .                            .....
   0.00...................                                      ........
       0---|---|---|---|---|---|---|---|---|---|---|---|---|---|---|---0
       0.00   12.50   25.00   37.50   50.00   62.50   75.00   87.50 100.00
       Domained:           0.00 to       100.00

---'CENTROID' defuzzification. Value: 53.125, [0.9688]
Model Solution:
  Risk        =      53.13
  CompIdx     =       0.97
  SurfaceHght =       1.00
```

Figure 5.50 Execution of the Second Policy (without comments)

The execution of the second fuzzy model produces a risk assessment somewhat lower than the risk developed from the first model. Both have approximately the same compatibility index. If the compatibility index values for the solution variables are significantly different, they could be used to scale the results, thus taking into account the degree of truth in the answer. Equation 5.7 shows how to adjust the solution for low compatibility scores.

$$R_i = \frac{\displaystyle\sum_{i=1}^{N} (S_i \times C_i) \times P_i}{\displaystyle\sum_{i=1}^{N} P_i}$$

Equation 5.7 Weighted (biased) averaging with compatibility scaling for combined systems

From a practical standpoint, however, care must be exercised in using the compatibility index in combination with the peer ranking since this process often results in an ordinal scaling that pushes the solution variables close to zero. A more constructive approach to solution truth management generally means monitoring the model output for acceptable degrees of compatibility—using the index as a filter on the utility of the model itself.

Combining Model Results Using Weighted Average

When both fuzzy policies have been executed, the results can be combined. Figure 5.51 shows the results of applying the peer adjusted weighted average to the model outcomes.

```
EXPERT PEER RANKINGS:
   Expert BILL.SMITH        Rank:       1.000
   Expert MARY.WILLIAMS     Rank:       1.000
INDIVIDUAL MODEL RESULTS:
   Expert BILL.SMITH        Risk:       75.78  [0.9980]
   Expert MARY.WILLIAMS     Risk:       53.13  [0.9688]
- - - - - - - - - - - - - - - - - - - - - - - - - - - - - - - - - -
   Average  Risk Assessment    :        64.45
   WgtdAvg  Risk Assessment    :        64.45
```

Figure 5.51 The weighted average combination with peer ranking=[1,1]

In this system execution, because the peer rankings are both [1.0], the average and the weighted average results are identical. When we change the peer rankings associated with each of the component fuzzy expert systems, the recommendation begins to reflect the preferred model. Figure 5.52 shows the results of executing the same risk assessment model with different peer ranking.

```
EXPERT PEER RANKINGS:
   Expert BILL.SMITH      Rank:      0.700
   Expert MARY.WILLIAMS   Rank:      0.400
INDIVIDUAL MODEL RESULTS:
   Expert BILL.SMITH      Risk:      75.78  [0.9980]
   Expert MARY.WILLIAMS   Risk:      53.13  [0.9688]
-----------------------------------------------
   Average  Risk Assessment   :      64.45
   WgtdAvg  Risk Assessment   :      67.54
```

Figure 5.52 The weighted average combination with peer ranking=[.7,.4]

By changing the peer weights we can bias the recommendation for or against a particular set of models. Figure 5.53, as an example, shows the results of making the first expert the most credible and the second expert minimally credible.

```
EXPERT PEER RANKINGS:
   Expert BILL.SMITH      Rank:      1.000
   Expert MARY.WILLIAMS   Rank:      0.400
INDIVIDUAL MODEL RESULTS:
   Expert BILL.SMITH      Risk:      75.78  [0.9980]
   Expert MARY.WILLIAMS   Risk:      53.13  [0.9688]
-----------------------------------------------
   Average  Risk Assessment   :      64.45
   WgtdAvg  Risk Assessment   :      69.31
```

Figure 5.53 The weighted average combination with peer ranking=[.1,.4]

The mean weighted risk now moves closer to the base recommendation from the first expert system. Figure 5.54 shows the results of reversing the expert peer ranking and, as you would expect, the expected risk value moves closer to the base risk developed from the second expert system.

```
EXPERT PEER RANKINGS:
   Expert BILL.SMITH      Rank:      0.400
   Expert MARY.WILLIAMS   Rank:      1.000
INDIVIDUAL MODEL RESULTS:
   Expert BILL.SMITH      Risk:      75.78  [0.9980]
   Expert MARY.WILLIAMS   Risk:      53.13  [0.9688]
-----------------------------------------------
   Average  Risk Assessment   :      64.45
   WgtdAvg  Risk Assessment   :      59.60
```

Figure 5.54 The weighted average combination with peer ranking=[.4,1]

Combination through Fuzzy Set Aggregation

In the weighted average method we combine the results from multiple fuzzy models after the defuzzification process. In other words, we have reduced the amount of available information in the model to a single scalar. This single point in the fuzzy hyperspace representing the cartesian product of the rule matrix carries only two dimensions of information: the expected domain value (the horizontal displacement in the fuzzy set) and the value's degree of membership in the output fuzzy set (the vertical displacement in the fuzzy set). Repeated combinations of fuzzy models at this level tends to increase the overall information entropy associated with the entire system. That is, the amount of disorder in the system (lost information) increases as we average the results of many independent fuzzy models. For a related topic, also see "Propagation of Fuzzy Entropy" on page 107.

The Combined Intelligence Approach

An alternate way of combining fuzzy models involves the maintenance of information in the complete system. This maintenance is achieved by combining the solution fuzzy regions using the additive aggregation method before defuzzification. In this way the complete topology of the fuzzy output space is preserved. The multiple fuzzy models or expert policies are executed, producing an output fuzzy region corresponding to the solution variables in their respective models. Instead of defuzzifying these solution fuzzy sets, they are scaled by the expert's peer ranking and then aggregated using the bounded-sum method of the additive implication method. Equation 5.8 shows how the solution fuzzy sets (S_i) are adjusted by the individual peer rankings (P_i).

$$\mu_{S_i}[x] = \bigvee_{i=1}^{N} \mu_{S_i}[x] \times P_i$$

Equation 5.8 Peer scaling of the solution fuzzy sets

After each solution set has been scaled by the peer ranking, the output fuzzy set containing the aggregation of all the solutions is formed. Equation 5.9 shows how this output fuzzy region is created.

$$\mu_{out_i}[x] = \bigvee_{i=1}^{n} \min((\mu_{out_i}[x] + \mu_{S_i}[x]), 1)$$

Equation 5.9 Aggregation of peer-scaled solution fuzzy sets

With this technique, the full width and height of the component fuzzy sets are maintained by the system and applied to the final solution. Defuzzification is performed on the combined results. Since the individual model solution fuzzy sets are scaled by the peer ranking before being aggregated into the combined output fuzzy sets, experts with low peer credibility have their contributions proportionally reduced. In this way, the combined intelligence method preserves expert knowledge and helps reduce the over-all information entropy of the system.

Combined Intelligence Policy Execution

Like the weighted average approach, these policies are executed independently of each other and the results combined to produce a final system risk recommendation. This combination, however, does not involve defuzzification of the individual solution fuzzy sets. Figure 5.55 shows the data elements in the weighted model execution. No ranking vector is specified so the expert weights are all set equal to one.

```
projrskl

PROJECT DATA
  Duration    :      110.00
  Budget      :      700.00
  Staffing    :       40.00
```

Figure 5.55 Execution data summary

The details of the actual model execution are not included in this discussion since they are similar to the rule execution logic in the weighted average approach (differing only by the fuzzy set placements due to slightly different data points). Figure 5.56 shows the solution fuzzy set from the first (Bill Smith) expert system.

```
------------------------------------------------------------------
 Risk Assessment Policy [Expert: BILL.SMITH] begins.
------------------------------------------------------------------

        FuzzySet:     RISK
     1.00                                              ...
     0.90                                           ..    ..
     0.80                                         ..        ..
     0.70                                        .            .
     0.60                                       .              .
     0.50                                      .                .
     0.40
     0.30                                    .                    .
     0.20                          ..........                      .......
     0.10                          .....
     0.00......................
        0---|---|---|---|---|---|---|---|---|---|---|---|---|---|---0
        0.00   12.50   25.00   37.50   50.00   62.50   75.00   87.50  100.00
        Domained:              0.00 to     100.00
        AlphaCut:              0.10
```

Figure 5.56 The risk solution fuzzy set for the first policy

Risk is centered around the high end of the scale with a small skew toward the left and the right. Figure 5.57 shows the solution fuzzy set from the second (Mary Williams) expert system.

```
------------------------------------------------------------------
Risk Assessment Policy [Expert: MARY.WILLIAMS] begins.
------------------------------------------------------------------

      FuzzySet:     RISK
 1.00                                    ...
 0.90                                 ..    ..
 0.80                              ..          ..
 0.70                            .                .
 0.60                          .                    .
 0.50                         .                      .
 0.40
 0.30                       .                          .
 0.20                .........                          .........
 0.10           .....                                           .....
 0.00........                                                        ........
     0---|---|---|---|---|---|---|---|---|---|---|---|---|---|---|---|---0
     0.00    12.50    25.00    37.50    50.00    62.50    75.00    87.50  100.00
     Domained:         0.00 to      100.00
     AlphaCut:         0.10
```

Figure 5.57 The risk solution fuzzy set for the second policy

Using the additive aggregation approach, the two fuzzy solution sets are combined to form a composite representation of the recommendation. Because no ranking vector was indicated, the fuzzy sets are not scaled before this composition. Figure 5.58 shows the results of merging the two solution fuzzy sets.

```
      FuzzySet:     CombinedRisk
      Description: Combined Risk Output Fuzzy Sets
 1.00                             .......................
 0.90                           .                          .
 0.80                          .                            .
 0.70                        .                                .
 0.60                      .                                    .
 0.50
 0.40
 0.30                    .                                        .
 0.20             .........                                        .......
 0.10        .....
 0.00........
     0---|---|---|---|---|---|---|---|---|---|---|---|---|---|---|---|---0
     0.00    12.50    25.00    37.50    50.00    62.50    75.00    87.50  100.00
     Domained:         0.00 to      100.00
     AlphaCut:         0.10
```

Figure 5.58 The aggregated combined risk fuzzy set (no peer ranking)

The two sets are added to indicate a general area of risk. By adding the fuzzy regions instead of adding the results, the total system information is available for use. This reduces loss of information over a larger number of individual contributing models. This final, combined fuzzy set is then defuzzified to produce the expected risk assessment. Figure 5.59 shows the results of the aggregation and defuzzification of the combined fuzzy set. The results of each expert policy are also shown.

```
04/30/1995  5.56pm---'CENTROID' defuzzification. Value: 60.938, [1.0000]
EXPERT PEER RANKINGS:
   Expert BILL.SMITH        Rank:      1.000
   Expert MARY.WILLIAMS     Rank:      1.000
INDIVIDUAL MODEL RESULTS:
   Expert BILL.SMITH        Risk:      72.66  [0.9824]
   Expert MARY.WILLIAMS     Risk:      50.00  [1.0000]
- - - - - - - - - - - - - - - - - - - - - - - - - - - - - -
   Average  Risk Assessment    :       61.33
   WgtdAvg  Risk Assessment    :       61.33
COMBINED MODEL RESULTS:
   Combined Risk Assessment    :       60.94  [1.0000]
   Combined Risk Height        :        1.0000
```

Figure 5.59 The combined intelligence risk assessment with peer ranking=[1,1]

In this particular example, with peer rankings equal to [1.0] for both expert systems, the results from combining and then defuzzifying the fuzzy sets are nearly the same as the weighted average risk assessment. This convergence is expected since the center of gravity finds the weighted average of the combined fuzzy set. The situation changes when we apply peer ranking to the source fuzzy sets. Figure 5.60 shows the combined fuzzy region when the individual peer rankings on the component fuzzy models are .8 and .3, respectively.

```
FuzzySet:    CombinedRisk
Description: Combined Risk Output Fuzzy Sets
1.00
0.90
0.80                                           .......
0.70                                   ..             ..
0.60                                ..                   .
0.50                             ..                        .
0.40                    ..........                          .
0.30                 ..                                      .
0.20              ..                                          .
0.10            .                                             ......
0.00.....................
    0---|---|---|---|---|---|---|---|---|---|---|---|---|---|---0
    0.00   12.50   25.00   37.50   50.00   62.50   75.00   87.50  100.00
    Domained:          0.00 to     100.00
    AlphaCut:          0.10
```

Figure 5.60 Combined fuzzy set with peer rankings (.8 and .3)

In this example, the composite, scaled fuzzy region is now skewed to the left. The center of gravity finds the expected risk value. Figure 5.61 shows the results of combining and defuzzifying the individual fuzzy sets.

```
---'CENTROID' defuzzification. Value: 67.969, [0.7278]
EXPERT PEER RANKINGS:
   Expert BILL.SMITH        Rank:      0.800
   Expert MARY.WILLIAMS     Rank:      0.300
INDIVIDUAL MODEL RESULTS:
   Expert BILL.SMITH        Risk:      72.66  [0.9824]
   Expert MARY.WILLIAMS     Risk:      50.00  [1.0000]
```

```
------------------------------------------------
   Average  Risk Assessment      :      61.33
   WgtdAvg  Risk Assessment      :      66.48
COMBINED MODEL RESULTS:
   Combined Risk Assessment      :      67.97  [0.7278]
   Combined Risk Height          :       0.8646
```

Figure 5.61 The combined intelligence risk assessment with peer ranking=[.8,.3]

Reversing the peer ranking on the individual fuzzy models simply changes the credibility of the experts. Figure 5.62 shows the composite output fuzzy set and the results of defuzzification for the system execution when the peer rankings are .3 and .8, respectively.

```
        FuzzySet:    CombinedRisk
        Description: Combined Risk Output Fuzzy Sets
    1.00
    0.90
    0.80                                .......
    0.70                             ..        ..
    0.60                           .              ..
    0.50                         .                  ..
    0.40                        .                      ...........
    0.30                       .                                  ...
    0.20                      .                                      .
    0.10             ............                                       .
    0.00........                                                   .......
        0---|---|---|---|---|---|---|---|---|---|---|---|---|---|---|---0
        0.00   12.50   25.00   37.50   50.00   62.50   75.00   87.50 100.00
        Domained:        0.00 to      100.00


---'CENTROID' defuzzification. Value: 55.078, [0.7914]
EXPERT PEER RANKINGS:
   Expert BILL.SMITH      Rank:     0.300
   Expert MARY.WILLIAMS   Rank:     0.800
INDIVIDUAL MODEL RESULTS:
   Expert BILL.SMITH      Risk:     72.66  [0.9824]
   Expert MARY.WILLIAMS   Risk:     50.00  [1.0000]
------------------------------------------------
   Average  Risk Assessment      :      61.33
   WgtdAvg  Risk Assessment      :      56.18
COMBINED MODEL RESULTS:
   Combined Risk Assessment      :      55.08  [0.7914]
   Combined Risk Height          :       0.8626
```

Figure 5.62 The combined intelligence risk assessment with peer ranking=[.3,.8]

Combined intelligence aggregation reflects the total information in the model. In the previous case (Figure 5.62) the result is close to but slightly less than the weighted average. Where the output fuzzy sets tend to be skewed, the use of the aggregated fuzzy set method provides a more consistently cohesive and reliable answer.

Adaptive and Feed-Back Fuzzy Models

The beatings will continue until morale improves.

Attributed to Zhuo Fu
(fl. ca. A.D. 905)
Provincial Governor,
Xinyang, Tongbai Shan Province

The models we have previously discussed in this book have been feed-forward fuzzy models. The result of the model evaluation is used by another component of the overall business system. In this chapter we take up the issues associated with fuzzy models having strong and weak feed-back loops. Models that evaluate their own performance provide the basis for adaptability and self-organization. We are concerned here with business models that dynamically interact with their own intelligence system and thus can alter their logic to reflect changes in their performance. As part of the investigation we examine the workings of two feed-back fuzzy systems: a model of a simple Just-in-Time inventory system and a model of organizational dynamics.

Feed-Forward, Feed-Back, and Adaptive Fuzzy Systems

Traditional feed-forward fuzzy systems follow a typical state-machine process (as illustrated in Figure 6.1). Input values are normalized and converted to fuzzy representations. The model's rule base is executed (in a parallel-like fashion) to produce a fuzzy region for each solution variable, and the solution fuzzy regions are defuzzified to find the expected value of each output variable. They are called *feed-forward* because the flow of control moved forward through the system from data input to result output.

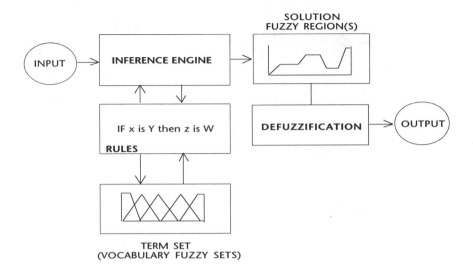

Figure 6.1 A typical feed-forward fuzzy system

Conventional feed-forward fuzzy systems currently constitute the bulk of the machine reasoning systems in business use. These systems provide analytical capabilities analogous to conventional backward and forward reasoning systems (for details on conventional machine intelligence and a comparison with fuzzy logic, see Chapter 2. Fuzzy Logic and Machine Reasoning, "Machine Reasoning Techniques" on page 61).

Feed-Back Fuzzy Models

Feed-forward systems find the expected values for their solution variables and pass them along to the next processing step in the system. In a feed-back fuzzy system, on the other hand, the results of the fuzzy model—as the name implies—are fed back into the model as part of the next execution. Feed-back fuzzy models are especially useful in systems involving time periods, process steps (such as assembly line management and production control), and other analytical models that need to converge toward a solution through iteration. Figure 6.2 shows the schematic for a typical feed-back fuzzy model through a number of execution periods.

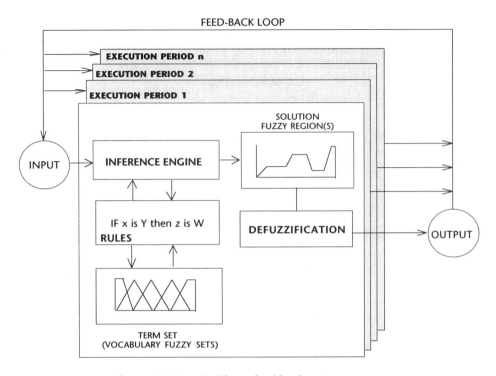

Figure 6.2 A typical fuzzy feed-back system

As Figure 6.2 indicates, feed-back models function as conventional feed-forward models during their execution. Their rule system, however, is designed to recognize and manipulate data generated from a previous generation of the model execution cycle (called the *lag period*). This often means the feed-back fuzzy model must have its data stream initialized so that the data in the initial lag period is available. As an example, consider a model with the following rule:

if avg(costs[t-4,*]) are high then price[t] is increased;

The rule is interpreted as "if the average costs in the previous four time periods is high, then product price in the current time period is increased." In order to run this model, processing begins in the fifth time period and the first four time periods are initialized to valid data. Since feed-back fuzzy models are using solution variable values in the predicate of their rules, they must be designed to differentiate between generations of a solution variable. That is, they must defuzzify a solution or dependent variable in a particular time period and consider all other time periods as unique and separate variables.

Adaptive Fuzzy Models

An adaptive system, like a pure feed-back model, also receives information about its processing from a previous execution generation. Adaptive fuzzy models attempt to modify their characteristics, such as the strength of their rules or the density, shape, or overlap of the fuzzy sets based upon model performance in reaching some objective function. Figure 6.3 shows the architecture of a typical adaptive fuzzy modelling system.

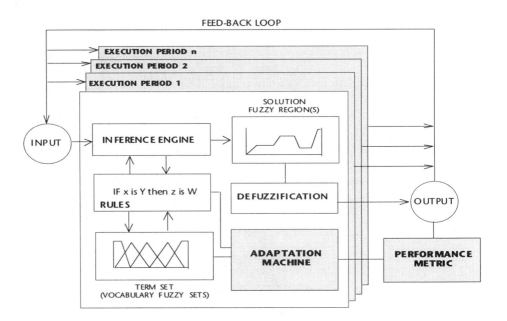

Figure 6.3 The organization of an adaptive fuzzy system

The principal characteristic that separates an adaptive from a feed-back fuzzy model is the adaptive system's ability to change its internal knowledge representation and knowledge processing capabilities based on exogenous information. This exogenous, or external, information can be in the form of feed-back from the model itself or information about the outside world that is fed directly into the model. In one form or another an adaptive fuzzy model has two important components: a performance measuring function and an adaptation machine or engine. The performance metric tracks the behavior of the model against a plan-of-attack generally cast as a set of objective functions. The adaptation machine actually changes the properties of the model consistent with the performance component's measurements against the objective function.

In many adaptive fuzzy systems, the performance metric and the adaptation machine are combined in a single training algorithm (such as a form of back-propagation). The training facility is employed in two distinct ways. In the first method, the fuzzy model itself is built using conventional if-then rules and the training algorithm adjusts the system parameters as well as the fuzzy set representation. In the second method, the training algorithm automatically generates the fuzzy system rules from data. The model becomes adaptive because the training algorithm can continuously generate new rules or modify existing rule bases. An approach to producing adaptive fuzzy systems through data mining is discussed in Chapter 4. *Knowledge Mining and Rule Discovery*. See "The Wang-Mendel Rule Discovery Method" on page 221 for complete details.

A Feed-Back Inventory Control Model

The purpose behind an intelligent inventory model is to maintain sufficient quantities of a product on hand to satisfy demand without incurring excessive stockage costs. The point at which new quantities of product are ordered to maintain the required inventory is called the *economic reorder point*. A relatively simple model of this process is represented by the economic lot size calculation. The inventory is assumed to be decreased continuously by a constant rate **g**. Replenishment stock is ordered in constant lots of size **R** which is also a measure of the current quantity-on-hand (QOH). Figure 6.4 illustrates the behavior of an idealized inventory model based on this function.

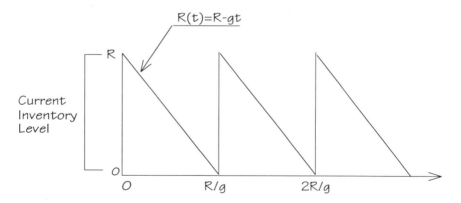

Figure 6.4 Inventory depletion and replenishment cycles

The basic costs are the initialization or setup costs, **S**, at the beginning of the model, the production (or purchase) costs of **p** dollars per unit, and a stockage or holding costs of **w** dollars per item per unit of time. The basic inventory management problem is: how often should new inventories be ordered and in what quantities so the cost per unit of time is minimized. In the standard model, the regularity of the prediction is based on the assumptions of a constant demand rate and a constant order quantity. This consistency allows a mathematical solution to a problem that does not exist in the real world. In actual production planning models, the inventory supply and demand graph typically has the characteristics illustrated in Figure 6.5.

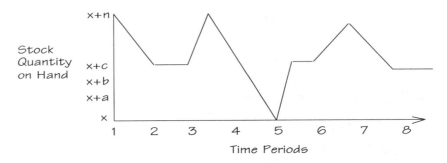

Figure 6.5 Real-world inventory stockage and depletion characteristics

The Fuzzy Model

Although quantitative methods exist to optimize the inventory process under conditions of varying demands, we examine another approach. In this simplified model we construct a fuzzy system that encodes the intelligence of the inventory manager. In place of optimality, we want a system that is more responsive to the uncertainties of the economy and can be easily adjusted. Figure 6.6 shows the organization of this model.

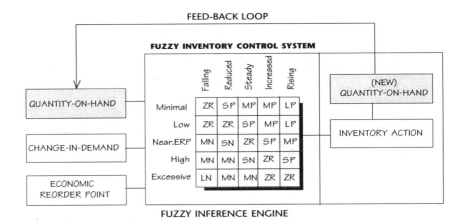

Figure 6.6 The fuzzy inventory model overview

This is a version of the Just-In-Time (JIT) system where we assume new inventories are ordered in response to demand. More specifically, the inventory quantity is in response to a change in the required demand (precipitated by sales orders.) Our model obeys the following heuristics:

> when demand is increasing or falling slightly and QOH is sufficient,
> > then do nothing
>
> when demand is falling significantly
> > then make a corresponding reduction to the QOH
>
> when demand is increasing significantly
> > then make corresponding increase to QOH

In this model we make the following two basic assumptions:

1. Excess inventories can be reduced in the immediate time period. If this is not the case then the cost of roll-over must be factored into the rules.
2. Reorder amount is a function of the previous change in demand levels.

Our model does not strive to optimize minimal carrying costs but simply attempts to maintain a proper inventory level given the current demand requirements. Refer to "fzyi-fam.cpp (The Fuzzy Inventory Control Program)" on page 501 for the complete program code.

The Fuzzy Rules

Our inventory stockage action in each time period is determined by the product quantity-on-hand [QOH] and the demand volume for the product. The product quantity on-hand can be minimal, low, near the currently estimated economic reorder point (near-erp), high, or excessive. The product demand can be falling, reduced, steady, increased, or rising. Based on the degree to which the quantity-on-hand is in one or more of these QOH states and the degree to which demand volume is in one or more of the demand states, the current inventory action can be:

> LN to make a large negative change.
> MN to make a moderate negative change.
> SN to to make a small negative change.
> ZR to take no action in this period.
> SP to make a small positive change.
> MP to make a moderate positive change.
> LP to make a large positive change.

We can combine these input and output states into a set of rules. The example of some inventory rule heuristics include:

*if Quantity-On-Hand is MINIMAL and DemandVolume is REDUCED
then OrderAction is SmallPositive;*

*if Quantity-On-Hand is MINIMAL and DemandVolume is STEADY
then OrderAction is ModeratePositive;*

*if Quantity-On-Hand is MINIMAL and DemandVolume is INCREASED
then OrderAction is ModeratePositive;*

This is a simple 2x1 fuzzy model. There are two inputs and one output. These relationships can be expressed in the form of an MxN matrix called the Fuzzy Associative Memory (FAM). The intersection of a row and column (the predicates of a fuzzy rule) indicate the action we should take when these conditions have some degree of truth. Table 6.1 is the FAM for the inventory model.

Table 6.1 The fuzzy associative memory [FAM]

		PERIOD UNIT DEMAND				
		FALLING	REDUCED	STEADY	INCREASED	RISING
QUANTITY-ON-HAND	MINIMAL	ZR	SP	MP	MP	LP
	LOW	ZR	ZR	SP	MP	LP
	NEAR.ERP	MN	SN	ZR	SP	MP
	HIGH	MN	MN	SN	ZR	SP
	EXCESSIVE	LN	MN	MN	ZR	ZR

All of these entries are fuzzy sets. Each row indicates a fuzzy state of the quantity on hand and each column indicates a fuzzy state of the item demand volume. The row and column intersections indicate a fuzzy set that contributes to the inventory action solution. These intersection fuzzy sets are combined by reducing their truth to the minimum of the row and column fuzzy set truths and taking the maximum of this correlated fuzzy region and the current output fuzzy set.

The Fuzzy Sets

Each of the primary control and solution variables in the inventory model is decomposed into a set of supporting fuzzy sets, known collectively as the *term set*. These fuzzy sets describe the underlying semantics of the variables in terms of regions that have particular meanings inside our model. In fact, we can only write rules for regions of the variables that have been described in terms of fuzzy set partitions. Each variable is decomposed into a set of over-lapping fuzzy regions. This over-lap is a very important feature of the fuzzy model. Figure 6.7 shows the fuzzy sets associated with the Item Demand variable.

```
ITEM.DEMAND
Domain [UofD]:      -30.00 to       30.00


     1.00..                    ***          ..            **                    ...
     0.90 .....              ** **        ... ..        ** ***                 ....
     0.80    ..             *        *       ..       ..  **      **         ..
     0.70      ..          *        *      . ..    ..  **        *         ...
     0.60     ..          **      **.        ..   *          *        ..
     0.50        ..        *            ..          *          **       ..
     0.40        .       *          .*           *            *      ..
     0.30     .. *         .*          * .         ** ..
     0.20      .*             ..  *          **  ..              ..
     0.10        *  ..         ..    *      **   ..           ...**
     0.00      ***        .......         *****      .........        ***
       0---|---|---|---|---|---|---|---|---|---|---|---|---|---|---|---0
       -30.00  -22.50  -15.00   -7.50    0.00    7.50   15.00   22.50   30.00

  .     FuzzySet:     FALLING
        Description: Significant decrease in product demand
        Domained:        -30.00 to      -10.00
  *     FuzzySet:     REDUCED
        Description: Moderate decrease in product demand
        Domained:        -20.00 to       0.00
  .     FuzzySet:     STEADY
        Description: More or less steady demand for product
        Domained:        -10.00 to      10.00
  *     FuzzySet:     INCREASED
        Description: Moderate increase in product demand
        Domained:         0.00 to      20.00
  .     FuzzySet:     RISING
        Description: Significant increase in product demand
        Domained:        10.00 to      30.00
```

Figure 6.7 The ITEM.DEMAND fuzzy sets

The Quantity-On-Hand fuzzy sets, unlike the demand volume sets, are not predetermined, but are calculated from the current economic reorder point (ERP). When we specify an estimated ERP for the inventory, the model creates a bell-shaped fuzzy set with a 10 percent diffusion width and centers it in the middle of a domain that extends plus twice the ERP to minus twice the ERP. Two neighboring fuzzy sets with 50 percent overlaps are created and then the shoulder sets are added. In this way the possible states of the quantity on hand are dynamically computed and always centered around the economic reorder point. Figure 6.8 shows the current collection of fuzzy sets for QOH given the initial model data values.

```
QTY-ON-HAND
Domain [UofD]:     112.00 to      208.00


    1.00..                     ***            **              ...
    0.90 .....              ** **      .... ..  ** ***        ....
    0.80   ..            *        *        ..   **    **        ..
    0.70     ..         *        *        . ..  **      *      ...
    0.60     ..        **       **.        . *         *       ..
    0.50       ..      *         ..        *         **       ..
    0.40        .     *         .*        *          *      ..
    0.30        .. *         . .*        *          **   ..
    0.20          .*         .. *       **        ..
    0.10          *  ..       .. *   **      **    ... **
    0.00        ***      .......   *****      ........  ***
      0---|---|---|---|---|---|---|---|---|---|---|---|---|---|---0
    112.00  124.00  136.00  148.00  160.00  172.00  184.00  196.00  208.00

   .    FuzzySet:    MINIMAL
        Description: Quantity on hand is near depletion levels
        Domained:        112.00 to      144.00
   *    FuzzySet:    LOW
        Description: Quantity on hand is below the reorder point
        Domained:        128.00 to      160.00
   .    FuzzySet:    NEAR.ERP
        Description: Quantity on hand is around the economic reorder point [ERP]
        Domained:        144.00 to      176.00
   *    FuzzySet:    HIGH
        Description: Quantity on hand is above the reorder point
        Domained:        160.00 to      192.00
   .    FuzzySet:    EXCESSIVE
        Description: Quantity on hand is well above required stockage
        Domained:        176.00 to      208.00
```

Figure 6.8 The QTY.ON-HAND fuzzy sets

To some extent, the meaning of large and small changes should be relative to the current value of the economic reorder point and we could do this with little difficulty, but for simplicity sakes in the example model, the actions are specified as static fuzzy regions from a decrease of 45 units to an increase of 45 units. Figure 6.9 shows the fuzzy sets for the inventory action variable.

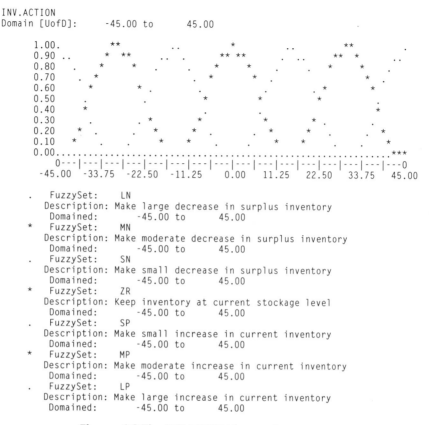

```
INV.ACTION
Domain [UofD]:      -45.00 to      45.00

      1.00.         **           ..          *          ..         **         .
      0.90 ..        *  **       ..         ** **       .  ..      ** *       ..
      0.80 .         *      *    . .        *     *     .     .    *    *     .
      0.70    .      *               .      *        *      .           *
      0.60       *          *   .          *          .           *
      0.50    .               .           *           *           .
      0.40    *                           .                       .
      0.30    .          .  *          *          *          .
      0.20    *   .          *          *         .  *          *       .
      0.10    *      .       .       *      *      .          *          .  *
      0.00...............................................................***
        0---|---|---|---|---|---|---|---|---|---|---|---|---|---|---|---0
      -45.00  -33.75  -22.50  -11.25   0.00   11.25   22.50   33.75   45.00
```

.   FuzzySet: LN
     Description: Make large decrease in surplus inventory
     Domained: -45.00 to   45.00
*   FuzzySet: MN
     Description: Make moderate decrease in surplus inventory
     Domained: -45.00 to   45.00
.   FuzzySet: SN
     Description: Make small decrease in surplus inventory
     Domained: -45.00 to   45.00
*   FuzzySet: ZR
     Description: Keep inventory at current stockage level
     Domained: -45.00 to   45.00
.   FuzzySet: SP
     Description: Make small increase in current inventory
     Domained: -45.00 to   45.00
*   FuzzySet: MP
     Description: Make moderate increase in current inventory
     Domained: -45.00 to   45.00
.   FuzzySet: LP
     Description: Make large increase in current inventory
     Domained: -45.00 to   45.00

Figure 6.9 The INV.ACTION fuzzy sets

Model Execution Logic

The inventory model reads a set of period demand values from an array. The model iterates from time period T_1 through T_n. In each period T_i, a product demand D_i is found coinciding with a current Quantity-on-Hand, QOH_i. We calculate a new recommended Quantity-on-Hand by finding and executing the rules that apply to the current values of D_i and QOH_i. When all rules have been fired, we solve for a current inventory adjustment action (invAction) by defuzzifying the output fuzzy set. When the inventory action is negative, we convert it to a fractional amount and when it is positive we convert it to a surplus percentage. This is called the adjustment factor (adjfactor) and is calculated as indicated in Equation 6.1.

$$
\begin{bmatrix}
invAction < 0 & 1 - \dfrac{abs(invAction)}{100} \\
invAction \geq 0 & 1 + \dfrac{invAction}{100}
\end{bmatrix}
$$

Equation 6.1 The inventory adjustment factor

From this adjustment factor calculation, a new quantity-on-hand amount is calculated from the current quantity-on-hand. The feed-back is accomplished with the transformation shown in Equation 6.2.

$$
QOH_{new} = QOH_{current} \times adjustfactor
$$

Equation 6.2 The Quantity-on-Hand feed-back calculation

Thus, if the invAction is -20, the adjustment factor is 1-(abs(-20)/100) or .80. When this is multiplied by the current Quantity-on-Hand, the result is a new QOH reduced by 20%. When the invAction is +20, the adjustment is 1+(20/100) or 1.20. When this is multiplied by the current Quantity-on-Hand, a new QOH that is 20% larger is produced. Thus QOH_i then becomes the QOH_{i+1}.

Model Processing

We start the execution of the model by initializing the fuzzy logic work area, creating the solution variable (invAction), and inserting it into the fuzzy model. The initial quantity on hand and preliminary economic reorder point values are also fixed at this time.

```
---Executing Inventory Management Policy
---MetusNote(003): Fuzzy Work Area Initialized
---Empty FuzzySet 'invAction' created.
---MetusNote(005): Output Variable 'invocation' added to Fuzzy Model.
Quantity On-Hand        [QOH]:     70.00
Economic Reorder Point [ERP]:    160.00
```

We start off the model with a demand in period T_1 of 10 units. Since the current (initial) quantity-on-hand is below the minimal left-hand edge of the variable's support set, the membership in the fuzzy set MINIMAL is [1.0]. That is, it is completely minimal. At the same time, a demand of 10 units falls at the center of the INCREASED bell-shaped fuzzy set for the demand volume. This has a value of [1.0]. As we can see, this means the FAM matrix intersection of [INCREASED,MINIMAL] fires specifying the output should be Moderate Positive (MP) to the degree that the antecedents are true. Figure 6.10 shows the model execution in the first time period.

```
   1. QOH:       70.00, Demand:       10.00, ChngDemand:       10.00

   1. Rule [INCREASED,MINIMAL]
FAM( 0, 3): if QOH is MINIMAL [1.000] and Demand is INCREASED [1.000]
                  then InvAction is MP [1.000];


        FuzzySet:     InvAction
        Description:
        1.00                                                          . .
        0.90                                                      . .   .
        0.80                                                   .      .
        0.70                                                 .        .
        0.60                                               .         .
        0.50                                             .
        0.40                                                       .
        0.30                                          .
        0.20                                       .            .
        0.10                                     .            .
        0.00.................................  .           ...
          0---|---|---|---|---|---|---|---|---|---|---|---|---|---0
        -45.00  -33.75  -22.50  -11.25   0.00  11.25  22.50  33.75  45.00
        Domained:         -45.00 to      45.00
        AlphaCut:          0.10

02/01/1994 11.43pm---'CENTROID'    defuzzification. Value:     29.883, [0.9999]
QOH       :        90.918
round(QOH) :       91.000
```

Figure 6.10 Inventory model execution in time period 1

An inventory action of +29.883 (with a certainty of .999) is resolved from defuzzifying the output fuzzy region. This change in inventory increases the current Quantity-on-Hand by 30 percent yielding a new rounded value of 91 units.

Effects of Multiple Rules

In the first time period only a single rule executed. The values happened to fall at the unity membership points in both predicate fuzzy regions. In general, however, a demand and a quantity-on-hand amount has memberships in two neighboring fuzzy sets. This causes more than one rule to fire and the output contains the aggregate from both rules. We can see this clearly in model period T_4, illustrated in the following execution trace.

```
   4. QOH:      167.00, Demand:       35.00, ChngDemand:        0.00
```

In looking for rules that apply to the current values of QOH and period demand, the model finds that the QOH is considered significantly close to the estimated economic reorder point and, a demand of zero, is absolutely steady. Applying the rule of correlation minimum, the fuzzy set Small Positive (SP) is reduced to a height of [.617] and moved to the output fuzzy region associated with InvAction (the solution variable.) Figure 6.11 illustrates this action.

```
   4. Rule [STEADY,NEAR.ERP]
FAM( 2, 2): if QOH is NEAR.ERP [0.617] and Demand is STEADY [1.000]
               then InvAction is SP [0.617];

      FuzzySet:    InvAction
      Description:
      1.00
      0.90
      0.80
      0.70
      0.60                                        . . . . . . . . . .
      0.50                                                         .
      0.40                                            .
      0.30                                                      .
      0.20                                        .
      0.10                                    .                .
      0.00. . . . . . . . . . . . . . . . . . . . . . . . . . . . . . . . . . . . . . . . . . . .
          0---|---|---|---|---|---|---|---|---|---|---|---|---|---|---|---|---0
        -45.00  -33.75  -22.50  -11.25   0.00  11.25  22.50  33.75  45.00
        Domained:           -45.00 to      45.00
```

Figure 6.11 Applying Rule FAM(2,2) in time period 4

The model continues looking for rules that apply to the current values of QOH and period demand, and finds that the QOH is also considered HIGH to a lesser extent (the demand of zero, remains absolutely steady). Applying the rule of correlation minimum, the fuzzy set Zero Action (ZR) is reduced to a height of [.383] and moved to the output fuzzy region associated with InvAction (the solution variable). This new fuzzy region is added to the output by taking the maximum of the truncate ZR set and existing SP set. Figure 6.12 shows the combination of the two contributing rules.

```
   4. Rule [STEADY,HIGH]
FAM( 3, 2): if QOH is HIGH [0.383] and Demand is STEADY [1.000]
               then InvAction is ZR [0.383];

      FuzzySet:    InvAction
      Description:
      1.00
      0.90
      0.80
      0.70
      0.60                                        . . . . . . . . . .
      0.50                                                         .
      0.40                                            .
      0.30                          . . . . . . . . .
      0.20                      .                              .
      0.10                  .                                .
      0.00. . . . . . . . . . . . . . . . . . . . .          . . . . . . . . . . . . .
          0---|---|---|---|---|---|---|---|---|---|---|---|---|---|---|---|---0
        -45.00  -33.75  -22.50  -11.25   0.00  11.25  22.50  33.75  45.00
        Domained:           -45.00 to      45.00
        AlphaCut:               0.10

---'CENTROID' defuzzification. Value:  8.789, [0.6172]
QOH        :        181.678
round(QOH) :        182.000
```

Figure 6.12 Applying Rule FAM(3,2) in Time Period 4

Using the combined fuzzy sets in this time period, the model defuzzifies the inventory action to reach an expected value of 8.8%; increasing the Quantity-on-Hand in this period to 182 units.

Highly Overlapping Rules and Alpha Thresholds

In a rule with a single predicate (such as *if x is Y then s is W*), the value 'x' may occur, in different degrees in two adjoining fuzzy regions. Thus, for a value of 'x', two rules can generally fire. When we have two predicates (such as *if x is Y and z is P then s is W*) then **x** can be in two states and **z** can be in two states, yielding a possibility that four rules might execute. In model period T_6 we see how this occurs and, at the same time, observe the affects of the alpha-cut threshold parameter. This period has a Quantity-on-Hand of 182 units and a current change in demand volume of -4.

```
6. QOH:      182.00, Demand:      29.00, ChngDemand:      -4.00
```

When the rules are searched, we find the demand volume is considered moderately reduced and that the quantity-on-hand is definitely considered high. The minimum of these two values is used to reduce the height of the Small Negative (SN) inventory action. This is used to create the working output region for `invAction` as illustrated in Figure 6.13.

```
    6. Rule [REDUCED,HIGH]
FAM( 3, 1): if QOH is HIGH [0.719] and Demand is REDUCED [0.330]
                then InvAction is SN [0.330];

        FuzzySet:    InvAction
        Description:
    1.00
    0.90
    0.80
    0.70
    0.60
    0.50
    0.40
    0.30                 ............
    0.20            .              .
    0.10          .                 .
    0.00...........          .................................
      0---|---|---|---|---|---|---|---|---|---|---|---|---|---0
    -45.00  -33.75  -22.50  -11.25   0.00  11.25  22.50  33.75  45.00
        Domained:         -45.00 to      45.00
        AlphaCut:          0.10
```

Figure 6.13 Executing the small negative Rule in time period 6

Now, the rule selector also finds that, to a very small degree, the quantity-on-hand is also considered excessive. But the truth in the proposition QOH$_i$ is EXCESSIVE is only slightly true. When the inference engine compares the truth of the rule's predicate with the alpha cut threshold of [.10] we find the rule has insufficient strength to actually fire. The model indicates the premise truth is below this threshold and the rule is by-passed.

```
    6. Rule [REDUCED,EXCESSIVE]
    02/01/1994 11.43pm---Rule fails. Premise truth is below alpha threshold: 0.1000
    FAM( 4, 1): if QOH is EXCESSIVE [0.070] and Demand is REDUCED [0.330]
                      then InvAction is MN [0.070];
```

The next rule looks once more at the demand volume and finds that, to a significant degree, it is considered STEADY. Taking the minimum of the memberships for HIGH and STEADY, the Zero Action (ZR) fuzzy set is truncated and applied to the invAction working fuzzy set. This is done, as before, by taking the maximum of the ZR and the existing (and already truncated) SN fuzzy sets. Figure 6.14 illustrates the application of the next rule in this time period.

```
    6. Rule [STEADY,HIGH]
    FAM( 3, 2): if QOH is HIGH [0.719] and Demand is STEADY [0.670]
                      then InvAction is ZR [0.670];

        FuzzySet:     InvAction
        Description:
        1.00
        0.90
        0.80
        0.70
        0.60                                  .........
        0.50                              .              .
        0.40
        0.30             ............              .
        0.20                    .                     .
        0.10         .                             .
        0.00...........                 ............................
          0---|---|---|---|---|---|---|---|---|---|---|---|---0
        -45.00  -33.75  -22.50  -11.25   0.00  11.25  22.50  33.75  45.00
        Domained:            -45.00 to      45.00
        AlphaCut:             0.10
```

Figure 6.14 Executing the ZERO Rule in time period 6

As we might expect, the rule selector also finds that a demand volume of steady is paired with the excessive Quantity-on-Hand state. But, as before, the truth in the proposition QOH_i is EXCESSIVE is only slightly true. The model indicates that the premise truth is below the alpha cut threshold and the rule is by-passed.

```
    6. Rule [STEADY,EXCESSIVE]
    02/01/1994 11.43pm---Rule fails. Premise truth is below alpha threshold: 0.1000
    FAM( 4, 2): if QOH is EXCESSIVE [0.070] and Demand is STEADY [0.670]
                      then InvAction is SN [0.070];
```

Thus, the final output from period T_6 is determined from the two rules with the most strength. Using the centroid, as in Figure 6.15, the center of gravity is slightly to the left of the zero position.

```
         FuzzySet:      InvAction
         Description:
       1.00
       0.90
       0.80
       0.70
       0.60                                    .........
       0.50                              .                 .
       0.40
       0.30                      ...........                .
       0.20                  .                               .
       0.10              .                                    .
       0.00.............                      ......................
         0---|---|---|---|---|---|---|---|---|---|---|---|---|---|---|---0
         -45.00  -33.75  -22.50  -11.25   0.00   11.25  22.50  33.75  45.00
         Domained:            -45.00 to      45.00
         02/01/1994 11.43pm---'CENTROID' defuzzification. Value: -5.273, [0.6699]
QOH        :       172.402
round(QOH) :       173.000
```

Figure 6.15 Defuzzifying the inventory action in time period 6

In each case where we defuzzify the invAction solution fuzzy set to find the current inventory action the new Quantity-on-Hand is rounded up to an integer amount. This corresponds to the notion that we cannot order fractional parts of an item, which might not be a safe assumption for some kinds of product.

Model Results

We have run the fuzzy inventory model for fifteen periods with varying values for period demands. Table 6.2 shows the inventory model results. This table indicates an initial QOH of 70 units, and a preliminary economic re-order point of 160 units.

Table 6.2 Results of fuzzy inventory model

	QOH	Period Demand	[+/-] Demand	invAction	CIX	adjfactor
1.	70.00	10.00	10.00	29.88	1.000	1.30
2.	91.00	15.00	5.00	29.88	1.000	1.30
3.	119.00	35.00	20.00	40.08	0.500	1.40
4.	167.00	35.00	0.00	8.79	0.500	1.09
5.	182.00	33.00	-2.00	0.00	0.617	1.00
6.	182.00	29.00	-4.00	-5.27	0.719	0.95
7.	173.00	28.00	-1.00	0.00	0.670	1.00
8.	173.00	17.00	-11.00	-15.12	0.930	0.85
9.	147.00	9.00	-8.00	14.77	0.930	1.15
10.	169.00	8.00	-1.00	5.63	0.924	1.06
11.	179.00	0.00	-8.00	-15.12	0.617	0.85
12.	152.00	0.00	0.00	22.50	0.924	1.23
13.	187.00	8.00	8.00	6.68	0.500	1.07
14.	200.00	25.00	17.00	8.44	0.236	1.08
15.	217.00	21.00	-4.00	-20.39	0.242	0.80

As demand generally increases in T_1 through T_4, the QOH is rapidly increased. The inventory amounts from that point on follow the demand lagged by one period. The Period Demand column indicates the demand vector, that is, we have a demand of 10 units in time period T_1, a demand of 15 units in T_2, of 35 units in T_3, and so forth. The value for QOH after period T_1 is computed by the fuzzy inventory model. The invAction column is the defuzzified value of the model solution variable with the CIX (compatibility Index) showing its strength relationship. The final column, adjfactor, is the actual adjustment factor used to alter the QOH for the next period.

A Model of Organizational Dynamics

In the early 1980's as part of his introduction to the *REVEAL* fuzzy logic modelling language, its designer and author, Peter Llewelyn Jones, introduced a feed-back system that modelled the management and supervisory dynamics of a mining company. This fuzzy system was based on Alvin Gouldner's 1954 book, *Patterns of Industrial Bureaucracy*. A variation of this psycho-social model has also been used more recently with the author's own Metus fuzzy logic modelling system as part of a company acquisitions and mergers systems (see Chapter 3. *Fuzzy SQL and Database Systems*, "Company Acquisition and Mergers" on page 199 for additional details.[1]) The organizational dynamic model is a feed-back fuzzy model that has a one and two period lag relationship between the cause and effect of some important model properties. Refer to "orgdyn1.cpp (The Organizational Dynamics Model Driver)" on page 506 for the complete main program and subordinate policy code.

The Model Philosophy and Design

Gouldner's organization model describes the relationship between supervision and worker performance. As the use of bureaucratic rules—the closeness of supervision—increases it is accompanied by a rise in the worker's hostility toward management. Continued hostility toward management results in a drop in the worker's productivity or performance. This feed-back model, employing multi-period lead and lag relationships, describes the inter-relationships between the level of supervisory control, the worker's awareness of acceptable behavior, and the impact of interpersonal tension on the worker's collective productivity. The following high level rules represent the essence of Gouldner's observations about the relationship between supervision and worker productivity:

1. If the level of supervisor-to-worker tension is high then existing bureaucratic rules are enforced or new rules are developed. This increase in management oversight takes two periods to be effective.

2. When the supervisory tension level is low, the use of bureaucratic rules decreases slightly.

3. A worker's minimum acceptable behavior—or his/her knowledge about this behavior— is related linearly to the degree to which bureaucratic rules are being enforced. The higher the degree of su-

---

1. Unfortunately, the organizational stability and productivity model developed as part of the company acquisitions and mergers system can not be discussed for reasons of ownership and client confidentiality.

pervision, the more aware the work force is of their minimum acceptable behavior.

4. The strength of the supervisor-to-worker tension is directly related to the observable or visible power structure between management and the work force. This effect takes one lead period to become effective.

5. If the supervisory tension level is relatively high, workers take advantage of their minimum acceptable behavior knowledge by reducing or otherwise restricting their output.

6. If worker performance is currently low and still declining, then management supervision increases.

7. When the current worker performance output level is not satisfactory, management supervision is sustained at or near its current level.

8. As performance levels reach a satisfactory level, the closeness of management supervision tends to decrease.

9. If the level of management supervision is moderately low, then the observation or visibility of the power relationship structure is inversely related to the over-all degree of supervision. However, when the level of management supervision is quite high, then the observable power structure relationships are proportional to the degree of management supervision.

In designing the organizational dynamics model, we decompose the critical knowledge components into a set of subordinate policies. Each policy executes a set of fuzzy rules that determines the expected value of a critical parameter in the current time frame. The model iterates across fifteen time frames, starting in the third period (since we must initialize the first two time periods in order to accommodate the two period lag relationship associated with supervisory tension and the increase in bureaucratic rules). Figure 6.16 shows the general, high-level organization of the model.

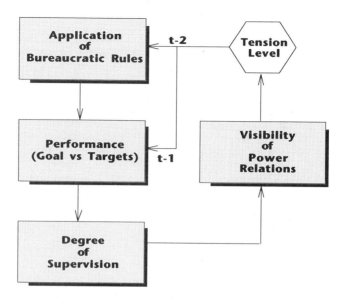

Figure 6.16 The organizational dynamics model (high-level overview)

Throughout the model, the initial conditions are fed back to produce a new set of initial state values for the next cycle. The model measures changes in the level of supervision, the degree of tension, and visibility of the power structure in the work force. This feed-back establishes the constraints for the next cycle in the fuzzy model. Although, as a general rule, the program code for applications in this book are collected separately (see Chapter 8. *C/C++ Code Listings* on page 373), the program code for the organizational dynamics model is sufficiently close to "technical" English that it can be generally understood even by nonprogrammers. Figure 6.17 is the core program code that produces the model analysis.

```
for(t=2;t<MAXPERIODS;t++)
    {
    printf("%s%3d\n","Time Period: ",t-1);
    /*--------------------------------------------------------*
    | First we assess the level at which bureaucratic rules |
    | are being applied. This depends on the tension level  |
    | two periods ago.                                       |
    *--------------------------------------------------------*/
    PDtension           =TensionLevel[t-2];
    RuleLevelChange[t]  =RulesPOLICY(t,PDtension);
    RuleLevel[t]        =RuleLevel[t-1]+RuleLevelChange[t];
    RuleLevel[t]        =max(min(RuleLevel[t],100),0);
    /*--------------------------------------------------------*
    | We now assess the level of performance against target.|
    | This depends on the current level of tension and the  |
    | worker's knowledge of minimum acceptable behavior.    |
    *--------------------------------------------------------*/
```

```
TensionLevel[t]        =RelationVisibility[t-1];
BehaviorAwareness[t]   =RuleLevel[t];
GoalShortfall[t]       =GoalPOLICY(t,BehaviorAwareness[t],TensionLevel[t]);
GoalChange[t]          =GoalShortfall[t]-GoalShortfall[t-1];
/*------------------------------------------------------*
| We now look at the change in supervision policy. This |
| depends on the performance (goal) shortfall.          |
*------------------------------------------------------*/
SVChange[t]            =SupervisionPOLICY(t,GoalShortfall[t],GoalChange[t]);
Supervision[t]         =Supervision[t-1]+SVChange[t];
Supervision[t]         =max(min(Supervision[t],100),0);
/*------------------------------------------------------*
| Finally we examine the visibility of power relations.  |
| This depends on the supervision level and the change   |
| in the application of bureaucratic rules.              |
*------------------------------------------------------*/
RelationVisibility[t]=
  RelationPOLICY(t,&PDChangeRV,Supervision[t],RuleLevel[t],RuleLevelChange[t]);
RelationVisibility[t]=RelationVisibility[t]+PDChangeRV;
}
```

Figure 6.17 The organizational dynamics model (C Code Listing)

The `for` statement causes the model to loop across the time horizon (MAXPERIODS) starting in the second period, incrementing the time period variable (t) in each instance. Each variable is represented as a time series variable subscripted by the current time period. This time subscript is also used on the right-hand side of the model to represent lag relations in such variables as TensionLevel and GoalShortfall.

Fuzzy Sets

The fuzzy sets in the organizational dynamics model are associated with a specific single variable in the model and with a broad class of nonspecific controls. Since the organizational model parameters are subjective and unitless, the model is constructed around the idea of parameter mapping along the psychometric scale. This is an arbitrary and (in this case) linear scale between 0 and 100 or between -100 and +100. Figure 6.18 shows the fuzzy sets associated with the supervisor to worker tension level parameter. It is the tension level parameter that drives most of the underlying dynamics in the model.

```
TENSION.LEVEL
Domain [UofD]:        0.00 to      100.00
    1.00...            ***                             ...          ***
    0.90   .....      **    **                      ..    ..      *****
    0.80       ...**           **                        ..    ..***
    0.70        *..                  *                    .    **.
    0.60       *    ..                *                    .  **   .
    0.50      *        ..              *                  **    .
    0.40                .                                *
    0.30      *          ..            *             . **       .
    0.20    **               ...        **         ***            ..
    0.10    *                   ...    *      .  ***                  .
    0.00************************************************************....
      0---|---|---|---|---|---|---|---|---|---|---|---|---|---|---0
      0.00  12.50  25.00  37.50  50.00  62.50  75.00  87.50  100.00
```

```
   .    FuzzySet:    LOW
        Support :          0.00,       25.00,      50.00
   *    FuzzySet:    LOWISH
        Support :         25.00,       25.00
   .    FuzzySet:    HIGHISH
        Support :         75.00,       25.00
   *    FuzzySet:    HIGH
        Support :         50.00,       75.00,     100.00
```

Figure 6.18 The TENSION.LEVEL fuzzy sets

In designing a way to measure changes in such parameters as supervision level and power structure visibility we constructed several fuzzy sets that approximate no movement, left-hand movements (a decrease), and right-hand movements (an increase.) Since we are measuring changes along the psychometric scale, bell-curves with moderate band widths provide an ideal way to represent these changes. Figure 6.19 shows the fuzzy sets used to implement changes in model parameters across this 100 unit interval scale.

```
CHANGE.METRICS
Domain [UofD]:     -100.00 to        100.00
      1.00                               .      *      .
      0.90                            .  .      * *  . .
      0.80                               .      *    *   . .
      0.70                            .    *              .
      0.60                         .                         .
      0.50                         *              *
      0.40                            .              .
      0.30                         .                    .
      0.20                            *     .    .  *
      0.10                         .        *          *     .
      0.00..................................................******...................
      0---|---|---|---|---|---|---|---|---|---|---|---|---|---|---0
    -100.00  -75.00  -50.00  -25.00   0.00   25.00   50.00   75.00  100.00


   .    FuzzySet:    DECREASE
        Support :        -20.00,       20.00
   *    FuzzySet:    NO.CHANGE
        Support :          0.00,       20.00
   .    FuzzySet:    INCREASE
        Support :         20.00,       20.00
```

Figure 6.19 The CHANGE.METRICS fuzzy sets

The organizational dynamics model uses a surprising few fuzzy sets. With the exception of supervisory-to-worker tension levels, all the model parameter rules measure movement in the model state through the three change metric fuzzy sets: DECREASE, NO.CHANGE, and INCREASE. Note that these are general utility fuzzy sets and are not members of the term set of any particular model variable.

Model Execution

The feed-back loop in the organizational dynamics model works in the same way as conventional feed-forward fuzzy systems. A glimpse inside the RulesPolicy execution indicates how the various components of the organization dynamics model use the current model parameter state to generate changes in the system. Figure 6.20 shows the start of the policy and the incoming parameter PDtension, the period tension that is actually the tension output from the model two periods in the past.

```
*-------------------------------------------------------------------*
*                                                                   *
*   Executing Policy: "RulesPolicy" in Time Period: 1               *
*                                                                   *
*-------------------------------------------------------------------*
Policy Parameters:
PDtension      : 20.00
---MetusNote(003): Fuzzy Work Area Initialized
---Empty FuzzySet 'RuleLevelChange' created.
---MetusNote(005): Output Variable 'RuleLevelChange' added to Model.
```

Figure 6.20 Starting the RulesPolicy in the organizational dynamics model

When the policy begins, a fuzzy set and a variable associated with the solution variable (RuleLevelChange) is created. Figure 6.21 shows the execution of rule [R1]. This rule contains a hedge reference (very) so the modelling system must create a new fuzzy set containing the linguistic variable very HIGH.

```
R1 if the PDtension is very high or the PDtension is highish
        then the RuleLevelChange is an increase
---Empty FuzzySet 'VERY.HIGH' created.
---Hedge 'very' applied to Fuzzy Set "HIGH"

        FuzzySet:     HIGH
        Description: very HIGH
   1.00                                                          ..
   0.90                                                       ....
   0.80                                                        ..
   0.70                                                      ..
   0.60                                                     .
   0.50                                                   ..
   0.40                                                  .
   0.30                                                ..
   0.20                                               ..
   0.10                                              ..
   0.00..........................................
      0---|---|---|---|---|---|---|---|---|---|---|---|---|---|---0
      0.00   12.50   25.00   37.50   50.00   62.50   75.00   87.50  100.00
    Domained:          0.00 to     100.00
```

```
---Membership of 'PDtension' (   20.00) in Fuzzyset 'very HIGH' is: m[0.000].
---Membership of 'PDtension' (   20.00) in Fuzzyset 'HIGHISH' is: m[0.000].
---RULE FAILS. Premise truth of 0.0000 is below alpha threshold: 0.1000
```

Figure 6.21 Executing Rule [R1] in the RulesPolicy

Neither of the predicate propositions in the first rule are true. Rule [R1] is not fired. The next rule, [R2], determines exactly how well the period tensions maps to the idea of high. Figure 6.22 shows how the first predicate proposition for the rule is evaluated.

```
R2 if the PDtension is not low and the PDtension is not very high
         then the RuleLevelChange is no.change
---Empty FuzzySet 'NOT.LOW' created.
---Hedge 'not' applied to Fuzzy Set "LOW"

        FuzzySet:    LOW
        Description: not LOW
        1.00                              ..................................
        0.90                          .....
        0.80                        ...
        0.70                       ..
        0.60                      ..
        0.50                     ..
        0.40                    .
        0.30                   ..
        0.20                 ...
        0.10              ...
        0.00.......
          0---|---|---|---|---|---|---|---|---|---|---|---|---|---|---|---0
          0.00  12.50  25.00  37.50  50.00  62.50  75.00  87.50 100.00
        Domained:            0.00 to      100.00

---Membership of 'PDtension' (   20.00) in Fuzzyset 'LOW' is: m[0.318].
```

Figure 6.22 Evaluating the first predicate in Rule [R1]

The hedge not must be applied to the fuzzy set LOW, producing a new linguistic variable. The rule is evaluated by finding the membership of the formal policy parameter PDtension in this fuzzy set. In this case, PDtension has a value of 20 with a membership of [.32] in the linguistic variable not LOW. Figure 6.23 shows the results of evaluating the second predicate proposition and executing the complete rule.

```
---Empty FuzzySet 'NOT.VERY.HI' created.
---Hedge 'not' applied to Fuzzy Set "HIGH"

        FuzzySet:    NOT.VERY.HIGH
        Description: not very HIGH
        1.00.......................................
        0.90                                    ......
        0.80                                         ..
        0.70                                           .
        0.60                                            ..
        0.50                                             .
        0.40                                              ..
        0.30                                                ..
        0.20                                                  .
        0.10                                                   ...
        0.00                                                      .....
          0---|---|---|---|---|---|---|---|---|---|---|---|---|---|---|---0
          0.00  12.50  25.00  37.50  50.00  62.50  75.00  87.50 100.00
        Domained:            0.00 to      100.00
---Membership of 'PDtension' (   20.00) in Fuzzyset 'HIGH' is: m[1.000].
---RULE FIRED--Premise truth of:0.3175
```

Figure 6.23 Executing Rule [R2] in the RulesPolicy

Since the linguistic variable very HIGH had been created for the first rule [R1], we can create the fuzzy set not very HIGH by simply applying the hedge *not* to this existing fuzzy set. The parameter PDtension has a membership of [1.0] in this new fuzzy region. A fuzzy conjunctive expression or intersection is evaluated by taking the minimum of the two membership values, the truth of the rule predicate (as seen in Equation 6.3).

$$P_{truth} = \min(\mu_A[x], \mu_B[x])$$

Equation 6.3 Computing the fuzzy AND

From this we see that the truth of the predicate is min(.32,1.0) or [.32]. Figure 6.24 shows how the consequent fuzzy set (NO.CHANGE) is correlated with the truth of the predicate and moved to the RuleLevelChange output fuzzy set.

```
FuzzySet:     RuleLevelChange
Description:
1.00
0.90
0.80
0.70
0.60
0.50
0.40
0.30                                      . . . . . . .
0.20                                  .              .
0.10                              .                       .
0.00. . . . . . . . . . . . . . . . . . . . . . . .              . . . . . . . . . . . . . . . . . . . . . . . . . . . .
    0---|---|---|---|---|---|---|---|---|---|---|---|---|---|---|---0
  -100.00  -75.00   -50.00   -25.00    0.00   25.00   50.00   75.00  100.00
   Domained:        -100.00 to      100.00
```

Figure 6.24 RuleLevelChange (NO.CHANGE) after executing Rule [R2]

The final rule, [R3], decreases the application of bureaucratic rules when the management to worker tension is on the low side. Note that the two predicate propositions in this rule are connected with the OR relation. A fuzzy OR is evaluated by taking the maximum of the two truth membership values (as seen in Equation 6.4).

$$P_{truth} = \max(\mu_A[x], \mu_B[x])$$

Equation 6.4 Computing the fuzzy OR

From this we see the truth of the predicate is max(.68,91.0) or [.91]. Figure 6.25 shows how the consequent fuzzy set (DECREASE) is correlated with the truth of the predicate and moved to the RuleLevelChange output fuzzy set. This action creates the final output fuzzy set associated with the solution variable.

```
R3 if the PDtension is low or the PDtension is lowish
       then then RuleLevelChange is a decrease
---Membership of 'PDtension' (   20.00) in Fuzzyset 'LOW' is: m[0.682].
---Membership of 'PDtension' (   20.00) in Fuzzyset 'LOWISH' is: m[0.917].
---RULE FIRED--Premise truth of:0.9175


       FuzzySet:   RuleLevelChange
       Description:
       1.00
       0.90                             ...
       0.80                            .
       0.70                                .
       0.60                         .
       0.50
       0.40                          .
       0.30                  .        ......
       0.20                                  .
       0.10               .              .
       0.00...................             ...........................
         0---|---|---|---|---|---|---|---|---|---|---|---|---|---|---|---0
       -100.00  -75.00  -50.00  -25.00   0.00   25.00   50.00   75.00 100.00
         Domained:        -100.00 to     100.00

---'CENTROID' defuzzification. Value: -14.063, [0.8237]
---MetusNote(009): Fuzzy Work Area Closed.
```

Figure 6.25 RuleLevelChange (DECREASE) after executing Rule [R3]

The two fuzzy sets around the NO.CHANGE and DECREASE regions are combined into a continuous fuzzy region. The centroid or center of gravity method finds a value of -14.1 for the degree of rule level change. This value is then used in the model to change the current level of rule application. Figure 6.26 (extracted from the complete model shown in Figure 6.17 on page 348) shows how the policy results are used.

```
[1] PDtension              =TensionLevel[t-2];
[2] RuleLevelChange[t]     =RulesPOLICY(t,PDtension);
[3] RuleLevel[t]           =RuleLevel[t-1]+RuleLevelChange[t];
[4] RuleLevel[t]           =max(min(RuleLevel[t],100),0);
```

Figure 6.26 Using the RulesPOLICY in the organizational dynamics model

In line [1], Tension level from two periods ago is stored in the PDtension scalar variable. This value along with the current time period variable are passed as formal parameters to the RulesPOLICY policy (line [2]). A new application of bureaucratic rules value (RuleLevel) in the current time period is found by adding the policy results to the RuleLevel value in the previous time period (line [3]). Finally, in line [4], we make sure that the value stays within the psychological metric scale of [0] to [100].

Model Analysis

The organizational dynamics module begins by "priming the pump"—we are required to specify the beginning state of the model. The values entered for the model are applied to the first two time periods (periods P_0 and P_1), although only period P_1 is displayed on the MxN tabular output. The allowed values range from 0 to 100, with values toward zero indicating a weak strength and values toward 100 indicating a strong strength for the model property. Figure 6.27 shows the execution of the model when all the model parameters have been set to a middle or neutral value.

```
FUZZY ORGANIZATIONAL BEHAVIOR MODEL. (c) 1994 Metus Systems Group.
from: Gouldner [1954] 'Patterns of Industrial Bureaucracy'
Initial Model Conditions:
Tension Level        : 50
Rule Level           : 50
Goal Shortfall       : 50
Supervision          : 50
Relation Visibility  : 50
```

	P1	P2	P3	P4	P5	P6	P7	P8	P9	P10	P11	P12
Effective Present tension Level	50	50	50	50	50	50	50	50	50	50	50	50
Change in Rule Application Level												
Rule Application Level	50	50	50	50	50	50	50	50	50	50	50	50
Behavior Awareness Level	50	50	50	50	50	50	50	50	50	50	50	50
Change in Goal Shortfall												
Achievement vs. Goal Shortfalls	50	50	50	50	50	50	50	50	50	50	50	50
Change in Supervision Level												
Active Supervision Level	50	50	50	50	50	50	50	50	50	50	50	50

Figure 6.27 Organizational dynamic model execution: neutral initial values

When the model is initialized with neutral values, (50 is the midpoint on the psychometric scale) its performance is completely stable across the execution horizon. This is both expected and encouraging since it provides significant reassurance that the model does not contain any positive or chaotic feed-back loops that would make the model's behavior unstable under normal operating conditions.

We can now explore the behavior of the model at different initial states. What happens when the model parameters are set to a low level—indicative of a good relationship between management and workers? Figure 6.28 and Figure 6.29 show the outcome when each of the initial parameters is set to 20 and then set slightly higher to 30, a very low and a moderately low value.

```
FUZZY ORGANIZATIONAL BEHAVIOR MODEL. (c) 1994 Metus Systems Group.
from: Gouldner [1954] 'Patterns of Industrial Bureaucracy'
Initial Model Conditions:
Tension Level        : 20
Rule Level           : 20
Goal Shortfall       : 20
Supervision          : 20
Relation Visibility  : 20
```

	P1	P2	P3	P4	P5	P6	P7	P8	P9	P10	P11	P12
Effective Present tension Level	20	94	97	97	60	41	21	15	42	56	72	77
Change in Rule Application Level	-14	-14	-14	20	20	20	5	-6	-14	-16	-5	2
Rule Application Level	6			20	39	59	64	58	44	27	23	25
Behavior Awareness Level	6			20	39	59	64	58	44	27	23	25
Change in Goal Shortfall	-2	-18		20	19	20	-10	-11	5	-16	-5	2
Achievement vs. Goal Shortfalls	18			20	39	58	48	38	43	27	23	25
Change in Supervision Level	-20	-20	-20	-20	-20			-20		-20	-20	-20
Active Supervision Level												

Figure 6.28 Organizational dynamic model: very low initial values

```
FUZZY ORGANIZATIONAL BEHAVIOR MODEL. (c) 1994 Metus Systems Group.
from: Gouldner [1954] 'Patterns of Industrial Bureaucracy'
Initial Model Conditions:
Tension Level       : 30
Rule Level          : 30
Goal Shortfall      : 30
Supervision         : 30
Relation Visibility : 30
```

	P1	P2	P3	P4	P5	P6	P7	P8	P9	P10	P11	P12
Effective Present tension Level	30	82	93	97	68	48	29	19	39	52	66	73
Change in Rule Application Level	-12	-12	-12	12	20	20	9		-12	-15	-7	
Rule Application Level	18	7		12	31	51	60	60	48	34	27	27
Behavior Awareness Level	18	7		12	31	51	60	60	48	34	27	27
Change in Goal Shortfall	-6	-18	-6	12	20	20	2	-8	4	-14	-7	
Achievement vs. Goal Shortfalls	24	6		12	31	51	52	44	48	34	27	27
Change in Supervision Level	-20	-20	-20	-20	-20					-20	-20	-20
Active Supervision Level	10											

Figure 6.29 Organizational dynamic model: moderately low initial values

In the case where the initial model state is set to a favorable relationship between management and the work force, the model displays an intricate oscillatory pattern representing the fundamental dynamics of the feed-back loops. Over-all performance begins to initially improve but can not be sustained. The improvement cycle decays and then starts to grow again.

What happens when the model parameters are set to a very high level—indicating a poor relationship between management and workers? Figure 6.30 shows the results of this model execution.

```
FUZZY ORGANIZATIONAL BEHAVIOR MODEL. (c) 1994 Metus Systems Group.
from: Gouldner [1954] 'Patterns of Industrial Bureaucracy'
Initial Model Conditions:
Tension Level       : 80
Rule Level          : 80
Goal Shortfall      : 80
Supervision         : 80
Relation Visibility : 80
```

	P1	P2	P3	P4	P5	P6	P7	P8	P9	P10	P11	P12
Effective Present tension Level	80	77	77	77	77	77	77	77	77	77	77	77
Change in Rule Application Level	12	12	12	11	11	11	11	11	11	11	11	11
Rule Application Level	92	100	100	100	100	100	100	100	100	100	100	100
Behavior Awareness Level	92	100	100	100	100	100	100	100	100	100	100	100
Change in Goal Shortfall	11	6										
Achievement vs. Goal Shortfalls	91	97	97	97	97	97	97	97	97	97	97	97
Change in Supervision Level	20	20										
Active Supervision Level	100	100	100	100	100	100	100	100	100	100	100	100

Figure 6.30 Organizational dynamic model: moderately low initial values

As we might expect, high levels of worker tension and the application of rules, leads to poor performance. The model stabilizes very rapidly in a steady-state with high goal shortfalls and extremely high supervisory levels. The model shows what intuition tells us and Gouldner observed. Enforcing trivial rules and closely supervising worker performance is unlikely to improve productivity and raise worker morale. An obvious improvement to the organizational dynamics model is the ability to "clamp" one or more of the parameters. Figure 6.31 shows the effect of making supervision a constant when initial conditions are fairly unfavorable.

```
FUZZY ORGANIZATIONAL BEHAVIOR MODEL. (c) 1994 Metus Systems Group.
from: Gouldner [1954] 'Patterns of Industrial Bureaucracy'
Initial Model Conditions:
Tension Level       :  80
Rule Level          :  80
Goal Shortfall      :  80
Supervision         :  30
Relation Visibility :  80
                                P1   P2   P3   P4   P5   P6   P7   P8   P9   P10  P11  P12
                                ---  ---  ---  ---  ---  ---  ---  ---  ---  ---  ---  ---
Effective Present tension Level 80    4    9    9   25   36   52   62   70   71   45   37
Change in Rule Application Level 12   12   12  -20  -20  -20  -13   -9         7    9   10
Rule Application Level          92  100  100   80   59   39   27   17   16   23   33   43
Behavior Awareness Level        92  100  100   80   59   39   27   17   16   23   33   43
Change in Goal Shortfall        11  -87    5        40  -11  -12  -10         7    9    9
Achievement vs. Goal Shortfalls 91    4    9    9   49   38   27   17   16   23   32   42
Change in Supervision Level
Active Supervision Level        30   30   30   30   30   30   30   30   30   30   30   30
```

Figure 6.31 Organizational dynamic model: high initial values/clamped supervision

The model seems to show that given highly unfavorable initial conditions, a policy of low supervision results in a movement toward an acceptable and satisfactory working productivity level. This is also in general accordance with Gouldner's observations and common sense. By clamping the values for various model parameters as well as varying the initial model state, we can observe a wide spectrum of relationships between management style and worker productivity. Refer to "orgdyn2.cpp (The "clamped" Organizational Dynamics Model Driver)" on page 523 for the program code associated with a version that allows you to specify one or more "clamped" parameter).

Fuzzy Cognitive Maps and Feed-Back Systems

Adaptive and feed-back fuzzy models can also be constructed using graphs in the form of a fuzzy cognitive map (FCM). The fuzzy cognitive map is a directed cognitive graph consisting of nodes with connections (edges) that describe the causal flow. The nodes are concepts—such as C_1, C_2, ... C_i, ... C_n — and the edges indicate the degree to which C_i causes or results from C_j. These edges can be viewed as rules if the form:

if C_i then C_j

And, since the edges have "fuzzy" strengths in the interval range [-1,+1] indicating the degree to which one event or concept affects another event or concept, the rule is generally interpreted as:

if C_i then C_j to D_{ij}

where $D(C_i, C_j)$ is the degree or strength of the connection. Associated with each concept (C_i) is an activation threshold ($C_i(t)$) specifying the minimum strength to which the incoming rule degrees must be aggregated in order to activate the concept. In a way similar to neural networks, a squashing function is used to combine the fuzzy rule (edge) weights. Figure 6.32 shows the organization of a typical fuzzy cognitive map.

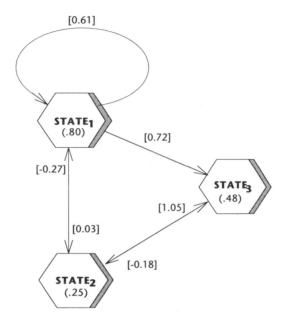

Figure 6.32 A Typical fuzzy cognitive map

As an abstract representation of expert knowledge fuzzy cognitive maps provide the knowledge engineer and business analyst with an expressive and flexible method of capturing and representing complex relationships. The relationships indicate that one concept increases the likelihood of another concept or decreases the likelihood of another concept. As an example, Figure 6.33 shows a (simplified) fuzzy cognitive map for the managed health care industry as developed by Dr. Rod Taber, one of the world's leading experts in the underlying mechanics and use of FCMs.

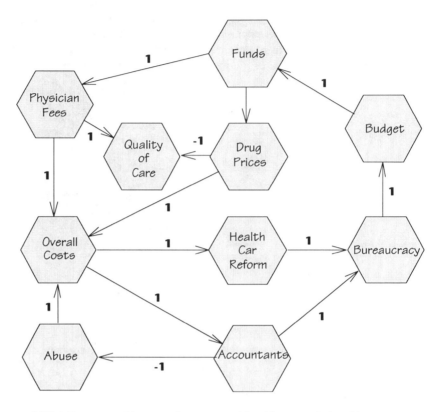

Figure 6.33 A Fuzzy cognitive map for managed health care relationships

The fuzzy cognitive map in Figure 6.33 is a *trivalent* map—the relationships can have one of three values: +1 indicating an increase in the effect, -1 indicating a decrease in the effect, and 0 indicating no relationship. As we can see from this map, drug prices cause a decrease in quality of care, overall costs causes a increase in the call for health care reform, and the work of accountants in reviewing claims leads to a decrease in managed health care abuse (but, of course, a increase in accountants as well as the call for reform leads to an increase in the size of bureaucracy, which leads to a increase in the budget, and so forth). The relationships in a fuzzy cognitive map (the rules or edges of the graph) are maintained in a simple NxM matrix. Figure 6.34 shows the FCM matrix for the managed health care map (the zero edges have been left blank.) The relationships are lead "from row to column."

	Fees	Costs	Abuse	Care	Drug	Funds	Accnts	Bureau	Budget	Reform
Fees		1.0		1.0						
Costs							1.0			1.0
Abuse		1.0								
Care										
Drug		1.0		-1.0						
Funds	1.0					1.0				
Accountants			-1.0					1.0		
Bureaucracy									1.0	
Budget						1.0				
Reform								1.0		

Figure 6.34 A three-valued state FCM for managed health care analysis

Since FCMs are essentially NxM matrices, multiple cognitive maps, representing multiple expert knowledge, can be directly combined. Equation 6.5 shows how many FCMs are combined into a new cognitive map.

$$F_{N+1} = \sum_{i=0}^{N} F_i$$

Equation 6.5 Combining fuzzy cognitive maps

Some experts have a higher peer ranking than others; that is, their knowledge is more valuable and their credibility is greater than other experts in the same domain. Fuzzy cognitive maps can be combined with a peer ranking in the rank [0,1] to yield a composite matrix that reflects the based aggregate experts. Equation 6.6 shows the method of combining FCMs weighted by the experts' peer ranking (P_i).

$$F_{N+1} = \sum_{i=0}^{N} p_i F_i$$

Equation 6.6 Combining fuzzy cognitive maps with peer rankings

As a real-world modelling tool, however, fuzzy cognitive maps have some significant drawbacks. These drawbacks, coupled with their general complexity as mathematical entities, make them difficult to use as production fuzzy systems. While these short-comings are not absolutes (some forms of FCM constructions incorporate weak capabilities in a few of these areas), they define the limitations of fuzzy cognitive maps as a broad class of modelling tools. Some of the more significant drawbacks include the following:

- **Separation of concept from actual model data**. Fuzzy cognitive maps represent the causal relationships between concepts. The model is run by following a feed-back loop through the directed graphs until a steady-state is achieved. But FCMs are detached from actual data in the underlying, physical model. To include data elements, ratios, and arithmetic, logical, and string expressions in the model—such as product prices, portfolio concentrations, market share growth, inventory stockage levels—and make the graph responsive to relationships between data and the fuzzy universe is not a feature of the fuzzy cognitive map. A fuzzy cognitive map is an expression of a cognitive state rather than an expression of a physical, data-driven process.

- **Difficulty in representing lead-lag relationships**. The edges (rules) in a fuzzy cognitive map represent the flow of causality between various concepts. Although we can construct feed-back loops to represent a flow from a previous concept state into the current state, the ability to describe complex lead-lag time relationships in a fuzzy cognitive map is very limited.

- **Limitation on the number of concept states**. In running a fuzzy cognitive map, the entire FCM state is evaluated and updated by following the bi-directional edges between concepts. This means the connection density roughly grows exponentially as the size of the FCM increases. For ordinary desktop personal computers, the machine resources necessary to solve the steady-state for a large fuzzy cognitive map can become prohibitive very quickly. The limitation on the size and complexity of a fuzzy cognitive map also extends to the problem of convergence and oscillations caused by undetected transients. If the convergence criteria of the FCM are not satisfied, or the implicit relationships in the model represent divergent or chaotic states, the FCM may never reach a steady state. The fuzzy cognitive map analysis program essentially runs forever.

Although they are often more difficult to design, construct, validate, and tune, conventional fuzzy expert systems incorporating lead and lag feed-back loops should be used to model business, scientific, and technical problems that require these capabilities. The conventional approach provides a top-down system design methodology along with a rule-based approach that provides extensibility, ease of comprehension, and a more robust and "deep" specification language that can directly incorporate advanced fuzzy reasoning techniques as well as, when necessary, other forms of machine intelligence such as backward and forward chaining, blackboard reasoning, and database access.

Planning and Building Fuzzy Models

Initiali;
Parms[0]
Parms [1;
sprint(s;
strncpy(;
FDBptr[M;
if(
Part om;
Part Dom;
(*F Bcnt;

7

No se pierde
El hacer bien, aun en sueños,
Don't relinquish right-doing, even in dreams
                    Pedro Calderón De La Barca (1600–1681)
                                La Vida es Sueño, dc. iv.

If you don't know where you're going, you can't get there.
                                                    Anonymous

In this relatively brief chapter we examine the nature of approaching fuzzy logic development projects. We look at such issues as finding the right initial project, structuring and managing the project, staffing the development and support team, and choosing the correct tools for the project. These are not hard-and-fast laws, but are guidelines and management heuristics in the design, development, validation, delivery, and maintenance of simple to complex fuzzy systems.

Selecting Appropriate Problems

Planning for an advanced technology project involves addressing several critical issues in human resource allocation and deployment, the resistance to organizational change, expectation management, and the risks associated with using technologies that are still evolving and for which a history of project case studies might not be available. Fuzzy Logic projects are inherently difficult and involve more risk than other similar projects due to the lack of significant project experience in the field, the sparseness of available and trained decision scientists, knowledge engineers, and business analysts, and the confusion that exists about the exact nature and capabilities of fuzzy logic. But, in the majority of business development efforts, the management of the over-all project involves the integration of advanced technology into a framework of conventional system analysis and design. Figure 7.1 shows the principle parts of a typical high technology project.

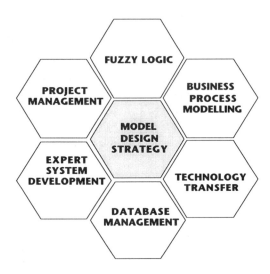

Figure 7.1 Components of a fuzzy logic design strategy

As we can see, fuzzy logic is only one component of the complete model design program. The other equally important parts include:

- **Business process modelling.** The analysis of how information is generated, flows, and is used in the organization as well as the isolation of intelligence[1] in the business model. This is the core of all modelling exercises and is the foundation for the design and development of working systems.

- **Technology transfer.** This component has several dimensions: the acquisition of advanced technology knowledge (such as fuzzy logic) by the technical and management team, the ability to relate project objectives and status in terms of meaningful features and benefits to senior management, and the transfer of operational and support knowledge to the client (the end user of the project.)

---

1. Intelligence has the same relationship to knowledge as knowledge has to information. Intelligence is the ability to decisively use knowledge in making decisions.

- **Database management.** Provides the essential link between the model process and the organization's data. Integrating this data into the model, either from corporate repositories on the main-frame, from distributed databases on workstations, or from local data sources such as spreadsheets, flat files, and private databases is a crucial part of completing the model development program.

- **Expert system development.** Involves the coupling of several disciplines: the knowledge acquisition and representation skills of knowledge engineers and business analysts, the organization of rule sets and inference methods by analysts familiar with intelligent systems, and, for fuzzy systems, the ability to break problems down into self-contained units that can use the parallel processing paradigm of approximate reasoning.

- **Project management.** The essential tool used to link all these concepts and methods together into a cohesive and workable process.

The lack of sound project management skills has lead to the failure of more advanced technology projects than nearly any other contributing cause. As a general rule, if you can't define the project in terms of necessary resources, well-defined tasks and a reasonable budget, then the risk of failure is extremely high.

Ideal Fuzzy Models

An ideal model not only provides a close representation of the underlying physical, real-word system, but communicates the underlying process to the user in a way that makes interpretation and decision-making easy, exploration of alternatives easy, and errors in execution or judgement difficult. Before addressing the issues associated with selecting a problem, we should examine what makes a model effective and the ideal properties of a fuzzy system model.

- **Over-all simplicity.** The design should follow *Occam's Razor*— include only the minimum rules and procedures necessary to adequately describe the problem. The client should be able to understand the model process easily and, if possible, intuitively. Add more detail to the model only when the client indicates the system fails to account for all observed phenomena or identifies other important properties of the system.

- **Ruggedness and robustness.** A model must gracefully accept erroneous, nonsensical, and bad data without causing a program state interrupt. As an example, if the model requests a number, it should not accept a nonnumeric value, a nonnumeric value should not cause the code to abort, and the system should insure the value of the number makes sense in the current context. In terms of context, the model should make it difficult for the user to produce errors or interpret erroneous results as correct results. Error messages should be in the user's, not in the model builder's vernacular (that is, "floating point mantissa overflow on program register" is not the same as "Too many decimal places on the current Product.Price value").

- **Process completeness and explanatory coherence.** The model must completely describe the underlying phenomena and the explanation must provide a coherent picture of the system. In a fuzzy system this is the core of the model design and knowledge representation activity. In many cases, the completeness issues of a model involve the development of subjective policies. Making the model too subjective in terms of the end user's world view might also make it less general and less usable across a wider spectrum of users.

- **Extensibility and adaptiveness.** This is a design and structure issue, but an ideal model should have an open architecture that allows easy incorporation of changes, rapid maintenance, and the addition of new intelligence as the outside world changes or as the client learns more about the nature of his/her problem.

Naturally, these ideal characteristics of an intelligent model extend to other technologies beside fuzzy logic. But fuzziness as the fundamental metaphor in the design of knowledge-based business models provides a closer approximation of the real-world than conventional experts systems, mathematical and statistical models, and models employing forms of Bayesian and frequentist probabilities. It is too easy, when approaching the development of a fuzzy model, to include too much information and encode too many rules. The ideal approach of computational simplicity embodied in Occam's Razor is the principle constraint in building workable, usable, and maintainable fuzzy systems.

Project Characteristics

Considering these constraints on the viability of fuzzy projects, the management team must exercise considerable care in the selection of the initial project. In general, projects should be carefully screened for definition, scope, and technical feasibility. The nature of building fuzzy models involves finding the correct balance between the ideal problem characteristics and the pragmatic choices associated with real-world problems. The following guidelines for fuzzy project characteristics address these issues of selecting the best initial project.

- **An expert exists.** Although it is possible and even necessary on some occasions to build an expert system without an expert, the initial fuzzy project should be anchored to the judgement of a single, well-regarded expert. This significantly improves the probability of success by providing an incremental development process using expert knowledge, ties the evolution process to a human expert, and provides a clear and recognizable way of validating the delivered model.

- **The project contains well-defined fuzzy properties.** Don't try to fit "a square peg in a round hole"—the variables in the project should have characteristics that map well into the domain of fuzzy systems. The variables should have a numeric basis with continuous values. Although experienced fuzzy modelers can build robust and reliable systems using discrete or boolean variables, the representational schemes necessary to handle these parameters make model development more difficult. You should not expect every independent and dependent variable to be fuzzy, but the majority of your controls should have significant fuzzy properties.

- **Reasonable visibility in the organization.** The project should have the support and interest of management, but, its political profile and urgency should not be so high that changes in the project plan, unanticipated delays, or rescaling of the end product cause serious problems.

- **Deliverables that provides benefits to the organization.** Too often managers select projects, as their initial prototype, that have little or no benefit to the organization. This approach is almost always guided by the underlying principle "if it fails, then it won't matter." However, unless the project actually contributes to the mission of the organization in some measurable way, neither success nor failure matters.

- **Objectives that are comprehensible and well-defined.** This involves two related concepts: technical feasibility and project definition. Fuzzy logic provides a means of building systems incorporating imprecise concepts—it is **not** a panacea for projects that are technically improbable or for which the goals and objects are "fuzzy" in the minds of the project or organization manager. It is also important to have a well-defined and understandable project objective. "Using fuzzy logic to cure cancer" is both ill-defined and not comprehensible as a realistic project. While this might appear obvious, the same constraints apply to ordinary business problems. "Develop a fuzzy logic program to identify good investment opportunities" or "Use fuzzy logic to find bugs in a computer program" are examples of projects that are probably too broad and too ill-defined. Initial projects must be concise, well understood, and technically achievable.

- **A moderate to short time frame.** This is an important property of the ideal fuzzy logic project—some recognizable product must be produced within a reasonable time frame. Long, complex projects are subject to staff attrition, changes in organizational priorities, changes in the end user requirements, political and management pressure, and a tendency to "wrap things up" just to finish the project. Project durations of less than sixty calendar days are the best way to insure the model is finished correctly.

When introducing advanced technologies, especially a concept as ill-understood as fuzzy logic, the consequences of project failure are often deep and long lasting. Failure, none-the-less, is a part of project management and organizational growth. You should be prepared to fail but failure should not necessarily be incorporated as one of the project objectives.

Project Management and Protocycling

Between 1980 and 1988—the early days of expert systems growth in business and industry—artificial intelligence, symbolic reasoning, rule-based expert systems, and frame-based reasoning were viewed by management, project team leaders, and the fresh cadre of young AI scientists that swept into corporate America as a world of its own, far removed from the stuffy, pedestrian universe of the company's production software systems. Sitting before banks of LISP machines, knowledge engineers tackled a bewildering array of problems involving human intelligence. While a few succeeded, many, many more failed. Some of this failure can be attributed to a mismatch between development and deployment technologies, some to a naive understanding by young PH.D.'s of the real problems faced by business executives, and some to the unexpected complexity of front-line business problems. But much of the failure is attributable to poor management (perhaps "lack of management" would be better) of project resources. Many knowledge engineers and computer scientists in those days felt that conventional project management techniques no longer applied to artificial intelligence projects where prototyping, incremental development, and "test-and-burn" techniques were not only the order of the day, but were the approved method of development taught at most colleges and universities.

Without a solid approach to project management, advanced technology projects, like any effort involving a mix of consumable resources that must be scheduled across time, will drift from the original objective. This project drift results in missed target deadlines, budget over-runs, and the improper use of critical skills and other resources.

Project Management Techniques

Project management and control involves basic decisions about how to structure a project (creating a reasonable work break-down structure), how to allocate resources, and how to organize the project into a set of activities with their precedence relationships—the construction of the critical path. Project plans are developed to place a logical framework around the design, development, testing, and delivery process. In building fuzzy models, we follow the orthodox approach to project management, except there is inherently (as previously mentioned) a slightly high risk factor associated with the project parameters. This risk is usually taken into account in one of several ways: through the elasticity associated with activity durations, through the reprioritization of events as the project unfolds, through the management of scarce resources, and through the practice of phased or staged deliverables.

Scheduling Analysis

It is generally a mistake to believe high technology projects cannot be approached through standard work break-down and critical path techniques. Certainly the level of certainty in many of the activity estimates may be low when the project begins. At a minimum a fuzzy logic project needs a clear definition of the tasks and the order in which they must be performed. The technique for doing this is called the Critical Path Method (CPM) and is based on the Project Evaluation and Review Technique (PERT) developed by the Navy for the Polaris submarine project. Figure 7.2 shows part of a network analysis using the critical path network analysis technique.

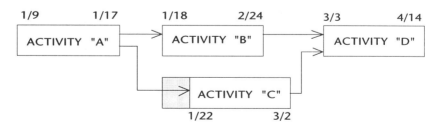

Figure 7.2 Part of a critical path network analysis

Each block in Figure 7.2 represents an activity in the project with any predecessor and successor events and has an estimated duration and (usually) an estimated resource requirement. The CPM and PERT scheduling techniques develop critical time frames for your project. These time frames include the early and late start and due dates as well as the amount of nonresource dependent slack in each event. The path through the network that has no slack is called the *Critical Path*. Any activity that slips along the critical path causes the entire project to slip. The results of a schedule are usually displayed on a bar or Gantt char. Figure 7.3 shows how a typical project gantt chart appears.

PROJECT TIMELINE

	JAN'98	FEB'98	MAR'98	APR'98	MAY'98	JUN'98
TASK1						
TASK2						
TASK3						
TASK4						
TASK5						
TASK6						

Figure 7.3 A project Gantt chart

The horizontal bar represents the duration of a task in the project. The bars that are shaded lie along the critical path. Actual project gantt charts carry additional information about project status, slippages, work done to-date, and so forth. In high technology projects the gantt chart, whether done formally through a project management program, or informally as an ad-hoc graph, provides a solid planning and analysis tool.

Resource Allocation and Staffing

An even more crucial factor in planning a project is the allocation and administration of critical and scarce resources. There are two issues here: the availability of resources and the staffing requirements for fuzzy logic projects. In the previous section on schedules we made reference to nonresource dependent slack. In actual project situations, the slack along the noncritical network paths may have a higher criticality in terms of the project completion schedule than the activities lying directly on the critical path. As an example,

Figure 7.4 shows the critical path through a portion of the project network. From this we can see that JONES is associated with activity "B" and has six (6) days of slack. This means Activity "B" can slip forward six days without impacting the due date of the project (since Activity "D" must wait until March 3rd for Activity "C" to finish.)

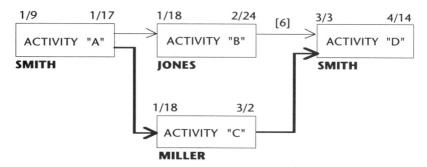

Figure 7.4 The critical path in a CPM network

But this resource-independent critical path is deceptive. It assumes we have unlimited access to JONES. The Resource requirements of higher priority projects, vacations, conferences, and meetings, as only a few examples, are not factored into the schedule. In fact, Figure 7.5 shows, shaded in grey, the remainder of Jones' assignments during the same time frame as Activity "B".

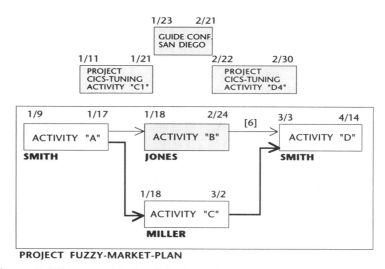

Figure 7.5 The true critical path in the project CPM network

From this more realistic view, we can see far from having six days of slack, it is highly unlikely that Jones completes more than one or two days worth of work on Activity "B". This problem of simultaneity of demand in allocating resources is responsible for many problems in high technology projects. This is especially exacerbated by the tendency of organizations to load critical staff officers and analysts to new technology projects without considering their total resource availability (spending 25% of your time on a fuzzy logic project is unrealistic if the demands on your total time exceed your actual weekly availability).

This leads to the issue of proper staffing for fuzzy projects. The issue of staffing is really two issues: the size of the project team and the skill sets required to effectively complete the project. Generally, the quality of a project and its ability to finish on-time and within budget is inversely proportional to the project team size. This makes sense when you consider the requirements for system design, programming, testing, documentation, and over-all project communication. The communication web density is generally $O(n^2)$, so assembling a large project team or adding staff to a project invariably retards progress.

The development team should be as small as possible consistent with the size of the effort and the need for specialized knowledge. As a rule, the project should consist of a project manager, a knowledge engineer, the principal system designer and architect, and the deployment specialist. In practice, and from experience, the first two are the most critical. The project manager is essential as the filter between the working project team and both the oversight requirements of management and the progress monitoring activities of the client. A project manager also needs to understand the implications of building products using new technologies such as fuzzy logic, but need not be a knowledge engineer or systems analyst. The knowledge engineer provides intelligence acquisition from the expert, structures the knowledge, and provides the over-all decision making framework. The system designer uses the available program coding and system building tools to actually construct the executable model. The deployment specialist is responsible for validation and testing of the delivered product, organizing the technology and operational knowledge transfer to the client, and managing the development of any written documentation.

Model Protocycling

The initial plan developed for a project should be considered tentative and speculative. Its purpose is structural rather than procedural. A large and detailed initial investment in the design phase is usually not productive since the scope of the project, the resolution of activity work contents and durations, as well as the nature of the model itself generally evolves as the knowledge acquisition, encoding, and preliminary testing continues. To reduce the probability that the model delivered is not what the client expects, a prototyping development methodology is used. This is an interactive process—each prototype is followed by a refinement of the model requirements and design that cycles back into the development of the final model. The cycle of prototype development is called protocycling. Figure 7.6 shows the nature of this development process.

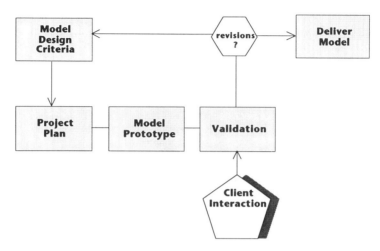

Figure 7.6 The model prototyping cycle

From the initial product design and project plan is developed a task list, the time relationships, skill requirements, and the budget. From this design, a model prototype is constructed representing as much of the system as reasonable given the model behavior characteristics described in the design. The client evaluates this model and provides both positive and negative feed-back. If revisions are necessary, changes to the design are made and the cycle begins again, otherwise we deliver the model. After some considerable usage, we may need to revalidate the model and start the cycle once more.

Tools and Support Requirements

Selecting a tool is also a critical issue in project development. There are fundamentally two kinds of tools: general development environments and code libraries. The general development environments provide, in most cases, a complete graphical user interface, such as HyperLogic's *CubiCalc*, Metus Systems' *Metus/Information Modelling System*, or a sophisticated command language shell such as Bill Siler's excellent *FLOPS* system from the Kemp-Carraway Heart Institute. Many of the development environments also generate program code so the resulting model can be embedded in application software. The graphical development environments usually provide point-and-click fuzzy set editors, rule compilers, multi-dimensional views of the fuzzy control surface, and other capabilities that provide the system designer with a rapid way of building and testing a fuzzy model.

The code libraries on the other hand generally consist of compiled programs collected in a relocatable library. Through an Application Program Interface (API) another program written in such common languages as C/C++, Pascal, Basic, Cobol, or Ada can access these functions. The fuzzy logic programs used throughout this book make use of this technique by calling on fuzzy logic functions stored in an object library (mtfzlib.lib). The use of code libraries coupled with compiled application code usually provides the best performance and the most compact execution module size. The trade-off, of course, is the necessity to work in compiled code, understand the library systems, and work without the assistance of a graphical development interface.

As a general rule, graphically hosted developed environments provide the best method of building, testing, and deploying a fuzzy logic model. The ability to quickly change the rule structure and visually follow the model execution helps both the system designer and the technically competent client. Where performance is an issue, the use of a development environment is still recommended as a method of prototyping the initial model. A translation into compiled code—either by hand, through a vendor supplied code library, or through a run-time code generator that is part of the environment—is done after the fundamental model operation has been validated.

C/C++ Code Listings

```
Initiali;
Parms[0]
Parms [1;
sprint(s)
strncpy(;
FDBptr[M;
if  si  t;
Par   om;
Pa   D
(*F    nt)
```
8

This chapter contains the C++ code listings for programs, demonstrations, and algorithms used throughout the book. The machine-readable source for these programs is located in the accompanying disk. The code description is arranged according to chapter location. If a program is referenced in several chapters it is shown under the chapter where it first appeared. Programs appear in roughly the same order that they appeared in the chapter.

The Code Relationships

The C/C++ code contained in this chapter has been compiled and tested under Microsoft's Visual C++ 1.0 and 1.5. Although every effort has been made to insure that the code is functioning correctly, these programs are basically intended for demonstration use and have not been put through the rigorous testing necessary for commercially durable software. You may find that some combination of input values produce unexpected results. I leave complete program robustness as an interesting and challenging project for the technically focused reader.

Compiling and Linking Code

The attached diskettes contain three sub-directories: *cppcode* contains the actual C++ source code, *hppcode* contains the header files necessary to compile the code (such as the symbolic constants, the prototype definitions, and the structures for objects like fuzzy sets), and *libcode* contains the four general object libraries needed to properly link and execute the code. An additional directory, *metus*, contains the error diagnostics files, and the fuzzy.ini file used to control the placement of audit files and the path to the error files. When the files have been retrieved, the demonstration programs can be compiled and linked. Figure 8.7 shows the general process.

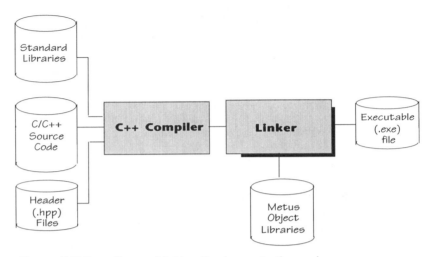

Figure 8.7 Compiling and linking the demonstration code

Note that in order to produce an executable (.exe) module, the Metus object libraries must be available to the linker. These are specified when you create your project file. Table 8.1 lists some of the compiler and linker options used in Microsoft Visual C++ to create the executables for the demonstration programs.

Table 8.1 Compiler and Linker Options

Compiler/Linker Option	Parameter Value
Memory Model	LARGE
Stack Size	32000
Max Segments	512
Private Libraries	MTDBLIB
	MTFZLIB
	MTGLLIB
	MTTLLIB

You should also be sure you are not using the Microsoft Foundation Libraries (MFC) and the compiler is producing a DOS executable. While the majority of the code is independent of the operating system, there are some specific links into the DOS operating system.

Demonstration .mak files

Included with the distribution disk in the *cppcode* subdirectory are a series of Microsoft Visual C++ make files (.mak). These files were created Microsoft Visual C++ and are enclosed simply as examples and specify directories used on the author's development machine (such as *metusmvc* as the principal code directory.) You can modify the make files, of course, to bring up and save a project with your own directory structure.

Directories and Code Placement

The distribution disks contain several directories containing the actual C/C++ source code, the include files, and the compiled object libraries (see "Compiling and Linking Code" on page 373). The distribution disk also contains a *metus* directory containing the error diagnostics files and the fuzzy system initialization file (which is discussed in the next section.) You are free to place the code, headers, and object libraries in any directory of your choosing. The actual names of these directories are unimportant and can be changed to suit your needs (although you will need to change the make files included with the demonstrations.)

However, the *metus* directory and its contents must be installed under the DOS root. To use the enclosed software, the underlying modelling software must have access to the *metus* directory.

Connecting to the Metus Modelling System

The fuzzy logic routines embedded in the application code are part of the Metus fuzzy logic object libraries. When an application program starts it **must** make a connection to the underlying library and its run-time utilities. This is done through the following program call:

SysConnecttoMetus(&status)

where *status* is a signed short integer. Connecting to the Metus software initializes the modelling environment. This process establishes the file names and paths for the system audit log (*syslog.fil*), the modelling audit log (*mdllog.fil*), and the error diagnostic file (*metus.edf*). By default, the model and system log files are placed on the A: disk drive. Figure 8.8 shows schematically how the *SysConnecttoMetus* function works.

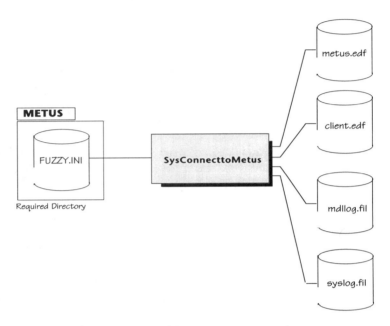

Figure 8.8 The SysConnecttoMetus program controls

Using the fuzzy.ini File

Since DOS is a unprotected operating system, writing files to your main hard disk during program development can be dangerous—a fault in logic can cause the C/C++ *fprintf* statement to write over existing data or parts of the operating system. When you install the code form the distribution disk, you create a Metus directory. Contained in the Metus directory is the *fuzzy.ini* file. This file contains the names and paths of the primary control files in the modelling environment. Listing 8.1 shows how a complete *fuzzy.ini* file appears.

```
systemfile=a:\syslog.fil
modelfile=a:\mdllog.fil
errorfile=c:\metus\metus.edf
clientfile=c:\metus\client.edf
```

Listing 8.1 A complete fuzzy.ini file

The *fuzzy.ini* file on the distribution disk is empty (it contains a comment header only). An empty file causes the system to use the default values shown in Listing 8.1. To change the name or location of any file, you can use the *fuzzy.ini* file to specify a new path or file name. You must use one or more the keywords shows in Listing 8.1, followed by an equal sign (or a space) and the complete path and file name of the file. You need not specify all of the keywords, and they can appear in any order. Note that if either the metus directory or the fuzzy.ini file do not exist, the fuzzy modelling software will not work.

Code for Chapter 2: Fuzzy Logic and Machine Reasoning

weight1.cpp (The Weight Estimator)

```
/*------------------------------------------------------------*
| (c) 1992 Metus Systems.      Proprietary software product. |
| Reproduction or unauthorized use is prohibited. Unauthorized|
| use is illegal. Violators will be prosecuted. This software |
| contains proprietary trade and business secrets.           |
/*------------------Procedure Description------------------*
| weight1.cpp   Earl Cox  11/18/92  The Weight Estimator    |
| This is the main driver routine that invokes the stand-alone|
| weight estimating model. This is an example of monotonic   |
| fuzzy reasoning using the low level fuzzy facilities.      |
*--------------Compiler and Operating Systems-------------*
| This program has been compiled under the Borland C++ 3.1   |
| compiler operating under DOS 5.1. It uses the Metus Low    |
| Level Fuzzy Service Libraries (Rel 1.0).                   |
*--------------Modification Audit/Change Log--------------*
| Rev  Sar              Metus                                |
| No   Code Date        Rellvl Mod  Description              |
| --   ----- --------   ------ ---  -----------------------  |
|                                                            |
|                                                            |
*------------------------------------------------------------*/
/*-------------D--I--S--C--L--A--I--M--E--R-------------*
| The Metus Systems Group provides the model example on a    |
| strictly "as is" basis and assumes no direct, indirect, or |
| consequential responsibility for its use. No warranties as |
| to its fitness for any particular use is made. * You are   |
| free to use, modify, and distribute this code so long as   |
| each recipient agrees to this waiver of responsibility.    |
*------------------------------------------------------------*/
#include <stdio.h>
#include "SFZYctl.hpp"
#include "SSYSctl.hpp"
#include "mtypes.hpp"
#include "mtsptype.hpp"
double Weight1Model(int,double,float*,int*);
void main(void)
  {
  double    inHeight[]={5.0,5.25,5.50,5.75,6,6.5};
  int       inHcnt=6;
  int       i,status;
  float     compidx;
  double    height=0,weight;
//
  MdlInitXSYSctl(&status);                    // Connect to Metus
```

```
     XSYSctl.XSYStrace[3]=TRUE;                // Turn plotting on
     for(i=0;i<inHcnt;i++)
        {
          height=inHeight[i];
          weight=Weight1Model(i,height,&compidx,&status);
          fprintf(stdout,"\n%s%8.2f%s%8.2f%s%8.3f\n",
            "Height: ",height,", Weight: ",weight,", CIX: ",compidx);
        }
     return;
   }
```

wgt1mod.cpp (The Weight Estimator Policy)

```
/*---------------------------------------------------------*
| (c) 1992 Metus Systems.       Proprietary software product. |
| Reproduction or unauthorized use is prohibited. Unauthorized|
| use is illegal. Violators will be prosecuted. This software |
| contains proprietary trade and business secrets.            |
/*------------------Procedure Description------------------*
| wgt1mod.cpp   Earl Cox  08/12/92  The Monotonic Weight Model|
|                                                             |
| ------------------------------------------------------------|
| See AI Expert, October 1992, "Problem Solving with Fuzzy    |
| Logic" by Earl Cox. This model develops an estimated weight |
| for an individual based on a single factor: the person's    |
| height. This shows the flexibility of a single rule fuzzy   |
| model using monotonic (proportional) reasoning.             |
*---------------Modification Audit/Change Log---------------*
| Rev  Sar         Metus                                      |
| No   Code  Date        Rellvl  Mod  Description             |
| --   ----  --------    ------  ---  -----------------------  |
|                                                             |
|                                                             |
*---------------------------------------------------------*/
#include <stdio.h>
#include <string.h>
#include "FDB.hpp"        // The Fuzzy Set descriptor
#include "XFZYctl.hpp"    // The fuzzy parallel processor work area
#include "XSYSctl.hpp"    // The Metus System control region
#include "mtypes.hpp"     // System constants and symbolics
#include "fuzzy.hpp"      // Fuzzy Logic constants and symbolics
#include "mtsptype.hpp"   // Metus function prototypes
//
//--These are the "logical" rules. In the high level fuzzy modelling
//--system we would enter these rules exactly as shown.
static const char *Rules[]=
  {
   "R1   if height is tall then weight is heavy"
  };
static const Rulemax=1;
//
double Weight1Model(int Cnt,double Height,float *PremiseTruth,int *statusPtr)
  {
   FDB     *TallFDBptr[2],
           *WeightFDBptr[2],
           *HeavyFDBptr[2];
   char    *PgmId="Weight1";
   char    strBuff[80];
   int     i,
           status,
           Index,
           Idxpos,
           Rulecnt;
```

```
   double   Weight,
            Domain[2],
            Parms [6];
   FILE    *mdllog;
   mdllog=MtsGetSystemFile(SYSMODFILE);     // Get default model log file
//--Describe the Model Parameters
//
   fprintf(mdllog,"%s\n",
     "Fuzzy Weight Estimation Model. (c) 1995 Metus Systems Group.");
   fprintf(mdllog,"%s%10.2f\n","Individual Height (feet): ",Height  );
   fprintf(mdllog,"%s\n","The Rules:");
   for(i=0;i<Rulemax;i++)     fprintf(mdllog,"%s\n",Rules[i]);
   fputc('\n',mdllog);
//
//--Create the basic fuzzy sets (Hi and Low for Weight)
//
   Domain[0]=5.0;
   Domain[1]=6.5;
   TallFDBptr[0]=FzyCreateSet("TALL",INCREASE,Domain,Parms,0,statusPtr);
   FzyDrawSet(TallFDBptr[0],SYSMODFILE,statusPtr);
//
   Domain[0]=150;
   Domain[1]=240;
   HeavyFDBptr[0]=FzyCreateSet("HEAVY",GROWTH,Domain,Parms,0,statusPtr);
   FzyDrawSet(HeavyFDBptr[1],SYSMODFILE,statusPtr);
//
//----------B E G I N    M O D E L    P R O C E S S I N G-------------
//
   Rulecnt=0;
//
//--Rule 1. If Height is TALL then Weight is HEAVY;
//
   fprintf(mdllog,"%s\n",Rules[Rulecnt]);
   Weight=FzyMonotonicLogic(
     TallFDBptr[0],HeavyFDBptr[0],Height,PremiseTruth,statusPtr);
   fprintf(mdllog,"%s\n","Model Solution:");
   fprintf(mdllog,"%s%10.2f\n","  Height       = ",Height       );
   fprintf(mdllog,"%s%10.2f\n","  Weight       = ",Weight       );
   fprintf(mdllog,"%s%10.6f\n","  Truth Grade = ",*PremiseTruth );
   Domain[0]=150;
   Domain[1]=240;
   WeightFDBptr[0]=FzyCreateSet("HEAVY",GROWTH,Domain,Parms,0,statusPtr);
   for(i=0;i<VECMAX;i++)
    if(WeightFDBptr[0]->FDBvector[i]>*PremiseTruth)
        WeightFDBptr[0]->FDBvector[i]=*PremiseTruth;
//
//
   FzyDrawSet(TallFDBptr[0],SYSMODFILE,statusPtr);
   sprintf(strBuff,"%s%03d%s","b:tal",Cnt,".txt");
   FzyStoreFuzzyData(TallFDBptr,1,strBuff,8,statusPtr);
//
   FzyDrawSet(HeavyFDBptr[0],SYSMODFILE,statusPtr);
   sprintf(strBuff,"%s%03d%s","b:hvy",Cnt,".txt");
   FzyStoreFuzzyData(HeavyFDBptr,1,strBuff,8,statusPtr);
//
   FzyDrawSet(WeightFDBptr[0],SYSMODFILE,statusPtr);
   sprintf(strBuff,"%s%03d%s","b:wgt",Cnt,".txt");
   FzyStoreFuzzyData(WeightFDBptr,1,strBuff,8,statusPtr);
   delete TallFDBptr[0];
   delete HeavyFDBptr[0];
   delete WeightFDBptr[0];
   return(Weight);
   }
```

wgtmodel.cpp (The Fuzzy Reasoning Weight Model)

```
/*-------------------------------------------------------------*
| Copyright (c) 1993 by The Metus Systems Group.              |
| All rights reserved. Proprietary Software Product.          |
| No part of this software may be reproduced or transmitted   |
| in any form or by any means, electronic or mechanical,      |
| including input into or storage in any information system   |
| for resale without permission in writing from Metus Systems.|
*-------------------------------------------------------------*
| wgtmodel1.cpp  Earl Cox  11/17/94  The fuzzy weight model   |
|                                                             |
*---------------Modification Audit/Change Log---------------* |
| Rev  Sar              Metus                                 |
| No   Code  Date      Rellvl  Mod  Description               |
| --   ----- --------  ------  ---  ------------------------  |
|                                                             |
*-------------------------------------------------------------*/
#include <stdio.h>
#include <string.h>
#include <math.h>
#include "PDB.hpp"
#include "FDB.hpp"
#include "SSYSctl.hpp"
#include "SFZYctl.hpp"
#include "fuzzy.hpp"
#include "mtypes.hpp"
#include "mtsptype.hpp"
static const Rulemax=5;
extern unsigned _stklen=50000;
PDB* MdlCreatePolicy(char*,int,int*);
#define MAXFZYSETS   8
void    CaptureFuzzySet(char*,FDB*,int*);
void    DisplayRule(char **,int,int);
//
char far * far hgtFDBnames[]= { "SHORT","MEDIUM","TALL"          };
char far * far sszFDBnames[]= { "SMALL","MEDIUM","BIG", "LARGE"  };
char far * far waiFDBnames[]= { "SMALL","MEDIUM","WIDE","LARGE"  };
char far * far wgtFDBnames[]= { "LIGHT","MEDIUM","HEAVY"         };
char far * far WgtRules[]    =
  {
  "[R1]  if height is Tall then weight is Heavy;        ",
  "[R2]  if height is Medium then weight is Medium;     ",
  "[R3]  if shoesize is Large then weight is Heavy;     ",
  "[R4]  if waistsize is Wide then weight is Heavy;     "
  };
//
//
void main(void)
  {
  FDB     *estwgtFDBptr,
          *hgtFDBptr[MAXFZYSETS],
          *sszFDBptr[MAXFZYSETS],
          *waiFDBptr[MAXFZYSETS],
          *wgtFDBptr[MAXFZYSETS];
  FSV     *wgtFSVptr;
  VDB     *wgtVDBptr;
  int      hgtFDBcnt=3,
           sszFDBcnt=4,
           waiFDBcnt=4,
           wgtFDBcnt=3;
  char    *PgmId="wgtmodel";
  int      i,j,t,status,TryCtl[2];
  int      idxpos,
```

```
                           thisCorrMethod,
                           thisDefuzzMethod;
          bool     trace,storfs;
          float    CompIDX,
                           Predtruth;
          double   Parms[4],
                           Domain[2],
                           estimatedWgt,
                           height,
                           shoesize,
                           waistsize;
          FILE     *mdlout;
//
//
   SysConnecttoMetus(&status);
   XSYSctl.XSYScurrPDBptr=NULL;
   XSYSctl.XSYSalfacut   =0.1;
   mdlout=MtsGetSystemFile(SYSMODFILE);
//
//
   printf("INITIALIZE MODEL\n");
   TryCtl[0]=5;
   TryCtl[1]=0;
   Domain[0]=  4;Domain[1]=  7;
   height=MtsAskforDBL(
     "height",   "Height      [4,7]      : ",Domain,TryCtl,&status);
   Domain[0]=  5;Domain[1]= 12;
   shoesize=MtsAskforDBL(
     "shoesize", "Shoe Size   [5,12]     : ",Domain,TryCtl,&status);
   Domain[0]= 28;Domain[1]= 50;
   waistsize=MtsAskforDBL(
     "waistsize", "Waist Size [28,50]    : ",Domain,TryCtl,&status);
   printf("SPECIFY MODEL ACTIONS\n");
   trace =MtsAskforBOOL(
     "fzySetTrace",   "Trace FuzzySets       : ",       TryCtl,&status);
   XSYSctl.XSYStrace[3]=trace;
   trace =MtsAskforBOOL(
     "RuleTrace",     "Trace Rule Actions    : ",       TryCtl,&status);
   XSYSctl.XSYStrace[2]=trace;
   storfs=MtsAskforBOOL(
     "StoreSets",     "Store FuzzySets       : ",       TryCtl,&status);
//
   fprintf(mdlout,"%s\n", "PARAMETERS:");
   fprintf(mdlout,"%s%10.2f\n", " Height    : ",height);
   fprintf(mdlout,"%s%10.2f\n", " Shoe Size : ",shoesize);
   fprintf(mdlout,"%s%10.2f\n", " Waist Size: ",waistsize);
   fprintf(mdlout,"%s\n\n",     "  ");
//
//=============================================================
//--HEIGHT FUZZY SETS. These sets define the semantics
//--associated with the individual's height.
//=============================================================
//
   for(i=0;i<hgtFDBcnt;i++)
     {
     if((hgtFDBptr[i]=new FDB)==NULL)
       {
       MtsSendError(2,PgmId,hgtFDBnames[i]);
       return;
       }
     FzyInitFDB(hgtFDBptr[i]);
     strcpy(hgtFDBptr[i]->FDBid,  hgtFDBnames[i]);
     hgtFDBptr[i]->FDBdomain[0]= 4;
     hgtFDBptr[i]->FDBdomain[1]= 7;
```

```
        }
    FzySCurve  (hgtFDBptr[0],  4.0, 4.75,5.5,DECLINE,&status); //SHORT
    FzyPiCurve (hgtFDBptr[1],  5.5, 1.00,            &status); //MEDIUM
    FzySCurve  (hgtFDBptr[2],  5.5, 6.25,7.0,GROWTH ,&status); //TALL
    FzyPlotSets("HEIGHT",hgtFDBptr,hgtFDBcnt,SYSMODFILE,&status);
    FzyStoreFuzzyData(hgtFDBptr,hgtFDBcnt,"b:wgtheigt.dat", 8,&status);
//
//=============================================================
//--SHOESIZE FUZZY SETS. The decomposition of the shoe sizes
//--based on various shoe sizes.
//=============================================================
//
    for(i=0;i<sszFDBcnt;i++)
      {
       if((sszFDBptr[i]=new FDB)==NULL)
         {
          MtsSendError(2,PgmId,sszFDBnames[i]);
          return;
         }
       FzyInitFDB(sszFDBptr[i]);
       strcpy(sszFDBptr[i]->FDBid,  sszFDBnames[i]);
       sszFDBptr[i]->FDBdomain[0]=  5;
       sszFDBptr[i]->FDBdomain[1]= 12;
      }
    FzySCurve  (sszFDBptr[0],  5,  6,    7,DECLINE,&status); //SMALL
    FzyPiCurve (sszFDBptr[1],  7,  2            ,&status); //MEDIUM
    FzyPiCurve (sszFDBptr[2],  9,  2            ,&status); //BIG
    FzySCurve  (sszFDBptr[3],  9, 10.5, 12,GROWTH ,&status); //LARGE
    FzyPlotSets("SHOE.SIZE",sszFDBptr,sszFDBcnt,SYSMODFILE,&status);
    FzyStoreFuzzyData(sszFDBptr,sszFDBcnt,"b:wgtshoes.dat", 8,&status);
//
//=============================================================
//--WAIST SIZE FUZZY SETS. These fuzzy sets describe the semantics
//--associated with the individuals's waist (belt) size.
//=============================================================
//
    for(i=0;i<waiFDBcnt;i++)
      {
       if((waiFDBptr[i]=new FDB)==NULL)
         {
          MtsSendError(2,PgmId,waiFDBnames[i]);
          return;
         }
       FzyInitFDB(waiFDBptr[i]);
       strcpy(waiFDBptr[i]->FDBid,  waiFDBnames[i]);
       waiFDBptr[i]->FDBdomain[0]= 28;
       waiFDBptr[i]->FDBdomain[1]= 48;
      }
    FzySCurve  (waiFDBptr[0],  28, 32, 36,DECLINE,&status); //SMALL
    FzyPiCurve (waiFDBptr[1],  36, 4            ,&status); //MEDIUM
    FzyPiCurve (waiFDBptr[2],  40, 4            ,&status); //WIDE
    FzySCurve  (waiFDBptr[3],  40, 44, 48,GROWTH ,&status); //LARGE
    FzyPlotSets("WAIST.SIZE",waiFDBptr,waiFDBcnt,SYSMODFILE,&status);
    FzyStoreFuzzyData(waiFDBptr,waiFDBcnt,"b:wgtshoes.dat", 8,&status);
//
//
//=============================================================
//--WEIGHT OUTPUT FUZZY SETS. These fuzzy sets describe the output
//--fuzzy region associated with the solution variable.
//=============================================================
//
    for(i=0;i<wgtFDBcnt;i++)
      {
       if((wgtFDBptr[i]=new FDB)==NULL)
```

```
         {
          MtsSendError(2,PgmId,wgtFDBnames[i]);
          return;
         }
      FzyInitFDB(wgtFDBptr[i]);
      strcpy(wgtFDBptr[i]->FDBid, wgtFDBnames[i]);
      wgtFDBptr[i]->FDBdomain[0]= 110;
      wgtFDBptr[i]->FDBdomain[1]= 210;
     }
  FzySCurve  (wgtFDBptr[0], 110,135,160,DECLINE,&status); //LIGHT
  FzyPiCurve (wgtFDBptr[1], 160, 25,             &status); //MEDIUM
  FzySCurve  (wgtFDBptr[2], 160,185,210,GROWTH ,&status); //HEAVY
  FzyPlotSets("WEIGHT",wgtFDBptr,wgtFDBcnt,SYSMODFILE,&status);
  FzyStoreFuzzyData(wgtFDBptr,wgtFDBcnt,"b:wgtweigt.dat", 8,&status);
//
  printf("Declare and Install 'EstimateWgt' output variable\n");
  Domain[0]=110; Domain[1]=210;
  wgtVDBptr=VarCreateScalar("EstimatedWgt",REAL,Domain,"0",&status);
  FzyInitFZYctl(&status);
  if(!(FzyAddFZYctl(wgtVDBptr,&estwgtFDBptr,&wgtFSVptr,&status)))
     {
      MtsSendError(12,PgmId,"estimatedWgt");
      exit(9);
     }
  thisCorrMethod  =wgtFSVptr->FzySVcorrMethod;
  thisDefuzzMethod=wgtFSVptr->FzySVdefuzzMethod;
//
//--if height is tall then weight is heavy;
//
  printf("Firing Rule[1]....\n");
  DisplayRule(WgtRules,0,1);
  Predtruth=FzyGetMembership(hgtFDBptr[2],height,&idxpos,&status);
  FzyCondProposition(wgtFDBptr[2],wgtFSVptr,thisCorrMethod,Predtruth,&status);
  FzyDrawSet(estwgtFDBptr,SYSMODFILE,&status);
  CaptureFuzzySet("b:wgtrule1.dat",estwgtFDBptr,&status);
//
//--if height is medium then weight is medium;
//
  printf("Firing Rule[2]....\n");
  DisplayRule(WgtRules,1,1);
  Predtruth=FzyGetMembership(hgtFDBptr[1],height,&idxpos,&status);
  FzyCondProposition(wgtFDBptr[1],wgtFSVptr,thisCorrMethod,Predtruth,&status);
  FzyDrawSet(estwgtFDBptr,SYSMODFILE,&status);
  CaptureFuzzySet("b:wgtrule2.dat",estwgtFDBptr,&status);
//
//--if shoesize is Large then weight is heavy;
//
  printf("Firing Rule[3]....\n");
  DisplayRule(WgtRules,2,1);
  Predtruth=FzyGetMembership(sszFDBptr[3],shoesize,&idxpos,&status);
  FzyCondProposition(wgtFDBptr[2],wgtFSVptr,thisCorrMethod,Predtruth,&status);
  FzyDrawSet(estwgtFDBptr,SYSMODFILE,&status);
  CaptureFuzzySet("b:wgtrule3.dat",estwgtFDBptr,&status);
//
//--if waistsize is Wide then weight is heavy;
//
  printf("Firing Rule[4]....\n");
  DisplayRule(WgtRules,3,1);
  Predtruth=FzyGetMembership(waiFDBptr[2],waistsize,&idxpos,&status);
  FzyCondProposition(wgtFDBptr[2],wgtFSVptr,thisCorrMethod,Predtruth,&status);
  FzyDrawSet(estwgtFDBptr,SYSMODFILE,&status);
  CaptureFuzzySet("b:wgtrule4.dat",estwgtFDBptr,&status);
//
//
  FzyDrawSet(estwgtFDBptr,SYSMODFILE,&status);
  CaptureFuzzySet("b:wgtfinal.dat",estwgtFDBptr,&status);
  printf("Defuzzify Output Fuzzy Region.....\n");
  estimatedWgt=FzyDefuzzify(estwgtFDBptr,thisDefuzzMethod,&CompIDX,&status);
```

```
      FzyCloseFZYctl(&status);
   return;
   }
//
//
void CaptureFuzzySet(char *FzyDataFile,FDB*FDBptr,int *statusPtr)
/*-------------------------------------------------------------*
| This routine is used to capture and store the fuzzy set      |
| membership array on disk for use in fine-point graphics.     |
*-------------------------------------------------------------*/
  {
   int       i,
             CompFactor= 8,
             MaxValues= 128,
             status,
             ExtCnt;
   double    DomValues[128];
   float     MemValues[128];
   FILE      *fzyout;
   *statusPtr=0;
   if((fzyout=fopen(FzyDataFile,"w"))==NULL)
     {
      *statusPtr=1;
      printf("Sorry. '%s' file was not created\n",FzyDataFile);
      return;
     }
   FzyExtractSetdata(FDBptr,CompFactor,DomValues,MemValues,&ExtCnt,&status);
   for(i=0;i<ExtCnt;i++)
      fprintf(fzyout,"%10.2f  %6.4f\n",DomValues[i],MemValues[i]);
   fclose(fzyout);
   return;
  }
//
//
void DisplayRule(char **Rules,int fromIDX,int forIDX)
  {
   int     i;
   FILE   *mdlout;
   mdlout=MtsGetSystemFile(SYSMODFILE);
//
   fprintf(mdlout,"%s\n","  ");
   for(i=fromIDX;i<fromIDX+forIDX;i++) fprintf(mdlout,"%s\n",Rules[i]);
   fprintf(mdlout,"%s\n","  ");
   return;
  }
```

soundex.cpp (The Soundex Main Program)

```
/*-------------------------------------------------------------*
| (c) 1995 Metus Systems.      Proprietary software product.  |
| Reproduction or unauthorized use is prohibited. Unauthorized|
| use is illegal. Violators will be prosecuted. This software |
| contains proprietary trade and business secrets.            |
*------------------Procedure Description--------------------*
| soundex.cpp  Earl Cox  01/12/95  The Soundex Phonetics      |
| This function takes a string and produces the soundex code  |
| that represents the equivalent phonetic representation for  |
| this collection of letters.                                 |
*--------------Modification Audit/Change Log---------------*
| Rev  Sar            Metus                                    |
| No   Code  Date     Rellvl  Mod  Description                |
| --   -----  --------  ------  ---  ------------------------- |
```

```
  |                                                                      |
  *----------------------------------------------------------------------*/
#include <stdio.h>
#include <stdlib.h>
#include <string.h>
#include "SSYSctl.hpp"
#include "mtsptype.hpp"
#include "mtypes.hpp"
#define MINSDX   4
void main(int argc,char **argv)
  {
   int     status;
   char  *inBuff,*outBuff;
//----------------------------------------------------------------------
   SysConnecttoMetus(&status);
   XSYSctl.XSYScurrPDBptr=NULL;
//----------------------------------------------------------------------
//
   switch(argc)
     {
      case 1:
       printf("ERROR. format is soundex <string>\n");
       exit(0);
      case 2:
       inBuff=argv[1];
       if(strlen(inBuff)<MINSDX)
          {
           printf("%s must have at least %3d characters.\n",inBuff,MINSDX);
           return;
          }
       break;
      default:
       printf("%s: extraneous argument\n", argv[2]);
       exit(1);
     }
   outBuff=MtsPhoneticAnalyzer(inBuff,&status);
   printf("%s%s%s%s\n","in: ",inBuff,", soundex: ",outBuff);
   return;
  }
```

mttlpan.cpp (The Phonetic Analyzer)

```
/*------------------------------------------------------------------*
| (c) 1994 Metus Systems.      Proprietary software product.      |
| Reproduction or unauthorized use is prohibited. Unauthorized|
| use is illegal. Violators will be prosecuted. This software |
| contains proprietary trade and business secrets.            |
*--------------------Procedure Description--------------------*
| mttlpan.cpp  Earl Cox  01/06/94 Phonetic Analyzer           |
| This routine computes the extended SOUNDEX value for a      |
| string. Through this technique we attempt to bring together |
| values that sound similar.                                  |
*----------------Modification Audit/Change Log----------------*
| Rev  Sar              Metus                                  |
| No   Code  Date     Rellvl  Mod  Description                |
| --   ----- --------  ------  ---  ------------------------|
|                                                             |
|                                                             |
*------------------------------------------------------------------*/
#include <ctype.h>
#include <string.h>
#include <stdlib.h>
#include "mtypes.hpp"
```

```
#include "mtsptype.hpp"
//
//
static  char *Alphabet    = "ABCDEFGHIJKLMNOPQRSTUVWXYZ";
static  char *CodeLetters = "BCDFGJKLMNPQRSTVXZ";
static  char *PgmId       = "mttlpan";
static  char  wrkBuff[128];
//
static void AdjustPrefixSound(char*,int*);
static void RemoveVowelsandOthers(char*,int*);
static void ReplaceLetters(char*,int*);
//
char *MtsPhoneticAnalyzer(char *String,int *StatusPtr)
  {
  char     FirstByte;
  char     *outBuff;
  int      i,k,N,buffsize,strsize;
  int      MaxSDX=4;
  long     SDXnum;
  strsize=strlen(String);
  if((outBuff=new char[strsize+2])==NULL)
     {
     *StatusPtr=1;
     MtsSendError(2,PgmId,String);
     return(NULL);
     }
  buffsize=strsize;
//
//-------------------------------------------------------------------
//--Step 1. Translate all characters to upper case
//-------------------------------------------------------------------
//
  memset(outBuff,'\0',strsize+1);
  for(i=0;i<strsize;i++) outBuff[i]=toupper(String[i]);
//
//-------------------------------------------------------------------
//--Step 2. Replace prefix sounds
//-------------------------------------------------------------------
//
  AdjustPrefixSound(outBuff,&strsize);
  FirstByte=outBuff[0];
//
//-------------------------------------------------------------------
//--Step 3. Remove all special characters and vowels
//-------------------------------------------------------------------
//
  RemoveVowelsandOthers(outBuff,&strsize);
//
//-------------------------------------------------------------------
//--Step 4. Replace remaining letters with numbers
//-------------------------------------------------------------------
//
  ReplaceLetters(outBuff,&strsize);
//
//-------------------------------------------------------------------
//--Step 5. Form phonetic classification pattern
//-------------------------------------------------------------------
//
  memset(wrkBuff,'\0',128);
  SDXnum=atol(outBuff);
  sprintf(wrkBuff,"%c%03ld",FirstByte,SDXnum);
  memset(outBuff,'\0',buffsize);
  strncpy(outBuff,wrkBuff,MaxSDX);
  return(outBuff);
```

```
    }
//
//========================================================================
//--------------SOUNDEX PHONETIC GENERATOR SERVICES-------------------
//========================================================================
//
void AdjustPrefixSound(char *outBuff,int *strsize)
/*-----------------------------------------------------------------*
| While individual letters have generally the same sound, some sets |
| of characters appearing at the start of words have a different    |
| sound. Here we convert these special cases to the corresponding   |
| phonetic representation.                                          |
*-----------------------------------------------------------------*/
  {
   int       i;
   /* An X sounds like a Z */
   if(outBuff[0]=='X')
     {
      outBuff[0]='Z';
      return;
     }
   memset(wrkBuff,'\0',128);
   if(strncmp(outBuff,"PH",2)==0)      wrkBuff[0]='F';
   if(strncmp(outBuff,"PS",2)==0)      wrkBuff[0]='S';
   if(strncmp(outBuff,"CH",2)==0)      wrkBuff[0]='G';
   if(strncmp(outBuff,"PN",2)==0
      ||strncmp(outBuff,"MN",2)==0
      ||strncmp(outBuff,"KN",2)==0)    wrkBuff[0]='N';
   if(wrkBuff[0]!='\0')
     {
      for(i=1;i<(*strsize);i++)
        {
         wrkBuff[i]=outBuff[i+1];
         wrkBuff[i+1]='\0';
        }
      strcpy(outBuff,wrkBuff);
      *strsize=strlen(outBuff);
      return;
     }
   if(strncmp(outBuff,"SCHW",4)==0)  strcpy(wrkBuff,"SHW");
   if(strncmp(outBuff,"SCHM",4)==0)  strcpy(wrkBuff,"SHM");
   if(wrkBuff[0]!='\0')
     for(i=3;i<(*strsize)-1;i++)
       {
        wrkBuff[i]=outBuff[i+1];
        wrkBuff[i+1]='\0';
        strcpy(outBuff,wrkBuff);
        *strsize=strlen(outBuff);
       }
   return;
  }
//
//
void RemoveVowelsandOthers(char *outBuff,int *strsize)
/*-----------------------------------------------------------------*
|  We now scrub the incoming string by removing all the special     |
|  characters and all the vowels. We loop across the input buffer    |
|  and build a temporary buffer by (1) inserting any byte that is    |
|  part of the proper alphabet and (2) removing any byte that is     |
|  a vowel or near-vowel (AEHIOUWY).                                 |
*-----------------------------------------------------------------*/
  {
   int  k,i,spos;
   spos=0;
```

```
   memset(wrkBuff,'\0',128);
   for(i=0;i<(*strsize);i++)
     {
      k=MtsStrIndex(CodeLetters,outBuff[i]);
      if(k!=NOTFOUND)
        {
         wrkBuff[spos]=outBuff[i];
         spos++;
        }
     }
   *strsize=spos;
   strcpy(outBuff,wrkBuff);
   return;
  }
//
//
void  ReplaceLetters(char *outBuff,int *strsize)
/*-------------------------------------------------------------------*
| We now have a string containing only non-vowels. Each character  |
| is now replaced by a number depending on its classification.     |
| After this we remove all values that occur in succession (such   |
| as LL, RR, etc.)                                                 |
*-------------------------------------------------------------------*/
  {
   int     i,spos;
   char    repByte;
   for(i=0;i<(*strsize);i++)
     {
      repByte=outBuff[i];
      //--Check for labials
      if(MtsStrIndex("BFPV",    outBuff[i])!=NOTFOUND) repByte='1';
      //--Check for sibilants and gutterals
      if(MtsStrIndex("CGJKQSXZ",outBuff[i])!=NOTFOUND) repByte='2';
      //--Check for dentals
      if(MtsStrIndex("DT",      outBuff[i])!=NOTFOUND) repByte='3';
      //--Check for long liquids
      if(MtsStrIndex("HL",      outBuff[i])!=NOTFOUND) repByte='4';
      //--Check for nasals
      if(MtsStrIndex("MN",      outBuff[i])!=NOTFOUND) repByte='5';
      //--Check for short liquids
      if(MtsStrIndex("WR",      outBuff[i])!=NOTFOUND) repByte='6';
      outBuff[i]=repByte;
     }
   spos=0;
   while(1)
     {
      if(outBuff[spos]==outBuff[spos+1])
        {
         for(i=spos;i<(*strsize);i++)
           {
            outBuff[i]=outBuff[i+1];
            outBuff[i+1]='\0';
           }
         (*strsize)--;
         spos--;
        }
      spos++;
      if(spos>(*strsize)) break;
     }
   return;
  }
```

dcmodel1.cpp (The Drug Concentration Model)

```
/*----------------------------------------------------------*
| (c) 1994 Metus Systems.        Proprietary software product. |
| Reproduction or unauthorized use is prohibited. Unauthorized|
| use is illegal. Violators will be prosecuted. This software |
| contains proprietary trade and business secrets.            |
*--------------------Procedure Description--------------------*
| dcmodel1.cpp  Earl Cox  11/17/94 Dosage Concentration       |
| This program calculates the concentration of a drug at a    |
| given dosage after "t" minutes. The concentration diffusion |
| rate is given by the expression,                            |
|                                                             |
|           C(t)=D*t*exp(-t/3)                                |
|                                                             |
| where "D" is the doage in units and "t" is the time in      |
| minutes after the initial injection.                        |
*---------------Modification Audit/Change Log----------------*
| Rev  Sar                   Metus                            |
| No   Code  Date     Rellvl Mod  Description                 |
| --   ----- -------- ------ ---  ------------------------    |
|                                                             |
*----------------------------------------------------------*/
#include <string.h>
#include <stdio.h>
#include <math.h>
#include "mttypes.hpp"
#define THREE     3
#define MAXTIME   36
#define MAXDOSES  10
//
double Concentration(double,double);
//
void main(void)
 {
  FILE   *Dataout;
  char   *DataFile="b:doselvl.dat";
  double dgUnits[]={100,120,140,160,180,200,220,240,260,280};
  double dgLevel,doseAmt[48][20];
  int    t,i,j,status;
  for(i=0;i<MAXDOSES;i++)
    for(t=0;t<MAXTIME;t++)
      {
       dgLevel=Concentration(dgUnits[i],t);
       doseAmt[t][i]=dgLevel;
      }
  printf("Capturing Data.\n");
  if((Dataout=fopen(DataFile,"w"))==NULL)
    {
     printf("Sorry. '%s' file was not created\n",DataFile);
     return;
    }
  for(i=0;i<MAXTIME;i++)
    {
     fprintf(Dataout,"%3d ",i);
     for(j=0;j<MAXDOSES;j++)
       fprintf(Dataout,", %11.3f  ",doseAmt[i][j]);
     fprintf(Dataout,"%c",'\n');
    }
  fclose(Dataout);
  printf("%s%s\n","Dosage Level data on: ",DataFile);
 }
//
//
```

```
double Concentration(double dgUnits,double t)
{
   double  texp,ConAmount;
   texp=-(t/THREE);
   ConAmount=(dgUnits*t)*pow(E,texp);
   return(ConAmount);
}
```

dcfuzzy1.cpp (The Fuzzy Drug Concentration Model)

```
/*------------------------------------------------------------*
| Copyright (c) 1995 by The Metus Systems Group.              |
| All rights reserved. Proprietary Software Product.          |
| No part of this software may be reproduced or transmitted   |
| in any form or by any means, electronic or mechanical,      |
| including input into or storage in any information system   |
| for resale without permission in writing from Metus Systems.|
*------------------------------------------------------------*
| dcfuzzy1.cpp  Earl Cox  11/17/94  The fuzzy dosage model.   |
| This model approximates the 1x1 fuzzy model of drug dosage  |
| concentration. This is the same model that is represented   |
| by the mathematical model C(t)=Dt*exp(-t/3). In this first  |
| fuzzy system we approximate the function at a high level    |
| of granularity.                                             |
|                                                             |
|             T0   T1   T2   T3   T4   T5   T6   T7           |
| Percent  +----+----+----+----+----+----+----+----+          |
| Change   | LN | LP | SP | ZR | SN | MN | LN | ZR |          |
| P(t)     +----+----+----+----+----+----+----+----+          |
|                                                             |
| In this first model, we approximate the nonlinear dosage    |
| concentration function using the change in blood level      |
| (as a percentage) from one period to the next.              |
|                                                             |
*---------------Modification Audit/Change Log---------------* |
| Rev  Sar                  Metus                             |
| No   Code  Date     Rellvl  Mod  Description                |
| --   ----- -------- ------  ---  ------------------------   |
|                                                             |
*------------------------------------------------------------*/
#include <stdio.h>
#include <string.h>
#include <math.h>
#include "FSV.hpp"
#include "FDB.hpp"
#include "VDB.hpp"
#include "SSYSctl.hpp"
#include "SFZYctl.hpp"
#include "fuzzy.hpp"
#include "mtypes.hpp"
#include "mtsptype.hpp"
static const Rulemax=5;
extern unsigned _stklen=50000;
#define MAXFZYSETS  26
#define MAXPERIODS  36
void    CaptureFuzzySet(char*,FDB*,int*);
//
char far * far tpdFDBnames[]= {"T0","T1","T2","T3","T4","T5","T6","T7"};
char far * far dosFDBnames[]= {"SMALL","MEDIUM","MODERATE","LARGE","COPIOUS"};
char far * far conFDBnames[]= {"LN","MN","SN","ZR","SP","MP","LP"};
char far * far conRules[]=
```

```
  {
  "if Time is T0 then Concentration is LN;    ",
  "if Time is T1 then Concentration is LP;    ",
  "if Time is T2 then Concentration is SP;    ",
  "if Time is T3 then Concentration is ZR;    ",
  "if Time is T4 then Concentration is SN;    ",
  "if Time is T5 then Concentration is MN;    ",
  "if Time is T6 then Concentration is LN;    ",
  "if Time is T7 then Concentration is ZR;    "
  };
static int NumRules=8;
//
void main(void)
 {
  FDB     *tpdFDBptr[MAXFZYSETS],
          *dosFDBptr[MAXFZYSETS],
          *conFDBptr[MAXFZYSETS],
          *OutConFDBptr;
  FSV     *OutConFSVptr;
  VDB     *OutConVDBptr;
  int      tpdFDBcnt=8,
           dosFDBcnt=5,
           conFDBcnt=7;
  char    *PgmId="dcfuzzy1";
  int      i,
           j,
           n,
           t,
           status,
           idxpos,
           TryCtl[2],
           thisCorrMethod,
           thisDefuzzMethod;
  bool     trace,storfs;
  float    predtruth,CompIDX;
  double   ConCurve [MAXPERIODS],
           ConChange[MAXPERIODS];
  double   Parms [4],
           Domain[2],
           timepd,
           dosage,
           dosChg,
           dosCon,
           dosConChg,
           PreviousDosage;
  FILE    *mdlout,
          *conout;
//
//
  SysConnecttoMetus(&status);
  XSYSctl.XSYScurrPDBptr=NULL;
  XSYSctl.XSYSalfacut   =0.1;
  mdlout=MtsGetSystemFile(SYSMODFILE);
//
  printf("INITIALIZE MODEL\n");
  TryCtl[0]=5;
  TryCtl[1]=0;
  Domain[0]=100;Domain[1]=300;
  dosage=MtsAskforDBL(
    "DosageAmount",  "Dosage Amt  [100,300]  : ",Domain,TryCtl,&status);
  printf("SPECIFY MODEL ACTIONS\n");
  trace =MtsAskforBOOL(
    "fzySetTrace",  "Trace FuzzySets      : ",        TryCtl,&status);
  XSYSctl.XSYStrace[3]=trace;
```

```
         trace =MtsAskforBOOL(
           "RuleTrace",    "Trace Rule Actions    : ",      TryCtl,&status);
         XSYSctl.XSYStrace[2]=trace;
         storfs=MtsAskforBOOL(
           "StoreSets",   "Store FuzzySets     : ",       TryCtl,&status);
    //
    //=======================================================================
    //--TIME PERIOD FUZZY SETS. The time goes from zero minutes to 36 minutes
    //--after drug introduction. we now semanically decopose the time span
    //--into a number of descriptive fuzzy sets.
    //=======================================================================
    //
       for(i=0;i<tpdFDBcnt;i++)
         {
         if((tpdFDBptr[i]=new FDB)==NULL)
           {
           MtsSendError(2,PgmId,tpdFDBnames[i]);
           return;
           }
         FzyInitFDB(tpdFDBptr[i]);
         strcpy(tpdFDBptr[i]->FDBid,  tpdFDBnames[i]);
         tpdFDBptr[i]->FDBdomain[0]= 0;
         tpdFDBptr[i]->FDBdomain[1]=36;
         }
      FzySCurve  (tpdFDBptr[0],   0,  1,  2,DECLINE,&status); //T0
      FzyPiCurve (tpdFDBptr[1],   2,  2          ,&status); //T1
      FzyPiCurve (tpdFDBptr[2],   4,  2          ,&status); //T2
      FzyPiCurve (tpdFDBptr[3],   6,  4          ,&status); //T3
      FzyPiCurve (tpdFDBptr[4],  10,  4          ,&status); //T4
      FzyPiCurve (tpdFDBptr[5],  14,  4          ,&status); //T5
      FzyPiCurve (tpdFDBptr[6],  18,  4          ,&status); //T5
      FzySCurve  (tpdFDBptr[7],  20, 23, 26,GROWTH ,&status); //T6
      FzyPlotSets("TIME.PERIOD",tpdFDBptr,tpdFDBcnt,SYSMODFILE,&status);
      FzyStoreFuzzyData(tpdFDBptr,tpdFDBcnt,"b:dcltime.dat", 8,&status);
    //
    //=======================================================================
    //--DOSAGE AMOUNT FUZZY SETS. The concentration, of course, depends on
    //--the initial dosage. The durg dosage can vary from 100 milligrams to
    //--a little over 300 milligrams.
    //=======================================================================
    //
       for(i=0;i<dosFDBcnt;i++)
         {
         if((dosFDBptr[i]=new FDB)==NULL)
           {
           MtsSendError(2,PgmId,dosFDBnames[i]);
           return;
           }
         FzyInitFDB(dosFDBptr[i]);
         strcpy(dosFDBptr[i]->FDBid,  dosFDBnames[i]);
         dosFDBptr[i]->FDBdomain[0]=100;
         dosFDBptr[i]->FDBdomain[1]=320;
         }
      FzySCurve  (dosFDBptr[0],100,110,120,DECLINE,&status); //SMALL
      FzyPiCurve (dosFDBptr[1],160, 50          ,&status); //MEDIUM
      FzyPiCurve (dosFDBptr[2],210, 50          ,&status); //MODERATE
      FzyPiCurve (dosFDBptr[3],260, 50          ,&status); //LARGE
      FzySCurve  (dosFDBptr[4],260,285,310,GROWTH ,&status); //COPIOUS
      FzyPlotSets("DRUG.DOSAGE",dosFDBptr,dosFDBcnt,SYSMODFILE,&status);
    //
    //=======================================================================
    //--CONCENTRATION CHANGE FUZZYSETS. These fuzzy sets describe the change
    //--in blood concentration (milligrams per milliliter). The change is
    //--represented as a positive or negative percentage.
```

```
//=======================================================================
//
   for(i=0;i<conFDBcnt;i++)
     {
      conFDBptr[i]=new FDB;
      FzyInitFDB(conFDBptr[i]);
      strcpy(conFDBptr[i]->FDBid,  conFDBnames[i]);
      conFDBptr[i]->FDBdomain[0]=-100;
      conFDBptr[i]->FDBdomain[1]= 100;
      }
   FzySCurve  (conFDBptr[0],-100,-80,-60,DECLINE,&status); //LN
   FzyPiCurve (conFDBptr[1], -50, 30             ,&status); //MN
   FzyPiCurve (conFDBptr[2], -20, 20             ,&status); //SN
   FzyPiCurve (conFDBptr[3],   0, 20             ,&status); //ZR
   FzyPiCurve (conFDBptr[4],  20, 20             ,&status); //SP
   FzyPiCurve (conFDBptr[5],  50, 30             ,&status); //MP
   FzySCurve  (conFDBptr[6],  60, 80,100,GROWTH ,&status); //LP
   FzyPlotSets("CONCENTRATION",conFDBptr,conFDBcnt,SYSMODFILE,&status);
   FzyStoreFuzzyData(conFDBptr,conFDBcnt,"b:dc1conc.dat", 8,&status);
//
//--This is a one dimensional FAM used to approximate the 1x1
//--concentration model.
//
   FDB *FAM[]=
     {
      conFDBptr[0],  // LN
      conFDBptr[6],  // LP
      conFDBptr[4],  // SP
      conFDBptr[3],  // ZR
      conFDBptr[2],  // SN
      conFDBptr[1],  // MN
      conFDBptr[0],  // LN
      conFDBptr[3]   // ZR
     };
//
//=======================================================================
//--Create the output solution variable and put it into the fuzzy work area.
//--This creates the output working fuzzy set and the fuzzy solution variable
//--block. We also extract the correlation and defuzzification methods.
//=======================================================================
//
   Domain[0]=-100; Domain[1]=100;
   OutConVDBptr=VarCreateScalar("Concentration",REAL,Domain,"0",&status);
   FzyInitFZYctl(&status);
   if(!(FzyAddFZYctl(OutConVDBptr,&OutConFDBptr,&OutConFSVptr,&status)))
     {
      MtsSendError(12,PgmId,"Concentration");
      exit(9);
      }
   thisCorrMethod  =OutConFSVptr->FzySVcorrMethod;
   thisDefuzzMethod=OutConFSVptr->FzySVdefuzzMethod;
//
//
   fprintf(mdlout,"%s\n",       "PARAMETERS:");
   fprintf(mdlout,"%s%7.2f\n"," Dosage   :",dosage);
   fprintf(mdlout,"%s\n",       "Running Fuzzy Associative Memory...");
//
   PreviousDosage=dosage;
   for(i=0;i<MAXPERIODS;i++)
     {
      ConChange[i]=0;
      ConCurve [i]=0;
      }
   for(t=0;t<MAXPERIODS;t++)
```

```
      {
      fprintf(mdlout,"\n%s%3d%s\n",
       "------------------------PERIOD: ",t,"----------------------------");
      for(j=0;j<NumRules;j++)
        {
        timepd=(double)t;
        predtruth=FzyGetMembership(tpdFDBptr[j],timepd,&idxpos,&status);
        if(predtruth<.05) predtruth=0;
        if(predtruth!=0)
          {
          fprintf(mdlout,"%s%3d,%s%s%6.3f%s\n",
           "FAM[",t,FAM[j]->FDBid,"] mem(",predtruth,")");
          FzyCondProposition(FAM[j],OutConFSVptr,thisCorrMethod,predtruth,&status);
          }
        }
      dosChg=FzyDefuzzify(OutConFDBptr,thisDefuzzMethod,&CompIDX,&status);
//
//--Now reset the output fuzzy set. We only have one output
//--variable so we do it directly instead of calling FzyResetFZYctl.
//
      for(n=0;n<VECMAX;n++) OutConFDBptr->FDBvector[n]=0;
      OutConFDBptr->FDBempty=TRUE;
//
//--Now store the results of this period's work in the concentration
//--and change arrays.
//
      dosConChg   =(dosChg/100);
      ConChange[t]=dosConChg;
      ConCurve [t]=max(PreviousDosage+(PreviousDosage*dosConChg),0);
      ConCurve [t]=min(dosage,ConCurve[t]);
      PreviousDosage=ConCurve[t];
      }
//
//
    fprintf(mdlout,"%s\n","BLOOD DOSAGE CONCENTRATION");
    fprintf(mdlout,"%s\n%s\n",
     "Time      +/-Chg       Concentration",
     "---    --------    -------------");
    for(i=0;i<MAXPERIODS;i++)
      fprintf(mdlout,"%4d.    %8.2f       %13.2f\n",i,ConChange[i],ConCurve[i]);
//
    if((conout=fopen("b:dcfuzzy1.dat","w"))==NULL)
      {
      printf("Sorry. '%s' file was not created\n","dcfuzzy1.dat");
      return;
      }
    for(i=0;i<MAXPERIODS;i++)
      fprintf(conout,"%5d, %10.2f\n",i,ConCurve[i]);
    fclose(conout);
    return;
//
//
  }
//
//
void CaptureFuzzySet(char *FzyDataFile,FDB *FDBptr,int *statusPtr)
/*------------------------------------------------------------*
 | This routine is used to capture and store the fuzzy set    |
 | membership array on disk for use in fine-point graphics.   |
 *------------------------------------------------------------*/
  {
  int     i,
          CompFactor= 16,
          MaxValues= 128,
```

```
                    status,
                    ExtCnt;
    double  DomValues[128];
    float   MemValues[128];
    FILE    *fzyout;
    *statusPtr=0;
    if((fzyout=fopen(FzyDataFile,"w"))==NULL)
      {
        *statusPtr=1;
        printf("Sorry. '%s' file was not created\n",FzyDataFile);
        return;
      }
    FzyExtractSetdata(FDBptr,CompFactor,DomValues,MemValues,&ExtCnt,&status);
    for(i=0;i<ExtCnt;i++)
        fprintf(fzyout,"%10.2f  %6.4f\n",DomValues[i],MemValues[i]);
    fclose(fzyout);
    return;
  }
```

dcfuzzy2.cpp (The Fuzzy Drug Concentration Model)

```
/*-------------------------------------------------------------*
| Copyright (c) 1995 by The Metus Systems Group.               |
| All rights reserved. Proprietary Software Product.           |
| No part of this software may be reproduced or transmitted    |
| in any form or by any means, electronic or mechanical,       |
| including input into or storage in any information system    |
| for resale without permission in writing from Metus Systems. |
*-------------------------------------------------------------*
| dcfuzzy2.cpp  Earl Cox  11/17/94  The fuzzy dosage model.    |
| This model approximates the 1x1 fuzzy model of drug dosage   |
| concentration. This is the same model that is represented    |
| by the mathematical model C(t)=Dt*exp(-t/3). In this second  |
| fuzzy system we approximate the function at a low level      |
| of granularity.                                              |
|                                                              |
|                                                              |
|                                                              |
| In this model, we approximate the nonlinear dosage           |
| concentration function using the change in blood level       |
| (as a percentage) from one period to the next.               |
|                                                              |
*---------------Modification Audit/Change Log---------------*
| Rev  Sar                Metus                                |
| No   Code  Date       Rellvl  Mod  Description               |
| --   ----- --------   ------  ---  ------------------------  |
|                                                              |
*-------------------------------------------------------------*/
#include <stdio.h>
#include <string.h>
#include <math.h>
#include "FSV.hpp"
#include "FDB.hpp"
#include "VDB.hpp"
#include "SSYSctl.hpp"
#include "SFZYctl.hpp"
#include "fuzzy.hpp"
#include "mtypes.hpp"
#include "mtsptype.hpp"
static const Rulemax=5;
extern unsigned _stklen=50000;
#define MAXFZYSETS  26
```

```
#define MAXPERIODS  36
void    CaptureFuzzySet(char*,FDB*,int*);
//
char far * far tpdFDBnames[]=
   {"T0","T1", "T2", "T3", "T4", "T5", "T6",
    "T7","T8", "T9","T10","T11","T12","T13"};
char far * far dosFDBnames[]=  {"SMALL","MEDIUM","MODERATE","LARGE","COPIOUS"};
char far * far conFDBnames[]=  {"LN","MN","SN","ZR","SP","MP","LP"};
char far * far conRules[]=
   {
   "if Time is T0    then Concentration is LN;    ",
   "if Time is T1    then Concentration is LP;    ",
   "if Time is T2    then Concentration is LP;    ",
   "if Time is T3    then Concentration is MP;    ",
   "if Time is T4    then Concentration is MP;    ",
   "if Time is T5    then Concentration is SP;    ",
   "if Time is T6    then Concentration is ZR;    ",
   "if Time is T7    then Concentration is ZR;    ",
   "if Time is T8    then Concentration is SN;    ",
   "if Time is T9    then Concentration is MN;    ",
   "if Time is T10   then Concentration is MN;    ",
   "if Time is T11   then Concentration is LN;    ",
   "if Time is T12   then Concentration is LN;    ",
   "if Time is T13   then Concentration is LN;    "
   };
static int NumRules=14;
//
void main(void)
   {
   FDB      *tpdFDBptr[MAXFZYSETS],
            *dosFDBptr[MAXFZYSETS],
            *conFDBptr[MAXFZYSETS],
            *OutConFDBptr;
   FSV      *OutConFSVptr;
   VDB      *OutConVDBptr;
   int      tpdFDBcnt=14,
            dosFDBcnt= 5,
            conFDBcnt= 7;
   char     *PgmId="dcfuzzy2";
   int      i,
            j,
            n,
            t,
            status,
            idxpos,
            TryCtl[2],
            thisCorrMethod,
            thisDefuzzMethod;
   bool     trace,storfs;
   float    predtruth,CompIDX;
   double   ConCurve [MAXPERIODS],
            ConChange[MAXPERIODS];
   double   Parms [4],
            Domain[2],
            timepd,
            dosage,
            dosChg,
            dosCon,
            dosConChg,
            PreviousDosage;
   FILE     *mdlout,
            *conout;
//
//
```

```
   SysConnecttoMetus(&status);
   XSYSctl.XSYScurrPDBptr=NULL;
   XSYSctl.XSYSalfacut   =0.1;
   mdlout=MtsGetSystemFile(SYSMODFILE);
//
//
   printf("INITIALIZE MODEL\n");
   TryCtl[0]=5;
   TryCtl[1]=0;
   Domain[0]=100;Domain[1]=300;
   dosage=MtsAskforDBL(
     "DosageAmount", "Dosage Amt [100,300] : ",Domain,TryCtl,&status);
   printf("SPECIFY MODEL ACTIONS\n");
   trace =MtsAskforBOOL(
     "fzySetTrace",  "Trace FuzzySets        : ",        TryCtl,&status);
   XSYSctl.XSYStrace[3]=trace;
   trace =MtsAskforBOOL(
     "RuleTrace",    "Trace Rule Actions     : ",        TryCtl,&status);
   XSYSctl.XSYStrace[2]=trace;
   storfs=MtsAskforBOOL(
     "StoreSets",    "Store FuzzySets        : ",        TryCtl,&status);
//
//=========================================================================
//--TIME PERIOD FUZZY SETS. The time goes from zero minutes to 36 minutes
//--after drug introduction. We now semantically decopose the time span
//--into a number of descriptive fuzzy sets.
//=========================================================================
//
   for(i=0;i<tpdFDBcnt;i++)
      {
      if((tpdFDBptr[i]=new FDB)==NULL)
         {
         MtsSendError(2,PgmId,tpdFDBnames[i]);
         return;
         }
      FzyInitFDB(tpdFDBptr[i]);
      strcpy(tpdFDBptr[i]->FDBid,  tpdFDBnames[i]);
      tpdFDBptr[i]->FDBdomain[0]= 0;
      tpdFDBptr[i]->FDBdomain[1]=36;
      }
   FzySCurve  (tpdFDBptr[ 0],  0,  .5,  1,DECLINE,&status); //T0
   FzyPiCurve (tpdFDBptr[ 1],  1,  1             ,&status); //T1
   FzyPiCurve (tpdFDBptr[ 2],  2,  1             ,&status); //T2
   FzyPiCurve (tpdFDBptr[ 3],  3,  1             ,&status); //T3
   FzyPiCurve (tpdFDBptr[ 4],  4,  1             ,&status); //T4
   FzyPiCurve (tpdFDBptr[ 5],  5,  1             ,&status); //T5
   FzyPiCurve (tpdFDBptr[ 6],  6,  1             ,&status); //T6
   FzyPiCurve (tpdFDBptr[ 7],  7,  1             ,&status); //T7
   FzyPiCurve (tpdFDBptr[ 8],  8,  1             ,&status); //T8
   FzyPiCurve (tpdFDBptr[ 9],  9,  1             ,&status); //T9
   FzyPiCurve (tpdFDBptr[10], 10,  1             ,&status); //T10
   FzyPiCurve (tpdFDBptr[11], 12,  2             ,&status); //T11
   FzyPiCurve (tpdFDBptr[12], 14,  2             ,&status); //T12
   FzySCurve  (tpdFDBptr[13], 16, 21, 26,GROWTH ,&status); //T13
   FzyPlotTermSet("TIME.PERIOD",tpdFDBptr,14,        SYSMODFILE,&status);
   FzyStoreFuzzyData(tpdFDBptr,tpdFDBcnt,"b:dc2time.dat", 8,&status);
//
//=========================================================================
//--DOSAGE AMOUNT FUZZY SETS. The concentration, of course, depends on
//--the initial dosage. The durg dosage can vary from 100 milligrams to
//--a little over 300 milligrams.
//=========================================================================
//
   for(i=0;i<dosFDBcnt;i++)
```

```
      {
       if((dosFDBptr[i]=new FDB)==NULL)
         {
          MtsSendError(2,PgmId,dosFDBnames[i]);
          return;
         }
       FzyInitFDB(dosFDBptr[i]);
       strcpy(dosFDBptr[i]->FDBid, dosFDBnames[i]);
       dosFDBptr[i]->FDBdomain[0]=100;
       dosFDBptr[i]->FDBdomain[1]=320;
      }
    FzySCurve  (dosFDBptr[0],100,110,120,DECLINE,&status); //SMALL
    FzyPiCurve (dosFDBptr[1],160, 50            ,&status); //MEDIUM
    FzyPiCurve (dosFDBptr[2],210, 50            ,&status); //MODERATE
    FzyPiCurve (dosFDBptr[3],260, 50            ,&status); //LARGE
    FzySCurve  (dosFDBptr[4],260,285,310,GROWTH ,&status); //COPIOUS
    FzyPlotTermSet("DRUG.DOSAGE",dosFDBptr,dosFDBcnt,SYSMODFILE,&status);
//
//===========================================================================
//--CONCENTRATION CHANGE FUZZYSETS. These fuzzy sets describe the change
//--in blood concentration (milligrams per milliliter). The change is
//--represented as a positive or negative percentage.
//===========================================================================
//
    for(i=0;i<conFDBcnt;i++)
      {
       conFDBptr[i]=new FDB;
       FzyInitFDB(conFDBptr[i]);
       strcpy(conFDBptr[i]->FDBid, conFDBnames[i]);
       conFDBptr[i]->FDBdomain[0]=-100;
       conFDBptr[i]->FDBdomain[1]= 100;
      }
    FzySCurve  (conFDBptr[0],-100,-80,-60,DECLINE,&status); //LN
    FzyPiCurve (conFDBptr[1], -50, 30            ,&status); //MN
    FzyPiCurve (conFDBptr[2], -20, 20            ,&status); //SN
    FzyPiCurve (conFDBptr[3],   0, 20            ,&status); //ZR
    FzyPiCurve (conFDBptr[4],  20, 20            ,&status); //SP
    FzyPiCurve (conFDBptr[5],  50, 30            ,&status); //MP
    FzySCurve  (conFDBptr[6],  60,  80,100,GROWTH,&status); //LP
    FzyPlotTermSet("CONCENTRATION",conFDBptr,conFDBcnt,SYSMODFILE,&status);
    FzyStoreFuzzyData(conFDBptr,conFDBcnt,"b:dc2conc.dat", 8,&status);
//
//--This is a one dimensional FAM used to approximate the 1x1
//--concentration model.
    FDB *FAM[]=
      {
       conFDBptr[0],   // LN
       conFDBptr[6],   // LP
       conFDBptr[6],   // LP
       conFDBptr[5],   // MP
       conFDBptr[5],   // MP
       conFDBptr[4],   // SP
       conFDBptr[3],   // ZR
       conFDBptr[3],   // ZR
       conFDBptr[2],   // SN
       conFDBptr[1],   // MN
       conFDBptr[1],   // MN
       conFDBptr[0],   // LN
       conFDBptr[0],   // LN
       conFDBptr[0]    // LN
      };
//
//===========================================================================
//--Create the output solution variable and put it into the fuzzy work area.
```

```
//--This creates the output working fuzzy set and the fuzzy solution variable
//--block. We also extract the correlation and defuzzification methods.
//===========================================================================
//
   Domain[0]=-100; Domain[1]=100;
   OutConVDBptr=VarCreateScalar("Concentration",REAL,Domain,"0",&status);
   FzyInitFZYctl(&status);
   if(!(FzyAddFZYctl(OutConVDBptr,&OutConFDBptr,&OutConFSVptr,&status)))
     {
      MtsSendError(12,PgmId,"Concentration");
      exit(9);
     }
   thisCorrMethod  =OutConFSVptr->FzySVcorrMethod;
   thisDefuzzMethod=OutConFSVptr->FzySVdefuzzMethod;
//
//
   fprintf(mdlout,"%s\n",     "PARAMETERS:");
   fprintf(mdlout,"%s%7.2f\n","  Dosage   :",dosage);
   fprintf(mdlout,"%s\n",     "Running Fuzzy Associative Memory...");
//
   PreviousDosage=dosage;
   for(i=0;i<MAXPERIODS;i++)
     {
      ConChange[i]=0;
      ConCurve [i]=0;
     }
   for(t=0;t<MAXPERIODS;t++)
    {
     fprintf(mdlout,"\n%s%3d%s\n",
      "------------------------PERIOD: ",t,"------------------------------");
     for(j=0;j<NumRules;j++)
       {
        timepd=(double)t;
        predtruth=FzyGetMembership(tpdFDBptr[j],timepd,&idxpos,&status);
        if(predtruth<.05) predtruth=0;
        if(predtruth!=0)
          {
           fprintf(mdlout,"%s%3d,%s%s%6.3f%s\n",
            "FAM[",t,FAM[j]->FDBid,"] mem(",predtruth,")");
           FzyCondProposition(FAM[j],OutConFSVptr,thisCorrMethod,predtruth,&status);
          }
       }
     dosChg=FzyDefuzzify(OutConFDBptr,thisDefuzzMethod,&CompIDX,&status);
//
//--Now reset the output fuzzy set. We only have one output
//--variable so we do it directly instead of calling FzyResetFZYctl.
//
     for(n=0;n<VECMAX;n++) OutConFDBptr->FDBvector[n]=0;
     OutConFDBptr->FDBempty=TRUE;
//
//--Now store the reslts of this period's work in the concentration
//--and change arrays.
//
     dosConChg   =(dosChg/100);
     ConChange[t]=dosConChg;
     ConCurve [t]=max(PreviousDosage+(PreviousDosage*dosConChg),0);
     ConCurve [t]=min(dosage,ConCurve[t]);
     PreviousDosage=ConCurve[t];
    }
//
//
   fprintf(mdlout,"%s\n","BLOOD DOSAGE CONCENTRATION");
   fprintf(mdlout,"%s\n%s\n",
    "Time      +/-Chg      Concentration",
```

```
        "---      --------        -------------");
     for(i=0;i<MAXPERIODS;i++)
       fprintf(mdlout,"%4d.    %8.2f        %13.2f\n",i,ConChange[i],ConCurve[i]);
//
     if((conout=fopen("b:dcfuzzy2.dat","w"))==NULL)
        {
         printf("Sorry. '%s' file was not created\n","dcfuzzy1.dat");
         return;
        }
     for(i=0;i<MAXPERIODS;i++)
       fprintf(conout,"%5d, %10.2f\n",i,ConCurve[i]);
     fclose(conout);
     return;
//
//
    }
//
//
void CaptureFuzzySet(char *FzyDataFile,FDB *FDBptr,int *statusPtr)
/*------------------------------------------------------------*
| This routine is used to capture and store the fuzzy set     |
| membership array on disk for use in fine-point graphics.    |
*------------------------------------------------------------*/
  {
   int       i,
             CompFactor= 16,
             MaxValues= 128,
             status,
             ExtCnt;
   double   DomValues[128];
   float    MemValues[128];
   FILE     *fzyout;
   *statusPtr=0;
   if((fzyout=fopen(FzyDataFile,"w"))==NULL)
      {
       *statusPtr=1;
       printf("Sorry. '%s' file was not created\n",FzyDataFile);
       return;
      }
   FzyExtractSetdata(FDBptr,CompFactor,DomValues,MemValues,&ExtCnt,&status);
   for(i=0;i<ExtCnt;i++)
      fprintf(fzyout,"%10.2f   %6.4f\n",DomValues[i],MemValues[i]);
   fclose(fzyout);
   return;
  }
```

dcfuzzy3.cpp (Weight-biased Drug Concentration Model)

```
#include <string.h>
#include <stdio.h>
#include <math.h>
#include "mttypes.hpp"
#define THREE    3
#define MAXTIME 36
//
double Concentration(double,double,double);
void CaptureDrugLevels(char*,double[],int,int*);
//
void main(void)
  {
   char   *outFile="b:DrugWgt.txt";
```

```
      char    weight[16];
      double  dgUnits=120;
      double  paWeight;
      double  dgLevel,doseAmt[48];
      int     t,status;
      printf("Enter Patient Weight: ");
      gets(weight);
      paWeight=atof(weight);
//
      for(t=0;t<MAXTIME;t++)
        {
         dgLevel=Concentration(dgUnits,paWeight,t);
         doseAmt[t]=dgLevel;
         printf("Time: %3d  BloodLevel: %8.3f\n",t,dgLevel);
        }
      printf("Capturing Data.\n");
      CaptureDrugLevels(outFile,doseAmt,MAXTIME,&status);
      if(status!=0) return;
     }
//
//
double Concentration(double dgUnits,double paWeight,double t)
    {
      double  texp,ConAmount;
      texp=-(t/log(paWeight*.20));
      ConAmount=((dgUnits*t)*pow(E,texp));
      return(ConAmount);
    }
//
//
void CaptureDrugLevels(
  char *DataFile,double Data[],int DataCnt,int *statusPtr)
/*------------------------------------------------------------*
| This routine is used to capture and store the fuzzy set     |
| membership array on disk for use in fine-point graphics.    |
*------------------------------------------------------------*/
   {
   FILE    *Dataout;
   int      i;
   *statusPtr=0;
   if((Dataout=fopen(DataFile,"w"))==NULL)
     {
      *statusPtr=1;
      printf("Sorry. '%s' file was not created\n",DataFile);
      return;
     }
   for(i=0;i<DataCnt;i++)
     fprintf(Dataout,"%3d  %9.3f\n",i,Data[i]);
   fclose(Dataout);
   printf("%s%s\n","Dosage Level data on: ",DataFile);
   return;
   }
```

Code for Chapter 3. FuzzySQL and Database Systems

FzySQL0 (A Fuzzy SQL database processor [version 0])

```
/*-------------------------------------------------------------*
| (c) 1995 Metus Systems.        Proprietary software product. |
| Reproduction or unauthorized use is prohibited. Unauthorized |
| use is illegal. Violators will be prosecuted. This software  |
| contains proprietary trade and business secrets.             |
*--------------------Procedure Description--------------------*
| fzysql0.cpp  Earl Cox  01/20/95 Fuzzy Database Operations    |
|                                                              |
| This program simulates fuzzy SQL query access against a      |
| relational database containing financial information. You    |
| specify a minimum alpha theshold as well as the type of      |
| membership aggregation you want. The records are selected    |
| and then ranked by their degree of compatibility with the    |
| request (high-to-low).                                       |
*-------------------------------------------------------------*
| CAVEATS: This program does not connect to a real relational  |
| database (but such a connection would obviously not be       |
| difficult), it does not support secondary fuzzy indexing,    |
| and the ranking methodology uses a very low performance      |
| sorting technique. And, of course, this version does not     |
| support hedges and other quantifiers.                        |
*---------------Modification Audit/Change Log----------------*
| Rev  Sar                  Metus                              |
| No   Code  Date       Rellvl  Mod  Description               |
| --   -----  --------   ------   ---   ------------------------ |
|                                                              |
*-------------------------------------------------------------*/
#include <stdlib.h>
#include <string.h>
#include <math.h>
#include "FDB.hpp"
#include "SSYSctl.hpp"
#include "mtypes.hpp"
#include "fuzzy.hpp"
#include "mtsptype.hpp"
//
//--------------------RELATIONAL DATABASE STRUCTURE--------------------
//--For purposes of simplicity and demonstration, we maintain our small
//--relational database as an in-memory array. This makes the database
//--easily transportable although we must simulate SQL statements.
//-------------------------------------------------------------------
//
struct fzyDBMS
   {
    char    *Company;
    long    Founded,
            Revenues,
            NumProducts,
            NumEmps,
            ProfitLoss;
    float   EarnPerShare;
   };
//
fzyDBMS  DBdata[]=
   {
//              SMALL MANUFACTURING COMPANIES
//          Year    1995     Num    Num  1995
// Company   Founded Revenues Prods Emps RetErn     EPS
```

```
//     -------     ------- --------- ----- ---- -------    ---
     {"CompA" ,     1948,     570,    1,  16,      3,  .20},
     {"CompB" ,     1972,     478,    3,  27,    243, 1.77},
     {"CompC" ,     1982,     401,    9,  58,     17, 1.02},
     {"CompD" ,     1997,     321,    3,   8,     25, 3.11},
     {"CompE" ,     1998,     650,    5,  33,    -87,  .44},
     {"CompF" ,     1994,     550,   16,   9,     99,  .79},
     {"CompG" ,     1992,     597,    4,  11,    -13,  .04},
     {"CompH" ,     1990,     602,    7,  41,     33, 2.14},
     {"CompI" ,     1991,     498,    5,  15,    207, 1.33},
     {"CompK" ,     1994,     501,    2,  57,    133, 2.83},
     {"CompL" ,     1985,     920,    8,   5,    201, 1.55},
     {"CompM" ,     1983,     555,    2,   9,    509, 1.05},
     {"CompN" ,     1988,    1050,   10,  25,    427, 2.94},
     {"CompO" ,     1990,     530,   14,  12,     22,  .30},
     {"CompP" ,     1988,     522,    4,  21,     62, 1.28},
     {"CompR" ,     1959,     900,    3,   5,     -8,  .00},
     {"CompS" ,     1964,     659,    2,   7,      0,  .10},
     {"CompT" ,     1979,     619,    5,  17,    280, 3.17},
     {"CompU" ,     1967,    1233,    2,  28,    322, 2.40},
     {"CompW" ,     1964,     973,   11,  48,    422, 2.88}
     };
const int fzyDBsize=20;
const int ColCnt  = 7;
const int DataCols = 6;
//
static  FILE    *DBlog;
const   char    *PgmId="fzySQLO";
const   int      FzyTermMax=11;
//
char far * far revFDBnames[]=
   {
     "HIGH",
     "LOW"
   };
char far * far ANDnames[]=
   {
     "MINIMUM",
     "AVERAGE"
   };
#define  MINIMUM    0
#define  AVERAGE    1
//
FDB*  FindFuzzySet(char*,FDB*[],int,int*);
float Membershipof(char*,double,float,FDB*);
void  SQLranking(int[],float[],int,int*);
//
void main()
  {
//
//----------------FUZZY SET DEFINTIONS AND CONTROLS--------------------
//--For purposes of simplicity and demonstration, we maintain our small
//--relational database as an in-memory array. This makes the database
//--easily transportable although we must simulate SQL statements.
//--------------------------------------------------------------------
//
    FDB      *revFDBptr[FzyTermMax];
    FDB      *Rev_FDBptr;
    int      revFDBcnt=2;
    int      ANDcnt   =2;
    char     *RevFS;
    float    RevMem;
```

```
//
//----------------------------------------------------------------------
//
   fzyDBMS *fzyRECptr;
   char    *DBAuditFile="b:DBaudit.fil";
   char     strBuff[32];
   int      TryCtl[2],minlen=4;
   int      i,j,idx,status;
   int      SelCnt,AlfaRejected,recIDX;
   int      SQLrecIDX[fzyDBsize];
   float    SQLrecDOM[fzyDBsize];
   float    AlfaCut,MemValues[fzyDBsize];
   double   Domain[2];
   double   dblSelCnt,dblDBsize;
//
   status=0;
//
   SysConnecttoMetus(&status);
   XSYSctl.XSYScurrPDBptr=NULL;
   XSYSctl.XSYSalfacut   =0.1;
   XSYSctl.XSYStrace[3]  =TRUE;
   XSYSctl.XSYStrace[2]  =TRUE;
//
//
   for(i=0;i<FzyTermMax;i++)    revFDBptr[i]=NULL;
//
//
//----------------------------------------------------------------------
//--REVENUES. These are the descriptions of the annual revenues in
//--dollars ($) adjusted for write-offs and other losses.
//----------------------------------------------------------------------
//
  for(i=0;i<revFDBcnt;i++)
    {
     if((revFDBptr[i]=new FDB)==NULL)
       {
        MtsSendError(2,PgmId,revFDBnames[i]);
        return;
       }
     FzyInitFDB(revFDBptr[i]);
     strcpy(revFDBptr[i]->FDBid,  revFDBnames[i]);
     revFDBptr[i]->FDBdomain[0]= 500;
     revFDBptr[i]->FDBdomain[1]=1200;
    }
  FzyLinearCurve(revFDBptr[0],  500, 1200,INCREASE,&status); //HIGH
  FzyLinearCurve(revFDBptr[1],  500, 1200,DECREASE,&status); //LOW
  FzyPlotTermSet("REVENUES",revFDBptr,revFDBcnt,SYSMODFILE,&status);
  FzyStoreFuzzyData(revFDBptr,revFDBcnt,"b:sql0rev.dat", 8,&status);
//
//
  if((DBlog=fopen(DBAuditFile,"w"))==NULL)
    {
     status=1;
     printf("Sorry. '%s' file was not created\n",DBAuditFile);
     return;
    }
//
//======================================================================
//--REQUEST THE ROW QUALIFIERS. We now prompt for the fuzzy set space
//--associated with each of the column domains. These would be for the
//--fuzzy WHERE statement in the SQL request.
//======================================================================
//
  memset(strBuff,'\0',32);
```

```
       TryCtl[0]=10;
       TryCtl[1]= 0;
       Domain[0]=0;
       Domain[1]=1;
       printf("\nFuzzySQL Database Processor\n");
       printf("------------------------\n");
       AlfaCut=MtsAskforDBL(
        "AlfaCut",
        "AlphaCut Threshold     : ",Domain,TryCtl,&status);
   //
       printf("%s\n%s\n%s\n",
         "select companies",
         "  from MfgDBMS",
         "  where: ");
       TryCtl[1]= 0;
       Rev_FDBptr=NULL;
       RevFS=MtsAskforVAL(
        "ANNUAL.REVENUES",
        "Annnual Revenues are : ",
         revFDBnames,revFDBcnt,minlen,&idx,TryCtl,&status);
       Rev_FDBptr=FindFuzzySet(RevFS,revFDBptr,revFDBcnt,&status);
       if(Rev_FDBptr!=NULL)
         sprintf(strBuff,"%s%s","Annual.Revenues are ",RevFS);
   //
   //=======================================================================
   //--PROCESS THE RELATIONAL DATABASE. Having found the fuzzy sets for
   //--each of the columns, we now read each record from the database and
   //--determine its degree of compatibility with the request.
   //=======================================================================
   //
       for(i=0;i<fzyDBsize;i++)
         {
          SQLrecIDX[i]=-1;
          SQLrecDOM[i]= 0;
          MemValues[i]= 0;
         }
   //
   //
       SelCnt=0;
       AlfaRejected=0;
       for(i=0;i<fzyDBsize;i++)
         {
          fzyRECptr=&DBdata[i];
          fprintf(DBlog,"\n%4d%s%s\n",i+1,". ",fzyRECptr->Company);
          RevMem=Membershipof(
            "ANNUAL.REVENUES",(double)fzyRECptr->Revenues,AlfaCut,Rev_FDBptr);
          MemValues[i]=RevMem;
          if(RevMem>=AlfaCut)
            {
             SQLrecIDX[SelCnt]= i;
             SQLrecDOM[SelCnt]= RevMem;
             SelCnt++;
            }
           else
            if(RevMem>0)
              {
               fprintf(DBlog,"%s%5.3f%s%5.3f\n",
                "        Alpha Cut Rejection: ",RevMem," < ",AlfaCut);
               AlfaRejected++;
              }
         }
```

```
//
//============================================================================
//--SHOW QUERY RESULTS. We now form and dispaly the actual fzySQL
//--query, rank the selected records by the composite truth value
//--(in descending order so highest truth appears first); and then
//--we print a report showing the companies selected.
//============================================================================
//
  fprintf(DBlog,"\n\n%s\n%s\n%s\n%s%s%s",
    "-----------------------------------------------------------",
    "select companies",
    "  from MfgDBMS",
    "  where  ",
     strBuff,";");
  //
  //
  SQLranking(SQLrecIDX,SQLrecDOM,SelCnt,&status);
  //
  //
  fprintf(DBlog,"\n\n\n%s\n%s\n",
   "Company          CompIDX    ",
    "----------------- ---------- ");
  for(i=0;i<SelCnt;i++)
    {
     recIDX=SQLrecIDX[i];
     fzyRECptr=&DBdata[recIDX];
     fprintf(DBlog,"%-16.16s  %10.3f\n",
                fzyRECptr->Company,SQLrecDOM[i]);
    }
  dblSelCnt=(double)SelCnt;
  dblDBsize=(double)fzyDBsize;
  fprintf(DBlog,"\n%s%10d\n%s%10d\n%s%10.2f\n",
   "Record Selected            : ",SelCnt,
   "Rejected due to AlphaCut   : ",AlfaRejected,
   "Percent (%) Found          : ",(dblSelCnt/dblDBsize)*100);
  return;
 }
//
//============================================================================
//-----------------FUZZY DATABASE SUPPORT SERVICES--------------------
//============================================================================
//
FDB* FindFuzzySet(char *FSid,FDB *FDBptr[],int FDBcnt,int *statusPtr)
/*--------------------------------------------------------------------*
| Given the name of a fuzzy set in the variable's Term Set, this      |
| function returns a pointer to the corresponding FDB structure.      |
*--------------------------------------------------------------------*/
 {
  FDB   *thisFDBptr;
  *statusPtr=0;
  if(!FSid) return(NULL);
  for(int i=0;i<FDBcnt;i++)
    {
     thisFDBptr=FDBptr[i];
     if(strcmp(FSid,thisFDBptr->FDBid)==0) return(thisFDBptr);
    }
  *statusPtr=1;
  return(NULL);
 }
//
//
float Membershipof(char *Colid,double DBColvalue,float AlfaCut,FDB *FDBptr)
```

```
/*----------------------------------------------------------------------*
| Given a column data value and a pointer into an FDB, this routine     |
| returns the value's grade of membership. If the grade is below        |
| the Alpha Cut threshold we return a zero. If the fuzzy set is NULL    |
| we indicate NOTFOUND. A message is also written to the audit log.     |
*----------------------------------------------------------------------*/
  {
   int    idx,status;
   float  memgrade;
   if(FDBptr==NULL) return(-1);
   memgrade=FzyGetMembership(FDBptr,DBColvalue,&idx,&status);
   fprintf(DBlog,"%s%-16.16s%s%s%s%7.2f%s%5.3f%s\n",
      "       ",Colid,"    in '",FDBptr->FDBid,"' (",DBColvalue,",",memgrade,")");
   return(memgrade);
  }
//
//
void  SQLranking(int SQLrecIDX[],float SQLrecDOM[],int SelCnt,int  *status)
/*----------------------------------------------------------------------*
| Perform a descending buddle sort on the record sector arrays. In      |
| this simple model we use a very low performance sorting algorithm     |
| for simplicity. In actual systems a version of quicksort coupled      |
| with an external sort/merge would be employed.                        |
*----------------------------------------------------------------------*/
  {
   int    i,j;
   int    tempIDX;
   float  tempDOM;
   bool   sortedFlag;
   if(SelCnt<2) return;
   for(j=0;j<SelCnt;j++)
     {
      sortedFlag=TRUE;
      for(i=0;i<(SelCnt-1);i++)
        {
         if(SQLrecDOM[i]<SQLrecDOM[i+1])
           {
            //----------------------------------------------------
            //--The i-th grade of membership is less than the i+1
            //--membership. We now save the current values and do a
            //--simple swap of the values.
            //----------------------------------------------------
            //
            tempIDX=SQLrecIDX[i];
            tempDOM=SQLrecDOM[i];
            SQLrecIDX[i]=SQLrecIDX[i+1];
            SQLrecDOM[i]=SQLrecDOM[i+1];
            SQLrecIDX[i+1]=tempIDX;
            SQLrecDOM[i+1]=tempDOM;
            sortedFlag=FALSE;
           }
        }
      if(sortedFlag==TRUE) return;
     }
   return;
  }
```

FzySQL1 (A Fuzzy SQL database processor [version 1])

```
/*------------------------------------------------------------*
| (c) 1995 Metus Systems.      Proprietary software product. |
| Reproduction or unauthorized use is prohibited. Unauthorized|
| use is illegal. Violators will be prosecuted. This software |
| contains proprietary trade and business secrets.            |
*-------------------Procedure Description--------------------*
| fzysql1.cpp  Earl Cox  01/20/95 Fuzzy Database Operations   |
|                                                             |
| This program simulates fuzzy SQL query access against a     |
| relational database containing financial information. You   |
| specify a minimum alpha theshold as well as the type of     |
| membership aggregation you want. The records are selected   |
| and then ranked by their degree of compatibility with the   |
| request (high-to-low).                                      |
*-------------------------------------------------------------*
| CAVEATS: This program does not connect to a real relational |
| database (but such a connection would obviously not be      |
| difficult), it does not support secondary fuzzy indexing,   |
| and the ranking methodology uses a very low performance     |
| sorting technique. And, of course, this version does not    |
| support hedges and other quantifiers.                       |
*----------------Modification Audit/Change Log---------------*
| Rev  Sar          Metus                                     |
| No   Code  Date   Rellvl  Mod  Description                  |
| --   -----  -------  ------  ---  --------------------------|
|                                                             |
*-------------------------------------------------------------*/
#include <stdlib.h>
#include <string.h>
#include <math.h>
#include "FDB.hpp"
#include "SSYSctl.hpp"
#include "mtypes.hpp"
#include "fuzzy.hpp"
#include "mtsptype.hpp"
//
//-------------------RELATIONAL DATABASE STRUCTURE-------------------
//--For purposes of simplicity and demonstration, we maintain our small
//--relational database as an in-memory array. This makes the database
//--easily transportable although we must simulate SQL statements.
//------------------------------------------------------------------
//
struct fzyDBMS
   {
    char   *Company;
    long   Founded,
           Revenues,
           NumProducts,
           NumEmps,
           ProfitLoss;
    float  EarnPerShare;
   };
//
fzyDBMS  DBdata[]=
   {
//              SMALL MANUFACTURING COMPANIES
//           Year   1995    Num   Num  1995
//  Company  Founded Revenues Prods Emps RetErn   EPS
//  -------  ------- -------- ----- ---- ---- ---  ---
    {"CompA" ,   1948,    570,   1,  16,    3,  .20},
    {"CompB" ,   1972,    478,   3,  27,  243, 1.77},
    {"CompC" ,   1982,    401,   9,  58,   17, 1.02},
```

```
      {"CompD" ,        1987,      321,    3,    8,      25, 3.11},
      {"CompE" ,        1988,      650,    5,   33,     -87,  .44},
      {"CompF" ,        1994,      550,   16,    9,      99,  .79},
      {"CompG" ,        1992,      597,    4,   11,     -13,  .04},
      {"CompH" ,        1990,      602,    7,   41,      33, 2.14},
      {"CompI" ,        1991,      498,    5,   15,     207, 1.33},
      {"CompK" ,        1994,      501,    2,   57,     133, 2.83},
      {"CompL" ,        1985,      920,    8,    5,     201, 1.55},
      {"CompM" ,        1983,      555,    2,    9,     509, 1.05},
      {"CompN" ,        1988,     1050,   10,   25,     427, 2.94},
      {"CompO" ,        1990,      530,   14,   12,      22,  .30},
      {"CompP" ,        1988,      522,    4,   21,      62, 1.28},
      {"CompR" ,        1959,      900,    3,    5,      -8,  .00},
      {"CompS" ,        1964,      659,    2,    7,       0,  .10},
      {"CompT" ,        1979,      619,    5,   17,     280, 3.17},
      {"CompU" ,        1967,     1233,    2,   28,     322, 2.40},
      {"CompW" ,        1964,      973,   11,   48,     422, 2.88}
      };
const int fzyDBsize=20;
const int ColCnt   = 7;
const int DataCols = 6;
//
static   FILE     *DBlog;
const    char     *PgmId="fzySQL1";
const    int       FzyTermMax=11;
//
char far * far ageFDBnames[]=
   {
    "NEW",
    "YOUNG",
    "RECENT",
    "MATURE",
    "ESTABLISHED",
    "OLD"
   };
char far * far revFDBnames[]=
   {
    "NONE",
    "LOW",
    "MODERATE",
    "MEDIUM",
    "HIGH"
   };
char far * far pnoFDBnames[]=
   {
    "FEW",
    "SOME",
    "SEVERAL",
    "MANY"
   };
char far * far enoFDBnames[]=
   {
    "SMALL",
    "MODERATE",
    "MEDIUM",
    "LARGE"
   };
char far * far pnlFDBnames[]=
   {
    "BIG.LOSS",
    "MODERATE.LOSS",
    "SMALL.LOSS",
    "BREAK.EVEN",
    "SMALL.GAIN",
```

```
    "MODERATE.GAIN",
    "BIG.GAIN"
  };
char far * far epsFDBnames[]=
  {
    "UNACCEPTABLE",
    "POOR",
    "ACCEPTABLE",
    "GOOD",
    "EXCELLENT"
  };
char far * far ANDnames[]=
  {
    "MINIMUM",
    "AVERAGE"
  };
#define   MINIMUM   0
#define   AVERAGE   1
//
FDB*  FindFuzzySet(char*,FDB*[],int,int*);
float Membershipof(char*,double,float,FDB*);
void  SQLranking(int[],float[],float[],int,int,int*);
bool  SQLrankingFault(int,int,float[],float[]);
//
void main()
  {
//
//---------------FUZZY SET DEFINTIONS AND CONTROLS--------------------
//--For purposes of simplicity and demonstration, we maintain our small
//--relational database as an in-memory array. This makes the database
//--easily transportable although we must simulate SQL statements.
//-------------------------------------------------------------------
//
    FDB      *ageFDBptr[FzyTermMax],
             *revFDBptr[FzyTermMax],
             *pnoFDBptr[FzyTermMax],
             *enoFDBptr[FzyTermMax],
             *pnlFDBptr[FzyTermMax],
             *epsFDBptr[FzyTermMax];
    FDB      *Age_FDBptr,
      .      *Rev_FDBptr,
             *Pno_FDBptr,
             *Eno_FDBptr,
             *Pnl_FDBptr,
             *Eps_FDBptr;
    int       ageFDBcnt=6,
              revFDBcnt=5,
              pnoFDBcnt=4,
              enoFDBcnt=4,
              pnlFDBcnt=7,
              epsFDBcnt=5;
    int      ANDcnt   =2;
    char     *AgeFS,*RevFS,*PnoFS,*EnoFS,*PnlFS,*EpsFS;
    float     AgeMem,RevMem,PnoMem,EnoMem,PnlMem,EpsMem;
//
//-------------------------------------------------------------------------
//
    fzyDBMS *fzyRECptr;
    char     *DBAuditFile="b:DBaudit.fil";
    char     *AggType;
    char     strBuff[8][32];
    int      TryCtl[2],minlen=4;
    int      i,j,idx,status;
    int      Wcnt,SelCnt,AlfaRejected,NumSets,AggOperator,recIDX;
```

```
    int       SQLrecIDX[fzyDBsize];
    float     SQLrecDOM[fzyDBsize];
    float     SQLrecAVG[fzyDBsize];
    float     AlfaCut,CompIDX,AvgGrade,CIX,MemValues[fzyDBsize][DataCols];
    double    Domain[2],CompAge,TotGrade;
    double    dblSelCnt,dblDBsize;
//
    status=0;
//
    SysConnecttoMetus(&status);
    XSYSctl.XSYScurrPDBptr=NULL;
    XSYSctl.XSYSalfacut   =0.1;
    XSYSctl.XSYStrace[3]  =TRUE;
    XSYSctl.XSYStrace[2]  =TRUE;
//
//
    for(i=0;i<FzyTermMax;i++)
      {
       ageFDBptr[i]=NULL;
       revFDBptr[i]=NULL;
       pnoFDBptr[i]=NULL;
       enoFDBptr[i]=NULL;
       pnlFDBptr[i]=NULL;
       epsFDBptr[i]=NULL;
      }
//
//=======================================================================
//--CREATE THE BASIC QUERY VOCABULARY. We now set up the underlying
//--fuzzy sets associated with each of the column domains in the
//--relational database. This forms the primary query vocabulary.
//=======================================================================
//
//
//-----------------------------------------------------------------------
//--COMPANY.AGE The company age is spread over sixty years indicating
//--the general perceived stability of the company.
//-----------------------------------------------------------------------
//
   for(i=0;i<ageFDBcnt;i++)
     {
       if((ageFDBptr[i]=new FDB)==NULL)
         {
          MtsSendError(2,PgmId,ageFDBnames[i]);
          return;
         }
       FzyInitFDB(ageFDBptr[i]);
       strcpy(ageFDBptr[i]->FDBid,  ageFDBnames[i]);
       ageFDBptr[i]->FDBdomain[0]= 0;
       ageFDBptr[i]->FDBdomain[1]=60;
     }
   FzySCurve  (ageFDBptr[0],  0,  2,  4,DECLINE,&status); //NEW
   FzyPiCurve (ageFDBptr[1],  4,  2           ,&status); //YOUNG
   FzyPiCurve (ageFDBptr[2],  8,  4           ,&status); //RECENT
   FzyPiCurve (ageFDBptr[3], 16,  8           ,&status); //MATURE
   FzyPiCurve (ageFDBptr[4], 24,  8           ,&status); //ESTABLISHED
   FzySCurve  (ageFDBptr[5], 24, 42, 60,GROWTH ,&status); //OLD
   FzyPlotTermSet("COMPANY.AGE",ageFDBptr,ageFDBcnt,SYSMODFILE,&status);
   FzyStoreFuzzyData(ageFDBptr,ageFDBcnt,"b:sqllage.dat", 8,&status);
//
//-----------------------------------------------------------------------
//--REVENUES. These are the descriptions of the annual revenues in
//--dollars ($) adjusted for write-offs and other losses.
//-----------------------------------------------------------------------
//
```

```
      for(i=0;i<revFDBcnt;i++)
        {
        if((revFDBptr[i]=new FDB)==NULL)
           {
           MtsSendError(2,PgmId,revFDBnames[i]);
           return;
           }
        FzyInitFDB(revFDBptr[i]);
        strcpy(revFDBptr[i]->FDBid,  revFDBnames[i]);
        revFDBptr[i]->FDBdomain[0]= 100;
        revFDBptr[i]->FDBdomain[1]=1800;
        }
     FzySCurve  (revFDBptr[0], 100, 150, 200,DECLINE,&status); //MINIMAL
     FzyPiCurve (revFDBptr[1], 300, 200          ,&status); //LOW
     FzyPiCurve (revFDBptr[2], 500, 200          ,&status); //MODERATE
     FzyPiCurve (revFDBptr[3], 700, 200          ,&status); //MEDIUM
     FzySCurve  (revFDBptr[4], 700, 850,1000,GROWTH ,&status); //HIGH
     FzyPlotTermSet("ANNUAL.REVENUES",revFDBptr,revFDBcnt,SYSMODFILE,&status);
     FzyStoreFuzzyData(revFDBptr,revFDBcnt,"b:sql1rev.dat", 8,&status);
//
//------------------------------------------------------------------------
//--PRODUCT.COUNT These are the quantity fuzzy sets associated with
//--number of products sold by the company.
//------------------------------------------------------------------------
//
     for(i=0;i<pnoFDBcnt;i++)
       {
       if((pnoFDBptr[i]=new FDB)==NULL)
          {
          MtsSendError(2,PgmId,pnoFDBnames[i]);
          return;
          }
       FzyInitFDB(pnoFDBptr[i]);
       strcpy(pnoFDBptr[i]->FDBid,  pnoFDBnames[i]);
       pnoFDBptr[i]->FDBdomain[0]=  0;
       pnoFDBptr[i]->FDBdomain[1]= 20;
       }
     FzySCurve  (pnoFDBptr[0],  0,  2,  4,DECLINE,&status); //FEW
     FzyPiCurve (pnoFDBptr[1],  4,  2          ,&status); //SOME
     FzyPiCurve (pnoFDBptr[2],  8,  4          ,&status); //SEVERAL
     FzySCurve  (pnoFDBptr[3],  8, 14, 20,GROWTH ,&status); //MANY
     FzyPlotTermSet("PRODUCT.COUNT",pnoFDBptr,pnoFDBcnt,SYSMODFILE,&status);
     FzyStoreFuzzyData(pnoFDBptr,pnoFDBcnt,"b:sql1pno.dat", 8,&status);
//
//------------------------------------------------------------------------
//--EMPLOYEE.COUNT These are the quantity fuzzy sets associated with
//--number of employees in the companies (also a measure of size).
//------------------------------------------------------------------------
//
     for(i=0;i<enoFDBcnt;i++)
        {
        if((enoFDBptr[i]=new FDB)==NULL)
           {
           MtsSendError(2,PgmId,enoFDBnames[i]);
           return;
           }
        FzyInitFDB(enoFDBptr[i]);
        strcpy(enoFDBptr[i]->FDBid,  enoFDBnames[i]);
        enoFDBptr[i]->FDBdomain[0]=  0;
        enoFDBptr[i]->FDBdomain[1]= 60;
        }
     FzySCurve  (enoFDBptr[0],  0,  5, 10,DECLINE,&status); //SMALL
     FzyPiCurve (enoFDBptr[1], 10,  5          ,&status); //MODERATE
     FzyPiCurve (enoFDBptr[2], 20, 10          ,&status); //MEDIUM
```

```
     FzySCurve (enoFDBptr[3],  20,  35,  60,GROWTH ,&status); //LARGE
     FzyPlotTermSet("EMPLOYEE.COUNT",enoFDBptr,enoFDBcnt,SYSMODFILE,&status);
     FzyStoreFuzzyData(enoFDBptr,enoFDBcnt,"b:sql1eno.dat", 8,&status);
  //
  //----------------------------------------------------------------------
  //--PROFIT.LOSS This is the effective retained earnings for the company
  //--during the past years. It can be either a profit or a loss.
  //----------------------------------------------------------------------
  //
     for(i=0;i<pnlFDBcnt;i++)
       {
        if((pnlFDBptr[i]=new FDB)==NULL)
          {
           MtsSendError(2,PgmId,pnlFDBnames[i]);
           return;
          }
        FzyInitFDB(pnlFDBptr[i]);
        strcpy(pnlFDBptr[i]->FDBid,  pnlFDBnames[i]);
        pnlFDBptr[i]->FDBdomain[0]=-500;
        pnlFDBptr[i]->FDBdomain[1]= 500;
       }
     FzySCurve  (pnlFDBptr[0],-500,-350,-200,DECLINE,&status); //BL
     FzyPiCurve (pnlFDBptr[1],-200,-100          ,&status); //ML
     FzyPiCurve (pnlFDBptr[2],-100,-100          ,&status); //SL
     FzyPiCurve (pnlFDBptr[3],   0,  50          ,&status); //BE
     FzyPiCurve (pnlFDBptr[4], 100, 100          ,&status); //SG
     FzyPiCurve (pnlFDBptr[5], 200, 100          ,&status); //MG
     FzySCurve  (pnlFDBptr[6], 200, 350, 500,GROWTH ,&status); //BG
     FzyPlotTermSet("PROFIT.LOSS",pnlFDBptr,pnlFDBcnt,SYSMODFILE,&status);
     FzyStoreFuzzyData(pnlFDBptr,pnlFDBcnt,"b:sql1pnl.dat", 8,&status);
  //
  //----------------------------------------------------------------------
  //--RETURNED.EPS This is the retained earnings per share for the company
  //--during the past year. It can range from zero to the maximum of after
  //--tax and after discount earnings.
  //----------------------------------------------------------------------
  //
     for(i=0;i<epsFDBcnt;i++)
       {
        if((epsFDBptr[i]=new FDB)==NULL)
          {
           MtsSendError(2,PgmId,epsFDBnames[i]);
           return;
          }
        FzyInitFDB(epsFDBptr[i]);
        strcpy(epsFDBptr[i]->FDBid,  epsFDBnames[i]);
        epsFDBptr[i]->FDBdomain[0]=  0;
        epsFDBptr[i]->FDBdomain[1]= 10;
       }
     FzySCurve  (epsFDBptr[0],  0, .5,  1,DECLINE,&status); //UNACCEPTABLE
     FzyPiCurve (epsFDBptr[1],  1,  1          ,&status); //POOR
     FzyPiCurve (epsFDBptr[2],  3,  2          ,&status); //ACCEPTABLE
     FzyPiCurve (epsFDBptr[3],  5,  2          ,&status); //GOOD
     FzySCurve  (epsFDBptr[4],  5, 7.5, 10,GROWTH ,&status); //EXCELLENT
     FzyPlotTermSet("RETURNED.EPS",epsFDBptr,epsFDBcnt,SYSMODFILE,&status);
     FzyStoreFuzzyData(epsFDBptr,epsFDBcnt,"b:sql1eps.dat", 8,&status);
  //
  //
     if((DBlog=fopen(DBAuditFile,"w"))==NULL)
       {
        status=1;
        printf("Sorry. '%s' file was not created\n",DBAuditFile);
        return;
       }
```

```
  //
  //======================================================================
  //--REQUEST THE ROW QUALIFIERS. We now prompt for the fuzzy set space
  //--associated with each of the column domains. These would for the
  //--fuzzy WHERE statement in the SQL request.
  //======================================================================
  //
    Wcnt=0;
    for(i=0;i<8;i++)
      memset(strBuff[i],'\0',32);
    TryCtl[0]=10;
    TryCtl[1]= 0;
    Domain[0]=0;
    Domain[1]=1;
    printf("\nFuzzySQL Database Processor\n");
    printf("--------------------------\n");
    AlfaCut=MtsAskforDBL(
     "AlfaCut",
     "AlphaCut Threshold    : ",Domain,TryCtl,&status);
    TryCtl[1]= 0;
    AggOperator=MINIMUM;
    AggType=MtsAskforVAL(
     "AND.Type",
     "AND operator Type     : ",
     ANDnames,ANDcnt,minlen,&idx,TryCtl,&status);
    AggOperator=idx;
  //
    printf("%s\n%s\n\n%s\n",
      "select companies",
      "  from MfgDBMS",
      "  where: ");
    TryCtl[1]= 0;
    Age_FDBptr=NULL;
    AgeFS=MtsAskforVAL(
     "COMPANY.AGE",
     "Company Age is        : ",
     ageFDBnames,ageFDBcnt,minlen,&idx,TryCtl,&status);
    Age_FDBptr=FindFuzzySet(AgeFS,ageFDBptr,ageFDBcnt,&status);
    if(Age_FDBptr!=NULL)
      sprintf(strBuff[Wcnt++],"%s%s","Company.Age is ",AgeFS);
    TryCtl[1]= 0;
    Rev_FDBptr=NULL;
    RevFS=MtsAskforVAL(
     "ANNUAL.REVENUES",
     "Annnual Revenues are : ",
     revFDBnames,revFDBcnt,minlen,&idx,TryCtl,&status);
    Rev_FDBptr=FindFuzzySet(RevFS,revFDBptr,revFDBcnt,&status);
    if(Rev_FDBptr!=NULL)
      sprintf(strBuff[Wcnt++],"%s%s","Annual.Revenues are ",RevFS);
    TryCtl[1]= 0;
    Pno_FDBptr=NULL;
    PnoFS=MtsAskforVAL(
     "PRODUCT.COUNT",
     "Product Count is      : ",
     pnoFDBnames,pnoFDBcnt,minlen,&idx,TryCtl,&status);
    Pno_FDBptr=FindFuzzySet(PnoFS,pnoFDBptr,pnoFDBcnt,&status);
    if(Pno_FDBptr!=NULL)
      sprintf(strBuff[Wcnt++],"%s%s","Product.Count is ",PnoFS);
    TryCtl[1]= 0;
    Eno_FDBptr=NULL;
    EnoFS=MtsAskforVAL(
     "EMPLOYEE.COUNT",
     "Employee Count is     : ",
     enoFDBnames,enoFDBcnt,minlen,&idx,TryCtl,&status);
```

```
          Eno_FDBptr=FindFuzzySet(EnoFS,enoFDBptr,enoFDBcnt,&status);
          if(Eno_FDBptr!=NULL)
            sprintf(strBuff[Wcnt++],"%s%s","Employee.Count is ",EnoFS);
          TryCtl[1]= 0;
          Pnl_FDBptr=NULL;
          PnlFS=MtsAskforVAL(
           "PROFIT.LOSS",
           "Profit or Loss is    : ",
            pnlFDBnames,pnlFDBcnt,minlen,&idx,TryCtl,&status);
          Pnl_FDBptr=FindFuzzySet(PnlFS,pnlFDBptr,pnlFDBcnt,&status);
          if(Eno_FDBptr!=NULL)
            sprintf(strBuff[Wcnt++],"%s%s","Profit.Loss is ",PnlFS);
          TryCtl[1]= 0;
          Eps_FDBptr=NULL;
          EpsFS=MtsAskforVAL(
           "RETURNED.EPS",
           "Returned EPS is      : ",
            epsFDBnames,epsFDBcnt,minlen,&idx,TryCtl,&status);
          Eps_FDBptr=FindFuzzySet(EpsFS,epsFDBptr,epsFDBcnt,&status);
          if(Eps_FDBptr!=NULL)
            sprintf(strBuff[Wcnt++],"%s%s","Returned.EPS is ",EpsFS);
     //
     //=========================================================================
     //--PROCESS THE RELATIONAL DATABASE. Having found the fuzzy sets for
     //--each of the columns, we now read each record form the database and
     //--determine its degree of compatibility with the request.
     //=========================================================================
     //
       for(i=0;i<fzyDBsize;i++)
          {
           SQLrecIDX[i]=-1;
           SQLrecDOM[i]= 0;
           SQLrecAVG[i]= 0;
           for(j=0;j<DataCols;j++)  MemValues[i][j]=0;
          }
     //
     //
       SelCnt=0;
       AlfaRejected=0;
       for(i=0;i<fzyDBsize;i++)
          {
           fzyRECptr=&DBdata[i];
           fprintf(DBlog,"\n%4d%s%s\n",i+1,". ",fzyRECptr->Company);
           //
           //----------------------------------------------------------------
           //--Now find the degree of membership in each of the specified
           //--fuzzy sets. These are stored in a working array for later use.
           //--We also calculate the age of the company from today's date.
           //----------------------------------------------------------------
           //
           CompAge=1995-(fzyRECptr->Founded);
           AgeMem=Membershipof(
             "COMPANY.AGE",CompAge,AlfaCut,Age_FDBptr);
           MemValues[i][0]=AgeMem;
           RevMem=Membershipof(
             "ANNUAL.REVENUES",(double)fzyRECptr->Revenues,AlfaCut,Rev_FDBptr);
           MemValues[i][1]=RevMem;
           PnoMem=Membershipof(
             "PRODUCT.COUNT",(double)fzyRECptr->NumProducts,AlfaCut,Pno_FDBptr);
           MemValues[i][2]=PnoMem;
           EnoMem=Membershipof(
             "EMPLOYEE.COUNT",(double)fzyRECptr->NumEmps,AlfaCut,Eno_FDBptr);
           MemValues[i][3]=EnoMem;
           PnlMem=Membershipof(
```

```
        "PROFIT.LOSS",(double)fzyRECptr->ProfitLoss,AlfaCut,Pnl_FDBptr);
      MemValues[i][4]=PnlMem;
      EpsMem=Membershipof(
        "RETURNED.EPS",(double)fzyRECptr->EarnPerShare,AlfaCut,Eps_FDBptr);
      MemValues[i][5]=EpsMem;
      //
      //----------------------------------------------------------------
      //--Now find the minimum of the truth memberships (this is the
      //--fuzzy AND operator applied to all the qualifiers). Note that
      //--statements that were not included in the expression, have a
      //--membership value of minus one (-1).
      //----------------------------------------------------------------
      //
      TotGrade=0;
      CompIDX=99999;
      NumSets=0;
      for(j=0;j<DataCols;j++)
         if(MemValues[i][j]!=NOTFOUND)
            {
            if(MemValues[i][j]<CompIDX) CompIDX=MemValues[i][j];
            TotGrade+=MemValues[i][j];
            NumSets++;
            }
      AvgGrade=(TotGrade/NumSets);
      //
      //----------------------------------------------------------------
      //--OK, if the composite truth membership is greater than the
      //--indicated alpha cut threshold for this query, then we select
      //--this record from the database. In our small model, this means
      //--saving the row index and the truth membership.
      //----------------------------------------------------------------
      //
      fprintf(DBlog,"%s%5.3f%s%5.3f\n",
         "         CompIDX: ",CompIDX,", AvgGrade: ",AvgGrade);
      if(AggOperator==MINIMUM)  CIX=CompIDX;
         else                   CIX=AvgGrade;
      if(CIX>=AlfaCut)
         {
         SQLrecIDX[SelCnt]= i;
         SQLrecDOM[SelCnt]= CompIDX;
         SQLrecAVG[SelCnt]= AvgGrade;
         SelCnt++;
         }
       else
        if(CIX>0)
           {
           fprintf(DBlog,"%s%5.3f%s%5.3f\n",
              "         Alpha Cut Rejection: ",CIX," < ",AlfaCut);
           AlfaRejected++;
           }
      }
//
//=====================================================================
//--SHOW QUERY RESULTS. We now form and dispaly the actual fzySQL
//--query, rank the selected records by the composite truth value
//--(in descending order so highest truth appears first); and then
//--we print a report showing the companies selected.
//=====================================================================
//
   fprintf(DBlog,"\n\n%s\n%s\n%s\n%s%s",
      "-----------------------------------------------------------",
      "select companies",
      "  from MfgDBMS",
      "  where  ",
```

```
            strBuff[0]);
      for(i=1;i<Wcnt;i++)
        fprintf(DBlog,"\n%s%s","     AND ",strBuff[i]);
      fprintf(DBlog,"%s\n",";");
      //
      //
      SQLranking(SQLrecIDX,SQLrecDOM,SQLrecAVG,AggOperator,SelCnt,&status);
      //
      //
      fprintf(DBlog,"\n\n\n%s\n%s\n",
       "Company          CompIDX     AvgIDX    ",
       "----------------  ----------  ----------");
      for(i=0;i<SelCnt;i++)
        {
        recIDX=SQLrecIDX[i];
        CompIDX=SQLrecDOM[i];
        AvgGrade=SQLrecAVG[i];
        fzyRECptr=&DBdata[recIDX];
        fprintf(DBlog,"%-16.16s  %10.3f  %10.3f\n",
                 fzyRECptr->Company,CompIDX,AvgGrade);
        }
      dblSelCnt=(double)SelCnt;
      dblDBsize=(double)fzyDBsize;
      fprintf(DBlog,"\n%s%10d\n%s%10d\n%s%10.2f\n",
       "Record Selected          : ",SelCnt,
       "Rejected due to AlphaCut  : ",AlfaRejected,
       "Percent (%) Found         : ",(dblSelCnt/dblDBsize)*100);
      return;
   }
//
//===========================================================================
//------------------FUZZY DATABASE SUPPORT SERVICES--------------------
//===========================================================================
//
FDB* FindFuzzySet(char *FSid,FDB *FDBptr[],int FDBcnt,int *statusPtr)
/*-------------------------------------------------------------------*
| Given the name of a fuzzy set in the variable's Term Set, this     |
| function returns a pointer to the corresponding FDB structure.     |
*-------------------------------------------------------------------*/
   {
   FDB  *thisFDBptr;
   *statusPtr=0;
   if(!FSid) return(NULL);
   for(int i=0;i<FDBcnt;i++)
     {
     thisFDBptr=FDBptr[i];
     if(strcmp(FSid,thisFDBptr->FDBid)==0) return(thisFDBptr);
     }
   *statusPtr=1;
   return(NULL);
   }
//
//
float Membershipof(char *Colid,double DBColvalue,float AlfaCut,FDB *FDBptr)
/*-------------------------------------------------------------------*
| Given a column data value and a pointer into an FDB, this routine  |
| returns the value's grade of membership. If the grade is below     |
| the Alpha Cut threshold we return a zero. If the fuzzy set is NULL |
| we indicate NOTFOUND. A message is also written to the audit log.  |
*-------------------------------------------------------------------*/
   {
   int    idx,status;
   float  memgrade;
   if(FDBptr==NULL) return(-1);
```

```
     memgrade=FzyGetMembership(FDBptr,DBColvalue,&idx,&status);
//if(memgrade<AlfaCut) memgrade=0;
     fprintf(DBlog,"%s%-16.16s%s%s%s%7.2f%s%5.3f%s\n",
       "       ",Colid,"    in '",FDBptr->FDBid,"' (",DBColvalue,",",memgrade,")");
     return(memgrade);
  }
//
//
void  SQLranking(
  int   SQLrecIDX[],float SQLrecDOM[],float SQLrecAVG[],
                int AggOperator,int SelCnt,int *status)
/*-----------------------------------------------------------------*
 | Perform a descending buddle sort on the record sector arrays. In  |
 | this simple model we use a very low performance sorting algorithm |
 | for simplicity. In actual systems a version of quicksort coupled  |
 | with an external sort/merge would be employed.                    |
 *-----------------------------------------------------------------*/
     {
     int    i,j;
     int    tempIDX;
     float  tempDOM,tempAVG;
     float  recCIX;
     bool   sortedFlag;
     if(SelCnt<2) return;
     for(j=0;j<SelCnt;j++)
       {
       sortedFlag=TRUE;
       for(i=0;i<(SelCnt-1);i++)
         {
         if(SQLrankingFault(AggOperator,i,SQLrecDOM,SQLrecAVG))
           {
           //---------------------------------------------------
           //--The i-th grade of membership is less than the i+1
           //--membership. We now save the current values and do a
           //--simple swap of the values.
           //---------------------------------------------------
           //
           tempIDX=SQLrecIDX[i];
           tempDOM=SQLrecDOM[i];
           tempAVG=SQLrecAVG[i];
           SQLrecIDX[i]=SQLrecIDX[i+1];
           SQLrecDOM[i]=SQLrecDOM[i+1];
           SQLrecAVG[i]=SQLrecAVG[i+1];
           SQLrecIDX[i+1]=tempIDX;
           SQLrecDOM[i+1]=tempDOM;
           SQLrecAVG[i+1]=tempAVG;
           sortedFlag=FALSE;
           }
         }
       if(sortedFlag==TRUE) return;
       }
     return;
     }
//
//
bool SQLrankingFault(int AggOperator,int i,float SQLrecDOM[],float SQLrecAVG[])
/*-----------------------------------------------------------------*
 | This, routine uses the current aggregation operator type to check |
 | whether or not the ordering of membership grades for the arary    |
 | that holds the specific values is out of order. If a fault is     |
 | found we return TRUE, otherwise we indicate FALSE.                |
 *-----------------------------------------------------------------*/
     {
     if(AggOperator==MINIMUM)
```

```
     {
      if(SQLrecDOM[i]<SQLrecDOM[i+1]) return(TRUE);
      return(FALSE);
      }
   if(AggOperator==AVERAGE)
     {
      if(SQLrecAVG[i]<SQLrecAVG[i+1]) return(TRUE);
      return(FALSE);
      }
   return(FALSE);
  }
```

FzySQL2 (A Fuzzy SQL database processor [version 2])

```
/*------------------------------------------------------------*
| (c) 1995 Metus Systems.       Proprietary software product. |
| Reproduction or unauthorized use is prohibited. Unauthorized|
| use is illegal. Violators will be prosecuted. This software |
| contains proprietary trade and business secrets.            |
*--------------------Procedure Description-------------------*
| fzysql2.cpp  Earl Cox  01/20/95 Fuzzy Database Operations   |
|                                                             |
| This program simulates fuzzy SQL query access against a     |
| relational database containing financial information. You   |
| specify a minimum alpha theshold as well as the type of     |
| membership aggregation you want. The records are selected   |
| and then ranked by their degree of compatibility with the   |
| request (high-to-low).                                      |
*-------------------------------------------------------------*
| This version of the fuzzySQL processor incoporates hedges   |
| into the query so that the we can say VERY FEW, etc. This    |
| means that we have to change the way we receive and parse    |
| the name of the linguistic variable.                        |
*-------------------------------------------------------------*
| CAVEATS: This program does not connect to a real relational |
| database (but such a connection would obviously not be      |
| difficult), it does not support secondary fuzzy indexing,   |
| and the ranking methodology uses a very low performance     |
| sorting technique. And, of course, this version does not    |
| support hedges and other quantifiers.                       |
*----------------Modification Audit/Change Log---------------*
| Rev  Sar              Metus                                 |
| No   Code  Date       Rellvl  Mod  Description              |
| --   -----  --------   ------   ---   ------------------------|
|                                                             |
|                                                             |
*-------------------------------------------------------------*/
#include <stdlib.h>
#include <string.h>
#include <math.h>
#include "FDB.hpp"
#include "SSYSctl.hpp"
#include "mtypes.hpp"
#include "fuzzy.hpp"
#include "mtsptype.hpp"
//
//------------------RELATIONAL DATABASE STRUCTURE------------------
//--For purposes of simplicity and demonstration, we maintain our small
//--relational database as an in-memory array. This makes the database
//--easily transportable although we must simulate SQL statements.
//-------------------------------------------------------------------
//
```

```
struct fzyDBMS
  {
  char    *Company;
  long    Founded,
          Revenues,
          NumProducts,
          NumEmps,
          ProfitLoss;
  float   EarnPerShare;
  };
//
fzyDBMS  DBdata[]=
  {
//              SMALL MANUFACTURING COMPANIES
//         Year    1995    Num   Num  1995
//  Company  Founded Revenues Prods Emps RetErn     EPS
//  -------  ------- -------- ----- ---- -------     ---
    {"CompA" ,   1948,    570,   1.  16,      3,  .20},
    {"CompB" ,   1972,    478,   3,  27,    243, 1.77},
    {"CompC" ,   1982,    401,   9.  58,     17, 1.02},
    {"CompD" ,   1987,    321,   3,   8,     25, 3.11},
    {"CompE" ,   1988,    650,   5,  33,    -87,  .44},
    {"CompF" ,   1994,    550,  16,   9,     99,  .79},
    {"CompG" ,   1992,    597,   4,  11,    -13,  .04},
    {"CompH" ,   1990,    602,   7,  41,     33, 2.14},
    {"CompI" ,   1991,    498,   5,  15,    207, 1.33},
    {"CompK" ,   1994,    501,   2,  57,    133, 2.83},
    {"CompL" ,   1985,    920,   8,   5,    201, 1.55},
    {"CompM" ,   1983,    555,   2,   9,    509, 1.05},
    {"CompN" ,   1988,   1050,  10,  25,    427, 2.94},
    {"CompO" ,   1990,    530,  14,  12,     22,  .30},
    {"CompP" ,   1988,    522,   4,  21,     62, 1.28},
    {"CompR" ,   1959,    900,   3,   5,     -8,  .00},
    {"CompS" ,   1964,    659,   2,   7,      0,  .10},
    {"CompT" ,   1979,    619,   5,  17,    280, 3.17},
    {"CompU" ,   1967,   1233,   2,  28,    322, 2.40},
    {"CompW" ,   1964,    973,  11,  48,    422, 2.88}
  };
const int fzyDBsize=20;
const int ColCnt  = 7;
const int DataCols = 6;
//
static  FILE    *DBlog;
static  HDB     *HDBptr,*HDBvector[HDBmax];
static  FDB     *FDBptr[FDBmax];
static  int     HDBcnt,FDBcnt;
const   char    *PgmId="fzySQL1";
const   int     FzyTermMax=11;
//
char far * far ageFDBnames[]=
  {
  "NEW",
  "YOUNG",
  "RECENT",
  "MATURE",
  "ESTABLISHED",
  "OLD"
  };
char far * far revFDBnames[]=
  {
  "NONE",
  "LOW",
  "MODERATE",
  "MEDIUM",
```

```
                 "HIGH"
            };
   char far * far pnoFDBnames[]=
            {
            "FEW",
            "SOME",
            "SEVERAL",
            "MANY"
            };
   char far * far enoFDBnames[]=
            {
            "SMALL",
            "MODERATE",
            "MEDIUM",
            "LARGE"
            };
   char far * far pnlFDBnames[]=
            {
            "BIG.LOSS",
            "MODERATE.LOSS",
            "SMALL.LOSS",
            "BREAK.EVEN",
            "SMALL.GAIN",
            "MODERATE.GAIN",
            "BIG.GAIN"
            };
   char far * far epsFDBnames[]=
            {
            "UNACCEPTABLE",
            "POOR",
            "ACCEPTABLE",
            "GOOD",
            "EXCELLENT"
            };
   char far * far ANDnames[]=
            {
            "MINIMUM",
            "AVERAGE"
            };
   #define  MINIMUM    0
   #define  AVERAGE    1
   //
   FDB*    FindFuzzySet(char*,FDB*[],int,int*);
   float   Membershipof(char*,double,float,FDB*);
   void    SQLranking(int[],float[],float[],int,int,int*);
   bool    SQLrankingFault(int,int,float[]);
   FDB    *FormLinguisticVariable(char*,char*,FDB**,int,char*,int*);
   void    ShowTermNames(char*,FDB**,int,int*);
   //
   void    FzyInsertHedges(HDB**,int*,int*);
   HDB*    FzyGetHedge(char*,HDB**,int,int*,int*);
   //
   void main()
    {
   //
   //---------------FUZZY SET DEFINTIONS AND CONTROLS--------------------
   //--For purposes of simplicity and demonstration, we maintain our small
   //--relational database as an in-memory array. This makes the database
   //--easily transportable although we must simulate SQL statements.
   //--------------------------------------------------------------------
   //
      FDB      *ageFDBptr[FzyTermMax],
               *revFDBptr[FzyTermMax],
               *pnoFDBptr[FzyTermMax],
```

```
                    *enoFDBptr[FzyTermMax],
                    *pnlFDBptr[FzyTermMax],
                    *epsFDBptr[FzyTermMax];
        FDB         *Age_FDBptr,
                    *Rev_FDBptr,
                    *Pno_FDBptr,
                    *Eno_FDBptr,
                    *Pnl_FDBptr,
                    *Eps_FDBptr;
        int         ageFDBcnt=6,
                    revFDBcnt=5,
                    pnoFDBcnt=4,
                    enoFDBcnt=4,
                    pnlFDBcnt=7,
                    epsFDBcnt=5;
        int         ANDcnt   =2;
        char        *AgeLV,*RevLV,*PnoLV,*EnoLV,*PnlLV,*EpsLV;
        float       AgeMem,RevMem,PnoMem,EnoMem,PnlMem,EpsMem;
//
//-----------------------------------------------------------------
//
        fzyDBMS *fzyRECptr;
        char        *DBAuditFile="b:DBaudit.fil";
        char        *AggType;
        char        strBuff[8][32];
        int         TryCtl[2],minlen=4,maxlen=80;
        int         i,j,idx,status;
        int         Wcnt,SelCnt,AlfaRejected,NumSets,AggOperator,recIDX;
        int         SQLrecIDX[fzyDBsize];
        float       SQLrecDOM[fzyDBsize];
        float       SQLrecAVG[fzyDBsize];
        float       AlfaCut,CompIDX,AvgGrade,CIX,MemValues[fzyDBsize][DataCols];
        double      Domain[2],CompAge,TotGrade;
        double      dblSelCnt,dblDBsize;
//
        status=0;
//
        SysConnecttoMetus(&status);
        XSYSctl.XSYScurrPDBptr=NULL;
        XSYSctl.XSYSalfacut   =0.1;
        XSYSctl.XSYStrace[3]  =TRUE;
        XSYSctl.XSYStrace[2]  =TRUE;
//
//
        for(i=0;i<FzyTermMax;i++)
          {
          ageFDBptr[i]=NULL;
          revFDBptr[i]=NULL;
          pnoFDBptr[i]=NULL;
          enoFDBptr[i]=NULL;
          pnlFDBptr[i]=NULL;
          epsFDBptr[i]=NULL;
          }
//
//================================================================
//--CREATE THE BASIC QUERY VOCABULARY. We now set up the underlying
//--fuzzy sets associated with each of the column domains in the
//--relational database. This forms the primary query vocabulary.
//================================================================
//
//
//-----------------------------------------------------------------
//--COMPANY.AGE The company age is spread over sixty years indicating
//--the general perceived stability of the company.
//-----------------------------------------------------------------
//
```

```
    for(i=0;i<ageFDBcnt;i++)
      {
        if((ageFDBptr[i]=new FDB)==NULL)
          {
            MtsSendError(2,PgmId,ageFDBnames[i]);
            return;
          }
        FzyInitFDB(ageFDBptr[i]);
        strcpy(ageFDBptr[i]->FDBid, ageFDBnames[i]);
        ageFDBptr[i]->FDBdomain[0]= 0;
        ageFDBptr[i]->FDBdomain[1]=60;
      }
    FzySCurve  (ageFDBptr[0],  0,  2,  4,DECLINE,&status); //NEW
    FzyPiCurve (ageFDBptr[1],  4,  2              ,&status); //YOUNG
    FzyPiCurve (ageFDBptr[2],  8,  4              ,&status); //RECENT
    FzyPiCurve (ageFDBptr[3], 16,  8              ,&status); //MATURE
    FzyPiCurve (ageFDBptr[4], 24,  8              ,&status); //ESTABLISHED
    FzySCurve  (ageFDBptr[5], 24, 42, 60,GROWTH ,&status); //OLD
    FzyPlotTermSet("COMPANY.AGE",ageFDBptr,ageFDBcnt,SYSMODFILE,&status);
    FzyStoreFuzzyData(ageFDBptr,ageFDBcnt,"b:sql2age.dat", 8,&status);
//
//-----------------------------------------------------------------------
//--REVENUES. These are the descriptions of the annual revenues in
//--dollars ($) adjusted for write-offs and other losses.
//-----------------------------------------------------------------------
//
    for(i=0;i<revFDBcnt;i++)
      {
        if((revFDBptr[i]=new FDB)==NULL)
          {
            MtsSendError(2,PgmId,revFDBnames[i]);
            return;
          }
        FzyInitFDB(revFDBptr[i]);
        strcpy(revFDBptr[i]->FDBid, revFDBnames[i]);
        revFDBptr[i]->FDBdomain[0]= 100;
        revFDBptr[i]->FDBdomain[1]=1800;
      }
    FzySCurve  (revFDBptr[0], 100, 150, 200,DECLINE,&status); //MINIMAL
    FzyPiCurve (revFDBptr[1], 300, 200              ,&status); //LOW
    FzyPiCurve (revFDBptr[2], 500, 200              ,&status); //MODERATE
    FzyPiCurve (revFDBptr[3], 700, 200              ,&status); //MEDIUM
    FzySCurve  (revFDBptr[4], 700, 850,1000,GROWTH ,&status); //HIGH
    FzyPlotTermSet("REVENUES",revFDBptr,revFDBcnt,SYSMODFILE,&status);
    FzyStoreFuzzyData(revFDBptr,revFDBcnt,"b:sql2rev.dat", 8,&status);
//
//-----------------------------------------------------------------------
//--PRODUCT.COUNT These are the quantity fuzzy sets associated with
//--number of products sold by the company.
//-----------------------------------------------------------------------
//
    for(i=0;i<pnoFDBcnt;i++)
      {
        if((pnoFDBptr[i]=new FDB)==NULL)
          {
            MtsSendError(2,PgmId,pnoFDBnames[i]);
            return;
          }
        FzyInitFDB(pnoFDBptr[i]);
        strcpy(pnoFDBptr[i]->FDBid, pnoFDBnames[i]);
        pnoFDBptr[i]->FDBdomain[0]=  0;
        pnoFDBptr[i]->FDBdomain[1]= 20;
      }
```

```
      FzySCurve  (pnoFDBptr[0],   0,   2,   4,DECLINE,&status); //FEW
      FzyPiCurve (pnoFDBptr[1],   4,   2                ,&status); //SOME
      FzyPiCurve (pnoFDBptr[2],   8,   4                ,&status); //SEVERAL
      FzySCurve  (pnoFDBptr[3],   8,  14,  20,GROWTH ,&status); //MANY
      FzyPlotTermSet("PRODUCT.COUNT",pnoFDBptr,pnoFDBcnt,SYSMODFILE,&status);
      FzyStoreFuzzyData(pnoFDBptr,pnoFDBcnt,"b:sql2pno.dat", 8,&status);
//
//-------------------------------------------------------------------------
//--EMPLOYEE.COUNT These are the quantity fuzzy sets associated with
//--number of employees in the companies (also a measure of size).
//-------------------------------------------------------------------------
//
   for(i=0;i<enoFDBcnt;i++)
     {
      if((enoFDBptr[i]=new FDB)==NULL)
        {
         MtsSendError(2,PgmId,enoFDBnames[i]);
         return;
        }
      FzyInitFDB(enoFDBptr[i]);
      strcpy(enoFDBptr[i]->FDBid,  enoFDBnames[i]);
      enoFDBptr[i]->FDBdomain[0]=   0;
      enoFDBptr[i]->FDBdomain[1]=  60;
     }
      FzySCurve  (enoFDBptr[0],   0,   5,  10,DECLINE,&status); //SMALL
      FzyPiCurve (enoFDBptr[1],  10,   5                ,&status); //MODERATE
      FzyPiCurve (enoFDBptr[2],  20,  10                ,&status); //MEDIUM
      FzySCurve  (enoFDBptr[3],  20,  35,  60,GROWTH ,&status); //LARGE
      FzyPlotTermSet("EMPLOYEE.COUNT",enoFDBptr,enoFDBcnt,SYSMODFILE,&status);
      FzyStoreFuzzyData(enoFDBptr,enoFDBcnt,"b:sql2eno.dat", 8,&status);
//
//-------------------------------------------------------------------------
//--PROFIT.LOSS This is the effective retained earnings for the company
//--during the past years. It can be either a profit or a loss.
//-------------------------------------------------------------------------
//
   for(i=0;i<pnlFDBcnt;i++)
     {
      if((pnlFDBptr[i]=new FDB)==NULL)
        {
         MtsSendError(2,PgmId,pnlFDBnames[i]);
         return;
        }
      FzyInitFDB(pnlFDBptr[i]);
      strcpy(pnlFDBptr[i]->FDBid,  pnlFDBnames[i]);
      pnlFDBptr[i]->FDBdomain[0]=-500;
      pnlFDBptr[i]->FDBdomain[1]= 500;
     }
      FzySCurve  (pnlFDBptr[0],-500,-350,-200,DECLINE,&status); //BL
      FzyPiCurve (pnlFDBptr[1],-200,-100                ,&status); //ML
      FzyPiCurve (pnlFDBptr[2],-100,-100                ,&status); //SL
      FzyPiCurve (pnlFDBptr[3],   0,  50                ,&status); //BE
      FzyPiCurve (pnlFDBptr[4], 100, 100                ,&status); //SG
      FzyPiCurve (pnlFDBptr[5], 200, 100                ,&status); //MG
      FzySCurve  (pnlFDBptr[6], 200, 350, 500,GROWTH ,&status); //BG
      FzyPlotTermSet("PROFIT.LOSS",pnlFDBptr,pnlFDBcnt,SYSMODFILE,&status);
      FzyStoreFuzzyData(pnlFDBptr,pnlFDBcnt,"b:sql2pnl.dat", 8,&status);
//
//-------------------------------------------------------------------------
//--RETURNED.EPS This is the retained earnings per share for the company
//--during the past year. It can range from zero to the maximum of after
//--tax and after discount earnings.
//-------------------------------------------------------------------------
//
```

```
        for(i=0;i<epsFDBcnt;i++)
          {
            if((epsFDBptr[i]=new FDB)==NULL)
              {
                MtsSendError(2,PgmId,epsFDBnames[i]);
                return;
              }
            FzyInitFDB(epsFDBptr[i]);
            strcpy(epsFDBptr[i]->FDBid,  epsFDBnames[i]);
            epsFDBptr[i]->FDBdomain[0]=  0;
            epsFDBptr[i]->FDBdomain[1]= 10;
          }
        FzySCurve  (epsFDBptr[0],  0,  .5,   1,DECLINE,&status); //UNACCEPTABLE
        FzyPiCurve (epsFDBptr[1],  1,  1          ,&status); //POOR
        FzyPiCurve (epsFDBptr[2],  3,  2          ,&status); //ACCEPTABLE
        FzyPiCurve (epsFDBptr[3],  5,  2          ,&status); //GOOD
        FzySCurve  (epsFDBptr[4],  5, 7.5,  10,GROWTH ,&status); //EXCELLENT
        FzyPlotTermSet("RETURNED.EPS",epsFDBptr,epsFDBcnt,SYSMODFILE,&status);
        FzyStoreFuzzyData(epsFDBptr,epsFDBcnt,"b:sql2eps.dat", 8,&status);
//
//
        if((DBlog=fopen(DBAuditFile,"w"))==NULL)
          {
            status=1;
            printf("Sorry. '%s' file was not created\n",DBAuditFile);
            return;
          }
        FzyInsertHedges(HDBvector,&HDBcnt,&status);
//
//=========================================================================
//--REQUEST THE ROW QUALIFIERS. We now prompt for the fuzzy set space
//--associated with each the column domains. These would for the
//--fuzzy WHERE statement in the SQL request.
//=========================================================================
//
        Wcnt=0;
        for(i=0;i<8;i++)
          memset(strBuff[i],'\0',32);
        TryCtl[0]=10;
        TryCtl[1]= 0;

        Domain[0]=0;
        Domain[1]=1;
        printf("\nFuzzySQL Database Processor\n");
        printf("--------------------------\n");
        AlfaCut=MtsAskforDBL(
          "AlfaCut",
          "AlphaCut Threshold    : ",Domain,TryCtl,&status);

        TryCtl[1]= 0;
        AggOperator=MINIMUM;
        AggType=MtsAskforVAL(
          "AND.Type",
          "AND operator Type     : ",
          ANDnames,ANDcnt,minlen,&idx,TryCtl,&status);
        AggOperator=idx;
//
        printf("%s\n%s\n%s\n",
          "select companies",
          "  from MfgDBMS",
          "  where: ");

        TryCtl[1]= 0;
        Age_FDBptr=NULL;
```

```
AgeLV=MtsAskforSTR(
 "COMPANY.AGE",
 "Company Age is        : ",
  maxlen,TryCtl,&status);
Age_FDBptr=FormLinguisticVariable(
  "COMPANY.AGE",AgeLV,ageFDBptr,ageFDBcnt,"b:sql2hage.dat",&status);
if(Age_FDBptr!=NULL)
   sprintf(strBuff[Wcnt++],"%s%s","Company.Age is ",AgeLV);

TryCtl[1]= 0;
Rev_FDBptr=NULL;
RevLV=MtsAskforSTR(
 "ANNUAL.REVENUES",
 "Annnual Revenues are : ",
  maxlen,TryCtl,&status);
Rev_FDBptr=FormLinguisticVariable(
  "ANNUAL.REVENUES",RevLV,revFDBptr,revFDBcnt,"b:sql2hrev.dat",&status);
if(Rev_FDBptr!=NULL)
   sprintf(strBuff[Wcnt++],"%s%s","Annual.Revenues are ",RevLV);

TryCtl[1]= 0;
Pno_FDBptr=NULL;
PnoLV=MtsAskforSTR(
 "PRODUCT.COUNT",
 "Product Count is     : ",
  maxlen,TryCtl,&status);
Pno_FDBptr=FormLinguisticVariable(
  "PRODUCT.COUNT",PnoLV,pnoFDBptr,pnoFDBcnt,"b:sql2hpno.dat",&status);
if(Pno_FDBptr!=NULL)
   sprintf(strBuff[Wcnt++],"%s%s","Product.Count is ",PnoLV);

TryCtl[1]= 0;
Eno_FDBptr=NULL;
EnoLV=MtsAskforSTR(
 "EMPLOYEE.COUNT",
 "Employee Count is    : ",
  maxlen,TryCtl,&status);
Eno_FDBptr=FormLinguisticVariable(
  "EMPLOYEE.COUNT",EnoLV,enoFDBptr,enoFDBcnt,"b:sql2heno.dat",&status);
if(Eno_FDBptr!=NULL)
   sprintf(strBuff[Wcnt++],"%s%s","Employee.Count is ",EnoLV);

TryCtl[1]= 0;
Pnl_FDBptr=NULL;
PnlLV=MtsAskforSTR(
 "PROFIT.LOSS",
 "Profit or Loss is    : ",
  maxlen,TryCtl,&status);
Pnl_FDBptr=FormLinguisticVariable(
  "PROFIT.LOSS",PnlLV,pnlFDBptr,pnlFDBcnt,"b:sql2hpnl.dat",&status);
if(Eno_FDBptr!=NULL)
   sprintf(strBuff[Wcnt++],"%s%s","Profit.Loss is ",PnlLV);

TryCtl[1]= 0;
Eps_FDBptr=NULL;
EpsLV=MtsAskforSTR(
 "RETURNED.EPS",
 "Returned EPS is      : ",
  maxlen,TryCtl,&status);
Eps_FDBptr=FormLinguisticVariable(
  "RETURNED.EPS",EpsLV,epsFDBptr,epsFDBcnt,"b:sql2heps.dat",&status);
if(Eps_FDBptr!=NULL)
   sprintf(strBuff[Wcnt++],"%s%s","Returned.EPS is ",EpsLV);
```

```
//
//==================================================================
//--PROCESS THE RELATIONAL DATABASE. Having found the fuzzy sets for
//--each of the columns, we now read each record form the database and
//--determine its degree of compatibility with the request.
//==================================================================
//
  for(i=0;i<fzyDBsize;i++)
     {
     SQLrecIDX[i]=-1;
     SQLrecDOM[i]= 0;
     SQLrecAVG[i]= 0;
     for(j=0;j<DataCols;j++)  MemValues[i][j]=0;
     }
//
//
  SelCnt=0;
  AlfaRejected=0;
  for(i=0;i<fzyDBsize;i++)
     {
     fzyRECptr=&DBdata[i];
     fprintf(DBlog,"\n%4d%s%s\n",i+1,". ",fzyRECptr->Company);
     //
     //----------------------------------------------------------------
     //--Now find the degree of membership in each of the specified
     //--fuzzy sets. These are stored in a working array for later use.
     //--We also calculate the age of the company from today's date.
     //----------------------------------------------------------------
     //
     CompAge=1995-(fzyRECptr->Founded);
     AgeMem=Membershipof(
         "COMPANY.AGE",CompAge,AlfaCut,Age_FDBptr);
     MemValues[i][0]=AgeMem;

     RevMem=Membershipof(
         "ANNUAL.REVENUES",(double)fzyRECptr->Revenues,AlfaCut,Rev_FDBptr);
     MemValues[i][1]=RevMem;

     PnoMem=Membershipof(
         "PRODUCT.COUNT",(double)fzyRECptr->NumProducts,AlfaCut,Pno_FDBptr);
     MemValues[i][2]=PnoMem;

     EnoMem=Membershipof(
         "EMPLOYEE.COUNT",(double)fzyRECptr->NumEmps,AlfaCut,Eno_FDBptr);
     MemValues[i][3]=EnoMem;

     PnlMem=Membershipof(
         "PROFIT.LOSS",(double)fzyRECptr->ProfitLoss,AlfaCut,Pnl_FDBptr);
     MemValues[i][4]=PnlMem;

     EpsMem=Membershipof(
         "RETURNED.EPS",(double)fzyRECptr->EarnPerShare,AlfaCut,Eps_FDBptr);
     MemValues[i][5]=EpsMem;
     //
     //----------------------------------------------------------------
     //--Now find the minimum of the truth memberships (this is the
     //--fuzzy AND operator applied to all the qualifiers). Note that
     //--statements that were not included in the expression, have a
     //--membership value of minus one (-1).
     //----------------------------------------------------------------
     //
     TotGrade=0;
     CompIDX=99999;
     NumSets=0;
```

```
        for(j=0;j<DataCols;j++)
           if(MemValues[i][j]!=NOTFOUND)
             {
              if(MemValues[i][j]<CompIDX) CompIDX=MemValues[i][j];
              TotGrade+=MemValues[i][j];
              NumSets++;
             }
        AvgGrade=(TotGrade/NumSets);
        //
        //---------------------------------------------------------------
        //--OK, if the composite truth membership is greater than the
        //--indicated alpha cut threshold for this query, then we select
        //--this record from the database. In our small model, this means
        //--saving the row index and the truth membership.
        //---------------------------------------------------------------
        //
        fprintf(DBlog,"%s%5.3f%s%5.3f\n",
           "       CompIDX: ",CompIDX,", AvgGrade: ",AvgGrade);

        if(AggOperator==MINIMUM)  CIX=CompIDX;
           else                   CIX=AvgGrade;
        if(CIX>=AlfaCut)
          {
           SQLrecIDX[SelCnt]= i;
           SQLrecDOM[SelCnt]= CompIDX;
           SQLrecAVG[SelCnt]= AvgGrade;
           SelCnt++;
          }
         else
          if(CIX>0)
            {
             fprintf(DBlog,"%s%5.3f%s%5.3f\n",
                "       Alpha Cut Rejection: ",CIX," < ",AlfaCut);
             AlfaRejected++;
            }
      }
   //
   //=========================================================================
   //--SHOW QUERY RESULTS. We now form and dispaly the actual fzySQL
   //--query, rank the selected records by the composite truth value
   //--(in descending order so highest truth appears first); and then
   //--we print a report showing the companies selected.
   //=========================================================================
   //
     fprintf(DBlog,"\n\n%s\n%s\n%s\n%s%s",
       "------------------------------------------------------------",
       "select companies",
       " from MfgDBMS",
       " where ",
       strBuff[0]);
     for(i=1;i<Wcnt;i++)
       fprintf(DBlog,"\n%s%s","       AND ",strBuff[i]);
     fprintf(DBlog,"%s\n",";");
     //
     //
     printf("Ranking %4d Rows.\n",SelCnt);
     SQLranking(SQLrecIDX,SQLrecDOM,SQLrecAVG,AggOperator,SelCnt,&status);
     printf("\nRanking Complete.\n");
```

```
    //
    //
    fprintf(DBlog,"\n\n\n%s\n%s\n",
     "Company          CompIDX     AvgIDX    ",
     "----------------  ----------  ----------");
    for(i=0;i<SelCnt;i++)
      {
        recIDX=SQLrecIDX[i];
        CompIDX=SQLrecDOM[i];
        AvgGrade=SQLrecAVG[i];
        fzyRECptr=&DBdata[recIDX];
        fprintf(DBlog,"%-16.16s  %10.3f  %10.3f\n",
                   fzyRECptr->Company,CompIDX,AvgGrade);
      }
    dblSelCnt=(double)SelCnt;
    dblDBsize=(double)fzyDBsize;
    fprintf(DBlog,"\n%s%10d\n%s%10d\n%s%10.2f\n",
     "Record Selected          : ",SelCnt,
     "Rejected due to AlphaCut  : ",AlfaRejected,
     "Percent (%) Found         : ",(dblSelCnt/dblDBsize)*100);
    return;
  }
//
//=========================================================================
//-----------------FUZZY DATABASE SUPPORT SERVICES--------------------
//=========================================================================
//
FDB* FindFuzzySet(char *LVid,FDB *FDBptr[],int FDBcnt,int *statusPtr)
/*-------------------------------------------------------------------*
| Given the name of a fuzzy set in the variable's Term Set, this     |
| function returns a pointer to the corresponding FDB structure.     |
*-------------------------------------------------------------------*/
  {
   FDB  *thisFDBptr;

   *statusPtr=0;
   if(!LVid) return(NULL);
   for(int i=0;i<FDBcnt;i++)
     {
       thisFDBptr=FDBptr[i];
       if(strcmp(LVid,thisFDBptr->FDBid)==0) return(thisFDBptr);
     }
   *statusPtr=1;
   return(NULL);
  }
//
//
float Membershipof(char *Colid,double DBColvalue,float AlfaCut,FDB *FDBptr)
/*-------------------------------------------------------------------*
| Given a column data value and a pointer into an FDB, this routine  |
| returns the value's grade of membership. If the grade is below     |
| the Alpha Cut threshold we return a zero. If the fuzzy set is NULL |
| we indicate NOTFOUND. A message is also written to the audit log.  |
*-------------------------------------------------------------------*/
  {
   int    idx,status;
   float  memgrade;

   if(FDBptr==NULL) return(-1);
   memgrade=FzyGetMembership(FDBptr,DBColvalue,&idx,&status);
//if(memgrade<AlfaCut) memgrade=0;
   fprintf(DBlog,"%s%-16.16s%s%s%s%7.2f%s%5.3f%s\n",
     "     ",Colid,"   in '",FDBptr->FDBid,"' (",DBColvalue,",",memgrade,")");
   return(memgrade);
  }
```

```
//
//
void  SQLranking(
 int SQLrecIDX[],float SQLrecDOM[],float SQLrecAVG[],
               int AggOperator,int SelCnt,int  *status)
/*-----------------------------------------------------------------*
 | Perform a descending buddle sort on the record sector arrays. In |
 | this simple model we use a very low performance sorting algorithm |
 | for simplicity. In actual systems a version of quicksort coupled  |
 | with an external sort/merge would be employed.                    |
 *-----------------------------------------------------------------*/
  {
   int    i,j;
   int    tempIDX;
   float  tempDOM,tempAVG;
   float  recCIX;
   bool   sortedFlag;

   if(SelCnt<2) return;

   for(j=0;j<SelCnt;j++)
     {
      sortedFlag=TRUE;
      printf(".");
      for(i=0;i<(SelCnt-1);i++)
        {
         if(SQLrankingFault(AggOperator,i,SQLrecDOM,SQLrecAVG))
           {
            printf("+");
            //----------------------------------------------------
            //--The i-th grade of membership is less than the i+1
            //--membership. We now save the current values and do a
            //--simple swap of the values.
            //----------------------------------------------------
            //
            tempIDX=SQLrecIDX[i];
            tempDOM=SQLrecDOM[i];
            tempAVG=SQLrecAVG[i];

            SQLrecIDX[i]=SQLrecIDX[i+1];
            SQLrecDOM[i]=SQLrecDOM[i+1];
            SQLrecAVG[i]=SQLrecAVG[i+1];

            SQLrecIDX[i+1]=tempIDX;
            SQLrecDOM[i+1]=tempDOM;
            SQLrecAVG[i+1]=tempAVG;
            sortedFlag=FALSE;
           }
        }
      printf("\n");
      if(sortedFlag==TRUE) return;
     }
   return;
  }
//
//
bool SQLrankingFault(int AggOperator,int i,float SQLrecDOM[],float SQLrecAVG[])
/*-----------------------------------------------------------------*
 | This routine uses the current aggregation operator type to check |
 | whether or not the ordering of membership grades for the array   |
 | that holds the specific values is out of order. If a fault is    |
 | found we return TRUE, otherwise we indicate FALSE.               |
 *-----------------------------------------------------------------*/
```

```
   {
    if(AggOperator==MINIMUM)
      {
       if(SQLrecDOM[i]<SQLrecDOM[i+1]) return(TRUE);
       return(FALSE);
      }
    if(AggOperator==AVERAGE)
      {
       if(SQLrecAVG[i]<SQLrecAVG[i+1]) return(TRUE);
       return(FALSE);
      }
    return(FALSE);
   }
//
FDB *FormLinguisticVariable(
    char    *varID,         // The variable Name
    char    *LVstring,      // The linguistic variable string
    FDB     **FDBterms,     // The term set for the variable
    int      FDBcnt,        // The number of fuzzy sets
    char    *HdgFSname,     // The Hedged Fuzzy Set file name
    int     *status)        // The status code
/*-----------------------------------------------------------------*
| A linguistic variable is a complex fuzzy expression that resolves |
| to a new fuzzy set with the general syntax of:                    |
|                                                                   |
|         <hedge1> <hedge2> ... <hedgeN> <fuzzyset>                 |
|                                                                   |
| such as POSITIVELY VERY TALL. The hedges are evaluated from the   |
| inside out to produce a new linguistic space that approximates    |
| an English adjective/adverb phrase.                               |
*-----------------------------------------------------------------*/
   {
    FDB     *inFDBptr,
            *outFDBptr,
            *FDBarray[2];
    HDB     *HDBptr;
    char    *tokens[21];
    char    wrkBuff[80];
    int     i,idx,tokcnt,maxtokens=21;

    *status=0;
    if(!LVstring) return(NULL);
    //
    //----------------------------------------------------------
    //--We now entoken the linguistic variable into its components.
    //--If we have more than one token, it means that the user entered
    //--a hedged fuzzy set.
    //----------------------------------------------------------
    //
    MtsEntoken(LVstring,tokens,maxtokens,&tokcnt,status);
    while(1)
      {
       inFDBptr=FindFuzzySet(tokens[tokcnt-1],FDBterms,FDBcnt,status);
       if(*status==0) break;
       if(inFDBptr==NULL)
         {
          ShowTermNames(varID,FDBterms,FDBcnt,status);
          fflush(stdin);
          printf("Enter Fuzzy Set Name : ");
```

```
                 gets(wrkBuff);
                 if(strcmp(wrkBuff,"//")==0) return(NULL);
                 tokens[tokcnt-1]=&wrkBuff[0];
              }
        }
    if(tokcnt>1)
       for(i=tokcnt-2;i>=0;i--)
          {
          //
          //------------------------------------------------------------
          //--Find the hedge in the installed system hedges.
          //------------------------------------------------------------
          //
          printf("----Applying the hedge '%s'\n",tokens[i]);
          HDBptr=FzyGetHedge(tokens[i],HDBvector,HDBcnt,&idx,status);
          if(*status!=0)
             {
             printf("----FzySQL ERROR: Item '%s' is not a hedge.\n",tokens[i]);
             return(NULL);
             }
          //
          //------------------------------------------------------------
          //--Allocate memory for a new output fuzzy set (the fuzzy set
          //--produced by the hedge.) We initialize this FDB and copy
          //--over the current fuzzy set.
          //------------------------------------------------------------
          //
          if((outFDBptr=new FDB)==NULL)
             {
             *status=1;
             MtsSendError(2,PgmId,HDBptr->HDBid);
             return(NULL);
             }
          FzyInitFDB(outFDBptr);
          FzyCopySet(inFDBptr,outFDBptr,status);
          //
          //------------------------------------------------------------
          //--Apply the hedge to produce a new, modified fuzzy set. We
          //--then plot the hedged fuzzy set, store the results in a file,
          //--and then swap the current in fuzzy set with the hedged
          //--output fuzzy set.
          //------------------------------------------------------------
          //
          FzyApplyHedge(inFDBptr,HDBptr,outFDBptr,status);
          FDBarray[0]=inFDBptr;
          FDBarray[1]=outFDBptr;
          FzyPlotVar(varID,FDBarray,2,SYSMODFILE,status);
          FzyCaptureFuzzySet(outFDBptr,HdgFSname,8,status);
          delete inFDBptr;
          inFDBptr=outFDBptr;
          }
    return(inFDBptr);
    }
//
//
void ShowTermNames(char *varID,FDB **FDBterms,int FDBcnt,int *status)
/*------------------------------------------------------------------*
| This procedure is used to display the names of the fuzzy sets in  |
| the variable's term set. We need this since the general string    |
| prompting method inbstead of the value promting method is used.   |
*------------------------------------------------------------------*/
```

```
     {
     FDB    *FDBptr;
     int    i;

     *status=0;
     printf("%s%4d%s%s%s\n",
       "There are ",FDBcnt," fuzzy set names for '",varID,"':");
     for(i=0;i<FDBcnt;i++)
       {
         FDBptr=FDBterms[i];
         printf("%4d%s%s\n",i+1,". ",FDBptr->FDBid);
       }
     return;
     }
```

cbrsiml.cpp (The CBR Similarity Function)

```
/*--------------------------------------------------------------*
| (c) 1995 Metus Systems.      Proprietary software product.   |
| Reproduction or unauthorized use is prohibited. Unauthorized|
| use is illegal. Violators will be prosecuted. This software |
| contains proprietary trade and business secrets.            |
*--------------------Procedure Description-------------------*
| cbrsiml.cpp  Earl Cox  01/11/95 CBR Similarity Function     |
| This function is used to compute the similarity coefficient |
| between two fuzzy sets. We return the degree of similarity. |
*--------------Modification Audit/Change Log---------------*
| Rev  Sar              Metus                                 |
| No   Code  Date       Rellvl  Mod  Description             |
| --   -----  --------   ------   ---  ------------------------|
|                                                            |
|                                                            |
*--------------------------------------------------------------*/
#include <stdlib.h>
#include <string.h>
#include <math.h>
#include "FDB.hpp"
#include "mtypes.hpp"
#include "fuzzy.hpp"
#include "mtsptype.hpp"
//
bool CDBcompatibleDomain(FDB*,FDB*);
//
float CBRsimilarity(FDB *xfdbptr,FDB *yfdbptr,float Alfacut)
  {
  int    i;
  float  simvec[VECMAX],maxmem;
  if(!CBRcompatibleDomain(xfdbptr,yfdbptr))
    {
      printf("ERROR: Incompatible Domains!\n");
      return(0);
    }
```

```
//
//-------------------------------------------------------------------
//--Create a similarity vector containing the minimum of the two
//--fuzzy numbers. This is the intersection of the two fuzzy sets.
//-------------------------------------------------------------------
//
for(i=0;i<VECMAX;i++)
  simvec[i]=min(xfdbptr->FDBvector[i],yfdbptr->FDBvector[i]);
//
//-------------------------------------------------------------------
//--Now find the maximum of the minimum membership values. This is
//--the degree of similarity (overlap) between the two fuzzy regions.
//--If this degree is less than the similarity alpha threshold,
//--we set the maximum membership to zero.
//-------------------------------------------------------------------
//
maxmem=0;
for(i=0;i<VECMAX;i++)
   if(simvec[i]>maxmem) maxmem=simvec[i];
 if(maxmem<Alfacut) maxmem=0;
 return(maxmem);
 }
//
//
bool CBRcompatibleDomain(FDB *FDBptr1,FDB *FDBptr2)
 {
  if(FDBptr1->FDBdomain[0]!=FDBptr2->FDBdomain[0]) return(FALSE);
  if(FDBptr1->FDBdomain[1]!=FDBptr2->FDBdomain[1]) return(FALSE);
  return(TRUE);
  }
```

similnum.cpp (Similarity Analysis Program)

```
/*------------------------------------------------------------*
 | (c) 1995 Metus Systems.       Proprietary software product. |
 | Reproduction or unauthorized use is prohibited. Unauthorized|
 | use is illegal. Violators will be prosecuted. This software |
 | contains proprietary trade and business secrets.            |
 *------------------Procedure Description------------------*
 | similnum.cpp Earl Cox  03/11/95 Fuzzy Similarity Function   |
 | This function takes two numbers and turns them into fuzzy   |
 | sets of a specific difussion width. We then request a       |
 | degree of similarity strength.                              |
 *---------------Modification Audit/Change Log---------------*
 | Rev  Sar              Metus                                 |
 | No   Code  Date       Rellvl  Mod  Description              |
 | --   ----- --------   ------  ---  ------------------------ |
 |                                                             |
 *------------------------------------------------------------*/
#include <stdio.h>
#include <string.h>
#include "PDB.hpp"
#include "FDB.hpp"
#include "SFZYctl.hpp"
#include "SSYSctl.hpp"
#include "fuzzy.hpp"
#include "mtypes.hpp"
#include "mtsptype.hpp"
//
bool  CBRcompatibleDomain(FDB*,FDB*);
float CBRsimilarity(FDB*,FDB*,float);
void main(void)
 {
```

```
FDB       *FDBptr[2];
char      strBuff[80];
int       FDBcnt=2;
int       status,
          TryCtl[2];
float     alfacut,
          simil_level;
double    num1,
          num2,
          num1width,
          num2width,
          num1base,
          num2base,
          compLevel,
          Domain[2];
FILE      *mdlout;
SysConnecttoMetus(&status);
XSYSctl.XSYSalfacut=0.1;
alfacut=XSYSctl.XSYSalfacut;
//
  XSYSctl.XSYStrace[3]=TRUE;
  XSYSctl.XSYStrace[2]=TRUE;
//
  mdlout=MtsGetSystemFile(SYSMODFILE);
  TryCtl[0]=5;
  TryCtl[1]=0;
  //
  //----------------------------------------------------------------
  //--Fetch the values and the fuzzy difussion widths for the two
  //--numbers. The width is the percent of the number that forms the
  //--radius of the fuzzy bell-curve.
  //----------------------------------------------------------------
  //
  Domain[0]=0;  Domain[1]=100;
  num1    =MtsAskforDBL("NUM1",
     "Enter Number 1           : ",Domain,TryCtl,&status);
  TryCtl[1]=0;
  Domain[0]=0;  Domain[1]=1;
  num1width=MtsAskforDBL("NUM1width",
     "Enter Width of Number 1   : ",Domain,TryCtl,&status);
  //
  Domain[0]=0;  Domain[1]=100;
  num2    =MtsAskforDBL("NUM2",
     "Enter Number 2           : ",Domain,TryCtl,&status);
  TryCtl[1]=0;
  Domain[0]=0;  Domain[1]=1;
  num2width=MtsAskforDBL("NUM1width",
     "Enter Width of Number 2   : ",Domain,TryCtl,&status);
  //
  //----------------------------------------------------------------
  //--Now create the bell-shaped fuzzy sets with the numbers. These
  //--numbers lie at the center of the fuzzy sets.
  //----------------------------------------------------------------
  //
  num1base=num1*num1width;
  num2base=num2*num2width;
  FDBptr[0]=new FDB;
  FzyInitFDB(FDBptr[0]);
  FDBptr[0]->FDBdomain[0]=  0;
  FDBptr[0]->FDBdomain[1]=100;
  strcpy(FDBptr[0]->FDBid,"NUM1");
  sprintf(strBuff,"%s%8.2f%s%5.2f%s",
     "Number: '",num1,"' at ",num1width*100,"% width spread");
  strcpy(FDBptr[0]->FDBdesc,strBuff);
  FzyPiCurve(FDBptr[0],num1,num1base,&status);
```

```
        //
        FDBptr[1]=new FDB;
        FzyInitFDB(FDBptr[1]);
        FDBptr[1]->FDBdomain[0]=  0;
        FDBptr[1]->FDBdomain[1]=100;
        strcpy(FDBptr[1]->FDBid,"NUM2");
        sprintf(strBuff,"%s%8.2f%s%5.2f%s",
           "Number: '",num2,"' at ",num2width*100,"% width spread");
        strcpy(FDBptr[1]->FDBdesc,strBuff);
        FzyPiCurve(FDBptr[1],num2,num2base,&status);
        FzyPlotTermSet("FUZZY.NUMBERS",FDBptr,FDBcnt,SYSMODFILE,&status);
        //
        Domain[0]=0;  Domain[1]=1;
        compLevel=MtsAskforDBL("SIMILARITY",
           "Enter Similarity Strength   : ",Domain,TryCtl,&status);
        simil_level=CBRsimilarity(FDBptr[0],FDBptr[1],(float)compLevel);
        fprintf(mdlout," Number 1: %10.2f (%6.4f)\n",num1,num1width);
        fprintf(mdlout," Number 2: %10.2f (%6.4f)\n",num2,num2width);
        fprintf(mdlout,
          "SIMILARITY: %10.2f to %10.2f at strength %5.4f is: %5.4f\n",
                     num1,num2,compLevel,simil_level);
        return;
      }
    //
    //
```

Code for Chapter 4: Knowledge Mining and Rule Discovery

xwmctls.hpp (The Wang-Mendel Control Area)

```
//--xwmctls.hpp [EDC Rev 1.0 01/01/95] (c)1995 Metus Systems Group
//--These are the various structures used by the WM rule discovery
//--facilities to process data and produce a fuzzy associative
//--memory (FAM).
#ifndef __xwmctls
#define __xwmctls
#include "mtypes.hpp"
#include "wmvar.hpp"
extern struct
  {
   WMvar *XWMnames[VTSmax];
   int    XWMvarcnt;
  } XWMctl;
//
#endif
```

wmcode.hpp (Prototype declaration for Wang Mendel)

```
#include <stdio.h>
#include "FDB.hpp"
#include "wmvar.hpp"
//
//===========================================================================
//------------------THE WANG-MENDEL RULE DISCOVERY FACILITIES-----------------
//===========================================================================
//
void    WMcreateTermSet(
            FILE*,char*,double[],FDB**,int,char*,int,int*,int*);        //wpartv
WMvar*  WMFindTermSet(char*,int*);                                      //wmfndvr
void    WMgenerateRules(char*,char**,int,float,int*);                   //wmgenrl
void    WMcreateFAM(char*,char**,int,int*);                             //wmcrfam
void    WMstoreTermSet(char*,FDB**,int,int*);                          //wmstofs
//---------------------------------------------------------------------------
```

wmvar.hpp (The Fuzzy Term Set for each Variable)

```
//--wmvar.hpp [EDC Rev 1.0 01/01/95] (c)1995 Metus Systems Group
//--The WMvar structure is used to hold the variables and their
//--term sets during the rule discovery process.
#ifndef __wmvar
#define __wmvar
#include "FDB.hpp"
#include "mtypes.hpp"
struct WMvar
  {
   char    WMvarid[IDENLEN+1];
   FDB    *WMtermset[FDBmax];
   int     WMtermcnt;
```

```
       WMvar *WMvarnext;
     };
   //
   #endif
```

wmdriver.cpp (The Wang-Mendel Main Program Driver)

```
   /*----------------------------------------------------------------*
   | (c) 1995 Metus Systems.      Proprietary software product.    |
   | Reproduction or unauthorized use is prohibited. Unauthorized|
   | use is illegal. Violators will be prosecuted. This software |
   | contains proprietary trade and business secrets.            |
   *-------------------Procedure Description-------------------*
   | wmdriver.cpp Earl Cox  01/12/95 The Wang-Mendel Driver      |
   | This routine drives the basic Wang-Mendel rule discovery    |
   | facility. It is used to take a set of model data points and |
   | output the fuzzy model.                                      |
   *---------------Modification Audit/Change Log---------------*
   | Rev  Sar                 Metus                              |
   | No   Code  Date      Rellvl  Mod  Description               |
   | --   ----- --------  ------  ---  ------------------------  |
   |                                                             |
   |                                                             |
   *----------------------------------------------------------------*/
   #include <stdio.h>
   #include <string.h>
   #include <math.h>
   #include "PDB.hpp"
   #include "FDB.hpp"
   #include "SSYSctl.hpp"
   #include "SFZYctl.hpp"
   #include "fuzzy.hpp"
   #include "mtypes.hpp"
   #include "mtsptype.hpp"
   #include "wmcode.hpp"
   #include "wmvar.hpp"
   //
   //------------------------------------------------------------------
   //
   struct
    {
     WMvar *XWMnames[VTSmax];
     int    XWMvarcnt;
    } XWMctl;
   //
   //------------------------------------------------------------------
   //
   void main()
    {
     FDB     *timFDBptr[21],
             *prcFDBptr[21],
             *salFDBptr[21];
     char     varID[IDENLEN+1];
     char    *DataFile;
     double   varDomain[2];
     float    AlfaCut=.10;
     int      i,N,FDBcnt,status;
     int      TryCtl[2];
     char    *WMAuditFile="b:WMaud01.fil";
     char    *WMRuleFile ="B:WMrules.FIL";
     FILE    *WMlog;
   //
```

```
   char    *varnames[]={"time","price","sales"};
   int      varCnt   =3;
   int      wmFDBmax =21;
   bool     storfs   =TRUE;
//
//
//-----------------------------------------------------------------
//--Make a connection to the Metus Modelling system and establish all
//--the operational and diagnostic controls. We also open the audit
//--log file used to hold information about inprogress processing.
//-----------------------------------------------------------------
//
   SysConnecttoMetus(&status);
   XSYSctl.XSYScurrPDBptr=NULL;
   XSYSctl.XSYSalfacut   =0.1;
//
   XSYSctl.XSYStrace[3]=TRUE;
   XSYSctl.XSYStrace[2]=TRUE;
   for(i=0;i<VTSmax;i++) XWMctl.XWMnames[i]=NULL;
   XWMctl.XWMvarcnt=0;
//
   if((WMlog=fopen(WMAuditFile,"w"))==NULL)
     {
      printf("Sorry. Audit file '%' was not created\n",WMAuditFile);
      return;
     }
//
   TryCtl[0]=10;
   TryCtl[1]=0;
   DataFile=MtsAskforSTR(
     "DataFile","Enter name of Data File: ",80,TryCtl,&status);
//
//-----------------------------------------------------------------
//--Step 1. Decompose the variables into a set of fuzzy sets. Each
//--variable set is broken down into an odd number of sets (N). The
//--fuzzy sets are S-curves at the shoulders and PI curves across
//--the width of the domain.
//-----------------------------------------------------------------
   N=5;
   for(i=0;i<wmFDBmax;i++)
     {
      timFDBptr[i]=NULL;
      prcFDBptr[i]=NULL;
      salFDBptr[i]=NULL;
     }
//
   printf(" 1.0--Partition Variables into Fuzzy Sets.\n");
   N=9;
   strcpy(varID,"time");
   varDomain[0]= 0;
   varDomain[1]=30;
   WMcreateTermSet(
     WMlog,varID,varDomain,timFDBptr,wmFDBmax,"TIM",N,&FDBcnt,&status);
   FzyPlotTermSet(varID,timFDBptr,FDBcnt,SYSMODFILE,&status);
   WMstoreTermSet(varID,timFDBptr,FDBcnt,&status);
   fflush(WMlog);
//
   N=9;
   strcpy(varID,"price");
   varDomain[0]=  8;
   varDomain[1]=200;
   WMcreateTermSet(
```

```
        WMlog,varID,varDomain,prcFDBptr,wmFDBmax,"PRC",N,&FDBcnt,&status);
    FzyPlotTermSet(varID,prcFDBptr,FDBcnt,SYSMODFILE,&status);
    WMstoreTermSet(varID,prcFDBptr,FDBcnt,&status);
    fflush(WMlog);
//
    N=17;
    strcpy(varID,"sales");
    varDomain[0]=    0;
    varDomain[1]=40000;
    WMcreateTermSet(
        WMlog,varID,varDomain,salFDBptr,wmFDBmax,"SAL",N,&FDBcnt,&status);
    FzyPlotTermSet(varID,salFDBptr,FDBcnt,SYSMODFILE,&status);
    WMstoreTermSet(varID,salFDBptr,FDBcnt,&status);
    fclose(WMlog);
//
//-----------------------------------------------------------------
//--Step 2. Generate Intermediate fuzzy rules from the fuzzy sets and
//--the a data file of independent variable values and the dependent
//--(solution) variables. This file contains the triplets with the
//--maximum degree of truth in the corresponding term sets. The file
//--also contains, for each record, the 'degree' as a product of the
//--individual membership as well as the record confidence weight.
//-----------------------------------------------------------------
    varCnt=3;
    printf(" 2.0--Generate Intermediate Rules from Training Data.\n");
    WMgenerateRules(DataFile,varnames,varCnt,AlfaCut,&status);
//
//-----------------------------------------------------------------
//--Step 3. Generate the Combined Fuzzy Associative Memory (FAM).
//--We now read the rule output from Step 2. Using the rule Degree
//--values, we map rules with the same predicate into cells based
//--on the maximum Degree. The end result is a combined FAM with the
//--most powerful rules dominating the rule matrix.
//-----------------------------------------------------------------
    printf(" 3.0--Create Combined FAM and write Production Rules.\n");
    WMcreateFAM(WMRuleFile,varnames,varCnt,&status);
//
    return;
    }
```

wmpartv.cpp (Create the Fuzzy Set Term Set for Variable)

```
/*-------------------------------------------------------------*
| (c) 1995 Metus Systems.      Proprietary software product.  |
| Reproduction or unauthorized use is prohibited. Unauthorized|
| use is illegal. Violators will be prosecuted. This software |
| contains proprietary trade and business secrets.            |
*------------------Procedure Description------------------*
| wmpartv.cpp  Earl Cox  01/03/95 Wang-Mendel Rule Discovery  |
| Package. This file contains the function that decomposes a   |
| variable into a set of underlying fuzzy sets (the Term set).|
*------------Modification Audit/Change Log---------------*
| Rev  Sar          Metus                                      |
| No   Code Date    Rellvl Mod  Description                    |
| --   ----- ------- ------ ---  ------------------------------|
|                                                             |
*-------------------------------------------------------------*/
#include <stdlib.h>
#include <string.h>
#include <math.h>
```

```
#include "FDB.hpp"
#include "mtypes.hpp"
#include "fuzzy.hpp"
#include "mtsptype.hpp"
#include "wmcode.hpp"
//
static  char    Setid[IDENLEN+1];
static  char    strBuff[280];
static  double  Width;
static  double  Parms[4];
//
//------------------------------------------------------------------
FDB* InsertSCurve(int,int,char*,char*,double[2],double[2],int*);
FDB* InsertPICurve(int,char*,char*,double[2],double[2],int*);
void FuzzyInitialize(int,char*,char*,char*);
void InitializeParms(void);
//------------------------------------------------------------------
//
void WMcreateTermSet(
   FILE    *WMlog,            // Current audit file
   char    *varID,            // Name of the variable
   double  varDomain[2],      // Domain of the variable
   FDB     **FDBptr,          // Pointer to array of FDB pointers
   int     wmFDBmax,          // Maximum of FDB objects in array
   char    *SetPrefix,        // Prefix for the fuzzy set names
   int     N,                 // Initial Partition estimate
   int     *FDBcnt,           // Count of actual fuzzy sets created
   int     *statusPtr)        // Status condition code
 {
   FDB    *currFDBptr;
   char   *PgmId="wmpack";
   int    i,
          status,
          MidPtSet,
          Partitions;
   int    FZmax,FZnum;
   double Lo,
          Hi,
          DomRange,
          MidPoint,
          PartWidth,
          PartDomain[FDBmax][2],
          SegmentDomain[2];
   *statusPtr=0;
   printf(" 1.1----Generating Term Set for '%s'.\n",varID);
   sprintf(strBuff,"\f\n\n%s\n%s\n%s%s\n%s%10.2f%s%10.2f",
     "------------------------------------------------------------------",
     "RD---[001]: Rule Discovery. Fuzzy Term Set Generation",
     "    Variable  :    ",varID,
     "    Domain    :    ",varDomain[0]," to ",varDomain[1]);
   fprintf(WMlog,"%s\n",strBuff);
   fflush(WMlog);
//
//------------------------------------------------------------------
//--Initialize the control variables by computing the variable's
//--scope (Universe of Discource), the center of the control region,
//--and the initial base line width of each fuzzy set.
//------------------------------------------------------------------
//
   Lo          =varDomain[0];        //Get the low domain value
   Hi          =varDomain[1];        //Get the high domain value
   DomRange    =Hi-Lo;               //Compute domain range
   MidPoint    =Lo+(DomRange/2);     //Computer domain midpoint
```

```
   Partitions   =N;                          //Store number of partitions
   if(fmod((double)N,2)==0)                   //See if partitions are equal
       Partitions =N+1;                       //--if so, make it odd number
   PartWidth   =1.5*(DomRange/Partitions);//Calculate partition width
   Width       =PartWidth/2;                  //Compute half width of partition
   SegmentDomain[0]=MidPoint-Width;           //Compute left side of segment
   SegmentDomain[1]=MidPoint+Width;           //Compute right side of segment
   //
   //
   sprintf(strBuff,"%s\n%s%10.2f\n%s%10.2f\n%s%10d\n%s%10.2f",
      "     INITIAL PARAMETERS",
      "     DomRange   :    ",DomRange,
      "     MidPoint   :    ",MidPoint,
      "     Partitions:     ",Partitions,
      "       PartWidth :    ",PartWidth);
   fprintf(WMlog,"%s\n",strBuff);
   fflush(WMlog);
   if(Partitions>wmFDBmax)
     {
       sprintf(strBuff,"%5d  %5d",Partitions,N);
       MtsSendError(187,PgmId,strBuff);
       return;
     }
//
//------------------------------------------------------------------
//--Now, for each partition create a fuzzy set with a 50% overlap.
//--In this process we differ from WM by using PI (bell-shaped)
//--fuzzy regions instead of triangles.
//------------------------------------------------------------------
//
   *FDBcnt=0;
   MidPtSet=((Partitions/2)+1)-1;
   for(i=0;i<wmFDBmax;i++) FDBptr[i]=NULL;
//
//------------------------------------------------------------------
//--Define the center of the variable space as a fuzzy set. This is
//--The starting point for the term set generation. After inserting
//--the center, the branch out left and right from this fuzzy set.
//------------------------------------------------------------------
//
   InitializeParms();
   Parms[0] =MidPoint;
   Parms[1] =Width;
   sprintf(strBuff,"%s%s",SetPrefix,"_CE");
   strncpy(Setid,strBuff,16);
   FDBptr[MidPtSet]=FzyCreateSet(Setid,PI,varDomain,Parms,2,statusPtr);
   if(*statusPtr!=0) return;
   PartDomain[MidPtSet][0]=SegmentDomain[0];
   PartDomain[MidPtSet][1]=SegmentDomain[1];
   (*FDBcnt)++;
//
//==================================================================
//--CREATE FUZZY TERM SET. We now populate the fuzzy term set for this
//--variable in two steps: we add the fuzzy sets to the left of the
//--midpoint and then add the fuzzy sets to the right of the midpoint.
//==================================================================
//
   FZnum=0;
   FZmax=Partitions-1;
   for(i=MidPtSet+1;i<Partitions;i++)
     {
       InitializeParms();
       SegmentDomain[0]=SegmentDomain[0]+Width;
```

```
            SegmentDomain[1]=SegmentDomain[1]+Width;
            FZnum++;
            if(i==FZmax)
              {
                SegmentDomain[1]=varDomain[1];
                FDBptr[i]=InsertSCurve(
                  GROWTH,FZnum,SetPrefix,"B",varDomain,SegmentDomain,&status);
              }
             else
                FDBptr[i]=InsertPICurve(
                  FZnum,SetPrefix,"B",varDomain,SegmentDomain,&status);
            if(status!=0) return;
            PartDomain[i][0]=SegmentDomain[0];
            PartDomain[i][1]=SegmentDomain[1];
            (*FDBcnt)++;
          }
//
//------------------------------------------------------------------
//--Now reset the domain to the region of the midpoint. We then move
//--backwards from the midpoint inserting fuzzy sets.
//------------------------------------------------------------------
//
    FZnum=0;
    SegmentDomain[0]=MidPoint-Width;
    SegmentDomain[1]=MidPoint+Width;
    for(i=MidPtSet-1;i>=0;i--)
      {
        InitializeParms();
        SegmentDomain[0]=SegmentDomain[0]-Width;
        SegmentDomain[1]=SegmentDomain[1]-Width;
        FZnum++;
        if(i==0)
          {
            SegmentDomain[0]=varDomain[0];
            FDBptr[i]=InsertSCurve(
              DECLINE,FZnum,SetPrefix,"S",varDomain,SegmentDomain,&status);
          }
         else
            FDBptr[i]=InsertPICurve(
              FZnum,SetPrefix,"S",varDomain,SegmentDomain,&status);
        if(status!=0) return;
        PartDomain[i][0]=SegmentDomain[0];
        PartDomain[i][1]=SegmentDomain[1];
        (*FDBcnt)++;
      }
//
//------------------------------------------------------------------
//--We have now completely filled in the term set for this variable. We
//--now open the audit file and write out all the fuzzy set information.
//--This is a trace report showing how all the fuzzy sets are laid out.
//------------------------------------------------------------------
//
    sprintf(strBuff,"\n\n\n%s\n%s\n%s",
      "                          Curve Edges        Curve Surface Parameters    ",
      "    FuzzySet              Left    Right    P1        P2        P3        ",
      "    ----------------      ------  ------   --------  --------  --------");
    fprintf(WMlog,"%s\n",strBuff);
    for(i=0;i<(*FDBcnt);i++)
      {
        currFDBptr=FDBptr[i];
        if(currFDBptr!=NULL)
          {
            sprintf(strBuff,
```

```
                            "%3d. %-16.16s  %10.2f %10.2f %10.2f %10.2f %10.2f",
                            i+1,
                            currFDBptr->FDBid,
                            PartDomain[i][0],
                            PartDomain[i][1],
                            currFDBptr->FDBparms[0],
                            currFDBptr->FDBparms[1],
                            currFDBptr->FDBparms[2]);
                       fprintf(WMlog,"%s\n",strBuff);
                       fflush(WMlog);
                     }
              }
     return;
   }
//
//===============================================================================
//--------------------FUZZY SET PLACEMENT MANAGER--------------------
//===============================================================================
//
FDB* InsertSCurve(
     int      CurveType,
     int      FZnum,
     char     *SetPrefix,
     char     *SetType,
     double   varDomain[2],
     double   SegmentDomain[2],
     int      *statusPtr)
   {
     FDB    *scFDBptr;
     *statusPtr=0;
     FuzzyInitialize(FZnum,strBuff,SetPrefix,SetType);
     Parms[0]=SegmentDomain[0];
     Parms[1]=SegmentDomain[0]+((SegmentDomain[1]-SegmentDomain[0])/2);
     Parms[2]=SegmentDomain[1];
     scFDBptr=FzyCreateSet(Setid,CurveType,varDomain,Parms,3,statusPtr);
     return(scFDBptr);
   }
//
//
FDB* InsertPICurve(
     int      FZnum,
     char     *SetPrefix,
     char     *SetType,
     double   varDomain[2],
     double   SegmentDomain[2],
     int      *statusPtr)
   {
     FDB    *piFDBptr;
     *statusPtr=0;
     FuzzyInitialize(FZnum,strBuff,SetPrefix,SetType);
     Parms[0]=SegmentDomain[0]+((SegmentDomain[1]-SegmentDomain[0])/2);
     Parms[1]=Width;
     piFDBptr=FzyCreateSet(Setid,PI,varDomain,Parms,2,statusPtr);
     return(piFDBptr);
   }
//
//
void FuzzyInitialize(int FZnum,char *strBuff,char *SetPrefix,char *SetType)
   {
     int j;
     InitializeParms();
```

```
      sprintf(strBuff,"%s%s%s%03d",SetPrefix,"_",SetType,FZnum);
      strncpy(Setid,strBuff,16);
      return;
     }
//
//
void InitializeParms(void)
    {
     int i;
     for(i=0;i<4;i++) Parms[i]=0;
    }
```

wmgenrl.cpp (Generate Intermediate Rule Set)

```
/*-------------------------------------------------------------------*
 | (c) 1995 Metus Systems.       Proprietary software product.       |
 | Reproduction or unauthorized use is prohibited. Unauthorized      |
 | use is illegal. Violators will be prosecuted. This software       |
 | contains proprietary trade and business secrets.                  |
 *-------------------Procedure Description--------------------*
 | wmgenrl.cpp  Earl Cox  01/03/95 Wang-Mendel Rule Discovery        |
 | Package. This file contains the function that generates the       |
 | initial rule set by applying the training data values to          |
 | the underlying term sets for each variable. The data is           |
 | organized into n-tuples to describe the behavior of the           |
 | function:                                                         |
 |                                                                   |
 |                  f:(x1,x2,x3) ---> y                              |
 |                                                                   |
 | The file format is x1, x2,... xn, y{; W} in free format and       |
 | comma delimited lines. The independent variables preceed          |
 | the dependent variable. The record can end with a semicolon       |
 | followed by the Degree Weight for the rule. This explicit         |
 | degree is used to measure the goodness of the data.               |
 |                                                                   |
 *---------------Modification Audit/Change Log---------------*
 | Rev  Sar             Metus                                         |
 | No   Code  Date      Rellvl  Mod  Description                      |
 | --   -----  --------  ------  ---  -------------------------       |
 |                                                                   |
 *-------------------------------------------------------------------*/
#include <stdlib.h>
#include <string.h>
#include <math.h>
#include "FDB.hpp"
#include "mtypes.hpp"
#include "fuzzy.hpp"
#include "mtsptype.hpp"
#include "wmcode.hpp"
//
#define MAXTOKS  32
#define RECSIZE  180
static char inrec   [RECSIZE+1],
            outrec  [RECSIZE+1];
static char fpPath  [_MAX_PATH];
static char fpDrive [_MAX_DRIVE];
static char fpDir   [_MAX_DIR];
static char fpFName [_MAX_FNAME];
static char fpExt   [_MAX_EXT];
//
static char *PgmId="wmgenrl";
```

```
//
//---------------------------------------------------------------------
float MaximumMembership(char*,double,char*,float,int*);
float gradeOf(double,FDB*,float);
float DegreeofRule(float[],float,int);
bool  isComment(char*);
//---------------------------------------------------------------------
//
void WMgenerateRules(
  char *WMDataFile,char **Varnames,int Vcnt,float AlfaCut,int *statusPtr)
 {
  int      i,tokcnt,sepPos,numtype,status;
  bool     WgtExists;
  int      RuleCnt;
  int      RecCnt;
  float    RuleWgt,
           RuleDegree;
  float    maxMem    [128];
  char     *tokens   [32];
  double   colValue  [32];
  char     FzyID     [IDENLEN+1];
  char     Fzynames  [32][IDENLEN+1];
  char     strBuff   [180];
  char     rulBuff   [RECSIZE+1];
  char     *WMAuditFile ="b:WMaud02.fil";
  char     *WMRuleFile  ="b:WMrules.fil";
  FILE     *WMdata,*WMlog,*WMrule;
//
  char     *theDate,*theTime,*fmtDate,*fmtTime;
  char     wrkBuff[16];
  int      dhow=5,thow=3;
  long     currDate,currTime;
//
//---------------------------------------------------------------------
//--Get and format the current data and time.
//---------------------------------------------------------------------
//
  theDate=MtsGetDate(wrkBuff,&status);
  theTime=MtsGetTime(&status);
  fmtDate=MtsFormatDate(theDate,dhow,&status);
  fmtTime=MtsFormatTime(theTime,thow,&status);
  currDate=atoi(theDate);
  currTime=atoi(theTime);
//
//---------------------------------------------------------------------
//--The rule generator uses three files: an audit file containing the
//--basic data from the generator (value and membership rank for each
//--variable), a rule file contaning the actual rules produced by the
//--generator in executable format, and finally the data file holding
//--the actual training data from which the rules are induced.
//---------------------------------------------------------------------
//
  *statusPtr=0;
  printf(" 2.1----Learning Rules from Data File: '%s'\n",WMDataFile);
  if((WMlog=fopen(WMAuditFile,"w"))==NULL)
     {
      *statusPtr=1;
      printf("Sorry. Audit file '%s' was not created\n",WMAuditFile);
      return;
     }
  if((WMrule=fopen(WMRuleFile,"w"))==NULL)
     {
      *statusPtr=1;
```

```
          printf("Sorry. Rule file '%s' was not created\n",WMRuleFile);
          return;
          }
     if((WMdata=fopen(WMDataFile,"r"))==NULL)
        {
        *statusPtr=1;
        printf("Sorry. Data file '%s' was not opened\n",WMDataFile);
        return;
        }
    sprintf(strBuff,"%s%s%s\n%s\n%s%s\n%s%s\n%s%s",
     fmtDate," ",fmtTime,
     "RD---[002]: Rule Discovery. Initial Rule Generation",
     "     Data  File :      ",WMDataFile,
     "     Rule  File :      ",WMRuleFile,
     "     Audit File :      ",WMAuditFile);
    fprintf(WMlog,"%s\n",strBuff);
    fflush(WMlog);
//
//------------------------------------------------------------------
//--The rule generator works by creating rules from the data cases. We
//--now open the input file and read each physical record. The record
//--is entokened into its comma delimited fields which are converted to
//--double precision floating point numbers. These are then used to
//--find their membership grades in the associated fuzzy term set.
//------------------------------------------------------------------
//
  RuleCnt=0;
  RecCnt =0;
  while(fgets(inrec,RECSIZE,WMdata))
    {
    //
    //------------------------------------------------------------------
    //--We log this physical record to the audit file so that we can
    //--link all the subsequent trace output to this record.
    //------------------------------------------------------------------
    RecCnt++;
    sprintf(strBuff,"%5d. %s\n",RecCnt,inrec);
    fprintf(WMlog,"%s",strBuff);
    fflush(WMlog);
    //
    RuleWgt  =1.0;
    WgtExists=FALSE;
    if(isComment(inrec)) continue;
    sepPos=MtsStrIndex(inrec,';');
    //
    //------------------------------------------------------------------
    //--We now break the record down into comma delimited tokens. These
    //--correspond to the data element (plus the optional degree weight)
    //------------------------------------------------------------------
    //
    MtsEntoken(inrec,tokens,MAXTOKS,&tokcnt,statusPtr);
    if(*statusPtr!=0) return;
    if(sepPos!=NOTFOUND)
      {
      WgtExists=TRUE;
      tokcnt--;
      }
    if(Vcnt!=tokcnt)
      {
      *statusPtr=9;
      MtsSendError(198,PgmId,inrec);
      return;
```

```
   }
//
//-----------------------------------------------------------------
//--Now, for each token, make sure it is numeric and convert it
//--into a double number. This maximum grade of this number in
//--any of the underlying term sets is returned (along with the
//--name of the term (fuzzy) set.
//-----------------------------------------------------------------
//
sprintf(strBuff,"%s",
 "RD---[003]: Rule Generation Statistics from Data:");
fprintf(WMlog,"%s\n",strBuff);
fflush(WMlog);
for(i=0;i<tokcnt;i++)
   {
   if(!(MtsIsNumeric(tokens[i],&numtype)))
      {
      *statusPtr=3;
      MtsSendError(199,PgmId,tokens[i]);
      return;
      }
   colValue[i]=atof(tokens[i]);
   maxMem[i]=MaximumMembership(Varnames[i],colValue[i],FzyID,AlfaCut,statusPtr);
   if(*statusPtr!=0) return;
   strcpy(Fzynames[i],FzyID);
   sprintf(strBuff,
      "           '%-16.16s' (%10.2f) has max m[%6.4f] in termset '%-16.16s'",
                          Varnames[i],colValue[i],maxMem[i],FzyID);
   fprintf(WMlog,"%s\n",strBuff);
   fflush(WMlog);
   }
if(WgtExists==TRUE) RuleWgt=atof(tokens[tokcnt]);
RuleDegree=DegreeofRule(maxMem,RuleWgt,tokcnt);
sprintf(strBuff,
   "         Unit ConfWeight: %6.4f, RuleDegree: %6.4f",
                          RuleWgt,RuleDegree);
fprintf(WMlog,"%s\n",strBuff);
fflush(WMlog);
//
//-----------------------------------------------------------------
//--We now have the maximum grade of the training data in each of
//--the fuzzy sets corresponding to the independent and dependent
//--variables. This file contains column data with the maximum
//--membership value. Eventually this data wil be processed to
//--produce a combined FAM with executable rules. Note that we
//--only need the RuleDegree, but the membership grades are also
//--written for diagnostic and system validation purposes.
//-----------------------------------------------------------------
//
memset(rulBuff,'\0',RECSIZE);
sprintf(strBuff,"%s, %s, %6.4f, ",Varnames[0],Fzynames[0],maxMem[0]);
strcpy(rulBuff,strBuff);
for(i=1;i<Vcnt;i++)
   {
   sprintf(strBuff,"%s, %s, %6.4f, ",Varnames[i],Fzynames[i],maxMem[i]);
   strcat(rulBuff,strBuff);
   }
sprintf(strBuff," %6.4f",RuleDegree);
strcat(rulBuff,strBuff);
fprintf(WMrule,"%s\n",rulBuff);
fflush(WMrule);
RuleCnt++;
} // end-of-file
```

```
//
//
   printf(" 2.2----Formed %5d Rules.\n",RuleCnt);
   sprintf(strBuff,"%s\n%s%10d",
    "RD---[003]: Rule Discovery. Rule Generation Complete",
    "       Rule Count :      ",RuleCnt);
   fprintf(WMlog,"%s\n",strBuff);
   fflush(WMlog);
//
//-----------------------------------------------------------------
//--Now close all the open files for this phase. This wil flush all the
//--data (and is also necessary due to DOS' restrictions on the number
//--of active files.)
//-----------------------------------------------------------------
//
   fclose(WMrule);
   fclose(WMlog);
   fclose(WMdata);
   return;
  }
//
//=================================================================
//--------RULE GENERATION AND MEMBERSHIP MANAGEMENT FUNCTIONS----------
//=================================================================
//
float MaximumMembership(
    char *varID,double colValue,char *FzyID,float AlfaCut,int *statusPtr)
/*----------------------------------------------------------------*
| Since a single data value (x) can have a grade of membeship in  |
| more than one fuzzy set, we must find the fuzzy set that has the |
| maximum degree of membership. This is the fuzzy set that will be |
| encoded into the rule. We now return the membership as well as   |
| the name of the fuzzy set itself.                                |
*----------------------------------------------------------------*/
  {
   FDB      *FDBptr;
   WMvar    *WMptr;
   int      i;
   float    memrank,memval;
   *statusPtr=0;
//
//-----------------------------------------------------------------
//--Find the variable in the XWMctl data dictionary. Associated with
//--each variable is an array of fuzzy sets stored in the order that
//--they were created by the system.
//-----------------------------------------------------------------
//
   WMptr=WMFindTermSet(varID,statusPtr);
   if(*statusPtr!=0)
     {
      MtsSendError(200,PgmId,varID);
      return(NOTFOUND);
     }
//
//-----------------------------------------------------------------
//--Now find the fuzzy set with the maximum memebrship grade for this
//--variable's current value. We do this by setting the maximum grade
//--equal to the current value's membership in the first term set. We
//--then loop through the others uuntil a higher grade is discovered.
//-----------------------------------------------------------------
//
   memrank=0;
```

```
      FDBptr=WMptr->WMtermset[0];
      strcpy(FzyID,FDBptr->FDBid);
      memrank=gradeOf(colValue,WMptr->WMtermset[0],AlfaCut);
      for(i=1;i<WMptr->WMtermcnt;i++)
        {
        FDBptr=WMptr->WMtermset[i];
        memval=gradeOf(colValue,WMptr->WMtermset[i],AlfaCut);
        if(memval>memrank)
          {
          memrank=memval;
          strcpy(FzyID,FDBptr->FDBid);
          }
        }
     return(memrank);
    }
//
//
float gradeOf(double ColValue,FDB *FDBptr,float Alfacut)
/*-------------------------------------------------------------------*
| Find the grade of membership for <colvalue> in the specified Fuzzy |
| Set. This value is also clipped by a standard alpha threshold cut  |
| to screen memberships that fall below the model tolerance.         |
*-------------------------------------------------------------------*/
   {
    float memval;
    int   vecpos,status;
    memval=FzyGetMembership(FDBptr,ColValue,&vecpos,&status);
    if(memval<Alfacut) memval=0;
    return(memval);
   }
//
//
bool  isComment(char *physline)
/*-------------------------------------------------------------------*
| This function examines the current physical record. If the record |
| is empty, begins with an asterisk or a double slash then it is a   |
| comment and we can skip it.                                        |
*-------------------------------------------------------------------*/
   {
    if(strlen(physline)==0) return(TRUE);
    if(physline[0]=='*')    return(TRUE);
    if(physline[0]=='/'
       && physline[1]=='/') return(TRUE);
    return(FALSE);
   }
//
//
float DegreeofRule(float maxMem[],float ConfDegree,int colCnt)
/*-------------------------------------------------------------------*
| The rule degree is the product of the individual premise and       |
| consequent membership values as well as the user data confidence   |
| ranking. If a user ConfDegree was not supplied, then [1] is always |
| assumed (and, of course, has no affect on the rule degree.)        |
*-------------------------------------------------------------------*/
   {
    float  ruleDegree;
    int    i;
    ruleDegree=maxMem[0];
    for(i=1;i<colCnt;i++) ruleDegree=ruleDegree*maxMem[i];
    ruleDegree=ruleDegree*ConfDegree;
    return(ruleDegree);
   }
```

wmcrfam.cpp (Create the Consolidated FAM structure)

```
/*-------------------------------------------------------------*
| (c) 1995 Metus Systems.      Proprietary software product.  |
| Reproduction or unauthorized use is prohibited. Unauthorized|
| use is illegal. Violators will be prosecuted. This software |
| contains proprietary trade and business secrets.            |
*-------------------Procedure Description-------------------*
| wmcrfam.cpp  Earl Cox  01/03/95 Wang-Mendel Rule Discovery  |
| Package. This file contains the function that assigns a      |
| degree to rules. The degree of a rule is the product of the |
| membership functions. We also allow the user to include a   |
| degree with each record indicating the reative confidence   |
| of the underlying data.                                     |
|                                                             |
| This function reads the output file generated by the base   |
| rule generator to produce a n intermediate FAM (Fuzzy       |
| Associative Memory). From this NxMxKx...Z matrix, we can     |
| produce the final rule set. Note that we use the FAM to     |
| reduce the rules by only storing a rule with the highest     |
| degree. The input to this function is the intermediate rule |
| output from the previous step with the following format:    |
|                                                             |
|   var,fzyset,mem(x),var,fzyset,mem(x),... ,degree           |
|                                                             |
| the triplet (var,fzyset,mem(x)) is repeated for each of the |
| rule's variables. The degree is is the product of each      |
| membership values as well as the user's noise degree.       |
*---------------Modification Audit/Change Log---------------*
| Rev  Sar            Metus                                   |
| No   Code  Date     Rellvl  Mod  Description                |
| --   ----- -------- ------  ---  ------------------------   |
|                                                             |
*-------------------------------------------------------------*/
#include <stdlib.h>
#include <string.h>
#include <math.h>
#include "FDB.hpp"
#include "mtypes.hpp"
#include "fuzzy.hpp"
#include "mtsptype.hpp"
#include "wmcode.hpp"
//
#define MAXTOKS  32
#define MAXFAM   32
#define RECSIZE  255
static char inrec[RECSIZE+1],outrec[RECSIZE+1];
static char fpPath  [_MAX_PATH];
static char fpDrive [_MAX_DRIVE];
static char fpDir    [_MAX_DIR];
static char fpFName [_MAX_FNAME];
static char fpExt    [_MAX_EXT];
//
static char  *nameptr;
static char  *PgmId="wmcrfam";
//
//-----------------------------------------------------------------
void FormFAMAxis(char*,char**,int*,int*);
//-----------------------------------------------------------------
//
void WMcreateFAM(
```

```
       char *RuleFile,char **Varnames,int Vcnt,int *statusPtr)
   {
   int     i,j,tokcnt,status;
   int     NumElements,recIDX;
   int     RuleCnt;
   int     RecCnt;
   int     RuleRejected;
   double  RuleRatio;
   float   memGrade,RuleDegree;
   char    varID    [IDENLEN+1];
   char    fzyID    [IDENLEN+1];
   char    ruleMsg  [16];
   char    *tokens  [32];
   char    strBuff  [256];
//
//-------------2x1 FAM Storage Declarations-------------------------
//
   char    *vertNames [MAXFAM];
   char    *horzNames [MAXFAM];
   char    *famNames  [MAXFAM][MAXFAM];
   float   famDegree  [MAXFAM][MAXFAM];
   int     vertCnt,horzCnt;
   int     vertFamCell,horzFamCell;
//
//-----------------------------------------------------------------
//
   char    *WMAuditFile ="b:WMaud03.fil";
   char    *WMFamFile   ="b:WMfam.fil";
   FILE    *WMlog,*WMinrule,*WMfam;
//
   char    *theDate,*theTime,*fmtDate,*fmtTime;
   char    wrkBuff[16];
   int     dhow=5,thow=3;
   long    currDate,currTime;
//
//--Get and format the current data and time.
//
   theDate=MtsGetDate(wrkBuff,&status);
   theTime=MtsGetTime(&status);
   fmtDate=MtsFormatDate(theDate,dhow,&status);
   fmtTime=MtsFormatTime(theTime,thow,&status);
   currDate=atoi(theDate);
   currTime=atoi(theTime);
//
//-----------------------------------------------------------------
//--The rule generator uses three files: an audit file containing the
//--basic data from the generator (value and membership rank for each
//--variable), a rule file contaning the actual rules produced by the
//--generator in executable format, and finally the data file holding
//--the actual training data from which the rules are induced.
//-----------------------------------------------------------------
//
   *statusPtr=0;
   printf(" 3.1----Generating FAM from Rule File: '%s'.\n",RuleFile);
   if((WMlog=fopen(WMAuditFile,"w"))==NULL)
      {
      *statusPtr=1;
      printf("Sorry. Audit file '%s' was not created\n",WMAuditFile);
      return;
      }
   if((WMfam=fopen(WMFamFile,"w"))==NULL)
      {
      *statusPtr=1;
```

```
      printf("Sorry. FAM file '%s' was not created\n",WMFamFile);
      return;
      }
   sprintf(strBuff,"%s\n%s%s\n%s%s\n%s%s",
    "RD---[003]: Rule Discovery. Combined FAM Generation",
    "     Audit File :    ",WMAuditFile,
    "     Rule  File :    ",RuleFile,
    "     FAM   File :    ",WMFamFile);
   fprintf(WMlog,"%s\n",strBuff);
   fflush(WMlog);
//
//----------------------------------------------------------------
//--Create the initial FAM matrix. Since we have a 2x1 model, we
//--need to construct a two dimensional rectangular FAM.
//----------------------------------------------------------------
//
   for(i=0;i<MAXFAM;i++)
      {
      vertNames [i]=NULL;
      horzNames [i]=NULL;
      for(j=0;j<MAXFAM;j++)
         {
         famNames[i][j] =NULL;
         famDegree[i][j]=0;
         }
      }
   vertCnt=0;
   horzCnt=0;
   strcpy(varID,Varnames[0]);
   FormFAMAxis(varID,vertNames,&vertCnt,statusPtr);
   if(*statusPtr!=0) return;
   strcpy(varID,Varnames[1]);
   FormFAMAxis(varID,horzNames,&horzCnt,statusPtr);
   if(*statusPtr!=0) return;
//
//----------------------------------------------------------------
//--We now read through the production rule file generated in the last
//--step. This file contains the basic rule components in the form of
//--<variable, fuzzy set,membership> triplets. The composite rule degree
//--is also calculated and saved.
//----------------------------------------------------------------
//
   RuleCnt=0;
   RecCnt=0;
   RuleRejected=0;
   NumElements=(Vcnt*3)+1;
   //
   if((WMinrule=fopen(RuleFile,"r"))==NULL)
      {
      *statusPtr=1;
      printf("Sorry. Rule file '%s' was not opened\n",RuleFile);
      return;
      }
   rewind(WMinrule);
   if(fseek(WMinrule,0L,SEEK_SET)!=0)
      {
      printf("Unable to reset Rule file '%s'\n",RuleFile);
      }
   //
   while(fgets(inrec,RECSIZE,WMinrule))
      {
      RecCnt++;
```

```
MtsEntoken(inrec,tokens,MAXTOKS,&tokcnt,statusPtr);
if(*statusPtr!=0) return;
//
if(tokcnt!=NumElements)
  {
   *statusPtr=9;
   MtsSendError(198,PgmId,inrec);
   return;
  }
//
//----------------------------------------------------------------
//--We now find the term set on the vertical and the horizontal
//--axes. This will tell us were to place the solution variable
//--term set name. Using the computed rule degree, we can enforce
//--a sieve that eliminates duplicate rules. [From a software
//--engineering perspective, we could encode this as a nested
//--loop to reduce redundancy].
//----------------------------------------------------------------
recIDX=0;
//
//--Pick up vertical fuzzy set name and find where it
//--lies on the FAM axis.
//
strcpy(varID,tokens[recIDX]);
 recIDX++;
strcpy(fzyID,tokens[recIDX]);
 recIDX++;
memGrade=atof(tokens[recIDX]);
 recIDX++;
vertFamCell=0;
for(i=0;i<vertCnt;i++)
  if(strcmp(fzyID,vertNames[i])==0) vertFamCell=i;
//
//--Pick up horizontal fuzzy set name and find where it
//--lies on the FAM axis.
//
strcpy(varID,tokens[recIDX]);
 recIDX++;
strcpy(fzyID,tokens[recIDX]);
 recIDX++;
memGrade=atof(tokens[recIDX]);
 recIDX++;
horzFamCell=0;
for(i=0;i<horzCnt;i++)
  if(strcmp(fzyID,horzNames[i])==0) horzFamCell=i;
//
//--Now pick up the solution variable fuzzy set. We want to
//--place it at the interesection of the vertical and horizontal
//--FAM axis. We only place this term name when its RuleDegree
//--is larger than the existing RuleDegree (that is, this is
//--a more powerful rule.
//
strcpy(varID,tokens[recIDX]);
 recIDX++;
strcpy(fzyID,tokens[recIDX]);
 recIDX++;
memGrade=atof(tokens[recIDX]);
 recIDX++;
RuleDegree=atof(tokens[recIDX]);
//
if(RuleDegree>famDegree[vertFamCell][horzFamCell])
  {
   j=strlen(fzyID);
```

```
           if((nameptr=new char[j+1])==NULL)
             {
              *statusPtr=1;
              MtsSendError(2,PgmId,fzyID);
              return;
             }
           strcpy(nameptr,fzyID);
           strcpy(ruleMsg,"ADDED:     ");
           if(famDegree[vertFamCell][horzFamCell]>0)
             {
              strcpy(ruleMsg,"UPDATES:  ");
              RuleRejected++;
             }
            else
             RuleCnt++;
           famNames[vertFamCell][horzFamCell] =nameptr;
           famDegree[vertFamCell][horzFamCell]=RuleDegree;
           sprintf(strBuff,"%s%5d. %s%s%sx%s: %s  (%6.4f)",
            "RD---[005]: Record: ",RecCnt,"Rule ",ruleMsg,
              vertNames[vertFamCell],horzNames[horzFamCell],nameptr,
               RuleDegree);
           fprintf(WMlog,"%s\n",strBuff);
           fflush(WMlog);
          }
         else
          {
           sprintf(strBuff,"%s%5d. %s%sx%s: %s  (%6.4f versus %6.4f)",
            "RD---[007]: Record: ",RecCnt,"Rule REJECTED: ",
              vertNames[vertFamCell],horzNames[horzFamCell],nameptr,
               RuleDegree,famDegree[vertFamCell][horzFamCell]);
           fprintf(WMlog,"%s\n",strBuff);
           fflush(WMlog);
           RuleRejected++;
          }
       } //end-of-file
     printf(" 3.2----Combined FAM contains %5d Rules.\n",RuleCnt);
     RuleRatio=((double)RuleCnt/(double)RecCnt)*100;
     sprintf(strBuff,"%s\n%s%10d\n%s%10d\n%s%10d\n%s%10.2f",
      "RD---[003]: Rule Discovery. FAM Generation Complete",
      "       Record Count  :   ",RecCnt,
      "       Rule Used      :   ",RuleCnt,
      "       Rule Rejected :   ",RuleRejected,
      "       Rule Use Ratio:   ",RuleRatio);
     fprintf(WMlog,"%s\n",strBuff);
     fflush(WMlog);
//
//---------------------------------------------------------------
//--OK, the fuzzy associative memory (FAM) has been constructed. We
//--want to generate a set of rules that can be fed into the fuzzy
//--modelling system.
//---------------------------------------------------------------
//
     fprintf(WMlog,"\n%s","             ");
     for(i=0;i<horzCnt;i++) fprintf(WMlog,"%-8.8s ",horzNames[i]);
     fprintf(WMlog,"\n%s","             ");
     for(i=0;i<horzCnt;i++)
        fprintf(WMlog,"%s","-------- ");
     fputc('\n',WMlog);
     for(i=0;i<vertCnt;i++)
       {
        fprintf(WMlog,"%-8.8s|",vertNames[i]);
        for(j=0;j<horzCnt;j++)
```

```
          {
           if(famNames[i][j])
             fprintf(WMlog,"%-8.8s ",famNames[i][j]);
           else
             fprintf(WMlog,"%-8.8s ","             ");
          }
        fputc('\n',WMlog);
       }
    fputc('\n',WMlog);
    fflush(WMlog);
//
    fclose(WMinrule);
//
//----------------------------------------------------------------------
//--Ok, now we have a Combined FAM with only the rules that maximally
//--contribute to the model process. The FAM must be converted into
//--rules that can be loaded and compiled by the fuzzy modelling system.
//----------------------------------------------------------------------
//
    RuleCnt=0;
    for(i=0;i<vertCnt;i++)
      for(j=0;j<horzCnt;j++)
        {
         if(famNames[i][j])
           {
            RuleCnt++;
            sprintf(strBuff,"%s%03d%s%s%s%s%s%s%s%s%s%s%s%s%s%s",
             "[R",RuleCnt,"]: ",
             "if ",Varnames[0]," is ",vertNames[i],  " and ",
                  Varnames[1]," is ",horzNames[j],   " then ",
                  Varnames[2]," is ",famNames[i][j],";");
            fprintf(WMfam,"%s\n",strBuff);
            fflush(WMfam);
           }
        }
    fclose(WMfam);
    fclose(WMlog);
    return;
  }
//
//
void FormFAMAxis(char *varID,char **AxisArray,int *AxisCnt,int *statusPtr)
/*--------------------------------------------------------------------*
| This function exracts the term set for the specified variable and   |
| creates an array of fuzzy set names. These are the names that will  |
| be along the horizontal or vertical axis of the fuzzy memory (FAM)  |
*--------------------------------------------------------------------*/
  {
   FDB     *FDBptr;
   WMvar   *WMptr;
   int     i,j;
   *statusPtr=0;
//
//----------------------------------------------------------------------
//--Locate the variable in the WM rule discovery hash discionary. Each
//--variable node contains the term set in the proper defined order.
//----------------------------------------------------------------------
//
   WMptr=WMFindTermSet(varID,statusPtr);
   if(*statusPtr!=0) return;
//
//----------------------------------------------------------------------
```

```
//--We now move through the variable's term set. For each fuzzy set we
//--allocate a name buffer, move in the fuzzy set identifier, and store
//--the buffer pointer in the axis array.
//----------------------------------------------------------------
//
  for(i=0;i<WMptr->WMtermcnt;i++)
    {
     FDBptr=WMptr->WMtermset[i];
     j=strlen(FDBptr->FDBid);
     if((nameptr=new char[j+1])==NULL)
        {
         *statusPtr=1;
         MtsSendError(2,PgmId,FDBptr->FDBid);
         return;
        }
     strcpy(nameptr,FDBptr->FDBid);
     AxisArray[i]=nameptr;
    }
  *AxisCnt=WMptr->WMtermcnt;
  return;
 }
//
//
```

wmstofs.cpp (Store Fuzzy Sets Generated for each Variable)

```
/*------------------------------------------------------------*
| (c) 1995 Metus Systems.      Proprietary software product. |
| Reproduction or unauthorized use is prohibited. Unauthorized|
| use is illegal. Violators will be prosecuted. This software |
| contains proprietary trade and business secrets.           |
*-------------------Procedure Description-------------------*
| wmstofs.cpp  Earl Cox  01/03/95 Wang-Mendel Rule Discovery |
| Package. This file contains the function that stores all the|
| fuzzy sets for a specified variable.                       |
*--------------Modification Audit/Change Log---------------*
| Rev  Sar            Metus                                   |
| No   Code  Date     Rellvl  Mod  Description               |
| --   -----  --------  ------  ---  ------------------------- |
|                                                            |
|                                                            |
*------------------------------------------------------------*/
#include <stdlib.h>
#include <string.h>
#include <math.h>
#include "FDB.hpp"
#include "XWMctls.hpp"
#include "mtypes.hpp"
#include "fuzzy.hpp"
#include "mtsptype.hpp"
#include "wmcode.hpp"
//
//----------------------------------------------------------------
WMvar* WMLinkVariable(char*,int*);
WMvar* MakeWMvar(char*,int*);
//----------------------------------------------------------------
//
void WMstoreTermSet(
  char    *varID,              // Name of the variable
  FDB     **FDBptr,            // Pointer to array of FDB pointers
```

```
    int       FDBcnt,          // Count of actual fuzzy sets created
    int      *statusPtr)       // Status condition code
  {
   WMvar *WMvarptr;
   char  *PgmId="wmstof";
   int    i;
   WMvarptr=WMLinkVariable(varID,statusPtr);
   if(*statusPtr!=0) return;
   for(i=0;i<FDBcnt;i++) WMvarptr->WMtermset[i]=FDBptr[i];
   WMvarptr->WMtermcnt=FDBcnt;
   return;
  }
//
//-------------------------------------------------------------------
//--This function returns the address of a WMvar block for the named
//--variable. If one does not exist, it is created and inserted.
//-------------------------------------------------------------------
//
WMvar* WMLinkVariable(char *varID,int *statusPtr)
  {
   WMvar  *WMvarptr,*thisWMvarptr;
   char   *PgmId="wmstofs";
   long    slot;
   *statusPtr=0;
   slot=MtsHashString(varID,VTSmax);
   if(slot<0||slot>(VTSmax-1))
     {
      *statusPtr=1;
      MtsSendError(97,PgmId,varID);
      return(NULL);
     }
   WMvarptr=XWMctl.XWMnames[slot];
   if(WMvarptr==NULL)
     {
      WMvarptr=MakeWMvar(varID,statusPtr);
      if(*statusPtr!=0) return(NULL);
      XWMctl.XWMnames[slot]=WMvarptr;
      return(WMvarptr);
     }
   while(1)
     {
      if(strcmp(WMvarptr->WMvarid,varID)==0) return(WMvarptr);
      if(WMvarptr->WMvarnext==NULL)
        {
         thisWMvarptr=MakeWMvar(varID,statusPtr);
         WMvarptr->WMvarnext=thisWMvarptr;
         return(thisWMvarptr);
        }
      WMvarptr=WMvarptr->WMvarnext;
     }
   return(NULL);
  }
//
//-------------------------------------------------------------------
//--This routine creates and initializes a new WMvar variable block.
//-------------------------------------------------------------------
//
WMvar* MakeWMvar(char *varID,int *statusPtr)
  {
   WMvar   *WMptr;
   char    *PgmId="wmstofs";
   int      i;
   *statusPtr=0;
```

```
    if((WMptr=new WMvar)==NULL)
      {
       *statusPtr=2;
       MtsSendError(2,PgmId,varID);
       return(NULL);
      }
    memset(WMptr->WMvarid,'\0',IDENLEN+1);
    strcpy(WMptr->WMvarid,varID);
    for(i=0;i<FDBmax;i++) WMptr->WMtermset[i]=NULL;
    WMptr->WMtermcnt=0;
    WMptr->WMvarnext=NULL;
    XWMctl.XWMvarcnt++;
    return(WMptr);
  }
```

wmfndvr.cpp (Find Variable and Fuzzy Set Block)

```
/*-------------------------------------------------------------*
| (c) 1995 Metus Systems.      Proprietary software product. |
| Reproduction or unauthorized use is prohibited. Unauthorized|
| use is illegal. Violators will be prosecuted. This software|
| contains proprietary trade and business secrets.           |
*--------------------Procedure Description-------------------*
| wmfndvr.cpp  Earl Cox  01/03/95 Wang-Mendel Rule Discovery |
| Package. This file contains the function that searches the |
| Wang-Mendel variable space for the indicated variable.     |
*---------------Modification Audit/Change Log---------------*
| Rev  Sar            Metus                                   |
| No   Code  Date     Rellvl  Mod  Description               |
| --   ----- -------- ------- ---  ------------------------- |
|                                                            |
|                                                            |
*-------------------------------------------------------------*/
#include <stdlib.h>
#include <string.h>
#include <math.h>
#include "FDB.hpp"
#include "XWMctls.hpp"
#include "mtypes.hpp"
#include "fuzzy.hpp"
#include "mtsptype.hpp"
#include "wmcode.hpp"
//
//
WMvar* WMFindTermSet(char *varID,int *statusPtr)
  {
    WMvar  *WMvarptr;
    char   *PgmId="wmfndvr";
    long    slot;
   *statusPtr=0;
   slot=MtsHashString(varID,VTSmax);
   if(slot<0||slot>VTSmax)
     {
       *statusPtr=1;
       MtsSendError(97,PgmId,varID);
```

```
        return(NULL);
      }
  *statusPtr=3;
  WMvarptr=XWMctl.XWMnames[slot];
  if(WMvarptr==NULL) return(NULL);
//
//-------------------------------------------------------------
//--Now search through the dictionary to find the variable name
//--entry. When found, return a pointer to the WMvar block.
//-------------------------------------------------------------
//
  *statusPtr=5;
  while(1)
    {
    if(strcmp(WMvarptr->WMvarid,varID)==0)
      {
        *statusPtr=0;
        return(WMvarptr);
      }
    if(WMvarptr->WMvarnext==NULL) return(NULL);
    WMvarptr=WMvarptr->WMvarnext;
    }
  return(NULL);
  }
```

Code for Chapter 5. Fuzzy Multi-Criteria/Expert Decision Making

invest1.cpp (The Peer-Ranked Investment Policy Advisor)

```
/*-----------------------------------------------------------*
| (c) 1995 Metus Systems.      Proprietary software product. |
| Reproduction or unauthorized use is prohibited. Unauthorized|
| use is illegal. Violators will be prosecuted. This software |
| contains proprietary trade and business secrets.           |
*--------------------Procedure Description-------------------*
| invest1.cpp  Earl Cox  01/12/95 Investment Strategy        |
| This program combines the investment strategies of multiple|
| experts. The experts have their own peer ranking. From each |
| expert we receive a recommended strategy in the range from |
| -100 (very conservative) to +100 (very aggressive).        |
*--------------Modification Audit/Change Log----------------*
| Rev  Sar              Metus                                |
| No   Code  Date       Rellvl  Mod  Description             |
| --   -----  --------  ------  ---  -----------------------  |
|                                                            |
*------------------------------------------------------------*/
#include <stdlib.h>
#include <string.h>
#include <math.h>
#include "mtypes.hpp"
#include "mtsptype.hpp"
#define    XPMAX    16
void main(void)
  {
  int      i,status,TryCtl[2];
  long     NumofExps;
  double   rankno,
```

```
                Strategy,
                Domain[2];
    char     *namestr;
    char     *ISAuditfile="b:invest1.fil";
    char     *XPid      [XPMAX];
    double   XPrank     [XPMAX],
             XPstrategy[XPMAX];
    double   Wgtstrategy,
             Wgtweight,
             RecStrategy;
    FILE     *Auditfp;
    status=0;
    printf("%s\n","The Peer-Ranked Investment Policy Advisor");
    printf("%s\n","(c) 1995 The Metus Systems Group          ");
//
    if((Auditfp=fopen(ISAuditfile,"w"))==NULL)
      {
      status=1;
      printf("Sorry. '%s' file was not created\n",ISAuditfile);
      return;
      }
    TryCtl[0]=5;
    TryCtl[1]=0;
    Domain[0]=1; Domain[1]=XPMAX;
    NumofExps=MtsAskforINT(
     "NumofExps",
     "Number of Experts       : ",Domain,TryCtl,&status);
//
//----------------------------------------------------------------------
//--We now ask for the name (identification) for each of the expert
//--as well as its peer ranking among the set of experts in this group
//----------------------------------------------------------------------
//
    printf("Enter Expert Rankings   :\n");
    for(i=0;i<NumofExps;i++)
      {
      TryCtl[1]=0;
      printf("%4d. ",i+1);
      namestr=MtsAskforSTR(
       "ExpertID",
       "Identification of Expert: ",16,TryCtl,&status);
      XPid[i]=namestr;
      TryCtl[1]=0;
      Domain[0]=0; Domain[1]=1;
      rankno=MtsAskforDBL(
       "ExpertRANK",
       "    Ranking of Expert [0,1] : ",Domain,TryCtl,&status);
      XPrank[i]=rankno;
      }
//
//----------------------------------------------------------------------
//--We now loop through the experts and pick up their investment strategy
//--recommendations on a scale of [-100] to [+100]
//----------------------------------------------------------------------
//
    printf("Enter Expert Strategies :\n");
    for(i=0;i<NumofExps;i++)
      {
      printf("%4d. %-16.16s",i+1,XPid[i]);
      TryCtl[1]=0;
      Domain[0]=-100; Domain[1]=100;
      Strategy=MtsAskforDBL(
```

```
        "Strategy",
        "Investment Strategy       : ",Domain,TryCtl,&status);
      XPstrategy[i]=Strategy;
      }
//
//------------------------------------------------------------------
//--Now we calculate the weighted strategy value based on the expert's
//--recommendation adjusted by the expert's peer ranking.
//------------------------------------------------------------------
//
  Wgtstrategy=0;
  Wgtweight=0;
  for(i=0;i<NumofExps;i++)
     {
     Wgtstrategy+=(XPstrategy[i]*XPrank[i]);
     Wgtweight+=(XPrank[i]);
     }
  RecStrategy=Wgtstrategy/Wgtweight;
//
  fprintf(Auditfp,"%s\n%s\n",
   "Expert          Peer Rank        Strategy",
   "---------------  -------------  ------------");
  for(i=0;i<NumofExps;i++)
    fprintf(Auditfp,
      "%-16.16s  %12.2f  %12.0f\n",XPid[i],XPrank[i],XPstrategy[i]);
  fprintf(Auditfp,
   "Strategy Recommendation: %8.2f\n",RecStrategy);
  fclose(Auditfp);
  return;
}
```

invest2.cpp (The Fuzzy Investment Strategy Advisor [version 2])

```
/*---------------------------------------------------------*
| (c) 1995 Metus Systems.      Proprietary software product. |
| Reproduction or unauthorized use is prohibited. Unauthorized|
| use is illegal. Violators will be prosecuted. This software |
| contains proprietary trade and business secrets.          |
*-----------------Procedure Description-------------------*
| invest2.cpp  Earl Cox  01/12/95 Investment Strategy      |
| This is a simple fuzzy investment policy advisor that makes |
| a recommendation based on the prime rate movement. The    |
| ranking weight is added to the predicate truth as the     |
| membership multiplier.                                    |
*--------------Modification Audit/Change Log---------------*
| Rev  Sar              Metus                               |
| No   Code  Date      Rellvl  Mod  Description             |
| --   -----  --------   ------  ---  ------------------------|
|                                                           |
*----------------------------------------------------------*/
#include <stdlib.h>
#include <string.h>
#include <math.h>
#include "FDB.hpp"
#include "FSV.hpp"
#include "VDB.hpp"
#include "SFZYctl.hpp"
#include "SSYSctl.hpp"
#include "fuzzy.hpp"
#include "mtypes.hpp"
```

```
#include "mtsptype.hpp"
#define   XPMAX   16
//
char far * far invRules[]=
  {
   "if PrimeRate is MovingDOWN then InvestmentPolicy is Aggressive;  ",
   "if PrimeRate is MovingUP   then InvestmentPolicy is Conservative;"
  };
char far * far invExperts[]=
  {
   "Peter",
   "Mary"
  };
char far * far invFDBnames[]=
  {
   "CONSERVATIVE",
   "AGGRESSIVE"
  };
char far * far invFDBdesc[]=
  {
   "Conservative Investment Policy",
   "Aggressive Investment Policy"
  };
char far * far chgFDBnames[]=
  {
   "MOVEUP",
   "MOVEDOWN"
  };
char far * far chgFDBdesc[]=
  {
   "Prime Rate PctDiff in Upward Movement",
   "Prime Rate PctDiff in Downward Movement"
  };
//
//
void main(void)
  {
  FDB      *invFDBptr[FDBmax],
           *chgFDBptr[FDBmax],
           *StrategyFDBptr;
  VDB      *VDBptr;
  FSV      *FSVptr;
  char     *namestr;
  char     *PgmId="invest2";
  int       invFDBcnt=2,
            chgFDBcnt=2,
            invRulecnt=2;
  int       i,status,TryCtl[2];
  int       Idxpos,
            Rulecnt,
            NumofExps,
            thisCorrMethod,
            thisDefuzzMethod;
  double    rankno,
            PrimeRateChg,
            Domain[2];
  char     *XPid      [XPMAX];
  double    XPrank    [XPMAX];
  double    RecStrategy,
            PremiseTruth;
  float     CIX,fsetheight;
  FILE     *mdllog;
```

```
    status=0;
    printf("%s\n","The Fuzzy Investment Policy Advisor");
    printf("%s\n","(c) 1995 The Metus Systems Group          ");
    SysConnecttoMetus(&status);
    XSYSctl.XSYSalfacut=0.1;
//
    XSYSctl.XSYStrace[3]=TRUE;
    XSYSctl.XSYStrace[2]=TRUE;
    mdllog=MtsGetSystemFile(SYSMODFILE);
    Domain[0]=-100;
    Domain[1]= 100;
    VDBptr=VarCreateScalar("STRATEGY",REAL,Domain,"0",&status);
    FzyInitFZYctl(&status);
    if(!(FzyAddFZYctl(VDBptr,&StrategyFDBptr,&FSVptr,&status)))
      {
      status=1;
      MtsSendError(12,PgmId,"STRATEGY");
      return;
      }
    strcpy(StrategyFDBptr->FDBdesc,"Combined Investment Strategy");
    thisCorrMethod  =FSVptr->FzySVimplMethod;
    thisDefuzzMethod=FSVptr->FzySVdefuzzMethod;
//
//=====================================================================
//--------------DEFINE INVESTMENT POLICY FUZZY SETS--------------------
//=====================================================================
//
    for(i=0;i<FDBmax;i++)
      {
      invFDBptr[i]=NULL;
      chgFDBptr[i]=NULL;
      }
//
//---------------------------------------------------------------------
//--The degree of change fuzzy set measure the movement of the prime
//--rate as the absolute difference between the rate in two periods.
//---------------------------------------------------------------------
//
    for(i=0;i<chgFDBcnt;i++)
      {
      chgFDBptr[i]=new FDB;
      FzyInitFDB(chgFDBptr[i]);
      strcpy(chgFDBptr[i]->FDBid,  chgFDBnames[i]);
      strcpy(chgFDBptr[i]->FDBdesc,chgFDBdesc[i]);
      chgFDBptr[i]->FDBdomain[0]=-100;
      chgFDBptr[i]->FDBdomain[1]= 100;
      }
    FzySCurve (chgFDBptr[0],-100,  0, 100,GROWTH ,&status); //MoveUp
    FzySCurve (chgFDBptr[1],-100,  0, 100,DECLINE,&status); //MoveDown
    FzyPlotVar("PRIMERATE.CHANGE",chgFDBptr,chgFDBcnt,SYSMODFILE,&status);
//
//---------------------------------------------------------------------
//--The investment strategy fuzzy sets are mapped across the same
//--range of values (-100 to 100) as sigmoid functions.
//---------------------------------------------------------------------
//
    for(i=0;i<invFDBcnt;i++)
      {
      invFDBptr[i]=new FDB;
      FzyInitFDB(invFDBptr[i]);
      strcpy(invFDBptr[i]->FDBid,  invFDBnames[i]);
      strcpy(invFDBptr[i]->FDBdesc,invFDBdesc[i]);
      invFDBptr[i]->FDBdomain[0]=-100;
```

```
      invFDBptr[i]->FDBdomain[1]= 100;
      }
   FzySCurve (invFDBptr[0],-100,  0, 100,DECLINE,&status); //Conservative
   FzySCurve (invFDBptr[1],-100,  0, 100,GROWTH ,&status); //Aggressive
   FzyPlotVar("INVEST.POLICY",invFDBptr,invFDBcnt,SYSMODFILE,&status);
//
//
   TryCtl[0]=5;
   TryCtl[1]=0;
   NumofExps=invRulecnt;
   printf("There are %3d experts in this model.\n",NumofExps);
//
//------------------------------------------------------------------
//--We now ask for the name (identification) for each of the expert
//--as well as its peer ranking among the set of experts in this group.
//------------------------------------------------------------------
//
   printf("Enter Expert Rankings   :\n");
   for(i=0;i<NumofExps;i++)
     {
      TryCtl[1]=0;
      printf("%4d. ",i+1);
      namestr=MtsAskforSTR(
       "ExpertID",
       "Identification of Expert       : ",16,TryCtl,&status);
      XPid[i]=namestr;
      TryCtl[1]=0;
      Domain[0]=-1; Domain[1]=1;
      rankno=MtsAskforDBL(
       "ExpertRANK",
       "     Ranking of Expert [0,1]       : ",Domain,TryCtl,&status);
      XPrank[i]=rankno;
      }
//
//------------------------------------------------------------------
//--We now loop through the experts and pick up their investment strategy
//--recommendations on a scale of [-100] to [+100].
//------------------------------------------------------------------
//
   TryCtl[1]=0;
   Domain[0]=-100; Domain[1]=100;
   PrimeRateChg=MtsAskforDBL(
    "PrimeRateChg",
    "PctDiff Change in Prime Rate  : ",Domain,TryCtl,&status);
//
   fprintf(mdllog,"PctDiff in Prime Rate: %8.2f\n",PrimeRateChg);
//
   fprintf(mdllog,"%s\n%s\n",
    "Expert          Peer Rank    Rule                               ",
    "---------------- ------------ --------------------------------------");
   for(i=0;i<NumofExps;i++)
     fprintf(mdllog,
      "%-16.16s  %12.2f  %-36.36s\n",XPid[i],XPrank[i],invRules[i]);
   Rulecnt=0;
//
//--Rule 1.  if PrimeRate is MovingDOWN
//           then InvestmentPolicy is Aggressive;
//
   fprintf(mdllog,"\n\n%s\n",invRules[Rulecnt]);
   fprintf(mdllog,
    "Expert '%s'. Ranking: %5.2f\n",XPid[Rulecnt],XPrank[Rulecnt]);
   PremiseTruth=FzyGetMembership(chgFDBptr[1],PrimeRateChg,&Idxpos,&status);
```

```
      fprintf(mdllog,"%s%10.2f\n","[Base] PremiseTruth= ",PremiseTruth);
      PremiseTruth=PremiseTruth*(1+XPrank[Rulecnt]);
      if(PremiseTruth>1.0) PremiseTruth=1.0;
      fprintf(mdllog,"%s%10.2f\n","[Rank] PremiseTruth= ",PremiseTruth);
      FzyCondProposition(
        invFDBptr[1],FSVptr,thisCorrMethod,PremiseTruth,&status);
      FzyDrawSet(StrategyFDBptr,SYSMODFILE,&status);
      Rulecnt++;
//
//--Rule 2.  if PrimeRate is MovingUP
//               then InvestmentPolicy is Conservative;
//
      fprintf(mdllog,"%s\n",invRules[Rulecnt]);
      fprintf(mdllog,
        "Expert '%s'. Ranking: %5.2f\n",XPid[Rulecnt],XPrank[Rulecnt]);
      PremiseTruth=FzyGetMembership(chgFDBptr[0],PrimeRateChg,&Idxpos,&status);
      fprintf(mdllog,"%s%10.2f\n","[Base] PremiseTruth= ",PremiseTruth);
      PremiseTruth=PremiseTruth*(1+XPrank[Rulecnt]);
      if(PremiseTruth>1.0) PremiseTruth=1.0;
      fprintf(mdllog,"%s%10.2f\n","[Rank] PremiseTruth= ",PremiseTruth);
      FzyCondProposition(
        invFDBptr[0],FSVptr,thisCorrMethod,PremiseTruth,&status);
      FzyDrawSet(StrategyFDBptr,SYSMODFILE,&status);
//
//--------------------------------------------------------------
//--Now we calculate the weighted strategy value based on the expert's
//--recommendation adjusted by the expert's peer ranking.
//--------------------------------------------------------------
//
      RecStrategy=FzyDefuzzify(StrategyFDBptr,thisDefuzzMethod,&CIX,&status);
      fsetheight=FzyGetHeight(StrategyFDBptr);
      fprintf(mdllog,"%s\n","Model Solution:");
      fprintf(mdllog,"%s%10.2f\n","  Strategy    = ",RecStrategy );
      fprintf(mdllog,"%s%10.2f\n","  CompIdx     = ",CIX          );
      fprintf(mdllog,"%s%10.2f\n","  SurfaceHght = ",fsetheight   );
//
      FzyCloseFZYctl(&status);
      fclose(mdllog);
      return;
    }
```

invest3.cpp (The Fuzzy Investment Strategy Advisor [version 3])

```
/*-------------------------------------------------------------*
| (c) 1995 Metus Systems.      Proprietary software product.  |
| Reproduction or unauthorized use is prohibited. Unauthorized|
| use is illegal. Violators will be prosecuted. This software |
| contains proprietary trade and business secrets.            |
*-------------------Procedure Description--------------------*
| invest2.cpp  Earl Cox  01/12/95  Investment Strategy        |
| This is a simple fuzzy investment policy advisor that makes |
| a recommendation based on the prime rate movement. The      |
| ranking weight is added to the predicate truth as the       |
| membership multiplier.                                      |
*---------------Modification Audit/Change Log---------------*
| Rev  Sar                Metus                               |
| No   Code  Date     Rellvl  Mod  Description                |
| --   ----- -------- ------  ---  ------------------------   |
|                                                             |
|                                                             |
*-------------------------------------------------------------*/
#include <stdlib.h>
#include <string.h>
```

```c
#include <math.h>
#include "FDB.hpp"
#include "FSV.hpp"
#include "VDB.hpp"
#include "SFZYctl.hpp"
#include "SSYSctl.hpp"
#include "fuzzy.hpp"
#include "mtypes.hpp"
#include "mtsptype.hpp"
#define    XPMAX   16
//
char far * far invRules[]=
 {
  "if PrimeRate is MovingDOWN then InvestmentPolicy is Aggressive;  ",
  "if PrimeRate is MovingUP   then InvestmentPolicy is Conservative;"
 };
char far * far invExperts[]=
 {
  "Peter",
  "Mary"
 };
char far * far invFDBnames[]=
  {
   "CONSERVATIVE",
   "AGGRESSIVE"
  };
char far * far invFDBdesc[]=
  {
   "Conservative Investment Policy",
   "Aggressive Investment Policy"
  };
char far * far chgFDBnames[]=
  {
   "MOVEUP",
   "MOVEDOWN"
  };
char far * far chgFDBdesc[]=
  {
   "Prime Rate PctDiff in Upward Movement",
   "Prime Rate PctDiff in Downward Movement"
  };
//
//
void main(void)
  {
   FDB     *invFDBptr[FDBmax],
           *chgFDBptr[FDBmax],
           *FDBarray [FDBmax],
           *StrategyFDBptr,
           *wrkFDBptr;
   VDB     *VDBptr;
   FSV     *FSVptr;
   char    *namestr;
   char    *PgmId="invest2";
   int      invFDBcnt=2,
            chgFDBcnt=2,
            invRulecnt=2;
   int      i,status,TryCtl[2];
   int      Idxpos,
            Rulecnt,
            NumofExps,
            thisCorrMethod,
```

```
             thisDefuzzMethod;
   double    rankno,
             PrimeRateChg,
             Domain[2];
   char      *XPid     [XPMAX];
   double    XPrank    [XPMAX];
   double    RecStrategy,
             PremiseTruth;
   float     CIX,fsetheight;
   FILE      *mdllog;
   status=0;
   printf("%s\n","The Fuzzy Investment Policy Advisor");
   printf("%s\n","(c) 1995 The Metus Systems Group          ");
   SysConnecttoMetus(&status);
   XSYSctl.XSYSalfacut=0.1;
//
   XSYSctl.XSYStrace[3]=TRUE;
   XSYSctl.XSYStrace[2]=TRUE;
   mdllog=MtsGetSystemFile(SYSMODFILE);
   Domain[0]=-100;
   Domain[1]= 100;
   VDBptr=VarCreateScalar("STRATEGY",REAL,Domain,"0",&status);
   FzyInitFZYctl(&status);
   if(!(FzyAddFZYctl(VDBptr,&StrategyFDBptr,&FSVptr,&status)))
      {
      status=1;
      MtsSendError(12,PgmId,"STRATEGY");
      return;
      }
   strcpy(StrategyFDBptr->FDBdesc,"Combined Investment Strategy");
   thisCorrMethod  =FSVptr->FzySVimplMethod;
   thisDefuzzMethod=FSVptr->FzySVdefuzzMethod;
//
//==============================================================================
//---------------DEFINE INVESTMENT POLICY FUZZY SETS--------------------
//==============================================================================
//
   for(i=0;i<FDBmax;i++)
      {
      invFDBptr[i]=NULL;
      chgFDBptr[i]=NULL;
      }
//
//----------------------------------------------------------------------
//--The degree of change fuzzy set measure the movement of the prime
//--rate as the absolute difference between the rate in two periods.
//----------------------------------------------------------------------
//
   for(i=0;i<chgFDBcnt;i++)
      {
      chgFDBptr[i]=new FDB;
      FzyInitFDB(chgFDBptr[i]);
      strcpy(chgFDBptr[i]->FDBid,  chgFDBnames[i]);
      strcpy(chgFDBptr[i]->FDBdesc,chgFDBdesc[i]);
      chgFDBptr[i]->FDBdomain[0]=-100;
      chgFDBptr[i]->FDBdomain[1]= 100;
      }
   FzySCurve (chgFDBptr[0],-100,  0, 100,GROWTH ,&status); //MoveUp
   FzySCurve (chgFDBptr[1],-100,  0, 100,DECLINE,&status); //MoveDown
   FzyPlotVar("PRIMERATE.CHANGE",chgFDBptr,chgFDBcnt,SYSMODFILE,&status);
//
//----------------------------------------------------------------------
//--The investment strategy fuzzy sets are mapped across the same
```

```
//--range of values (-100 to 100) as sigmoid functions.
//-------------------------------------------------------------------
//
  for(i=0;i<invFDBcnt;i++)
    {
     invFDBptr[i]=new FDB;
     FzyInitFDB(invFDBptr[i]);
     strcpy(invFDBptr[i]->FDBid,  invFDBnames[i]);
     strcpy(invFDBptr[i]->FDBdesc,invFDBdesc[i]);
     invFDBptr[i]->FDBdomain[0]=-100;
     invFDBptr[i]->FDBdomain[1]= 100;
    }
   FzySCurve (invFDBptr[0],-100,  0, 100,DECLINE,&status); //Conservative
   FzySCurve (invFDBptr[1],-100,  0, 100,GROWTH ,&status); //Aggressive
   FzyPlotVar("INVEST.POLICY",invFDBptr,invFDBcnt,SYSMODFILE,&status);
//
//
   TryCtl[0]=5;
   TryCtl[1]=0;
   NumofExps=invRulecnt;
   printf("There are %3d experts in this model.\n",NumofExps);
//
//-------------------------------------------------------------------
//--We now ask for the name (identification) for each of the expert
//--as well as its peer ranking among the set of experts in this group.
//-------------------------------------------------------------------
//
   printf("Enter Expert Rankings   :\n");
   for(i=0;i<NumofExps;i++)
     {
      TryCtl[1]=0;
      printf("%4d. ",i+1);
      namestr=MtsAskforSTR(
       "ExpertID",
       "Identification of Expert     : ",16,TryCtl,&status);
      XPid[i]=namestr;
      TryCtl[1]=0;
      Domain[0]=-1; Domain[1]=1;
      rankno=MtsAskforDBL(
       "ExpertRANK",
       "      Ranking of Expert [0,1]     : ",Domain,TryCtl,&status);
      XPrank[i]=rankno;
     }
//
//-------------------------------------------------------------------
//--We now loop through the experts and pick up their investment strategy
//--recommendations on a scale of [-100] to [+100].
//-------------------------------------------------------------------
//
   TryCtl[1]=0;
   Domain[0]=-100; Domain[1]=100;
   PrimeRateChg=MtsAskforDBL(
    "PrimeRateChg",
    "PctDiff Change in Prime Rate  : ",Domain,TryCtl,&status);
   fprintf(mdllog,"PctDiff in Prime Rate: %8.2f\n",PrimeRateChg);
//
   fprintf(mdllog,"%s\n%s\n",
    "Expert            Peer Rank     Rule                                    ",
    "----------------  -----------   ------------------------------------------");
   for(i=0;i<NumofExps;i++)
     fprintf(mdllog,
      "%-16.16s  %12.2f  %-36.36s\n",XPid[i],XPrank[i],invRules[i]);
```

```
        Rulecnt=0;
//
//--Rule 1.  if PrimeRate is MovingDOWN
//               then InvestmentPolicy is Aggressive;
//
   fprintf(mdllog,"\n\n%s\n",invRules[Rulecnt]);
   fprintf(mdllog,
     "Expert '%s'. Ranking: %5.2f\n",XPid[Rulecnt],XPrank[Rulecnt]);
//
//----------------------------------------------------------------------
//--Now we modify the shape of the associated predicate fuzzy set using
//--the expert's ranking. We add this to one [1.0] so that it approaches
//--[2.0], the intensification level of the ordinary VERY hedge.
//----------------------------------------------------------------------
//
   wrkFDBptr=new FDB;
   FzyInitFDB(wrkFDBptr);
   FzyCopySet(chgFDBptr[1],wrkFDBptr,&status);
   sprintf(wrkFDBptr->FDBdesc,"%s%s%s%s",
    "'",XPid[Rulecnt],"'--",chgFDBptr[1]->FDBdesc);
   for(i=0;i<VECMAX;i++)
     wrkFDBptr->FDBvector[i]=pow(wrkFDBptr->FDBvector[i],(1-XPrank[Rulecnt]));
   FDBarray[0]=chgFDBptr[1];
   FDBarray[1]=wrkFDBptr;
   FzyPlotVar("PRIMERATE.CHANGE",FDBarray,2,SYSMODFILE,&status);
//
//----------------------------------------------------------------------
//--OK, execute the actual rule by finding he premise truth and issuing
//--the conditional fuzzy proposition.
//----------------------------------------------------------------------
//
   PremiseTruth=FzyGetMembership(wrkFDBptr,PrimeRateChg,&Idxpos,&status);
   fprintf(mdllog,"%s%10.2f\n","PremiseTruth= ",PremiseTruth);
   FzyCondProposition(
      invFDBptr[1],FSVptr,thisCorrMethod,PremiseTruth,&status);
   FzyDrawSet(StrategyFDBptr,SYSMODFILE,&status);
   Rulecnt++;
//
//--Rule 2.  if PrimeRate is MovingUP
//               then InvestmentPolicy is Conservative;
//
   fprintf(mdllog,"%s\n",invRules[Rulecnt]);
   fprintf(mdllog,
     "Expert '%s'. Ranking: %5.2f\n",XPid[Rulecnt],XPrank[Rulecnt]);
//
//----------------------------------------------------------------------
//--Now we modify the shape of the associated predicate fuzzy set using
//--the expert's ranking. We add this to one [1.0] so that it approaches
//--[2.0], the intensification level of the ordinary VERY hedge.
//----------------------------------------------------------------------
//
   wrkFDBptr=new FDB;
   FzyInitFDB(wrkFDBptr);
   FzyCopySet(chgFDBptr[0],wrkFDBptr,&status);
   sprintf(wrkFDBptr->FDBdesc,"%s%s%s%s",
    "'",XPid[Rulecnt],"'--",chgFDBptr[0]->FDBdesc);
   for(i=0;i<VECMAX;i++)
     wrkFDBptr->FDBvector[i]=pow(wrkFDBptr->FDBvector[i],(1-XPrank[Rulecnt]));
   FDBarray[0]=chgFDBptr[0];
   FDBarray[1]=wrkFDBptr;
   FzyPlotVar("PRIMERATE.CHANGE",FDBarray,2,SYSMODFILE,&status);
//
//----------------------------------------------------------------------
```

```
//--OK, execute the actual rule by finding he premise truth and issuing
//--the conditional fuzzy proposition.
//-----------------------------------------------------------------
//
  PremiseTruth=FzyGetMembership(chgFDBptr[0],PrimeRateChg,&Idxpos,&status);
  fprintf(mdllog,"%s%10.2f\n","PremiseTruth= ",PremiseTruth);
  FzyCondProposition(
     invFDBptr[0],FSVptr,thisCorrMethod,PremiseTruth,&status);
  FzyDrawSet(StrategyFDBptr,SYSMODFILE,&status);
//
//-----------------------------------------------------------------
//--Now we calculate the weighted strategy value based on the expert's
//--recommendation adjusted by the expert's peer ranking.
//-----------------------------------------------------------------
//
  RecStrategy=FzyDefuzzify(StrategyFDBptr,thisDefuzzMethod,&CIX,&status);
  fsetheight=FzyGetHeight(StrategyFDBptr);
  fprintf(mdllog,"%s\n","Model Solution:");
  fprintf(mdllog,"%s%10.2f\n","  Strategy    = ",RecStrategy );
  fprintf(mdllog,"%s%10.2f\n","  CompIdx     = ",CIX          );
  fprintf(mdllog,"%s%10.2f\n","  SurfaceHght = ",fsetheight   );
//
  FzyCloseFZYctl(&status);
  fclose(mdllog);
  return;
}
```

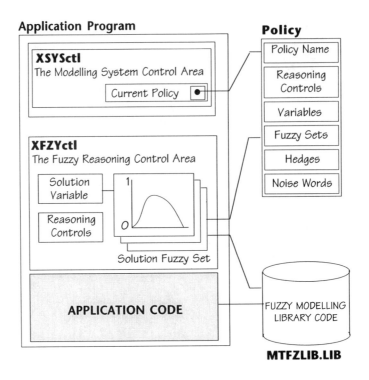

Figure 8.9 The Program Code Layout of The Fuzzy Pricing Model

Price1.cpp (The Fuzzy Pricing Model Main Module)

```
/*--------------------------------------------------------------*
| Copyright (c) 1995 by The Metus Systems Group.               |
*-------------------Procedure Description-------------------*
| price1.cpp    Earl Cox  04/01/93  The Pricing Model         |
| The pricing model is an example of a fuzzy system drawing    |
| on the knowledge and advise of multiple experts to define    |
| the price of a new product.                                  |
*----------------Modification Audit/Change Log---------------*
| Rev  Sar                                                      |
| No   Code  Date      Rellvl  Mod  Description               |
| --   -----  --------  ------   ---  ------------------------  |
|                                                              |
|                                                              |
*--------------------------------------------------------------*/
#include <stdio.h>
#include <string.h>
#include "FDB.hpp"
#include "SFZYctl.hpp"
#include "SSYSctl.hpp"
#include "fuzzy.hpp"
#include "mtypes.hpp"
```

```
#include "mtsptype.hpp"
//
//
static const char *Rules[]=
  {
   "Rule1   our price must be HIGH",
   "Rule2   our price must be LOW",
   "Rule3   our price must be AROUND 2*MFGCOSTS",
   "Rule4   if the competition.price is NOT VERY HIGH",
   "        then our price must be AROUND the COMPETITION.PRICE"
  };
//
//-----------------------------------------------------------------
double Price1Policy   (const char**,double,double,float*,int*);
PDB*   MdlCreatePolicy(char*,int,int*);
//-----------------------------------------------------------------
//
#define FDBvecmax 16
void main(void)
  {
  PDB       *PDBptr;
  FDB       *FDBptr[FDBvecmax];
  VDB       *VDBptr;
  int       i,
            status,
            FDBcnt,
            Hdgcnt,
            TryCtl[2];
  int       Rulemax=5;
  float     priceCIX;
  double    TwoTimesMfgCosts,
            MfgCosts=0,
            CompetitionPrice=0,
            ProductPrice;
  double    Domain[2],
            Parms[4];
  FILE      *mdlout;
//
//-----------------------------------------------------------------
//---Initailize the fuzzy modelling environment. We allocate storage
//--for a policy structure and link it into the model control block.
//-----------------------------------------------------------------
//
  SysConnecttoMetus(&status);
  XSYSctl.XSYSalfacut=0.1;
//
  XSYSctl.XSYStrace[3]=TRUE;
  XSYSctl.XSYStrace[2]=TRUE;
  PDBptr=MdlCreatePolicy("PRICING",MODELADD,&status);
  XSYSctl.XSYScurrPDBptr=PDBptr;
  MdlInsertHedges(PDBptr,&Hdgcnt,&status);
  mdlout=MtsGetSystemFile(SYSMODFILE);
//
//-----------------------------------------------------------------
//--create a variable descriptor block for the output variable (PRICE)
//-----------------------------------------------------------------
//
  Domain[0]= 4;
  Domain[1]=48;
  VDBptr=VarCreateScalar("PRICE",REAL,Domain,"0",&status);
  MdlLinkVDB(VDBptr,PDBptr,&status);
//
```

```
//------------------------------------------------------------------
//--Create the basic fuzzy sets (High and Low for Price) and store them
//--in the policy's fuzzy set dictionary. Also display their shape.
//------------------------------------------------------------------
//
   FDBptr[0]=FzyCreateSet("HIGH",INCREASE,Domain,Parms,0,&status);
   strcpy(FDBptr[0]->FDBdesc,"High for Price");
   MdlLinkFDB(FDBptr[0],PDBptr,&status);
   FDBptr[1]=FzyCreateSet("LOW", DECREASE,Domain,Parms,0,&status);
   strcpy(FDBptr[1]->FDBdesc,"Low for Price");
   MdlLinkFDB(FDBptr[1],PDBptr,&status);
   FDBcnt=2;
   FzyPlotVar("PRICE",FDBptr,FDBcnt,SYSMODFILE,&status);
//
//------------------------------------------------------------------
//--Create an empty fuzzy set as a working area. This area is used as
//--as scratch area for applying hedges and other fuzzy operators.
//------------------------------------------------------------------
//
   FDBptr[0]=FzyCreateSet("NULL",EMPTYSET,Domain,Parms,0,&status);
   MdlLinkFDB(FDBptr[0],PDBptr,&status);
//
//------------------------------------------------------------------
//--We now read in the basic model parameters. These include the
//--current manufacturing costs and the average competition price for
//--the product in the target demographic area.
//------------------------------------------------------------------
//
   TryCtl[0]=8;
   TryCtl[1]=0;
   printf("Enter the Model Parameters:\n");
   Domain[0]=2;Domain[1]=24;
   MfgCosts=MtsAskforDBL(
     "MfgCosts",
     "(MfgCosts) Base Manufacturing Costs : ",
     Domain,TryCtl,&status);
   if(status!=0) return;
   Domain[0]= 4;Domain[1]=48;
   CompetitionPrice=MtsAskforDBL(
     "CompPrice",
     "(CompPrice) Mean Competition's Price: ",
     Domain,TryCtl,&status);
   if(status!=0) return;
//
//------------------------------------------------------------------
//--Create the dynamic fuzzy sets tied into the exogenous variables.
//--These are fuzzy numbers with varying band widths (degrees of
//--noise or certainty in their center of measure)..
//------------------------------------------------------------------
//
   Domain[0]= 8;Domain[1]=48;
   TwoTimesMfgCosts=2*MfgCosts;
   Parms[0]=TwoTimesMfgCosts;
   Parms[1]=TwoTimesMfgCosts*.25;
   FDBptr[0]=FzyCreateSet("Near.2*MfgCosts",PI,Domain,Parms,2,&status);
   strcpy(FDBptr[0]->FDBdesc,"Near (Around) Twice MfgCosts");
   MdlLinkFDB(FDBptr[0],PDBptr,&status);
   FzyDrawSet(FDBptr[0],SYSMODFILE,&status);
   FDBcnt++;
//
//------------------------------------------------------------------
//--Now create the fuzzy number for around CompetitionPrice
//------------------------------------------------------------------
```

```
//
   Parms[0]=CompetitionPrice;
   Parms[1]=CompetitionPrice*.15;
   FDBptr[0]=FzyCreateSet("Near.CompPrice",PI,Domain,Parms,2,&status);
   strcpy(FDBptr[0]->FDBdesc,"Near (Around) Competition Price");
   MdlLinkFDB(FDBptr[0],PDBptr,&status);
   FzyDrawSet(FDBptr[0],SYSMODFILE,&status);
//
//========================================================================
//--------------EXECUTE THE FUZZY PRICING MODEL----------------------
//========================================================================
//
fprintf(mdlout,"%s\n",
   "FUZZY NEW PRODUCT PRICING MODEL. (c) 1995 Metus Systems Group.");
fprintf(mdlout,"%s%10.2f\n",
   "[Mean] Competition Price: ",CompetitionPrice);
fprintf(mdlout,"%s%10.2f\n",
   "Base Manufacturing Costs: ",MfgCosts );
//
   fprintf(mdlout,"%s\n","The Rules:");
   for(i=0;i<Rulemax;i++) fprintf(mdlout,"%s\n",Rules[i]);
   fputc('\n',mdlout);
//
//-----------------------------------------------------------------
//--The actual fuzzy reasoning is performed in a separately compiled
//--procedural policy. This is called as a subroutine to return the
//--estimated product price along with its ocmpatibility index.
//-----------------------------------------------------------------
//
   ProductPrice=Price1Policy(
       Rules,MfgCosts,CompetitionPrice,&priceCIX,&status);
   fprintf(stdout,"\n\n\n%s%8.2f%s%8.3f\n",
    "The Recommended Price is: ",ProductPrice," with CIX: ",priceCIX);
   return;
  }
```

price1pl.cpp (The Fuzzy Pricing Model's Reasoning Policy)

```
/*-------------------------------------------------------------*
| Copyright (c) 1995 by The Metus Systems Group.              |
*-------------------Procedure Description-------------------*
| price1pl.cpp  Earl Cox  02/01/95  The Pricing Policy       |
|                                                            |
| This is the core fuzzy rasoning policy used by the new     |
| product pricing model to develop a recommended price based |
| on the expertise of multiple experts in finance, sales,    |
| marketing, and manufacturing. The policy contains both     |
| conditional and unconditional fuzzy rules. For more details |
| see AI Expert, October 1992, "Problem Solving with Fuzzy   |
| Logic" by Earl Cox.                                        |
*--------------Modification Audit/Change Log---------------*
| Rev  Sar                                                   |
| No   Code  Date     Rellvl Mod  Description                |
| --   ----- --------  ------  ---  ------------------------ |
|                                                            |
|                                                            |
*-------------------------------------------------------------*/
#include <stdio.h>
#include <string.h>
#include "PDB.hpp"        // The Policy descriptor
#include "FDB.hpp"        // The Fuzzy Set descriptor
```

```cpp
#include "HDB.hpp"        // The Hedge descriptor
#include "VDB.hpp"        // A Variable descriptor
#include "XFZYctl.hpp"    // The fuzzy parallel processor work area
#include "XSYSctl.hpp"    // The System control region
#include "mtypes.hpp"     // System constants and symbolics
#include "fuzzy.hpp"      // Fuzzy Logic constants and symbolics
#include "mtsptype.hpp"   // Function prototypes
//
double Price1Policy(const char **Rules,
    double MfgCosts,double CompPrice,float *CIXptr,int *statusPtr)
  {
  PDB     *PDBptr;
  FDB     *High_FDBptr,
          *Low_FDBptr,
          *MfgCost_FDBptr,
          *CompPrice_FDBptr,
          *Price_FDBptr,
          *wkFDBptr,
          *FDBarray[8];
  HDB     *very_HDBptr;
  VDB     *VDBptr;
  FSV     *FSVptr;
  char    *PgmId="pricep11";
  int      FDBcnt,
           status,
           CellIDXpos,
           Rulecnt,
           thisCorrMethod,
           thisDefuzzMethod;
  float    fsetheight;
  double   Price,
           NoPrice=0,
           PremiseTruth;
  FILE    *mdlout;
  *statusPtr=0;
  mdlout=MtsGetSystemFile(SYSMODFILE);
  fprintf(mdlout,"%s\n",
  "(Price1Policy) New Product Pricing Estimation Policy Begins....");
  PDBptr=XSYSctl.XSYScurrPDBptr;
  VDBptr=MdlFindVDB("PRICE",PDBptr,statusPtr);
  FzyInitFZYctl(statusPtr);
  if(!(FzyAddFZYctl(VDBptr,&Price_FDBptr,&FSVptr,statusPtr)))
     {
     *statusPtr=1;
     MtsSendError(12,PgmId,"PRICE");
     return(NoPrice);
     }
  strcpy(Price_FDBptr->FDBdesc,"The Estimated Product Price");
  FzyDrawSet(Price_FDBptr,SYSMODFILE,statusPtr);
  thisCorrMethod  =FSVptr->FzySVimplMethod;
  thisDefuzzMethod=FSVptr->FzySVdefuzzMethod;
  printf("thisCorrMethod  :  %5d\n",thisCorrMethod);
  printf("thisDefuzzMethod:  %5d\n",thisDefuzzMethod);
//
//-----------------------------------------------------------------
//--The main pricing model driver stored the system fuzzy sets in the
//--dictionary associated with the policy. We now have to find them
//--and resolve their dictionary addresses into working pointers.
//-----------------------------------------------------------------
//
  High_FDBptr     =MdlFindFDB("HIGH",            PDBptr,statusPtr);
  Low_FDBptr      =MdlFindFDB("LOW",             PDBptr,statusPtr);
  MfgCost_FDBptr  =MdlFindFDB("Near.2*MfgCosts",PDBptr,statusPtr);
```

```
    CompPrice_FDBptr=MdlFindFDB("Near.CompPrice" ,PDBptr,statusPtr);
    wkFDBptr        =MdlFindFDB("NULL",           PDBptr,statusPtr);
//
//------------------------------------------------------------------
//--Find the hedge very in the poilcy dictionary.
//------------------------------------------------------------------
//
    very_HDBptr=MdlFindHDB("very",PDBptr,statusPtr);
//
//==================================================================
//----------B E G I N   M O D E L   P R O C E S S I N G-------------
//==================================================================
//
    Rulecnt=0;
    fprintf(mdlout,"%s\n","Start Policy Rule Execution....");
//
//------------------------------------------------------------------
//--Rule1. Our Price must be High
//------------------------------------------------------------------
//
    fprintf(mdlout,"%s\n",Rules[Rulecnt]);
    FzyUnCondProposition(High_FDBptr,FSVptr);
    FzyDrawSet(Price_FDBptr,SYSMODFILE,statusPtr);
    Rulecnt++;
//
//------------------------------------------------------------------
//--Rule2. Our Price must be Low
//------------------------------------------------------------------
//
    fprintf(mdlout,"%s\n",Rules[Rulecnt]);
    FzyUnCondProposition(Low_FDBptr,FSVptr);
    FzyDrawSet(Price_FDBptr,SYSMODFILE,statusPtr);
    Rulecnt++;
//
//------------------------------------------------------------------
//--Rule3. Our Price must be around 2*MfgCosts
//------------------------------------------------------------------
//
    FDBcnt=2;
    FDBarray[0]=MfgCost_FDBptr;
    FDBarray[1]=Price_FDBptr;
    FzyPlotVar("",FDBarray,FDBcnt,SYSMODFILE,&status);
    fprintf(mdlout,"%s\n",Rules[Rulecnt]);
    FzyUnCondProposition(MfgCost_FDBptr,FSVptr);
    FzyPlotVar("",FDBarray,FDBcnt,SYSMODFILE,&status);
    FzyDrawSet(Price_FDBptr,SYSMODFILE,statusPtr);
    Rulecnt++;
//
//------------------------------------------------------------------
//--Rule4. If the Competition.price is not very high,
//            then our price should be near the competition.price
//------------------------------------------------------------------
//
    fprintf(mdlout,"%s\n",Rules[Rulecnt]);
    fprintf(mdlout,"%s\n",Rules[Rulecnt+1]);
    FzyInitFDB(wkFDBptr);
//
//--------------Evaluate Predicate of rule--------------------------
//
//--Apply the hedge VERY to the High fuzzy set
//
    FzyApplyHedge(High_FDBptr,very_HDBptr,wkFDBptr,statusPtr);
    FzyDrawSet(wkFDBptr,SYSMODFILE,statusPtr);
//
//--Apply the operator NOT to the hedged fuzzy set
```

```
//
   FzyApplyNOT(ZADEHNOT,0,wkFDBptr,statusPtr);
   FzyDrawSet(wkFDBptr,SYSMODFILE,statusPtr);
//
//--computed membership of competiton price in this fuzzy region
//
   PremiseTruth=FzyGetMembership(wkFDBptr,CompPrice,&CellIDXpos,statusPtr);
   fprintf(mdlout,"%s%10.2f\n","PremiseTruth= ",PremiseTruth);
//
//-------------Perform consequent proposition--------------------
//
   FDBcnt=2;
   FDBarray[0]=CompPrice_FDBptr;
   FDBarray[1]=Price_FDBptr;
   FzyPlotVar("",FDBarray,FDBcnt,SYSMODFILE,&status);
   FzyCondProposition(
      CompPrice_FDBptr,FSVptr,thisCorrMethod,PremiseTruth,statusPtr);
   FzyDrawSet(Price_FDBptr,SYSMODFILE,statusPtr);
//
//----------------------------------------------------------------------
//--Defuzzify to find expected value for price
//----------------------------------------------------------------------
//
   Price=FzyDefuzzify(Price_FDBptr,thisDefuzzMethod,CIXptr,statusPtr);
   fsetheight=FzyGetHeight(Price_FDBptr);
   fprintf(mdlout,"%s\n","Model Solution:");
   fprintf(mdlout,"%s%10.2f\n","  Price        = ",Price       );
   fprintf(mdlout,"%s%10.2f\n","  CIX          = ",*CIXptr );
   fprintf(mdlout,"%s%10.2f\n","  SurfaceHght  = ",fsetheight  );
//
   FzyCloseFZYctl(statusPtr);
   return(Price);
  }
```

price1.mak (The Visual C++ 1.5 Make File for Price1.cpp)

```
# Microsoft Visual C++ generated build script - Do not modify
PROJ = PRICE1
DEBUG = 1
PROGTYPE = 6
CALLER =
ARGS =
DLLS =
D_RCDEFINES = -d_DEBUG
R_RCDEFINES = -dNDEBUG
ORIGIN = MSVC
ORIGIN_VER = 1.00
PROJPATH = C:\METUSMVC\
USEMFC = 0
CC = cl
CPP = cl
CXX = cl
CCREATEPCHFLAG =
CPPCREATEPCHFLAG =
CUSEPCHFLAG =
CPPUSEPCHFLAG =
FIRSTC =
FIRSTCPP = PRICE1.CPP
RC = rc
CFLAGS_D_DEXE = /nologo /Zr /G2 /Zp1 /W3 /Zi /AL /Gt16 /Od /D "_DEBUG" /D "_DOS" /FR
/Fd"PRICE1.PDB"
CFLAGS_R_DEXE = /nologo /Gs /G2 /W3 /AM /Ox /D "NDEBUG" /D "_DOS" /FR
```

```
                     LFLAGS_D_DEXE = /NOLOGO /NOI /STACK:32000 /SEG:512 /ONERROR:NOEXE /CO
                     LFLAGS_R_DEXE = /NOLOGO /NOI /STACK:5120 /ONERROR:NOEXE
                     LIBS_D_DEXE = oldnames llibce
                     LIBS_R_DEXE = oldnames mlibce
                     RCFLAGS = /nologo
                     RESFLAGS = /nologo
                     RUNFLAGS =
                     OBJS_EXT =
                     LIBS_EXT = MTDBLIB.LIB MTFZLIB.LIB MTGLLIB.LIB MTTLLIB.LIB
                     !if "$(DEBUG)" == "1"
                     CFLAGS = $(CFLAGS_D_DEXE)
                     LFLAGS = $(LFLAGS_D_DEXE)
                     LIBS = $(LIBS_D_DEXE)
                     MAPFILE = nul
                     RCDEFINES = $(D_RCDEFINES)
                     !else
                     CFLAGS = $(CFLAGS_R_DEXE)
                     LFLAGS = $(LFLAGS_R_DEXE)
                     LIBS = $(LIBS_R_DEXE)
                     MAPFILE = nul
                     RCDEFINES = $(R_RCDEFINES)
                     !endif
                     !if [if exist MSVC.BND del MSVC.BND]
                     !endif
                     SBRS = PRICE1.SBR \
                                     PRICE1PL.SBR
                     PRICE1_DEP = c:\metusmvc\fdb.hpp \
                             c:\metusmvc\mtypes.hpp \
                             c:\metusmvc\adb.hpp \
                             c:\metusmvc\sfzyctl.hpp \
                             c:\metusmvc\fsv.hpp \
                             c:\metusmvc\vdb.hpp \
                             c:\metusmvc\edb.hpp \
                             c:\metusmvc\llnode.hpp \
                             c:\metusmvc\ssysctl.hpp \
                             c:\metusmvc\bsd.hpp \
                             c:\metusmvc\lru.hpp \
                             c:\metusmvc\tdb.hpp \
                             c:\metusmvc\cdb.hpp \
                             c:\metusmvc\ddb.hpp \
                             c:\metusmvc\rpnnode.hpp \
                             c:\metusmvc\mtdbms.hpp \
                             c:\metusmvc\mdb.hpp \
                             c:\metusmvc\msb.hpp \
                             c:\metusmvc\pdb.hpp \
                             c:\metusmvc\rdb.hpp \
                             c:\metusmvc\rab.hpp \
                             c:\metusmvc\rfs.hpp \
                             c:\metusmvc\hdb.hpp \
                             c:\metusmvc\ndb.hpp \
                             c:\metusmvc\rxb.hpp \
                             c:\metusmvc\udt.hpp \
                             c:\metusmvc\fuzzy.hpp \
                             c:\metusmvc\mtsptype.hpp \
                             c:\metusmvc\cix.hpp \
                             c:\metusmvc\rpd.hpp \
                             c:\metusmvc\ppb.hpp \
                             c:\metusmvc\psv.hpp \
                             c:\metusmvc\sio.hpp \
                             c:\metusmvc\tdd.hpp \
                             c:\metusmvc\mdbdd.hpp \
                             c:\metusmvc\rcsblk.hpp \
                             c:\metusmvc\eqrnode.hpp \
                             c:\metusmvc\toknode.hpp
                     PRICE1PL_DEP = c:\metusmvc\pdb.hpp \
```

```
                             c:\metusmvc\vdb.hpp \
                             c:\metusmvc\rdb.hpp \
                             c:\metusmvc\llnode.hpp \
                             c:\metusmvc\adb.hpp \
                             c:\metusmvc\rpnnode.hpp \
                             c:\metusmvc\rab.hpp \
                             c:\metusmvc\mtypes.hpp \
                             c:\metusmvc\rfs.hpp \
                             c:\metusmvc\fdb.hpp \
                             c:\metusmvc\hdb.hpp \
                             c:\metusmvc\ndb.hpp \
                             c:\metusmvc\edb.hpp \
                             c:\metusmvc\xfzyctl.hpp \
                             c:\metusmvc\fsv.hpp \
                             c:\metusmvc\xsysctl.hpp \
                             c:\metusmvc\bsd.hpp \
                             c:\metusmvc\lru.hpp \
                             c:\metusmvc\tdb.hpp \
                             c:\metusmvc\cdb.hpp \
                             c:\metusmvc\ddb.hpp \
                             c:\metusmvc\mtdbms.hpp \
                             c:\metusmvc\mdb.hpp \
                             c:\metusmvc\msb.hpp \
                             c:\metusmvc\rxb.hpp \
                             c:\metusmvc\udt.hpp \
                             c:\metusmvc\fuzzy.hpp \
                             c:\metusmvc\mtsptype.hpp \
                             c:\metusmvc\cix.hpp \
                             c:\metusmvc\rpd.hpp \
                             c:\metusmvc\ppb.hpp \
                             c:\metusmvc\psv.hpp \
                             c:\metusmvc\sio.hpp \
                             c:\metusmvc\tdd.hpp \
                             c:\metusmvc\mdbdd.hpp \
                             c:\metusmvc\rcsblk.hpp \
                             c:\metusmvc\eqrnode.hpp \
                             c:\metusmvc\toknode.hpp
MTDBLIB_DEP =
MTFZLIB_DEP =
MTGLLIB_DEP =
MTTLLIB_DEP =
all:     $(PROJ).EXE $(PROJ).BSC
PRICE1.OBJ:     PRICE1.CPP $(PRICE1_DEP)
         $(CPP) $(CFLAGS) $(CPPCREATEPCHFLAG) /c PRICE1.CPP
PRICE1PL.OBJ:   PRICE1PL.CPP $(PRICE1PL_DEP)
         $(CPP) $(CFLAGS) $(CPPUSEPCHFLAG) /c PRICE1PL.CPP
$(PROJ).EXE::   PRICE1.OBJ PRICE1PL.OBJ $(OBJS_EXT) $(DEFFILE)
         echo >NUL @<<$(PROJ).CRF
PRICE1.OBJ +
PRICE1PL.OBJ +
$(OBJS_EXT)
$(PROJ).EXE
$(MAPFILE)
c:\msvc\lib\+
c:\msvc\mfc\lib\+
MTDBLIB.LIB+
MTFZLIB.LIB+
MTGLLIB.LIB+
MTTLLIB.LIB+
$(LIBS)
$(DEFFILE);
<<
         link $(LFLAGS) @$(PROJ).CRF
run: $(PROJ).EXE
         $(PROJ) $(RUNFLAGS)
$(PROJ).BSC: $(SBRS)
         bscmake @<<
/o$@ $(SBRS)
<<
```

projrsk1.cpp (The Weighted Average Risk Model)

```
/*---------------------------------------------------------------*
| (c) 1995 Metus Systems.      Proprietary software product.    |
| Reproduction or unauthorized use is prohibited. Unauthorized  |
| use is illegal. Violators will be prosecuted. This software   |
| contains proprietary trade and business secrets.              |
*--------------------Procedure Description--------------------* |
| projrsk1.cpp Earl Cox  11/13/94 A Combined Fuzzy System       |
| In this model we follow two strategies for combining fuzzy    |
| systems: (1) by combining the output using a weighted mean    |
| and (2) by combining the throughput of the system before      |
| defuzzification.                                              |
*---------------------------------------------------------------*
| We employ a simple two-expert fuzzy system where the weight   |
| of each expert is entered at execution time.  Although we     |
| construct a policy architecture for the model, the fuzzy      |
| sets are defined as statics so we can use them directly.      |
*---------------Modification Audit/Change Log---------------*   |
| Rev  Sar                 Metus                                |
| No   Code  Date          Rellvl  Mod  Description             |
| --   ----- --------      ------  ---  -----------------------  |
|                                                               |
*---------------------------------------------------------------*/
#include <stdio.h>
#include <string.h>
#include "PDB.hpp"
#include "FDB.hpp"
#include "SFZYctl.hpp"
#include "SSYSctl.hpp"
#include "fuzzy.hpp"
#include "mtypes.hpp"
#include "mtsptype.hpp"
//
//---------------------------------------------------------------------
//--These are the symbolic constants that tie an FDB array slot to the
//--underlying semantic (fuzzy) concept.
//---------------------------------------------------------------------
//
#define BRIEFduration      0
#define SHORTduration      1
#define MODERATEduration   2
#define EXTENDEDduration   3
#define LONGduration       4
#define MINORbudget        0
#define LOWbudget          1
#define MEDIUMbudget       2
#define HIGHbudget         3
#define MAJORbudget        4
#define SPARSEstafffing    0
#define AUSTEREstaffing    1
#define ROBUSTstaffing     2
#define FULLstaffing       3
#define HEAVYstaffing      4
#define LOWrisk            0
#define MODERATErisk       1
#define ACCEPTABLErisk     2
#define ELEVATEDrisk       3
#define HIGHrisk           4
//
//---------------------------------------------------------------------
//--These are the function prototypes for procedures not declared as
```

```
//--part of the standard modelling system environment.
//-----------------------------------------------------------------------
//
void InitializeTermSet(FDB*[],int,char**,double[],int*);
PDB* MdlCreatePolicy(char*,int,int*);
double ProjectRisk1(float,FDB**,double,double,double,float*,int*);
double ProjectRisk2(float,FDB**,double,double,double,float*,int*);
//
//-----------------------------------------------------------------------
//--We make all the fuzzy set descriptors static so that the policy
//--code modules can reference them without the necessity of passing
//--them as formal parameters.
//-----------------------------------------------------------------------
//
char        *PgmId="combfzy1";
//
FDB   *durFDBptr[8],
      *budFDBptr[8],
      *stfFDBptr[8],
      *rskFDBptr[8];
char  *expNames[2];
//
void main(int argc,char **argv)
  {
  int  durFDBcnt=5,
       budFDBcnt=5,
       stfFDBcnt=5,
       rskFDBcnt=5;
//
  char *durFDBnames[]=
    {
     "BRIEF",
     "SHORT",
     "MODERATE",
     "EXTENDED",
     "LONG"
    };
  char *budFDBnames[]=
    {
     "MINOR",
     "LOW",
     "MEDIUM",
     "HIGH",
     "MAJOR"
    };
  char *stfFDBnames[]=
    {
     "SPARSE",
     "AUSTERE",
     "ROBUST",
     "FULL",
     "HEAVY"
    };
  char *rskFDBnames[]=
    {
     "LOW",
     "MODERATE",
     "ACCEPTABLE",
     "ELEVATED",
     "HIGH"
    };
//
  PDB     *rskPDBptr;
```

```
       FDB    *riskout1FDBptr,
              *riskout2FDBptr;
       char   *strBuff;
       int    i,j,status,NumType,TryCtl[2];
       double Domain[2],
              PJduration,
              PJbudget,
              PJstaffing,
              PJrisk1,
              PJrisk2;
       float  expWgt1,
              expWgt2,
              alfacut,
              CIX1,
              CIX2;
       FILE   *mdlout;
//
//----------------------------------------------------------------------
//--Get and format the current data and time.
//----------------------------------------------------------------------
//
   char   *theDate,*theTime,*fmtDate,*fmtTime;
   char   wrkBuff[16];
   int    dhow=5,thow=3;
   long   currDate,currTime;
   theDate =MtsGetDate(wrkBuff,&status);
   theTime =MtsGetTime(&status);
   fmtDate =MtsFormatDate(theDate,dhow,&status);
   fmtTime =MtsFormatTime(theTime,thow,&status);
   currDate=atoi(theDate);
   currTime=atoi(theTime);
//
//----------------------------------------------------------------------
//--We now examine the program parameters, picking up each argument. The
//--arguments contain the weights of the experts in serial order.
//----------------------------------------------------------------------
//
   switch(argc)
     {
      case 1:
       expWgt1=1.0;
       expWgt2=1.0;
       break;
      case 2:
       if(!MtsIsNumeric(argv[1],&NumType))
         {
          fprintf(stderr, "%s: is not a valid number\n", argv[1]);
          exit(1);
         }
       expWgt1=atof(argv[1]);
       expWgt2=1.0;
       break;
      case 3:
       if(!MtsIsNumeric(argv[1],&NumType))
         {
          fprintf(stderr, "%s: is not a valid number\n", argv[1]);
          exit(1);
         }
       expWgt1=atof(argv[1]);
       if(!MtsIsNumeric(argv[2],&NumType))
         {
          fprintf(stderr, "%s: is not a valid number\n", argv[2]);
          exit(1);
```

```
          }
          expWgt2=atof(argv[2]);
          break;
        default:
          fprintf(stderr, "%s: extraneous argument\n", argv[3]);
          exit(1);
      }
    SysConnecttoMetus(&status);
    XSYSctl.XSYSalfacut=0.1;
    alfacut=XSYSctl.XSYSalfacut;
//
    XSYSctl.XSYStrace[3]=TRUE;
    XSYSctl.XSYStrace[2]=TRUE;
//
    rskPDBptr=MdlCreatePolicy("PROJECT_RISK",MODELADD,&status);
    XSYSctl.XSYScurrPDBptr=rskPDBptr;
    mdlout=MtsGetSystemFile(SYSMODFILE);
//
//----------------------------------------------------------------------
//--PROJECT.DURATION is the length of the project in working days.
//----------------------------------------------------------------------
//
    Domain[0]=0; Domain[1]=200;
    InitializeTermSet(durFDBptr,durFDBcnt,durFDBnames,Domain,&status);
    FzySCurve  (durFDBptr[0],    0,    5,   10,DECLINE,&status); //BRIEF
    FzyPiCurve (durFDBptr[1],   10,    5             ,&status); //SHORT
    FzyPiCurve (durFDBptr[2],   40,   30             ,&status); //MODERATE
    FzyPiCurve (durFDBptr[3],   90,   50             ,&status); //EXTENDED
    FzySCurve  (durFDBptr[4],   90,  120,  150,GROWTH ,&status); //LONG
    FzyPlotTermSet("PROJECT.DURATION",durFDBptr,durFDBcnt,SYSMODFILE,&status);
//
//----------------------------------------------------------------------
//--PROJECT.BUDGET is the cost of the project in dollars (x000).
//----------------------------------------------------------------------
//
    Domain[0]=0; Domain[1]=1200;
    InitializeTermSet(budFDBptr,budFDBcnt,budFDBnames,Domain,&status);
    FzySCurve         (budFDBptr[0],    0,   50,  100,DECLINE,&status); //MINOR
    FzyTrapezoidCurve (budFDBptr[1],   50,  100,  200,  250  ,&status); //LOW
    FzyTrapezoidCurve (budFDBptr[2],  200,  250,  500,  550  ,&status); //MEDIUM
    FzyTrapezoidCurve (budFDBptr[3],  500,  550,  800,  850  ,&status); //HIGH
    FzySCurve         (budFDBptr[4],  800,  900, 1000,GROWTH ,&status); //MAJOR
    FzyPlotTermSet("PROJECT.BUDGET",budFDBptr,budFDBcnt,SYSMODFILE,&status);
//
//----------------------------------------------------------------------
//--PROJECT.STAFFING is staffing size of the project.
//----------------------------------------------------------------------
//
    Domain[0]=0; Domain[1]= 150;
    InitializeTermSet(stfFDBptr,stfFDBcnt,stfFDBnames,Domain,&status);
    FzySCurve  (stfFDBptr[0],    0,    5,   10,DECLINE,&status); //SPARSE
    FzyPiCurve (stfFDBptr[1],   10,    5             ,&status); //AUSTERE
    FzyPiCurve (stfFDBptr[2],   30,   20             ,&status); //ROBUST
    FzyPiCurve (stfFDBptr[3],   60,   30             ,&status); //FULL
    FzySCurve  (stfFDBptr[4],   60,   90,  120,GROWTH ,&status); //HEAVY
    FzyPlotTermSet("PROJECT.STAFFING",stfFDBptr,stfFDBcnt,SYSMODFILE,&status);
//
//----------------------------------------------------------------------
//--PROJECT.RISK is risk associated with the project.
//----------------------------------------------------------------------
//
    Domain[0]=0; Domain[1]= 100;
    InitializeTermSet(rskFDBptr,rskFDBcnt,rskFDBnames,Domain,&status);
```

```
                  FzySCurve  (rskFDBptr[0],   0,  25,  50,DECLINE,&status); //LOW
                  FzyPiCurve (rskFDBptr[1],  25,  25           ,&status); //MODERATE
                  FzyPiCurve (rskFDBptr[2],  50,  25           ,&status); //ACCEPTABLE
                  FzyPiCurve (rskFDBptr[3],  75,  25           ,&status); //ELEVATED
                  FzySCurve  (rskFDBptr[4],  50,  75, 100,GROWTH ,&status); //HIGH
                  FzyPlotTermSet("PROJECT.RISK",rskFDBptr,rskFDBcnt,SYSMODFILE,&status);
              //
                strBuff=new char[80];
                strcpy(strBuff,"BILL.SMITH");
                expNames[0]=strBuff;
                strBuff=new char[80];
                strcpy(strBuff,"MARY.WILLIAMS");
                expNames[1]=strBuff;
              //
                printf("THE PROJECT RISK ASSESSMENT MODEL  (c)1995 Metus Systems\n");
                printf("Enter Project Properties:\n");
                TryCtl[0]=5;
                TryCtl[1]=0;
                Domain[0]=0; Domain[1]=200;
                PJduration=MtsAskforDBL("PROJECT.DURATION",
                   "Enter the Project Duration    :",Domain,TryCtl,&status);
                TryCtl[1]=0;
                Domain[0]=0; Domain[1]=2400;
                PJbudget  =MtsAskforDBL("PROJECT.BUDGET",
                   "Enter the Project Budget      :",Domain,TryCtl,&status);
                TryCtl[1]=0;
                Domain[0]=0; Domain[1]=150;
                PJstaffing=MtsAskforDBL("PROJECT.STAFFING",
                   "Enter the Project Staffing    :",Domain,TryCtl,&status);
                fprintf(mdlout,"%s\n%s%10.2f\n%s%10.2f\n%s%10.2f\n",
                  "PROJECT DATA ",
                  "  Duration      : ",PJduration,
                  "  Budget        : ",PJbudget,
                  "  Staffing      : ",PJstaffing);
              //
              //-------------------------------------------------------------------
              //--RUN RISK ASSESSMENT POLICIES. We now run the two risk policies to
              //--develop the project based on the rules of the two experts.
              //-------------------------------------------------------------------
              //
                PJrisk1=ProjectRisk1(
                   expWgt1,&riskout1FDBptr,PJduration,PJbudget,PJstaffing,&CIX1,&status);
                PJrisk2=ProjectRisk2(
                   expWgt2,&riskout2FDBptr,PJduration,PJbudget,PJstaffing,&CIX2,&status);
                //
                fprintf(mdlout,"\n\n%s\n","EXPERT PEER RANKINGS:");
                fprintf(mdlout,
                  "%s%-16.16s%s%10.3f\n%s%-16.16s%s%10.3f\n",
                  "  Expert ",expNames[0]," Rank: ",expWgt1,
                  "  Expert ",expNames[1]," Rank: ",expWgt2);
                fprintf(mdlout,"\n%s\n","INDIVIDUAL MODEL RESULTS:");
                fprintf(mdlout,
                  "%s%-16.16s%s%10.2f%s%6.4f%s\n%s%-16.16s%s%10.2f%s%6.4f%s\n",
                  "  Expert ",expNames[0]," Risk: ",PJrisk1,"  [",CIX1,"]",
                  "  Expert ",expNames[1]," Risk: ",PJrisk2,"  [",CIX2,"]");
                fprintf(mdlout,"%s\n%s%10.2f\n%s%10.2f\n",
                  "----------------------------------------",
                  "  Average  Risk Assessment   : ",(PJrisk1+PJrisk2)/2,
                  "  WgtdAvg  Risk Assessment   : ",
                     ((PJrisk1*expWgt1)+(PJrisk2*expWgt2))/(expWgt1+expWgt2));
                printf("Model Finished.\n");
                return;
                }
```

```
//
//=============================================================================
//------------------SUPPORT AND MAINTENANCE FUNCTIONS-------------------
//=============================================================================
//
void InitializeTermSet(
   FDB *FDBptr[],
     int FDBcnt,char **FDBnames,double Domain[],int *statusPtr)
 {
  int i;
  for(i=0;i<FDBcnt;i++)
    {
     if((FDBptr[i]=new FDB)==NULL)
       {
        MtsSendError(2,PgmId,FDBnames[i]);
        return;
       }
     FzyInitFDB(FDBptr[i]);
     strcpy(FDBptr[i]->FDBid,FDBnames[i]);
     FDBptr[i]->FDBdomain[0]=Domain[0];
     FDBptr[i]->FDBdomain[1]=Domain[1];
     }
  return;
 }
//
//=============================================================================
//----------------------FUZZY REASONING POLICIES----------------------
//=============================================================================
//
double ProjectRisk1(
     float    expWgt,          // the peer ranking of this expert
     FDB     **riskoutFDBptr,   // pointer to the output fuzzy set
     double   PJduration,       // project duration
     double   PJbudget,         // project budget
     double   PJstaffing,       // project staffing
     float   *CIX,              // compatibility index
     int     *statusPtr)        // status code
 {
  FDB     *RiskFDBptr;
  VDB     *VDBptr;
  FSV     *FSVptr;
  int      Idxpos,
           Rulecnt,
           thisCorrMethod,
           thisDefuzzMethod;
  float    CompIDX,
           fsetheight,
           PremiseTruth;
  double   Domain[2],Risk,NoRisk=0;
  FILE    *mdlout;
  char *projRules[]=
    {
    "[R1]  if project.duration is long then risk is acceptable;",
    "[R2]  if project.duration is extended then risk is elevated;",
    "[R3]  if project.budget is high then risk is elevated;",
    "[R4]  if project.staffing is full then risk is high;"
    };
  *statusPtr=0;
  mdlout=MtsGetSystemFile(SYSMODFILE);
  fprintf(mdlout,"%s\n%s%s%s\n%s\n\n",
    "----------------------------------------------------------------",
    " Risk Assessment Policy [Expert: ",expNames[0],"] begins.",
    "----------------------------------------------------------------");
```

```
        Domain[0]=  0;
        Domain[1]=100;
        VDBptr=VarCreateScalar("RISK",REAL,Domain,"0",statusPtr);
        FzyInitFZYctl(statusPtr);
        if(!(FzyAddFZYctl(VDBptr,&RiskFDBptr,&FSVptr,statusPtr)))
          {
           *statusPtr=1;
           MtsSendError(12,PgmId,"RISK");
           return(NoRisk);
          }
       thisCorrMethod  =CORRPRODUCT;
       thisDefuzzMethod=FSVptr->FzySVdefuzzMethod;
       Rulecnt=0;
       fprintf(mdlout,"%s\n","Rule Execution....");
//
//--------------------------------------------------------------------
//--[R1]  if project.duration is long then risk is acceptable;",
//--------------------------------------------------------------------
//
       fprintf(mdlout,"%s\n",projRules[Rulecnt]);
//
//--Compute membership of project duration in this fuzzy region, and
//--then use the truth of this to compute the output (solution) set.
//
       PremiseTruth=FzyGetMembership(
            durFDBptr[LONGduration],PJduration,&Idxpos,statusPtr);
       fprintf(mdlout,"%s%10.2f\n","PremiseTruth= ",PremiseTruth);
       FzyCondProposition(
            rskFDBptr[ACCEPTABLErisk],FSVptr,thisCorrMethod,PremiseTruth,statusPtr);
       FzyDrawSet(RiskFDBptr,SYSMODFILE,statusPtr);
//
//--------------------------------------------------------------------
//--[R2]  if project.duration is extended then risk is elevated;",
//--------------------------------------------------------------------
//
       Rulecnt++;
       fprintf(mdlout,"%s\n",projRules[Rulecnt]);
//
//--Compute membership of project duration in this fuzzy region, and
//--then use the truth of this to compute the output (solution) set.
//
       PremiseTruth=FzyGetMembership(
            durFDBptr[EXTENDEDduration],PJduration,&Idxpos,statusPtr);
       fprintf(mdlout,"%s%10.2f\n","PremiseTruth= ",PremiseTruth);
       FzyCondProposition(
            rskFDBptr[ELEVATEDrisk],FSVptr,thisCorrMethod,PremiseTruth,statusPtr);
       FzyDrawSet(RiskFDBptr,SYSMODFILE,statusPtr);
//
//--------------------------------------------------------------------
//--[R3]  if project.budget is high then risk is elevated;
//--------------------------------------------------------------------
//
       Rulecnt++;
       fprintf(mdlout,"%s\n",projRules[Rulecnt]);
//
//--Compute membership of project budget in this fuzzy region, and
//--then use the truth of this to compute the output (solution) set.
//
       PremiseTruth=FzyGetMembership(
            budFDBptr[HIGHbudget],PJbudget,&Idxpos,statusPtr);
       fprintf(mdlout,"%s%10.2f\n","PremiseTruth= ",PremiseTruth);
       FzyCondProposition(
            rskFDBptr[ELEVATEDrisk],FSVptr,thisCorrMethod,PremiseTruth,statusPtr);
```

```
    FzyDrawSet(RiskFDBptr,SYSMODFILE,statusPtr);
//
//-------------------------------------------------------------------------
//--[R4]  if project.staffing is full then risk is high;"
//-------------------------------------------------------------------------
//
   Rulecnt++;
   fprintf(mdlout,"%s\n",projRules[Rulecnt]);
//
//--Compute membership of project staff size in this fuzzy region, and
//--then use the truth of this to compute the output (solution) set.
//
   PremiseTruth=FzyGetMembership(
      stfFDBptr[FULLstaffing],PJstaffing,&Idxpos,statusPtr);
    fprintf(mdlout,"%s%10.2f\n","PremiseTruth= ",PremiseTruth);
   FzyCondProposition(
      rskFDBptr[HIGHrisk],FSVptr,thisCorrMethod,PremiseTruth,statusPtr);
   FzyDrawSet(RiskFDBptr,SYSMODFILE,statusPtr);
//
//-------------------------------------------------------------------------
//--Defuzzify to find expected value for price.
//-------------------------------------------------------------------------
//
   *riskoutFDBptr=RiskFDBptr;
   Risk=FzyDefuzzify(RiskFDBptr,thisDefuzzMethod,&CompIDX,statusPtr);
   fsetheight=FzyGetHeight(RiskFDBptr);
   fprintf(mdlout,"%s\n","Model Solution:");
   fprintf(mdlout,"%s%10.2f\n","  Risk       = ",Risk        );
   fprintf(mdlout,"%s%10.2f\n","  CompIdx    = ",CompIDX     );
   fprintf(mdlout,"%s%10.2f\n","  SurfaceHght = ",fsetheight );
//
   *CIX=CompIDX;
   FzyCloseFZYctl(statusPtr);
   return(Risk);
  }
//
//
//
double ProjectRisk2(
     float     expWgt,        // the peer ranking of this expert
     FDB     **riskoutFDBptr, // pointer to the output fuzzy set
     double    PJduration,    // project duration
     double    PJbudget,      // project budget
     double    PJstaffing,    // project staffing
     float    *CIX,           // compatibility index
     int      *statusPtr)     // status code
  {
  FDB     *RiskFDBptr;
  VDB     *VDBptr;
  FSV     *FSVptr;
  int      Idxpos,
           Rulecnt,
           thisCorrMethod,
           thisDefuzzMethod;
  float    CompIDX,
           fsetheight,
           PremiseTruth;
  double  Domain[2],Risk,NoRisk=0;
  FILE    *mdlout;
  char *projRules[]=
    {
    "[R1]  if project.duration is long then risk is elevated;",
    "[R2]  if project.budget is high then risk is acceptable;",
```

```
          "[R3]  if project.staffing is full then risk is elevated;"
      };
    *statusPtr=0;
    mdlout=MtsGetSystemFile(SYSMODFILE);
    fprintf(mdlout,"%s\n%s%s%s\n%s\n\n",
      "-----------------------------------------------------------------",
      " Risk Assessment Policy [Expert: ",expNames[1]," begins.",
      "-----------------------------------------------------------------");
    Domain[0]=   0;
    Domain[1]=100;
    VDBptr=VarCreateScalar("RISK",REAL,Domain,"0",statusPtr);
    FzyInitFZYctl(statusPtr);
    if(!(FzyAddFZYctl(VDBptr,&RiskFDBptr,&FSVptr,statusPtr)))
      {
        *statusPtr=1;
        MtsSendError(12,PgmId,"RISK");
        return(NoRisk);
      }
    thisCorrMethod  =CORRPRODUCT;
    thisDefuzzMethod=FSVptr->FzySVdefuzzMethod;
    Rulecnt=0;
    fprintf(mdlout,"%s\n","Rule Execution....");
//
//-------------------------------------------------------------------------
//--[R1]  if project.duration is long then risk is elevated;
//-------------------------------------------------------------------------
//
    fprintf(mdlout,"%s\n",projRules[Rulecnt]);
//
//--Compute membership of project duration in this fuzzy region, and
//--then use the truth of this to compute the output (solution) set.
//
    PremiseTruth=FzyGetMembership(
    durFDBptr[LONGduration],PJduration,&Idxpos,statusPtr);
    fprintf(mdlout,"%s%10.2f\n","PremiseTruth= ",PremiseTruth);
    FzyCondProposition(
        rskFDBptr[ELEVATEDrisk],FSVptr,thisCorrMethod,PremiseTruth,statusPtr);
    FzyDrawSet(RiskFDBptr,SYSMODFILE,statusPtr);
//
//-------------------------------------------------------------------------
//--[R2]  if project.budget is high then risk is acceptable;
//-------------------------------------------------------------------------
//
    Rulecnt++;
    fprintf(mdlout,"%s\n",projRules[Rulecnt]);
//
//--Compute membership of project budget in this fuzzy region, and
//--then use the truth of this to compute the output (solution) set.
//
    PremiseTruth=FzyGetMembership(
        budFDBptr[HIGHbudget],PJbudget,&Idxpos,statusPtr);
    fprintf(mdlout,"%s%10.2f\n","PremiseTruth= ",PremiseTruth);
    FzyCondProposition(
        rskFDBptr[ACCEPTABLErisk],FSVptr,thisCorrMethod,PremiseTruth,statusPtr);
    FzyDrawSet(RiskFDBptr,SYSMODFILE,statusPtr);
//
//-------------------------------------------------------------------------
//--[R3]  if project.staffing is full then risk is elevated;
//-------------------------------------------------------------------------
//
    Rulecnt++;
    fprintf(mdlout,"%s\n",projRules[Rulecnt]);
//
```

```
//--Compute membership of project staff size in this fuzzy region, and
//--then use the truth of this to compute the output (solution) set.
//
   PremiseTruth=FzyGetMembership(
        stfFDBptr[FULLstaffing],PJstaffing,&Idxpos,statusPtr);
   fprintf(mdlout,"%s%10.2f\n","PremiseTruth= ",PremiseTruth);
   FzyCondProposition(
        rskFDBptr[ELEVATEDrisk],FSVptr,thisCorrMethod,PremiseTruth,statusPtr);
   FzyDrawSet(RiskFDBptr,SYSMODFILE,statusPtr);
//
//--Defuzzify to find expected value for price
//
   *riskoutFDBptr=RiskFDBptr;
   Risk=FzyDefuzzify(RiskFDBptr,thisDefuzzMethod,&CompIDX,statusPtr);
   fsetheight=FzyGetHeight(RiskFDBptr);
   fprintf(mdlout,"%s\n","Model Solution:");
   fprintf(mdlout,"%s%10.2f\n","  Risk       = ",Risk        );
   fprintf(mdlout,"%s%10.2f\n","  CompIdx     = ",CompIDX     );
   fprintf(mdlout,"%s%10.2f\n","  SurfaceHght = ",fsetheight  );
//
   *CIX=CompIDX;
   FzyCloseFZYctl(statusPtr);
   return(Risk);
  }
?
```

projrsk2.cpp (The Combined Intelligence Project Risk Model)

```
/*-------------------------------------------------------------*
| (c) 1995 Metus Systems.      Proprietary software product.  |
| Reproduction or unauthorized use is prohibited. Unauthorized|
| use is illegal. Violators will be prosecuted. This software |
| contains proprietary trade and business secrets.            |
*-------------------Procedure Description-------------------*
| projrsk2.cpp Earl Cox  11/13/94 A Combined Fuzzy System    |
| In this model we follow two strategies for combining fuzzy |
| systems: (1) by combining the output using a weighted mean |
| and (2) by combining the throughput of the system before   |
| defuzzification.                                           |
*-------------------------------------------------------------*
| We employ a simple two-expert fuzzy system where the weight |
| of each expert is entered at execution time.  Although we   |
| construct a policy architecture for the model, the fuzzy    |
| sets are defined as statics so we can use them directly.    |
*---------------Modification Audit/Change Log---------------*
| Rev  Sar              Metus                                 |
| No   Code  Date      Rellvl  Mod  Description               |
| --   -----  --------   ------   ---   ------------------------|
|                                                            |
|                                                            |
*-------------------------------------------------------------*/
#include <stdio.h>
#include <string.h>
#include "PDB.hpp"
#include "FDB.hpp"
#include "SFZYctl.hpp"
#include "SSYSctl.hpp"
#include "fuzzy.hpp"
#include "mtypes.hpp"
#include "mtsptype.hpp"
//
//--------------------------------------------------------------------
//--These are the symbolic constants that tie an FDB array slot to the
```

```
//--underlying semantic (fuzzy) concept.
//-----------------------------------------------------------------------
//
#define BRIEFduration     0
#define SHORTduration     1
#define MODERATEduration  2
#define EXTENDEDduration  3
#define LONGduration      4
#define MINORbudget       0
#define LOWbudget         1
#define MEDIUMbudget      2
#define HIGHbudget        3
#define MAJORbudget       4
#define SPARSEstafffing   0
#define AUSTEREstaffing   1
#define ROBUSTstaffing    2
#define FULLstaffing      3
#define HEAVYstaffing     4
#define LOWrisk           0
#define MODERATErisk      1
#define ACCEPTABLErisk    2
#define ELEVATEDrisk      3
#define HIGHrisk          4
//
//-----------------------------------------------------------------------
//--These are the function prototypes for procedures not declared as
//--part of the standard modelling system environment.
//-----------------------------------------------------------------------
//
void    InitializeTermSet(FDB*[],int,char**,double[],int*);
void    ScalebyExpertRanking(float,FDB*,int*);
PDB*    MdlCreatePolicy(char*,int,int*);
double  ProjectRisk1(float,FDB**,double,double,double,float*,int*);
double  ProjectRisk2(float,FDB**,double,double,double,float*,int*);
//
//-----------------------------------------------------------------------
//--We make all the fuzzy set descriptors static so that the policy
//--code modules can reference them without the necessity of passing
//--them as formal parameters.
//-----------------------------------------------------------------------
//
char *PgmId="projrsk2";
//
FDB   *durFDBptr[8],
      *budFDBptr[8],
      *stfFDBptr[8],
      *rskFDBptr[8];
char  *expNames[2];
//
void main(int argc,char **argv)
 {
  int  durFDBcnt=5,
       budFDBcnt=5,
       stfFDBcnt=5,
       rskFDBcnt=5;
//
  char *durFDBnames[]=
   {
    "BRIEF",
    "SHORT",
    "MODERATE",
    "EXTENDED",
    "LONG"
```

```
      };
    char *budFDBnames[]=
     {
      "MINOR",
      "LOW",
      "MEDIUM",
      "HIGH",
      "MAJOR"
     };
    char *stfFDBnames[]=
     {
      "SPARSE",
      "AUSTERE",
      "ROBUST",
      "FULL",
      "HEAVY"
     };
    char *rskFDBnames[]=
     {
      "LOW",
      "MODERATE",
      "ACCEPTABLE",
      "ELEVATED",
      "HIGH"
     };
//
    PDB    *rskPDBptr;
    FDB    *riskout1FDBptr,
           *riskout2FDBptr,
           *combFDBptr;
    char   *strBuff;
    int    i,j,status,NumType,TryCtl[2];
    int    thisDefuzzMethod;
    double Domain[2],
           combRisk,
           PJduration,
           PJbudget,
           PJstaffing,
           PJrisk1,
           PJrisk2;
    float  combHeight;
    float  expWgt1,
           expWgt2,
           alfacut,
           CCIX,
           CIX1,
           CIX2;
    FILE   *mdlout;
//
//------------------------------------------------------------------------
//--Get and format the current data and time.
//------------------------------------------------------------------------
//
    char   *theDate,*theTime,*fmtDate,*fmtTime;
    char   wrkBuff[16];
    int    dhow=5,thow=3;
    long   currDate,currTime;
    theDate =MtsGetDate(wrkBuff,&status);
    theTime =MtsGetTime(&status);
    fmtDate =MtsFormatDate(theDate,dhow,&status);
    fmtTime =MtsFormatTime(theTime,thow,&status);
    currDate=atoi(theDate);
    currTime=atoi(theTime);
```

```
//
//---------------------------------------------------------------------
//--We now examine the program parameters, picking up each argument. The
//--arguments contain the weights of the experts in serial order.
//---------------------------------------------------------------------
//
  switch(argc)
    {
      case 1:
       expWgt1=1.0;
       expWgt2=1.0;
       break;
      case 2:
       if(!MtsIsNumeric(argv[1],&NumType))
          {
            fprintf(stderr, "%s: is not a valid number\n", argv[1]);
            exit(1);
          }
       expWgt1=atof(argv[1]);
       expWgt2=1.0;
       break;
      case 3:
       if(!MtsIsNumeric(argv[1],&NumType))
          {
            fprintf(stderr, "%s: is not a valid number\n", argv[1]);
            exit(1);
          }
       expWgt1=atof(argv[1]);
       if(!MtsIsNumeric(argv[2],&NumType))
          {
            fprintf(stderr, "%s: is not a valid number\n", argv[2]);
            exit(1);
          }
       expWgt2=atof(argv[2]);
       break;
      default:
       fprintf(stderr, "%s: extraneous argument\n", argv[3]);
       exit(1);
    }
  SysConnecttoMetus(&status);
  XSYSctl.XSYSalfacut=0.1;
  alfacut=XSYSctl.XSYSalfacut;
//
  XSYSctl.XSYStrace[3]=TRUE;
  XSYSctl.XSYStrace[2]=TRUE;
//
  rskPDBptr=MdlCreatePolicy("PROJECT_RISK",MODELADD,&status);
  XSYSctl.XSYScurrPDBptr=rskPDBptr;
  mdlout=MtsGetSystemFile(SYSMODFILE);
//
//---------------------------------------------------------------------
//--PROJECT.DURATION is the length of the project in working days.
//---------------------------------------------------------------------
//
  Domain[0]=0; Domain[1]=200;
  InitializeTermSet(durFDBptr,durFDBcnt,durFDBnames,Domain,&status);
  FzySCurve  (durFDBptr[0],   0,   5,  10,DECLINE,&status); //BRIEF
  FzyPiCurve (durFDBptr[1],  10,   5            ,&status); //SHORT
  FzyPiCurve (durFDBptr[2],  40,  30            ,&status); //MODERATE
  FzyPiCurve (durFDBptr[3],  90,  50            ,&status); //EXTENDED
  FzySCurve  (durFDBptr[4],  90, 120, 150,GROWTH ,&status); //LONG
  FzyPlotTermSet("PROJECT.DURATION",durFDBptr,durFDBcnt,SYSMODFILE,&status);
//
```

```
//-------------------------------------------------------------------
//--PROJECT.BUDGET is the cost of the project in dollars (x000)
//-------------------------------------------------------------------
//
  Domain[0]=0; Domain[1]=1200;
  InitializeTermSet(budFDBptr,budFDBcnt,budFDBnames,Domain,&status);
  FzySCurve        (budFDBptr[0],   0,  50, 100,DECLINE,&status); //MINOR
  FzyTrapezoidCurve (budFDBptr[1],  50, 100, 200, 250   ,&status); //LOW
  FzyTrapezoidCurve (budFDBptr[2], 200, 250, 500, 550   ,&status); //MEDIUM
  FzyTrapezoidCurve (budFDBptr[3], 500, 550, 800, 850   ,&status); //HIGH
  FzySCurve        (budFDBptr[4], 800, 900,1000,GROWTH ,&status); //MAJOR
  FzyPlotTermSet("PROJECT.BUDGET",budFDBptr,budFDBcnt,SYSMODFILE,&status);
//
//-------------------------------------------------------------------
//--PROJECT.STAFFING is staffing size of the project.
//-------------------------------------------------------------------
//
  Domain[0]=0; Domain[1]= 150;
  InitializeTermSet(stfFDBptr,stfFDBcnt,stfFDBnames,Domain,&status);
  FzySCurve (stfFDBptr[0],   0,   5,  10,DECLINE,&status); //SPARSE
  FzyPiCurve (stfFDBptr[1],  10,   5              ,&status); //AUSTERE
  FzyPiCurve (stfFDBptr[2],  30,  20              ,&status); //ROBUST
  FzyPiCurve (stfFDBptr[3],  60,  30              ,&status); //FULL
  FzySCurve (stfFDBptr[4],  60,  90, 120,GROWTH ,&status); //HEAVY
  FzyPlotTermSet("PROJECT.STAFFING",stfFDBptr,stfFDBcnt,SYSMODFILE,&status);
//
//-------------------------------------------------------------------
//--PROJECT.RISK is risk associated with the project.
//-------------------------------------------------------------------
//
  Domain[0]=0; Domain[1]= 100;
  InitializeTermSet(rskFDBptr,rskFDBcnt,rskFDBnames,Domain,&status);
  FzySCurve (rskFDBptr[0],   0,  25,  50,DECLINE,&status); //LOW
  FzyPiCurve (rskFDBptr[1],  25,  25              ,&status); //MODERATE
  FzyPiCurve (rskFDBptr[2],  50,  25              ,&status); //ACCEPTABLE
  FzyPiCurve (rskFDBptr[3],  75,  25              ,&status); //ELEVATED
  FzySCurve (rskFDBptr[4],  50,  75, 100,GROWTH ,&status); //HIGH
  FzyPlotTermSet("PROJECT.RISK",rskFDBptr,rskFDBcnt,SYSMODFILE,&status);
//
  strBuff=new char[80];
  strcpy(strBuff,"BILL.SMITH");
  expNames[0]=strBuff;
  strBuff=new char[80];
  strcpy(strBuff,"MARY.WILLIAMS");
  expNames[1]=strBuff;
//
  printf("THE PROJECT RISK ASSESSMENT MODEL  (c)1995 Metus Systems\n");
  printf("Enter Project Properties:\n");
  TryCtl[0]=5;
  TryCtl[1]=0;
  Domain[0]=0; Domain[1]=200;
  PJduration=MtsAskforDBL("PROJECT.DURATION",
    "Enter the Project Duration      :",Domain,TryCtl,&status);
  TryCtl[1]=0;
  Domain[0]=0; Domain[1]=2400;
  PJbudget =MtsAskforDBL("PROJECT.BUDGET",
    "Enter the Project Budget        :",Domain,TryCtl,&status);
  TryCtl[1]=0;
  Domain[0]=0; Domain[1]=150;
  PJstaffing=MtsAskforDBL("PROJECT.STAFFING",
    "Enter the Project Staffing      :",Domain,TryCtl,&status);
  fprintf(mdlout,"%s\n%s%10.2f\n%s%10.2f\n%s%10.2f\n",
   "PROJECT DATA ",
```

```
   "   Duration     : ",PJduration,
   "   Budget       : ",PJbudget,
   "   Staffing     : ",PJstaffing);
//
//------------------------------------------------------------------
//--RUN RISK ASSESSMENT POLICIES. We now run the two risk policies to
//--develop the project based on the rules of the two experts.
//------------------------------------------------------------------
//
   PJrisk1=ProjectRisk1(
      expWgt1,&riskout1FDBptr,PJduration,PJbudget,PJstaffing,&CIX1,&status);
   PJrisk2=ProjectRisk2(
      expWgt2,&riskout2FDBptr,PJduration,PJbudget,PJstaffing,&CIX2,&status);
   //
   ScalebyExpertRanking(expWgt1,riskout1FDBptr,&status);
   ScalebyExpertRanking(expWgt2,riskout2FDBptr,&status);
   //
   combFDBptr=new FDB;
   FzyInitFDB(combFDBptr);
   strcpy(combFDBptr->FDBid,   "CombinedRisk");
   strcpy(combFDBptr->FDBdesc,"Combined Risk Output Fuzzy Sets");
   combFDBptr->FDBdomain[0]=    0;
   combFDBptr->FDBdomain[1]= 100;
   for(i=0;i<VECMAX;i++)
      {
      combFDBptr->FDBvector[i]=
        min(1,(riskout1FDBptr->FDBvector[i]+riskout2FDBptr->FDBvector[i]));
      }
   FzyDrawSet(combFDBptr,SYSMODFILE,&status);
   thisDefuzzMethod=CENTROID;
   combRisk=FzyDefuzzify(combFDBptr,thisDefuzzMethod,&CCIX,&status);
   combHeight=FzyGetHeight(combFDBptr);
   //
   fprintf(mdlout,"\n\n%s\n","EXPERT PEER RANKINGS:");
   fprintf(mdlout,
     "%s%-16.16s%s%10.3f\n%s%-16.16s%s%10.3f\n",
     "  Expert ",expNames[0]," Rank: ",expWgt1,
     "  Expert ",expNames[1]," Rank: ",expWgt2);
   fprintf(mdlout,"\n%s\n","INDIVIDUAL MODEL RESULTS:");
   fprintf(mdlout,
     "%s%-16.16s%s%10.2f%s%6.4f%s\n%s%-16.16s%s%10.2f%s%6.4f%s\n",
     "  Expert ",expNames[0]," Risk: ",PJrisk1,"  [",CIX1,"]",
     "  Expert ",expNames[1]," Risk: ",PJrisk2,"  [",CIX2,"]");
   fprintf(mdlout,"%s\n%s%10.2f\n%s%10.2f\n",
     "------------------------------------------",
     "  Average  Risk Assessment    : ",(PJrisk1+PJrisk2)/2,
     "  WgtdAvg  Risk Assessment    : ",
        ((PJrisk1*expWgt1)+(PJrisk2*expWgt2))/(expWgt1+expWgt2));
   fprintf(mdlout,"\n\n%s\n","COMBINED MODEL RESULTS:");
   fprintf(mdlout,"%s%10.2f%s%6.4f%s\n%s%10.4f\n",
     "  Combined Risk Assessment    : ",combRisk,"  [",CCIX,"]",
     "  Combined Risk Height        : ",combHeight);
   printf("Model Finished.\n");
   return;
   }
//
//==================================================================
//-----------------SUPPORT AND MAINTENANCE FUNCTIONS----------------
//==================================================================
//
void InitializeTermSet(
   FDB *FDBptr[],
     int FDBcnt,char **FDBnames,double Domain[],int *statusPtr)
```

```
  {
   int i;
   for(i=0;i<FDBcnt;i++)
     {
      if((FDBptr[i]=new FDB)==NULL)
        {
         MtsSendError(2,PgmId,FDBnames[i]);
         return;
        }
      FzyInitFDB(FDBptr[i]);
      strcpy(FDBptr[i]->FDBid,FDBnames[i]);
      FDBptr[i]->FDBdomain[0]=Domain[0];
      FDBptr[i]->FDBdomain[1]=Domain[1];
     }
   return;
  }
//
void ScalebyExpertRanking(float expWgt,FDB *FDBptr,int *statusPtr)
  {
   int i;
   *statusPtr=0;
   if(expWgt==1.0) return;
   for(i=0;i<VECMAX;i++)
      FDBptr->FDBvector[i]=FDBptr->FDBvector[i]*expWgt;
   return;
  }
//
//==================================================================
//----------------------FUZZY REASONING POLICIES--------------------
//==================================================================
//
double ProjectRisk1(
      float     expWgt,          // the peer ranking of this expert
      FDB       **riskoutFDBptr,  // pointer to the output fuzzy set
      double    PJduration,       // project duration
      double    PJbudget,         // project budget
      double    PJstaffing,       // project staffing
      float     *CIX,             // compatibility index
      int       *statusPtr)       // status code
  {
   FDB     *RiskFDBptr;
   VDB     *VDBptr;
   FSV     *FSVptr;
   int     Idxpos,
           Rulecnt,
           thisCorrMethod,
           thisDefuzzMethod;
   float   CompIDX,
           fsetheight,
           PremiseTruth;
   double  Domain[2],Risk,NoRisk=0;
   FILE    *mdlout;
   char *projRules[]=
     {
      "[R1]  if project.duration is long then risk is acceptable;",
      "[R2]  if project.duration is extended then risk is elevated;",
      "[R3]  if project.budget is high then risk is elevated;",
      "[R4]  if project.staffing is full then risk is high;"
     };
   *statusPtr=0;
   mdlout=MtsGetSystemFile(SYSMODFILE);
   fprintf(mdlout,"%s\n%s%s%s\n%s\n\n",
     "---------------------------------------------------------------",
```

```
      " Risk Assessment Policy [Expert: ",expNames[0],"] begins.",
      "--------------------------------------------------------------");
    Domain[0]=  0;
    Domain[1]=100;
    VDBptr=VarCreateScalar("RISK",REAL,Domain,"0",statusPtr);
    FzyInitFZYctl(statusPtr);
    if(!(FzyAddFZYctl(VDBptr,&RiskFDBptr,&FSVptr,statusPtr)))
      {
       *statusPtr=1;
       MtsSendError(12,PgmId,"RISK");
       return(NoRisk);
      }
    thisCorrMethod  =CORRPRODUCT;
    thisDefuzMethod=FSVptr->FzySVdefuzMethod;
    Rulecnt=0;
    fprintf(mdlout,"%s\n","Rule Execution....");
//
//------------------------------------------------------------------
//--[R1]  if project.duration is long then risk is acceptable;",
//------------------------------------------------------------------
//
    fprintf(mdlout,"%s\n",projRules[Rulecnt]);
//
//--Compute membership of project duration in this fuzzy region, and
//--then use the truth of this to compute the output (solution) set.
//
    PremiseTruth=FzyGetMembership(
        durFDBptr[LONGduration],PJduration,&Idxpos,statusPtr);
    fprintf(mdlout,"%s%10.2f\n","PremiseTruth= ",PremiseTruth);
    FzyCondProposition(
        rskFDBptr[ACCEPTABLErisk],FSVptr,thisCorrMethod,PremiseTruth,statusPtr);
    FzyDrawSet(RiskFDBptr,SYSMODFILE,statusPtr);
//
//------------------------------------------------------------------
//--[R2]  if project.duration is extended then risk is elevated;",
//------------------------------------------------------------------
//
    Rulecnt++;
    fprintf(mdlout,"%s\n",projRules[Rulecnt]);
//
//--Compute membership of project duration in this fuzzy region, and
//--then use the truth of this to compute the output (solution) set.
//
    PremiseTruth=FzyGetMembership(
        durFDBptr[EXTENDEDduration],PJduration,&Idxpos,statusPtr);
    fprintf(mdlout,"%s%10.2f\n","PremiseTruth= ",PremiseTruth);
    FzyCondProposition(
        rskFDBptr[ELEVATEDrisk],FSVptr,thisCorrMethod,PremiseTruth,statusPtr);
    FzyDrawSet(RiskFDBptr,SYSMODFILE,statusPtr);
//
//------------------------------------------------------------------
//--[R3]  if project.budget is high then risk is elevated;
//------------------------------------------------------------------
//
    Rulecnt++;
    fprintf(mdlout,"%s\n",projRules[Rulecnt]);
//
//--Compute membership of project budget in this fuzzy region, and
//--then use the truth of this to compute the output (solution) set.
//
    PremiseTruth=FzyGetMembership(
        budFDBptr[HIGHbudget],PJbudget,&Idxpos,statusPtr);
    fprintf(mdlout,"%s%10.2f\n","PremiseTruth= ",PremiseTruth);
```

```
     FzyCondProposition(
        rskFDBptr[ELEVATEDrisk],FSVptr,thisCorrMethod,PremiseTruth,statusPtr);
     FzyDrawSet(RiskFDBptr,SYSMODFILE,statusPtr);
   //
   //----------------------------------------------------------------------
   //--[R4]  if project.staffing is full then risk is high;"
   //----------------------------------------------------------------------
   //
     Rulecnt++;
     fprintf(mdlout,"%s\n",projRules[Rulecnt]);
   //
   //--Compute membership of project staff size in this fuzzy region, and
   //--then use the truth of this to compute the output (solution) set.
   //
     PremiseTruth=FzyGetMembership(
          stfFDBptr[FULLstaffing],PJstaffing,&Idxpos,statusPtr);
     fprintf(mdlout,"%s%10.2f\n","PremiseTruth= ",PremiseTruth);
     FzyCondProposition(
        rskFDBptr[HIGHrisk],FSVptr,thisCorrMethod,PremiseTruth,statusPtr);
     FzyDrawSet(RiskFDBptr,SYSMODFILE,statusPtr);
   //
   //----------------------------------------------------------------------
   //--Defuzzify to find expected value for risk.
   //----------------------------------------------------------------------
   //
     *riskoutFDBptr=RiskFDBptr;
     Risk=FzyDefuzzify(RiskFDBptr,thisDefuzzMethod,&CompIDX,statusPtr);
     fsetheight=FzyGetHeight(RiskFDBptr);
     fprintf(mdlout,"%s\n","Model Solution:");
     fprintf(mdlout,"%s%10.2f\n","  Risk        = ",Risk        );
     fprintf(mdlout,"%s%10.2f\n","  CompIdx      = ",CompIDX      );
     fprintf(mdlout,"%s%10.2f\n","  SurfaceHght = ",fsetheight  );
   //
     *CIX=CompIDX;
     FzyCloseFZYctl(statusPtr);
     return(Risk);
    }
   //
   //
   //
   double ProjectRisk2(
       float     expWgt,         // the peer ranking of this expert
       FDB      **riskoutFDBptr, // pointer to the output fuzzy set
       double    PJduration,     // project duration
       double    PJbudget,       // project budget
       double    PJstaffing,     // project staffing
       float    *CIX,            // compatibility index
       int      *statusPtr)      // status code
    {
     FDB     *RiskFDBptr;
     VDB     *VDBptr;
     FSV     *FSVptr;
     int      Idxpos,
              Rulecnt,
              thisCorrMethod,
              thisDefuzzMethod;
     float    CompIDX,
              fsetheight,
              PremiseTruth;
     double   Domain[2],Risk,NoRisk=0;
     FILE    *mdlout;
     char *projRules[]=
      {
```

```
        "[R1]  if project.duration is long then risk is moderate;",
        "[R2]  if project.budget is high then risk is acceptable;",
        "[R3]  if project.staffing is full then risk is low;"
       };
     *statusPtr=0;
     mdlout=MtsGetSystemFile(SYSMODFILE);
     fprintf(mdlout,"%s\n%s%s%s\n%s\n\n",
       "-------------------------------------------------------------------",
       " Risk Assessment Policy [Expert: ",expNames[1]."] begins.",
       "-------------------------------------------------------------------");
     Domain[0]=  0;
     Domain[1]=100;
     VDBptr=VarCreateScalar("RISK",REAL,Domain,"0",statusPtr);
     FzyInitFZYctl(statusPtr);
     if(!(FzyAddFZYctl(VDBptr,&RiskFDBptr,&FSVptr,statusPtr)))
       {
        *statusPtr=1;
        MtsSendError(12,PgmId,"RISK");
        return(NoRisk);
        }
     thisCorrMethod  =CORRPRODUCT;
     thisDefuzzMethod=FSVptr->FzySVdefuzzMethod;
     Rulecnt=0;
     fprintf(mdlout,"%s\n","Rule Execution....");
//
//-------------------------------------------------------------------------
//--[R1]  if project.duration is long then risk is moderate;
//-------------------------------------------------------------------------
//
     fprintf(mdlout,"%s\n",projRules[Rulecnt]);
//
//--Compute membership of project duration in this fuzzy region, and
//--then use the truth of this to compute the output (solution) set.
//
     PremiseTruth=FzyGetMembership(
     durFDBptr[LONGduration],PJduration,&Idxpos,statusPtr);
     fprintf(mdlout,"%s%10.2f\n","PremiseTruth= ",PremiseTruth);
     FzyCondProposition(
       rskFDBptr[MODERATErisk],FSVptr,thisCorrMethod,PremiseTruth,statusPtr);
     FzyDrawSet(RiskFDBptr,SYSMODFILE,statusPtr);
//
//-------------------------------------------------------------------------
//--[R2]  if project.budget is high then risk is acceptable;
//-------------------------------------------------------------------------
//
     Rulecnt++;
     fprintf(mdlout,"%s\n",projRules[Rulecnt]);
//
//--Compute membership of project budget in this fuzzy region, and
//--then use the truth of this to compute the output (solution) set.
//
     PremiseTruth=FzyGetMembership(
        budFDBptr[HIGHbudget],PJbudget,&Idxpos,statusPtr);
     fprintf(mdlout,"%s%10.2f\n","PremiseTruth= ",PremiseTruth);
     FzyCondProposition(
       rskFDBptr[ACCEPTABLErisk],FSVptr,thisCorrMethod,PremiseTruth,statusPtr);
     FzyDrawSet(RiskFDBptr,SYSMODFILE,statusPtr);
//
//-------------------------------------------------------------------------
//--[R3]  if project.staffing is full then risk is low;
//-------------------------------------------------------------------------
//
     Rulecnt++;
```

```
        fprintf(mdlout,"%s\n",projRules[Rulecnt]);
//
//--Compute membership of project staff size in this fuzzy region, and
//--then use the truth of this to compute the output (solution) set.
//
    PremiseTruth=FzyGetMembership(
        stfFDBptr[FULLstaffing],PJstaffing,&Idxpos,statusPtr);
    fprintf(mdlout,"%s%10.2f\n","PremiseTruth= ",PremiseTruth);
    FzyCondProposition(
        rskFDBptr[LOWrisk],FSVptr,thisCorrMethod,PremiseTruth,statusPtr);
    FzyDrawSet(RiskFDBptr,SYSMODFILE,statusPtr);
//
//--Defuzzify to find expected value for risk
//
    *riskoutFDBptr=RiskFDBptr;
    Risk=FzyDefuzzify(RiskFDBptr,thisDefuzzMethod,&CompIDX,statusPtr);
    fsetheight=FzyGetHeight(RiskFDBptr);
    fprintf(mdlout,"%s\n","Model Solution:");
    fprintf(mdlout,"%s%10.2f\n","   Risk        = ",Risk       );
    fprintf(mdlout,"%s%10.2f\n","   CompIdx      = ",CompIDX     );
    fprintf(mdlout,"%s%10.2f\n","   SurfaceHght = ",fsetheight  );
//
    *CIX=CompIDX;
    FzyCloseFZYctl(statusPtr);
    return(Risk);
  }
```

Code for Chapter 6. Adaptive and Feed-Back Fuzzy Models

fzyifam.cpp (The Fuzzy Inventory Control Program)

```
/*------------------------------------------------------------*
| (c) 1995 Metus Systems.      Proprietary software product. |
| Reproduction or unauthorized use is prohibited. Unauthorized|
| use is illegal. Violators will be prosecuted. This software |
| contains proprietary trade and business secrets.           |
*--------------------Procedure Description--------------------*
| fzyifam.cpp  Earl Cox  07/12/93 The Inventory FAM           |
|                                                             |
| This is a simple fuzzy inventory model based on a supply    |
| and demand model. We have rules that adjust the inventory   |
| base on the product demand and the current quantity in      |
| stock. The model  is cast in  the form a FAM.               |
|                                                             |
|                         product demand volume               |
| qoh      FALLING   REDUCED   STEADY   INCREASED   RISING     |
|         +--------+--------+--------+-----------+--------+    |
| MINIMAL |  ZR    |  SP    |  MP    |    MP     |  LP    |    |
|         +--------+--------+--------+-----------+--------+    |
| LOW     |  ZR    |  SP    |  MP    |    LP     |  LP    |    |
|         +--------+--------+--------+-----------+--------+    |
| NEAR.ERP|  SN    |  ZR    |  SP    |    MP     |  LP    |    |
|         +--------+--------+--------+-----------+--------+    |
| HIGH    |  MN    |  SN    |  ZR    |    SP     |  MP    |    |
|         +--------+--------+--------+-----------+--------+    |
| EXCESS  |  LN    |  MN    |  SN    |    ZR     |  SP    |    |
|         +--------+--------+--------+-----------+--------+    |
|                                                             |
|  As we execute each inventory action, this changes the      |
|  current quantity on-hand that leads to a change in the     |
|  system state for the next interation of the rule analysis. |
|                                                             |
*---------------Modification Audit/Change Log----------------*
| Rev  Sar           Metus                                    |
| No   Code  Date    Rellvl  Mod  Description                 |
| --   ----- -------- ------  ---  ------------------------    |
|                                                             |
*------------------------------------------------------------*/
#include <string.h>
#include <stdio.h>
#include <stdlib.h>
#include <math.h>
#include "FDB.hpp"
#include "FSV.hpp"
#include "VDB.hpp"
#include "SSYSctl.hpp"
#include "SFZYctl.hpp"
#include "fuzzy.hpp"
#include "mtypes.hpp"
#include "mtsptype.hpp"
char far * far dmdFDBnames[]=
   {
    "FALLING",
    "REDUCED",
    "STEADY",
    "INCREASED",
    "RISING"
   };
char far * far dmdFDBdesc[]=
```

```
          {
          "Significant decrease in product demand",
          "Moderate decrease in product demand",
          "More or less steady demand for product",
          "Moderate increase in product demand",
          "Significant increase in product demand"
          };
        char far * far qtyFDBnames[]=
          {
          "MINIMAL",
          "LOW",
          "NEAR.ERP",
          "HIGH",
          "EXCESSIVE"
          };
        char far * far qtyFDBdesc[]=
          {
          "Quantity on hand is near depletion levels",
          "Quantity on hand is below the reorder point",
          "Quantity on hand is around the economic reorder point [ERP]",
          "Quantity on hand is above the reorder point",
          "Quantity on hand is well above required stockage"
          };
        char far * far invFDBnames[]=
          {
          "LN",
          "MN",
          "SN",
          "ZR",
          "SP",
          "MP",
          "LP"
          };
        char far * far invFDBdesc[]=
          {
          "Make large decrease in surplus inventory",
          "Make moderate decrease in surplus inventory",
          "Make small decrease in surplus inventory",
          "Keep inventory at current stockage level",
          "Make small increase in current inventory",
          "Make moderate increase in current inventory",
          "Make large increase in current inventory"
          };
        const int FzyTermMax=9;
        //            FALLING   REDUCED   STEADY  INCREASED  RISING
        double dmdPoint[]={-30, -10,  -20, 0, -10, 10,  0, 20,  10, 30};
        double invPoint[]=
        // ---LN--- ---MN--- ---SN--- ---ZR--- ---SP--- ---MP--- ---LP---
          {-45, -30, -45, -15, -30,  0, -15, 15, 0,  30, 15,  45, 30,  45};
        void main(void)
          {
          FDB    *dmdFDBptr[FzyTermMax],
                 *qtyFDBptr[FzyTermMax],
                 *invFDBptr[FzyTermMax];
          int    dmdFDBcnt=5,
                 qtyFDBcnt=5,
                 invFDBcnt=7;
          char   *PgmId="fzyifam";
          int    i,j,k,n,status;
          double ERP,
                 ERPwidth,
                 PIcenter,
                 SCstart,
                 SCmidpt,
```

```
          SCend;
  FILE  *mdllog;
  status=0;
  printf("%s\n","The Fuzzy Inventory Supply and Demand Model");
  printf("%s\n","(c) 1995 The Metus Systems Group          ");
  SysConnecttoMetus(&status);
  XSYSctl.XSYSalfacut=0.1;
//
  XSYSctl.XSYStrace[3]=TRUE;
  XSYSctl.XSYStrace[2]=TRUE;
//
  mdllog=MtsGetSystemFile(SYSMODFILE);
//
//
/*-------------------------------------------------------------*
|            QUARTERLY PRODUCT DEMAND VOLUMES                   |
|  These fuzzy sets (for the QtrlyDemand variable) define the   |
|  meaning for positive, negative or steady sakes orders/       |
*-------------------------------------------------------------*/
  fprintf(mdllog,"%s\n","---Creating quarterly demand volume fuzzy sets");
  k=0;
  for(i=0;i<dmdFDBcnt;i++)
    {
    dmdFDBptr[i]=new FDB;
    FzyInitFDB(dmdFDBptr[i]);
    strcpy(dmdFDBptr[i]->FDBid,  dmdFDBnames[i]);
    strcpy(dmdFDBptr[i]->FDBdesc,dmdFDBdesc[i]);
    dmdFDBptr[i]->FDBdomain[0]=dmdPoint[k];
    dmdFDBptr[i]->FDBdomain[1]=dmdPoint[k+1];
    k+=2;
    }
  FzySCurve (dmdFDBptr[0],-30,-20,-10,DECLINE,&status); //FALLING
  FzyPiCurve(dmdFDBptr[1],-10, 10         ,&status); //REDUCED
  FzyPiCurve(dmdFDBptr[2],  0, 10         ,&status); //STEADY
  FzyPiCurve(dmdFDBptr[3], 10, 10         ,&status); //INCREASED
  FzySCurve (dmdFDBptr[4], 10, 20, 30,GROWTH ,&status); //RISING
  FzyPlotVar("ITEM.DEMAND",dmdFDBptr,dmdFDBcnt,SYSMODFILE,&status);
//
//
/*-------------------------------------------------------------*
|            CURRENT WAREHOUSE ON-HAND QUANTITIES               |
|  These fuzzy sets (for the QntyOnHand variable) define the    |
|  meaning  for stockage levels that are above or below the     |
|  current economic reorder point for the product.              |
*-------------------------------------------------------------*/
  fprintf(mdllog,"%s\n","---Creating on-hand quantities fuzzy sets");
  ERP=160;
  ERPwidth     =ERP*.10;
  for(i=0;i<qtyFDBcnt;i++)
    {
    qtyFDBptr[i]=new FDB;
    FzyInitFDB(qtyFDBptr[i]);
    strcpy(qtyFDBptr[i]->FDBid,  qtyFDBnames[i]);
    strcpy(qtyFDBptr[i]->FDBdesc,qtyFDBdesc[i]);
    }
//--Define the center of the fuzzy region.
    qtyFDBptr[2]->FDBdomain[0]=ERP-ERPwidth;
    qtyFDBptr[2]->FDBdomain[1]=ERP+ERPwidth;
  FzyPiCurve(qtyFDBptr[2],ERP,    ERPwidth,           &status);
//
//--Define the right pi region
    qtyFDBptr[3]->FDBdomain[0]=ERP;
    qtyFDBptr[3]->FDBdomain[1]=ERP+(2*ERPwidth);
  PIcenter=ERP+ERPwidth;
```

```
      FzyPiCurve(qtyFDBptr[3],PIcenter,ERPwidth,                &status);
//
//--Define the right S-curve region
   SCstart=PIcenter; SCend=PIcenter+(2*ERPwidth);
   SCmidpt=SCstart+((SCend-SCstart)/2);
      qtyFDBptr[4]->FDBdomain[0]=SCstart;
      qtyFDBptr[4]->FDBdomain[1]=SCend;
   FzySCurve (qtyFDBptr[4],SCstart,SCmidpt,SCend,GROWTH ,&status);
//
//--Define the left pi region
      qtyFDBptr[1]->FDBdomain[1]=ERP;
      qtyFDBptr[1]->FDBdomain[0]=ERP-(2*ERPwidth);
   PIcenter=ERP-ERPwidth;
   FzyPiCurve(qtyFDBptr[1],PIcenter,ERPwidth,                &status);
//
//--Define the left S-curve region
   SCstart=PIcenter-(2*ERPwidth); SCend=PIcenter;
   SCmidpt=SCstart+((SCend-SCstart)/2);
      qtyFDBptr[0]->FDBdomain[0]=SCstart;
      qtyFDBptr[0]->FDBdomain[1]=SCend;
   FzySCurve (qtyFDBptr[0],SCstart,SCmidpt,SCend,DECLINE,&status);
   FzyPlotVar("QTY.ON-HAND",qtyFDBptr,qtyFDBcnt,SYSMODFILE,&status);
//
//
/*-------------------------------------------------------------*
|           SURPLUS OR SHORTAGE INVENTORY ACTIONS             |
|   These fuzzy sets (for the TakeInvAction variable) define  |
|   the action we should take for combinations of quarterly   |
|   demand and on-hand stockage. The action specifies a percent|
|   change in the current inventory stockage level.           |
*-------------------------------------------------------------*/
   fprintf(mdllog,"%s\n","---Creating inventory action fuzzy sets");
   k=0;
   for(i=0;i<invFDBcnt;i++)
     {
      invFDBptr[i]=new FDB;
      FzyInitFDB(invFDBptr[i]);
      strcpy(invFDBptr[i]->FDBid,invFDBnames[i]);
      strcpy(invFDBptr[i]->FDBdesc,invFDBdesc[i]);
      invFDBptr[i]->FDBdomain[0]= -45;
      invFDBptr[i]->FDBdomain[1]=  45;
      k+=2;
     }
   FzySCurve (invFDBptr[0],-45,-37.5,-30,DECLINE,&status); //LN
   FzyPiCurve(invFDBptr[1],-30,  15,          &status); //MN
   FzyPiCurve(invFDBptr[2],-15,  15,          &status); //SN
   FzyPiCurve(invFDBptr[3],  0,  15,          &status); //ZR
   FzyPiCurve(invFDBptr[4], 15,  15,          &status); //SP
   FzyPiCurve(invFDBptr[5], 30,  15,          &status); //MP
   FzySCurve (invFDBptr[6], 30, 37.5, 45,GROWTH ,&status); //LP
   FzyPlotVar("INV.ACTION",invFDBptr,invFDBcnt,SYSMODFILE,&status);
/*-------------------------------------------------------------*
|        EXECUTE THE FAM-BASED FUZZY INVENTORY MODEL          |
|                                                             |
|   In this mdoel we start at a base quantity on-hand [QOH] and|
|   an economic reorder point [ERP]. Each cycle of the model  |
|   reads a new product demand value and calculates a new QOH |
|   from the inventory action.                                |
*-------------------------------------------------------------*/
   FDB     *ivaFDBptr,*rsltFDBptr;
   FSV     *FSVptr;
   VDB     *invVDBptr;
   double  DemandDeltas[45];
   double  ProductDemand[]=
```

```
                    {10,15,35,35,33,29,28,17,9,8,0,0,8,25,21};
       double  PrevDemand=0;
       int     MAXdemands=15;
       int     thisCorrMethod,thisDefuzzMethod,idx;
       double  QOH,pdQOH[24],Domain[2],currDemand,invAction[24],adjfactor[24];
       float   dmdmem,qtymem,rsltmem,CIX,pdCIX[24];
       FDB *FAM[5][5]=
        {
         {invFDBptr[3],invFDBptr[4],invFDBptr[5],invFDBptr[5],invFDBptr[6]},
         {invFDBptr[3],invFDBptr[4],invFDBptr[5],invFDBptr[6],invFDBptr[6]},
         {invFDBptr[2],invFDBptr[3],invFDBptr[4],invFDBptr[5],invFDBptr[6]},
         {invFDBptr[1],invFDBptr[2],invFDBptr[3],invFDBptr[4],invFDBptr[5]},
         {invFDBptr[0],invFDBptr[1],invFDBptr[2],invFDBptr[3],invFDBptr[4]}
        };
       fprintf(mdllog,"%s\n","---Executing Inventory Management Policy");
       QOH= 70;
       Domain[0]=-45;Domain[1]=45;
       invVDBptr=VarCreateScalar("InvAction",REAL,Domain,"0",&status);
       FzyInitFZYctl(&status);
       if(!(FzyAddFZYctl(invVDBptr,&ivaFDBptr,&FSVptr,&status)))
         {
          MtsSendError(12,PgmId,"InvAction");
          exit(9);
         }
       thisCorrMethod  =FSVptr->FzySVcorrMethod;
       thisDefuzzMethod=FSVptr->FzySVdefuzzMethod;
//--Inventory management model. How much inventory should we keep
//--based on demand and the amount already in-stock? This model
//--generates an inventory action based on these factors that is
//--used to produce a new quantity-on-hand for the next cycle.
//
       if(QOH<1.0)
         {
          fprintf(mdllog,"%s\n",
           "Caution. Current QOH negative or zero. QOH=1 assumed.");
          QOH=1;
         }
       fprintf(mdllog,"%s%10.2f\n",
        "Quantity On-Hand        [QOH]: ", QOH);
       fprintf(mdllog,"%s%10.2f\n",
        "Economic Reorder Point  [ERP]: ", ERP);
       pdQOH[0]=QOH;
       pdCIX[0]=1.0;
       for(i=0;i<MAXdemands;i++)
         {
          currDemand=ProductDemand[i]-PrevDemand;
          DemandDeltas[i]=currDemand;
          fprintf(mdllog,"%3d. %s%10.2f%s%10.2f%s%10.2f\n",
           i+1,"QOH: ",QOH,". Demand: ",ProductDemand[i],
              ", ChngDemand: ",currDemand);
          fprintf(mdllog,"\n%s\n","--------------------------------");
          dmdmem=0;
//
//--Look at each demand fuzzy region and find the degree of
//--membership for the current demand in these FAM columns/
          for(j=0;j<dmdFDBcnt;j++)
            {
             qtymem=0;
             dmdmem=FzyGetMembership(dmdFDBptr[j],currDemand,&idx,&status);
             if(dmdmem>0)
               for(k=0;k<qtyFDBcnt;k++)
                 {
                  qtymem=FzyGetMembership(qtyFDBptr[k],QOH,&idx,&status);
                  if(qtymem!=0)
```

```
            {
            fprintf(mdllog,"%3d. %s%s%s%s%s\n",i+1,"Rule [",
            dmdFDBptr[j]->FDBid,",",qtyFDBptr[k]->FDBid,"]");
            rsltmem=min(dmdmem,qtymem);
            rsltFDBptr=FAM[k][j];
            FzyCondProposition(
              rsltFDBptr,FSVptr,thisCorrMethod,rsltmem,&status);
            fprintf(mdllog,
              "%s%2d%s%2d%s%s%s%5.3f%s%s%s%s%5.3f%s\n%s%s%s%5.3f%s\n",
              "FAM(",k,",",j,"): if QOH is ",
                qtyFDBptr[k]->FDBid," [",qtymem,"] and ",
              "Demand is ",dmdFDBptr[j]->FDBid," [",dmdmem,"]",
              "                    then InvAction is ",
                rsltFDBptr->FDBid," [",rsltmem,"];");
            FzyDrawSet(ivaFDBptr,SYSMODFILE,&status);
            }
          }
        }
    invAction[i]=FzyDefuzzify(ivaFDBptr,thisDefuzzMethod,&CIX,&status);
    if(invAction[i]<0) adjfactor[i]=1-(fabs(invAction[i])/100);
       else           adjfactor[i]=1+(invAction[i]/100);
     fprintf(mdllog,"%s%12.3f\n","invAction   : ",invAction);
    QOH*=adjfactor[i];
     fprintf(mdllog,"%s%12.3f\n","QOH         : ",QOH);
    QOH=ceil(MtsRound(QOH,1,&status));
     fprintf(mdllog,"%s%12.3f\n","round(QOH)  : ",QOH);
    pdQOH[i+1]=QOH;
    pdCIX[i+1]=CIX;
//--Now reset the output fuzzy set. We only have one output
//--variable so we do it directly instead of calling FzyResetFZYctl.
    for(n=0;n<VECMAX;n++) ivaFDBptr->FDBvector[n]=0;
    ivaFDBptr->FDBempty=TRUE;
    PrevDemand=ProductDemand[i];
    }
  fprintf(mdllog,"%s\n%s\n%s\n",
    "                Period    [+/-] ",
    "      QOH      Demand    Demand     invAction   CIX    adjfactor",
    "---    --------   --------   --------   ---------   -----   --------- ");
  for(i=0;i<MAXdemands;i++)
    fprintf(mdllog,"%2d.   %8.2f   %8.2f   %8.2f   %9.2f   %5.3f   %9.2f\n",
     i+1,pdQOH[i],ProductDemand[i],
       DemandDeltas[i],invAction[i],pdCIX[i],adjfactor[i]);
  fprintf(mdllog,"%s\n"," ");
  return;
  }
```

orgdyn1.cpp (The Organizational Dynamics Model Driver)

```
*-------------------------------------------------------------*/
#include <stdio.h>
#include <string.h>
#include <math.h>
#include "PDB.hpp"
#include "FDB.hpp"
#include "SSYSctl.hpp"
#include "fuzzy.hpp"
#include "mtypes.hpp"
#include "mtsptype.hpp"
static const Rulemax=5;
extern unsigned _stklen=50000;
PDB* MdlCreatePolicy(char*,int,int*);
#define MAXFZYSETS  16
#define MAXPERIODS  16
double   RulesPOLICY(int,double);
double   GoalPOLICY(int,double,double);
double   SupervisionPOLICY(int,double,double);
double   RelationPOLICY(int,double*,double,double,double);
void     CaptureFuzzySet(char*,FDB*,int*);
//
void main(void)
 {
  PDB      *orgPDBptr;
  FDB      *FDBptr[MAXFZYSETS];
  int      j,t,status,Hdgcnt,TryCtl[2];
  bool     trace,storfs;
  double   Parms[4],
           Domain[2],
           tenlvl,
           rullvl,
           gsfall,
           suplvl,
           relvis;
  FILE     *mdlout,
           *rptout;
//
//
//===============================================================
//--The TIME SERIES and PERIOD Variables. These are the variables used
//--to hold the values of the organizational dynamics model in each
//--successive time period.
//===============================================================
//
//
//                                              R A N G E
//                                         Minimum      Maximum
//                                         -------      -------
  double   TensionLevel    [MAXPERIODS], //      0          100
           RuleLevelChange  [MAXPERIODS], //    -20           20
           RuleLevel        [MAXPERIODS], //      0          100
           BehaviorAwareness [MAXPERIODS], //     0          100
           GoalShortfall    [MAXPERIODS], //      0          100
           GoalChange       [MAXPERIODS], //      0          100
           SVChange         [MAXPERIODS], //   -100          100
           Supervision      [MAXPERIODS], //   -100          100
           RelationVisibility[MAXPERIODS]; //  -100          100
  double   PDtension,
           PDChangeRV;
  SysConnecttoMetus(&status);
  orgPDBptr=MdlCreatePolicy("ORGDYNS",MODELADD,&status);
  XSYSctl.XSYScurrPDBptr=orgPDBptr;
  XSYSctl.XSYSalfacut   =0.1;
//
  XSYSctl.XSYStrace[3]=TRUE;
```

```
  XSYSctl.XSYStrace[2]=TRUE;
//

  MdlInsertHedges(orgPDBptr,&Hdgcnt,&status);
  mdlout=MtsGetSystemFile(SYSMODFILE);
//
//
  printf("INITIALIZE MODEL\n");
  TryCtl[0]=5;
  TryCtl[1]=0;
  Domain[0]=0;Domain[1]=100;
  tenlvl=MtsAskforDBL(
    "TensionLevel",  "Tension Level       : ",Domain,TryCtl,&status);
  rullvl=MtsAskforDBL(
    "RuleLevel",     "Rule Level          : ",Domain,TryCtl,&status);
  gsfall=MtsAskforDBL(
    "Goal Shortfall","Goal Shortfall      : ",Domain,TryCtl,&status);
  suplvl=MtsAskforDBL(
    "Supervision",   "Supervision         : ",Domain,TryCtl,&status);
  relvis=MtsAskforDBL(
    "RelationVis",   "RelationVisibility : ",Domain,TryCtl,&status);
  printf("SPECIFY MODEL ACTIONS\n");
  trace =MtsAskforBOOL(
    "fzySetTrace",   "Trace FuzzySets     : ",         TryCtl,&status);
  XSYSctl.XSYStrace[3]=trace;
  trace =MtsAskforBOOL(
    "RuleTrace",     "Trace Rule Actions : ",         TryCtl,&status);
  XSYSctl.XSYStrace[2]=trace;
  storfs=MtsAskforBOOL(
    "StoreSets",     "Store FuzzySets     : ",         TryCtl,&status);
//
//============================================================================
//--The TENSION LEVEL fuzzy regions. These represent relative degrees
//--of tension in the organization on a scale from 0 (none) to 100 (high).
//============================================================================
//
  Domain[0]=  0;Domain[1]= 100;
   Parms[0]=0;   Parms[1]=  25;   Parms[2]=50;
  FDBptr[0]=FzyCreateSet("LOW", DECLINE,Domain,Parms,3,&status);
  if(storfs)
    CaptureFuzzySet("b:low.txt",FDBptr[0],&status);
  MdlLinkFDB(FDBptr[0],orgPDBptr,&status);
  Domain[0]=  0;Domain[1]= 100;
   Parms[0]=25;  Parms[1]=  25;
  FDBptr[1]=FzyCreateSet("LOWISH", PI,Domain,Parms,2,&status);
  if(storfs)
    CaptureFuzzySet("b:lowish.txt",FDBptr[1],&status);
  MdlLinkFDB(FDBptr[1],orgPDBptr,&status);
  Domain[0]=  0;Domain[1]= 100;
   Parms[0]= 75; Parms[1]=  25;
  FDBptr[2]=FzyCreateSet("HIGHISH", PI,Domain,Parms,2,&status);
  if(storfs)
    CaptureFuzzySet("b:highish.txt",FDBptr[2],&status);
  MdlLinkFDB(FDBptr[2],orgPDBptr,&status);
  Domain[0]=  0;Domain[1]= 100;
   Parms[0]= 50; Parms[1]=  75;   Parms[2]=100;
  FDBptr[3]=FzyCreateSet("HIGH", GROWTH,Domain,Parms,3,&status);
  if(storfs)
    CaptureFuzzySet("b:high.txt",FDBptr[3],&status);
  MdlLinkFDB(FDBptr[3],orgPDBptr,&status);
  FzyPlotTermSet("TENSION.LEVEL",FDBptr,4,SYSMODFILE,&status);
//
//============================================================================
//--The MODEL STATE CHANGE fuzzy regions. These represent relative degrees
```

```
//--of changes of such factors as rule enforcement, supervision, etc. This
//---is measured on a scale from -100 (extremely weak) to +100 (very strong)
//=============================================================================
//
  Domain[0]=-100;Domain[1]=100;
   Parms[0]= -20; Parms[1]= 20;
  FDBptr[0]=FzyCreateSet("DECREASE", PI,     Domain,Parms,2,&status);
  if(storfs)
    CaptureFuzzySet("b:decrease.txt",FDBptr[0],&status);
  MdlLinkFDB(FDBptr[0],orgPDBptr,&status);
  Domain[0]=-100;Domain[1]=100;
   Parms[0]=   0; Parms[1]= 20;
  FDBptr[1]=FzyCreateSet("NO.CHANGE", PI,     Domain,Parms,2,&status);
  if(storfs)
    CaptureFuzzySet("b:nochng.txt",FDBptr[1],&status);
  MdlLinkFDB(FDBptr[1],orgPDBptr,&status);
  Domain[0]=-100;Domain[1]=100;
   Parms[0]=  20; Parms[1]= 20;
  FDBptr[2]=FzyCreateSet("INCREASE", PI,     Domain,Parms,2,&status);
  if(storfs)
    CaptureFuzzySet("b:increase.txt",FDBptr[2],&status);
  MdlLinkFDB(FDBptr[2],orgPDBptr,&status);
  FzyPlotTermSet("CHANGE.METRICS",FDBptr,3,SYSMODFILE,&status);
//
//=============================================================================
//--The MODEL INITIALIZATION PHASE. We loop through the time horizons and
//---set each value to zero. We then go back and initialize the first two
//---time periods (since the model as a [-2] lag architecture).
//=============================================================================
//
  for(t=0;t<MAXPERIODS;t++)
     {
     TensionLevel        [t]=0;
     RuleLevelChange     [t]=0;
     RuleLevel           [t]=0;
     BehaviorAwareness   [t]=0;
     GoalShortfall       [t]=0;
     GoalChange          [t]=0;
     SVChange            [t]=0;
     Supervision         [t]=0;
     RelationVisibility[t]=0;
     }
//
  for(t=0;t<2;t++)
     {
     TensionLevel        [t]=tenlvl;
     RuleLevel           [t]=rullvl;
     GoalShortfall       [t]=gsfall;
     Supervision         [t]=suplvl;
     RelationVisibility[t]=relvis;
     }
//
//=============================================================================
//--The MODEL EXECUTION PROCESS. This is the main logic of the organizational
//---dynamics model. We start in period three of the time frame and loop over
//---each time frame invoking the fuzzy policies to compute the period data.
//=============================================================================
//
  for(t=2;t<MAXPERIODS;t++)
     {
     printf("%s%3d\n","Time Period: ",t-1);
     /*-------------------------------------------------------*
     | First we assess the level at which bureaucratic rules |
     | are being applied. This depends on the tension level  |
```

```
| two periods ago.                                                |
*----------------------------------------------------------------*/
    PDtension               =TensionLevel[t-2];
    RuleLevelChange[t]      =RulesPOLICY(t,PDtension);
    RuleLevel[t]            =RuleLevel[t-1]+RuleLevelChange[t];
    RuleLevel[t]            =max(min(RuleLevel[t],100),0);
    /*----------------------------------------------------------*
    | We now assess the level of performance against target.|
    | This depends on the current level of tension and the  |
    | worker's knowledge of minimum acceptable behavior.    |
    *----------------------------------------------------------*/
    TensionLevel[t]         =RelationVisibility[t-1];
    BehaviorAwareness[t]    =RuleLevel[t];
    GoalShortfall[t]        =GoalPOLICY(t,BehaviorAwareness[t],TensionLevel[t]);
    GoalChange[t]           =GoalShortfall[t]-GoalShortfall[t-1];
    /*----------------------------------------------------------*
    | We now look at the change in supervision policy. This |
    | depends on the performance (goal) shortfall.          |
    *----------------------------------------------------------*/
    SVChange[t]             =SupervisionPOLICY(t,GoalShortfall[t],GoalChange[t]);
    Supervision[t]          =Supervision[t-1]+SVChange[t];
    Supervision[t]          =max(min(Supervision[t],100),0);
    /*----------------------------------------------------------*
    | Finally we examine the visibility of power relations. |
    | This depends on the supervision level and the change  |
    | in the application of bureaucratic rules.             |
    *----------------------------------------------------------*/
    RelationVisibility[t]=
        RelationPOLICY(t,&PDChangeRV,Supervision[t],RuleLevel[t],RuleLevelChange[t]);
    RelationVisibility[t]=RelationVisibility[t]+PDChangeRV;
    //
    //--Now we take a snap shot of the mode state in this time frame and
    //--post it to the model log. We may want to discontinue this or make
    //--it conditional in a production system.
    //
    fprintf(mdlout,"\n%s%4d\n",  "Model State. Time:",t-1);
    fprintf(mdlout,"%s%7.2f\n",  " Previous Tension      : ",PDtension);
    fprintf(mdlout,"%s%7.2f\n",  " Tension Level         : ",TensionLevel[t]);
    fprintf(mdlout,"%s%7.2f\n",  " Rule Level            : ",RuleLevel[t]);
    fprintf(mdlout,"%s%7.2f\n",  " Rule LevelChange      : ",RuleLevelChange[t]);
    fprintf(mdlout,"%s%7.2f\n",  " Goal Shortfall        : ",GoalShortfall[t]);
    fprintf(mdlout,"%s%7.2f\n",  " Goal Change           : ",GoalChange[t]);
    fprintf(mdlout,"%s%7.2f\n",  " Supervision           : ",Supervision[t]);
    fprintf(mdlout,"%s%7.2f\n",  " Supervision Change    : ",SVChange[t]);
    fprintf(mdlout,"%s%7.2f\n",  " Relation Visibility   : ",RelationVisibility[t]);
    fprintf(mdlout,"%s%7.2f\n",  " Visibility Change     : ",PDChangeRV);
    fprintf(mdlout,"%s\n\n",     "         ");
    }
//
//
//==============================================================================
//--The MODEL REPORT PHASE. When the model is complete, we open a new file
//--and write a report that shows the model data in each time frame. In this
//--report, time period (P1) is actually time frame three in the horizon.
//==============================================================================
//
//
  if((rptout=fopen("b:odrpt.fil","w"))==NULL)
    {
    printf("Sorry. 'b:orgrpt.fil' file was not created\n");
    return;
    }
  fprintf(rptout,"%s\n%s\n",
    "FUZZY ORGANIZATIONAL BEHAVIOR MODEL. (c) 1994 Metus Systems Group.",
```

```
                 "from: Gouldner [1954] 'Patterns of Industrial Bureaucracy'");
            fprintf(rptout,"%s\n","Initial Model Conditions:");
            fprintf(rptout,"%s%3.0f\n",  "Tension Level           : ",tenlvl);
            fprintf(rptout,"%s%3.0f\n",  "Rule Level              : ",rullvl);
            fprintf(rptout,"%s%3.0f\n",  "Goal Shortfall          : ",gsfall);
            fprintf(rptout,"%s%3.0f\n",  "Supervision             : ",suplvl);
            fprintf(rptout,"%s%3.0f\n",  "Relation Visibility : ",relvis);
            fprintf(rptout,"\n%s\n%s\n",
            "                                       P1  P2  P3  P4  P5  P6  P7  P8  P9
   P10  P11  P12",
            "                                       --- --- --- --- --- --- --- --- --- -
-- --- ---");
          fprintf(rptout,"%-32.32s  ","Effective Present tension Level");
          for(j=2;j<14;j++)
            if((fabs(TensionLevel[j]))<1)  fprintf(rptout,"%.3s  "," ");
             else fprintf(rptout,"%3.0f  ",TensionLevel[j]);
          fprintf(rptout,"%c",'\n');
          fprintf(rptout,"%-32.32s  ","Change in Rule Application Level");
          for(j=2;j<14;j++)
            if((fabs(RuleLevelChange[j]))<1)  fprintf(rptout,"%.3s  "," ");
             else fprintf(rptout,"%3.0f  ",RuleLevelChange[j]);
          fprintf(rptout,"%c",'\n');
          fprintf(rptout,"%-32.32s  ","Rule Application Level");
          for(j=2;j<14;j++)
            if((fabs(RuleLevel[j]))<1)  fprintf(rptout,"%.3s  "," ");
             else fprintf(rptout,"%3.0f  ",RuleLevel[j]);
          fprintf(rptout,"%c",'\n');
          fprintf(rptout,"%-32.32s  ","Behavior Awareness Level");
          for(j=2;j<14;j++)
            if((fabs(BehaviorAwareness[j]))<1)  fprintf(rptout,"%.3s  "," ");
             else fprintf(rptout,"%3.0f  ",BehaviorAwareness[j]);
          fprintf(rptout,"%c",'\n');
          fprintf(rptout,"%-32.32s  ","Change in Goal Shortfall");
          for(j=2;j<14;j++)
            if((fabs(GoalChange[j]))<1)  fprintf(rptout,"%.3s  "," ");
             else fprintf(rptout,"%3.0f  ",GoalChange[j]);
          fprintf(rptout,"%c",'\n');
          fprintf(rptout,"%-32.32s  ","Achievement vs. Goal Shortfalls");
          for(j=2;j<14;j++)
            if((fabs(GoalShortfall[j]))<1)  fprintf(rptout,"%.3s  "," ");
             else fprintf(rptout,"%3.0f  ",GoalShortfall[j]);
          fprintf(rptout,"%c",'\n');
          fprintf(rptout,"%-32.32s  ","Change in Supervision Level");
          for(j=2;j<14;j++)
            if((fabs(SVChange[j]))<1) fprintf(rptout,"%.3s  "," ");
             else fprintf(rptout,"%3.0f  ",SVChange[j]);
          fprintf(rptout,"%c",'\n');
          fprintf(rptout,"%-32.32s  ","Active Supervision Level");
          for(j=2;j<14;j++)
            if((fabs(Supervision[j]))<1)  fprintf(rptout,"%.3s  "," ");
             else fprintf(rptout,"%3.0f  ",Supervision[j]);
          fprintf(rptout,"%c",'\n');
          fprintf(rptout,"%c",'\n');
          fclose(rptout);
          return;
         }
//
//
void CaptureFuzzySet(char *FzyDataFile,FDB *FDBptr,int *statusPtr)
/*-----------------------------------------------------------*
| This routine is used to capture and store the fuzzy set    |
| membership array on disk for use in fine-point graphics.   |
*-----------------------------------------------------------*/
 {
```

```
int      i,
         CompFactor= 16,
         MaxValues= 128,
         status,
         ExtCnt;
double   DomValues[128];
float    MemValues[128];
FILE     *fzyout;
*statusPtr=0;
if((fzyout=fopen(FzyDataFile,"w"))==NULL)
   {
   *statusPtr=1;
   printf("Sorry. '%s' file was not created\n",FzyDataFile);
   return;
   }
FzyExtractSetdata(FDBptr,CompFactor,DomValues,MemValues,&ExtCnt,&status);
for(i=0;i<ExtCnt;i++)
   fprintf(fzyout,"%10.2f  %6.4f\n",DomValues[i],MemValues[i]);
fclose(fzyout);
return;
}
```

orgglpd.cpp (The Organizational Dynamics Goal Policy)

```
/*--------------------------------------------------------------*
 | Copyright (c) 1993 by The Metus Systems Group.               |
 | All rights reserved. Proprietary Software Product.           |
 | No part of this software may be reproduced or transmitted    |
 | in any form or by any means, electronic or mechanical,       |
 | including input into or storage in any information system    |
 | for resale without permission in writing from Metus Systems. |
 *-------------------Procedure Description--------------------*
 | orgglpd.cpp   Earl Cox 04/01/93  Organizational dynamics    |
 *---------------Modification Audit/Change Log----------------*
 | Rev  Sar                                                     |
 | No   Code  Date      Rellvl  Mod  Description                |
 | --   ----- --------  ------  ---  ------------------------   |
 |                                                              |
 *--------------------------------------------------------------*/
#include <stdio.h>
#include <string.h>
#include "PDB.hpp"
#include "FDB.hpp"
#include "FSV.hpp"
#include "HDB.hpp"
#include "VDB.hpp"
#include "XFZYctl.hpp"
#include "XSYSctl.hpp"
#include "fuzzy.hpp"
#include "mtypes.hpp"
#include "mtsptype.hpp"
static const Rulemax=6;
#define MAXFZYSETS  16
#define MAXPERIODS  24
void PolicyHeader(int,char*);
void DisplayRule(char**,int,int);
double GoalPOLICY(int t,double PDbehavior,double PDtensionlvl)
  {
  char  *RPrules[]=
    {
    "R1 if the PDtensionlvl is not low                            ",
    "         then the GoalShortfall is about PDbehavior;         ",
```

```
           "R2 if the PDtensionlvl is low                                      ",
           "          then the GoalShotfall is about PDtensionlvl;             ",
       };
       PDB     *orgPDBptr;
       FDB     *gsfFDBptr,
               *loFDBptr,
               *notLoFDBptr,
               *nbehFDBptr,
               *ntenFDBptr;
       FSV     *gsfFSVptr;
       HDB     *nearHDBptr,
               *notHDBptr;
       VDB     *gsfVDBptr;
       char    *PgmId="orgglpd";
       int     status,
               Idxpos,
               Rulecnt,
               thisCorrMethod,
               thisDefuzzMethod;
       float   CompIDX,Predtruth;
       double  GoalShortfall,
               Parms[4],
               Domain[2];
       FILE    *mdlout;
       Rulecnt=0;
       printf("....Goal Policy.\n");
       PolicyHeader(t,"GoalPolicy");
       mdlout=MtsGetSystemFile(SYSMODFILE);
       fprintf(mdlout,"%s\n","Policy Parameters:");
       fprintf(mdlout,"%s%5.2f\n",   "PDbehavior     : ",PDbehavior);
       fprintf(mdlout,"%s%5.2f\n",   "PDtensionlvl   : ",PDtensionlvl);
//
//========================================================================
//--Create the output solution variable and put it into the fuzzy work area.
//--This craetes the output woprking fuzzy set and the fuzzy solution variable
//--block. We also extract the correlation and defuzzification methods.
//========================================================================
//
       Domain[0]=0; Domain[1]=100;
       gsfVDBptr=VarCreateScalar("GoalShortfall",REAL,Domain,"0",&status);
       FzyInitFZYctl(&status);
       if(!(FzyAddFZYctl(gsfVDBptr,&gsfFDBptr,&gsfFSVptr,&status)))
          {
           MtsSendError(12,PgmId,"RuleLevelChange");
           exit(9);
          }
       thisCorrMethod  =gsfFSVptr->FzySVcorrMethod;
       thisDefuzzMethod=gsfFSVptr->FzySVdefuzzMethod;
//
//========================================================================
//--Fetch the base fuzzy set from the policy dictionary, and fetch the needed
//--Hedges from the policy hedge dictionary.
//========================================================================
//
       orgPDBptr=XSYSctl.XSYScurrPDBptr;
       loFDBptr  =MdlFindFDB("LOW",        orgPDBptr,&status);
       nearHDBptr=MdlFindHDB("about",      orgPDBptr,&status);
       notHDBptr =MdlFindHDB("not",        orgPDBptr,&status);
//
//========================================================================
//--Now execute the rules by forming any dynamic fuzzy sets and finding the
//--appropriate membership values and then applying the correlation method.
//========================================================================
//
```

```
//-- R1 if the PDtensionlvl is not low
//           then the GoalShortfall is about PDbehavior;
//
  DisplayRule(RPrules,0,2);
  Domain[0]=loFDBptr->FDBdomain[0];
  Domain[1]=loFDBptr->FDBdomain[1];
  notLoFDBptr=FzyCreateSet("NOT.LOW",EMPTYSET,Domain,Parms,0,&status);
  FzyApplyHedge(loFDBptr,notHDBptr,notLoFDBptr,&status);
  FzyDrawSet(notLoFDBptr,SYSMODFILE,&status);
  Predtruth=FzyGetMembership(notLoFDBptr,PDtensionlvl,&Idxpos,&status);
  FzyDisplayMembership("PDtensionlvl",PDtensionlvl,notLoFDBptr,Predtruth);
//
  Domain[0]=0;Domain[1]=100;
  Parms[0]=PDbehavior;
  Parms[1]=PDbehavior*.10;
  nbehFDBptr=FzyCreateSet("ABOUT.PDBEHAVIOR",PI,Domain,Parms,2,&status);
  FzyDrawSet(nbehFDBptr,SYSMODFILE,&status);
  FzyCondProposition(nbehFDBptr,gsfFSVptr,thisCorrMethod,Predtruth,&status);
//
//-- R2 if the PDtensionlvl is low
//--           then the GoalShotfall is about PDtensionlvl;
//
  DisplayRule(RPrules,2,2);
  Predtruth=FzyGetMembership(loFDBptr,PDtensionlvl,&Idxpos,&status);
  FzyDisplayMembership("PDtensionlvl",PDtensionlvl,loFDBptr,Predtruth);
//
  Domain[0]=0;Domain[1]=100;
  Parms[0]=PDtensionlvl;
  Parms[1]=PDtensionlvl*.10;
  ntenFDBptr=FzyCreateSet("ABOUT.PDTENSION",PI,Domain,Parms,2,&status);
  FzyDrawSet(ntenFDBptr,SYSMODFILE,&status);
  FzyCondProposition(ntenFDBptr,gsfFSVptr,thisCorrMethod,Predtruth,&status);
//
//=============================================================================
//---Conclude. Defuzzify the output fuzzy region to get the actual rule change.
//---Clear the fuzzy work area and then release storage for the temporary variables.
//=============================================================================
//
  FzyDrawSet(gsfFDBptr,SYSMODFILE,&status);
  GoalShortfall=FzyDefuzzify(gsfFDBptr,thisDefuzzMethod,&CompIDX,&status);
  FzyCloseFZYctl(&status);
  delete gsfVDBptr;
  delete gsfFDBptr,notLoFDBptr,nbehFDBptr,ntenFDBptr;
  delete gsfFSVptr;
  return(GoalShortfall);
  }
```

orgpolh.cpp (Organizational Dynamics Print Policy Header)

```
/*------------------------------------------------------------*
| (c) 1994 Metus Systems.       Proprietary software product. |
| Reproduction or unauthorized use is prohibited. Unauthorized|
| use is illegal. Violators will be prosecuted. This software |
| contains proprietary trade and business secrets.            |
/*-----------------Procedure Description-------------------*
| orgpolh.cpp  Earl Cox  06/18/94 Print policy header         |
| When a policy is initiated we print a banner on the output  |
| audit log showing the current time period and policy name.  |
*---------------Modification Audit/Change Log--------------*
| Rev  Sar              Metus                                 |
| No   Code  Date       Rellvl  Mod  Description              |
| --   ----- --------   ------  ---  ----------------------- |
|                                                             |
*------------------------------------------------------------*/
```

```
#include <stdio.h>
#include <string.h>
#include "mtypes.hpp"
#include "mtsptype.hpp"
void PolicyHeader(int t,char *policyid)
  {
  FILE  *mdlout;
  mdlout=MtsGetSystemFile(SYSMODFILE);
//
  fprintf(mdlout,"%s\n%s\n%s%-16.16s%s%3d%s\n%s\n\n%s\n\n",
   "*----------------------------------------------------------------*",
   "*                                                                *",
   "*    Executing Policy: \"",policyid,"\" in Time Period: ",t-1,"    *",
   "*                                                                *",
   "*----------------------------------------------------------------*");
  return;
  }
```

orgrlpd.cpp (Organizational Dynamics Rule Application Policy)

```
/*----------------------------------------------------------------*
| Copyright (c) 1993 by The Metus Systems Group.                  |
| All rights reserved. Proprietary Software Product.              |
| No part of this software may be reproduced or transmitted       |
| in any form or by any means, electronic or mechanical,          |
| including input into or storage in any information system       |
| for resale without permission in writing from Metus Systems.    |
*--------------------Procedure Description--------------------*
| orgrlpd.cpp   Earl Cox  04/01/93  Organizational dynamics       |
*----------------Modification Audit/Change Log---------------*
| Rev  Sar                                                        |
| No   Code  Date     Rellvl  Mod  Description                    |
| --   ----- --------  ------  ---  -------------------------      |
|                                                                 |
*----------------------------------------------------------------*/
#include <stdio.h>
#include <string.h>
#include "PDB.hpp"
#include "FDB.hpp"
#include "FSV.hpp"
#include "HDB.hpp"
#include "VDB.hpp"
#include "SFZYctl.hpp"
#include "XSYSctl.hpp"
#include "fuzzy.hpp"
#include "mtypes.hpp"
#include "mtsptype.hpp"
static const Rulemax=6;
#define MAXFZYSETS  16
#define MAXPERIODS  24
void  PolicyHeader(int,char*);
void  DisplayRule(char**,int,int);
double RulesPOLICY(int t,double PDtension)
  {
  char  *RPrules[]=
    {
    "R1 if the PDtension is very high or the PDtension is highish   ",
    "          then the RuleLevelChange is an increase              ",
    "R2 if the PDtension is not low and the PDtension is not very high",
    "          then the RuleLevelChange is no.change               ",
    "R3 if the PDtension is low or the PDtension is lowish          ",
    "          then then RuleLevelChange is a decrease             "
```

```
      };
PDB       *orgPDBptr;
FDB       *hiFDBptr,
          *loFDBptr,
          *hsFDBptr,
          *lsFDBptr,
          *icFDBptr,
          *dcFDBptr,
          *ncFDBptr,
          *rlcFDBptr,
          *veryHiFDBptr,
          *notLoFDBptr,
          *notveryHiFDBptr;
FSV       *rlcFSVptr;
HDB       *veryHDBptr,
          *notHDBptr;
VDB       *rlcVDBptr;
char      *PgmId="orgrlpd";
int        status,
           Idxpos,
           Rulecnt,
           thisCorrMethod,
           thisDefuzzMethod;
float     CompIDX,Pred1,Pred2,Predtruth;
double    RlChange,
          Parms[4],
          Domain[2];
FILE      *mdlout;
Rulecnt=0;
printf("....Rules Policy.\n");
PolicyHeader(t,"RulesPolicy");
mdlout=MtsGetSystemFile(SYSMODFILE);
fprintf(mdlout,"%s\n","Policy Parameters:");
fprintf(mdlout,"%s%5.2f\n",    "PDtension       : ",PDtension );
//
//=============================================================================
//--Create the output solution variable and put it into the fuzzy work area.
//--This creates the output working fuzzy set and the fuzzy solution variable
//--block. We also extract the correlation and defuzzification methods.
//=============================================================================
//
  Domain[0]=-100; Domain[1]=100;
  rlcVDBptr=VarCreateScalar("RuleLevelChange",REAL,Domain,"0",&status);
  FzyInitFZYctl(&status);
  if(!(FzyAddFZYctl(rlcVDBptr,&rlcFDBptr,&rlcFSVptr,&status)))
    {
    MtsSendError(12,PgmId,"RuleLevelChange");
    exit(9);
    }
  thisCorrMethod =rlcFSVptr->FzySVcorrMethod;
  thisDefuzzMethod=rlcFSVptr->FzySVdefuzzMethod;
//
//=============================================================================
//--Fetch the base fuzzy set from the policy dictionary, and fetch the needed
//--Hedges from the policy hedge dictionary.
//=============================================================================
//
  orgPDBptr=XSYSctl.XSYScurrPDBptr;
  hiFDBptr=MdlFindFDB ("HIGH",     orgPDBptr,&status);
  loFDBptr=MdlFindFDB ("LOW",      orgPDBptr,&status);
  hsFDBptr=MdlFindFDB ("HIGHISH",  orgPDBptr,&status);
  lsFDBptr=MdlFindFDB ("LOWISH",   orgPDBptr,&status);
  icFDBptr=MdlFindFDB ("INCREASE", orgPDBptr,&status);
  dcFDBptr=MdlFindFDB ("DECREASE", orgPDBptr,&status);
```

```
        ncFDBptr=MdlFindFDB  ("NO.CHANGE",orgPDBptr,&status);
        veryHDBptr=MdlFindHDB("very",     orgPDBptr,&status);
        notHDBptr =MdlFindHDB("not",      orgPDBptr,&status);
//
//=============================================================================
//--Now execute the rules by forming any dynamic fuzzy sets and finding the
//--appropriate membership values and then applying the correlation method.
//=============================================================================
//
//-- R1 if the PDtension is very high or the PDtension is highish
//            then the RuleLevelChange is an increase
//
   DisplayRule(RPrules,0,2);
   veryHiFDBptr=FzyCreateSet("VERY.HIGH",EMPTYSET,Domain,Parms,0,&status);
   FzyApplyHedge(hiFDBptr,veryHDBptr,veryHiFDBptr,&status);
   FzyDrawSet(veryHiFDBptr,SYSMODFILE,&status);
   Pred1=FzyGetMembership(veryHiFDBptr,PDtension,&Idxpos,&status);
   FzyDisplayMembership("PDtension",PDtension,veryHiFDBptr,Pred1);
   Pred2=FzyGetMembership(hsFDBptr,    PDtension,&Idxpos,&status);
   FzyDisplayMembership("PDtension",PDtension,hsFDBptr,Pred2);
   Predtruth=max(Pred1,Pred2);
   FzyCondProposition(icFDBptr,rlcFSVptr,thisCorrMethod,Predtruth,&status);
//
//-- R2 if the PDtension is not low and the PDtension is not very high
//--           then the RuleLevelChange is no.change
//
   DisplayRule(RPrules,2,2);
   notLoFDBptr=FzyCreateSet("NOT.LOW",EMPTYSET,Domain,Parms,0,&status);
   FzyApplyHedge(loFDBptr,notHDBptr,notLoFDBptr,&status);
   FzyDrawSet(notLoFDBptr,SYSMODFILE,&status);
   Pred1=FzyGetMembership(notLoFDBptr,PDtension,&Idxpos,&status);
   FzyDisplayMembership("PDtension",PDtension,notLoFDBptr,Pred1);
   notveryHiFDBptr=FzyCreateSet("NOT.VERY.HI",EMPTYSET,Domain,Parms,0,&status);
   FzyApplyHedge(veryHiFDBptr,notHDBptr,notveryHiFDBptr,&status);
   FzyDrawSet(notveryHiFDBptr,SYSMODFILE,&status);
   Pred2=FzyGetMembership(notveryHiFDBptr,PDtension,&Idxpos,&status);
   FzyDisplayMembership("PDtension",PDtension,notveryHiFDBptr,Pred2);
   Predtruth=min(Pred1,Pred2);
   FzyCondProposition(ncFDBptr,rlcFSVptr,thisCorrMethod,Predtruth,&status);
//
//-- R3 if the PDtension is low or the PDtension is lowish
//--           then then RuleLevelChange is a decrease
//
   DisplayRule(RPrules,4,2);
   Pred1=FzyGetMembership(loFDBptr,PDtension,&Idxpos,&status);
   FzyDisplayMembership("PDtension",PDtension,loFDBptr,Pred1);
   Pred2=FzyGetMembership(lsFDBptr,PDtension,&Idxpos,&status);
   FzyDisplayMembership("PDtension",PDtension,lsFDBptr,Pred2);
   Predtruth=max(Pred1,Pred2);
   FzyCondProposition(dcFDBptr,rlcFSVptr,thisCorrMethod,Predtruth,&status);
//
//=============================================================================
//--Conclude. Defuzzify the output fuzzy region to get the actual rule change.
//--Clear the fuzzy work area and then release storage for the temporary variables.
//=============================================================================
//
   FzyDrawSet(rlcFDBptr,SYSMODFILE,&status);
   RlChange=FzyDefuzzify(rlcFDBptr,thisDefuzzMethod,&CompIDX,&status);
   FzyCloseFZYctl(&status);
   delete rlcVDBptr;
   delete rlcFDBptr,veryHiFDBptr,notLoFDBptr,notveryHiFDBptr;
   delete rlcFSVptr;
   return(RlChange);
   }
```

orgruld.cpp (Organizational Dynamics Print Current Rule)

```
/*-------------------------------------------------------------*
| (c) 1994 Metus Systems.       Proprietary software product.  |
| Reproduction or unauthorized use is prohibited. Unauthorized |
| use is illegal. Violators will be prosecuted. This software  |
| contains proprietary trade and business secrets.             |
*---------------------Procedure Description-------------------*
| orgruld.cpp  Earl Cox  06/18/94 Print current Rule           |
*---------------Modification Audit/Change Log----------------*
| Rev  Sar                   Metus                             |
| No   Code  Date         Rellvl  Mod  Description             |
| --   ----- --------     ------  ---  --------------------    |
|                                                              |
|  \                                                           |
*-------------------------------------------------------------*/
#include <stdio.h>
#include <string.h>
#include "mtypes.hpp"
#include "mtsptype.hpp"
void DisplayRule(char **Rules,int fromIDX,int forIDX)
  {
  int    i;
  FILE   *mdlout;
  mdlout=MtsGetSystemFile(SYSMODFILE);
//
  fprintf(mdlout,"%s\n"," ");
  for(i=fromIDX;i<fromIDX+forIDX;i++) fprintf(mdlout,"%s\n",Rules[i]);
  fprintf(mdlout,"%s\n"," ");
  return;
  }
```

orgrvpd.cpp (Organizational Dynamics Relation Visibility Policy)

```
/*-------------------------------------------------------------*
| Copyright (c) 1993 by The Metus Systems Group.               |
| All rights reserved. Proprietary Software Product.           |
| No part of this software may be reproduced or transmitted    |
| in any form or by any means, electronic or mechanical,       |
| including input into or storage in any information system    |
| for resale without permission in writing from Metus Systems. |
*---------------------Procedure Description-------------------*
| orgrvpd.cpp  Earl Cox  04/01/93  Organizational dynamics     |
*---------------Modification Audit/Change Log----------------*
| Rev  Sar                                                     |
| No   Code  Date         Rellvl  Mod  Description             |
| --   ----- --------     ------  ---  --------------------    |
|                                                              |
|                                                              |
*-------------------------------------------------------------*/
#include <stdio.h>
#include <string.h>
#include "PDB.hpp"
#include "FDB.hpp"
#include "FSV.hpp"
#include "HDB.hpp"
#include "VDB.hpp"
#include "XFZYctl.hpp"
#include "XSYSctl.hpp"
#include "fuzzy.hpp"
#include "mtypes.hpp"
#include "mtsptype.hpp"
static const Rulemax=6;
#define MAXFZYSETS  16
```

```
#define MAXPERIODS  24
void PolicyHeader(int,char*);
void DisplayRule(char**,int,int);
double RelationPOLICY(
  int t,double *PDChangeRV,
    double PDSupervision,double PDRuleLevel,double PDRlChange)
 {
  char   *RPrules[]=
   {
    "R1 if PDSupervision is not low                                         ",
    "           then the RelVisibility is about PDSupervision;              ",
    "R2 if PDSupervision is low or PDSupervision is lowish                  ",
    "           then the RelVisibility is about (100-PDRuleLevel);          ",
    "R3 if the PDRlChange is an increase                                    ",
    "           then theh PDChangeRV is a decrease;                         "
   };
  PDB      *orgPDBptr;
  FDB      *rviFDBptr,
           *crvFDBptr,
           *loFDBptr,
           *lsFDBptr,
           *icFDBptr,
           *dcFDBptr,
           *notLoFDBptr,
           *nsupFDBptr,
           *nrulFDBptr;
  FSV      *rviFSVptr,
           *crvFSVptr;
  HDB      *nearHDBptr,
           *notHDBptr;
  VDB      *rviVDBptr,
           *crvVDBptr;
  char     *PgmId="orgglpd";
  int       status,
            Idxpos,
            Rulecnt,
            thisCorrMethod,
            thisDefuzzMethod;
  float    CompIDX,Pred1,Pred2,Predtruth;
  double   RelVisibility,
           AboutRL,
           Parms[4],
           Domain[2];
  FILE     *mdlout;
  Rulecnt=0;
  printf("....Relation Policy.\n");
  PolicyHeader(t,"RelationPOLICY");
  mdlout=MtsGetSystemFile(SYSMODFILE);
  fprintf(mdlout,"%s\n","Policy Parameters:");
  fprintf(mdlout,"%s%5.2f\n",    "PDSupervision      : ",PDSupervision);
  fprintf(mdlout,"%s%5.2f\n",    "PDRuleLevel        : ",PDRuleLevel );
  fprintf(mdlout,"%s%5.2f\n",    "PDRuleLevelChange  : ",PDRlChange );
//
//==============================================================================
//--Create the output solution variable and put it into the fuzzy work area.
//--This creates the output working fuzzy set and the fuzzy solution variable
//--block. We also extract the correlation and defuzzification methods.
//==============================================================================
//
  Domain[0]=0; Domain[1]=100;
  rviVDBptr=VarCreateScalar("RelVisibility",REAL,Domain,"0",&status);
  Domain[0]=-100; Domain[1]=100;
  crvVDBptr=VarCreateScalar("ChangeInRV",REAL,Domain,"0",&status);
  FzyInitFZYctl(&status);
```

```
    if(!(FzyAddFZYctl(rviVDBptr,&rviFDBptr,&rviFSVptr,&status)))
      {
      MtsSendError(12,PgmId,"RuleLevelChange");
      exit(9);
      }
    if(!(FzyAddFZYctl(crvVDBptr,&crvFDBptr,&crvFSVptr,&status)))
      {
      MtsSendError(12,PgmId,"ChangeInRV");
      exit(9);
      }
   thisCorrMethod  =rviFSVptr->FzySVcorrMethod;
   thisDefuzzMethod=rviFSVptr->FzySVdefuzzMethod;
//
//==================================================================
//--Fetch the base fuzzy set from the policy dictionary, and fetch the needed
//--Hedges from the policy hedge dictionary.
//==================================================================
//
   orgPDBptr=XSYSctl.XSYScurrPDBptr;
   loFDBptr=MdlFindFDB  ("LOW",       orgPDBptr,&status);
   lsFDBptr=MdlFindFDB  ("LOWISH",    orgPDBptr,&status);
   icFDBptr=MdlFindFDB  ("INCREASE",  orgPDBptr,&status);
   dcFDBptr=MdlFindFDB  ("DECREASE",  orgPDBptr,&status);
   nearHDBptr=MdlFindHDB("about",     orgPDBptr,&status);
   notHDBptr =MdlFindHDB("not",       orgPDBptr,&status);
//
//==================================================================
//--Now execute the rules by forming any dynamic fuzzy sets and finding the
//--appropriate membership values and then applying the correlation method.
//==================================================================
//
//-- R1 if PDSupervision is not low
//--           then the RelVisibility is about PDSupervision;
//
   DisplayRule(RPrules,0,2);
   Domain[0]=loFDBptr->FDBdomain[0];
   Domain[1]=loFDBptr->FDBdomain[1];
   notLoFDBptr=FzyCreateSet("NOT.LOW",EMPTYSET,Domain,Parms,0,&status);
   FzyApplyHedge(loFDBptr,notHDBptr,notLoFDBptr,&status);
   FzyDrawSet(notLoFDBptr,SYSMODFILE,&status);
   Predtruth=FzyGetMembership(notLoFDBptr,PDSupervision,&Idxpos,&status);
   FzyDisplayMembership("PDSupervision",PDSupervision,notLoFDBptr,Predtruth);
//
   Domain[0]=0;Domain[1]=100;
   Parms[0]=PDSupervision;
   Parms[1]=PDSupervision*.10;
   nsupFDBptr=FzyCreateSet("NEAR.SUPERVISION",PI,Domain,Parms,2,&status);
   FzyDrawSet(nsupFDBptr,SYSMODFILE,&status);
   FzyCondProposition(nsupFDBptr,rviFSVptr,thisCorrMethod,Predtruth,&status);
//
//-- R2 if PDSupervision is low or PDSupervision is lowish
//--           then the RelVisibility is about (100-PDRuleLevel);
//
   DisplayRule(RPrules,2,2);
   Pred1=FzyGetMembership(loFDBptr,PDSupervision,&Idxpos,&status);
   FzyDisplayMembership("PDSupervision",PDSupervision,loFDBptr,Pred1);
   Pred2=FzyGetMembership(lsFDBptr,PDSupervision,&Idxpos,&status);
   FzyDisplayMembership("PDSupervision",PDSupervision,lsFDBptr,Pred2);
   Predtruth=max(Pred1,Pred2);
//
   AboutRL=100-PDRuleLevel;
   Domain[0]=0;Domain[1]=100;
   Parms[0]=AboutRL;
   Parms[1]=AboutRL*.10;
```

```
  nrulFDBptr=FzyCreateSet("ABOUT.100-RLLVL",PI,Domain,Parms,2,&status);
  FzyDrawSet(nrulFDBptr,SYSMODFILE,&status);
  FzyCondProposition(nrulFDBptr,rviFSVptr,thisCorrMethod,Predtruth,&status);
//
//-- R3 if the PDRlChange is an increase
//--          then the PDChangeRV is a decrease;
//
  DisplayRule(RPrules,4,2);
  Pred1=FzyGetMembership(icFDBptr,PDRlChange,&Idxpos,&status);
  FzyDisplayMembership("PDRlChange",PDRlChange,icFDBptr,Pred1);
  FzyCondProposition(dcFDBptr,crvFSVptr,thisCorrMethod,Pred1,&status);
//
//
//===========================================================================
//--Conclude. Defuzzify the output fuzzy region to get the actual rule change.
//--Clear the fuzzy work area and then release storage for the temporary variables.
//===========================================================================
//
  FzyDrawSet(rviFDBptr,SYSMODFILE,&status);
  RelVisibility=FzyDefuzzify(rviFDBptr,thisDefuzzMethod,&CompIDX,&status);
  FzyDrawSet(crvFDBptr,SYSMODFILE,&status);
  *PDChangeRV =FzyDefuzzify(crvFDBptr,thisDefuzzMethod,&CompIDX,&status);
  FzyCloseFZYctl(&status);
  delete rviVDBptr,crvVDBptr;
  delete rviFDBptr,crvFDBptr,notLoFDBptr,nsupFDBptr,nrulFDBptr;
  delete rviFSVptr,crvFSVptr;
  return(RelVisibility);
  }
```

orgsppd.cpp (Organizational Dynamics Supervision Level Policy)

```
/*-----------------------------------------------------------*
| Copyright (c) 1993 by The Metus Systems Group.            |
| All rights reserved. Proprietary Software Product.        |
| No part of this software may be reproduced or transmitted |
| in any form or by any means, electronic or mechanical,    |
| including input into or storage in any information system |
| for resale without permission in writing from Metus Systems.|
*-------------------Procedure Description-------------------*
| orgsppd.cpp   Earl Cox  04/01/93  Organizational dynamics |
*---------------Modification Audit/Change Log---------------*
| Rev  Sar                                                  |
| No   Code  Date      Rellvl  Mod  Description             |
| --   ----- --------  ------  ---  ----------------------- |
|                                                           |
|                                                           |
*-----------------------------------------------------------*/
#include <stdio.h>
#include <string.h>
#include "PDB.hpp"
#include "FDB.hpp"
#include "FSV.hpp"
#include "HDB.hpp"
#include "VDB.hpp"
#include "XFZYctl.hpp"
#include "XSYSctl.hpp"
#include "fuzzy.hpp"
#include "mtypes.hpp"
#include "mtsptype.hpp"
static const Rulemax=6;
#define MAXFZYSETS  16
#define MAXPERIODS  24
void PolicyHeader(int,char*);
```

```
void DisplayRule(char**,int,int);
double SupervisionPOLICY(int t,double PDGoalShortfall,double PDGoalChange)
  {
  char   *RPrules[]=
    {
    "R1 if the PDGoalShortfall is high and PDGoalChange is a decrease      ",
    "          then the SupervisionChange is no.change;                    ",
    "R2 if the PDGoalShortfall is low and PDGoalShortfall is high          ",
    "          then the SupervisionChange is no.change;                    ",
    "R3 if the PDGoalShortfall is low then SupervisionChange is decrease;  ",
    "R4 if the PDGoalChange is an increase and PDGoalShortfall is high     ",
    "          then the SupervisionChange is an increase;                  "
    };
  PDB      *orgPDBptr;
  FDB      *hiFDBptr,
           *loFDBptr,
           *icFDBptr,
           *dcFDBptr,
           *ncFDBptr,
           *spcFDBptr;
  FSV      *spcFSVptr;
  VDB      *spcVDBptr;
  char     *PgmId="orgrlpd";
  int       status,
            Idxpos,
            Rulecnt,
            thisCorrMethod,
            thisDefuzzMethod;
  float    CompIDX,Pred1,Pred2,Predtruth;
  double   SUChange,
           Domain[2];
  FILE     *mdlout;
  Rulecnt=0;
  printf("....Supervise Policy.\n");
  PolicyHeader(t,"SupervisePolicy");
  mdlout=MtsGetSystemFile(SYSMODFILE);
  fprintf(mdlout,"%s\n","Policy Parameters:");
  fprintf(mdlout,"%s%5.2f\n",    "PDGoalShortfall  : ",PDGoalShortfall);
  fprintf(mdlout,"%s%5.2f\n",    "PDGoalChange     : ",PDGoalChange);
//
//=============================================================================
//--Create the output solution variable and put it into the fuzzy work area.
//--This creates the output working fuzzy set and the fuzzy solution variable
//--block. We also extract the correlation and defuzzification methods.
//=============================================================================
//
  Domain[0]=-100; Domain[1]=100;
  spcVDBptr=VarCreateScalar("SuperviseChange",REAL,Domain,"0",&status);
  FzyInitFZYctl(&status);
  if(!(FzyAddFZYctl(spcVDBptr,&spcFDBptr,&spcFSVptr,&status)))
    {
    MtsSendError(12,PgmId,"RuleLevelChange");
    exit(9);
    }
  thisCorrMethod   =spcFSVptr->FzySVcorrMethod;
  thisDefuzzMethod=spcFSVptr->FzySVdefuzzMethod;
//
//=============================================================================
//--Fetch the base fuzzy set from the policy dictionary, and fetch the needed
//--Hedges from the policy hedge dictionary.
//=============================================================================
//
  orgPDBptr=XSYSctl.XSYScurrPDBptr;
  hiFDBptr=MdlFindFDB ("HIGH",      orgPDBptr,&status);
```

```
      loFDBptr=MdlFindFDB   ("LOW",      orgPDBptr,&status);
      icFDBptr=MdlFindFDB   ("INCREASE", orgPDBptr,&status);
      dcFDBptr=MdlFindFDB   ("DECREASE", orgPDBptr,&status);
      ncFDBptr=MdlFindFDB   ("NO.CHANGE",orgPDBptr,&status);
    //
    //=============================================================================
    //--Now execute the rules by forming any dynamic fuzzy sets and finding the
    //--appropriate membership values and then applying the correlation method.
    //=============================================================================
    //
    //-- R1 if the PDGoalShortfall is high and PDGoalChange is a decrease
    //--         then the SupervisionChange is no.change;
    //
      DisplayRule(RPrules,0,2);
      Pred1=FzyGetMembership(hiFDBptr,PDGoalShortfall,&Idxpos,&status);
      Pred2=FzyGetMembership(dcFDBptr,PDGoalChange,&Idxpos,&status);
      Predtruth=min(Pred1,Pred2);
      FzyCondProposition(ncFDBptr,spcFSVptr,thisCorrMethod,Predtruth,&status);
    //
    //-- R2 if the PDGoalShortfall is low and PDGoalShortfall is high
    //--         then the SupervisionChange is no.change;
    //
      DisplayRule(RPrules,2,2);
      Pred1=FzyGetMembership(loFDBptr,PDGoalShortfall,&Idxpos,&status);
      Pred2=FzyGetMembership(hiFDBptr,PDGoalShortfall,&Idxpos,&status);
      Predtruth=min(Pred1,Pred2);
      FzyCondProposition(ncFDBptr,spcFSVptr,thisCorrMethod,Predtruth,&status);
    //
    //-- R3 if the PDGoalShortfall is low then SupervisionChange is decrease;
    //
      DisplayRule(RPrules,4,1);
      Predtruth=FzyGetMembership(loFDBptr,PDGoalShortfall,&Idxpos,&status);
      FzyCondProposition(dcFDBptr,spcFSVptr,thisCorrMethod,Predtruth,&status);
    //
    //-- R4 if the PDGoalChange is an increase and PDGoalShortfall is high
    //--         then the SupervisionChange is an increase;
    //
      DisplayRule(RPrules,5,2);
      Pred1=FzyGetMembership(icFDBptr,PDGoalChange,&Idxpos,&status);
      Pred2=FzyGetMembership(hiFDBptr,PDGoalShortfall,&Idxpos,&status);
      Predtruth=min(Pred1,Pred2);
      FzyCondProposition(icFDBptr,spcFSVptr,thisCorrMethod,Predtruth,&status);
    //
    //=============================================================================
    //--Conclude. Defuzzify the output fuzzy region to get the actual rule change.
    //--Clear the fuzzy work area and then release storage for the temporary variables.
    //=============================================================================
    //
      FzyDrawSet(spcFDBptr,SYSMODFILE,&status);
      SUChange=FzyDefuzzify(spcFDBptr,thisDefuzzMethod,&CompIDX,&status);
      FzyCloseFZYctl(&status);
      delete spcVDBptr;
      delete spcFDBptr;
      delete spcFSVptr;
      return(SUChange);
     }
```

orgdyn2.cpp (The "clamped" Organizational Dynamics Model Driver)

```
/*-------------------------------------------------------------*
| Copyright (c) 1993 by The Metus Systems Group.              |
| All rights reserved. Proprietary Software Product.         |
```

```
| No part of this software may be reproduced or transmitted |
| in any form or by any means, electronic or mechanical,    |
| including input into or storage in any information system |
| for resale without permission in writing from Metus Systems.|
*--------------------Procedure Description--------------------*
| orgdyn1.cpp   Earl Cox  04/01/93  Organizational dynamics  |
*---------------Modification Audit/Change Log----------------*
| Rev  Sar                                                   |
| No   Code  Date     Rellvl  Mod  Description               |
| --   ----- -------- ------  ---  ------------------------- |
|                                                            |
*------------------------------------------------------------*/
#include <stdio.h>
#include <string.h>
#include <math.h>
#include "PDB.hpp"
#include "FDB.hpp"
#include "SSYSctl.hpp"
#include "fuzzy.hpp"
#include "mtypes.hpp"
#include "mtsptype.hpp"
static const Rulemax=5;
extern unsigned _stklen=50000;
PDB* MdlCreatePolicy(char*,int,int*);
#define MAXFZYSETS  16
#define MAXPERIODS  16
double  RulesPOLICY(int,double);
double  GoalPOLICY(int,double,double);
double  SupervisionPOLICY(int,double,double);
double  RelationPOLICY(int,double*,double,double,double);
void    CaptureFuzzySet(char*,FDB*,int*);
//
#define  TENSIONLEVEL     0
#define  RULELEVEL        1
#define  GOALSHORTFALL    2
#define  SUPERVISION      3
#define  RELATION         4
#define  FIELDQUIT        5
//
void main(void)
  {
  PDB      *orgPDBptr;
  FDB      *FDBptr[MAXFZYSETS];
  char     *fldNames[]=
    {
    "TensionLevel",
    "RuleLevel",
    "Goal Shortfall",
    "Supervision",
    "RelationVis",
    "quit"
    };
  char     *fldID;
  int      fldNCnt=6,fldClamped[5];
  int      fldMinLen=2,fldIDX,fldCNo;
  int      i,j,t,k,status,Hdgcnt,TryCtl[2];
  bool     trace,storfs;
  double   Parms[4],
           Domain[2],
           tenlvl,
           rullvl,
           gsfall,
           suplvl,
           relvis;
```

```
       FILE    *mdlout,
               *rptout;
//
//
//==============================================================================
//--The TIME SERIES and PERIOD Variables. These are the variables used
//--to hold the values of the organizational dynamics model in each
//--successive time period.
//==============================================================================
//
//                                                   R  A  N  G  E
//                                              Minimum        Maximum
//                                              -------        -------
     double    TensionLevel     [MAXPERIODS], //       0           100
               RuleLevelChange  [MAXPERIODS], //     -20            20
               RuleLevel        [MAXPERIODS], //       0           100
               BehaviorAwareness[MAXPERIODS], //       0           100
               GoalShortfall    [MAXPERIODS], //       0           100
               GoalChange       [MAXPERIODS], //       0           100
               SVChange         [MAXPERIODS], //    -100           100
               Supervision      [MAXPERIODS], //    -100           100
               RelationVisibility[MAXPERIODS]; //   -100           100
     double    PDtension,
               PDChangeRV;
     SysConnecttoMetus(&status);
     orgPDBptr=MdlCreatePolicy("ORGDYNS",MODELADD,&status);
     XSYSctl.XSYScurrPDBptr=orgPDBptr;
     XSYSctl.XSYSalfacut    =0.1;
//
     XSYSctl.XSYStrace[3]=TRUE;
     XSYSctl.XSYStrace[2]=TRUE;
//
     MdlInsertHedges(orgPDBptr,&Hdgcnt,&status);
     mdlout=MtsGetSystemFile(SYSMODFILE);
//
//
     printf("INITIALIZE MODEL\n");
     TryCtl[0]=5;
     TryCtl[1]=0;
     Domain[0]=0;Domain[1]=100;
     tenlvl=MtsAskforDBL(
       "TensionLevel",  "Tension Level      : ",Domain,TryCtl,&status);
     rullvl=MtsAskforDBL(
       "RuleLevel",     "Rule Level         : ",Domain,TryCtl,&status);
     gsfall=MtsAskforDBL(
       "Goal Shortfall","Goal Shortfall     : ",Domain,TryCtl,&status);
     suplvl=MtsAskforDBL(
       "Supervision",   "Supervision        : ",Domain,TryCtl,&status);
     relvis=MtsAskforDBL(
       "RelationVis",   "RelationVisibility : ",Domain,TryCtl,&status);
//
     printf("CLAMP PARAMETER VALUES\n");
     for(i=0;i<fldNCnt;i++) fldClamped[i]=FALSE;
     fldCNo=0;
     while(1)
       {
       fldID= MtsAskforVAL(
         "ClampedField",
         "Parameter Name     : ",
           fldNames,fldNCnt,fldMinLen,&fldIDX,TryCtl,&status);
       if(fldIDX==FIELDQUIT) break;
       fldClamped[fldIDX]=TRUE;
       fldCNo++;
       }
```

```
      printf("SPECIFY MODEL ACTIONS\n");
      trace =MtsAskforBOOL(
         "fzySetTrace",    "Trace FuzzySets    : ",        TryCtl,&status);
      XSYSctl.XSYStrace[3]=trace;
      trace =MtsAskforBOOL(
         "RuleTrace",      "Trace Rule Actions : ",        TryCtl,&status);
      XSYSctl.XSYStrace[2]=trace;
      storfs=MtsAskforBOOL(
         "StoreSets",      "Store FuzzySets    : ",        TryCtl,&status);
//
//===============================================================================
//--The TENSION LEVEL fuzzy regions. These represent relative degrees
//--of tension in the organization on a scale from 0 (none) to 100 (high).
//===============================================================================
//
      Domain[0]=  0;Domain[1]= 100;
       Parms[0]=0;    Parms[1]= 25;  Parms[2]=50;
      FDBptr[0]=FzyCreateSet("LOW", DECLINE,Domain,Parms,3,&status);
      if(storfs)
         CaptureFuzzySet("b:low.txt",FDBptr[0],&status);
      MdlLinkFDB(FDBptr[0],orgPDBptr,&status);
      Domain[0]=  0;Domain[1]= 100;
       Parms[0]=25;  Parms[1]= 25;
      FDBptr[1]=FzyCreateSet("LOWISH", PI,Domain,Parms,2,&status);
      if(storfs)
         CaptureFuzzySet("b:lowish.txt",FDBptr[1],&status);
      MdlLinkFDB(FDBptr[1],orgPDBptr,&status);
      Domain[0]=  0;Domain[1]= 100;
       Parms[0]= 75; Parms[1]= 25;
      FDBptr[2]=FzyCreateSet("HIGHISH", PI,Domain,Parms,2,&status);
      if(storfs)
         CaptureFuzzySet("b:highish.txt",FDBptr[2],&status);
      MdlLinkFDB(FDBptr[2],orgPDBptr,&status);
      Domain[0]=  0;Domain[1]= 100;
       Parms[0]= 50; Parms[1]= 75;  Parms[2]=100;
      FDBptr[3]=FzyCreateSet("HIGH", GROWTH,Domain,Parms,3,&status);
      if(storfs)
         CaptureFuzzySet("b:high.txt",FDBptr[3],&status);
      MdlLinkFDB(FDBptr[3],orgPDBptr,&status);
      FzyPlotTermSet("TENSION.LEVEL",FDBptr,4,SYSMODFILE,&status);
//
//===============================================================================
//--The MODEL STATE CHANGE fuzzy regions. These represent relative degrees
//--of changes of such factors as rule enformcement, supervision, etc. This
//--is measured on a scale from -100 (extremely weak) to +100 (very strong).
//===============================================================================
//
      Domain[0]=-100;Domain[1]=100;
       Parms[0]= -20; Parms[1]= 20;
      FDBptr[0]=FzyCreateSet("DECREASE", PI,     Domain,Parms,2,&status);
      if(storfs)
         CaptureFuzzySet("b:decrease.txt",FDBptr[0],&status);
      MdlLinkFDB(FDBptr[0],orgPDBptr,&status);
      Domain[0]=-100;Domain[1]=100;
       Parms[0]=  0; Parms[1]= 20;
      FDBptr[1]=FzyCreateSet("NO.CHANGE", PI,    Domain,Parms,2,&status);
      if(storfs)
         CaptureFuzzySet("b:nochng.txt",FDBptr[1],&status);
      MdlLinkFDB(FDBptr[1],orgPDBptr,&status);
      Domain[0]=-100;Domain[1]=100;
       Parms[0]= 20; Parms[1]= 20;
      FDBptr[2]=FzyCreateSet("INCREASE", PI,     Domain,Parms,2,&status);
      if(storfs)
         CaptureFuzzySet("b:increase.txt",FDBptr[2],&status);
```

```
      MdlLinkFDB(FDBptr[2],orgPDBptr,&status);
      FzyPlotTermSet("CHANGE.METRICS",FDBptr,3,SYSMODFILE,&status);
//
//============================================================================
//--The MODEL INITIALIZATION PHASE. We loop through the time horizions and
//--set each value to zero. We then go back and initialize the first two
//--time periods (since the model as a [-2] lag architecture).
//============================================================================
//
   for(t=0;t<MAXPERIODS;t++)
     {
      TensionLevel       [t]=0;
      RuleLevelChange    [t]=0;
      RuleLevel          [t]=0;
      BehaviorAwareness  [t]=0;
      GoalShortfall      [t]=0;
      GoalChange         [t]=0;
      SVChange           [t]=0;
      Supervision        [t]=0;
      RelationVisibility[t]=0;
      if(fldClamped[TENSIONLEVEL ])  TensionLevel       [t]=tenlvl;
      if(fldClamped[RULELEVEL     ])  RuleLevel          [t]=rullvl;
      if(fldClamped[GOALSHORTFALL])  GoalShortfall      [t]=gsfall;
      if(fldClamped[SUPERVISION  ])  Supervision        [t]=suplvl;
      if(fldClamped[RELATION      ])  RelationVisibility[t]=relvis;
     }
//
   for(t=0;t<2;t++)
     {
      TensionLevel       [t]=tenlvl;
      RuleLevel          [t]=rullvl;
      GoalShortfall      [t]=gsfall;
      Supervision        [t]=suplvl;
      RelationVisibility[t]=relvis;
     }
//
//============================================================================
//--The MODEL EXECUTION PROCESS. This is the main logic of the organizational
//--dynamics model. We start in period three of the time frame and loop over
//--each time frame invoking the fuzzy policies to compute the period data.
//============================================================================
//
   for(t=2;t<MAXPERIODS;t++)
     {
      printf("%s%3d\n","Time Period: ",t-1);
      /*-------------------------------------------------------*
      | First we assess the level at which bureaucratic rules |
      | are being applied. This depends on the tension level  |
      | two periods ago.                                      |
      *-------------------------------------------------------*/
      PDtension             =TensionLevel[t-2];
      RuleLevelChange[t]    =RulesPOLICY(t,PDtension);
      RuleLevel[t]          =RuleLevel[t-1]+RuleLevelChange[t];
      RuleLevel[t]          =max(min(RuleLevel[t],100),0);
      /*-------------------------------------------------------*
      | We now assess the level of performance against target.|
      | This depends on the current level of tension and the  |
      | worker's knowledge of minimum acceptable behavior.    |
      *-------------------------------------------------------*/
      TensionLevel[t]       =RelationVisibility[t-1];
      BehaviorAwareness[t]  =RuleLevel[t];
      GoalShortfall[t]      =GoalPOLICY(t,BehaviorAwareness[t],TensionLevel[t]);
      GoalChange[t]         =GoalShortfall[t]-GoalShortfall[t-1];
      /*-------------------------------------------------------*
```

```
           | Finally we examine the visibility of power relations. |
           | This depends on the supervision level and the change  |
           | in the application of bureaucratic rules.             |
           *-------------------------------------------------------*/
           RelationVisibility[t]=
             RelationPOLICY(t,&PDChangeRV,Supervision[t],RuleLevel[t],RuleLevelChange[t]);
           RelationVisibility[t]=RelationVisibility[t]+PDChangeRV;
           //
           //--Now we take a snap shot of the mode state in this time frame and
           //--post it to the model log. We may want to discontinue this or make
           //--it conditional in a production system.
           //
           fprintf(mdlout,"\n%s%4d\n",   "Model State. Time:",t-1);
           fprintf(mdlout,"%s%7.2f\n",   "  Previous Tension     : ",PDtension);
           fprintf(mdlout,"%s%7.2f\n",   "  Tension Level        : ",TensionLevel[t]);
           fprintf(mdlout,"%s%7.2f\n",   "  Rule Level           : ",RuleLevel[t]);
           fprintf(mdlout,"%s%7.2f\n",   "  Rule LevelChange     : ",RuleLevelChange[t]);
           fprintf(mdlout,"%s%7.2f\n",   "  Goal Shortfall       : ",GoalShortfall[t]);
           fprintf(mdlout,"%s%7.2f\n",   "  Goal Change          : ",GoalChange[t]);
           fprintf(mdlout,"%s%7.2f\n",   "  Supervision          : ",Supervision[t]);
           fprintf(mdlout,"%s%7.2f\n",   "  Supervision Change   : ",SVChange[t]);
           fprintf(mdlout,"%s%7.2f\n",   "  Relation Visibility  : ",RelationVisibility[t]);
           fprintf(mdlout,"%s%7.2f\n",   "  Visibility Change    : ",PDChangeRV);
           fprintf(mdlout,"%s\n\n",      "  ");
         }
   //
   //
   //=========================================================================
   //--The MODEL REPORT PHASE. When the model is complete, we open a new file
   //--and write a report that shows the model data in each time frame. In this
   //--report, time period (P1) is actually time frame three in the horizon.
   //=========================================================================
   //
   //
     if((rptout=fopen("b:odrpt.fil","w"))==NULL)
       {
       printf("Sorry. 'b:orgrpt.fil' file was not created\n");
       return;
       }
     fprintf(rptout,"%s\n%s\n",
       "FUZZY ORGANIZATIONAL BEHAVIOR MODEL. (c) 1992 Metus Systems Group.",
       "from: Gouldner [1954] 'Patterns of Industrial Bureaucracy'");
     fprintf(rptout,"%s\n","Initial Model Conditions:");
     fprintf(rptout,"%s3.0f\n",   "Tension Level        : ",tenlvl);
     fprintf(rptout,"%s3.0f\n",   "Rule Level           : ",rullvl);
     fprintf(rptout,"%s3.0f\n",   "Goal Shortfall       : ",gsfall);
     fprintf(rptout,"%s3.0f\n",   "Supervision          : ",suplvl);
     fprintf(rptout,"%s3.0f\n",   "Relation Visibility  : ",relvis);
     fprintf(rptout,"\n%s\n%s\n",
       "                                    P1  P2  P3  P4  P5  P6  P7  P8  P9
   P10 P11 P12",
       "                                    --- --- --- --- --- --- --- --- ---
   -- --- ---");
     fprintf(rptout,"%-32.32s  ","Effective Present tension Level");
     for(j=2;j<14;j++)
       if((fabs(TensionLevel[j]))<1)  fprintf(rptout,"%.3s  ","   ");
       else fprintf(rptout,"%3.0f  ",TensionLevel[j]);
     fprintf(rptout,"%c",'\n');
     fprintf(rptout,"%-32.32s  ","Change in Rule Application Level");
     for(j=2;j<14;j++)
       if((fabs(RuleLevelChange[j]))<1)  fprintf(rptout,"%.3s  ","   ");
       else fprintf(rptout,"%3.0f  ",RuleLevelChange[j]);
     fprintf(rptout,"%c",'\n');
     fprintf(rptout,"%-32.32s  ","Rule Application Level");
```

```
     for(j=2;j<14;j++)
       if((fabs(RuleLevel[j]))<1) fprintf(rptout,"%.3s  ."   ");
         else fprintf(rptout,"%3.0f  ",RuleLevel[j]);
     fprintf(rptout,"%c",'\n');
     fprintf(rptout,"%-32.32s  ","Behavior Awareness Level");
     for(j=2;j<14;j++)
       if((fabs(BehaviorAwareness[j]))<1)  fprintf(rptout,"%.3s  ."   ");
         else fprintf(rptout,"%3.0f  ",BehaviorAwareness[j]);
     fprintf(rptout,"%c",'\n');
     fprintf(rptout,"%-32.32s  ","Change in Goal Shortfall");
     for(j=2;j<14;j++)
       if((fabs(GoalChange[j]))<1)  fprintf(rptout,"%.3s  ."   ");
         else fprintf(rptout,"%3.0f  ",GoalChange[j]);
     fprintf(rptout,"%c",'\n');
     fprintf(rptout,"%-32.32s  ","Achievement vs. Goal Shortfalls");
     for(j=2;j<14;j++)
       if((fabs(GoalShortfall[j]))<1)  fprintf(rptout,"%.3s  ."   ");
         else fprintf(rptout,"%3.0f  ",GoalShortfall[j]);
     fprintf(rptout,"%c",'\n');
     fprintf(rptout,"%-32.32s  ","Change in Supervision Level");
     for(j=2;j<14;j++)
       if((fabs(SVChange[j]))<1) fprintf(rptout,"%.3s  ."   ");
         else fprintf(rptout,"%3.0f  ",SVChange[j]);
     fprintf(rptout,"%c",'\n');
     fprintf(rptout,"%-32.32s  ","Active Supervision Level");
     for(j=2;j<14;j++)
       if((fabs(Supervision[j]))<1)  fprintf(rptout,"%.3s  ."   ");
         else fprintf(rptout,"%3.0f  ",Supervision[j]);
     fprintf(rptout,"%c",'\n');
     if(fldCNo>0)
       {
        fprintf(rptout,"\n%s\n",  "Clamped Parameters:");
        k=0;
        for(i=0;i<fldNCnt;i++)
          {
           if(fldClamped[i])
             {
              k++;
              fprintf(rptout,"%3d. %s",k,fldNames[i]);
             }
          }
       }
     fprintf(rptout,"%c",'\n');
     fprintf(rptout,"%c",'\n');
     fclose(rptout);
     return;
    }
//
//
void CaptureFuzzySet(char *FzyDataFile,FDB *FDBptr,int *statusPtr)
/*------------------------------------------------------------*
| This routine is used to capture and store the fuzzy set     |
| membership array on disk for use in fine-point graphics.    |
*------------------------------------------------------------*/
   {
   int     i,
           CompFactor= 16,
           MaxValues= 128,
           status,
           ExtCnt;
   double  DomValues[128];
   float   MemValues[128];
   FILE    *fzyout;
   *statusPtr=0;
```

```
if((fzyout=fopen(FzyDataFile,"w"))==NULL)
   {
    *statusPtr=1;
    printf("Sorry. '%s' file was not created\n",FzyDataFile);
    return;
   }
FzyExtractSetdata(FDBptr,CompFactor,DomValues,MemValues,&ExtCnt,&status);
for(i=0;i<ExtCnt;i++)
    fprintf(fzyout,"%10.2f  %6.4f\n",DomValues[i],MemValues[i]);
fclose(fzyout);
return;
}
```

Fuzzy Set Theory

This appendix briefly reviews the background of fuzzy set theory and then briefly covers the basic logical operations in fuzzy set theory: union, intersection, and negation. We also examine the Laws of the excluded middle and noncontradiction— areas where fuzzy logic departs significantly from ordinary Boolean logic.

The History of Fuzzy Logic

Fuzzy Logic had its formal start with the 1965 publication of "Fuzzy Sets" by Lotfi Zadeh in the journal *Information and Control*. Lotfi Zadeh, now a professor emeritus at the University of California in Berkeley, was interested in understanding complex, nonlinear systems in ways that made their behavior clearer and more understandable. In fact, Lotfi's next important paper, "Outline of a New Approach to the Analysis of Complex Systems and Decision Processes," published in 1973 in the journal *IEEE Transactions on Systems, Man, and Cybernetics*, spelled out his concern and how he thought fuzzy reasoning contributed to this understanding. One part of this paper states his *principle of incompatibility*:

> [A]s the complexity of a system increases, our ability to make precise and yet significant statements about its behavior diminishes until a threshold is reached beyond which precision and significance (or relevance) become almost mutually exclusive characteristics.

Lotfi Zadeh did not invent fuzzy logic out of an intellectual vacuum. History is rich in the exploration of alternatives to Boolean logic. This often comes as a surprise to many people who have been educated in the writings of Aristotle and George Boole. The ancient Greek philosophers such as Heraclitus and Anaximander developed logical systems of many states two hundred years before Aristotle. William of Ockham, famous for his Ockham's Razor, speculated, in the early 14th century, on logics that were neither absolutely

531

true nor absolutely false. In the early part of the twentieth century Max Black invented the first authentic fuzzy sets in his study of vagueness, and, in the mid 1930s, Jan Lukasiewicz (also famous as the inventor of *Polish notation* used in expression evaluation and compiler writing) developed a workable multi-state logic.

About the same time another Polish-born mathematician and logician, Alfred Tarski, in his paper *Der Wahheitsbefriff in den Formalisierten Sprachen*, or *The Concept of Truth in Formalized Languages,* provided one of the key understanding to a multi-state logic by breaking away from the idea that uncertainty or logical contingencies was somehow based on events occurring only the future. The unspoken tenet that the present is precise and only the future contains imprecision came down from Aristotle's *Prior Analytics* and influenced almost every logician until Tarski showed that degrees of truth can also be applied to present events in a consistent and formal manner.

What Is Fuzzy Logic?

So fuzzy logic has a deep pedigree. It is a logic that attempts to combine the imprecision associated with natural events with the computational power of the computer to produce highly intelligent, robust, and flexible reasoning systems. But fuzzy logic, in its everyday use, actually encompasses a much broader realm of disciplines. These different faces are shown in Figure A.9.

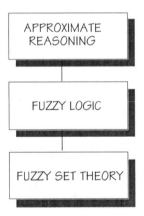

Figure A.9 The various aspects of fuzzy logic

At the bottom rung is fuzzy set theory, which describes the mechanics of how fuzzy sets are organized and what operations are allowed. Fuzzy logic itself is the process of making logical inferences from a collection of fuzzy sets. For many applications in control and process engineering this is the top of the ladder—no other technology is needed. At the top is approximate reasoning, a combination of mathematically precise logic and powerful heuristics. Approximate reasoning is the tool used by fuzzy expert and decision support systems and includes such heuristics as fuzzy sets hedges, rule contribution weights, and alternate forms of set operators.

We now turn our attention to the nature of fuzzy logic and why its is fuzzy. Fuzzy Logic is about the properties of imprecise events. It is concerned with the imprecision associated with the description of an event instead of the imprecision associated with the occurrence of an event The former is intrinsic to the event and cannot be removed, while the latter, often called the probability of the event, is contingent upon the event's future history. When we talk about fuzzy imprecision in this context, we mean the uncertainty or vagueness inherent in how we can describe or characterize an object or event. As we will see, nearly everything in the real world is fuzzy to some degree.

Fuzzy Sets

The basic component of fuzzy logic is the *fuzzy set*. Fuzzy sets are called "fuzzy" because they have indistinct boundaries. Conventional, or crisp, sets, on the other hand, have clearly defined boundaries. Conventional sets can be represented as lists or expressions showing what belongs and what does not belong to the set. Venn or Euler diagrams, familiar to every high school algebra student, is a convenient way to express a crisp set. Fuzzy sets cannot be drawn this way. As Figure A.10 shows, fuzzy set consists of three parts, the horizontal axis representing the members of the set, the vertical axis representing the degree of membership in the set, and a curve that connects each point in the membership with its appropriate degree of membership.

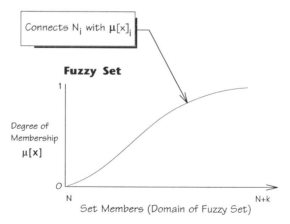

Figure A.10 The structure of a fuzzy set

The classical illustration of a fuzzy set is the idea of TALL. In crisp or boolean logic we must make a decision about exactly who is tall, such as the definition "everyone six feet and over is tall." This appears, in formal terms, as the discrimination function for the set:

$$\mu_{TALL}[x] = \{height \geq 6\,feet\}$$

Figure A.11 shows how this kind of definition produces a set with very sharp boundaries.

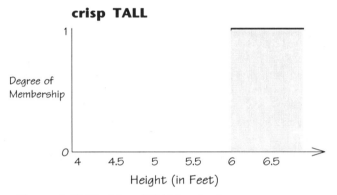

Figure A.11 The idea of TALL in crisp terms

In the crisp version of a set the boundary between TALL and not TALL is fully dichotomized—everyone over six feet is TALL. There is no degree of tallness. Mike's height is five feet eleven and three-quarters inches, so he is SHORT. Arnold's height is six feet exactly, and so he is TALL. In a fuzzy set, however, membership is based on degrees. A fuzzy set measures to what degree something is a member of a particular set. Figure A.12 shows the concept of TALL as a fuzzy set.

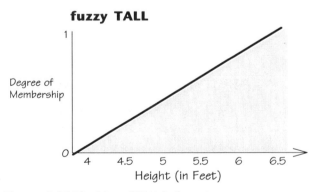

Figure A.12 The idea of TALL in fuzzy terms

From this fuzzy set we can see that a height of four feet has no membership in the set of TALL people while someone six feet and six inches is absolutely representative of the concept TALL. Heights in between these points have different degrees of membership in the set TALL. This degree of membership tells us how compatible a particular height is with the idea of TALL. As you can also see from this example, fuzzy sets are not absolute but are dependent on the semantics of the model. The idea of TALL for men and women differ, the idea of TALL in Japan is, to some extent, different than the idea of TALL in the United States.

Fuzzy Set Operations

Fuzzy logic operations include those familiar to users of crisp logic: union, intersection, and the set complement. In fuzzy logic these operations work on the degrees of membership and can produce some surprising results. Consider the collection of fuzzy sets describing the variable Customer.Age shown in Figure A.13. The group of overlapping fuzzy sets underlying the complete range of values for a variable is called the *term set* and the full range of values is known as the *universe of discourse*.

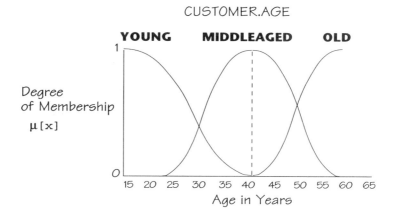

Figure A.13 The term set for the variable Customer.Age

The *union* or logical OR of two fuzzy sets is found by taking the maximum of the membership values at each point across their common domains. This is expressed mathematically as:

$$\mu_{YOUNG \cup MIDDLEAGED}[X] = \bigvee_{i=0}^{N} MAX(\mu_{YOUNG}[x]_i, \mu_{MIDDLEAGED}[x]_i)$$

For each membership value in the two fuzzy sets we construct a new fuzzy region that is the maximum of the grades of membership in the base sets. The resulting fuzzy region is shown in Figure A.14.

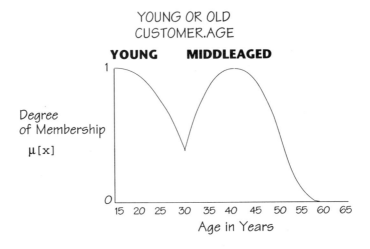

Figure A.14 Young OR MiddleAged

The *intersection* or logical AND of two fuzzy sets is found by taking the minimum of the membership values at each point across their common domains. This is expressed mathematically as:

$$\mu_{YOUNG \cap MIDDLEAGED}[X] = \bigvee_{i=0}^{N} MIN(\mu_{YOUNG}[x]_i, \mu_{MIDDLEAGED}[x]_i)$$

In the same manner as the union operator, we construct a new fuzzy region from the maximum grades of membership in the base set. The resulting fuzzy region is shown in Figure A.15.

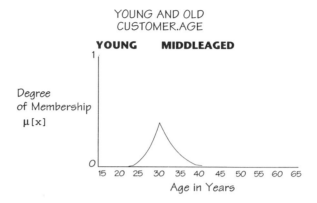

Figure A.15 Young AND MiddleAged

The *complement* or logical NOT of a fuzzy set is a significant departure from the idea of complementarity in Boolean logic. Instead of forming a set of elements outside the domain of the fuzzy set, a fuzzy complement is found by inverting the truth membership. This is expressed mathematically as:

$$\mu_{\sim MIDDLEAGED}[X] = \bigvee_{i=0}^{N} 1 - \mu_{MIDDLEAGED}[x]_i)$$

Thus, for each membership value we take the difference between absolute membership in the set and the element's actual degree of membership. Figure A.16 shows how Not MiddleAged appears.

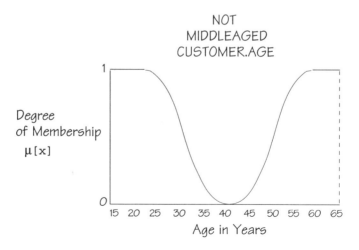

Figure A.16 Not MiddleAged

Fuzzy Rules of Noncontradiction

As consequence of the way in which set complements are determined, fuzzy logic only weakly obeys Aristotle's *law of the excluded middle* and *law of noncontradiction*. These are the foundations of Boolean logic (from them all of the rules of Boolean logic can be derived) and they describe the behavior of contradictory propositions. In particular, the law of noncontradiction says that the intersection of a set with its complement—the collection of elements that are both in the set and not in the set—is an empty set. The set cannot have any members! In Boolean logic something either *is* something or *is not* something. This appears mathematically as:

$$S_1 \cap \sim S_1 = \varnothing$$

But, if we examine the intersection of a fuzzy set with itself, it is immediately apparent that this law is not obeyed (except, perhaps, at the very edges). Since fuzzy sets are based on degrees of membership, a fuzzy set intersected with its complement produces a set that is not empty. We can see this clearly by going back to the TALL fuzzy set. What is the intersection of TALL and NOT TALL? The shaded area in Figure A.17 shows the fuzzy region formed by the proposition TALL AND NOT TALL.

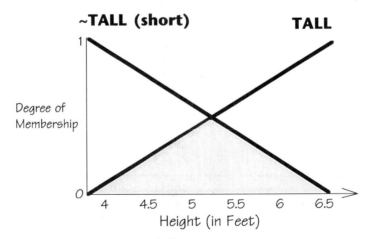

Figure A.17 The intersection of TALL and SHORT

This set is not empty, in fact, it contains elements that are to some degree complementary. Now why is this behavior in fuzzy logic important? Actually, this is one of the most important properties of fuzzy logic. Without this ability to represent partial complements we cannot define the semantics of a model's variables, we cannot execute rules that accumulate evidence, and we cannot approximate arbitrary functions. Figure A.13 shows how the fuzzy sets describing the broad range of meanings in the variable Client.Age have overlapping regions. These overlaps are areas of complementary meaning—an age has some degree of membership in YOUNG and, at the same time, has some degree of membership in MIDDLEAGED.

Fuzzy Resource Guide

```
Initiali:
Parms[0]
Parms [1,
sprint(s)
strncpy(:
FDBptr[M:
i       at;
Pa     om;
Pa t   m,
(        nt.
```

B

This appendix contains selected software listings, internet sites, miscellaneous items, and conferences related to the topic of fuzzy logic, and, specifically its wide spectrum of applications in business and industry. The compilation is based on information requests posted on the comp.ai *and the* comp.ai.fuzzy *usenet forums. We are grateful to those who responded, and we will continue to update this guide in subsequent printings.*

Disclaimer

Inclusion in this guide does not represent an endorsement of any kind by either the author or the publisher. Although every effort has been taken to ensure the accuracy of product and service descriptions, addresses, phone numbers, and so forth, including the updating of recent software releases and web sites, neither the author nor the publisher are responsible for any misrepresentation of information, errors, loss of revenue, or any claim, based on the information contained in this guide.

Software Listings

AGENT_CLIPS 1.0

Multi-agent tool, multiple copies of CLIPS can run simultaneously, handles incoming commands automatically, requires knowledge of CLIPS 6.0. Macintosh. Free. For additional information contact:

Yilmaz Cengeloglu
73313.755@compuserve.com
ftp://ftp.cs.cmu.edu/user/ai/areas/expert/systems/clips/agent/

APOLLO, ATHENA, and DIANA

Nonlinear decision tools, developed by NeuWorld Financial. These investment systems combine neural networks, genetic algorithms, fuzzy logic and expert systems, as well as more traditional statistical techniques, to provide outstanding investment performance. For information, contact:

NeuWorld Financial
16516 Bernardo Center Drive
Suite 330
San Diego, CA 92128

CubiCalc and CubiCalc RTC

CubiCard, CubiCalc Fuzzy Logic Shell, CubiCalc RTC system-building tools, Cubi-Card fuzzy logic shell with integral I/O card, and Rule Maker, an automatic system-generation utility. Windows, DOS. For more info, see the descriptions in the FAQ for the newsgroup *comp.ai.fuzzy*, or write to:

HyperLogic Corporation
P.O. Box 300010
Escondido, CA 92030

DataEngine

DataEngine is a software package for intelligent data analysis. It includes fuzzy clustering, fuzzy rule based methods and neural networks. Additionally mathematical transformations, signal processing and data visualization are provided. The graphical user interface allows efficient handling of the software. Available for Windows and Sun Workstations, other platforms on request.

DataEngine V.i. is an extension module for National Instruments' LabVIEW. It provides virtual instruments for fuzzy clustering and neural networks. Available for Windows and Macintosh, other platforms on request.

DataEngine ADL is a C++ library that enables users to include solutions worked out with DataEngine or DataEngine V.i into their own programs. It provides a runtime engine for fuzzy clustering, fuzzy rule based methods and neural networks. Available for Windows and Sun Workstations, other platforms on request.

For additional information on the DataEngine series:

MIT GmbH
Promenade 9
52076 Aachen, Germany
Phone: 49-2408-94580
Fax: 49-2408-94582
email: info@mitgmbh.de

DYNACLIPS

DYNAamic CLIPS Utilities, a set of blackboard, dynamic knowledge exchange, and agent tools for CLIPS 5.1 and 6.0. UNIX. Free.

ftp://ftp.cs.cmu.edu/user/ai/areas/expert/systems/clips/dyna/
yil@engr.ucf.ed

FCMeans Clustering Package

Package contains the FCMeans Clustering algorithm implemented in C language for MATLAB V4.0 or higher. UNIX. Free.

ftp://ftp.neuronet.pitt.edufile/pub/bogdan/dist/fcmc.v1-2.tar.Z
ftp://ftp.neuronet.pitt.edufile/pub/bogdan/dist/fcmc.v1-2.tar
http://www.neuronet.pitt.edu/~bogdan/FTP/dist.html

Fismatpc

This collection of files can be used as subroutines in MATLAB to design a fuzzy logic controller. DOS, UNIX. Free.

ftp://ftp.mathworks.com/pub/contrib/misc/fismatpc

FlexTool(GA) v M1.1 for MATLAB

A modular genetic algorithm optimization toolbox. FlexTool(EFM) Version M1.1 for MATLAB, a modular Evolutionary Fuzzy Modeling (EFM) Toolbox.

Flexible Intelligence Group, L.L.C.
P. O. Box 1477
Tuscaloosa, AL 35486-1477
FIGLLC@AOL.COM

FLIPC v1.1

A simulation of the behavior of an inverted pendulum using Fuzzy Logic. PC with FP3000 (Omron) processor. Shareware.

> ftp://oak.oakland.edu/SimTel/msdos/ai/flipc11.zip
> Michelangelo Sebastiani
> msebast@cs.unitn.it

FLOPS

A comprehensive fuzzy modelling and execution system that operates in command and full-screen mode under DOS. Provides a powerful control language, complete fuzzy representations, a nonmonotonic reasoning capability, a blackboard reasoning facility, and a wide array of fuzzification and defuzzification features. An ideal system for medical, business, and commercial fuzzy modelling.

> Dr. William Siler
> Kemp-Carraway Heart Institute
> 1901 Hoke Avenue
> Birmingham, AL 35217
> (205) 841-4925

FOOL (Fuzzy Organizer OLdenburg)

Also the FOX (Fuzzy Organizers eXecutor). FOOL is a graphical user interface to build fuzzy engine databases. These databases can be read and executed by the fuzzy engine FOX. UNIX. Free.

> ftp://ftp.informatik.uni-oldenburg.de
> FOOL c/o Ronald Hartwig
> Haareneschstrasse 2
> D-26121 Oldenburg
> Germany

Fril

A logic programming language that incorporates a consistent method for handling fuzzy and probabilistic uncertainty, based on Baldwin's theories of support logic, mass assignments, and evidential reasoning. Macintosh, Windows 3.1, Motif, UNIX.

Fril Systems Ltd.
Bristol Business Centre, Maggs House,
78 Queens Road, Bristol BS8 1QX, UK
Tel: 44117-9713481

FuNeGen 1.0

Based on the concept of fuzzy-neural system that can generate a fuzzy classifier system from sample data (training file) for real world applications. PC. Free.

ftp://obelix.microelectronic.e-technik.th-darmstadt.de/pub/neurofuzzy
Saman K. Halgamuge
Darmstadt University of Technology
Institute of Microelectronic Systems
Karlstr. 15
D-64283 Darmstadt
Germany
Tel: 49-6151-16-5136

FUZZLE

Shell for building fuzzy algorithms. Has a generic executable fuzzy engine and generates C and FORTRAN source codes. DOS, Windows.

MODiCO Inc.
Fax: (615) 584-4934

Fuzzy Cognitive Maps v1.1a

Modelling Tool. PC. Free.

ftp://ftp.wordperfect.com/3rdparty/scen11a.zip
Harm Verbeek
hverbeek@knoware.nl

FuzzyCLIPS

Version of the CLIPS rule-based expert system shell with extensions for representing and manipulating fuzzy facts and rules. UNIX, Macintosh, PC. Free.

http://ai.iit.nrc.ca/fuzzy/fuzzy.html
Bob Orchard
National Research Council of Canada
Knowledge Systems Laboratory
Montreal Road, Bldg M-50
Ottawa, Ontario
Canada K1A 0R6

FUZzySTAT, v.3.1

Calculates fuzzy subset relations such as inclusion and logical implication, fuzziness, fuzzy probabilities. Macintosh.

Dr. Michael Smithson
Behavioural Sciences
James Cook University
Queensland Australia 4811
Tel: 61-77-814-150

Fuzzy Studio 1.0/2.0

Software development tool for W.A.R.P. 1.0 processor and Application Development Board. Fuzzy Studio 2.0, Software development tool for W.A.R.P. 2.0 processor and Application Development Board. Rule-based modeler (RBM) software tool for automatic synthesis of fuzzy controllers based on neuro-fuzzy algorithm. W.A.R.P.-SIM, Software tool for simulation of closed-loop W.A.R.P.-based control systems and stability analysis based on cell-to-cell algorithm.

SGS-Thomson Microelectronics
via C. Olivetti 2
20041 Agrate Brianza (MI)
Italy
casa@agr04.st.it

Fuzzy Thought Amplifier

Provides an intuitively helpful interface for modeling, capturing and exercising thought models through Fuzzy Cognitive Maps. Windows 3.1.

Fuzzy Systems Engineering
12223 Wilsey Way
Poway, CA 92064
(619) 748-7384

LFLC-edu 1.5

Linguistic Fuzzy Logic Controller that differs from the classical Max-t-norm interpolation concept. DOS, Windows.

Vilem Novak
University of Ostrava
Department of Mathematics
Brafova 7
70100 Ostrava 1
Czech Republic
Vilem.Novak@osu.cz

MATLAB Fuzzy Logic Toolbox 1.0 (requires MATLAB 4.2c)

An intuitive software environment that combines easy-to-use fuzzy logic modelling with practical engineering design tools to streamline the development of intelligently-controlled products and processes. Windows, Macintosh, UNIX.

The MathWorks, Inc.
24 Prime Park Way
Natick, MA 01760
(508) 653-1415

METUS/IMS Information Modelling System

A client-server modelling facility for designing and deploying advanced machine intelligence applications in business and industry using fuzzy logic as well as backward and forward chaining. Metus/IMS contains an integrated relational repository, a blackboard reasoning system, ODBC connectivity to external databases, synchronous and asynchronous task control, complex, nested if-then-else rules, a knowledge mining facility for rule discovery and automatic fuzzy set generation, and a procedure scripting language.

METUS Machine Reasoning Class Libraries

A collection of C++ class libraries supporting approximate reasoning (fuzzy logic plus hedges and usuality quantifiers), backward and forward chaining, genetic algorithms, data mining, and supervised fuzzy system generation using several relationship discovery techniques. Includes a visual interface for fuzzy set creation and modification.

The Metus Systems Group
1 Griggs Lane
Chappaqua, NY 10514
Tel: (914) 238-0647
Fax: (914) 238-0837
ecox@paltech.com

NEFCLASS PC

Software to develop and train a neuro-fuzzy classifier based on the NEFCLASS model. The model learns by a supervised training procedure, and develops fuzzy sets and fuzzy rules to classify a data set. DOS.

> ftp://ftp.ibr.cs.tu-bs.de/pub/local/nefclass/nefclass.zip
> Dr. Detlef Nauck
> Technical University of Braunschweig
> Dept. of Computer Science
> Bueltenweg 74–75
> D-38106 Braunschweig
> Germany
> Tel: 49-531-391-3155

NEFCON–I

A graphical simulation environment to create, train, and test a neuro-fuzzy controller based on the NEFCON model. UNIX.

> ftp://ftp.ibr.cs.tu-bs.de/pub/local/nefcon
> Dr. Detlef Nauck
> Technical University of Braunschweig
> Dept. of Computer Science
> Bueltenweg 74 - 75
> D-38106 Braunschweig
> Germany
> Tel: 49-531-391-3155

O'INCA Design Framework

An integrated platform for design, simulation, and C code generation of fuzzy logic and neural net systems.

> Intelligent Machines, Inc.
> 1153 Bordeaux Drive
> Sunnyvale, CA 94089
> (408) 745-0881

OWL Neural Network Library

OWL Neural Network Library, CubiCalc Fuzzy Logic Shell, CubiCalc RTC system-building tools, CubiCard fuzzy logic shell with integral I/O card, and Rule Maker, an automatic system-generation utility. Descriptions in the FAQ for the newsgroup comp.ai.fuzzy.

> HyperLogic Corp.
> P.O. Box 300010
> Escondido, CA 92030

RTFCM 1.4

A fuzzy cognitive maps modelling and exploration system for Windows 3.1. Developed by Rod Taber one of the principal experts in fuzzy cognitive map technology, RTFCM combines an easy-to-use graphical interface with a wide spectrum of modelling capabilities.

> Rod Taber, Ph.D.
> Ring Technology
> Route 1, Box 69AA
> Ridgeley, WV 26753
> (304) 738-3603

SCENARIO

A modelling tool that uses fuzzy cognitive maps. Windows. Free.

> ftp://ftp.uni-paderborn.de/ftp/aminet/pub/new
> Harm Verbeek
> Rozenpad 14
> 2651 XA Berkel en Rodenrijs
> The Netherlands

Sonalysts, Inc.

Providing fuzzy logic solutions to government and industry, including mission effectiveness, automatic helmsman, and multi-sensor data fusion applications.

> Sonalysts, Inc.
> 215 Parkway North
> PO Box 280
> Waterford, CT 06385
> (800) 526-8091

Internet Sites

WWW Sites

http://analogy.ie.utoronto.ca/fuzzy.html
>The Intelligent Fuzzy Systems Laboratory at the University of Toronto.

http://ai.iit.nrc.ca/home_page.html
>Knowledge Systems Lab Server.

http://csv.warwick.ac.uk/~esrlj/Research/Finance.html
>Relating to research on stock market trading with neural networks.

http://http.cs.berkeley.edu/projects/Bisc
>List of fuzzy logic institutions that are affiliates of BISC (at University of California-Berkeley).

http://larry.texsci.edu
>Fuzzy Logic Group of the College of Textiles and Science.

http://rtm.science.unitn.it/
>About Reactive Memory Search, University of Trento, Italy.

http://seraphim.csee.usf.edu/nafips.html
>The North American Fuzzy Information Processing Society.

http://www.cs.cmu.edu:8001/Web/Groups/AI/html/faqs/ai/fuzzy/part1/faq.html
>Answers to questions about fuzzy logic and fuzzy expert systems.

http://www.cs.unitn.it/Mail/Fuzzy-ML/
>All of the mail coming from the fuzzy-mail mailing list in separate html documents.

http://www.cse.ucsd.edu/users/elkan/
>"The Paradoxical Success of Fuzzy Logic" by Charles Elkan.

http://www.dice.ucl.ac.be/neural-nets/NPL/NPL.html
>Abstracts of papers published in Neural Processing Letters.

http://www.dsi.unimi.it/Users/Labs/LAC/softcomp/convegni/index.html
List of Workshops, call for papers, and seminars about fuzzy logic & soft computing.

http://www.mcs.net/~jorn/html/ai.html
"An opinionated overview of AI" by Jorn Barger.

http://www.neuronet.pitt.edu/~bogdan/FTP/dist.html
FCMeans Clustering Package software.

http://www.quadralay.com/www/Fuzzy/Fuzzy.html

FTP (File Transfer Protocol)

ftp://ftp.dice.ucl.ac.be/pub/neural-nets/NPL
Abstracts of papers published in Neural Processing Letters.

ftp://ftp.cs.cmu.edu/user/ai/
Carnegie Mellon AI Repository.

ftp://ftp.ibr.cs.tu-bs.de/pub/local/papers/fuzzy-nn.bib
The Neuro-Fuzzy Bibliography, over 130 references to neuro-fuzzy papers.

ftp://ftp.informatik.uni-oldenburg.de
FOOL and FOX software.

ftp://ftp.mathworks.com/pub/contrib/misc/fismatpc
Fismatpc software.

ftp://mira.dbai.tuwien.ac.at/pub/slany
Various information files including the who-is-who in fuzzy directory, a bibliography on fuzzy-scheduling, and many others.

ftp://ftp.neuronet.pitt.edufile/pub/bogdan/dist/fcmc.v1-2.tar.Z
FCMeans Clustering Package software.

ftp://oak.oakland.edu/SimTel/msdos/ai/flipc11.zip
FLIPC v1.1 software.

ftp://obelix.microelectronic.e-technik.th-darmstadt.de/pub/neurofuzzy
FuNe (fuzzy neural software) and papers.

ftp://ftp.uni-paderborn.de/ftp/aminet/pub/new
SCENARIO software.

ftp://ftp.wordperfect.com/3rdparty/scen11a.zip
Fuzzy Cognitive Maps v1.1a.

Mailing Lists

73313.775@compuserve.com
For users of AGENT_CLIPS software.

fuzzy-mail@vexpert.dbai.tuwien.ac.at
Fuzzy systems mailing list.

Green Eggs Report
A monthly post of URLs spotted within the newsgroup comp.ai.fuzzy. Send mail to: rick@ar.com.

maiser@pz-oekosys.uni-kiel.d400.de
Fuzzy topics in ecology.

Majordomo@mcs.anl.gov
Application of neural networks to the solution of problems in medicine and biology; include message: subscribe Biomedical-SIG-INNS.

Newsgroups

comp.ai
The primary artificial intelligence forum. Discussions here range over the entire spectrum of issues in machine intelligence.

comp.ai.fuzzy
A forum for the discussion of fuzzy logic, fuzzy expert systems, and other issues associated with fuzzy logic. Since this is a usenet news group on the internet, its contents tend to be very academic and technical.

Compuserve:
Go AIEXPERT, a forum on Artificial Intelligence systems, and related topics. The FUZZY LOGIC section provides a continual dialog on the many business and software development issues associated with fuzzy logic. The messages on this forum tend be slightly less technical than those on the comp.ai.fuzzy usenet forum.

alt.books.technical	Often contains listing of books on fuzzy logic and related issues of machine reasoning.
biz.books.technical	Business books that occasionally cover expert system and system design topics.
misc.books.technical	A discussion of various technical books, infrequently covers books dealing with artificial intelligence, fuzzy logic, and related technical topics.

Miscellaneous Fuzzy Items

Courses and Lectures

Neural and Fuzzy Systems
Signal and Image Processing Institute
Electrical Engineering Department
University of Southern California

Fuzzy Fundamentals—Two courses
University of California at San Diego
San Diego, CA

Neural and Fuzzy Systems
Signal and Image Processing Institute
Electrical Engineering Department
University of Southern California

Fuzzy Sets Course and Intelligent Systems course
Department of Computer Science and Engineering
University of South Florida
Tampa, FL

Fuzzy Sets and Systems
Computer Science Department
Philadelphia College of Textiles and Science
Philadelphia, PA

Intelligent Systems with Fuzzy Sets
Department of Computer Science and Engineering
University of South Florida
Tampa, FL

Modeling and Management of Uncertainty
Electrical and Computer Engineering Department
University of Missouri
Columbia, MO

Oregon Graduate Institute of Science and Technology (OGI)
Ph.D. programs in the areas of Neural Networks, Learning,
Signal Processing, Time Series, Control, Speech, Language, Vision,
and Computational Finance

IEEE Standards

To obtain electronic copies of the latest drafts of the IEEE standards on computational intelligence, neural networks, evolutionary systems, or virtual reality contact:

Bob Labelle
IEEE Standards
445 Hoes Lane
Piscataway, NJ 08855
Tel: (908) 526-3800
Fax: (908) 562-1571
r.labelle@ieee.org
For questions or details, contact mpadgett@eng.auburn.edu

Groups

Fuzzy logic research group at the University of Missouri, Columbia. Interests are in computer vision/pattern recognition, decision making, and intelligent automation.

Jim Keller
Electrical and Computer Engineering Department
University of Missouri, Columbia
Columbia, MO 65211
Tel: (314) 882-7339
Fax: (314) 882-0397
keller@sun1.ece.missouri.edu

Italian fuzzy logic group at the Qualitative Reasoning Working Group of the Italian Association for AI (AI*IA).

Andrea Bonarini
Politecnico di Milano—Dip. di Elettronica e Informazione
Politecnico di Milano AI & Robotics Project
Piazza Leonardo da Vinci, 32
I–20133 Milano, Italy
Tel: 39-2-2399-3525

Manuscripts

Fuzziness and Probability by S. F. Thomas. To obtain an email copy of the manuscript in postscript, send email to:

book@decan.gate.net

The email response will consist of 20 parts, none exceeding 62Kbytes. The total size of the unencoded compressed tar file is 1.2Mbytes.

Newsletters

Apollo Small Cap Stock Report. Monthly newsletter based on the Apollo Stock Selection System (see software listings) that uses fuzzy logic, neural nets, and other computing technology to select stocks most likely to out-perform the market. For more information, contact:

16516 Bernardo Center Drive, Suite 330
San Diego, CA 92128
(800) 261-3811

NeuroVe$t Journal. A bimonthly journal which publishes original papers and information in the collective fields of finance, advanced technologies and techniques. Contact:

P.O. Box 764
Haymarket, VA 22069
(703) 754-0696

Videotapes and Training

FuzzyTape is a set of instructional videos, tailored to different audiences, including technical managers, engineers, and computer scientists. These tapes introduce both fuzzy theory and applications. For more information, contact:

The Schwartz Associates
801 West El Camino Real, Suite 150
Mountain View, CA 94040

Conferences (July 95–April 96)

North American Fuzzy Information Processing Society (NAFIPS)

The Joint Third International Symposium on Uncertainty Modelling and Analysis (ISUMA). Special session on fuzzy sets and systems in signal processing applications. *September 17–20, 1995. College Park, MD*

Mathematical Methods in Economics, 13th MME '95 Symposium

Opinions and experiences of macro- and micro-economic models using fuzzy sets theory and other techniques. *September 18–20, 1995. Ostrava, VSB—Technical University, Czech Republic*

Second Annual Joint Conference on Information Sciences

Fourth International Conference on Fuzzy Theory and Technology, Second International Conference on Computer Theory and Informatics, and First International Conference on Computational Intelligence and Neurosciences. *September 28–October 1, 1995. Wrightsville Beach, NC*

Seventh Portuguese Conference on Artificial Intelligence

Devoted to all areas of artificial intelligence, parallel workshops on expert systems, fuzzy logic and neural networks, and applications of artificial intelligence to robotics and vision systems. *October 3–6, 1995. Funchal, Madeira Island, Portugal*

IEEE International Conference on Systems, Man and Cybernetics

Intelligent systems for the 21st century. *October 22–25, 1995. Vancouver, British Columbia, Canada*

International ICSC Symposium on Soft Computing

Fuzzy logic (approximate reasoning), artificial neural networks and genetic algorithms. *October 24–27, 1995. Rochester, NY*

Digital Image Storage and Archiving Systems

Fuzzy, object-oriented, feature-based, neural network, and information theoretic approaches to image and video storage indexing and retrieval. *October 26–27, 1995. Philadelphia, PA*

Fuzzy Logic '95

International conference on fuzzy-neural applications, systems and tools. A technical users conference on the design and application of intelligent information and control systems. This year's conference includes a special presentation of *The Meeting of Minds: A Discussion of Models of Reality*, hosted by Steve Allen. *November 7–9, 1995. Burlingame, CA*

EXPERSYS

Seventh International Conference on Artificial Intelligence and Expert Systems Applications (EXPERSYS). Fundamental aspects as well as industrial applications of artificial intelligence and expert systems. *November 9–10, 1995. San Francisco, CA*

Artificial Neural Networks in Engineering

The conference will cover the theory of artificial neural networks, fuzzy logic, and evolutionary programming, and their applications in the engineering domain. *November 12–15, 1995. St. Louis, MO*

International Joint Conference of CFSA/IFIS/SOFT

A joint conference on fuzzy theory and applications with emphasis on the technology and applications of fuzzy systems. *December 7–9, 1995. Taipei, Taiwan, R.O.C.*

Fifth International Conference on User Modelling

All aspects of user modeling and user-adapted interaction, including intelligent/adaptive user interfaces, student modeling and intelligent tutoring systems, and other applications. *January 2–5, 1996. Kailua-Kona, HI*

International Fuzzy Systems and Intelligent Control Conference '96

Devoted primarily to computer-based feedback control systems that rely on fuzzy logic, neural network theory, probabilistic reasoning, genetic algorithms, chaos theory, learning theory, and other soft computing and artificial techniques. *April 8–11, 1996. Maui, HI*

Second IEEE International Conference on Requirements Engineering

Aimed at bringing together practitioners and researchers to discuss software requirements, engineering related problems, and results. *April 15–18, 1996. Colorado Springs, CO*

The Fuzzy Standard Additive Model

By Bart Kosko

This appendix presents the mathematical details of the most popular family of fuzzy models. These fuzzy systems convert an input x *into an output* F(x) *by adding the scaled outputs of the fired rules and then taking their centroid or center of gravity. The output* F(x) *is this center of gravity and has a simple form:*

$$F(x) \quad = \quad \frac{\sum\limits_{j=1}^{m} a_j(x)\, V_j\, c_j}{\sum\limits_{j=1}^{m} a_j(x)\, V_j} \qquad\qquad . \qquad (1)$$

These models are the so-called *standard additive models* (SAMs) and account not only for the fuzzy systems used in this book but for those used in most fuzzy applications. They are universal function approximators and also reduce to the radial basis function nets used in neural network applications. This appendix derives the SAM equation and shows how it reduces to the center-of-gravity models of this text. The Appendix is based on the additive system results in Kosko's *Neural Networks and Fuzzy Systems* and related publications.

An *additive* fuzzy system $F: R^n \rightarrow R^p$ stores m if-then rules of the word form "If $X = A_j$, then $Y = B_j$" or patch form $A_j \times B_j \subset R^n \times R^p$ and then *adds* or sums the "fired" then-parts $B'_j \subset R^p$ to give te set term B. The additive fuzzy system is a *standard additive model* or SAM if it computes the output value $F(x) \in R^p$ from B as the centroid of B and if the vector input $x \in R^n$ fires each rule through scaling or product-correlation inference:

$$F(x) \quad = \quad Centroid(B) \quad = \quad Centroid(\sum_{j=1}^{m} w_j\, a_j(x)\, B_j) \qquad (2)$$

559

The rule weights cancel out of (2) (and out of (1)) if they all equal the same value: $w_1 = ... = w_j$. This appendix assumes the rules weights have the same values and thus ignores them. In general learning schemes can tune the rule weights.

In (2) $a_j : R^n \to [0, 1]$ is the set function of the *multivalued* or "fuzzy" if-part set $A_j \subset R^n$ and $b_j : R^p \to [0, 1]$ is the set function of the then-part set $B_j \subset R^p$. The input x belongs to A_j to the degree $a_j(x)$ (or degree $\mu_{A_j}(x)$). In practice fuzzy designers often work with scalar systems $F : R^n \to R$ with $b_j : R \to [0, 1]$ and with factored if-part sets $A_j = A_j^1 \times ... \times A_j^n$. The factored sets allow one to work with their n coordinate projections A_j^i as scalar fuzzy sets on n indepenent input axes as in the fuzzy systems in this book. The SAM equation (1) allows one to replace the then-part set B_j with just its area or volume V_j and its centroid c_j and these terms one can compute in advance. The next section defines these terms.

SAM Theorem

Suppose the fuzzy system $F : R^n \to R^p$ is a *standard additive model*:

$$F(x) = Centroid(B) = Centroid(\sum_{j=1}^{m} a_j(x) B_j).$$ Then $F(x)$ is a convex sum of

the m then-part set centroids:

$$F(x) = \frac{\sum_{j=1}^{m} a_j(x) V_j c_j}{\sum_{j=1}^{m} a_j(x) V_j} \tag{3}$$

$$= \sum_{j=1}^{m} p_j(x) c_j \tag{4}$$

The convex coefficients or discrete probability weights $p_1(x), ..., p_m(x)$ depend on the input x through

$$p_j(x) \;=\; \frac{a_j(x)\,V_j}{\displaystyle\sum_{j=1}^{m} a_j(x)\,V_j} \qquad\qquad . \qquad (5)$$

V_j is the finite positive volume (or area if $p = 1$) and c_j is the centroid of then-part set B_j:

$$V_j \;=\; \int_{R^p} b_j(y_1,\dots,y_p)\,dy_1\dots dy_p \quad > 0 \qquad (6)$$

$$c_j \;=\; \frac{\displaystyle\int_{R^p} y\,b_j(y_1,\dots,y_p)\,dy_1\dots dy_p}{\displaystyle\int_{R^p} b_j(y_1,\dots,y_p)\,dy_1\dots dy_p} \qquad\qquad . \qquad (7)$$

Proof. There is no loss of generality to prove the theorem for the scalar-output case $p = 1$ when $F{:}R^n \to R$. This simplifies the notation. We need but replace the scalar integrals over R with the p-multiple or volume integrals over R^p in the proof to prove the general case. The scalar case $p = 1$ gives (6) and (7) as

$$V_j \;=\; \int_{-\infty}^{\infty} b_j(y)\,dy \qquad (8)$$

$$c_j \;=\; \frac{\displaystyle\int_{-\infty}^{\infty} y\,b_j(y)\,dy}{\displaystyle\int_{-\infty}^{\infty} b_j(y)\,dy} \qquad\qquad . \qquad (9)$$

Then the theorem follows by expanding the centroid of B and invoking the SAM or sum-of-products assumption (2) to rearrange terms:

$$F(x) \;=\; \text{Centroid}(B) \qquad (10)$$

$$=\; \frac{\displaystyle\int_{-\infty}^{\infty} y\,b(y)\,dy}{\displaystyle\int_{-\infty}^{\infty} b(y)\,dy} \qquad (11)$$

$$=\; \frac{\displaystyle\int_{-\infty}^{\infty} y \sum_{j=1}^{m} b_j'(y)\,dy}{\displaystyle\int_{-\infty}^{\infty} \sum_{j=1}^{m} b_j'(y)\,dy} \qquad (12)$$

$$= \frac{\int_{-\infty}^{\infty} y \sum_{j=1}^{m} a_j(x) b_j(y)\, dy}{\int_{-\infty}^{\infty} \sum_{j=1}^{m} a_j(x) b_j(y)\, dy} \tag{13}$$

$$= \frac{\sum_{j=1}^{m} a_j(x) \int_{-\infty}^{\infty} y\, b_j(y)\, dy}{\sum_{j=1}^{m} a_j(x) \int_{-\infty}^{\infty} b_j(y)\, dy} \tag{14}$$

$$= \frac{\sum_{j=1}^{m} a_j(x)\, V_j \dfrac{\int_{-\infty}^{\infty} y\, b_j(y)\, dy}{V_j}}{\sum_{j=1}^{m} a_j(x)\, V_j} \tag{15}$$

$$= \frac{\sum_{j=1}^{m} a_j(x)\, V_j\, c_j}{\sum_{j=1}^{m} a_j(x)\, V_j} \; . \tag{16}$$

Q.E.D.

The SAM fuzzy system

$$F(x) \;=\; \frac{\sum_{j=1}^{m} a_j(x)\, V_j\, c_j}{\sum_{j=1}^{m} a_j(x)\, V_j} \tag{17}$$

$$F(x) \;=\; \frac{\sum_{j=1}^{m} a_j(x)\, V_j\, c_j}{\sum_{j=1}^{m} a_j(x)\, V_j} \tag{17}$$

reduces to the *center of gravity* or COG fuzzy model

$$F(x) \quad = \quad \frac{\displaystyle\sum_{j=1}^{m} m_j \, x_j}{\displaystyle\sum_{j=1}^{m} m_j} \tag{18}$$

if the modes or "peaks" x_j of the then-part sets $B_j \subset R^p$ equal the then-part set centroids c_j, if m stands for the compound if-part set function a, and if the then-part sets B_j all have the same areas or volumes V_j: $\quad x_j = c_j, \quad m_j = a_j(x)$, and $V_1 = ... = V_m > 0$. The COG model is Sugeno's refinement on the original Mamdani fuzzy model of the 1970s. Equation (18) uses the notation of the COG model in Chapter 1 of this book.

A simple Gaussian SAM gives both a COG model and the popular radial-basis-function (RBF) model of neural networks of Moody and Specht. Wang and Mendel have recently restated this RBF model in fuzzy notation as a simple scalar Gaussian SAM $F : R^n \to R$:

$$F(x) \quad = \quad \frac{\displaystyle\sum_{j=1}^{m} \bar{z}^j \left(\prod_{i=1}^{n} \mu_{A_i^j}(x_i) \right)}{\displaystyle\sum_{j=1}^{m} \left(\prod_{i=1}^{n} \mu_{A_i^j}(x_i) \right)} \tag{19}$$

The SAM equation (1) reduces to (19) if for Gaussian sets with product combination of if-part set values:

$$y \quad = \quad z \tag{20}$$

$$a_j(x) \quad = \quad \prod_{i=1}^{n} a_j^i(x_i) \tag{21}$$

$$= \quad \prod_{i=1}^{n} \mu_{A_i^j}(x_i) \tag{22}$$

$$V_j \quad = \quad 1 \tag{23}$$

$$c_j \quad = \quad \bar{z}^j \tag{24}$$

$$a_j^i(x_i) \quad = \quad s_i^j \exp\left[-\frac{1}{2} \left(\frac{x_i - \bar{x}_i^j}{\sigma_i^j} \right)^2 \right] \tag{25}$$

for scaling constant $0 < s_i^j \le 1$.

The unity volume follows in (23) since the m then-part Gaussian sets integrate to unity over all of R. The result still follows so long as the then-part sets have the same area. (38) follows because the mode of a Gaussian set equals its centroid and Wang and Mendel use the mode definition "$\bar{z}^j$ is the point in R at which $\mu_{B^j}(z)$ achieves its maximum value." John Moody arrived at (19) in his search for a neural network built from the m input-ouput pairs (x_j, y_j) with light computation. Donald Specht arrived arrived at (19) from the theory of Parzen density estimators and the use of conditional expectations as mean-squared optimal estimators. They all center a vector Gaussian set or ball at each input vector x_j and center a Gaussian bell curve at each output value y_j.

The Specht result holds for all SAM systems with arbitrary fuzzy sets: The fuzzy system F computes the conditional expectation $E[Y|X]$. This follows from the centroid structure in (10) - (11) and is important and simple enough to derive here. Note that each vector input x gives its own combined output set $B(x)$ and thus its own output $F(x)$:

$$F(x) \quad = \quad Centroid(B(x)) \tag{26}$$

$$= \quad \frac{\int_{R^p} y\, b(x, y)\, dy}{\int_{R^p} b(x, y)\, dy} \tag{27}$$

$$= \quad \int_{R^p} y\, p(y|x)\, dy \tag{28}$$

$$= \quad E[Y|X = x] \tag{29}$$

for each $x \in R^n$. This holds because the joint/marginal ratio in (27) defines a proper conditional probability

$$p(y|x) \quad = \quad \frac{b(x, y)}{\int_{R^p} b(x, y)\, dy} \tag{30}$$

even though $b(x,y) > 0$ may hold. The conditional mean is the optimal mean-squared estimator based on the available information in the if-part and then-part fuzzy sets. In this sense fuzzy systems are optimal but ultimately probabilistic systems.

Glossary

This is not a complete and detailed glossary of all the terms used in this book nor related to the concepts addressed in this book but is a list of some important terms and ideas. The definitions are intended to be brief and relatively nontechnical.

Adaptive Fuzzy System

A system that learns its behavior from the interactive between inputs and outputs. Adaptive systems can learn the relationships through supervised training or through unsupervised cluster analysis. An adaptive system is capable of interacting with the external environment to adjust its long-term behavior.

Agents

Autonomous software programs that operate independently and usually remotely. Agents can negotiate for information resources, cluster and classify knowledge, and spawn other agent activities. Agents are used on the Internet to seek out universal resource locators (URLs) and return information to the owner.

Alpha-level

A metric establishing the minimum degree of membership in a fuzzy set. The alpha-threshold level (or *alpha-cut*) is a truth membership value. There are two types of alpha thresholds, *strong* and *weak*. A strong threshold is indicated by $\mu_A[x] > A$, while the weak threshold is defined as $\mu_A[x] \geq A$. This slight change in the definition plays a significant role in the definition of other fuzzy control parameters, most notably, the idea of the underlying support set (where the alpha level is set to zero [0] and the strong alpha cut is applied to the fuzzy space).

Ambiguity

Ambiguity is generally distinct from fuzziness. Our everyday experiences tell us that an ambiguous statement involves a meaning with several distinct yet possible interpretations such as: the food is hot where the term *hot* could refer to the temperature of the food, to the amount of spices in the food, or to the current trendiness associated with a particular kind of food. However, the definition of a fuzzy concept, such as TALL, involves little ambiguity, only imprecision or uncertainty.

Antecedent

The state or processes preceding the current model state. Rule-based expert systems often use this term to define the premise or predicate of a rule. The antecedent in a fuzzy logic system defines the combined truth of the fuzzy region for a control or solution variable.

Approximation

The process of forming a fuzzy set from a scalar or nonfuzzy continuous variable. An approximation of a scalar generally results in a bell-shaped fuzzy space (such as a PI or Weibull curve). Approximations can be applied to both fuzzy sets (and fuzzy regions) as well as scalars. The hedges around, near {to}, close {to}, and about are used to approximate the fuzzy set or scalar.

Assertions

A fuzzy system model consists almost completely of assertions (or fuzzy propositions). These can be conditional or unconditional. Unconditional assertions establish a fuzzy region that acts as the support space for the solution. A statement such as our price must be high is an unconditional assertion. On the other hand, conditional fuzzy assertions update the solution space with a strength or degree that depends on the truth of their predicate (the "conditional" part). A statement such as if competition_price is not very high then our price should be near the competition_price is a conditional fuzzy assertion.

B*Tree

A balanced indexing scheme used in database systems to retrieve records based on nonunique keys. A B*tree grows from the bottom up and maintains rapid access to clusters of related records.

Backward Chaining

A machine reasoning technique that works from a goal backwards to all the supporting properties for the goal. Backward chaining recursively establishes a series of goals (called *subgoals*) as it works through a rule set looking for the value associated with the current goal state.

Bayes Theorem   A theorem of probability that says if you know the *a priori* probability of a hypothesis before examining the results of some test, the future test results can be used to modify the cumulative probability to predict the *a posteriori* probability. In practice, however, Bayes theorem has become a measure of subjective probability based on a scale of "rational belief" in the probability that an event will occur. The scale ranges from [0], absolute disbelief, and [1], absolute belief. Bayesian probabilities often diverge from frequentist or parametric probabilities in the sense that *a priori* observational histories are not required to establish the total probabilities.

Blackboard System   (also *blackboard reasoning*) A machine intelligence system that uses a high-level or meta-reasoning facility to control the reasoning of subordinate tasks. A blackboard system accumulates knowledge—often in a hierarchial or taxonomic fashion—and stores the knowledge in a way that is accessible to all of the individual tasks. Blackboard tasks are started synchronously or asynchronously.

Belief System   A belief system operation establishes a plausibility state for an object or a particular model state, thus projecting its domain into a set of candidate values. A belief system corresponds to the subjective intentions of the observer in confirming or denying the validity of a model assertion or proposition.

Cache   An in-memory buffer containing frequently used data. In database systems the page cache, known as the *least-recently used* (LRU) buffering system, holds all the pages that have been recently and frequently accessed by application code. Caches can be organized as complex data structures (such as binary trees or threaded hash tables) or as simple LIFO (last in, first out), FIFO (first in, first out) queues.

Case-Based Reasoning   A machine reasoning system based on the analysis of and extrapolation from previous examples in a common domain. A case-based reasoning (CBR) facility uses a similarity function to find cases with attributes that approximate each other to various degrees of cohesion. Once a set of similar cases have been collected, an action plan is extracted based on statistical, rule-based, and, in more modern CBR systems, neural network facilities.

Cellular Automata	mathematical representations of an ideal physical or conceptual system in which the dimensions of space and time have been quantized (made discrete). The behavior of cellular automata is dictated by a set of simple rules, usually completely determined by the current or immediately previous state of the system. Cellular automata systems are capable of assuming highly complex, highly nonlinear behaviors, and have immediate applicability to problems in marketing, economics, manufacturing, and asset allocation.
Certainty Factors	Measures of cumulative certainty or uncertainty in some early forms of expert systems (such as MYCIN). Certainty factors provide a consistent, but somewhat *ad hoc* means of combining evidence in rule-based expert systems. Since they are applied by the analyst on an external basis rather than being associated with and directly developed by the reasoning process, they have limited application is complex system.
Chaotic Systems	A mathematically or logically defined system employing nonlinear dynamics. Chaotic systems are typically associated with high sensitive to small changes in initial conditions.
Closure	The property, in database systems and linguistic variables, of forming new entities from operations on one or more entities. A relational join on two tables produces a new relation with its own physical and logical structure. The application of a hedge on a fuzzy set produces a new fuzzy set.
Column	Used in database technology to indicate a single data element in a physical record. A column has a single value, an underlying data type, and a domain of applicability (a possible set of data values.)
Compatibility	A central idea of fuzzy set theory representing the degree to which a control variable's value is compatible with the associated fuzzy set. In the view of some theorists, compatibility is the essence of fuzzy logic and possibility theory. When we encounter a fuzzy statement such as `if the temperature is hot then increase cool air about 2 units` the conditional fuzzy proposition `the temperature is hot` is a measure of the compatibility between the value for temperature and the fuzzy set `HOT`. The degree of membership value returned by evaluating the assertion is a measure of this compatibility.

Complement

The negation of a fuzzy set is the complement of the fuzzy set. The complement of a fuzzy space is usually produced by the operation, $1-\mu_A(x)$. The fuzzy complement indicates the degree to which an element (x) is not a member of the fuzzy set (A). Unlike conventional crisp sets, an element is not either in or out of a fuzzy set, thus the complement also contains members that have partial exclusions. See the law of the excluded middle for another feature of the fuzzy complement.

Conjunction

The process of applying the intersection operator (AND) to two fuzzy sets. For each point on the fuzzy set, we take the minimum of the membership functions for the two intersected sets.

Consequent

The action or right-side part of a rule. In a fuzzy modelling system the consequent defines each control fuzzy region that updates the specified solution variable. As an example in the rules, our price must be high if rotor.temperature is hot then rotor_speed must be reduced the control fuzzy sets HIGH and REDUCED are consequent sets. The variables price and rotor.temperature are solution variables (and are represented during the model processing as solution fuzzy sets).

Consistency Principle

A principle from possibility theory that says the possibility of event X is always at least as great as its probability, or stated formally, $\text{poss}(X) \geq \text{prob}(X)$.

Continuous Variables

A control variable whose possible values are not discrete. In statistical and probability models these are usually called *continuous random variables* and they play an important role in expectation based on their probability density function (PDF). Generally speaking, fuzzy spaces are continuous variables.

Contrast

A hedge operation that moves the truth function of a fuzzy set around the [.5] degree of membership. The contrast intensification process increases membership values above [.5], while the dilution process defuses or decreases membership below this value. The hedge positively implements the intensification capability and the hedge generally implements the defusing capability.

Correlation Rules

(also called *correlation encoding*) These rules couple the truth of the consequent assignment fuzzy region with the truth of the rule's premise. Predicated on the principle that the truth of consequent cannot be greater than the truth of the premise. In the fuzzy rule space, if FR_p then FR_c is FR_a it is the fuzzy region FR_a that is correlated with the premise fuzzy expression FR_p—the result of this correlated space is used to update the consequent fuzzy region FR_c. Both correlation rules reduce the height of the fuzzy region.

Correlation Minimum Rule

(also see *correlation product rule*) The method of implication that correlates the consequent fuzzy region with the antecedent (premise) fuzzy truth value by truncating the consequent fuzzy set at the limit of the premise's truth value. The formal implication space is defined as $\mu_R[xi] = \min(\mu_R[xi], \mu P_{tv})$. That is, the membership value of the current consequent fuzzy region (R) is the minimum of the fuzzy region and the truth of the premise (P_{tv}). The correlation maximum maintains the general dimensions of the fuzzy region but forms a plateau across the membership plane corresponding to the truth of the premise.

Correlation Product Rule

(also see *correlation minimum rule*) The method of implication that correlates the consequent fuzzy region with the antecedent (premise) fuzzy truth value by the taking the outer product of the membership values. The formal implication space is defined as $\mu_R[xi] = \mu_R[xi] \bullet \mu P_{tv}$. That is, the membership value of the current consequent fuzzy region (R) is the product of the fuzzy region and the truth of the premise (P_{tv}). This effectively scales the fuzzy space.

Crisp Set

The term, in fuzzy logic and approximate reasoning, usually applied to classical (Boolean) sets where membership is either [1] (totally contained in the set) or [0] (totally excluded from the set). As an example, the crisp representation for the concept TALL might have a discrimination function, $T = \{x \in U | \mu_t(x) \geq 6\}$ meaning that anyone with a height greater than or equal to six feet is a member of the TALL set. Crisp sets, unlike fuzzy sets, have distinct and sharply defined membership edges. Note that the vertical line connecting nonmembership with membership, unlike a fuzzy set, is dimensionless. An intrinsic property of a crisp set is the well-defined behavior of its members. In particular, crisp sets obey the geometry of Boolean and Aristotelian sets. This means that the universe of discourse for a set and its complete is always disjoint and complete. Thus the relation $A \cap \sim A \equiv \varnothing$ (also known as the law of the excluded middle) is always obeyed.

Database	(also *database management system* or *DBMS*) A formally structured repository for organizing, controlling, retrieving, and maintaining complex data structures and data relationships. Databases can have several organizations: network or hierarchical, relational, and object. Network and hierarchical databases (common in the mid 1960s through the early 1980s) maintain data through a series of physical pointers. Relationships are established and fixed when the database is designed and implemented through these pointers. Most modern databases systems are relational—information is stored in a series of independently maintained tables consisting of rows and columns. Relationships are established "in the data," that is, by sharing common data columns and can be specified dynamically. A new family of ObjectBases used the idea of object classes to store conceptual organizations. In their need to fix the organization of the database and its relationships, the object base systems have some of the same design and architecture features of the network systems of the 1960s and 1970s.

Data Mining	(also *knowledge mining*) The process of evaluating the data in large database to discover relationships. Data mining is used in fuzzy systems to discover rules as well as generate and tune fuzzy sets. Data Mining can be done through both supervised and unsupervised methods often involving a combination of fuzzy logic and neural networks.

Decision Support System (DSS)	A management system containing an operational, tactical, and/or strategic model of the enterprise. Decision support systems generally contain time-series based facilities combining statistics, linear or dynamic programming, and financial models with report generators, graphics, and visual interfaces. Modern decision support systems combine expert system technology with high-volume commercial databases.

Defuzzification	The process of deriving a scalar, representing a control variable's expected value, from a fuzzy set. Following one of several rules for selecting a point on the edge of the fuzzy region, the defuzzification process isolates a value on the fuzzy set's domain. Defuzzification is primarily a matter of selecting a point on the fuzzy region's boundary and then dropping a "plumb line" to the domain axis. The point of contact on this axis is the scalar's value. For further discussions, see *decomposition methods, composite mass, composite maximum,* and *composite moments.*

**Degree
of Membership**

In fuzzy set theory, this is the degree to which a variable's value is compatible with the fuzzy set. The degree of membership is a value between [0] (no membership) and [1] (complete membership) and is drawn from the truth function of the fuzzy set. While the values in the domain of a fuzzy set always increase as you go from left to right, the degree of membership follows the shape of the fuzzy set's surface (so that, as an example, membership values associated with a bell curve rise to a maximum value (usually [1]) and then fall back toward the zero [0] membership point). The term truth function is often used interchangeably with degree of membership.

Delphi Method

A consensus gathering method used predictively or prescriptively (as a diagnostic and analysis vehicle). The Delphi method uses blind voting, convergence and threshold analysis to evaluate a premise (hypothesis) and its possible configurations (outcomes). When knowledge is distributed among many experts or the knowledge is represented among different interlocking fields of expertise, the Delphi method is one important technique in knowledge acquisition and validation.

**Dempster-
Shafer
Theory**

A mathematical model of plausible belief systems based on frames of discernment, probability ranges, and evidential reasoning. Dempster-Shafer assumes that, in response to a hypothesis, a mutually exclusive set of possible solution states exist. In practice the Dempster-Shafer [DS] approach accumulates evidence (much in the same manner as Bayesian systems) except that here the belief in the evidence itself is under analysis. The total accumulated evidence or evidence measure (m) is treated as a mass function. The DS theory differs significantly from probability in its handling of uncertainty and especially ignorance. Unlike probability which assigns the value $(1/N)$ to an event with N outcomes—even if we have no information about the statistical behavior of the system—the Dempster-Shafer model treats the unknown state of a system as simple nonbelief. This means that if we only know S_1 with a probability of .80, then $p(\sim S_1)$ is held in a state of reserved judgment. Thus under Dempster-Shafer, $p(S_1) + p(\sim S_1) \geq 1$. Because this expression of probabilities is very close to the nature of fuzzy possibilities, and since both fuzzy systems and DS processes incorporate rules of evidence much research has recently gone into reconciling Dempster-Shafer's rules of evidence processing and possibility theory.

Dilution

A hedge operation, generally implemented by rather, quite, or somewhat, that moves the truth function of the fuzzy set so that its degrees of membership values are increased for each point along the line. This means that, for a given variable's membership rank, its value in a diluted fuzzy set will increase. The most common dilution mechanism changes the fuzzy surface by taking the square root of the membership function at each point along the original fuzzy set's limits. This has the effect of moving the surface to the left.

Disjoint Fuzzy Space

In fuzzy modeling a consequent fuzzy space with a discontinuous region. Disjoint solution sets produce "prohibited" zones that require special means of defuzzification.

Disjunction

The process of applying the union operator to two fuzzy sets. For each point on the fuzzy set, we take the maximum of the membership functions for the two combined sets.

Domain

There are two related kinds of domains: those associated with fuzzy sets and those associated with database table columns. A fuzzy set domain is the range of real numbers over which the fuzzy set is mapped and can be any set of positive or negative monotonic numbers. See the definition of *fuzzy sets* for more details on the domain of a fuzzy set. A column domain is the permissible range of values for the column. This set of values can be numeric or alphanumeric (as an example, the STATE_of_RESIDENCE column has a domain of the possible 50 state identifiers).

Expected Value

The singleton value derived from "defuzzifying" a fuzzy region that represents the model's value for a solution or control variable. An expected value is derived from a fuzzy set by applying one of the methods of decomposition. This value represents the central measure of the fuzzy space according to the type of defuzzification technique. See *composite moments*, *composite maximum*, or *composite mass* for additional details.

Expert System	A software system that uses some form of machine intelligence to approximate the reasoning process of an expert in some domain of competence. Expert systems use rules in the form of *if-then-else* to represent knowledge along with an inference engine that manipulates the rules to express the embedded intelligence. Expert systems use such machine reasoning techniques as backward chaining, forward chaining, and fuzzy logic.
Feed-Back Systems	Control or information systems that base their current action on the output from some previous execution state of the same model. A marketing model that develops a product price in period T, feeds that price into the same model in period T+1 to calculate the demand (which, in turn will formulate a new product price in T+1). A feed-back loop supports adaptive as well as self-organizing systems.
Forward Chaining	A data-driven machine reasoning strategy that continually loops through the rule set in cycle 1 through N, firing rules and accumulating data. As data is accumulated, rules that failed to fire in cycle k, might fire in k+1. Forward chaining is often used in configuration, production planning, and marketing systems.
Forward Firing	(often called *opportunistic forward firing*) The process of scanning ahead in the rule set to find rules that can be fired as a result of instantiating a variable in the consequent of a currently fired rule. Thus, when a rule if A > B then C=X is executed, we can find a candidate and eligible rule in the knowledge base such as if C=X then S=T that can be fired even though it is not a direct part of the reasoning process. Forward firing is an important method of rapidly accumulating knowledge in a backward chaining process.
Fuzziness	The degree or quality of imprecision (or, perhaps, vagueness) intrinsic in a property, process, or concept. The measure of the fuzziness and its characteristic behavior within the domain of the process is the semantic attribute captured by a fuzzy set. Fuzziness is not ambiguity nor is it the condition of partial or total ignorance; rather, fuzziness deals with the natural imprecision associated with everyday events. When we measure temperature against the idea of hot, or height against the idea of tall, of speed against the idea of fast, we are dealing with imprecise concepts. There is no sharp boundary at which a metal is precisely cold, then precisely cool, then precisely warm, and finally, precisely hot. Each state transition occurs continuously and gradually, so that, at some given measurement, a metal rod may have some properties of warm as well as hot.

Fuzzy Approximation Theory

(also *FAT*) A fundamental theory of fuzzy logic attributed to Bart Kosko that defines the ways in which an additive fuzzy system using the correlation product method can approximate to any degree of detail any continuous function.

Fuzzy Associative Memory

(also *FAM*) An [MxN] array of fuzzy conditions and actions. FAM arrays are used principally in process control environments where a correspondence exists between a [2x2] antecedent array and a solution variable.

Fuzzy Cognitive Map

(also *FCM*) A connectionist system that expresses the relationship between concepts (nodes) in terms of positive and negative affects. A fuzzy cognitive map represents a dynamic-state relationship between the concepts. These states are continuously evaluated until a steady state is found. FCMs are important tools in strategic policy analysis, prototyping, knowledge acquisition, and system dynamics analysis.

Fuzzy Logic

A class of multivalent, generally continuous-valued logics based on the theory of fuzzy sets initially proposed by Lotfi Zadeh in 1965, but that has its roots in the multivalued logic of Lukasiewicz and Gödel. Fuzzy logic is concerned with the set theoretic operations allowed on fuzzy sets, how these operations are performed and interpreted, and the nature of fundamental fuzziness. Most fuzzy logics are based on the min-max or the bounded arithmetic sum rules for set implication.

Fuzzy Memberships

See *truth memberships*.

Fuzzy Numbers

Numbers that have fuzzy properties. Models deal with scalars by treating them as fuzzy regions through the use of hedges. A fuzzy number generally assumes the space of a bell curve with the most probable value for the space at the center of the bell. Fuzzy numbers obey the rules for conventional arithmetic but also have some special properties (such as the ability to subsume each other or to obey the laws of fuzzy set geometry). For more information see *approximation*.

Fuzzy Operators	The class of connecting operators, notably AND and OR, that combines antecedent fuzzy propositions to produce a composite truth value. The traditional Zadeh fuzzy operators use the min-max rules, but several other alternative operator classes exist, such as the classes described by Yager, Schweizer and Sklar, Dubois and Prade, and Dombi. Fuzzy operators determine the nature of the implication and inference process and thus also establish the nature of fuzzy logic for that implementation.
Fuzzy Region	Another term for a fuzzy space.
Fuzzy Sets	A fuzzy set differs from conventional or crisp sets by allowing partial or gradual memberships. A fuzzy set has three principal properties: the range of values over which the set is mapped, this is called the *domain* and must be monotonic real numbers in the range $[-\infty, +\infty]$; the degree of membership axis that measures the value's membership in the set; and the actual surface of the fuzzy set—the points that connect the degree of membership with the underlying domain. The fuzzy set's degree of membership value is a consequence of its intrinsic truth function. This function returns a value between [0] (not a member of the set) and [1] (a complete member of the set) depending on the evaluation of the fuzzy proposition X is a member of fuzzy set A. In many interpretations, fuzzy logic is concerned with the compatibility between a domain's value and the fuzzy concept. This can be expressed as How compatible is X with fuzzy set A?
Fuzzy Space	A region in the model that has intrinsic fuzzy properties. A fuzzy surface simply differs from a fuzzy set in its dynamic nature and composite characteristics. In modelling terms, we view the fuzzy sets created by set theoretic operations, as well as the consequent sets produced by the approximate reasoning mechanism, as fuzzy spaces. This distinction remains one of semantics, enabling the model builder to draw a distinction between the sets that are created as permanent parts of the system and those that have a lifetime associated with the active model.
Goal	In backward chaining, a variable whose value is sought through rule execution. Thus, for a rule, if A > B then C= X, a backward chaining inference engine might be invoked to find the value of variables A, B, and X. Each of these variables becomes a goal. Finding a goal is a recursive process. For the goal A, we are looking for a rule such as if M = R then A = K (that is, a rule that establishes the value for A). In this case the backward chaining inference engine makes the variables M, R, and K the next level goals (often called *subgoals*.)

Graph

A network of nodes and edges. Graphs represent process that can be cyclical (they have repeating paths) or acyclical (they have no repeating paths). Graphs are used in decision support systems in a variety of ways from fuzzy cognitive maps to critical path networks.

Hashing

A technique for generating an address from a key. Hashing is a very rapid mechanism of supporting direct access into a dictionary (or, for databases, into the page space). Hashing usually (but not always) converts data, either numbers or string data, into chunks that are manipulated to form a bit string that is interpreted as a number. The number is adjusted for the maximum possible address spaces to produce a slot address. Hashing is very fast, but can produce a large number of collisions (different keys produce the same hash address) if not carefully designed.

Hedge

A term, basically linguistic in nature, that modifies the surface characteristics of a fuzzy set. A hedge has an adjectival or adverbial relationship with a fuzzy set, such that the natural specification of a hedge with a fuzzy set acts in the same fashion as its English language counterpart. Hedges can approximate a scalar or another fuzzy set (near, close to, around, about, approaching); intensify a fuzzy set (very, extremely); dilute a fuzzy set (quite, rather, somewhat), create the complement of a fuzzy set (not), and intensify or diffuse through contrasting (positively, generally). The definition and calibration of hedges play an important part in the construction and validation of fuzzy systems. In functional fuzzy systems, users define their own hedge vocabularies and the way each hedge will change the surface of a fuzzy set.

Heuristics

Rules of thumb. A heuristic is not based generally on a mathematical foundation and is not derived from "first principles" but from some approach that appears to work well and provides a satisfactory solution to complex or poorly understood problems. The use and development of hedges, as an example, is based on a commonly understood set of heuristics.

Implication Rules

Implication is a formal method of assigning truth to fuzzy propositions and assertions involved in a logical implication process. This sounds a little like a tautology, but, in fact, it means that when we use the fuzzy implication operators—AND and OR. There are rules about the nature of truth they imply. In most fuzzy systems there are two rules of implication—the min-max and the bounded arithmetic sums.

Imprecision   The degree of intrinsic imprecision associated with an event, process or concept is a measure of the overall system fuzziness (see *fuzziness*). In this respect imprecision is a characteristic of fuzzy systems. We note that fuzziness and imprecision are intransitive phenomena; that is, a fuzzy system is always imprecise, but an imprecise system is not always fuzzy. The latter definition of imprecision is based on the evident role of granularity in our measurements. Within some systems, the resolution of the control variables moves toward greater and greater precision as we increase our level of detail. (As an example, the imprecision associated with measuring the edge of a cube diminishes as we change measuring tools from our finger, to a ruler marked in 1/16 inches, to a ruler marked in millimeters, to an optical sensor [laser] that can read in angstrom units. At some arbitrary level of detail, the measurement falls below the smallest unit of measurement in our model, thus becoming, for all purposes, absolutely precise).

Intelligence   A poorly understood concept of being intelligent, but generally, the processing of using knowledge in manner that we might attribute to a living creature if it occurred in nature.

Intensification   A hedge operation, usually implemented by very or extremely, that moves the truth function of a fuzzy set so that its degrees of membership values are decreased for each point along the line. This means that, for a given variable's membership rank, its value in the intensified fuzzy set will decrease. The most common intensification mechanism changes the fuzzy surface by squaring the membership function at each point along the original fuzzy set's limits. This has the effect of moving the surface to the right.

Intersection   The conjunction of two fuzzy sets.

Intrinsic Fuzziness

(or *imprecision*) The property of fuzziness that is an inseparable characteristic of a concept, event, or process. The universe at large consists of mostly fuzzy processes, that is, measurable events that cannot be calibrated or separated into distinct groups. The simplest and most commonly used example is the concept of tall associated with height. At what precise point does a height measurement move from short, to average, to tall? We can demonstrate the ineluctable notion of imprecision by attempting to separate tallness from non-tallness. Let set T be the set of all tall people. At any chance division point $[S]$, we note that the adjoining value $[S]$-$\in$ (where $\in$ is any arbitrarily small number approaching $[S]$) is excluded from the set, yet this point, if sufficiently close to $[S]$, shares nearly all the properties of set T. We can solve this problem by moving the division point left by $\in$. Applying the same separability analysis to this new division point $[S_1]$ we find the same indistinctness. Now, we can resolve this by moving the separation point continuously to the left. At some point, however, the membership of set T no longer represents its semantic property of tall. Thus, in attempting to resolve imprecision we are forced to abandon any precise separability. This means that tallness is an intrinsic imprecise or fuzzy characteristic of height.

Join

In database technology, the process of connecting two or more tables to produce a new table based on common data values in columns that share the same implicit or explicit domain. A join also has the property of closure.

Knowledge Base

In an expert system, the collection of rules, objects, and procedures that represent the acquired knowledge and implicit intelligence of the source (the human expert, as an example.) A knowledge base is a structured collection stored in the native file system of the expert system tool (this can be a formal database or a proprietary file organization).

Knowledge Engineer

A business analyst specially trained in the acquisition, analysis, and structuring of knowledge in an expert system environment. Knowledge engineers are also skilled in the interview techniques necessary to acquire raw process knowledge from experts and cast this knowledge in a form that can be used by an inference engine. Knowledge engineering has recently become a skill used by conventional systems, marketing, and engineering analysts.

Knowledge Mining	See *data mining*.
Knowledge-Based Systems	An information decision system using the techniques and structures associated with expert systems. Knowledge-based systems weave intelligence cognitive modelling with traditional mathematical and statistical modelling. The field of expert system design, development, and deployment has been subsumed by the general field of knowledge-based systems.
Kurtosis	The fourth moment in statistical analysis indicating the "look" or form of a bell-shaped distribution. Kurtosis is also an important property in · fuzzy logic. Kurtosis falls into three general categories: *leptokurtic*, indicating a narrow, sharp curve; *mesokurtic*, indicating a moderate, generally normal bell-shaped look; and *platykurtic*, indicating a wide or "squat" bell-shape.
Law of the Excluded Middle	In classical set theory an element has two states respective to its membership in a set: true [1], complete membership, or false [0], complete nonmembership. This means that the intersection of set A with its complement $\sim A$ is the null or empty set, expressed symbolically as $A \cap \sim A \equiv \varnothing$ indicating that an element cannot be, at the same time, a member of a set and its complement (which, by definition, says that $\sim A$ contains all the elements not in A). This is also the law of noncontradiction. Since fuzzy sets have partial membership characteristics we might expect that they behave differently in the presence of their complement.
Linguistic Variable	In the rule formulation language of fuzzy systems, the term applied to a fuzzy set or the combination of a fuzzy set and its associated hedges. Thus the rule our price must be positively very high the term `positively very high` is a linguistic variable. Since the effect of a hedged fuzzy set is a single fuzzy space, it is, conceptually, a single fuzzy set.
Linear Systems	A system where the outcomes are linearly proportional to the inputs. In general expert and decision support system parlance, *linear* has come to mean *able to be modelled*. Whereas, *nonlinear*, has come to mean any system that is *too difficult to model given current technologies*.

Machine Intelligence

Intelligent behavior encoded in a machine. The "machine" can be software, hardware, or a combination of the two.

Methods of Decomposition

The techniques employed to derive the expected value from a consequent fuzzy region. The methods of decomposition varying according to the type of expectation associated with the composite fuzzy region. For details on the more common methods see *composite moments*, *composite maximum*, and *composite mass*.

Min-Max Rule

The basic rule of implication and inference for fuzzy logic that follows the traditional Zadeh algebra of fuzzy sets. There are two statements of this rule pertaining to different elements in the fuzzy logic process.

The min-max rule of implication. This rule specifies how fuzzy unions and intersections are performed. When two fuzzy sets are combined with the intersection operator (AND), the resulting fuzzy space is found by taking the minimum of the truth functions across the compatible domains. When two fuzzy sets are combined with the union operator (OR), the resulting fuzzy space is found by taking the maximum of the truth functions across the compatible domains.

The min-max rule of inference. This rule specifies, in a fuzzy system, how conditional and unconditional fuzzy assertions (propositions) are combined. An unconditional assertion is applied to the consequent fuzzy region under generation by taking the minimum of the unconditional's fuzzy space and the consequent's fuzzy space at each point in the region. A conditional fuzzy proposition first has its truth reduced to the maximum truth of the rule's premise, then it is applied to the consequent fuzzy region under generation by taking the maximum of the conditional's fuzzy space and the consequent's fuzzy space at each point in the region.

Model

A logical or mathematical process that attempts to represent or closely approximate the behavior of a related set of physical phenomena.

Necessity

The degree to which we can say that an event must occur, that is, an ineluctable or inevitable event. Necessity is related to the Markov dependency in both probability and fuzzy systems in describing the extent that one event is dependent on another event. Bayesian systems often employ the concept of logical necessity (as well as logical sufficiency). Necessity in this context is the extent to which an observed phenomenon is said to be essential in order for another phenomenon or condition to exist.

Neural Network   A multi-layered connectionist architecture modelled after a biological neural system. Neural networks are not organized around rules or programming, but learn the underlying behaviors of a model by analyzing its input and output values and adjusting the weights between neuron layers. In this respect the behavior of a neural network is trained using supervised or unsupervised techniques. Supervised techniques tell the network whether is prediction from a set of input data is correct (and feeds back the degree of error.) Unsupervised training leaves the analysis of data relationships and the grouping of related data classes to the software system.

Nonlinear Systems   Models where the output of the system cannot be easily predicted from the initial conditions and/or where small changes in the initial conditions produce significantly different (and often unexpected) results. This is due to the nature of nonlinearity in the model. In common expert system parlance, *nonlinear* has come to mean any system that is too difficult to model, to complex to understand, or as an explanation of any system that fails.

Normal Form   In relational database terminology, one of several orthogonal relationships between data elements in a table. There are at least five normal forms, known as 1NF through 5NF, each one indicating a tighter restriction on the structural organization of a table. Normal forms insure that relational databases are organized in such a way that, for instance, every data column is completely and only dependent on the primary key, that columns contain only one data element (no arrays of data), that data columns are not dependent on each other, and so forth.

Normalization   The process of ensuring that the maximum truth value of a fuzzy set is one [1]. Fuzzy sets are normalized by readjusting all the truth membership values proportionally around the maximum truth value which is set to [1]. If the fuzzy sets defined as part of the model vocabulary are not in normal form, they cannot contribute properly to the implication and inference process. This affects not only the compatibility index associated with the final control variable regions, but dampens the fuzzy implication strength, thus producing spurious results.

**Object-
Oriented**

A general approach to system analysis, design and construction that places emphasis on the objects being modelled and the process that occur between objects rather on the code that manipulates data. Object-oriented systems support such capabilities as the definition of classes (the objects), the inheritance of properties between classes and special-izations of these classes (often called *subclasses*), the shielding of the user from the internal mechanisms or data representation in the class, and the definition of common procedures that can act across a family of classes.

**Objective
Function**

A function used to measure the solution progress of a system.

Ockham's Razor

The belief that the model with least number of assumptions and the least number of components that adequately explains a phenomena is the most desirable. Essentially a form of the KISS principle (from *keep it simple, stupid*). First expressed by William of Ockham as *essentia non sunt multiplicanda praeter necessiatem* (eh-sen-tea-ah nohn sunt mul-tea-plee-kan-dah pry-ter neh-kays-see-ah-tem), roughly translated, *don't screw around with simplicity.*

**Possibility
Theory**

Possibility theory evolved from the concept of fuzzy sets and provides a calculus of possibility analysis similar to the crisp calculus of probabil-ity (where the degrees of possibility can take only true or false values [1,0]). Developed and solidified by such researchers as Dider Dubois and Henri Prade, possibility theory embraces the entire spectrum of fuzzy logic and approximate reasoning by codifying the relationship between fuzzy interval analysis, event phenomena, and fuzzy spaces into a comprehensive mathematically sound discipline. What possibility theory attempts to do is provide a mathematical framework for the intru-sion of fuzzy logic into a wide spectrum of disciplines such as game the-ory, linear programming, operations research, and general decision theory.

**Predictive
Precision**

A concept used in the fuzzy verification and stability metrics and indi-cates the degree to which we can falsify or disprove a prediction (or proposition) of the system. Precise predictions are, naturally, highly fal-sifiable since they make specific predictions. On the other hand, impre-cise or approximate claims are less verifiable.

Premise   (also the *predicate*) The conditional or left-side part of a rule. In fuzzy modeling the premise is a series of fuzzy assertions (or propositions) connected by AND and OR operators. These are combined according to the nature of the AND or OR operators (using Zadeh's algebra, as an example, this is the min-max rule) to produce a final and total truth for the rule premise. See the definition of *rules* for more details.

Principle of   Zadeh's intuitive appeal to linguistic system modeling based on his
Incompatibility   belief that, as systems are defined in ever more rigorous mathematical terms, there is a point beyond which our understanding of the system as a whole and the mathematical representation are incompatible. Zadeh says, *as the complexity of a system increases, our ability to make precise yet significant statements about its behavior diminishes until a threshold is reached beyond which precision and significance (or relevance) become almost mutually exclusive characteristics.* (From L.A. Zadeh, Outline of a New Approach to the Analysis of Complex Systems and Decision Processes, *IEEE Transactions on Systems, Man, and Cybernetics,* Vol. SMC-3, No. 1, 1973.)

Probability   A quantitative method of dealing with uncertainty based on the measurement of behavior patterns for some selected set of properties in a large population. Probability provides a statistical inference process, since if we know the *a priori* chance of an event occurring, we can predict (within a prescribed confidence limit) the chance of that event occurring in the future. The basic classical probability formula is defined as $p(x) = [e/N]$, meaning that the probability of x is the number of observed x events (e) divided by the total number of equally possible events N. As an example, when you roll a single die, the probability of getting a one is $P(1) = [1/6] = .16666666667$. Probability, concerned with deterministic and nondeterministic (random) systems, attempts to quantify the behavior of these systems as we gain more and more knowledge about the underlying populations. See *Bayes theorem* for additional information on probabilities.

Randomness   A characteristic of a property or event such that, when we sample that property, any of its possible values is equally likely to occur. The principal characteristic of such a random event is that there is no way to predict its outcome. One view of fuzziness is coupled closely with randomness in the sense that fuzzy sets are considered as measurements "corrupted" by white or random noise. If we consider the bell-shaped fuzzy set `MIDDLE AGED` one interpretation of this is the number 40 surrounded by random noise. One way to view a fuzzy set is to consider the membership function as a random variable with noise around or near the true truth function values.

Relation   In relational database terminology, a storage form that resembles a table. A relation is a mathematically defined structure consisting of rows and columns. A rule in a relation is called a *tuple*. In a pure relation, the order of rows in the relation is not important (nor defined) and the order of columns in the relation is not important (and not defined). Relational databases usually modify this strict relation definition by giving some meaning to the order of columns. The first N columns become the primary identifier of the table.

Rules   Statements of knowledge that relate the compatibility of fuzzy premise propositions to the compatibility of one or more consequent fuzzy spaces. The rule *if temperature is high then friction is decreased*; is interpreted as a correlation between two fuzzy states such that the rule should be read *as [to the degree that] temperature is high friction is [proportionally] decreased* or, perhaps, in a slightly more formal statement considering the idea of fuzzy compatibility: *[to the degree that] temperature is [compatible with the concept] high make friction [compatible with the concept] decreased*. Of course, the proportionality need not be linear. In fact, the correspondence or compatibility function between an antecedent fuzzy region and a consequent fuzzy state is determined by (1) the shape of the fuzzy sets (2) the connector (implication) operators, (3) the preponderance of truth in the antecedent, and (4) the technique for transforming the consequent fuzzy region from the current fuzzy state. This means that fuzzy rules operate in a different manner than rules in conventional knowledge-based systems (which are concerned with pattern matching and the logical evaluation of discrete expressions).

Secondary Index

(also see *B*tree* and *hashing*) A structure that allows the rapid retrieval of records from a database when the record identifier is not the primary key. As an example, the expression FIND PROJECTS WHERE DEPTS = "ENGR"; uses the secondary index associated with the department (DEPT) column to retrieve all the records with the value ENGR.

Support Set

That part of a fuzzy set or fuzzy region defined by the strong alpha-cut threshold, $\mu_A[x] > 0$. The support set, since it contains the actual membership region for the set, is the area that actually participates in the fuzzy implication and inference process.

Truth Function

A view that the degree of membership axis of a fuzzy set or region acts as a function $\mu_A = T(x)$ for each unique value selected from the domain, the function returns a unique degree of membership in the fuzzy regions. We call this a "truth" function since it reflects the truth of the fuzzy proposition x is a member of fuzzy set A. For second-order sets, the truth function returns a vector containing the fuzzy region approximating the truth value. For third-order sets, the truth function returns an [NxM] matrix of vectors representing the possibility density at the truth region.

Undecidability

The degree to which the state of a control variable cannot be determined from the fuzzy space context. Undecidability is most generally associated with the fuzzy region bounded by two intersecting, complementary fuzzy sets (or fuzzy regions).

Union

The disjunction of two fuzzy sets.

Vagueness

A property closely allied with imprecision and thus a characteristic of fuzzy systems. Vague concepts approach fuzziness as we begin to calibrate them in terms of their compatibility with an overlying idea. To say *Bill is big* may be vague rather than fuzzy if the idea underlying big is not particularly correlated to any metric from which we could sample individual property points. On the other hand, if the attributes of Bill were defined in terms of height (TALL) and weight (HEAVY), then big becomes imprecise rather than vague. We should note that vagueness is distinct from ambiguity.

Bibliography

Initiali;
Parms[0]
Parms [1,
sprint(s)
strncpy(:
FDBptr[M?
if(*stat1
Part Dom;
Part Dom,
(*FDBcnt,

In the year since the publication of *The Fuzzy System Handbook*, a number of books have appeared addressing many important issues in fuzzy logic and fuzzy system modelling. Most however, continue to be written by academics and research scientists with little experience in the commercial business world. Most are deeply involved with control engineering. This control orientation in fuzzy logic carries with it much baggage that is not of immediate relevance to the business analyst and knowledge engineer. Highly sophisticated and complex business systems in marketing, portfolio optimization, asset allocation, project management, product pricing and risk assessment are neither time-critical systems, nor bound to the tight memory constraint of microprocessors used in controlling camcorders, antilock braking systems, and automatic subway systems. Today's fuzzy models are running on mainframes or high-speed 32-bit work stations with access to gigabytes of virtual (or even real) memory. Finding information about the use of fuzzy logic in business is therefore difficult. I have attempted to address this issue in the bibliography by eliminating the vast collection of papers on control engineering (most of these, in any case, tediously (and in my view, pointlessly) report on newly discovered ways to balance pendulums or back up trucks using 2 less bytes of memory or 3 less cycles of machine time.)

Recommended Reading

Deciding how to get started in fuzzy logic and fuzzy modelling is often difficult. This especially true for business analysts concerned about issues of representation, flexibility, and over-all machine intelligence. The following eight books are, I believe, especially important, well written, and accessible to the nonscientist.

Altrock, Constantin von (1995). *Fuzzy Logic and NeuroFuzzy Applications Explained*, Prentice Hall PTR, Englewood Cliffs, NJ.

587

Cox, Earl D. (1994). *The Fuzzy Systems Handbook: A Practitioner's Guide to Building, Using, and Maintaining Fuzzy Systems,* AP Professional, Cambridge, MA.

Jones, Peter L., and Graham, Ian (1988). *Expert Systems: Knowledge, Uncertainty and Decision.* Chapman and Hall, London.

Klir, George J., and Folger, Tina A. (1988). *Fuzzy Sets, Uncertainty, and Information.* Prentice Hall, Englewood Cliffs, NJ.

Kosko, Bart (1993). *Fuzzy Thinking: The New Science of Fuzzy Logic*, Hyperion, New York, NY.

Masters, Timothy (1993). *Practical Neural Network Recipes in C++.* Academic Press, San Diego, CA.

Smithson, Michael (1987). *Fuzzy Set Analysis for Behavioral and Social Sciences.* Springer-Verlag, New York.

Terano, T., Asai, K., and Sugeno, Michio (1991). *Fuzzy Systems Theory and Its Applications.* Academic Press, San Diego, CA.

Main Bibliography

Fuzzy Logic References

Cox, Earl D., and Goetz, Martin (1991). "Fuzzy Logic Clarified." *Computerworld* (March 11, 1991), 69–71.

Cox, Earl D. (1991). "Approximate Reasoning: The Use of Fuzzy Logic in Expert Systems and Decision Support." Proceedings of the Conference on Expert Systems in the Insurance Industry (April 24–25), Institute for International Research, New York.

——— (1991) "Company Acquisition Analysis: Formulating Queries with Imprecise Domains." Proceedings of the First International Conference on Artificial Intelligence Applications on Wall Street (October 9–11), IEEE Computer Society Press, Los Alamos, CA. 19–199.

——— (1992). "The Great Myths of Fuzzy Logic." *AI Expert* (January), 40–45.

—— (1992). "Solving Problems with Fuzzy Logic." *AI Expert* (March), 28–37.

—— (1992). "Integrating Fuzzy Logic into Neural Nets." *AI Expert* (June), 43–47.

—— (1992). "Fuzzy Fundamentals." *IEEE Spectrum* (October), 58–61.

—— (1992). "Effectively Using Fuzzy Logic and Fuzzy Expert System modeling—in Theory and Practice." Proceedings of the Conference on Advanced Technologies to Re-Engineer the Insurance Process (September 17–18), Institute for International Research, New York.

—— (1992). "Fuzzy Logic and Fuzzy System Modeling." Proceedings of the Fourth Annual IBC Conference on Expert Systems in Insurance (October 28–29), IBC USA Conferences, Southborough, MA.

—— (1992) "Applications of Fuzzy System Models." *AI Expert* (October), 34-39.

—— (1992) "A Close Shave with Occam's Razor: Fuzzy-Neural Hetero-Genetic Object-Oriented Knowledge-Based Nano-Synthetic Reasoning Models: Throwing the Kitchen Sink at Problem Solving." *A Workshop in the Industrial Applications of Philosophy and Epistemology to AI.* Proceedings of the Third Annual Symposium of the International Association of Knowledge Engineers (November 16–19), Software Engineering Press, Kensington, MD.

—— (1993). "Adaptive Fuzzy Systems." *IEEE Spectrum* (February), 67–70.

—— (1993). "A Fuzzy Systems Approach to Detecting Anomalous Risk Behaviors in Portfolio Management Strategies." Proceedings of the Second International Conference on Artificial Intelligence Applications on Wall Street (April 19–22), Software Engineering Press, Gaithersburg, MD. 144–148.

—— (1993). "Fuzzy Information Systems with Multiple Conflicting Experts." Proceedings of the Computer Design Magazine's Fuzzy Logic '93 Conference (March), M223–1–13.

—— (1993). "A Model-Free Trainable Fuzzy System for the Analysis of Financial Time-Series Data." Proceedings of the Computer Design Magazine's Fuzzy Logic '93 Conference (March), A124–1–7.

Dubois, Didier, and Prade, Henri (1980). *Fuzzy Sets and Systems: Theory and Applications. Mathematics in Science and Engineering, vol 144.* Academic Press, San Diego, CA.

———— (1988). *Possibility Theory, An Approach to Computerized Processing of Uncertainty.* Plenum Press, New York.

Jamshidi, M., Vadiee, N., and Ross, Timothy J., Eds. (1993). *Fuzzy Logic and Control.* Prentice Hall, Englewood Cliffs, NJ.

Kosko, Bart (1992). *Neural Networks and Fuzzy Systems, A Dynamical Systems Approach to Machine Intelligence.* Prentice Hall, Englewood Cliffs, NJ.

Kosko, Bart and Isaka, Satoru (1993). "Fuzzy Logic." *Scientific American* (July), 76–81.

McNeil, Martin F. and Thro, Ellen (1994). *Fuzzy Logic: A Practical Approach*, AP Professional, Cambridge, MA.

Pedrycz, Witold (1993). *Fuzzy Control and Fuzzy Systems.* 2nd ed. John Wiley and Sons, New York.

Schmucker, Kurt J. (1984). *Fuzzy Sets, Natural Language Computations, and Risk Analysis.* Computer Science Press, Rockville, MD.

Wang, Li-Xin, and Mendel, Jerry M. (1991). "Generating Fuzzy Rules from Numerical Data, with Applications." USC-SIPI Report No. 169. Signal and Image Processing Institute, University of Southern California, Los Angeles, CA.

Wang, Zhenyuan, and Klir, George J. (1992). *Fuzzy Measure Theory.* Plenum Press, New York.

Yager, Ronald E., and Zadeh, Lotfi A. Eds. (1992). *An Introduction to Fuzzy Logic Applications in Intelligent Systems.* Kluwer Academic Publishers, Norwell, MA.

Yager, R.R., Ovchinnikov, S., Tong, R.M., and Nguyen, H.T. (1987). *Fuzzy Sets and Applications: Selected Papers by L.A. Zadeh.* John Wiley and Sons, New York.

Zadeh, Lotfi A., and Kacprzyk, Janusz, Eds. (1992). *Fuzzy Logic for the Management of Uncertainty.* John Wiley and Sons, New York.

Zimmerman, Hans J. (1985). *Fuzzy Set Theory—and Its Applications.* Kluwer Academic Publishers, Norwell, MA.

Zimmerman, Hans J. (1987). *Fuzzy Sets, Decision Making, and Expert Systems.* Kluwer Academic Publishers, Norwell, MA.

Database Management Systems

Date, C.J. (1983). *Database: A Primer*, Addison-Wesley Publishing Company, Reading, MA.

——— (1982). *An Introduction to Database Systems*, 3rd ed., volumes I and II. Addison-Wesley Publishing Company, Reading, MA.

Kerschberg, Larry, Ed. (1989). *Expert Database Systems*, The Benjamin/Cummings Publishing Company, Redwood City, CA.

Kroenke, David (1978). *Database: A Professional's Primer*, Science Research Associates, Palo Alto, CA.

Ullman, Jeffrey D. (1989). *Principles of Database and Knowledge-Base Systems*, volumes I and II, Computer Science Press, Rockville, MD.

Wiederhold, Gio (1983). *Database Design*, 2nd ed., McGraw-Hill Book Company, New York.

Expert and Decision Support System References

Bennett, John L. (1983). *Building Decision Support Systems*, Addison-Wesley Publishing Company, Reading, MA.

Buchanan, Bruce G. and Shortliffe, Edward H. (1984). *Rule Based Expert Systems: The MYCIN Experiments of the Stanford Heuristic Programming Project*, Addison-Wesley Publishing Company, Reading, MA.

Giarrantano, Joseph and Riley, Gary (1989). *Expert Systems: Principles and Programming*, PWS-Kent Publishing Company, Boston, MA.

Goonatilake, Suran and Khebbal, Sukhdev, Eds. (1995). *Intelligent Hybrid Systems*, John Wiley and Sons, New York.

Haromon, Paul and Sawyer, Brian (1990). *Creating Expert Systems for Business and Industry*, John Wiley and Sons, New York.

Keen, Peter and Scott, Michael (1978). *Decision Support Systems: An Organizational Perspective*, Addison-Wesley Publishing Company, Reading, MA.

Liebowitz, Jay, Ed.(1990). *Expert Systems for Business and Management*, Prentice Hall, Englewood Cliffs, NJ.

Maus, Rex and Keyes, Jessica, Eds. (1991). *Handbook of Expert Systems in Manufacturing*, McGraw-Hill, New York.

Parsaye, Kamran and Chignell, Mark (1988). *Expert Systems for Experts*, John Wiley and Sons, New York.

Reitman, Walter, Ed. (1984). *Artificial Intelligence Applications for Business: Proceedings of the NYU Symposium, May, 1983*, Ablex Publishing, Norwood, NJ.

Watkins, Paul R. and Eliot, Lance B., Eds. (1993). *Expert Systems in Business and Finance: Issues and Applications*, John Wiley and Sons, New York.

General Modeling

Cellier, Francois E. (1991). *Continuous System Modeling*, Springer-Verlag, New York.

Smets, P., Mamdani, E.H., Dubois, D., and Prade, Henri (1988). *Non-Standard Logics for Automated Reasoning.* Academic Press Limited, London.

White, David A., and Sofge, Donald A. (1992). *Handbook of Intelligent Control, Neural, Fuzzy, and Adaptive Approaches.* Van Nostrand Reinhold, New York.

Weinberg, Gerald M. (1975). *An Introduction to General Systems Thinking*, John Wiley and Sons, New York.

Zurek, Wojciech H., Ed. (1990). *Complexity, Entropy and the Physics of Information.* vol. VIII. Santa Fe Institute, Studies in the Sciences of Complexity. Addison-Wesley Publishing Company, Redwood City, CA.

Knowledge Management

Wiig, Karl M. (1993). *Knowledge Management Foundations: Thinking about Thinking—How People and Organizations Create, Represent, and Use Knowledge*, Schema Press, Arlington, TX.

———— (1994). *Knowledge Management: The Central Management Focus for Intelligent-Acting Organizations*, Schema Press, Arlington, TX.

Index

A